If Only We Could See

If Only We Could See

Mystical Vision and Social Transformation

Gary Commins

CASCADE *Books* • Eugene, Oregon

IF ONLY WE COULD SEE
Mystical Vision and Social Transformation

Copyright © 2015 Gary Commins. All rights reserved. Except for brief quotations in critical publications or reviews, no part of this book may be reproduced in any manner without prior written permission from the publisher. Write: Permissions, Wipf and Stock Publishers, 199 W. 8th Ave., Suite 3, Eugene, OR 97401.

Cascade Books
An Imprint of Wipf and Stock Publishers
199 W. 8th Ave., Suite 3
Eugene, OR 97401

www.wipfandstock.com

ISBN 13: 978-1-62564-495-4

Cataloguing-in-Publication Data

Commins, Gary

> If only we could see : mystical vision and social transformation / Gary Commins.
>
> xiv + 502 p. ; 23 cm. Includes bibliographical references and indexes.
>
> ISBN 13: 978-1-62564-495-4
>
> 1. Mysticism—Social aspects. 2. Religion and social problems. I. Title.

BV5082 .C63 2015

Manufactured in the U.S.A.   10/09/2015

For Zac

Contents

Permissions | ix
Preface | xi
Acknowledgments | xiii

  1 Introduction: Sparks | 1
  2 Wakers on Earth | 41
  3 With Moaning and with Mourning | 88
  4 A Great Light | 133
  5 Footprints on the Water | 185
  6 Wounds, Forever Fresh | 232
  7 Harijans | 277
  8 Holy Communists | 323
  9 The Unseeable One Glory | 373
10 The Peace that is No Peace | 414

Glossary of Names | 451
Bibliography | 467
Names Index | 485
Subject Index | 491
Scripture Index | 497

Permissions

Excerpt from "The Quickening of St. John the Baptist" by Thomas Merton from *The Collected Poems of Thomas Merton*, copyright © 1949 by Our Lady of Gethsemani Monastery. Reprinted by permission of New Directions Publishing Corp.

Excerpts from "Hagia Sophia" and "Macarius and The Pony" by Thomas Merton, from *The Collected Poems of Thomas Merton*, copyright © 1963 by The Abbey of Gethsemani. Reprinted by permission of New Directions Publishing Corp.

Excerpt from "Prayers of God" in *Darkwater: Voices from Within the Veil* by W. E. B. DuBois, copyright © 1999. Used by permission of Dover Publications, Inc.

Excerpt from "The Dry Salvages" from *Four Quartets* by T. S. Eliot. Copyright © 1941 by T. S. Eliot; copyright © renewed 1969 by Esme Valerie Eliot. Reprinted by permission of Houghton Mifflin Harcourt Publishing Company. American rights reserved.

Excerpt from "The Dry Salvages" from *Four Quartets* by T. S. Eliot. Copyright © 1941 by T. S. Eliot. Used by permission of Faber and Faber Limited. Non-exclusive English language permission throughout the world excluding North America.

Excerpts from "The Mad Farmer Manifesto: The First Amendment," "The Contrariness of the Mad Farmer," "Manifesto: The Mad Farmer Liberation Front," and "The Mad Farmer Revolution" from *The Collected Poems of Wendell Berry, 1957–1982* by Wendell Berry. Used by permission of Counterpoint LLC.

Excerpts from "Harlem" from *The Collected Poems of Langston Hughes* by Langston Hughes, edited by Arnold Rampersad with David Roessel, copyright © 1994 by the Estate of Langston Hughes. Used by permission of Alfred A. Knopf, an imprint of the Knopf Doubleday Publishing Group, a division of Random House LLC. All American rights reserved.

Excerpts from "Harlem" from *The Collected Poems of Langston Hughes* by Langston Hughes, edited by Arnold Rampersad with David Roessel, copyright © 1994 by the Estate of Langston Hughes. Used by permission of Harold Ober Associates Incorporated for electronic and UK and Commonwealth.

Excerpts from "Transfiguration" from *The Collected Poems of Edwin Muir* by Edwin Muir, copyright © 1957. Used by permission of Oxford Publishing Limited, USA.

Excerpts from "Transfiguration" from *The Collected Poems of Edwin Muir* by Edwin Muir, copyright © 1957. Used by permission of Faber and Faber Limited. Non-exclusive English language permission throughout the world excluding North America.

Preface

Ideas for this book began gyrating in my mind twenty years ago. For quite some time, I wondered if it would be one of several projects that a lack of time or fluctuations in focus would abort, but the subject matter is so dear to my soul that it weathered the many changes and chances of life. In ways hard to describe, it kept clamoring for my attention. Five years ago I finally had time to funnel notes, sift ideas, and scratch out drafts of chapters. So this book has had a long gestation period, and like anyone going through all of the annoying discomforts and giddy anticipations of a pregnancy, I hope the end product brings life.

During the past two decades, I have not been blissfully daydreaming about writing a book. As scholars go, I am an amateur. I read and write in my spare time. As a parish priest, I am busy. As a human being, I am a father. For the past twenty years and more, I've been engaged in ministry. I've been reading. I've been thinking. I've been praying. I've been a parent. I've been living. Before entering the priesthood, I abandoned the scholar's path. It is my road not taken. Yet it stays in my blood. I do not approach this subject matter as a seasoned academic or a full-time activist. Yet mysticism and activism mold my theology, ministry, and faith.

To me, mysticism and activism are like loose-leaf canons, as Scripture once was, of people's experiences of God. That precious wisdom, while open to examination and interpretation, is ultimately more than can be weighed, measured, boxed, catalogued, itemized, or even fully digested. This book creates an arena for a collective call and response, something akin to an anarchist's convention, between mystics and activists. It connects dots. It identifies patterns. It reveals conflicts, sometimes to resolve them, sometimes to let them rest in the integrity of an unsettled paradox or an unsettling contradiction. As in any intellectual exercise, coherence is desirable. As in life, it is often not achievable. Scripture's uncounted voices refute each other. Neither mysticism nor activism, each with a passion for truth and a yearning to love, ever speak with what Woody Allen long ago mocked as a single, resonant, well-modulated voice.

Instead, two very human voices shape the spirit and method of this book. Over twenty-five years ago, I heard Gustavo Gutierrez say, "If you start with pastoral questions, you get theological answers. If you start with theological questions, all you get are books!" As a priest moonlighting as a scholar, I can't escape the practical, pastoral ramifications of theology. I can't, I won't, pretend to be spiritually or emotionally disengaged. The stakes of prayer and justice are too high. From my perspective, this engagement does not dampen the demand for intellectual integrity; it lends it two more dimensions.

That is the spirit in which I write. What of the method? Twenty-five years ago I heard a presentation by William J. Bouwsma on his book about John Calvin. When complimented for his rigorous research, he quipped, "You don't have to lick the bottom of a lake to know how the water tastes." The twin literatures on the history of mysticism and modern social activism are vast, and my day job is not conducive to time off for research. But I read, write, pray, and participate. I have sipped and tasted. Like Howard Thurman, I find the same spark in myself that I find in mystics and activists. And I believe that the experiential meditations that bookend each chapter ground the academic—the study of other people, places, and times—in the personal, our place and time, because this book is not only about them. It's about us.

This book is about us, but it is dedicated specifically to my son Zac. When his mother Karla gave birth to him, I discovered that, for me, becoming a parent was like falling in love but better because I wanted and needed nothing in return. His childhood, adolescence, and adulthood have been one long, deep, breathtaking, and life-giving epiphany, as powerful as any mystical experience. When he was a child, I was proud of him. Now that he is an adult, I respect him. The love that I felt on Day One of his life has expanded beyond those first horizons in ways I could not have foreseen. His very existence has infused in me an ever-greater urgency to pray, and to do more for peace, justice, and the well-being of all of God's beloved children.

As I write this, Zac is a young adult. As I told him on his twentieth birthday, his first twenty years have magically coincided with my best twenty years. Even if I weren't his father, I would look upon him as a reason to be joyful and as cause to give God nonstop thanks.

Acknowledgments

I would like to thank the Lilly Foundation for a grant that gave me time to gather thoughts, read new materials, and re-examine books I had read before, all of which jump-started my writing. I am even more grateful to the parishioners of St. Luke's, Long Beach, California for never complaining (nor being overly or overtly joyful!) about me taking a sabbatical every few years without which I could not have started or finished this book.

I would like to thank the editors at Wipf and Stock Publishers for working with me to complete this book. Their input has improved and polished the final product.

Throughout the past five years, my old friend (and when I say old, I mean old!) Tim Vivian has been an engaged reader and editor, correcting errors, tightening up ideas, and applauding the overall content. He is a stickler about grammar, an incredibly knowledgeable historian, and an astute theologian who combines intellectual rigor, spiritual depth, and a passion for justice. His belief in the integrity and uniqueness of this book mean more to me than I can say. Thanks, Coach!

1

Introduction

Sparks

The real discovery consists not in seeking new landscapes, but in having new eyes.
 —Marcel Proust[1]

Abba Bessarion, at the point of death, said, "The monk ought to be as the Cherubim and the Seraphim: all eye."[2]

No one can see the kingdom of God without being born from above.
 —John 3:3

Dissolve your whole body into Vision: become seeing, seeing, seeing!
 —Rumi[3]

1. Lane, *Landscapes of the Sacred*, 227.
2. Ward, *Sayings of the Desert*, 42.
3. Rumi, *Poet and Mystic*, 38.

I have seen that all those sparks sparkle from the High Spark,
Hidden of all Hidden!
... All those lights are connected: this light to that light, that light to this light,
One shining into the other,
Inseparable, one from the other.
—The Zohar[4]

When the Savior came, he awakened the soul and kindled the spark
...
—Clement of Alexandria[5]

With most of us there is only a spark, whilst with them it is a long flame; but in us as in them alike, the same fire burns.
—Howard Thurman[6]

A MEANINGFUL WORD

"How does God make skin?"

It was my niece Marcia, now an adult, then almost five years old, who asked this. It was one of her first theological questions and my brother David thought he could rely on my professional training and pastoral experience to provide a satisfying answer. So they dialed me up long-distance on a convenient, conversational, technologically enhanced virtual pilgrimage.

When I heard her question, all of the accumulated acumen I had gained from years of telling stories to preschool children immediately and inexplicably evaporated. Suddenly I felt like Aquinas equipped only with a single off-white crayon. I babbled and fumbled for an explanation, then grasped for words Marcia could not understand—"chemicals," "molecules," "atoms." After several halting attempts, and beginning to wonder if all theology was not an illusory chasing after wind, I finally surrendered and tried to point her toward the timeless Gehenna where the answers to such questions have long ago been left to decompose.

"No one knows," I said. "It's a mystery."

She was, to put it mildly, dissatisfied. "Hey!" she shouted into the phone. "I thought you worked at a church!" My ignorance had been

---

4. Zohar, *Book of Enlightenment*, 186.
5. McGinn, *Foundations of Mysticism*, 102–3.
6. Thurman, "Mysticism," 10.

unveiled. Whatever credibility I had built up in four years had been obliterated. She threw down the phone with the same disgust she exhibited in the same act three years later when I told her that her as-yet-unborn cousin was going to be a *boy*.

But all was not lost, at least for me. If I had no answer, I could at least share her question. Shortly after that phone call, I included her question in a sermon on the last Sunday of Epiphany, a Sunday in the Episcopal Church when we annually tilt our liturgical celebration in the direction of the transfiguration. In Matthew's Gospel, Jesus' face glistens like the sun. "How does God make skin?" I asked—Jesus' skin, our skin, my niece's skin. I had been reading Thomas Traherne's *Centuries* and, on reflection, I thought that he had answered Marcia's question far better than I ever could. "Boys and girls tumbling in the street," he writes, "were moving jewels."[7] So *that* is how God makes skin! God carefully selects creation's most precious materials and uses them to craft our skin and cover our bodies.

Such spiritual clear-sightedness was typical of Traherne, whose vision regularly penetrated the world's opaque features to unearth discretely hidden treasures:

> O what venerable and revered creatures did the aged seem! Immortal Cherubims! And young men glittering and sparkling Angels, and maids strange seraphic pieces of life and beauty! . . . Eternity was manifest in the Light of the Day, and something infinite behind everything appeared. . . . The city seemed to stand in Eden, or to be built in Heaven. The streets were mine, the temple was mine, the people were mine, their clothes and gold and silver were mine, as much as their sparkling eyes, fair skins, and ruddy faces. The skies were mine, and so were the sun and moon and stars, and all the World was mine; and I the only spectator and enjoyer of it.[8]

This is how Traherne saw *every* person, place, and thing—in its full glory, a divine light streaming through everyone and everything. But what did it mean to be able to see all creation unveiled and awash in divine light? How would it affect the seer? How would it affect the seen—that is, the neighbor, society, and the world? Traherne delights to exclaim, "What a holy and blessed life would people lead, what joys and treasures would they be to each other, in what a sphere of excellency would every person move, how sublime and glorious would their estate be, how full of peace and quiet would the world be, yea of joy and honor, order and beauty, did people

---

7. Traherne, *Centuries*, 110.
8. Ibid.

perceive this of themselves and had they this esteem for one another!"[9] If only we could perceive the world in its transfigured state, Traherne says, our lives would be transformed, blissful, and blessed. In my sermon, Marcia's question intersected with the transfiguration and Traherne's awakened observation, the personal, the mystical, and the gospel interacting, each of the three reference points bringing the others to life.

But my sermon had a fourth reference point. It was early 1991. I was preaching during the Gulf War, when American bombs rained death down on hapless teenaged soldiers and defenseless civilians. It was yet another minor, easily dwarfed episode in a series of twentieth-century holocausts: another quasidivine cause and another new world order, a kinder gentler Reich. This war featured carefully marketed smart bombs, a self-prostituting media, and strutting superstar generals. For me it was a horrific reawakening: for all of its blessings and ideals and good intentions, the nation in which I live doesn't know who or what it is unless it demonizes other nations and peoples, and kills and kills and kills. Every few years it needs to resurrect its self-image as the divinely appointed creator-destroyer, a Shiva-nation, a power that creates by destroying, that gives birth by bombing, a power whose bombs are the labor pains of a "new" world order that is as ancient as the first empire. As much as I have been outwardly and visibly blessed by this nation, I am unsure that it has blessed me inwardly and spiritually. However many people this nation has blessed, it has cursed many as well, and there will never be a body-and-soul count to determine whether it has cursed or blessed more.

This nation wanted to avoid, needed to avoid, had to avoid my niece's question. No one could ask my niece's question if they were going to repeat the mantra "war is good." As long as smart bombs and genius generals worked together to make war quick and winnable, as convenient as fast food, with a smattering, a garnish, of casualties to feed the nation's hunger for martyr-heroes, there would be no significant antiwar movement. Such movements require a gestation period, when the few who oppose war on moral grounds find allies among those who turn against it because it has become impractical, expensive, unwinnable, destructive of the wrong people (our people) or the wrong economy (our economy). These, the shifting restless majority, oppose war not because of morality, but because of a short attention span or a limited commitment or a miniscule sense of sacrifice. There is often a belated awakening, a grim reaper of a reminder, that war is never peace. This majority turns the political tide, if it turns, joins the moral minority, and becomes a movement.

9. Ibid., 101.

Introduction

To ask Marcia's question in the midst of a popular war might pop the premise that God is on our side. "How does God make skin?" I asked in my sermon. I let Traherne provide the answer. "How does God make my niece Marcia's olive Arab skin, and her mother's skin, and the olive Arab skin of the people *we* are killing?" Her olive Arab skin was the anti-skin du jour, the off-putting suspected skin color of our generation. People covered with this skin were assumed to be ignorant, inscrutable, irrational, irredeemable, fanatical, maniacal, murderous savages, as were their predecessors—Vietnamese, Chinese, Japanese, Native Americans, African Americans, and Huns—in our national collective imagination. These barbarians are ever outside the gate, with only one goal in mind: the destruction of everyone living inside and everything those people hold dear. We Americans stereotype reflexively. Whatever the anti-skin du jour, we have the same Pavlovian responses to condescend, dominate, domesticate, or exterminate. Whoever "they" are, all they understand is violence. Whoever they are, we know how to show them our capacity for violence since they understand nothing else.

Traherne's vision reminded me of Thomas Merton. Merton had been reading the seventeenth-century epiphanies of Traherne[10] shortly after he had a similar experience on the streets of Louisville in 1958. He reflected on his awakening in Traherne-like terms: "I was suddenly overwhelmed with the realization that I loved all those people, that they were mine and I theirs, that we could not be alien to one another even though we were total strangers." How, he mused, could he tell people "that they are all walking around shining like the sun?" Like Traherne, Merton wondered what life would be like, what the world would be like, "If only they could all see themselves as they really *are*. If only we could see each other that way all the time. There would be no more war, no more hatred, no more cruelty, no more greed." The only problem he could imagine "would be that we would fall down and worship each other."[11]

The mystical, the personal, the gospel, and a war had met together in my sermon. If the sermon had a fifth reference point it was an extenuation of my personal anguish that began the afternoon I took communion to a parishioner in her home, when I first heard voices on the radio announce that bombs were falling on Baghdad. Feeling heartsick and ill, I returned to the church, and made my way into the chapel to vomit my angry and grieving prayers into a sacred space. My anguish continued that first night as I made my way to the Federal Building to save or salve my soul or at least stand

---

10. Merton, *Search for Solitude*, 384.

11. Merton, *Conjectures*, 156–8, italics his; this account is his rewriting of the epiphany in Merton, *Dancing in the Water*, 298.

with others in visible opposition to the war, Thoreau's friction against the machine, smoothed sandpaper trying to stop shiny bombs. Our place on the sidewalk as traffic passed by, many drivers honking their horns in support, symbolized our place in the political order— the side of the road. We might as well have been in a ditch watching a military parade. We were completely unable or unwilling to do anything to stop the bombs from falling.

From the first day of the war, I thought again and again of Traherne and Merton. "If only we perceived" what Traherne perceived, "if only we could see" what Merton saw, what would we believe about the Gulf War? What would we do about it? What would we do about poverty in our communities and violence in our neighborhoods and abuse in our homes? If only we understood the precious materials, the sacred *stuff* God uses to create us, how delicately, intricately, and lovingly we and our friends and our allies and our enemies are made. If only we could see this as true of ourselves and of all others, no one could order one child of God to point a weapon at another child of God. No shots would be fired. No bombs would be dropped. No orders would be issued. How could someone kill another being whose face was shining like the sun? Or if someone failed to see, especially those with the most power and the least acute vision, if orders were issued, no one would obey. There would be no need to remind the ones who were supposed to respond with trained genuflection and ingrained obedience of the Nuremburg trials: no one would follow malign orders anyway. We would be possessed—and freed—by a spirit entirely antithetical to war, injustice, exploitation, domination, and greed. We would have no need to restore and burnish our national identity, like a tarnished bronze, by calling mass murder a patriotic triumph.

If only we could perceive this. If only we could see. If only . . . If . . .

A sermon is only a sermon, and at this point in my ministry I have preached well over a thousand. Not one of them has stopped a war, but for me the intersection that day was complete—the personal, the mystical, the gospel, the political. I said—together *they* said—all that needed to be said in a sermon about the transfiguration during a popular war. It was all I needed to say when I was heartsick because the wholesale destruction of human life is called "collateral damage," as if murder were an accidental tourist. It was all I could say when I was anguished because my country was at it *again* and I'd been reading Thomas Traherne, remembering Thomas Merton, and my four-year-old niece asked me a question I couldn't answer.

I didn't answer her question. But I preached a sermon. I don't know how many in the congregation appreciated it. But on that day, in my anguish, I said what this intersection inspired me to say. I thought it added up to a meaningful word, better than most sermons. Smarter, like the bombs I hated.

The political, social, and economic ramifications of Traherne's mystical vision have stayed with me. If only we could perceive what he perceived, if only we could see the world constantly transfigured, *we* would be transfigured. What in the world would be the same if we could see how God makes skin, how God makes hearts, how God makes children and the elderly and everyone in between, if we could see how and of what we are made? If we could share that mystical vision, what social transformation would follow?

It was the first spark.

DANGEROUS ORTHODOXY

"Have you ever heard of al-Hallaj?" It was my brother David. It was another long-distance phone call. Because David teaches Middle Eastern history, sometimes—with his knowledge of Islam—we have talked shop, discussed theologies, compared saints, and traced spiritual paths.

"No," I said, this time confessing my ignorance without equivocation. "Who was he?"

"He said, 'God and I are one.'"

"Sounds like Meister Eckhart," I said.[12] "What did they do to him?"

I knew nothing of al-Hallaj. I had admitted that. But I knew that when anyone says something like *that* publicly, there would be a *they* and that *they*, whoever *they* are, would not let someone say such a thing without, to understate the case, ramifications. *They* must have done something to him. Eckhart, after all, was tried for heresy and died before a verdict was reached. *Jesus,* after all, according to John, made the same claim and was convicted and crucified. My brother offered a few details of al-Hallaj's torture and death, a punishment even more hideously gruesome than Jesus' crucifixion.[13] Ah! So that was what *they* did to him.

Throughout history, mystics of many religious traditions, mystics like al-Hallaj, have been labeled, branded, judged, and condemned as dangerous—people whose religious experiences and subsequent explanations challenge fossilized patterns of thought and enshrined habits of institutions. Such people break rules. They don't even play by rules. They don't play ball. They don't even play. Or they play when they are supposed to be perpetually solemn. Their witness itself mocks the institutional game. Mystics don't bow

---

12. Massignon, *Passion of al-Hallaj*, lvi. Massignon makes the same comparison.
13. Ibid., 601–7.

often enough, or quite deeply enough, or sincerely enough, or at all to the reigning hierarchy or its managed symbols of authority.

During that conversation with David it struck me how consistently mystics have been perceived as a threat, like revolutionaries, reformers, prophets, heretics, and witches. Traherne says that those with sight and insight are blessed beyond anything they could imagine. But clearly there is a perpendicular reality. Those with sight and insight are diagnosed, dismissed, hated, cursed, excommunicated, persecuted, tortured, killed, and damned. And when they are not damned to hell, they are damned with faint praise or thorny scorn as deluded or misguided or eccentric or irrelevant. Theirs is the climactic blessing of the Beatitudes: blessed are *you* when you are hated for the sake of truth, love, life, Christ, or the realm of God (Matt 5:11). Traherne is right *and* al-Hallaj's cruel execution is but an extreme instance of a banal norm. Blessings come in violently contradictory forms. Mystics are dangerous to the "world-as-it-is,"[14] to its defenders and its apologists.

Dangerous mysticism. This was the second spark.

But it is a spark seldom recognized. At the dawn of the twentieth century, William James expounded a common rationalist-Protestant opinion that mystics disengage from history, politics, and social responsibility, from working for a better earth because they are preoccupied with the things of heaven.[15] Two decades later, Walter Rauschenbusch, from his activist perspective, wrote that a mystic "shuts out the world" in order to seek the selfish "tranquillity and forgetfulness of mystic absorption."[16] Two decades after that Reinhold Niebuhr, sitting on the same neo-orthodox judgment seat from which he would dismiss Rauschenbusch as naïvely optimistic (the deadliest in Niebuhr's catalogue of mortal sins), convicted mystics for engaging in the "practical absurdity of becoming obsessed with self."[17] To these thinkers mystics are dangerous only inasmuch as they distract people of faith away from personal ethics and social justice—for them, the *real* work of faith. To them, mysticism is a slow form of spiritual self-destruction masked in a fog of self-delusion—Marx's opiate, a spiritual placebo, a self-administered medication ingested at the suggestion of external powers-that-be.

But true mysticism does not result in a benignly pleasant numbing gaze into a cosmic navel. In spite of Plotinus's famous description of contemplation as "the flight of the alone to the Alone,"[18] few mystics find that

---

14. Stringfellow, *Dissenter*, 161.
15. James, *Religious Experience*, 7.
16. Rauschenbusch, *Social Gospel*, 103, 155.
17. Niebuhr, *Moral Man*, 55–56.
18. Ruffing, *Mysticism and Social Transformation*, 163.

Introduction

snappy slogan consistent with their experience. Birgitta of Sweden hears God tell her, "For I do not speak to you for your sake alone, but the sake of the salvation of others."[19] Likewise, Julian of Norwich realizes that her revelation is for the common good: "I was humbly moved in love towards my fellow Christians, that they might all see and know the same as I saw, for I wished it to be a comfort to them all, as it is to me, for this vision was shown for all people, and not for me alone."[20] Aquinas says that Paul tells the story of his rapture (2 Cor 12:2–4) as a "witness to beatitude."[21] Even the most intimate revelation has an evangelical dimension. A single epiphany, like a loaf of bread, can feed multitudes.

The accusation of mystical irrelevance butts up against empirical evidence. Are mystics truly so harmless? Are they really so safely and wastefully irrelevant, so self-secluding and impractical—voluntarily sitting in the world's corners whether or not they don the dunce's cap? If so, why do *they*, whoever *they* are in every religious institution, society, culture, and generation, feel compelled to seek mystics out or hunt them down—to anathematize them, to condemn them to death, or to besmirch them with ridicule? Why, when mystics are not stoned to death, are they stoned with scorn? Why, when they are not under arrest, are they so often placed in some kind of ecclesiastical quarantine or philosophical solitary confinement? Why do war-makers and war-worshipers need protection from them? How do mystics present such a threat to almost-almighty institutions? Why did al-Hallaj meet such a gruesome end? Why was Eckhart accused? If mysticism is truly countermagnetic to history and politics, why was Traherne the perfect inspiration for a sermon during the Gulf War?

Why was Merton, a monk, silenced by his order when he wrote about peace? Why were his books burned, if not as an official act of the institution, by the people the institution had thoroughly institutionalized? The institutional church, he said, wanted the monk to be "an eye that sees nothing except what is carefully selected for him to see. An ear that hears nothing except what it is advantageous for the managers for him to hear." Why close the eyes of those who see? Why make people deaf? Merton concludes, "We know what Christ said about such ears and eyes."[22] Why are political and ecclesiastical institutions and their leaders—like Ahab, like Herod—so easily threatened by voices crying in the wilderness, by monks and mystics so far from the corridors of power, their shouts heard—if at all—as barely

---

19. Birgitta, *Life and Selected Revelations*, 78.
20. Julian, *Showings*, 136.
21. McGinn, *Varieties of Vernacular Mysticism*, 180.
22. Merton, *Cold War Letters*, 133–34.

audible whispers in the wind? To ask why monks and mystics are dangerous is like asking, "Why is *peace* dangerous?" Why did the British government charge Muriel Lester with treason for speaking about peace during World War II? Why did the FBI target Dorothy Day, A. J. Muste, and Martin Luther King, Jr.? Why are *pacifists* threats? Whom and what do they threaten? It makes more immediate sense to silence activists who more directly and loudly question the social order, but why mystics?

And are these two groups, mystics and activists—people Evelyn Underhill calls spiritual and social pioneers[23]—so irreconcilably different from each other? Or is there a connection between the two? Why was Underhill, one of the foremost modern students of mysticism and one of the wisest spiritual teachers of the twentieth century, also a founding member of the Fellowship of Reconciliation, the first and oldest international movement committed to nonviolent action? Why did she remain committed to nonviolence to her dying day, even after the English pacifist movement imploded beneath the rubble of bombs and the panic that followed the fall of France? Why did Louis Massignon, a committed Roman Catholic and a scholar of Islam who felt that al-Hallaj had reached out to him through time,[24] inaugurate a ministry to Arabs living in France and form an organization called the Friends of Gandhi?[25] Did Oscar Romero's academic background in ascetical theology[26] or his experience of the oneness of creation[27] cultivate in him the values and conviction he needed to carry out his ministry and face his martyrdom? Why is it that those who *study and practice* mysticism find themselves drawn toward activism? Didn't Catherine of Siena engage in the politics of her age *because* she was a mystic? What, then, is the connection, if any, between mystical vision and social transformation? Is it intrinsic or accidental, occasional or eternal?

Certainly not all activists are closet mystics nor are all mystics closet activists, but some activists with the greatest spiritual depth—Desmond Tutu, Gandhi, Lester, Muste, Day—had profound insights into the issues of their time because of their faith. They helped others to see. They acted tirelessly to stop war and do justice and inspired many to do the same in ordinary ways in their ordinary lives. Their witness scarcely fits the simplistic

---

23. Underhill, *Modern Guide,* 16, 208.
24. Massignon, *Passion of al-Hallaj,* xix.
25. Ibid., xxxiv–xxxv; Merton, *Witness to Freedom,* 280.
26. Brockman, *Word Remains,* 34.
27. Ibid., 169.

and dismissive James-Rauschenbusch-Niebuhr mystic profiling, a common enough Protestant caricature of mysticism.[28]

If mysticism and activism do not stand in diametrically opposed corners of the community of faith, or even if they do, what do they have in common? Al-Hallaj, like Eckhart and Merton, like Tutu, King, Romero, and Gandhi, like Jesus, and so many, many others, *was* dangerous. *They*—the people in power, the Roman Empire and first-century Palestinian Jewish religious authorities and all of their spiritual descendants—*know* that both mystics and activists are dangerous, and they know what they have to do to them. Even if mystics and activists had nothing else in common, they would have this mark, they would bear this stigma. They cannot be controlled. They will not be deafened or blinded or silenced. What they say and do will directly challenge the social and religious status quo.

Some argue that mysticism and activism are symbiotic, that social activism needs a contemplative dimension and that mysticism is incomplete without prophetic social engagement. Activism can seem like the hands and feet of faith and mysticism its heart. Charles Péguy's quotable aphorism about the relationship of spirituality to activism makes it sound simple: "Everything begins in mysticism and ends in politics."[29] Péguy makes it sound simple, but any serious dialogue between mystics and activists reveals anything but an uncomplicated formula. Rather, it is a complex cross-pollination and indefinable interaction that can create what Gandhi called satyagraha, "truth force," "love-force," or "soul-force."[30] At the dawn of the nuclear age, A. J. Muste declared provocatively that God had given birth to a force as creatively powerful in faith-based nonviolence as the destructiveness of nuclear weapons.[31] How we connect God and the spirit with this irresistible revolutionary force—that is the question.

Although I agree that contemplation is truncated without action and action ungrounded without contemplation, that is not my primary argument. My argument is, in a sense, an extension of Kenneth Leech's consistent witness: there is an intrinsic connection between prayer and social action because Christian spirituality is always incarnational. The incarnation, he says, "is the basis both of Christian mysticism and of Christian social theology."[32] Like Leech, I argue that a truly mystical vision *always* leads

---

28. McGinn, *Foundations of Mysticism*, 268–70.

29. Péguy, "Politics and Mysticism," 109. However, assumptions about the meaning of this sentence don't neatly fit the caricature of his complex argument.

30. Gandhi, *Non-violent Resistance*, 3, 6. "Truth" was Gandhi's preferred name for God.

31. Muste, "Look Around," 5.

32. Leech, *Social God*, 26.

to social transformation because a clear view of God and the world *always* becomes a burr to an anguished passion for a new earth. But my argument is also that, for people of faith, social transformation is always undergirded, encompassed, and made *more* urgent by transcendence. But I begin with an empirical observation—mystics and activists are deemed threatening because they *are* dangerous to every empire, every religious, political, and economic system, and every status quo of any kind, because no status quo is ever the realm of God.[33] Their experiences of God and their faith in God make them all dangerous.

Leech, in fact, contends that the mystic can be more foundationally dangerous than the activist: "The contemplative who can stand back from a situation and see it for what it is is more threatening to an unjust social system than the frenzied activist who is so involved in the situation that they cannot see clearly at all."[34] There is no way to test this assertion, yet partly because of this intriguing claim, I use Merton, first among equals in a cloud of witnesses, as a human thread throughout this book. Merton says that contemplatives do not seek "fiery visions of the cherubim carrying God on their imagined chariot," but people who "risk their minds in the desert beyond language and beyond ideas where God is encountered in the nakedness of pure trust."[35] Thus, Jean Leclerq calls Merton a "prophet," a "person of vision—not of visions."[36] It is said that he saw the world through "rinsed eyes."[37] In one of Merton's most illuminating personal essays, this finished product of English boarding schools, Cambridge, and Columbia uses a term from the Old West—"outlaw"—to describe the contemplative.[38] Using the lingo of spy movies and super-patriots, he brands the solitary a "traitor."[39] He labels his monastic vocation a protest,[40] an existential, cultural, and political critique of society's delicious, seductive, addictive, and poisonous illusions.

---

33. See below for my preference for "realm of God" and "revolution of God" in place of "kingdom of God."

34. Leech, *True Prayer*, 85.

35. Merton, *Monastic Journey*, 222–23.

36. Leclerq, "Merton and History," 231. This distinction is not entirely true, as will be seen below.

37. de Waal, *Celtic Way*, 96, 221.

38. Merton, *Raids on the Unspeakable*, 14.

39. Ibid., 22.

40. Merton, *Hidden Ground*, 85–86, and *Nonviolent Alternative*, 260: his meditation at a retreat he hosted was entitled "Monastic Protest; The Voice in the Desert" or "Voice in the Wilderness."

> By my monastic life and vows I am saying NO to all the concentration camps, the aerial bombardments, the staged political trials, the judicial murders, the racial injustices, the economic tyrannies, and the whole socio-economic apparatus which seems geared for nothing but global destruction in spite of all its fair words in favor of peace. I make monastic silence a protest against the lies of politicians, propagandists and agitators, and when I speak it is to deny that my faith and my Church can ever seriously be aligned with these forces of injustice and destruction.[41]

In the sorting of wheat from chaff that characterizes much of Merton's monastic life, he also affirms the world's goodness: "If I say NO to all these secular forces," he also says "YES to all that is good in the world and in people. I say YES to all that is beautiful in nature. . . . I say YES to all the men and women who are my brothers and sisters in the world. . . . It is because I want to be more to them than a friend that I become, to all of them, a stranger."[42]

If mystics and activists are dangerous, it is—in part—because they share in the controversial work and the inherently dangerous nature of Jesus. Writing in opposition to some traditional apologetics that insist not only on Jesus' sinlessness, but also his legal innocence, William Stringfellow—an attorney as well as a theologian—argues that Jesus was *guilty as charged*.[43] Jesus was guilty of treason, and that was enough for the Romans. He was guilty of heresy,[44] and that was enough for the Sanhedrin. Anyone who does not find Christian orthodoxy dangerous has not paid sufficient attention to, of all people, *Jesus*. Anyone who follows Jesus' spiritual direction, teaching, and command to "seek first the kingdom"—God's realm—will have, at least, discordant or disloyal thoughts toward ecclesiastical and national institutions because all other fealties will come second or third, or be found absolutely unworthy of a pinch of incense or pledge of allegiance. Anyone who is faithful to the person of Jesus of Nazareth will, at the least, be accused of proactive noncooperation with religious structures and social order. According to Stringfellow's logic, Dostoevsky's Grand Inquisitor has it right. Jesus was—and is—too dangerous to the institutional church and the regime du jour to be allowed to freely roam the streets preaching, teaching,

---

41. Merton, *Introductions*, 45–46.

42. Ibid., 46.

43. Stringfellow and Towne, *Suspect Tenderness*, 61; Stringfellow makes this observation in a sermon defending friend, fellow agitator, and accused felon Daniel Berrigan.

44. Noel, *Jesus the Heretic*, 25; Jesus "was condemned for heresy; but in him the world has found the supreme note of orthodoxy" (ibid.).

and healing.⁴⁵ Institutions do not allow such unpredictability and disorder to disturb *their* peace. It doesn't matter if the Grand Inquisitor is Pontius Pilate, Torquemada, or Joe McCarthy. In an observation that in our time would have to be tempered by memories of Joseph Stalin, Mao Zedong, and Pol Pot, Walter Rauschenbusch says, "it takes religion to put a steel edge on social intolerance."⁴⁶ Such anarchy—as those in power (and those who lust for it) perceive the realm of God—invites imprisonment. Such perceived anarchy led religious leaders to scold Martin Luther King, Jr. as he sat in the Birmingham jail.⁴⁷ The Pax Romana and the Pax Americana and all forms of "peace" that do not surpass understanding cannot, do not, and will not peacefully coexist with Pax Christi.

In his analysis of South African politics in 1963, British Ambassador Sir John Maud proved prescient, even prophetic. At a time when the apartheid regime—like its Western allies that laced their civilly muted criticisms of institutionalized racism alongside weightier global strategic considerations—continually raised the specter of Communism, Maud said Christianity was a far more dangerous threat to apartheid than Communism would ever be.⁴⁸ At the same moment in history, in the United States, segregationists and apologists for that peculiar institution felt threatened by a conspiracy that they identified as Communist. In reality, the civil rights movement was a loose, disorganized, conflicted movement, but the outside and grassroots agitators who threatened the advocates of inequality, their values, and their way of life were Christians and Jews and their allies—people of faith, conviction, and *vision*. There were indeed a handful of Communists in a mix of hundreds of thousands, but the primary threat to Southern culture and American politics arose from people with dreams, people seeking a semblance of God's realm, people with faith, people who could see.

The anti-apartheid and civil rights movements were not the products of mass mystical visions, although journalist Pat Watters argues that the evening rallies in African American churches were spiritually transforming—if only white Americans could see, he said, even on television, the "mystical, ecstatic" quality of those gatherings, they would join the movement they opposed.⁴⁹ Even among mystics, visions and ecstatic experiences are controversial—necessary to some and counterproductive to others. Within

---

45. Dostoevsky, *Brothers Karamazov*, 297–319.
46. Rauschenbusch, *Social Gospel*, 249.
47. See ch. 10 below, "The Peace that is No Peace."
48. Sampson, *Mandela*, 186.
49. Watters, *Down to Now*, 226, 191.

the desert tradition, there is an "anti-mystical strain."[50] So Abba Poemen warns that if you have visions or hear voices, do not tell your neighbor, for a delusion is in progress.[51] There are as many visionless mystics—Eckhart, John of the Cross, the author of *The Cloud of Unknowing*—as there are those who have visions. Rudolph Otto describes such writers as practitioners of "teaching mysticism," mystics whose primary purpose is to clarify mystical truths rather than seek mystical experience.[52] Eckhart, as much as any modern Protestant scholar, activist, or social critic, dismisses those who lose themselves in a single-minded pursuit of contemplative bliss. They are mistaken, he says, to believe they are closer to God "when sunk in rapture" or in "extravagant emotion" than when they sit each day "by hearth and in the stable."[53]

Some mystics have *visions*; others do not; but—to use Leclerq's distinction—all of them have *vision*. This is not to airbrush the content of mystical visions. On the contrary, many ecstatic visions have profound ramifications for daily life in the real world. For some it *is* a vision or a series of visions, a singular revelation or a string of epiphanies, that enable them to see. For others it is a contemplative awareness cultivated in silence. Still others distill their political acumen from a low-key, even-keel relationship with God that deepens wisdom, perspective, insight, awareness, or love. By *mystical vision*, then, I do not mean—or rule out—the content of specific visions of a few mystics. Rather, mystical vision is a by-product of mystical insight, whether or not it is gained in visions. Vision*s* can have meaning in and of themselves, but ultimately they give *vision*. Mysticism is a *way*, several ways actually, of seeing the world in relationship to God, ways that often share common intuitions with some of the most important peacemakers and social reformers of the modern era. Mystics, like activists, are dangerous because they have a vision of God, the world, and human nature that will not fit the straitjacket of hierarchical structures or preestablished theological fabrications.

Mysticism and activism are bound together partly because both are *dangerous*.[54] They are also bound together because both are completely *orthodox*. There is absolutely nothing esoteric about either one. They may bear an especially distinctive flavor of the transcendent and/or the incarnational, but there ought to be nothing astounding about those foundations in Chris-

---

50. Vivian, *Becoming Fire*, 19.
51. Ward, *Sayings of the Desert*, 187.
52. Otto, *Mysticism*, 49.
53. Ibid., 92.
54. See Leech, *Subversive Orthodoxy*. I prefer the word "dangerous" because it is perceived more viscerally.

tian theology. Neither requires an asterisk as if to be a Christian mystic* or a Christian activist* is any different from being an ordinary Christian. There is nothing esoteric in the beliefs of mystics and activists, but there might well be something more personal and concrete, or at least undeniable, like the ingredients in human skin. They are bound together because true orthodoxy is always transcendent and therefore dangerous and because it presents an alternative possibility for human life and civil society. True orthodoxy is always incarnational and therefore subversive because, like the vocation of the prophet Jeremiah, it cannot help but pluck up and pull down as well as build up and plant (Jer 1:10). As it was for Jeremiah, there is always a mystical dimension that gives the prophet a particular angle on historical, political, economic, and social realities. The experience of the transcendent always leads to a new way of seeing life and living in history. To be truly orthodox is not to renew one's subscription to a set of beliefs or to sign a loyalty oath or to repeat a creed *ad nauseam*. Orthodoxy is fealty to a person—Jesus, guilty-of-treason, guilty-of-heresy Jesus. The static, brittle, often fossilized beliefs of a dictatorship, a democracy, or an ecclesiastical system are, in truth, paralyzed by their stasis and unable to follow the historical, canonical, risen, and living Jesus. Orthodoxy means literally to blaze with the right glory.[55] It is that glory that the Grand Inquisitor—every grand inquisitor—senses, fears, and condemns as a nihilistic tornado.

Yet nihilism is not truly the issue. Underhill denies that mystics are "spiritual anarchists."[56] Rather, she says, they are completely grounded in the communion of saints and the community of faith. All true mystics are rooted and nurtured in a spiritual tradition and a living religious community. Their experiences reinforce, refresh, reform, and sometimes resurrect orthodoxy. As a modern Sufi says, "Sufism without Islam is like a candle burning in the open without a lantern."[57] Without the glass to protect the flame, the candle is extinguished. Without the faith community's experience, the individual's experience—no matter how powerful—will dissipate or lose direction.[58]

Rather than being untethered, mysticism is profoundly rooted. Vladimir Lossky discerns a "deep and indissoluble bond between theology and mysticism, between doctrinal tradition and spirituality" with "doctrine and experience mutually conditioning each other."[59] Underhill insists that

---

55. McNamara, *Earthy Mysticism*, 88.
56. Underhill, *Mysticism*, 95–96.
57. Fadiman and Frager, *Essential Sufism*, 4.
58. Underhill, *Modern Guide*, 123.
59. Lossky, *Mystical Theology*, 236.

all Christian mystics are fed with the "common food of the great Christian family"[60] and that all mystical experiences have to be "tested and corrected by the general good sense" of the faith community.[61] As long as it is "good sense," it is necessary. But some mystics like Teresa of Ávila cautiously shape, quibble, and qualify their writings knowing that inquisitors—grand and small—are always made anxious by too enlivening and lively an experience of God.[62] John of the Cross, who felt firsthand the scars of other people's theological anxieties, exegeted his own mystical poems into conventional theological terms perhaps as much to suit doctrinal norms as to elucidate the experiences he describes in his poetry.[63]

What is true of mystics is also true of activists. Dorothy Day was a *true* theological conservative (unlike those wolves in sheep's clothing who identify themselves as conservatives today), and her theological conservatism, her knowledge of and devotion to Scripture and tradition, spurred her social radicalism. Ultimately, all Christian mystics and activists have a spiritual umbilical cord that connects them to the spirit, wisdom, and experience of Jesus of Nazareth. That is what worries and sometimes terrifies the powers that be.

The bond between mysticism and theology cannot be dissolved. In the Orthodox tradition, a theologian is *not* a theologian unless he or she is also a mystic. As Lossky writes, "All truly dogmatic work has a basis in mystical experience. . . . If a purely 'mystical' author like St. Symeon was named 'the New Theologian,' this indicates that mysticism is considered to be theology *par excellence.*"[64] Symeon himself asks, how do you dare to speculate about God, much less speak of God unless you experience God?

> But if you have not discerned that the eye
> of your mind has been opened, and that it has seen the light,
> if you have not perceived the sweetness of the divinity,
> if you have not been enlightened by the divine Spirit,
> if you have not shed tears without feeling any pain,
> if you have not contemplated that your soul has been cleansed,
> if you have not known that your heart has been purified,
> that it has shone with its luminous reflections,
> if you have not found the Christ within yourself, contrary to all expectations,

---

60. Underhill, *Mystics of the Church*, 18.
61. Ibid., 16.
62. Teresa, *Interior Castle*, 24.
63. See Kieran Kavanaugh's comments in John of the Cross, *Collected Works*, 402.
64. Lossky, *Mystical Theology*, 9; see also 7–11 and Lossky, *Image and Likeness*, 50.

if you have not been struck with stupor on seeing the divine beauty,
and have not forgotten human nature
on seeing yourself completely transformed,
how do you not tremble, tell me, to speak of God?[65]

Evagrius put it more succinctly: "If you are a theologian you truly pray. If you truly pray you are a theologian."[66] Mysticism in the Orthodox tradition, then, is *experienced orthodoxy*, what Lossky calls "theology *par excellence*,"[67] a direct encounter with God.[68] The mystic experiences God immediately in ways that make even the most florid tongue stammer.

If the Orthodox tradition's claim is true, it is also fair to ask, can you truly be a theologian unless you are actively engaged in social transformation? Can one walk humbly with God without doing justice (Mic 6:8)? Can one speak of God, and of loving God, without loving one's neighbor (Lev 19:18, Deut 6:5, Matt 22:37)? The First Epistle of John declares the two loves as inseparable as conjoined twins (1 John 4:20). Teresa of Ávila says that the surest sign that we love God is that we love our neighbor; it is hard to know if we love God, she says—what would be the visible criteria—but "we can know quite well if we are loving our neighbor."[69] Building on the saying in 1 John, a spiritual director for the *Catholic Worker* declared that we love God only as much as the people we love the least.[70] There is nothing odd, exotic, or theologically extraordinary about loving God and neighbor. Those who claim to love God without loving their neighbor are liars. Theology must be both *doxa* and praxis.

Liberation theologians argue that all theologians must make a "commitment to liberation,"[71] take "effective participation" in "transforming the conditions of human life," or drop their claim of being theologians.[72] They insist that it is impossible to know God without doing justice. Segundo Galilea asserts that "authentic Christian contemplation" transforms

---

65. Symeon, *Hymns*, 98–99.

66. McGinn, *Foundations of Mysticism*, 150.

67. Lossky, *Mystical Theology*, 9.

68. "Mysticism, according to its historical and psychological definitions, is the direct intuition or experience of God; and a mystic is a person who has, to a greater or lesser degree, such a direct experience" (Underhill, *Mystics of the Church*, 9).

69. Teresa, *Interior Castle*, 115.

70. Day, *By Little*, 301.

71. Segundo, *Liberation of Theology*, 84.

72. Gutierrez, *Theology of Liberation*, 269; Geffré and Gutierrez, *Mystical and Political*, 11, 57.

Introduction

contemplatives into prophets and "militants into mystics."[73] Rauschenbusch questions the intellectual integrity of theologians who have no interest in "redeeming humanity from the reign of tyranny and fear," who fail to combat "the Kingdom of Evil," who feel no compunction at leaving the "naked unclothed, the hungry unfed, and the prisoners uncomforted."[74] Such a theologian, he implies, is a fraud. Further, he questions the veracity of a theologian's God who has no interest in justice. Such a deity, he says, is a fake and an idol.[75] Centuries earlier, Eckhart came to the same conclusion and perhaps went a step further: if *God* did not care for justice, Eckhart would not care a "bean" for such a God.[76]

Such fervent statements seem out of synch with the elastic spirit of our times, when a growing number of North Americans walk paths self-professed to be "spiritual but not religious." While not advocating the efficacy of organized religion (or judging whether institutional religion is truly organized!), I wonder if they are in effect attempting to live a hermit's life without benefit of even a disembodied community; and if they are practicing a gated-community spirituality in an ocean of human suffering. As Abba Longinus says, "If you have not first of all lived rightly with others, you will not be able to live rightly in solitude."[77] Still, one can conceivably claim to be spiritual but not religious. But there is almost universal agreement across religious boundaries that there is no such thing as spiritual but not ethical. Students of ascetical theology like Underhill, Leech, and Romero have found such a separation impossible; even if doable, it would lead to a maimed spirit and a crippled life.

If mysticism, then, is *experienced orthodoxy*, activism is *enacted orthodoxy*, as deep, direct, and profound an experience of God as that of the mystic yet known primarily through social movements, neighbors, allies, and enemies. Like mystics, Christian activists are often marginalized in their religious communities, humored, tolerated, discounted as fanatics within the fold; yet they—like mystics—*directly experience*, see, and know what others ought to know by faith. They blaze with the right glory; they are truly orthodox.

If Christian mystics and social activists are right that theologians ought to be those who experience God and seek the realm of God, what would happen if we took their *experiences* of God and the world as the

---

73. Galilea, "Liberation as Encounter," 28.
74. Rauschenbusch, *Social Gospel*, 174.
75. Ibid., 174, 178.
76. Eckhart, *Sermons & Treatises II*, 132.
77. Ward, *Sayings of the Desert*, 122.

primary data in doing theology? One thing is sure: a conversation between mystics and activists does not lead to a distinct, discreet, decent, orderly, or coherent systematic theology. There is, in reality, no such neat summation of sacred and secular mysteries. Experiences of light and darkness, cross and transfiguration, seen and unseen—whether mystical or political—cannot be smoothly adjusted, by design or by chance, until each piece finds its place and fits satisfactorily together like a Rubik's Cube. Theology, at its best, is always intuitive, impressionistic, amorphous, and applicable to daily life in the real world. In some ways, discerning a mystical-political theology is like writing a biblical theology. There simply isn't *one* biblical theology. There are many. They hold some things in common; they hold others in tension; they find themselves in creative conflict. Theological pluralism, after all, begins in Scripture, and finds continuing, living, Spirit-breathing expression in pluralistic political spiritualities and mystical-political theologies.

What might we gain from this cacophonous dialogue? First, it is worthwhile to discover what mystics and activists might say to each other. But second, theological insights will spin off of the interaction of mysticism and activism like sparks from a burning wheel. They will form new insights and sharpen theological accents. Sometimes the voices of mystics and activists will harmonize; sometimes they will be contrapuntal, and just as often dissonant. Sometimes they will complement and complete each other. Sometimes they will refute each other. Sometimes they will bring light to the other. Yet they must always be in relationship. Mysticism, like activism, is a loose-leaf canon—a Talmud—that extends and expands on the hardbound canon of Scripture; it is an informal, living, lived, and growing orthodoxy. Simply put, mystical vision and social transformation—loving God and neighbor—have always been the two primary starting points for doing theology. And the *doing* of theology means less pondering and writing it than living, praying, and embodying it.

Underhill approves of a saying: all mystics are from the same country and they all speak the same language.[78] If I am making an argument about the connection between traditional mystics and historical activists, it is this: they are *both* from the same country—known in John's Gospel as "the world." They hunger and thirst for another country—the realm of God—to which they are on pilgrimage. They speak the same experiential language that runs the gamut from wilderness to mountaintop and from trauma to ecstasy. Even after all the contradictions they embody are laid bare, they share a vision of God and a passion for creation. Together they reveal the ramifications of mystical ethics and the dimensions of activist spirituality.

---

78. Underhill, *Mysticism*, 80.

They have experienced and enacted a mystical-political, ascetical-social, transcendent-incarnational orthodoxy (God's glory). And those spiritual and political experiences make them dangerous.

FALSE STEPS ON TRUE PATHS

Even in a life of amazing grace, there are many dangers, toils, and snares. Mysticism and activism, as two primal gifts of grace, are as susceptible to missteps and misdirection as any part of the human journey. False mystics and pseudoactivists are more preoccupied with their internal psychospiritual issues than with Gandhi's experiment with truth. As such, they are perfectly capable of spewing their internal conflicts projectile-like onto spiritual, societal, and cosmic landscapes. These may be the people James, Rauschenbusch, and Niebuhr experienced when they tarred all mystics with that brush. Even an advocate for mysticism like Underhill admits that some mystics can be guilty of "excessive or distorted" opinions and actions.[79] Some, she says, have in their self-serving and self-centered delusions "put barbed wire round the edges" of their souls.[80] Eckhart admonishes the spiritually self-absorbed for seeking "great experiences" out of "self-will."[81] John of the Cross cautions against spiritual gluttony,[82] a greed that treats the Creator as coinage, an objectivizing lust that, like anonymous sex, seeks fleeting ecstasy instead of sustaining relationship. This "panhedonism"[83] is merely a form of spiritual onanism. Some mystics are also drawn to pantheism (the overidentification of God with creation) and autotheism (the overidentification of *oneself* with God).[84] Autotheism is al-Hallaj's ecstatic statement *without* a simultaneous self-differentiation that mystics go to great lengths to delineate—we can be at one with God in spirit, life, and love, but we never perfectly share God's nature; we remain "distinct."[85] Psychologically, pseudomysticism's great temptation is narcissism—an all-encompassing self-absorption that uses its claim of single-minded love of God to avoid life's grittiness and God's demands.[86]

79. Ibid., 16.
80. Underhill, *Modern Guide*, 109.
81. Otto, *Mysticism*, 93.
82. John of the Cross, *Collected Works*, 307–9.
83. Kirk, *Vision of God*, 49–50, 90, 120, 180–82, 192.
84. See Richard Woods's comment in the introduction of Ruusbroec, *Spiritual Espousals*, 27.
85. Ibid., 241.
86. "Narcissism and self-centeredness are dangers inherent in nearly any form of

Spiritually, false activists often yield to a self-righteousness that numbs self-awareness and mutes self-criticism. The activist's spiritual gluttony—a hidden hunger for self-importance or a lust for results that validate the work (and ego) of the activist—distorts both the means and ends of reforms and revolutions.[87] Activists are also susceptible to simplistic, mathematically precise moral formulas. This leads to the Zealot's dualism that obsessively separates people based on ideology or nation, the Pharisee's dualism that compulsively divides righteous from sinners, and the Essene's tidy dualism that sees oh so clearly where darkness ends and light begins. None of these is so very different from the dualism of the disciples who believe they can, with but a cursory glance, sort sheep from goats. Such dualisms blur the complex interaction of cosmic, systemic, and personal evils, and project devilry onto particular persons, institutions, ideologies, and nations.

Another activist temptation is the collective narcissism that attaches itself to something even as worthy as La Raza, La Causa, liberation of the oppressed, or solidarity with the poor, and, in the eyes of the activist, inflates proximate goals into ultimate concerns. When this happens, activists so focus on a new earth that they lose sight of the new heaven (Isa 65:17–25) as if there can be incarnation without transcendence, a moment without eternity, a *here* without a *there*, a *now* without a *then*. Secular movements may indeed launch creative social experiments but there cannot be a realm of God without God. Sometimes, because of the superhuman effort, energy, and single-mindedness required for reform or revolution, activists succumb to Pelagianism. *We* shall overcome, instead of whatever happens to us in our particular struggle today, whether it succeeds or fails, and whether we feel fulfilled or defeated, God shall overcome.[88] Activists that begin as Pelagians invariably end as Sisyphus, pushing another cause up another hill only to see it roll down and feel its dead weight crushing hope.

Particular prescriptions can assist activists if and when they are overcome by a hyperventilating zeal. César Chávez says that farmworkers, even labor organizers, if given the power of a land-owning grower would quickly act like the growers they oppose.[89] In one nutshell, he recognizes the doggedness of sin, the systemic nature of oppression, and the temptation of self-righteousness. Meditating on the parable of the Pharisee and the Tax

---

spiritual practice. If these dangers are to be minimized, *it is vital that one locate oneself within the context of one's history and one's community*" (May, *Pilgrimage Home*, 2, italics his).

87. Merton, *Hidden Ground*, 294–96, 594. Merton consistently counsels against the need for results.

88. Merton, *Nonviolent Alternative*, 75.

89. Dalton, *Moral Vision*, 81.

Collector, A. J. Muste warns that pacifists should not deem themselves better in God's eyes than fascists or Nazis;[90] a humble member of the military, he says, is closer to God than a self-righteous pacifist.[91] Underhill goes further when she calls an embittered pacifist a "poisoned chalice."[92] In his letters to activists, Merton consistently warns against projecting evil onto others and elevating principles—like a spiritualized form of profits—over people.[93] As if to underline Merton's warnings, John Cassian writes that it is easier to perform an *exorcism* on someone else than to root sin out of oneself.[94]

King's activist midrash on First Corinthians 13 makes a wise mantra for anyone seeking social transformation, and it became—posthumously—a poignant testimony to King's life:

> You may give your goods to feed the poor, you may bestow great gifts to charity, and you may tower high in philanthropy, but if you have not love, your charity means nothing. You may give your body to be burned, and die the death of a martyr, and your spilled blood may be a symbol of honor for generations yet unborn, and thousands may praise you as one of history's supreme heroes; but even so, if you have not love, your blood is spilled in vain.[95]

Underhill redirects King's idea toward the mystic when she cautions: "vision without love-impelled action should always be held suspect."[96] Likewise Ruusbroec warns: "Those who wish only to turn inward in contemplation and so leave their neighbor in need do not live a recollected and contemplative life but are deceived to the core of their being. Above all things," he says, "beware of such persons."[97] Thomas Kelly addresses both groups. He says that the mystical pilgrimage toward God must lead back into "the furrows of the world's suffering"[98] or fulfill the rationalist-Protestant stereotype. True mysticism, he says, "opens our eyes to the old world and shows it to us in

---

90. Muste, "Pacifist Way," 199.
91. Muste, *Non-violence*, 126.
92. Underhill, *Modern Guide*, 200.
93. Merton, *Disputed Questions*, 115, *Faith and Violence*, 163, *Nonviolent Alternative*, 211.
94. Cassian, *Conferences*, 180.
95. King, *Strength to Love*, 145.
96. Underhill, *Modern Guide*, 126.
97. Ruusbroec, *Spiritual Espousals*, 227. He was probably referring to the Free Spirit movement, *Spiritual Espousals*, 9.
98. Kelly, *Eternal Promise*, 56.

a new way."[99] Likewise, activists must ground their action in God: "Facts remain facts, when brought into the Presence," but "their significance is wholly realigned."[100]

Even if not tainted by autotheistic or Pelagian narcissism, the temptation to grandiosity can prove irresistible as mystics and activists alike create imaginary grids of mythic importance to rate and rank religious paths. Richard Rolle's claim that the contemplative life is "superior" to the active life is precisely the kind of arrogance that can infect both mysticism and activism.[101] A similar desert saying calls the person who practices the commandments good but prefers the contemplative "who has risen from active works to the spiritual sphere and has left it to others to be anxious about earthly things."[102] Yet in the Hegelian nature of tradition the desert offers its own multiple antitheses with stories of ordinary saints living in cities—the ancient equivalent of finding ascetics in corporate America, zaddikim at Exxon Mobil, holy men and holy women at Halliburton—who are as righteous as the *abbas*. Abba Daniel meets Eulogius the stonecutter who, at the end of each day, takes foreigners home, feeds them, and even gives leftovers to the dogs.[103] Antony discovers that a doctor in the city gives whatever he has beyond his needs to the poor, and "every day he sang the Sanctus with the angels."[104] Activists embroiled in the city's agony and injustices often turn the same dismissive edge toward the contemplative. In the 1960s many well-meaning civil rights and antiwar activists accused Merton of wasting his gifts in the monastery, a way of life they piously deemed inferior, irrelevant, or worthless.[105] Such spiritual one-upmanship is always an inkling of immaturity. Even within their preferred spheres, some have been foolish enough to rate and rank certain forms of social and spiritual transformation—advocacy over charity, charity over advocacy, contemplation over intercession, intercession over contemplation—more highly than others instead of seeing every form of action and prayer as part of a holistic life.

One of the roots of these unnecessary, unfortunate, distracting, and disturbing arguments lies in the partition of doing justice from walking humbly with God. In 1968, mutual friends tried to arrange a meeting

---

99. Ibid., 37.
100. Kelly, *Testament of Devotion*, 36.
101. Rolle, *Fire of Love*, 55.
102. Vivian, *Becoming Fire*, 276.
103. Vivian, *Witness to Holiness*, 77–82.
104. Ward, *Sayings of the Desert*, 6.
105. Griffin, "Controversial Merton," 83; Merton, *Hidden Ground*, 502.

between Merton and King, but King felt compelled to go to Memphis.[106] The segregation of mysticism from activism goes deep into Hebrew Scripture to what Walter Brueggemann describes as "trajectories" in the Old Testament—one seeking holiness to heal existential disorder, the other justice to alleviate the suffering of the dispossessed:[107] one trajectory inspired the priestly tradition; the other gave birth to the Law. All too often, these opposing camps in a theological tug-of-war become walleyed, concentrating only on a single primary truth, unable to take in the breadth and fullness of the one, holy, and living God. The Greek roots of this spiritual segregation are found in Aristotle's dissection of *theoria* from praxis; like those who favor Mary over Martha, Aristotle deems contemplation superior. Through it, he believes, we become like the gods[108] as if we are not equally sanctified by loving our neighbor. Such comparisons and competitions always reek of self-exaltation in a faith tradition founded on Jesus' repeated mantra: humility, humility, humility. They stink of Gnosticism, as if someone (mystic or activist or scholar or philosopher) has attained an esoteric knowledge (the mind's holy grail) of a privileged elite.

To a degree, we can understand the source of these divisions. Both experiences of God—spiritual and social—have a spellbinding power and their intoxicating sway stirs an enthusiastic advocacy for their beauty and significance. The idea of spiritual inebriation is normative across religious traditions;[109] borrowing from the Song of Songs (5:1), Catherine of Siena says she is drunk in her love for God and that God is equally drunk in divine love for us.[110] Activists are equally intoxicated by their political hopes and achievements. In the Pentecost story, of course, observers accuse the disciples of being drunk on cheap wine (Acts 2:13). To an outsider, the two kinds of intoxication are indistinguishable. Of course, in the mystical tradition, this intoxication is true sobriety. Yet this inebriation does not equate with self-anointing, self-preoccupation, or autotheism: Symeon, describing himself as aflame like the burning bush, adds humbly that he is nothing but "straw."[111] True mysticism never glorifies the mystic. True activism never glorifies the activist. The only glory is God's.

---

106. Mott, *Seven Mountains,* 490, 511, 519–20; Merton, *Hidden Ground,* 451.

107. Brueggemann, *Theology,* 190–96.

108. Ruffing, *Mysticism and Social Transformation,* 163.

109. Underhill, *Mysticism,* 287; Ruusbroec, *Spiritual Espousals,* 82; Rumi, *Poet and Mystic,* 52–53.

110. Catherine, *Dialogue,* 202.

111. Lossky, *Mystical Theology,* 18.

The fallacies and frailties of self-absorbed mystics and self-avoiding activists are in many ways interchangeable. Their temptations are cut from the same theological, psychological, and spiritual cloth. Both seek escape—one from the world, the other from the self. Both cling to a dualistic separation of the spiritual from the material and relish an anti-incarnationalism that strips the integrity from their yearnings for God and the realm. Yet for each of these temptations there is a prescription or a preventive medicine. The Hasidic tradition describes a rabbi so caught up in intimacy with God that he has to read the Psalms to reawaken his relationships with people.[112] It does not matter whether it is with the Psalms or Merton's Louisville epiphany or simply a love that grows from prayer, spiritual experience pushes mystics to love their neighbor more intensely just as true activism leads one to depend more deeply on God.

Gregory of Nyssa gives both activism and mysticism their due in a creative and insightful synthesis. Avoiding the already hackneyed dichotomy of Mary and Martha as surrogate boxers in a heavyweight fight between contemplation and ministry, Gregory turns to another pair of sisters—Leah and Rachel—as a metaphor for the relationship of prayer and action. Reflecting personally, he says, "I loved the beauty of the contemplative life just as if it were the sterile Rachel—beautiful and keen of sight, though of fewer children because of her repose, but seeing the light with a keener vision. Because of some decision or other, however, I was married to Leah in the night, she of the active life, fertile but poor-sighted, the one who sees less but is more fruitful."[113] Contemplation sees, but bears less fruit. Activism impacts the world, but lets beauty slip through its busy fingers and clarity elude its jumpy vision.

Charles de Foucauld offers his own resolution. It is not a question of one vocation being the holiest, one type of prayer the best, or one plan of action the brightest. God "does not ask all souls to show their love by the same works," he says, nor "to climb to heaven by the same ladder, to achieve goodness in the same way."[114] Mysticism and activism are two vocations, two spiritual temperaments. There are examples, of course, of those who link both arcs. The Hebrew prophets embody a synthesis of mystical vision and social transformation as the Bible's twin trajectories meet in their very being. Their experiences of God and their passion for the world, begun in Moses and consummated in Jesus, were united. Rauschenbusch and Gutier-

---

112. Buber, *Tales: Early Masters*, 51.

113. McGinn, *Growth of Mysticism*, 36. In this otherwise helpful dichotomy, Gregory ignores Jacob's concubines who bear his other children, thus extending tradition's common slap of Hagar to Bilhah and Zilpah.

114. Foucauld, *Writings*, 69.

rez in one arc, and Evagrius and Symeon in another, were already joined in the prophets.

Ruusbroec uses the homely metaphor of a bee to describe a grounded disposition for the true mystic.[115] As a bee extracts raw materials from a flower to make honey and wax, so in a direct experience of God mystics find sweetness for themselves *and* wax that they return to the hive for the common good. A true mystic—like Birgitta or Julian—may well experience ecstatic union with God, but the mystic's experience, if genuine, will always benefit the community of faith and spill over into the world. It is little different for the activist who finds a similar sweetness in working for the common good. Activists must acknowledge that they do not act out of a chaste altruism as if they taste in their ministry no sense of satisfaction, reward, or blessing. The bee not only acts to benefit the hive; the bee enjoys the sweetness.

The parable of the Sower and its explanation (Mark 4:3–8, 14–20) offer spiritual direction to both the self-absorbed mystic and the self-avoiding activist, and to any and all of the theological, psychological, and spiritual "traps"[116] that can captivate, corrupt, or capture them. The seed—the truth within both mysticism and activism—can fall on a path, rocky ground, among thorns, or in good soil. Only if the seed takes root does it yield fruit. The mystic's and activist's insight and passion—if not rooted—can be scattered by external factors, rooted in shallow ideology or carefully controlled "spiritual" experiences, or choked on their own temptations. Without roots *in worldly reality*, the truths of mysticism become ethereal—mere vapor. False mystics can be so caught up in their own cares that their faith becomes disembodied, and their lives—unlike Ruusbroec's bee—offer nothing to others. Without roots in *transcendence*, activism becomes a transient mood. It brings an immediate rush of satisfaction that cannot endure conflict or ever-lurking defeat. It becomes choked on its own ideological precision or its strategic minutiae, and its power to transform implodes. The tests for both mystics and activists, the signs that they are alive, are the gifts and the fruits of the Spirit. And the greatest single sign of their truth is, as King reminds us, love. If love is made visible, then they are indeed rooted in both transcendent and worldly reality, heaven and earth.

There are many prescriptions and solutions for immature, undeveloped, or wrong-headed mysticism and activism. Just as certainly, there are quirky, self-absorbed, and self-avoiding people of faith who sense no pull to either mysticism or activism. False activists and mystics are anything

---

115. Ruusbroec, *Spiritual Espousals*, 84.
116. Maslow, *Religions*, viii.

but unique when it comes to neuroses, stunted spiritual development, or theological boo-boos. Nor are people who profess no faith immune from the same narcissism, intolerance, and self-righteousness. The failures of those who seek spiritual or social transformation in no way undermine the integrity of those who experience and enact orthodoxy. False mystics and activists do not negate the witness of true mystics and activists any more than false messiahs and false prophets (Matt 24:24) negate the truth of the Word of God made flesh in Jesus of Nazareth (John 1:14).

The best touchstone is, again, as always, Jesus. The greatest failure—and indicator—for people who take any false path is that, unlike Jesus, they are not dangerous.

THE SAME FIRE BURNS

In a series of lectures on "Mysticism and Social Change," Howard Thurman prefaces his theological observations with a personal reflection.

> I do not claim to have scaled the heights of rarefied illumination so vivid to the mystics in their moments of clarity, but I have lived for a long time in the stream of the mystic's experience and am convinced that there is available to me some significant and relevant clues as to their interpretation. [It] has been necessary for me to participate both passively and actively in what is generally known as the social struggle . . . I do not speak as an expert in either but always as a seeker after the truth, after a deeper insight and a greater knowledge.[117]

A few, Thurman says, are most deeply engaged in social struggle or spiritual practice. Others, like him, feel drawn in both directions. But the difference between them is in degree of intensity, not in direction or insight: "With most of us there is only a spark, whilst with them it is a long flame; but in us as in them alike, the same fire burns."[118] There are differences between Meister Eckhart and Julian of Norwich on the one hand, and us. There are distinctions between Desmond Tutu and Dorothy Day on another hand, and us. But Day—we must recall—was almost dyspeptically disgusted with people who crowned or canonized her as an exception to be admired instead of an example to be emulated.[119] Few, if any, of us will be remembered

---

117. Thurman, "Mysticism," 3.

118. Ibid., 10. He is quoting from Kenneth Kirk, *Vision of God*, 533–34, who in turn is quoting Henri Bremond.

119. Cuneen, "Dorothy Day," 290: when asked if she had a saint's visions, Day replied, "Horseshit! Just visions of unpaid bills" (ibid.).

for our spiritual prowess or the social reforms we bring into being. Few of us—a tiny fraction of the human race—will be remembered for more than a generation except in the mind of God. But the spark within us contains the same fire that burns in the most ecstatic, insightful, and wise mystic and the most effective, inspired, and inspiring revolutionary.

The language of the "spark" preceded Thurman by many centuries and is shared by numerous traditions. Dante describes God in Paradise as a "river of fire" and deified souls as "ardent sparks therein."[120] Medieval Flemish and Rhenish mystics often write of a "spark of the soul," a speck within an inner abyss in each person where God dwells.[121] Ruusbroec is typical when he speaks of the "brilliant, burning sparks which, in the fire of love, touch and enflame the heart and senses, the will and desires, and all the powers of the soul."[122] It is here, he says in language akin to Eckhart's ever-begetting spiritual incarnation, that God begets Christ and "their mutual love flows forth in a fathomless way."[123] Muriel Lester asserts that there is a "manifestation of God," "the spark of living flame" in everyone.[124] The kabbalistic tradition speaks even more gratuitously of divine sparks littered lavishly over every inch of creation, sparks in all things, sparks freed and redeemed whenever someone becomes aware of them.[125] Teilhard de Chardin says that his spiritual journey began "from the point at which a spark was first struck, a point that was built into me congenitally." He was born, he believed, to observe these sparks. From this early awakening, Teilhard says, "the world gradually caught fire for me, burst into flames."[126] For him, as for others, all of creation becomes a burning bush.

In his reflection on his Louisville epiphany, Merton describes the same spark:

> At the center of our being is a point of nothingness which is untouched by sin and by illusion, a point of pure truth, a point or spark which belongs entirely to God, which is never at our disposal . . . , which is inaccessible to the fantasies of our own mind or the brutalities of our own will. This little point of nothingness and of *absolute poverty* is the pure glory of God in us. . . . It is like a pure diamond, blazing with the invisible light of

---

120. Dante, *Divine Comedy*, Paradiso xxx.64.
121. Woods, *Eckhart's Way*, 59–60.
122. Ruusbroec, *Spiritual Espousals*, 238.
123. Ibid., 240.
124. Wallis, *Mother of World Peace*, 76.
125. Matt, *Essential Kabbalah*, 97.
126. Teilhard, *Writings*, 31.

heaven. It is in everybody, and if we could see it we would see these billions of points of light coming together in the face and blaze of a sun that would make all the darkness and cruelty of life vanish completely.[127]

This spark, he later wrote, is "not so much a stable entity . . . but an event, an explosion which happens as all opposites clash within oneself."[128]

Such sparks are extraordinarily breathtaking in their uniqueness but even more so in their ordinariness. When writing of a spark within us, Dorotheos of Gaza says that when God created the human race, God breathed something divine into us, something like "a hot and bright spark added to reason, which lit up the mind and showed [us] the difference between right and wrong." But this "conscience," this original mind and heart, the very law and guide of our nature, could not sustain itself. Following the natural flow of the deep riverbed of traditional Christian theology, Dorotheos says that there came a time—the fall—when this spark of conscience became scattered and lost: "We needed the instruction of our Master, Jesus Christ, to reveal it and raise it up and bring to life through the observance of the Commandments that buried spark. It is our power to bury it again, or, if we obey it, to allow it to shine and illuminate us."[129] The sparks Thurman describes are not an esoteric discovery or a hidden treasure, the special gift of a privileged few or a Gnostic elite. Dorotheos says God gives these sparks to everyone; they are revived for anyone who learns from Jesus.

Some may be—to use traditional words—specially *blessed, chosen,* or *called* to be a mystic. Some may also be called, or—like King (and as Gregory of Nyssa implies)—"thrust," "pushed," "trapped," or "shamed" into an activist life.[130] Some are blessed with a vision of God that evokes an ardor unmatched even by sexual ecstasy. Others are blessed with a vision of the world's hidden potential that taps a well of passion to alleviate suffering, create just societies, or quench violence in the hotter flame of ahimsa. One may boil with holy passion while another simmers, but it is the same spark, the same flame, that heats both.

Many are not so blessed, chosen, or called, nor thrust, pushed, or trapped, yet the kindling of this spiritual flame is nothing unusual. Friedrich Cristoph Oetinger, part of an eighteenth-century Pietism that treasured conversions and epiphanies, swims upstream against his own tradition:

127. Merton, *Conjectures*, 158.
128. Merton, *Love and Living*, 10.
129. Dorotheos, *Discourses*, 104.
130. King says "thrust," Garrow, *Bearing the Cross*, 125, 355; Andrew Young says "pushed," "trapped," and "shamed," Raines, *My Soul*, 425–26.

"if one has many revelations, visions, and dreams, one's heart is still not as firmly rooted as by faith."[131] Spiritual experiences can be wonderful, astounding, and transforming, but they cannot be predicted, prefabricated, or preordered. The only surefire "method" of experiencing God is through faith. Writing two centuries earlier from an entirely different theological perspective, John of the Cross concurs: "the likeness between faith and God is so close that no other difference exists" between *"believing in"* God and *"seeing"* God.[132] Meditating on the disciples' need to see and touch their risen Lord's wounds in order to believe in the resurrection, the Gospel of John concludes: we are more blessed when faith helps us to see than when seeing helps us to believe (20:29). In other words, experiencing the divine flame may be incidental to the spark of faith; it is as good to be grounded in the soil of conviction as to inhale the more rarefied air of the mystic or to bear the martyr's stigmata. In short, *dangerous orthodoxy* is *ordinary orthodoxy*.

Discerning a spark consistent with mysticism and activism relies on the delicate and inexact spiritual art of discernment. The Jesus Seminar uses the criterion of *dissimilarity* to differentiate the sayings of the *historical Jesus* from the *canonical Jesus*. According to its criteria, to ascribe a saying to the historical Jesus requires that the saying be unique, unlike the common received religious wisdom of his age. Such a method opposes the theological logic of the incarnation—that Jesus was fully human, and fully part of his society, culture, religion, and age. It may well be antihistorical in its bias—could any person *not* absorb, adopt, and adapt received cultural and religious wisdom? What kind of sui generis angelic being would be so cut off from their surroundings? Nevertheless, such a method may be useful as a point of reference.

To find sparks of dangerous orthodoxy, it is preferable to invert the process and seek *similarity* to discern when social and spiritual pioneers share the same spark, when ascetical and political theologies overlap, reinforce, and even, on occasion, merge. This inclusion or exclusion of sources is not made from a Himalayan height with pristine objectivity and perfect discrimination. Mystics and activists—those in whom the long flame burns—are the primary resources of theologies based on experiences of God, neighbor, society, and creation, but the fire burns in others as well—poets, philosophers, scholars, and storytellers. Essays, histories, poetry, fiction, and legends can contain a mystical/activist spark; each has the capacity to reveal truth. While the Jesus Seminar carries out its work with a kind of intellectual purity code, we seek sparks wherever they may be.

---

131. Erb, ed., *Pietists*, 285.
132. John of the Cross, *Collected Works*, 129, italics mine.

In his otherwise stunning record of a mystical experience that he recorded on a scrap of paper and sewed into his coat, a note found only after his death, Blaise Pascal makes an unnecessary over-against, different-from, better-than distinction.

> From about half past ten in the evening to about half an hour after midnight.
>   Fire.
> God of Abraham, God of Isaac, God of Jacob.
> Not the God of philosophers and scholars.
> Absolute Certainty: Beyond reason. Joy. Peace.
> Forgetfulness of the world and everything but God.
> The world has not known you, but I have known you.
>   Joy! Joy! Joy! Tears of joy![133]

In deference to his experience, in deference to the mystical, Pascal dismisses and demeans scholars and philosophers. One cannot say that he is wrong, per se, or that, for him, this experience did not dwarf any academic discovery. But is this a necessary competition? Nicholas of Cusa seems to reply when he says, "our intellectual spirit has the power of fire within."[134] And as part of his conversion from being a scholar to becoming a mystic, Rumi sees flames leap from his books.[135] They contain more than knowledge; they host sparks that can burst into spiritual fire. So in seeking sparks, why pit the God of mystics against the God of activists, or the God of mystics against the God of the philosophers, or the God of activists against the God of theologians? Rather, let us seek the spark wherever it burns.

Martin Buber found the spark in terse sayings, fragments of memory, and simple stories. In the introduction to his two-volume collection of Hasidic writings, he unveils his purpose in collecting hundreds of short stories, anecdotes, aphorisms, and legends: "By the term short story I mean the recital of a destiny which is represented in a single incident; by anecdote the recital of a single incident which illumines an entire destiny. The legendary anecdote goes one step beyond: the single incident in question conveys the meaning of life."[136] This is why desert Christian stories, Sufi stories, and Hasidic stories—as succinct as parables—are much more than charming fables. In this observation, Buber makes sense of the episodic and often disjointed nature of biblical narrative; it is the preferred way to discover and convey the meaning of life. This is the power of Jesus' parables—silver

---

133. Happold, *Mysticism*, 39.
134. Nicholas of Cusa, *Selected Spiritual Writings*, 228.
135. Harvey, *Way of Passion*, 25.
136. Buber, *Tales: Early Masters*, ix.

on the outside and gold on the inside.[137] With an incredible economy of language, Jesus reveals a universe in a few obviously artistic or seemingly artless verbal strokes. Whether a verbal Monet or an aural Zen drawing, these stories contain sparks of eternal wisdom that *cannot* be molded together into one great iconic Truth. Efforts to combine, compare, synthesize, and systematize them can easily turn them—after the flames have gone out—into a golden calf.

Contradicting the James-Rauschenbusch-Niebuhr bias and disassembling any spiritual golden calf, Thurman says: "Christian mystics go beyond mere pantheistic insight. They see the pain, the struggle, the frustration" of the world and "the moral struggle of human life."[138] True mystics do not turn away from the world. A healthy and holy mysticism does not lead to disengagement from politics, economics, or culture; it is a particular set of ways to engage positively and creatively with the world as it is so that the world may be reformed, restored, reconciled, and transfigured to conform to God's original intention. If mystics are truly of God and possessed by the Spirit, they must—like God, like the Spirit—turn ever and always towards the world and, like God's Word, enter it. Thurman insists: "the greatest mystic-ascetics in the Christian tradition have turned the whole stream of Christian thought and achievement into new and powerful channels of practical living."[139] They are what Underhill calls "practical mystics," those who reveal to others their experiences of "a world of higher truth and greater reality than the world of concrete happenings in which we seem to be immersed." Rather than dampening or diminishing mystics' care for the world, this higher truth increases their desire and need to respond to the "overwhelming disharmonies and sufferings of the present time." Mystics, Underhill says, do not experience a divine hiatus or a cosmic silence during times of intense or horrifying strife. Just the opposite: mystics do not get wrapped up "in a selfish and otherworldly calm," nor do their experiences "isolate them from the pain and effort of the common life. Quite the contrary, direct experiences of God give them renewed vitality" for social action.[140] Vietnam in the 1960s gave birth to Engaged Buddhism, a movement among Buddhists to use their vision of reality as the basis for political action. Rufus Jones writes of a similar movement in the Christian tradition

---

137. Eckhart, *Essential Sermons,* 92, quoting Moses Maimonides.
138. Thurman, "Mysticism," 16.
139. Ibid., 24.
140. Underhill, *Practical Mysticism,* xiii–iv.

among "affirmation mystics"—those "concerned with working out in a social frame of reference the realism of their mystic experience."[141]

Thurman gave his lectures on mysticism and social change in 1939; Merton entered the monastery in 1941. Without knowing anything of Merton, Thurman presciently charts in a remarkably succinct summary the arc of Merton's monastic-mystical journey: "Many a monastic ascetic, fleeing from the world to the wilderness, discovered that in the barren waste of his own solitariness were present all the things from which he had fled."[142] As a young man, Merton wrote eloquently but melodramatically of his first entrance into the monastery: "Presently the key turned in the door. I passed inside. The door closed quietly behind me. I was out of the world . . . I had entered into a solitude that was an impregnable fortress."[143] With the benefit of hindsight, maturity, and wisdom, he writes: "the first place in which to go looking for the world is not outside us but in ourselves."[144] He had learned that the monastic life's detachment from the world is simply a paradoxical way of engaging the world. According to Thurman, Merton's journey is the mystic's *norm*. It is also congruent with the activist's relationship with the world. In a sagacious quip, activist-anarchist Ammon Hennacy, upbraided for the apparently foolish presumption of his one-man protests, says: I don't protest to change the world, but to keep the world from changing me.[145] In other words, the protester begins from the same starting point as the monk or the mystic, the same starting point of all Christians. The mystic prays. The activist acts. And these daily disciplines keep them from being conformed to the world so that they can transform it (Rom 12:2).

In answer to a novice's question, Theophan the Recluse describes the true purpose of monastic life and mystical vision. When asked, "What is a monk?" the teacher responds, "Do you mean in the daytime or at night? . . . A monk, like everyone else, is a creature of contraction and expansion. During the day he is contracted—behind his cloister walls, dressed in a habit like all the others, doing the routine things you expect a monk to do. At night he expands. The walls cannot contain him. He moves throughout the world and he touches the stars." While the world judges by a geographically constricted daytime existence, Theophan says, "we tend to measure a monk by the number of persons he touches at night, and the number of stars."[146]

---

141. Jones, *Essential Writings*, 89; also Thurman, "Mysticism," 27.
142. Thurman, "Mysticism," 28.
143. Merton, *Seven Storey Mountain*, 320.
144. Merton, *Love and Living*, 120.
145. Dorothy Day cites this saying in the Foreword to Hennacy, *Book of Ammon*.
146. Theophan, *Tales*, 28.

Introduction

This was people's experience of Merton. He was often frustratingly out of touch with day-to-day sociopolitical realities because of his geographical isolation and semisolitary self-confinement. At the same time, he saw realities much more clearly *because* of the distance he kept from them, and was able to touch people's lives—and the stars, sustaining a sense of the transcendent—far from his hermitage. Merton, like Thurman's generic ascetic, like Theophan's typical monk, ultimately found for himself that by turning toward God in isolation, one can touch a greater number of people more deeply than in a more "active" life. The effects of a contemplative-mystical-monastic life, surprisingly, have as good a chance of circumnavigating the globe as the lives of Gandhi, King, or Tutu.

Thurman also anticipates what Merton would call his "conjectures of a guilty bystander." In Thurman's view mystics "shared consciously and unconsciously in the collective guilt of their age, of their society, of their race, and their problem is how to work out an atonement for this guilt in ways that would be redemptive."[147] Merton writes of his lifetime, "That I should have been born in 1915, that I should be the contemporary of Auschwitz, Hiroshima, Vietnam, and the Watts riots, are things about which I was not first consulted. Yet they are also events in which, whether I like it or not, I am deeply and personally involved."[148] But mysticism—through prayer and contemplation—leads to liberation theology's solidarity. John Howard Griffin said that Merton "had the deepest sense of empathy with the oppressed and the bullied that I had ever encountered."[149] According to Thurman, any "affirmative mystic" would endorse the creed of the socialist Eugene Debs: "While there is a lower class, I am in it. While there is a criminal element, I am of it. While there is a man in jail, I am not free."[150] In Thurman's analysis, mystics not only empathize with Debs' position; they anticipate it. Merton's monastic-mystical journey came to fruition in his Louisville epiphany. It was, he says, like "waking from a dream of separateness, of spurious self-isolation in a special world."[151] In this discovery, he took the spiritual step Thurman predicts for every contemplative.

Thurman offers the same step to every Christian. He extols the virtues of those in whom the long flame burns, but he is more passionate to preach that ordinary people of faith need not warm themselves in another's flame but seek first and foremost a tiny spark within. For us as for Dorotheos of

---

147. Thurman, "Mysticism," 33.
148. Merton, *Contemplation in World*, 161.
149. Griffin, "Controversial Merton," 86.
150. Thurman, "Mysticism," 28.
151. Merton, *Conjectures*, 156.

Gaza, it is the experience of having the inner spark rekindled by a dangerous orthodoxy, an ordinary orthodoxy, by a person—Jesus Christ.

THE REALMS OF THE SPIRIT

Jean-Pierre de Caussade displays a profound lack of interest in theory, a scarcely disguised disdain for a learned, secondhand knowledge of the Spirit. His is the Buddhist skepticism embodied in a story in which a man felled with a poisoned arrow refuses to allow anyone to remove it. First, he insists, he must have all of his questions answered about who, what, how, and why someone targeted him. In his stubborn inquisitiveness, he forgets that unless someone acts quickly, he will die, and his questions will become moot.[152]

De Caussade is part of a school of spiritual thought that cares less for systemic dissection and theoretical precision than for personal and social transformation. A passion for love and fidelity trumps an obsession with logic and consistency. In times and places and persons, the spirit of the Buddha penetrates and suffuses itself into Christian faith and practice. It shares the cynicism of Sufis: "Like an ass laden with books: heavy is the knowledge that is not inspired by God."[153] At times, this tradition has strayed into a suspicion of reason and even education. At times, it has devolved into anti-intellectualism and know-nothingism. Taken to an extreme, it becomes a contradiction to read—let alone write—a book. More moderately, if one is going to read or write, the reading or writing must lead to prayer and action. As mystical, liberation, and social gospel theologies maintain, theology without practice—faith without works—is dead (Jas 2:17). Theoretically, if a book is orthodox, it should blaze. It is not that de Caussade and his spiritual kin are universal book burners. He wrote, after all. It is that the mind has a higher calling—to love God and neighbor. To be true to the Spirit, reading and writing *must* lead to spiritual and social revolution. Even the Logos, the Word, is of little value to the world unless it becomes flesh. In that light, de Caussade's words express my invitation to the reader.

> Come, I say, come, not to study the map of the realms of the spirit, but to possess it so that you can walk freely about it and never be afraid of getting lost. Come, not to study the record of God's grace, not to learn what it has done down all the centuries and is still doing but come and be the trusting subject of its operation. There is no need for you to understand the lessons it

---

152. Nhat Hanh, *Old Path White Clouds*, 299.
153. Rumi, *Poet and Mystic*, 98.

has taught others, nor to repeat them cleverly. You will be taught matters which are for you alone.[154]

Dorotheos of Gaza parses things somewhat differently. He teaches that we gain access to wisdom through "the lessons [the Spirit] has taught others." For Dorotheos, there are two parts to the Christian life: "to sit in the solitude of the cell is one half, and to sit with the elders is the other half."[155] When we read or write a book like this one we sit at the feet of the elders; we feel the sparks in our hearts ignite in response to their long and living flame. When we read we absorb wisdom from *their* experience. One's cell, our daily mundane existence and the self-knowledge that comes from discerning the movement of the Spirit in our own life, is a way of learning from *our personal* experience. As William Stringfellow says, we are, each of us, "parables,"[156] stories of incredible complexity and infinite meaning. From the early centuries of Christian faith, it has been so. We learn from those who go before us—our ancestors. We learn from those around us—our community. We learn from our own daily life.

The gifts of the elders are unmistakable. The desert Christians believed that you could smell sanctity. Holiness emits a distinctive, recognizable odor.[157] Not even death diminishes holiness, its scent, or its ability to touch others, like holy hands rising up from the earth to heal, an inversion of the raising of Lazarus. The Tomb of the Five Saints narrates this truth: Because of their holy lives, even in death the bodies of these saints bestow "numerous gifts of healing while lying in the same tomb." Their tomb "unceasingly poured forth oil for healing so that it covered the slab on top of the tomb."[158] This underground tomb was filled to the brim and beyond with healing oil that flowed from the corpses of the saints. The tomb overflowed with healing and pilgrims came to the tomb, this Lourdes, to be healed or to stare in rapture as they saw God work through the righteous dead.

Of course, as in any garden, there were complications in this healing oasis and, as in many a biblical tale the narrative explains these in contradictory ways. In part, it blames the devil, "the enemy and corrupter of our race," who has a lamplighter—the Judas-style scapegoat of the story—arrange it so that "the saints no longer poured forth oil for healing."[159] The faithful grieve as the power of healing is dammed at its source. But the story also blames

---

154. de Caussade, *Abandonment,* 56.
155. Dorotheos, *Discourses,* 245.
156. Stringfellow, *Simplicity of Faith,* 20.
157. Waddell, *Desert Fathers,* 189–201, especially 195.
158. Anthony of Choziba, *Life of St. George,* 102.
159. Ibid., 102–3.

human fickleness and, nixing the scapegoat, holds the whole community collectively responsible for their lax faith. The interruption achieved by the enemy was merely an "excuse" for people to ignore the holy tomb. As years passed, people began to take the tomb for granted and it lost its power to heal.

Whatever the cause—the work of the enemy and an accomplice, and/or the people's complacent faith—healing no longer flowed as a constant river but sputtered and spurted as an occasional gusher. God's grace could be interrupted by open opposition and undermined by subtle infidelities, but it would never be permanently extinguished: "Even now they [the five saints] do not stop unceasingly providing bounteous gifts of kindness and healing for those who ask in faith."[160] In spite of obstacles, when faith responds to grace, the work of grace is consummated.

Too often, like those who took the tomb's healing oil for granted, we casually or listlessly leaf through the wisdom of the past as if in a hurry to reach a destination we think we can find without its guidance. Those who study the mystics, or who sit at the feet of activists, are today's pilgrims seeking the tomb of the saints. They bathe in the wisdom (and witness) of mystics and the witness (and wisdom) of activists who have come before us, all of whom have known God directly in ecstatic experience and ordinary action, all of whom have *practiced* dangerous, ordinary orthodoxy. To ignore them is to be like the lamplighter's generation that came to take the saints' tomb for granted.

It is easy to lose touch with the power that remains in the lives of mystics and activists. Like Thurman, we need to recall that the long flame of their lives rekindles the tiny spark in ours. They inspire us to seek within ourselves the passion that drives activists to risk their lives. King often fantasized about turning away from activism to something—pastoral ministry, academia—almost anything less chaotic and stressful, less life-threatening, to a life more serene, quiet, and *normal*. He was often tempted to consider his activism merely one phase in what *could* have been—had he made that choice—a life of longevity; he could have chosen to become an elder. Teresa of Ávila knew that to record her mystical experiences in writing put her in danger. Her writings were as controversial as the reforms she brought to her order and sought for her church, as controversial as being an activist in the 1960s. Yet King did not turn; Teresa refused to be silent. Many mystics and activists have thought about exchanging their vocation for security, perhaps even for the twin temptations of acclaim and prosperity, but what would they have if they gained the whole world and lost the life God intended

---

160. Ibid., 103.

them to live? Their experience of orthodoxy refused to allow them the comforts and security we normally crave.

In part, we read books to *bathe* in the dangerous orthodoxy of our elders. We bathe in it because it heals us of our cynicism, our helplessness, our passivity, our self-pity, and our self-absolving apathy. We bathe in it because we know that it is far too easy to become like Bethsaida's paralytic sitting by the healing pool for thirty-eight years without finding a way to get in when its healing waters move (John 5:2–9). We bathe in the wisdom of the past, in part because we are afraid Jesus will ask us the questions he asks and implies of the paralytic: Do you *want* to be healed? Do you *want* to be fully alive? Or do you *prefer* to be paralyzed? Do you *prefer* to be helpless and hopeless and passive? We are invited to bathe in the healing power of those who have experienced the divine directly in God and *equally* directly in their neighbors, their societies, in the midst of the daily dehumanizing grind of poverty, in small-minded, small-town cruelty, in wars and rumors of wars, at the heart of the injustice and corruption and bleakness of the world. They rekindle that spark infused in us at creation. They resurrect our ordinary faith.

But *we* cannot revel in *their* holiness. In the story of the Tomb of the Five Saints, a sixth person is found worthy to be buried in their tomb. If we bathe in the wisdom of our elders, not only will there come a day when others are healed by our witness; if we bathe in their holiness, the smell of sanctity should be discernible on us *now*. As Day said, they are not exceptions, but examples. They unveil the potential for holiness in everyone in whom is found the divine spark.

One well-known desert Christian story[161] parallels two Gospel stories and embodies this truth. Abba Lot goes to Abba Joseph as the lawyer (Luke 10:25–37) and the rich young man (Mark 10:17–21) go to Jesus. Each seeker first describes his spiritual practice. Abba Lot tells Abba Joseph that he fasts, prays, and meditates: "I live in peace and, as far as I can, I purify my thoughts." The lawyer tells Jesus that to inherit eternal life we must love God and neighbor. The rich young man also wants to know how to inherit eternal life. When in response Jesus cites the commandments directed towards one's neighbor, the rich young man affirms, "I have kept all these since my youth."

These seekers yearn for, and deserve, commendation. But the stories do not end there. There is—in each story—another question, another statement, another step. Abba Lot asks, "What else can I do?" Jesus tells the rich young man, "You lack one thing." The lawyer, apparently, lacks nothing, in

---

161. Ward, *Sayings of the Desert*, 103.

theory! Jesus tells the lawyer, "Do this and you will live." He does not need to do anything else. But Jesus has something else in mind for the rich young man: "Sell all you own, and give the money to the poor . . . *then* come and follow me." The lawyer, perhaps too pleased with his rhetorical skills, or possessed by his need for self-justification, foolishly reopens the case: "but who is my neighbor?" Jesus tells him the parable of the Good Samaritan and says again, "Go and do likewise."

Abba Joseph, like Jesus, has something else to say, one more lesson to impart, one more suggestion to make, one more way of leading by example. So Abba Joseph "stood up and stretched his hands towards heaven. His fingers became like ten lamps of fire and he said to [Abba Lot], 'If you will, you can become all flame.'" Jesus stretches the lawyer and the rich young man beyond their capacity to respond. Jesus may as well ask them to walk on water or be turned into flame. Perhaps he does. The rich young man's quest snaps. The lawyer's? Abba Lot's? We will never know.

Abba Joseph makes the same invitation to us. We may well be healed through our elders by the wisdom of dangerous orthodoxy. We may be happily scented and soaked in their witness and words. We may well have a spark of their long flame within us. But why settle for a spark? Why not be changed into fire? Books are not only for reading. When they contain the long flame—directly or indirectly—they set us on fire. As de Caussade says, be less concerned with what the Spirit can teach you in the abstract than with what the Spirit can do with you: "You will be taught matters which are for you alone."[162]

Alone? Yes and no. For though very intimate, what we learn, how we burn, is for us as for Birgitta and Julian, through us, and for all.

---

162 de Caussade, *Abandonment*, 56.

2

Wakers on Earth

The soul has two eyes, one inward and one outward.
 —Meister Eckhart[1]

I saw moreover that it did not so much concern us what objects were before us, as with what eyes we beheld them.... All people see the same objects, but do not equally understand them.
 —Thomas Traherne[2]

We believe that we are in a new historical era. This era requires clarity in order to see, lucidity in order to diagnose, and solidarity in order to act.
 —Medellín Conference[3]

And when [the Samaritan] saw him, he was moved with pity.
 —Luke 10:33

---

1. Eckhart, *Sermons & Treatises II*, 141.
2. Traherne, *Centuries*, 146.
3. Hennelly, *Liberation Theology*, 91.

You know what time it is, how it is now the moment for you to wake from sleep.
—ROMANS 13:11

We try many ways to be awake, but our society still keeps us forgetful.
—THICH NHAT HANH[4]

Christian! You must awake, through God, from your deep sleep;
If you don't rouse yourself, you'll stay fixed in your dream.
—ANGELUS SILESIUS[5]

The angel who talked with me came again, and wakened me, as one is wakened from sleep.
—ZECHARIAH 4:1

The Wakers rejoice today
for the Wakeful One has come to wake us up:
on this night who shall sleep
when all creation is awake?
—EPHREM THE SYRIAN[6]

Open, open the eye of your mind, and sleep no more in such blindness.
—CATHERINE OF SIENA[7]

You have to wake people up . . . to their humanity, to their own worth, and to their heritage.
—MALCOLM X[8]

---

4. Nhat Hanh, *Love in Action*, 111.
5. Silesius, *Cherubinic Wanderer*, 125.
6. Brock, *Luminous Eye*, 140–41.
7. Catherine, *Saint Catherine*, 288.
8. Dyson, *Making Malcolm*, 175.

> I am just beginning to awaken and to realize how much more awakening is to come.
> —Thomas Merton[9]

> [Jesus said] And what I say to you I say to all: Keep awake.
> —Mark 13:37

MEDITATION: LINCOLN AND VENICE

I was waiting on a street corner to meet Anna, a friend and colleague, for breakfast. As I slowly paced back and forth to avoid sitting on a dirty concrete bench, I looked at the tiny slice of the world around me. It was not the best of neighborhoods. It was not the worst of neighborhoods. My preternaturally privileged eyes noticed the dusty, dirty sidewalks. Someone appearing to be homeless sat down on the bench I had shunned.

Even though I had worked in a neighborhood not quite as nice as this for a decade, the privileged eyes of my childhood, unaccustomed to urban grime and human grit, momentarily seized the day as the minor topographical decay and the world-weariness on people's faces grabbed me like a sociological revelation. Then, remembering where I had been since my youth, it all became normal again. Most of the people, ordinary people, God's people I would have supposed if I had thought about it, were on their way to work—the habit of survival worn on their faces like a uniform. The lush racial mix of Latinos, African Americans, Anglos, and Asians—in numerically descending order—reflected the neighborhood. As an Anglo, I hardly stood out. No one did. No one could. Wearing my standard off-duty clothes, jeans and a T-shirt, my priesthood was safely hidden.

Standing next to a bus stop, I considered a sign of LA's class division—a privilege marked even by my sixteen-year-old car parked a few spaces away. Even *that* car separated my experience from the daily habits of the people riding the bus. A young Latina exiting the bus, leaned over to say something (in Spanish?) to an elderly man in a wheelchair, and then pushed him across the street, an almost invisible, no-trumpet-sounding act of simple courtesy or sacred charity. The lights changed. Pedestrians crossed the wide streets. There were more pedestrians in this part of town than in most, another sign of working-class predominance.

---

9. Merton, *Dancing in the Water*, 195.

Then I saw him coming. He was slightly taller than me, an Anglo, maybe thirty. His curly black hair fell down over his forehead, a clump of it springing up and down between his eyebrows. His eyes were wide open. I guessed that they were glazed. He hadn't shaved for a few days, the black stubble a shadow across his cheeks and chin. His clothes were improbable in their combinations of color and design—a conjunction of thrift store basic and thrift store classic. He wore no shoes or socks. His feet were dark with soot. Instead of pants, he wore what looked like a potato sack tied around his waist, but his movements belied the possibility of a picnic race. He lurched back and forth as he walked; whether medicated or self-medicated or needing to be medicated I could not diagnose.

He was not going to walk by me, two ships passing in the morning on an urban street corner. He was approaching me. We were going to meet. I prepared myself for the familiar interaction. Did I have any change? Good question. How much change did I have? None. Was I feeling generous enough to reach into my wallet? Would I ask him to wait a minute while I walked fifty feet to my car where I knew there were fistfuls of change? Would I smile and decline his request? Would I act on my faith or out of a well-fed, well-tended urban lethargy—so many requests, so little change? At least he didn't know that I was a priest, a pigeon, a sitting duck. At least I wasn't officially representing the divine. He would ask—one human being to another, one in need, the other not, both sharing the same collective innocence and guilt. I would choose how to respond.

He was a few feet away when he said, "God bless you."

It was not the interaction I had expected. That one sometimes *ended* with "God bless you," after cash had exchanged hands, but it never started that way; and it was never said in place of the request. Surprised, I smiled to myself, the priest being blessed by the stranger on a street corner. "God bless *you*," I replied, an ironic smile breaking across my lips.

"God bless you and your family!" he said more emphatically, walking past me having delivered his message, no other business on his agenda.

I turned and watched him as he walked up the busy street. He didn't speak to anyone else. He continued to lurch from side to side, each step more work than it ought to be, as if he were walking uphill or through sand, as if he might lose his balance, or as if he were avoiding stepping on or in something, real or imagined.

Anna arrived, another priest working in another urban church. I told her about my morning interaction, the blessing that *was* the transaction. I asked, "How often does *that* happen?"

AWAKENINGS

We expect the language of permanent revolution from Lenin, Trotsky, or Mao, but not from Evelyn Underhill. We are not surprised that someone reading *The Communist Manifesto* might extract one radical ideology or another, but Underhill drew her inspiration from the Lord's Prayer. The prim Victorian student of mysticism, retreat leader, writer, and spiritual director to the becalmed early-twentieth-century Church of England struck a dissonant, seemingly incongruous chord in her meditations on the Christian faith's most beloved prayer. The Lord's Prayer, she says, teaches us "the real Christian is always a revolutionary, belongs to a new race, and has been given a new name and a new song."[10] At the heart of Jesus' spiritual teaching she found the seeds of social revolution.

God's realm, the "kingdom" for which Christians work and wait and pray, and *God's revolution*, the process through which that "kingdom" comes, is the vital core of prayer. God's realm is an annunciation, God's revolution a partial, sputtering incarnation. Both are the "kingdom," already and not yet. The revolution of God seeks the complete transformation of all that is—unjust systems and the chaotic, twitching, random movements and countermovements of politics and economics—into all that can be: God's will done on earth. We await the realm. We take part in the revolution. The realm is the mustard plant, the revolution the seed. The revolution never ends until the realm is established. The revolution is the Spirit's activity in the world working through people of faith as it once worked through Jesus, making the blind see, the deaf hear, the lame leap, and the dumb sing. It is practical, pragmatic, and immediate good news to the poor. It subverts and inverts the social order.

Reflecting on major revolutions from 1776 to 1919—American, French, and Russian—Andre Trocmé says that the revolution begun in Moses and expanded through Jesus is far more radical than anything the modern world has produced.[11] Eberhard Arnold calls the revolution based on the Sermon on the Mount "the revolution of all revolutions."[12] It requires more than regime change or social change, although it embodies both top-down and grassroots connotations. It is *world change*. Underhill says that God's ultimate victory is not signified by the triumph of the institutional—or invisible—church, nor of a particular ecclesiastical or social order. It means "something far more deep, subtle and costly: the reign of

---

10. Underhill, *Abba*, 33–34.
11. Trocmé, *Jesus and the Nonviolent*, 16.
12. Arnold, *Writings*, 58.

God, the all-demanding and all-loving, individual hearts, over-ruling all the 'adverse powers' which dominate human life . . . —fear and anger, greed and self-assertion, jealousy, impatience and discontent. It means the re-ordering, the quieting, the perfecting of our turbulent interior life, the conquest of our rampant individualism," massive social change and complete spiritual revolution.[13]

The revolution of God is this wholesale conversion of William Stringfellow's "world as it is"[14] into the realm of God. Some will always experience the Christian's rapacious hunger for justice as nihilism, yet it is no more accurate to call it *anarchy* than to brand any regime or government true *order*. That is the error Martin Luther King, Jr. corrects with his "Letter from Birmingham Jail": religious leaders conflate God's will with an existing social order, even one blatantly unjust, virulently racist, and impulsively violent.[15] Peter Maurin pronounces any and every existing order "chaos."[16] Both King and Maurin tried to awaken the church from its self-absorbed self-importance as it all too often and too comfortably abrogated its role in God's revolution and sundered its connection with God's realm.

When Underhill calls "real" Christians revolutionaries, she is rebelling against a staid status quo church. But she also announces, like a gentle prophet, that no Christian can fully embrace a social order envisioned by human minds or created by human hands. The true Christian always thirsts for the *not yet* of God's realm, and in pursuing it, brings about the *already* of God's revolution. The Christian, she says, "belongs to a new race," an *international* that transcends race and racism, nation and nationalism, and that unites the followers of Jesus. All other allegiances are secondary, tertiary, ephemeral, and dying. Augustine, expanding on a New Testament theme (1 Cor 7:31, 1 John 2:17, Rev 21:4), writes, "The world is passing away, the world is losing its grip, the world is short of breath."[17]

Underhill insists that a person's Christian identity and purpose belong to a God who is "with the future."[18] It is not only the real activist or mystic who is the revolutionary, but the real *Christian*—whether or not drawn by character or charism to activism or contemplation. The *real* Christian seeks the transformation of all on earth that is not of God's will. The *real* Christian no longer belongs—heart, soul, mind, and strength—to an identity defined

---

13. Underhill, *Abba*, 34–35.
14. Stringfellow, *Dissenter*, 161.
15. King, *Testament of Hope*, 290.
16. Maurin, *Easy Essays*, 83.
17. Brown, *Augustine of Hippo*, 298.
18. Underhill, *Abba*, 33.

by tribe, nation, class, gender, or ideology. The *real* Christian no longer builds a fortress around family, clan, culture, or language. A new *name* has been gifted and the old identity shed. *Real* Christians offer no pinch of incense to emperors; they sing no national anthems; they bow only to the cross and sing only the hymns of the citizens of heaven.

Underhill calls the work of the realm we pray for "perpetual. Again and again freshness, novelty, power from beyond the world, break in by unexpected paths, bringing unexpected change." Many in church and society stubbornly and tragically "cling to tradition and fear all novelty." By doing so they "deny the creative activity of the Holy Spirit, and forget that what is now tradition was once innovation."[19] The "pioneers" of this revolution are mystics and pacifists, the prayerful and the nonviolent.[20] Mystics are awake, sometimes to glory and ecstasy, sometimes to inadequacy and desolation, but always to God. They see with what Eckhart calls the "inner eye,"[21] an eye attuned to God at the center of one's being. Experiences, occasionally profound, more often trivial, may awaken them, but both vision-based and vision-antagonistic mystics share a way of seeing, an awareness, a *consciousness*,[22] and by virtue of that consciousness, a compassionate yearning for everything in creation. Using language more often associated with Buddhism, Ephrem the Syrian writes, "The Wakeful One . . . has come to make us wakers on earth,"[23] not only awake, but "awakeners," people given the vocation to awaken others.[24]

Activism is also first and foremost a consciousness. Activists are awake to God through the world, often inspired by potential, often shaken by misery—misogyny, bigotry, and poverty; degradation, dehumanization, and violence; suffering, injustice, and oppression. They see with what Eckhart calls the "outer eye."[25] They find God and godlessness in institutions, nations, and peoples, in urban, cosmopolitan, and agrarian systems. They align themselves "against" all that is lofty and proud, all pyramids and pockets of pride, all idolatry and human self-exaltation, all militarized fortifications and centralized wealth.[26] They are alive to a God who announces a

---

19. Ibid., 33–34.
20. Underhill, *Modern Guide*, 16, 208.
21. Eckhart, *Sermons & Treatises II*, 141.
22. McGinn, *Foundations of Mysticism*, xviii.
23. Brock, *Luminous Eye*, 140.
24. Ephrem, *Hymns*, 71.
25. Eckhart, *Sermons & Treatises II*, 141.
26. Isaiah 2:12–16 uses the word "against" ten times.

new order where all live in secure interdependence where none shall make them afraid (Mic 4:4).

The real Christian is incomplete without both sets of eyes, inner and outer, alighting on and aligning the spiritual and the material, and the spiritual *in* the material. The real Christian cannot help but see the breathtaking goodness of creation and the defiling evil of systemic turmoil, the spark of holiness at the core of our being and the "eggs" of death hatching in human hearts.[27] Each eye can be pried open for moments at a time, but the real Christian prays to *be* awake. Like Paul's oft ill-explained koan about praying "without ceasing" (1 Thess 5:17), an apparently offhand comment-cum-spiritual principle, the person of faith is constantly conscious of God and the world.

Such a consciousness relies on revelation. The Abrahamic faiths assert that, arrhythmically but indelibly, God chooses to unveil the nature of the divinity. While proclaiming that God can be discovered in creation and the divine activity bubbling up hourly in the midst of life, singular revelations occur in events set apart from the ordinary—in a burning bush, parting waters, a voice from heaven, an empty tomb. Sometimes with voice, sometimes in silence, sometimes in visions, sometimes in blindness, intimations of divine presence suggest fluidity between heaven and earth too slippery for definition and too amorphous for rationalism. These awakenings are called many things—epiphanies, illuminations, revelations, openings, conversions, and breakthroughs. They are gentle. They are shattering. They require no confirmation. They demand further review. They are rare and intense. They are omnipresent and subtle.[28] Merton describes a constant shower of seeds present in every moment of every person's life. A few are noticed, observed, received, and treasured. Most, however, are lost.[29] Martin Buber focuses on "ecstatic" experiences,[30] Rudolph Otto on involuntary shudders of dread, bewilderment, terror, and shame.[31] These moments are sometimes claimed as the aerie of mystics, but some activists know them equally well. They can also be the experiences of people who identify as neither, even those who proclaim no faith at all. They caress, assault, spin, and resurrect our relationship with God. They renew and realign our comprehension of and our commitment to the world. Sometimes they are utterly transcendent. Sometimes they are so earthy and earthly that their transcendence is at first hidden.

---

27. Merton, *Hidden Ground*, 283.
28. Otto, *Idea of the Holy*, 12–13.
29. Merton, *New Seeds*, 14.
30. See Buber, *Ecstatic Utterances*.
31. Otto, *Idea of the Holy*, 13–17.

Long before she became a friend of Gandhi, before she dreamed of founding Kingsley Hall in one of the poorest sections of London, before she became the Traveling Secretary of the International Fellowship of Reconciliation, Muriel Lester had such an awakening. In her autobiography, the first childhood story she tells that takes place outside of her home occurs on a train ride through the "unsalubrious neighborhood of East London." On the train, passengers bang windows shut and cover their noses to protect themselves from "the foul smell that pervaded the whole atmosphere." The odor comes from the factories that produce "sweet-smelling soap out of bone manure. The West End [her neighborhood] enjoyed the pleasant perfumed delicacy. The East End perpetually reeked of its manufacture." People from her neighborhood "habitually commiserated with each other over the fact that their railway line ran through this malodorous area." The fact that others endured it every moment of every day did not matter. The chronic stench and daily injustice did not disturb them as much as their own occasional discomfort. At age eight as Lester stared down "at the rabbit-warren of unsavory dwelling-houses, gardenless, sordid, leaking," and asked her nurse, "Do people live down there?" Her nurse replied, "Oh yes. Plenty of people live down there but you needn't worry about them. They don't mind it. They're not like you. They enjoy it." A year later, another adult reaffirmed her nurse's verdict: "It's all right. They don't feel things the same way as we do."[32]

Lester's later commitment to East London marks her train revelation as a formative epiphany. It tears a curtain in two that veiled social inequality and a smug self-serving class prejudice. It was her first lesson in economics—free market capitalism indulges some with the luxury of sweet-smelling soaps while it curses others with the factories' stench. Generations away in El Salvador, in another political context, Ignacio Ellacuría, theologian and martyr, describes the same economic and social "necessity": "the necessity that many suffer so a few many enjoy, that many be dispossessed so that a few may possess."[33]

Only a child, Lester was now awake to that so-called "necessity." She speculates but does not overanalyze her nurse's outlook: "Perhaps she had orders not to let any of us become unhappy." An inquiring eight-year-old's awakening has no impact on her socially dulled adult companion. The nurse is like the English butler in Kazuo Ishiguro's *Remains of the Day,* who is so singularly devoted to his duties that he stays at his post even as his father, also a butler, is dying, believing rightly that his father would be proud of

---

32. Lester, *It Occurred to Me,* 4–5.
33. Ellacuría, "Crucified People," 266.

him for putting responsibility first. Both the fictitious butler and Lester's nurse are singularly loyal to a class system that exploits them. The nurse identifies with the Lester family rather than the factory workers. Like house slaves in the antebellum South, she believes that because she belongs to the *house* she is somehow less a *slave*. She has sold herself down a river with a common delusion; she has inhaled the secondhand smoke of another class's opiate; she has happily poured their Kool-Aid down her own throat. She has not been awakened like James Baldwin, who wrote of his own maturation in words reminiscent of Paul's contrast of childish and adult thinking (1 Cor 13:11). When Baldwin was a child he pledged allegiance to the flag. He later discovered that, as a gay African-American, for him it spelled spiritual death to "pledge allegiance to a flag that had pledged no allegiance to you."[34] The nurse's soul belongs to an economic system that silently mocks her fidelity and gladly abuses her loyalty. The child was awakened. The adult was not.

According to common parlance, Lester's was not a religious awakening. She says nothing of God in these pages, but the contemplative seeds of permanent revolution had been planted. In this, she was not unique. As a fourteen-year-old with no discernible religious inclination, Dorothy Day made a solemn secular vow to work with the poor.[35] Her adult conversion was both emotional dismemberment and reintegration, initially tearing her away from everything she considered precious—her partner (common-law husband), bohemian lifestyle, and commitment to the poor. Nothing in her superficial experience of the church gave her the slightest inkling that Christian faith could be linked to social justice; the church she observed blessed the convenient blindness of the privileged. Only later would Day integrate prayer and politics, as her inner and outer eyes focused as one. The youthful awakenings of Lester and Day were distinctively earthly and political. Awakened to the world, they were unknowingly awakened to God.

At a different moment in a different place another awakening occurred in the life of the Mahatma who would become Lester's friend. Thoroughly religious and political, Gandhi describes it as a singular experience. Asleep in prison at midnight, he was awakened by a whisper "within or without, I cannot say." The voice told him to start a twenty-one-day fast the next morning to purify himself before launching a new campaign to abolish India's caste system. He assented and went back to sleep. Later, like a mystic, he tries to describe the inexplicable:

> I saw no form. I have never tried to, for I have always believed God to be without form. But what I did hear was like a voice

---

34. Troupe, *James Baldwin*, 249.
35. Day, *Loaves and Fishes*, 8.

from afar and yet quite near. It was as unmistakable as some human voice, definitely speaking to me, and irresistible. I was not dreaming at the time I heard the voice. The hearing of the voice was preceded by a terrific struggle within me. Suddenly the voice came upon me. I listened, made certain that it was a voice and the struggle ceased. I was calm. The determination was made accordingly, the date and the hour of the fast fixed. Joy came over me . . . I felt refreshed.

No external evidence, he says, could validate or corroborate the experience. A skeptic, he admits, could dismiss his claim as "self-delusion or hallucination." But he was as certain of its reality as anything he could taste, touch or see: "not the unanimous verdict of the whole world against me could shake me from the belief that what I heard was the true voice of God."[36] In the middle of a spiritual-activist life, Gandhi was awakened. Even the mature Gandhi was only half-awake stuck, as Merton would say, in "the half-tied vision of things."[37] The voice Gandhi heard, like the vow Day made, was an awakening.

For Merton, the purpose of contemplation is to be awake. Try as he had and try as he might, he knew he could not fully escape the delusions of his deviously, devilishly, self-distracted society. Western civilization, he believed—and he in it—is "involved in the deepest and most restless, and most stupid sleep."[38] Even after fifteen years in the monastery, "only now I am getting down to waking up."[39] Again and again, Merton links inner and outer eyes, spiritual and social awareness. Churches sleep; civilizations are comatose; social classes bask in self-centered slumber. If only we could see, Merton insists, we would see God *and* the world and God *in* the world.

To be unaware of injustice is a spiritual malady as malignant as ignorance of God. Walter Rauschenbusch says "an unawakened person" ignores how broad economic trends and personal financial investments adversely affect the poor.[40] In such societies, the gospel has the power to awaken people to the truth. To Oscar Romero, good preaching "enlightens." Like a light turned on in a dark room, it "awakens and of course annoys a sleeper." To preach Christ, Romero says, is to consistently call others to "Wake up!

---

36. Gandhi, *Way to God* 96–97, *Prayer* 68–70.
37. Merton, *Other Side*, 323.
38. Merton., *Search for Solitude*, 264.
39. Ibid., 207.
40. Rauschenbusch, *Social Gospel*, 19.

Be converted!"[41] Day bemoans the fact that others are "calmed down" by the Eucharist. She found herself "worked up" and "excited."[42]

No less than divine epiphanies, awakenings to the world are fraught with angst. While some mystics describe their experiences in poetic pastels, others are ravaged. The mystical experience gives birth to bewilderment as often as it nurtures bliss.[43] In his luminous essay "Fire Watch," Merton finds the translucence of the divine in each footfall, yet in his encounter with a tender but forthright God, God offers little reward and even less sympathy for Merton's sincerity.

> God, my God, God Whom I meet in darkness. With You it is always the same thing! Always the same question that nobody knows how to answer!
> I have prayed to You in the daytime with thoughts and reasons, and in the nighttime You have confronted me, scattering thought and reason. I have come to You in the morning with light and with desire, and You have descended upon me, with great gentleness, with most forbearing silence, in this inexplicable night, dispersing light, defeating all desire. I have explained to You a hundred times my motives for entering the monastery and You have listened and said nothing, and I have turned away and wept with shame.
> Is it true that all my motives have meant nothing? Is it true that all my desires were an illusion?
> While I am asking questions which You do not answer, You ask me a question which is so simple that I cannot answer. I do not even understand the question.[44]

A gentle God strips him of self-justification and spiritual clarity and leaves him to feel naked and a fool.

Whether one awakens quickly or gradually, there is a dramatic difference between spiritual wakefulness and a socially induced sleep. Rumi says, "When you have become awake, your ears are so sensitive they can hear the cries of a sparrow ten thousand miles away."[45] The Hasidic rabbi Mordecai of Neskhizh observes that you are not worthy to be called a "zaddik" (righteous one) until you can feel the pain of a woman in labor fifty

---

41. Romero, *Violence of Love*, 38.
42. Coles, *Dorothy Day*, 77.
43. al-Kalabadhi, *Doctrine of the Sufis*, 138–39.
44. Merton, *Sign of Jonas*, 342–43.
45. Rumi, *Say I Am You*, 47.

miles away.[46] To be awake is to be hyperaware and hyperempathetic. This is the measured lawyer *becoming* the merciful Samaritan in order to love his neighbor as himself. This is the rich young man selling his possessions and distributing the profits to the poor. This is the desert pilgrim becoming the flame. This is what it is to be awake, to lose the life we have in order to gain the life we envision.

One of Rumi's stories sheds a prismatic light on losing life to gain it and on Jesus' invitations to the lawyer, the rich young man, and Nicodemus (John 3:1–21). Someone tries to coax a fetus out of the womb with a kerygma of wonder: the world has "a thousand delights," glorious starlight, countless stars, sunshine, moonbeams, sky, seas, mountains, plains, fields, orchards, and gardens. Why, given all this, the voice asks, would you stay in the womb, that "dungeon"? But the fetus rejects the proposition: "There is no 'other world.' I only know what I've experienced. You must be hallucinating."[47] If only it could see it would want to be born. If only the lawyer, the rich young man, and Nicodemus could see, they would enter a new life. If only. That is the lament. That is also the hope.

Symeon the New Theologian describes a similar scene. Someone born in a dark prison feebly lit by a single lamp cannot imagine beauty. Through a crack in the wall the prisoner catches a glimpse of a landscape bathed in sunlight. At first, nearly blinded, he is ecstatic, and slowly he becomes accustomed to the brilliance. The soul no longer needs to be sustained by external joy. "Instead it has the constant experience of the divine reality in which it lives."[48] People of faith need only to be sustained by the truth. Whether it is Lester on a train, Gandhi on his bed, or Merton on fire watch, it is no longer unusual to be awake to heaven and earth. Epiphanies do their work. We are not trapped in a prison. We do not grow old in a womb. We need no further signs and wonders, much less facts or proof. We are awake.

MISSISSIPPI AND ASSISI EYES

Stringfellow branded it an antibiblical heresy—the narcissistic theology that shaves and shears the Christian faith until it pares its ultimate concern to a tiny fragment of its former self, a personal relationship with God.[49] To him, a God-and-me faith desecrates the kerygma that calls the Christian community a body and hails the impending salvation of the world. We cannot

---

46. Buber, *Tales: Early Masters*, 164.
47. Rumi, *Essential Rumi*, 71.
48. Lossky, *Mystical Theology*, 209.
49. Stringfellow, *My People*, 150.

be faithful to God nor be awake to ourselves *or* to God unless we are aware of the world as it is. Some epiphanies lead the eye in one direction, some in another; some employ the inner eye, others the outer. The two eyes together, however, lead to a holy and holistic mystical-political awakening. Perhaps by inclination, and certainly according to stereotype, mystics are primarily oriented to the divine, activists to the human, the mystical eye drawn to creation and the Creator, the activist eye attentive to sin and redemption. All of this is, of course, prosaic and simplistic, barely scratching the surface of mysticism or activism.

Certainly activists develop eyes sensitive to interpersonal malevolence and the fury of cold, calculating, systemic indifference. A handful of white activists left their homes to work for African American voting rights in the sixties South and developed what they called "Mississippi eyes."[50] Afterwards, when they went to California, they were surprised that their newly focused eyes enabled them to see Mississippi in the Golden State's oppression, exploitation, and disenfranchisement of farmworkers. Like many of their generation, they thought that the worst evils were *out there*. Then, eureka! They discovered that injustice begins at home.

Mystics might be inclined to see what Merton calls "a hidden wholeness,"[51] all created things less in their fragmentation than in their unifying relationship to God. Francis of Assisi's *Canticle of Creation* presents an ordered, linear, and rhapsodic rendering of creation, praising first the cosmological, then creatures, and finally even death in a descending journey from the ethereal to the material, the accessible, and even the destructive.[52] Francis's *Canticle* puts flesh on Abraham Maslow's theory that from the perspective of a "peak-experience" "the world is seen as acceptable and beautiful . . . [even] the bad things about life are accepted more totally."[53] Another of Maslow's descriptions aptly fits Francis's ministry: an "all-embracing love for everybody and for everything, leading to an impulse to do something good for the world, an eagerness to repay, even a sense of obligation and dedication."[54] *Mississippi eyes* see all that is balkanized, violence woven into the daily ruin of the innocent. *Assisi eyes* see all things held together by Christ. *Both* ignite the impulse to do something *for* the world. *Both* unveil the world which, like God, according to a classic theological distinction, is known through its *energies*, but whose *essence* remains a mystery.

50. Ferriss and Sandoval, *Fight in the Fields*, 103.
51. Merton, *Collected Poems*, 363.
52. Leclerc, *Canticle of Creatures*, 30.
53. Maslow, *Religions*, 64.
54. Ibid., 68.

In Christian political and ascetical theology, the word "world," like the word "God," is simultaneously overloaded with freight and exasperatingly elusive. Ideologically conditioned terms like *domination system*[55] or *locus imperii*[56] describe norms of power relationships. As suggested by the broader term *antimerciful world*, there is something in the world's nature that makes room for personal healing and familial happiness as long as they remain within a structural framework of debilitating oppression.[57] But while the world includes destructive systems, it is more than that. Merton writes of the West gazing out at the world as a "one-eyed giant," its functioning eye attuned to techniques and technology, know-how less than knowledge, and blind to human complexities and holy mysteries.[58] Reinhold Niebuhr complains of the hubris of modern ideologies that lack "the humility to accept the fact that the whole drama of history is enacted in a frame of meaning too large for human comprehension or management."[59] Trying to fathom patterns in history is like reading tea leaves. Gregory of Nyssa asks: how could it be otherwise? Just as God is inherently a mystery, an "essential incomprehensibility," the same is true for everything God has made because there is something of God in all things.[60] It is erroneous, dangerous, or both, to believe that we can intellectually grasp the course of history or succinctly define the nature of the world. From Gregory's perspective, then, Marx, Freud, and Jung no less than Augustine, Aquinas, and Luther are cartographers mapping mists, clouds, and bogs.

The Gospel of John, the "mystical" gospel,[61] provides a more nuanced definition of the world. The political landscape of first-century Palestine was a prototype of an imperial domination system perfectly embodying an antimerciful world. But the Fourth Gospel also attributes an inborn, unpredictable quality to the cosmos. The world spurns the Word. It hates Jesus and his disciples, *and* God sends Christ (and the disciples) into the world because God loves the world. John's Gospel opens and never closes an apparently intentional paradox about salvation: is it intended for believers (John 1:12, 3:16), for the world (John 3:17), or for believers as the first fruits of the final harvest? In the Fourth Gospel, salvation—and damnation—are part of the creative chaos of the universe. Salvation does not calm chaos and quell

---

55. Wink, *Engaging the Powers*, 13–104.
56. Myers, *Who Will Roll*, 15.
57. Sobrino, *Principle of Mercy*, 23.
58. Merton, *Gandhi*, 1.
59. Niebuhr, *Irony of American History*, 88.
60. Otto, *Idea of the Holy*, 194.
61. Countryman, *Mystical Way*, and Rensberger, *Johannine Faith*, 16–17.

wickedness as much as it massages every good and evil nook and cranny of life with divine love.

There may be a spiritual link, though not an exegetical one, between John's "world" and God's answer to Job. God's speech confronts "the limits of Job's imagination" and "the inadequacy of any merely human calculus."[62] No equations or creative improvisations can encapsulate the mystery of the world. God's words silence Job's demands, all demands, that life be sensible, predictable, or comprehensible, or even peaceful or just. Like Francis's orderly *Canticle* tornado-tossed and gloriously disheveled, God's whirlwind soliloquy passes swiftly through the cosmological and the meteorological to the wild, fierce, free creatures of nature to even more uncontrollable mythological forces. All of this renders Job's previous arguments about scales of justice a quaint preoccupation and a pitiable pittance of an argument.

In Job's direct, one might say "mystical," experience of God, God gives him Otto's *mysterium tremendum* treatment extraordinaire. Creation is both wild and good. The world is as untidy and marvelous as a never-ending birth, as unmanageable as a volcanic eruption. It is an irretrievably unruly, torrentially active, terrifying, awe-inspiring, constant crescendo of movement, whether chaos or chiaroscuro or both, one cannot tell and it may not matter. Job's speeches evolve from "God and me" to "God and us."[63] God responds that God and us is but a tiny splinter of God and us *and* creation. Job, like the activist, seeks justice, but when he asks for it, God reveals creation as a crashing, clashing, dissonant, but magnificent canticle. Even the *locus imperii*, its hobnailed boots weighing heavily on the masses, is but a loose dirt clod in the hurricane of the cosmos. Testifying during the apartheid era before a commission investigating the potentially treasonous activities of the South African Council of Churches, Desmond Tutu reiterated his prophecy that racist South Africa would one day take its place alongside other tyrannical regimes in "the flotsam and jetsam" of history.[64] Even as the world often disappoints activists as cosmic forces dwarf justice, tyrants inevitably suffer defeat as they idolize their own puny power. In a creation as alive and complex as God's answer to Job, no one can extricate the power of destruction from the vitality of creation.

In such a dizzying world, we are tempted to try to control the pandemonium with the Tinkertoy tools of logic and reason, as if the human mind were not one more swirling dust devil in the whirlwind. In fact, the attempt (or temptation) to rely on reason is a symptom and manifestation of the

---

62. Alter, *Art of Biblical Poetry*, 102, 106.
63. Gutierrez, *On Job*, 39, 48.
64. Tutu, *Hope and Suffering*, 158.

turmoil. Using his Mississippi eyes, Merton wrote "A Devout Meditation in Memory of Adolf Eichmann." In the essay he unveils disquieting twists not only in the ways dictatorial, genocidal regimes manipulate definitions of sanity and normalcy but the ways democratically elected officials use the same apparently rational touchstones as they prepare for criminally insane megamurder. To Merton, the court's assessment of Eichmann's sanity raised deeper questions about the slickly lubricated interrelationship of rationality, normalcy, morality, and carnage. As he wrote during the Cold War,

> The sanity of Eichmann is disturbing. We equate sanity with a sense of justice, with humaneness, with prudence, with the capacity to love and understand other people. We rely on the sane people of the world to preserve it from barbarism, madness, destruction. And now it begins to dawn on us that it is precisely the *sane* ones who are the most dangerous.
>
> It is the sane ones, the well-adapted ones, who can without qualms and without nausea aim the missiles and press the buttons that will initiate the great festival of destruction that they, *the sane ones*, have prepared . . . and the sane ones will have *perfectly good reasons*, logical, well-adjusted reasons, for firing the shot. They will be obeying sane orders that have come sanely down the chain of command. And because of their sanity they will have no qualms at all. When the missiles take off, then, *it will be no mistake*.[65]

In verifying the rationality of totalitarianism and holocaust, Merton exposes the logic of a democracy capable of planning a solution more final than any Hitler had imagined. Merton writes repeatedly: pragmatic policies are criminal, craven immorality is normal. Just as the commandant at Auschwitz could spend his workday liquidating Jews, then go home to his family as if he worked in any ordinary industry, so American leaders could pamper their families and plan genocide.[66]

When definitions of the world are elusive and chaotic, it is natural that the question and quest of how best to engage the world will be, at best, muddled. H. R. Niebuhr's mid-twentieth-century essay, *Christ and Culture*, while time-bound and Eurocentric, summarizes various plausible relationships communities of faith may have with the social systems of the world. Some argue that the Christian community best serves the world's deepest interests by withdrawing into alternative communities that model, however

---

65. Merton, *Raids on the Unspeakable*, 46–47 (italics his), *Nonviolent Alternative*, 161.

66. Merton, *Nonviolent Alternative* 156–59, *Collected Poems*, 345–48.

imperfectly, a just society—a light to the nations, and a partial realization of God's realm. In this quasi-utopian tradition honored by monks and Anabaptists, the Catholic Worker and the Koinonia Community, the temptation is to overidentify the remnant with God's realm. At the opposite end of a broad spectrum is a spirituality of incarnational social engagement in which Christians and their communities actively seek to transform cultures. In this lineage of engaged, incarnational social transformation, from abolitionism to human rights movements, the temptation is to write political prescriptions for society without practicing them as a faith community.

In his typically passionate language, William McNamara sides with incarnational involvement. The spiritually alive are always drawn into the realities of society. To him, the mystic withdraws from the world's antimerciful values in order to address its injustices. Because they are mystics, they are activists. Their sacred passion enlivens them "to be wholly, totally, fascinatingly, captivatingly engaged by God and therefore simultaneously by humanity, by the social, political world."[67] McNamara, like Kenneth Leech, insists that spirituality is always manifested in the paradoxical and dynamic world of John and Job. In their eyes, as in Merton's, desert, monastic, and mystical detachment is a necessary precursor to healthy participation in the world.

Gandhi's personal embodiment of Hinduism paralleled this Christian incarnational spirituality and sixties Vietnam's Engaged Buddhism. To Gandhi, "whatever awakens people to a sense of their wrongs and whatever gives them strength for disciplined and peaceful resistance and habituates them to [purposeful] corporate suffering brings us nearer Swaraj" [self-rule, freedom].[68] Seeing colonized India through Mississippi-Assisi eyes, Gandhi offered a spiritual-political prescription: 1) understand how people are wronged and wrong others, 2) find spiritual strength for social action, and 3) risk suffering to give birth to a new order. To Gandhi, India's freedom meant more than political independence from the British Empire, the *locus imperii* of his era; it meant interfaith cooperation, the abolition of the caste system, and the demise of the exploitative class system.

Regardless of his activist orientation, Gandhi never lost a sense of wonder undimmed by evil. While the world may be a swirling mixture of good and evil, Assisi eyes perceive God everywhere. Charles de Foucauld, living a harsh, modern desert life, was naturally awakened to beauty in the world, and to its Source:

---

67. McNamara, *Earthy Mysticism*, 11.
68. Bondurant, *Conquest of Violence*, 53–54.

> All created beauty, all beauty of Nature, the beauty of the sunset, of the sea lying like a mirror beneath the blue sky, of the dark forest, of the garden of flowers, of the mountains and the great spaces of the desert, of the snow and the ice, the beauty of a rare soul reflected in a beautiful face, all these beauties are but the palest reflection of yours, My God. All that has ever charmed my eyes in this world is but the poorest, the humblest reflection of your infinite Beauty.[69]

Foucauld perceives Beauty through beauty, the divine through creation, God *in* all things. In contrast, Augustine stresses the transcendent over the material, God *above* all things.

> What then do I love, when I love You? . . . I love a certain light, and a certain voice, a certain fragrance, a certain food, a certain embrace when I love my God: a light, voice, fragrance, food, embrace of the inner person. Where that shines upon my soul which space cannot contain, that sounds which time cannot sweep away, that is fragrant which is scattered not by the breeze, that tastes sweet which when fed upon is not diminished, that clings close which no satiety disparts. This is what I love, when I love my God.[70]

As mystics belie cleanly wrapped and neatly folded preconceptions, so do activists. As mystics have an activist dimension, many activists have a deep mystical awareness. Day was as pointed a prophet as any in the twentieth century. Yet she reveled in every tree in Manhattan, praised the beauty of farms, and edited traditional liturgical forms to create personal songs of praise for all that was beautiful, including her grandchildren: "All ye works of the Lord, bless ye the Lord. Oh ye ice and snow, oh ye cold and wind, oh ye winter and summer, oh ye trees in the woods, oh ye fire in the stove, oh ye Beckie and Susie and Eric, bless ye the Lord!"[71] Mystics, likewise, do not merely praise God like distant and diffident choirs of sanctimonious seraphim. They also offer prophetic warnings and vivid denunciations. In the fourteenth century, Birgitta of Sweden, as much an apocalyptic prophet as a mystic, not only denounced ecclesiastical corruption and the gluttonous abuse of wealth, she also condemned sex trafficking that sometimes drove female slaves to suicide.[72]

---

69. Foucauld, *Writings*, 107–8.
70. Augustine, *Confessions*, 10.6.
71. Day, *On Pilgrimage*, 2.
72. Birgitta, *Life and Selected Revelations*, 212–13.

As Eckhart says there are two eyes, Traherne says there are two worlds—one created by God, the other produced by humans. What God designs is "great and beautiful," "Adam's joy and the Temple of his Glory." What people manufacture is a "Babel of Confusions: Invented Riches, Pomps and Vanities." To Traherne, condemning and enjoying the world are two movements of one spirit. Traherne's spiritual counsel, in synchronicity with the wisdom of the far-off desert, is to "leave the one that you may enjoy the other."[73] When one word—*world*—has two meanings (as in Traherne), or contradictory realities (as in John), or is a twitching, spinning, agitating, aggravating object (God's answer to Job), it can be difficult to know exactly how to relate to it. Niebuhr charts different answers. Traherne offers a single classical monastic-desert prescription. In opposition to modern love-it-or-leave-it jingoism, he says to leave it *so as to* love it. In a different way, this is also the activist's answer. Their convictions meet, like steadfast love and faithfulness, righteousness and peace (Ps 85:10), in Paul's admonition: do not be conformed to the world but be transformed by the renewing of your mind (Rom 12:2). An activist like A. J. Muste shed the antimerciful values of the world in a spiritual flight as dramatic and complete as Merton's. And like Christ and his disciples, Muste and Merton found themselves sent into the world in a way that is at once a sign of spiritual freedom and an incarnational engagement.

Sharing Traherne's view of social structures produced by human hands, Muste sums up much of what was amiss in mid-twentieth-century America, his world, as "conformity" to economic exploitation, racist laws, and war. He compares the moral impact of conformity to the traditional Chinese practice of binding women's feet. In the end, to conform is to become deformed.[74] In a spirit consistent with fourth-century monks, Muste praises "holy disobedience" as a "necessary and indispensable measure of self-preservation, in a day when the impulse to conform, to acquiesce, to go along, is used as an instrument to subject people to totalitarian rule and involve them in permanent war."[75] As an informal spiritual director to the nonviolent faith community, Muste calls pacifists to be transformed by cultivating an inner desert and withdrawing from the habits of an antimerciful world. To him, this means more than philanthropy, electoral politics, labor organizing, political advocacy, or violent revolution. The "inner revolution," as Muste calls it,[76] means a wholesale metanoia, a transformation

---

73. Traherne, *Centuries*, 5.
74. Muste, "Pacifist Way," 198.
75. Muste, *Essays*, 372.
76. Muste, "Religious Basis," 5; Merton calls conversions "inner revolutions" (*Life*

in principles, outlook, and behavior. Like the immature monk who tries to escape from the world with a geographical solution, the shallow activist finds it equally ineffective to try to elude the world through an ideological conversion. Neither superficial rejection has the power to free us from a world that is deeply implanted and cannot be extracted by sweat, strategy, philosophy, or wishful thinking.

The world as it is must be seen with both Mississippi and Assisi eyes— full of horrific human evil, nature's cataclysmic indifference, *and* God's glory. Julian of Norwich saw the world as it is in the hazelnut she held in the palm of her hand. In that hazelnut, she saw three essential truths about "everything" in creation. God made it. God loves it. God preserves it.[77] God does not merely love the world's goodness. God loves the antimerciful Johannine world. God loves both of Traherne's worlds, the one made by God's hand and the one marred by human hands.

Yet it is not enough that God loves the world. God gave Catherine of Siena a theological insight when teaching her to love the world. She heard God tell her, "I ask you to love me with the same love with which I love you" but this is impossible because "I loved you without being loved." Whatever love we give to God, it cannot be original, uncreated, or unbegotten. But God shows us a way to love without being loved. "This," God says, "is why I have put you among your neighbors: so that you can do for them what you cannot do for me . . . love them without any concern for thanks and without looking for any profit for yourself. And whatever you do for them I will consider done for me." We can, God says, love our neighbors "with the same pure love with which I love you," without regard to self-interest, blessing, or reward.[78] We can love others without them first loving us.

The only answer to the world as it is, marred by human hands, is a power that can cut the visible Gordian knots of exploitation, oppression, and degradation, and the invisible ones of selfishness, hopelessness, and powerlessness. The only power that can sever those knots is love. Day liked to quote from *The Brothers Karamazov* that love is sweet only in dreams. In reality, it is a "harsh and dreadful thing."[79] Also disdaining a romantic sentimentality, Merton describes love as "the resetting of a Body of broken bones."[80] Expanding on such antiromantic notions, William McNamara

---

and Holiness, 117), and speaks of "a total interior revolution" (*Nonviolent Alternative*, 112); Day speaks of a "revolution of the heart" (*Loaves and Fishes*, 210).

77. Julian, *Showings*, 131.

78. Catherine, *Dialogue*, 121, 165.

79. Dostoevsky, *Brothers Karamazov*, bk. 2 ch. 4.

80. Merton, *New Seeds*, 72.

says, "Love is not a bromide. It is a revolution. That is why chattering about it is so absurd, cuddling up to it so silly, and a casual approach so bizarre."[81] Underhill asserts the centrality of love in social transformation: "You cannot redeem, help, or save anything you despise, *only* that which you love."[82] Such a love is severe, painful, and revolutionary. Whatever one might call the world—the domination system, the *locus imperii*, an antimerciful reality—it cannot be transformed by brute force, ingenious strategy, or sheer determination. Whatever the particular means in a given situation, social transformation will not be of a piece with the revolution of God unless it is rooted in loving the unlovable.

Such love comes into being only through a profound transformation. In a poem about abandoning the world's dehumanization, Rumi describes a worm "addicted" to eating grape leaves. One day, it wakes up and realizes that it no longer has to live by devouring. Suddenly it is no longer a worm. It has become "the entire vineyard, the fruit, the trunks, a growing wisdom and joy that doesn't need to devour."[83] This is not mere metaphor. Martin Luther King, Jr. once compared capitalism's power to impoverish to cannibalism.[84] For Ellacuría, devouring is a social necessity in an antimerciful world. The person of faith no longer devours and so becomes one with the new creation. This is what the mystic does with enchanted Assisi eyes. This is what the activist does with judicious Mississippi eyes. This is how Gandhi and Day and Muste left the world, taking the transcendent path of voluntary poverty and the incarnational path of God's apostles. This is how Underhill and Julian and Catherine engaged the world. Both mystic and activist start like Rumi's worm and end as the vineyard. They stop devouring and become the garden.

CONSCIENTIZATION AND CONTEMPLATION

According to John Ruusbroec, the spiritual life begins when Christ says "see."[85] If only we see and stop devouring, we can become sources of mercy. If only we see, we would become revolutionaries. But *how* do our eyes become adjusted to the intrinsic and infinite value of everything in creation? And how do we become equally aware of the systems that are the skeletal infrastructure of human agony?

81. McNamara, *Earthy Mysticism*, 79.
82. Underhill, *Ways of the Spirit* (italics hers), 114.
83. Rumi, *Essential Rumi*, 265.
84. King, *Where Do We Go*, 194.
85. Ruusbroec, *Spiritual Espousals*, 71.

Every religious tradition seeks to cultivate awareness. The *shema* keeps alive the primal memory that constitutes and reconstitutes an unshakable Jewish identity. *Dhikr* is the Muslim practice of being mindful of a single, almighty divinity; you either use this memory as a compass or wander aimlessly as an amnesiac. The root of buddha, *buddh,* means "to be awake"; a *boddhisattva* is someone awake to the world. The fruit of Zen practice, like all contemplation, is to live in constant touch with a grounded level of consciousness; good deeds without that awareness are artificial flowers without a scent.[86] The liturgical *anamnesis* performs a similar role as a remembrance and re-membering of Christ that recenters the lives of Christians. The personal practice of *lectio divina*, like Protestantism's persistent insistence on the primacy of the Word and the centrality of Bible study, infuses a spiritual pulse into human hearts transfusing the Word into the veins of history. There can be no outward revolution without this constant introspective conversion.

In Deuteronomy, Moses announces that God's Word is not found in distant lands, in an inaccessible heaven, or in esoteric knowledge, but in the common parlance of language, in the everyday life of people, in their own mouths and hearts (Deut 30:11–14). Building on this insight, Ephrem of Syria meditated on the ironies of the incarnation:

> They sought You above on high; they saw You below in the depth.
> They sought You in heaven; they saw You in the abyss.
> They considered You as divine; they found You in the creation.[87]

In the same era, Abba Moses enshrined the desert tradition's antipilgrimage prescription to seekers when he taught a pilgrim the way to God: "Go, sit in your cell, and your cell will teach you everything."[88] A fourth-century desert cell, like Merton's hermitage, no larger than an urban studio apartment, contains a galaxy of wisdom. Abba Moses's statement reaches beyond the monastery. Zen-like, it teaches that our daily routine, our *place* in life, is our greatest spiritual teacher—Lester's train, or Gandhi's bed, yes; but also Lester's nurse, and Gandhi's imprisonment. The empty delusions speak as articulately as the epiphanies. All are found in one's cell.

Later tradition stretched Abba Moses's idea of the cell as a fixed place. Francis of Assisi sometimes spent days in his cell,[89] but his incarnational the-

---

86. *Dhammapada* 4:51; Gandhi, *Prayer*, 57; 1 John 3:18.
87. Ephrem, *Hymns*, 244.
88. Ward, *Sayings of the Desert*, 139.
89. Celano, *Saint Francis*, 177, 181.

ology and evangelical fervor committed his ministry to mendicant mobility. In the Franciscan tradition, one's cell travels; it is less like Jerusalem's temple than God's wilderness tent. In many ways, Merton's vocational restlessness was a yearning for the right cell; ironically, his hermitage became what he often felt compelled to seek elsewhere. As he spent more time in solitude, he saw more clearly. From his cell, he observed God's glory in Kentucky's hills.

> Marvelous vision of the hills at 7:45 a.m. The same hills as always, as in the afternoon, but now catching the light in a totally new way, at once very earthly and very ethereal, with delicate cups of shadow and dark ripples and crinkles where I had never seen them before, the whole slightly veiled in mist so that it seemed to be a tropical shore, a newly discovered continent. A voice in me seemed to be crying, "Look! Look!" For these are the discoveries, and it is for this that I am high on the mast of my ship (have always been) and I know that we are on the right course, for all around is the sea of paradise.[90]

Merton saw creation with Assisi eyes[91] and he credited his cell with his newfound sight.

> Happy Sunday morning in cell—which does all that tradition says it does! How eloquent all these four walls and the landscapes of hills and woods and crazy barns outside my window! I am high up as a stylite, the window goes down to the floor, my head almost touches the low ceiling, birds fly past below me. I sit on the edge of the sky, the sunlight drenches my feet. I have a stool here, an old one, and a desk . . . by the bed—three ikons and a small crucifix which [Ernesto] Cardenal made. Reading in here is a totally different experience from anywhere else, as if the silence and the four walls enriched everything with great significance. One is alone, not on guard, utterly relaxed and receptive, having four walls and silence all around enables you to listen, so to speak, with the pores of your skin and to absorb truth through every part of your being.[92]

Enclosure broadened Merton's horizons. Yet the cell and its ability to grace him with an Assisi vision did not blind him to the horrors of history. The same monastic eyes that made him aware of God's presence in creation also enabled him to see with Mississippi eyes, stirring his anguish at the sheer primordial force of evil.

90. Merton, *Turning Toward the World*, 321–22.
91. Merton, *Sign of Jonas*, 208: he believed his monastic life fed his inner Franciscan.
92. Merton, *Search for Solitude*, 387.

This stable, almost static, life enables one to see. Near the alpha of the Thousand Year Reich, Eberhard Arnold had a premonition of the new regime's omega in the seeds of war all over the world and asked rhetorically and repeatedly, "Isn't that war?" When a government has killed a thousand without trial, when hundreds of thousands "are robbed of their freedom and stripped of their dignity," isn't that war? Yet as great as his anxiety about events in Germany was, he knew it held no monopoly on war. When hundreds of thousands are sent to Siberia in forced labor camps, when wheat is stockpiled while millions die of hunger in Asia, isn't that war? When people are forced to work for low wages, when women are forced into prostitution, when the wealthy live in villas while others are without shelter, when some hoard fortunes while others cannot afford the basic necessities of life, "isn't that war?"[93]

Thirty years later, Merton's monastic life helped him discern the *meaning* of events,[94] to see—like Arnold—war woven into the fabric of everyday life. The nuclear weapons Merton decried were merely the tip of a much more sinister iceberg. Nuclear war was the logical outcome of a superstitious reverence for violence. American culture was more than a domination system or a *locus imperii* with winners and losers; it was viral, toxic, an all-consuming way of death. On Holy Saturday in 1965, Merton's thoughts turned to the multifaceted and multifarious ways his society distorted and destroyed life.

> Fetishism of power, machines, possessions, medicines, sports, clothes, etc., all kept going by greed for money and power. The bomb is only one accidental aspect of the cult. Indeed, the bomb is not the worst. We should be thankful for it as a sign, a revelation of what all the rest of our civilization points to. The self-immolation of people to their own greed and their own despair. And behind it all are the principalities and powers whom we serve in this idolatry.[95]

In the scum and scrum of terror, Merton found a blossom of hope as an improbable gift and an ironic, prophetic sign. Nuclear weapons are an extraordinarily visible "sign," writ large, of the destructive core of American civilization. Yet God can take the most unpromising, malevolent raw material, even nuclear weapons, any evil, and use it to spur contrition. Even in the midst of foreign crises (the Cold War, the Cuban Missile Crisis, and the Vietnam War) and domestic chaos (civil rights, race riots, and cultural

---

93. Arnold, *Writings*, 38.
94. Merton, *Search for Solitude*, 231.
95. Merton, *Dancing in the Water*, 230.

revolution), God offers redemption. In those most terrifying moments, God mercifully inserts the possibility of hope for those with eyes to see the whole truth: "the most terrible situation in the world today is a vivid sign in which the mercy of God seeks to spell out the truth of our sins and win us to repentance."[96] As clearly as Merton saw the glories of creation, he sifted through "seeds of destruction"[97] for signs of redemption.

The idea of learning from daily experience belongs equally to the contemplative tradition and to the process of social awakening: conscientization. The goals, methods, and purpose of one mirror the other. Conscientization focuses Mississippi eyes, as contemplation does Assisi eyes. Conscientization helps us to understand our place in society, contemplation our place in the cosmos. Conscientization is a way of knowledge that leads to justice and love, contemplation a way of love that leads to knowledge and justice. Contemplation rains down from the transcendent, conscientization rises up from the grassroots (Isa 55:10–11). Both deconstruct and reconstruct the world. Both seek personal and social transformation, partly by clarifying one's place in the social order—consumer and/or consumed—partly by understanding that it is equally dehumanizing to consume or be consumed. The goal is reached when you no longer need to prey or devour, when you identify with the whole vineyard, orchard, garden, creation.

Paulo Freire's conscientization nurtures diagnosis and prescription through a sensate, Ignatian method. Merton's contemplative social criticism unmasks illusions by cutting through layers of Orwellian obfuscation and its loud, repetitive lies. Merton's contemplative criticisms functioned for his readers as conscientization, wrenching them out of their half-rational way of seeing. Freire's work of conscientization seeks to liberate the oppressed from internalized, dehumanizing, passive fatalism. Seeing ourselves and our society in a new light, we can engage the world as agents of change instead of inert objects. In some ways conscientization works like contemplation. In conscientization, one extracts the *housed oppressor*; in contemplation, one plucks out the *internalized world*. Likewise, contemplation functions like conscientization, creating new ways of perceiving the world. The traditional purpose of the desert, Merton says, is to create "a clear unobstructed vision of the true state of affairs, an intuitive grasp of one's own inner reality as anchored, or rather lost, in God through Christ."[98] The goal of the desert is to see the world, to know oneself, and to love. The twofold purpose of conscientization is to see and engage the world differently by re-envisioning

---

96. Merton, *Witness to Freedom*, 23.
97. The title of one of his books: Merton, *Seeds of Destruction*.
98. Merton, *Wisdom of the Desert*, 8.

oneself and others. Both ways protest dehumanization, and each frees people to construct a new creation.

Conscientization contains the seeds of the mystical path: purgation, illumination, and union. It uproots distorted and self-destructive self-images in the psyches of the oppressed (purgation), shines light on the world's corrupting and degrading systems (illumination), and offers a way to be reconciled to others on the basis of justice (union). Through spiritual awareness, contemplation seeks human liberation from the institutional forces that enslave people in body, mind, and spirit. In conscientization, people are purged from seeing themselves as "oppressed individuals," atomized and impotent. Purgation comes with the realization that one's poverty is not one's fault. Dorothy Day calls the psychological absorption of scorn one of the most debilitating effects of poverty, perhaps even harder to overcome than poverty's visible and physical damage.[99] With illumination, the oppressed come to see themselves as members of a "class," an organism, a community that has the collective competence to alter its future. People learn that they are not inert objects of oppression but human beings who have a hand in their own fate. They are not clay or, worse, filth, but potters. Conscientization illumines social, political, and economic realities. Instead of living in a sociologist's Petri dish, one leaves it—flees the world for the desert—and analyzes the network of social systems that create oppression.[100] Freire employs the language of contemplation when he says conscientization penetrates the totality of socioeconomic reality and helps people cultivate "an attitude of awareness." When fully developed, this becomes a consciousness of consciousness.[101]

In Freire's lexicon, the oppressed have been exploited by a "cultural invasion" of what John's gospel calls the "world."[102] Sometimes a cultural invasion is as obvious as when nineteenth-century mission schools forced Native American children to cut their hair and make their beds as if those social mores were divine commandments. Sometimes it is as clear as when Japanese Americans in internment camps started each day pledging allegiance to the flag of the nation that had stolen their property, impugned their integrity, stained their dignity, and imprisoned their loved ones.[103] More often than not, though, the cultural invasion is not the ham-handed work of the empire, the oligarchy, the dictator, or the corporation. It is ini-

---

99. Day, *All is Grace*, 134.
100. Freire, *Pedagogy of the Oppressed*, 175, 151–52, 158.
101. Ibid., 66–68, 95, 103, 101.
102. Ibid., 150.
103. Takaki, *Strangers*, 395–96.

tiated by the paternalistic big brother, the democratically elected government, purportedly "of the people, by the people, and for the people," leaving the poor confused and ashamed of their social status. It is essential to the domination system's viability that the *invaded* embrace the outlook of the *invaders*. The climactic moment of the *locus imperii*'s success comes when the *invaded* mimic the *invaders*. So Lester's nurse giddily surrenders to England's sheer-cliff class structure and scorns the poor of East London on its behalf. It is one thing when the oppressor proselytizes the oppressed in an ideology of paternalism[104]—Pharaoh, after all, wanted Israelite slaves to fear the anxiety-ridden freedom of the wilderness and to dismiss the promised land as a Shangri-la of their wishful thinking. It is another thing when the Israelites—any oppressed people—partially fulfill that wish.

The oppressed internalize their oppression in other ways as well. Writing during the apartheid era, Dennis Brutus describes a yet more insidious process by which the oppressed unknowingly internalize and mimic their antimerciful experience. Always at ease in his scathing denunciations of the agents of the white-dominated regime, Brutus reflects despondently that the oppressed majority ends up copycatting the behavior of their oppressors: everyone, he says, abuses power, if not in boardrooms, then in bedrooms; everyone, he says, takes things that belong to someone else; and everyone, he says, is at least tempted to victimize someone younger, older, smaller, sicker, or weaker. The monumental guilt of the oppressive minority is not as dissimilar from the oppressed majority as we, in the moral clarity our unconscious Manichean pipe dreams, want to believe. The moral dilemma of the oppressors is merely one dimension of a broader and more basic human predicament.[105] As apartheid waned, *their* behavior, white behavior, Afrikaner behavior, became *our* behavior, African behavior, as necklacing and internecine violence supplemented official state torture and law-and-order repression in an almost cataclysmic fugue of bloodshed.

Before Freire articulated the theory of conscientization, it was already embodied in the Catholic Worker movement. Freire's belief that traditional forms of education fail to educate because they "bank" information and numb reflective thinking was anticipated in Day's repugnant distaste for those who rely on statistics to describe poverty.[106] To her, statistics blot out a person's sacramental value. To help the privileged recognize the innate dignity of the poor, Day used thousands of words to sculpt three-dimensional figures of fragile young women snapped by unforgiving systems, and tough-

---

104. Freire, *Pedagogy of the Oppressed*, 150–52, 169, 107.
105. Brutus, *Simple Lust*, 79.
106. Coles, *Dorothy Day*, 98.

ened old bigots whose hearts housed demons. Conscientization was also the purpose of the Catholic Worker's roundtable discussions that brought workers and academics together for what Peter Maurin called the "clarification of thought."[107] The woodcuts of Fritz Eichenberg functioned both like icons for contemplatives and the drawings Freire used to help nonliterate people develop a new consciousness. But the iconic is not limited to particular movements. In a process Freire would have saluted, photographs spurred Martin Luther King, Jr.'s conversion to the antiwar movement. After measuring the political calculus in his first aborted foray into antiwar politics, his second great awakening—the irreversible one—began when he saw war photographs in a magazine.[108]

During the civil rights movement, contemplation and conscientization became complementary spiritual exercises. Journalist Pat Watters describes the movement's nightly mass meetings as "mystical, ecstatic." Such nights gave way to illuminating days when the movement inched forward in three-mile-an-hour marches, walking meditations on the realities of hatred, oppression, and poverty. To Watters, the civil rights movement had a "genius" for exposing the nation as it was in "existential flashes."[109] In that regard, the civil rights movement, as it traversed the nation's main streets and back roads, operated like a Franciscan cell.

Like conscientization, the civil rights movement acted as spiritual-political purgation and illumination in its work to end oppression and seek reconciliation. The leaders of the movement saw the oppressed as only the most visible victims of the domination system. So they sought the even more complicated liberation of the privileged, whose spiritual health contradicts their material self-interest. Their housed oppressor is not a house slave, but the slave's master. For the oppressed, spiritual and political liberation are knit together as one. The dehumanization of the overprivileged is counterintuitive; the very system that blesses them materially enslaves them spiritually. They are blind to their own privileges, often misinterpreting them as an economic justification by works. The civil rights movement's pedagogy of the oppressors helped people see privilege's intrinsic damage—to gain the world while losing their souls (Mark 8:36).

Already awake to her privilege and given Mississippi eyes on her childhood train ride, Lester later prescribed an urban contemplative habit, putting on Assisi eyes whenever you board a train, ride a bus, or enter a room

---

107. Ellis, "Peter Maurin," 22.
108. Oates, *Let the Trumpet Sound*, 427–28.
109. Watters, *Down to Now*, 191, 226, 247.

"to practice conscious reverence for the personality of each of those already there":

> The mystics used to take time to untie themselves with their environment, so that, whatever it was and however unpleasant, it had no power to oppress them.
>
> Our job is just as hard; it is to keep ourselves in harmony with our fellows, even in the crush of an overcrowded tube. We can do it by remembering the Presence of God, looking at our fellow passengers and reminding ourselves that each of them, though perhaps they have no idea of it, is near and dear to God.[110]

Ignorant of Lester's spiritual direction, Day nonetheless recalls a profound epiphany on a Manhattan bus. Reading the foreword of Merton's *Contemplative Prayer*, she found a quote from William Blake about "beams of love":

> Suddenly I remembered coming home from a meeting in Brooklyn many years ago, sitting in an uncomfortable bus seat facing a few poor people. One of them, a downcast, ragged man, suddenly epitomized for me the desolation, the hopelessness of the destitute, and I began to weep. I had been struck by one of those "beams of love," wounded by it in a most particular way.[111]

Contemplation and conscientization are two ways to develop Assisi and Mississippi eyes, two ways to refuse conformity to domination systems, and two ways to exorcise the housed oppressor. Our failure to see, whether willful blindness or collective delusion, turns people into worms who seek only to devour even if it means gorging on one another and oneself. Seeing, as Ruusbroec says, whether through contemplation or conscientization, begins a meandering path toward God and the realm.

KNITTING HEAVEN TO EARTH

Our consciousness of God, like our awareness of the world, can be awakened in multiple, complex, overlapping, and conflicting ways. If Merton calls them "seeds of contemplation,"[112] John Cassian dissects each seed. We can experience God, Cassian says, in the "magnificence" of creation and be astonished that God "keeps a count of the waves." We can be alerted to God's omniscience when "we meditate on the fact that the sands of the sea

---

110. Lester, *Ambassador of Reconciliation*, 125.
111. Day, *By Little*, 181.
112. The title of an essay in Merton, *New Seeds of Contemplation*, 14–20.

are numbered" and that God is aware of each drop of rain, every day and every hour, "everything past and everything to come." Likewise, we ought to be astounded at God's response to human wantonness in "the spectacle of God's justice" and in God's "unspeakable mercy" and "unfailing patience" in the face of humanity's "numberless crimes." We can also be, in C. S. Lewis's phrase, "surprised by joy" or, as Cassian puts it, awakened through an "eternity of happiness and of rewards."[113] We can be surprised awake by human sanctity, sensing God's presence in each generation's saints. Our awareness can even be spurred by the unknowable, "that astonished gaze at God's ungraspable nature." All of this—God's will, God's love, God's mercy, God's presence, God's creative power—is available to us from the time we are "in the cradle." As Paul announces defiantly that nothing in creation can separate us from God's love (Rom 8:35–39), Cassian proclaims joyfully that everything in creation can reveal God's love. To Cassian, it is next to impossible to find a godless time or godforsaken place. Only sloth or infidelity can keep us from discovering God; God *is* everywhere, in creation, in society, in everything seen and unseen.

Following Cassian's logic, Augustine kicks himself for having been obtusely unaware of God. Yet he lightly sloughs aside his self-flagellation with a praise that rolls from his pen like poetry from someone newly in love.

> How late I came to love you, O beauty so ancient and so fresh, how late I came to love you! You were within me while I had gone outside to seek you. Unlovely, myself, I rushed towards all those lovely things you had made. And always you were with me, I was not with you. All these beauties kept me far from you—although they would not have existed at all unless they had their being in you. You called, you cried, you shattered my deafness. You sparkled, you blazed, you drove away my blindness. You shed your fragrance, and I drew in my breath and I pant for you. I tasted and now I hunger and thirst. You touched me and now I burn with longing for your peace.[114]

Cassian insists it is easy to perceive God's presence, yet Augustine finds God "late," and many do not find God at all. It is a simple paradox: awakenings to God are constantly available and completely impossible—the most sustained efforts from the most profound minds and most mature hearts can be infuriatingly unrewarded, and yet God is even found when we forget to look.

---

113. Cassian, *Conferences*, 50–51.
114. Leech, *Experiencing God*, 324–25; Augustine, *Confessions* 10.27.

Augustine's awakening led to a passionate proclamation of love, but to be awake to God is not always ecstatic, consoling, blissful, or radiant. Otto's *mysterium tremendum* evokes knee-buckling awe, thought-dissolving bewilderment, and heart-quivering terror. This is the terror felt in tremors on Mt. Sinai of the dangerous God of thunder and lightning. This is Isaiah's experience in the temple of a dazzling brilliance that accentuates his sense of frailty. To a lesser extent, it is Merton's confounded rawness in "Fire Watch." C. S. Lewis aptly captures the dread of the holy in his Space Trilogy when Ransom, the first-person narrator, monitors his emotions as he approaches something other and otherworldly: "My fear was now of another kind. I felt sure that the creature was what we call 'good,' but I wasn't sure whether I liked 'goodness' so much as I had supposed. This is a very terrible experience. As long as what you are afraid of is something evil, you may still hope that the good may come to your rescue. But suppose you struggle through to the good and find that it also is dreadful?"[115] For Otto, the holy is beyond goodness. It is an "other" category that makes us shudder merely because it is so different.[116]

Cassian stresses experiences of life and love and joy, but if alertness to God inevitably led to bliss, an endless stream of pilgrims would willingly risk almost unendurable spiritual discipline and physical hardship to reach it. Being aware of God is similar to being awake to a complex and self-contradictory world. God transcends light and darkness (Isa 45:7). God is knowable and unknowable. The theological distinction between God's *energies* (through which divine self-revelation occurs) and God's *essence* (which remains devoutly hidden) melts clarity into a bubbling brew of bliss and anxiety. Being awake to God opens us to height, breadth, and unfathomable depth. It penetrates every abyss and opens us to a more multidimensional life. But is it pleasant? Sometimes.

If God can be perceived anywhere, as Cassian says, there can be no distinctions about *where* you would experience God or *who* would have that encounter. Epiphanies can take place in light or darkness. They can be nurtured by an elder's lifetime of spiritual discipline or come completely unbidden to a child. In his late twenties, during the Montgomery bus boycott, King had what has been called the most significant epiphany of his life.[117] His family was asleep when he answered the phone and heard someone bark yet another death threat into his ear. His mind numbed by one too many verbal blows and his confidence sapped, he sat alone in his kitchen, his cup

---

115. Lewis, *Perelandra*, 19.
116. Otto, *Idea of the Holy*, 15, 17.
117. Garrow, *Bearing the Cross*, 57–58.

of coffee untouched. He felt drained of his capacity to encourage others; he had no inner resources to rouse himself from despair. In that godless moment, "I experienced the presence of the Divine as I had never experienced God before. It seemed as though I could hear the quiet assurance of an inner voice saying, 'Stand up for righteousness, stand up for truth; and God will be at your side forever.' Almost at once my fears began to go."[118] King told and retold this story of God's welcome intrusion. In the face of vulgar hatred and bald-faced violence, God comforted him with words of renewal and empowerment.[119] King was both prepared for and dumbfounded by that moment. All of his life, he had been nurtured in faith. Under extreme pressure, his faith had feebly ebbed away. Suddenly it was rejuvenated.

Knowing the ebb and flow of faith and life, spiritual masters recommend that we cultivate a constant state of watchfulness. Theophan the Recluse compares the awareness of God to the chronic consciousness of a toothache:[120] how can you not be aware of that pain? How can you be aware of anything else? Thich Nhat Hanh describes consciousness as a "non-toothache":[121] how can you become as aware of something as if it were a toothache without the pulsing pain to remind you? King hears God's voice when he is *not* looking, *not* listening, *not* waiting, *not* ready. Even in what might be considered dubious conditions for an awakening, King felt delivered, honored, and loved.

The contemplative tradition adamantly maintains that God initiates every epiphany, opening, and awakening. Any and every revelation is a gift. Eckhart, whose accusers suspected that he blurred sanctification with deification, says that we should not imagine that we have to call out to God in far-off heaven, nor think that *we* are pilgrims seeking a distant or elusive deity (cf. Deut 30:11–14). God, he says, "can hardly wait for you to open up."[122] Similarly, one of the hadith declares that every time we walk toward God, God runs toward us.[123] According to Eckhart God longs for each person "a thousand times more than you long" for God; and when God touches us, "the opening and the entering are a single act."[124] Like Eckhart, Teresa of Ávila stresses the anti-Pelagian character of mystical experience. God, she says, transports the human spirit as easily as a giant might move a piece of

---

118. King, *Stride Toward Freedom*, 134–35.
119. King, *Strength to Love*, 113.
120. Bloom, *Beginning to Pray*, 24.
121. Nhat Hanh, *Touching Peace*, 7–8.
122. Eckhart, *Sermons & Treatises I*, 44.
123. Cleary, *Wisdom of Prophet*, 84.
124. Eckhart, *Sermons & Treatises I*, 44.

straw. Using another homely metaphor, she says, "when God has willed that a toad should fly," God does not wait for it to sprout wings. The initiative and impetus belong to God.[125] An incredulous Merton mocked the notion that people could manipulate contemplative methods to yield predictable results.[126] His personal epiphanies were the fruit of faith, prayer, and solitude, but they were given, not achieved.[127] He could say *what* he saw; with less precision he could guess what it meant; he knew nothing of *how* his eyes were opened. Ruusbroec credits "the light of God's grace" over "exterior works" or "fervent interior zeal."[128] As Gregory Palamas explains, God has planted something within us—Dorotheos's divine spark?—inherently receptive to truth. Adam possessed an abundance of "natural wisdom," he says, "more so than his descendants."[129] Meditation or contemplation may ignite or rekindle the spark, but there is no well-charted, smoothly paved path to enlightenment.

God is omnipresent (Cassian), yet epiphanies are surprising (King). The intent of Merton's contemplative life was to create a spiritual environment that nurtured breakthroughs, but he understood the paradoxical gift in his most powerful revelations. Even before he entered the monastery, Merton had what he would later describe as an unforgettable epiphany.[130] As he sat in a church service in Havana in 1940, external distractions were unfavorable to an illumination. The church doors open, street noise, bells, car horns, and the cries of newsboys pierced the liturgy's sanctity and obscured the ring of the communion bell. But suddenly, as the prayer of consecration began, Merton felt something inside himself "like a thunderclap." His eyes fixed only on the Eucharist, "the priest seemed to be standing in the exact center of the universe."

> I knew with the most absolute and unquestionable certainty that before me, between me and the altar, somewhere in the center of the church, up in the air (or any other place because in no place), but directly before my eyes, or directly present to some apprehension or other of mine which was above that of the sense, was at the same time God in all God's essence, all God's power, God in the flesh and God in God's self and God surrounded by the radiant faces of the thousand million uncountable numbers

---

125. Teresa, *Life of Teresa*, 217, 251–52.
126. Merton, *Inner Experience*, 2, 5.
127. Merton, *Conjectures*, 158.
128. Ruusbroec, *Spiritual Espousals*, 71–72.
129. Palamas, *Triads*, 30.
130. Merton, *Courage for Truth*, 236.

of saints contemplating God's Glory and praising God's Holy Name.[131]

Merton's eyes had grazed the hem of God's garment. This awareness that heaven was in front of him "struck me like a thunderbolt and went through me like a flash of lightning and seemed to lift me clean up off the earth."[132] In a later reflection on this awakening, he said he had thought, "Heaven is right here in front of me: Heaven, Heaven!"[133] Such an epiphany, Merton says, is entirely a gift, pure grace.

Revelation does not demand such a jarring experience. Following John of the Cross, Merton believes that we can apprehend the same mystery through the simplicity of faith. As John writes, "believing in" God is the same as "seeing" God.[134] For Merton, Havana crystallized his conversion. He had found heaven in the church, a foreshadowing of his elation when he arrived at Gethsemani.[135] He had begun the mystic's journey Thurman describes.

Eighteen years later, Merton had a second epiphany in a decidedly secular setting. His attitude to the city of Louisville embodied his love-hate relationship with the world, but his perception of the city had slowly and haltingly changed. He had been accused of having "stomped" on Louisville,[136] and at times he loathed it.[137] Sometimes his visits reinforced this revulsion, but he gradually came to the realization Thurman predicted. Even before his epiphany, he wrote of a visit to Louisville,

> I met the world and I found it no longer so wicked after all. Perhaps the things I had resented about the world when I left it were defects of my own that I had projected upon it. Now, on the contrary, I found that everything stirred me with a deep and mute sense of compassion. . . . I went through the city, realizing for the first time in my life how much good are all the people in the world and how much value they have in the sight of God.[138]

The spiritual groundwork laid, with astonishing swiftness a tidal wave of compassion overwhelmed his cultivated skepticism. Walking through the

---

131. Merton, *Run to the Mountain*, 218.
132. Ibid.
133. Merton, *Seven Storey Mountain*, 285.
134. John of the Cross, *Collected Works*, 129.
135. Merton, *Seven Storey Mountain*, 320.
136. Merton, *Introductions*, 44.
137. Merton, *Search for Solitude*, 316.
138. Merton, *Sign of Jonas*, 97–98.

commercial district of Louisville in 1958, "[I] suddenly realized that I loved all the people and that none of them were or could be totally alien to me. As if waking from a dream—the dream of my separateness, of the 'special' vocation to be different."[139] Solitude had enabled him to see "such things with a clarity that would be impossible to anyone completely immersed in" the world.[140] Because he was no longer enmeshed in the world he could now love it. The arc of the conversion Thurman described had reached its hairpin turn. Like his experience in Havana, Merton considered this vision sheer gift, generous grace—"this seeing . . . is only given." In Havana, he saw heaven in church. Now he realized that "the gate of heaven is everywhere."[141]

Ten years later, on his Asian pilgrimage, Merton stood as a spiritual tourist before Buddhist statues at Polonnaruwa in Sri Lanka. Days earlier, he had surveyed Hindu shrines only to be distracted by secular tourists and youths hawking spiritual knickknacks. At first, Merton took in the Buddhist statues through his photographer's eye, astonished by the sculptures' aesthetic beauty. Then, "Looking at these figures, I was suddenly, almost forcibly, jerked clean out of the habitual, half-tied vision of things, and an inner clearness, clarity, as if exploding from the rocks themselves, became evident and obvious." Writing in the Asian religious lexicon with which he was experimenting, he realized, "there is no puzzle, no problem, and really no 'mystery.' All problems are resolved and everything is clear, simply because what matters is clear. The rock, all matter, all life, is charged with *dharmakaya*—everything is emptiness and everything is compassion."[142]

As startlingly profound as Merton's epiphanies were, they primarily reinforced things he already knew. Before Havana, he knew that he could find God in church. Before Louisville, he knew that people were holy. Polonnaruwa confirmed what he had written in an essay, "Everything That Is Is Holy."[143] He had used the same theme in a conference just before coming to Asia: "you have to . . . see God in God's creation and creation in God . . . everything manifests God . . . God is in everything."[144] Echoing Cassian, years before he had written, "thus as we go about the world, everything we meet and everything we see and hear and touch, far from defiling, purifies us and plants in us something more of contemplation and of heaven."[145]

139. Merton, *Search for Solitude*, 182.
140. Merton, *Conjectures*, 158.
141. Ibid.
142. Merton, *Other Side*, 323.
143. Merton, *New Seeds*, 21–28.
144. Merton, *Merton in Alaska*, 139–40.
145. Merton, *New Seeds*, 25.

Even in his early sin-obsessed days, Merton anticipated this later discovery in tones with which Traherne would have resonated.

> Since everything that is, is good, and since the world is full of things that are good in themselves and which all proclaim the infinite goodness and power of God: if we rejoiced in the good that is possessed by others, formally as possessed by them, we would not be able to look at a flower or a blade of grass or an insect or a drop of water or a grain of sand or a leaf, let alone a whole tree, or a bird, or a living animal, or a human being, without exploding with exultation.[146]

Merton's spiritual journey had completed its turn. His first awakening to God led him into the church and into the monastery; his second made him embrace the human race and creation.

The arc of Merton's journey, while *a* norm, is not *the* norm. It was inverted in the life of A. J. Muste. Described in 1940 as America's Number One Pacifist,[147] Muste took a circuitous path in which he lost interest in heaven while remaining passionate about a new earth. From a theologically and politically conservative upbringing, he swung to Protestantism's liberal wing. An ordained Presbyterian minister, he resigned his pastoral position during World War I because he believed his pacifism kept him from being an effective pastor with parishioners whose sons had been killed in the war. He became a Quaker and a labor leader. Even though epiphanies had graced his early years, his disillusionment with the church's blithe indifference to injustice eroded his faith. The church Rauschenbusch decried for having lost its "radical ethical spirit" and "its revolutionary consciousness"[148] alienated Muste. The church Dorothy Day feared—moored and mired in a distant and disconnected heaven—was the sin-stained church from which Muste fled with the same fervor that impelled Merton to abandon the corrupt world. Always seeking personal integrity, when Muste abandoned the institution he also abandoned its faith, the body and the person of Christ. His restless pilgrimage led him first to labor organizing and then to radical Leftist politics. He became a socialist and finally a Marxist. His impatience with each new ideology kept him on an endless exodus. One experiment followed another as he moved further from the church and, he believed, God. But as with Augustine, when it seemed "late," a powerful opening redirected his life.

---

146. Merton, *Thomas Merton Reader*, 316.
147. Robinson, *Abraham Went Out*, xiii.
148. Rauschenbusch, *Social Gospel*, 26.

In Paris in 1936, he entered St. Sulpice Church as a self-identified Trotskyite tourist: "When you go sightseeing in Europe, you go to see churches even if you believe it would be better if there were no churches for anyone to visit." Cluttered with statues and overpopulated by saints, St. Sulpice did not suit his Quaker tastes. This was not Merton's aesthetic enthrallment at Polonnaruwa. But as Muste entered the church, "Without the slightest premonition of what was going to happen, I was saying to myself: 'This is where you belong,'" inside the church, not outside. When he stood up to leave, he had been reconverted to Christian pacifism.[149] His wandering was over, his exodus fulfilled. Like Merton, his journey had taken a hairpin curve as he rediscovered a discarded pattern of religious activism that would guide him for the rest of his life.

If Thurman foresaw the arc of Merton's life, no one traced Muste's. He had been as disdainful of the church as Merton had been of the world. Merton left the world to find God and then discovered God in the world. Muste left God to find the revolution and then rediscovered God. If Merton trekked from church to human race to creation, Muste's mid-life experience in St. Sulpice was his "Havana" *after* his "Louisville." Together, their back-and-forth consciousness mirrored the prophets in being directed at one moment to God's divinity and the next to society's reality. Their crisscrossing paths knit together church and world, heaven and earth, spiritual and material, mystical and political.

Hairpin turns and crisscrossing paths, though, are not unique to Merton and Muste. Kneading into a unified pastoral wisdom the traditions that offer spiritual discipline even as they rely on proactive grace, Symeon the New Theologian says that God reveals the divine to us only to the extent that we are ready to absorb it.[150] If God were not constantly veiled, al-Hallaj warns, we would be so entranced that we would be driven insane. Yet in the next instant he declares, "there is no longer a veil between God and me, not even a wink."[151] The interweaving journeys of Merton and Muste, then, tell us as much about what they were *ready* to see as what they saw.

As Cassian says, we can see God in the magnificence of creation, in the quest for justice, and in human sanctity. Day made an adolescent commitment to justice, *then* an adult commitment to God. Muste started with faith, lost it in his quest for justice and then, like Day, found the God of peace. Nurtured in faith, King felt it quiver beneath an onslaught of hatred, then

---

149. Muste, "True International," 667–68, "Steamer Letter," 109; Robinson, *Abraham Went Out*, 63–64.

150. Symeon, *Discourses*, 356.

151. Massignon, *Passion of Al-Hallaj*, 284.

had it breathed back into him. In the end, Day, Muste, King, and Merton found that awareness of God awakened them to the world, and their awareness of the world awakened them to God. The relationship of the transcendent and the earthly, the mystical and the political, is much more sinuous than they had imagined. A never-to-be-severed cord links heaven to earth. And when the link weakens in our perception, imagination, or faith, God knits them back together and, in that knitting, pulls heaven closer to earth.

AN AWAKENED HEART AND A NEW EARTH

Sounding apocalyptic, like a purveyor of science fiction dystopia or many a chapter of modern history, Abba Anthony predicted, "A time is coming when people will go mad, and when they see someone who is not mad, they will attack saying, 'You are mad, you are not like us.'"[152] Hannah Arendt describes Nazi Germany's inversion of norms, a time when madness became normalcy and normalcy madness. In civilized countries, she writes, one assumes "that the voice of conscience tells everybody 'Thou shalt not kill.'" But "the law of Hitler's land demanded that the voice of conscience tell everybody 'Thou shalt kill.'" "Evil in the Third Reich," she says, "had lost the quality by which most people recognize it—the quality of temptation. Many Germans and many Nazis, probably an overwhelming majority of them, must have been tempted *not* to murder, *not* to rob, *not* to let their neighbors go off to their doom . . . and not to become accomplices in all these crimes by benefiting from them. But, God knows, they had learned how to resist temptation."[153] In Muste's words, they had conformed. In Merton's vocabulary, they were all too sane.

People tend to associate inversions of justice and perversions of decency with totalitarianism, but *any and every* systemic injustice enshrines an inversion of God's realm, turns sanctity to madness and reason to murder. Nazi Germany, it turns out, was no more than an extreme form of the norm. As Merton points out, however horrific the Holocaust, less than two decades later the democratically elected government of the United States calmly created a coherent plan for genocide. Merton debunked the voice of civilization, the very same voice Rumi describes that denies other possibilities: this world, this dungeon, this war, this injustice is all there is; there is no other way, truth, or life. Those addicted to the benefits, deprivations, and "necessities" (Ellacuría) of the status quo always accuse those filled by the Spirit of being foolish, crazy, or drunk (Acts 2:13). Those awake to God will

---

152. Ward, *Sayings of the Desert*, 6.
153. Arendt, *Eichmann in Jerusalem*, 150 (italics hers).

practice, in King's words, "creative maladjustment"[154] and become "transformed nonconformists."[155] The world will always accuse them of being outside agitators, troublemakers, Communists. And, like those who said that Jesus was guilty, they will be right. Jesus *was* dangerous; those who see *are* subversive. Oscar Romero calls it an irrevocable but oft-forgotten part of the church's vocation to use the sword of truth to cut through an unjust society's deceptions: "A church that doesn't provoke any crises, a gospel that doesn't unsettle, a word of God that doesn't get under anyone's skin, a word of God that doesn't touch the real sin of the society in which it is being proclaimed, what gospel is that?"[156] The gospel that had won Romero's heart was the Word of a new heaven and a new earth, the end goal of the revolution envisioned by the Hebrew prophets—laborers paid justly, the sick healed quickly, infants and the aged dancing joyfully, prayers answered before being uttered (Isa 65:17–25). Rauschenbusch cautions in one breath that there will never be a "perfect" society, but proclaims or prays in the next, "Perhaps these nineteen centuries of Christian influence have been a long preliminary state of growth, and now the flower and fruit are almost here. If at this juncture we can rally sufficient religious faith and moral strength to snap the bonds of evil . . . the generations yet unborn will mark this as that great day of the Lord for which the ages waited."[157] For at least a glimmering instant, the new earth unveiled itself so powerfully in Rauschenbusch's imagination that the world as it is, with its myriad detours, dead ends, cul-de-sacs, sand traps, and death traps, had been obscured.

Yet in the world as it is, God's revolution is still announced—every vision a prophecy, every story a gospel, and every poem a beatitude—whenever the first are last and the last first. Flannery O'Connor describes a vision of the revolution of God in her short story "Revelation."[158] In it, Mrs. Turpin shares the social location, predisposition, and desperate need of Lester's nurse to identify with the privileged that would, if they paid her any heed, scoff at the notion that she was one of their own. Mrs. Turpin pledges allegiance to a racist, classist social order. Like Rumi's embryo, she does not want to—she cannot—envision another world. She is content with her tiny stale slice of the status quo. For her, the revolution of God is nonexistent. Even her imagined conversations with Jesus merely help her to express her social and racial prejudices against white trash and blacks. Her

---

154. King, *Strength to Love*, 24.
155. Ibid., 17–25; cf. Paul's fools for Christ (1 Cor 1:18–31).
156. Romero, *Violence of Love*, 54.
157. Rauschenbusch, *Christianity and the Social*, 422.
158. O'Connor, "Revelation," 191–218.

sleepy musings lead her to dream that everyone beneath her social station can be "crammed together in a box car... [and] ridden off to be put in a gas oven."[159] In a doctor's office waiting room, Mrs. Turpin plays a mental game of one-upmanship, labeling an ugly girl a "lunatic," as she hyperactively scorns her neighbor. Back home before sunset, a vision sparked by a streak in the sky rips away her dull and dulled perceptions.

> A visionary light settled in her eyes. She saw the streak as a vast swinging bridge extending upward from the earth through a field of living fire. Upon it a vast horde of souls were rumbling toward heaven. There were whole companies of white-trash, clean for the first time in their lives, and the bands of black n-----s in white robes, and battalions of freaks and lunatics shouting and clapping and leaping like frogs. And bringing up the end of the procession was a tribe of people whom she recognized at once as those who, like herself and [her husband] Claud, had always had a little of everything and the God-given wit to use it right. She leaned forward to observe them closer. They were marching behind the others with great dignity, accountable as they had always been for good order and common sense and respectable behavior. They alone were on key. Yet she could see by their shocked and altered faces that even their virtues were being burned away. She lowered her hands and gripped the rail of the hog pen, her eyes small but fixed unblinkingly on what lay ahead. In a moment the vision faded but she remained where she was, immobile.
> ... In the woods around her the invisible cricket choruses had struck up, but what she heard were the voices of the souls climbing upward into the starry field and shouting hallelujah.[160]

Mrs. Turpin reacts to her vision as much of white America responded to King's beloved community and as many white South Africans reacted to Desmond Tutu's "rainbow people of God."[161] In the envisioned heavenward procession, Mrs. Turpin has lost her place. The last *have* become first, and the first last. Hers is a fictionalized version of Merton's Louisville epiphany and Traherne's world in which even society's dregs are shining lights and glittering jewels. For a split second, Mrs. Turpin sees.

According to Abba Anthony, if only we could see, we would be mad. In his "Mad Farmer" poems, Wendell Berry breathes life into revolutionary madness. The Mad Farmer is always and everywhere contrary and

159. Ibid., 196.
160. Ibid., 218.
161. Tutu, *Rainbow People of God*.

subversive. His is the Sermon on the Mount's "mysticism of action,"[162] the logic of the Beatitudes, the madness of Anthony, the creative maladjustment of King, the holy disobedience of Muste, and the Desert Protest[163] of Merton that rebels against the forces of the market and the sanity of Eichmann. The "Mad Farmer's Manifesto" says,

> To be sane in a mad time
> is bad for the brain, worse
> for the heart.

All the same,

> The world
> is a holy vision, had we clarity to see it.[164]

Given such a vision, society's "yes" becomes the poet's "no"; and society's propriety yields to the poet's maladjusted eye.

> If I have been caught
> so often laughing at funerals, that was because
> I knew the dead were already slipping away,
> preparing a comeback . . .
> "Dance," they told me,
> and I stood still, and while they stood
> quiet in line at the gate of the Kingdom, I danced.
> "Pray," they said, and I laughed, covering myself
> in the earth's brightnesses, and then stole off gray
> into the midst of a revel, and prayed like an orphan.
> When they said, "I know that my Redeemer liveth,"
> I told them, "He's dead." And when they told me,
> "God is dead," I answered, "He goes fishing every day
> in the Kentucky River. I see him often."[165]

The Mad Farmer parodies the aphorisms of world-as-it-is wisdom: "Love the quick profit . . . want more/of everything ready-made. Be afraid to know your neighbors and to die."[166] Instead the Mad Farmer Liberation Front calls people to complete contrarianism:

> . . . every day do something

---

162. Happold, *Mysticism*, 102.
163. Merton, *Hidden Ground*, 85–86, *Nonviolent Alternative*, 260.
164. Berry, "Mad Farmer Manifesto: The First Amendment," in *Collected Poems*, 154.
165. Berry, "Contrariness of Mad Farmer," in *Collected Poems*, 121.
166. Berry, "Manifesto: Mad Farmer Liberation," in *Collected Poems*, 151.

that won't compute. Love the Lord.
Love the world. Work for nothing.
Take all that you have and be poor.
Love someone who does not deserve it.
. . . Ask the questions that have no answers.
Invest in the millennium. Plant sequoias.
Say that your main crop is the forest
that you did not plant,
that you will not live to harvest. . . . Be joyful
though you have considered all the facts. . . . Be like the fox
who makes more tracks than necessary,
some in the wrong direction.
Practice resurrection.[167]

Like the zaddikim of Hasidic lore that have herbs leap up and cling to them as they pass by,[168] the Mad Farmer plants "a forest of little pines" in a parking lot only to find that

Pumpkins
ran out to the ends of their vines
to follow him. Ripe plums
and peaches reached into his pockets.
Flowers sprang up in his tracks
everywhere he stepped.[169]

The Mad Farmer, *because* he is mad, is righteous. He no longer devours. He is one with the orchard. And the Mad Sower who inspires the Mad Farmer is Jesus.

Yet even among those who seek truth, temptations lurk. Like John Bunyan's pilgrim, one can fall asleep near the end of the journey.[170] One can be a self-proclaimed revolutionary—a Christian—and yet be uncomfortable with God's realm as it will be. Those who dream of alternatives to the current social chaos do not necessarily seek first the realm of God; often they merely imagine a new social disorder. One does not have to be Mrs. Turpin, hating so many and loving so few, to know that the realm will break all molds. If it is truly of God, it will not even conform to our most radical dreams.

---

167. Berry, "Manifesto: Mad Farmer Liberation," in *Collected Poems*, 151.
168. Buber, *Tales: Later Masters*, 217.
169. Berry, "Mad Farmer Revolution," in *Collected Poems*, 120.
170. Bunyan, *Pilgrim's Progress*, 285.

The climax of Sembene Ousmane's novella *Xala*[171] pictures this disjunction between one's not-yet-new heart and a truly new earth with an outbreak of mayhem/riot/revolution as uncontainable as the vortex of God's whirlwind answer to Job. When that vortex enters Traherne's world made by human hands, as Mrs. Turpin's vision invades her contented misery, a melee unveils the hopes and fears of those who seek a world in which the mentally ill, physically deformed, and spiritually bedraggled meet the privileged on equal terms. It is one thing to envision how the human race will enter heaven (O'Connor); it is another to see the last becoming first on earth (Ousmane).

In *Xala*, the wealthy and powerful El Hadji is about to marry his third wife when he finds he is victimized by a curse, a *xala*, that makes him impotent. El Hadji's daughter, Rama, and her boyfriend—adult children of privilege—have anointed themselves aptly suited to lead the poor in a revolution of their design. When a street beggar leads an invasion of El Hadji's mansion, it creates a hubbub like the climactic scene in the controversial 1930s movie *Freaks* when all of the circus show "freaks" turn against a beautiful woman who has humiliated one of their own. *Xala*'s conclusion is an off-kilter retelling of Israelite slaves plundering Egypt as they depart for the promised land, a surrealistic reworking of the Magnificat, the poor lifted up and the mighty cast down.

> Walking abreast across the entire width of the road came a procession of lame and blind people, lepers, legless cripples, one-legged cripples, men, women and children, led by the beggar. There was something repulsive about the procession, which gave off a fetid smell of ragged clothes....
>
> [T]he beggar rang the bell. Then rang again. A pause. The maid opened the door. She drew back startled, nearly falling over onto the steps. Leading the way, the beggar pushed open the door, followed by his retinue. Some struggled crawling on to the verandah. They went into the sitting-room and settled themselves down as if it belonged to them. A legless cripple, his palms and knees covered with black soil from the garden, printed a black trail on the floor like a giant snail. With his strong arms he hoisted himself up into a red velvet armchair, where he sat with a foolish, triumphant grin that revealed his broken teeth and his pendulous lower lip. Another with a maggoty face and a hole where his nose had been, his deformed, scarred body visible through his rags, grabbed a white shirt and putting it on admired himself in a mirror, roaring with laughter at the reflection of his own antics. A woman with twins, emboldened by the

---

171. Ousmane, *Xala*, 108–12.

others, tore open a cushion on the settee and wrapped one of her babies in the material. On the other cushion she rested a foot with a cloven heel and stunted toes....

A cripple with a degenerate's head and runny eyes stuffed the crockery into a sling bag. Opposite him a one-armed man was using his remaining limb to heap in front of him all the shiny objects he could find....

Like the paralytic brought by his friends to Jesus, the "moving trunk" encourages his friends to throw him onto a bed where he bounces up and down "emitting incoherent shouts of joy each time he fell back." The rioting guests rummage through the kitchen finding alcohol, forbidden in a Muslim household. When El Hadji protests, the beggar calmly replies he is there to collect reparations for a crime the rich man has committed. When El Hadji threatens to phone the police, the beggar demands payment to remove the *xala*. The beggar then revives El Hadji's memory with a story reminiscent of Naboth's vineyard (1 Kgs 21:1–16): Falsifying the clan names of the beggar's family, El Hadji bought a large piece of land, and with his legal ruse won a case in a corrupt court. When the Lazarus-like beggar protested, the rich man had him arrested. When the beggar left prison and again approached the rich man he was beaten. El Hadji, the beggar says, has attained his wealth dishonestly, and his intermittent acts of charity have been vain attempts to scour his conscience. To cure the curse El Hadji must strip naked and let each person spit on him three times.

El Hadji's revolutionary daughter Rama has the opportunity she has eagerly anticipated. When a police officer pushes open the mansion door, she claims it is the day that comes once a month when her father gives alms to the poor. But does her deceit protect the riffraff or her father's reputation? "Rama herself was bursting with anger. Against whom? Against her father? Against these wretched people? She who was always ready with the words 'revolution' and 'new social order' felt deep within her breast something like a stone falling heavily onto her heart, crushing her."[172] The novel ends with external and internal standoffs.

What Otto writes about the mystic's shuddering dread before God is equally true of our anxieties about God's realm. The revolution of God goes hand in hand with revulsion, not only for the Mrs. Turpins of the world but also the Ramas who dream of justice but are repulsed when they discover that equality, like love, is a harsh and dreadful thing. Those who understand the need for congruence between our spiritual revolution and the realm to come anticipate Rama's failure of will. Recognizing a revolutionary prayer

---

172. Ibid., 111–12.

when he prays it, Leech says, to pray "Your Kingdom come" is to pray that one's own life will be transformed[173]: "Political depth and spirituality meet at the point where the inner revolution and the outer revolution are seen as one and indivisible. The fate of the soul is the fate of the social order."[174]

To us, in our half-tied, half-freed vision of things, the realm of God will appear unruly, misshapen, and terrifying. Only our personal metanoia, the expulsion of the world from our hearts, the conquest of our housed oppressor, allows us to seek social metanoia. Only an inner revolution prepares us to embrace God's revolution. Only when our deformed hearts conform to the realm of God can we wholeheartedly welcome a new earth. Then, and only then, the Christian becomes a wholehearted revolutionary.

MEDITATION: CONVALESCING

The regression was jarring. Everything drooped—her head, neck, and cheeks. Everything was dry—her hair, skin, and bones. The twinkle in her dancing eyes had become a blank, unmoving stare. Her charming smile had been wiped from her face, and from the earth. She showed no affect. Her head tilted down and to the right.

Two weeks earlier her eyes gleamed, her smile lit up the room, her wit ignited smiles, her face was bright, and she walked—not easily, but she walked—from room to room. Now she sat in her wheelchair dazed, not recognizing me or acknowledging my presence. Two weeks before, she could have remembered seeing the church being built in 1914. She knew the first three priests. One, she said, had stayed too long. Once when I teased her with a question, "have I been here too long?" she said, "not yet" and smiled mischievously. At age ninety-two, she provided a rare link with the birth of the congregation.

Winona and her friend Joy, both widows, came to the church's Senior Guild. They were deservedly beloved. In one week, both of them had been struck down, Joy by a stroke and—a week later—death. Winona's health had plunged, the cause undiagnosed, and her daughter placed her in an upscale convalescent facility half a city removed from her friends. The doctor at the facility refused to let her attend Joy's funeral. Winona could die, he explained. As I stared at her in the wheelchair, everything dry and drooping, I asked, what difference would that make?

My first visit was an uncomfortable trip to a barren landscape. The terrain had shifted. Everything that made Winona who she was was gone. I

---

173. Leech, *True Prayer*, 74.
174. Ibid., 89.

spoke with her as if it might matter, not believing that it would. I spoke with her as if she was in a coma and she might hear what I was saying. You could call it faith. You could call it hope. I knew I was bluffing.

I began with small talk. I told her about her friends, the church, and the funeral. I might as well have read to her from *Grimm's Fairy Tales* or a German theological dictionary. But there in front of me, as my words meandered meaninglessly, her neck straightened. She sat erect. She looked me in the eye, and her eyes skipped again. Color blushed across her cheeks. Sinews and flesh covered dry bones, and the breath entered her. She spoke as if two weeks had not passed, as if she had not moved, as if the undiagnosed problem was unreal. She was Winona.

Everything was the same, except now she felt "stuck in right field," exiled and forgotten—our bones are dried up, our hope lost; we are cut off. She always looked the same when I arrived—her head dangling, her eyes blank, no wink, no wit, no spark. Then I spoke. She awoke, always in a few minutes, always in the same way, always an accidental exercise in the Valley of Dry Bones.

The Senior Guild decided for the first time to move our meeting halfway across the city to see her. We made the one-hour drive in carpools. The first ones to arrive roused her. We celebrated the Eucharist—the presence of Christ—in her room, the sacrament feeling more sacred in the secular setting. We shared a light lunch and light conversation. A convalescent home staff person brought her food that must have been extraordinarily healthy because it looked like green gruel. She had already had a few bites of an ordinary, homemade sandwich that delighted her as much as a divine delicacy from the Great Banquet. The staff person returned and warned us that anything she ate had to be preapproved. As soon as she exited, one Senior Guild member closed the door, and another, a retired octogenarian nurse asked Winona, "Would you like a cookie?" Another taste of grace.

I have visited others equally cut off, an elderly man with a form of dementia, a once-brilliant woman who could no longer remember her name. And when I started the Lord's Prayer—that revolutionary prayer—they joined me at "who art in heaven." Their minds almost imprisoned, the universe almost dark, the words still awakened them to God.

I have visited others equally cut off, yet hers was the only resurrection I have seen: a voice crying, Winona! Come forth! The Senior Guild sharing sandwiches and cookies as the risen Jesus cooked fish and broke bread to open the eyes of his disciples. I spoke, and the scales fell from her eyes. How little it took to awaken her—a few minutes . . . a few words . . . a prayer.

3

With Moaning and with Mourning

I had heard of you by the hearing of the ear, but now my eye sees you.
 —Job 42:5

To see or not to see, that is the question.
 —Bernard McGinn[1]

Sometimes our hearts are so awakened . . .that we cannot confess them in any language but that of tears.
 —William Law[2]

Tears are the messengers that let you know whether life or death is in the heart.

1. McGinn, *Harvest of Mysticism*, 457.
2. Law, *Serious Call*, 171–72.

—Catherine of Siena[3]

Wash your face only with tears.
   —Symeon the New Theologian[4]

The duty of the monk is not to teach but to weep.
   —Bernard of Clairvaux[5]

I entered the village . . . and the place was filled with moaning and with mourning for the dead.
   —Black Elk[6]

. . . then Christ bears all alone the burden of us. And so he remains, moaning and mourning.
   —Julian of Norwich[7]

Blessed are those who mourn.
   —Matthew 5:4

MEDITATION: A HOSPITAL BED PSALM

It was Sunday night. Matthew was going to sleep in a bed that night, a hospital bed. He was going to sleep under a roof, and not the one the church provided in our gardening shed, nor the one I had given him in temporary dispensation—a couch in the church lounge when I thought he had pneumonia. Now things added up. He was a lifelong smoker in his late fifties suffering from congested lungs and physical exhaustion. This wasn't pneumonia.

I sat next to Matthew on the hospital bed—two gathered together in Jesus' name—as we read the psalm assigned for that morning. That morning the congregation read it by rote in a dignified, liturgical, devoid-of-life

---

3. Catherine, *Dialogue*, 175.
4. Symeon, *Divine Eros*, 49.
5. Bernard, *Song of Songs III*, 171.
6. Black Elk, *Black Elk Speaks*, 33.
7. Julian, *Showings*, 336.

monotone indistinguishable from boredom. Reading it with him that Sunday night, the psalm was resurrected. Whoever had written it, this was now *Matthew's* prayer, *his* life, *his* soul. The words soared, swooped, swayed, and shivered. His body shook. Tears fell. His nose ran like oil into his glistening Aaron's beard. Nothing was held back, not from him, not from the psalm—its life's blood fully squeezed.

A few minutes later, Matthew talked about the morphine he would be given after surgery. In the Navy thirty years before, "they said morphine made you feel mmmmmmMMMMMM!" His hum leapt an octave to symbolize the high he anticipated, his characteristic, contagious laugh breaking into a noncontagious cough. He regularly insisted he was a "recovered" alcoholic, but he still liked "a little weed" now and then. At that moment, morphine sounded like a field of weed.

Marx called religion an opiate, something far more powerful and pleasurable than alcohol or weed. Sometimes it is. You can see it almost everywhere across the American religious landscape—escape after escape after escape into raptures, blessings without responsibility, into the ever-blessed rest of hoped-for, dreamed-of, never-ending prosperity. The Christian faith is metamorphosed into a cheaper-than-cheap grace gospel, a consumer kerygma, a judgmental Pharisaism, and a zealous, fanatical, violent, expansionist, imperialistic, crusading Christian Zionism. All of these are part of a Kafkaesque, Americanized religion, something once divine and human now reduced to the self-centered instincts of a cockroach.

The US is a land of lotus-eaters with a menu of choices about what kind of buzz we want, from the cloisters of Wall Street to the razor wire of the inner city. Substances are only the beginning: the media, entertainment, sports, fashion, consumerism, the mall, diversion after distraction after delusion. Pascal's point made centuries ago, truer here, that we are constantly unhappy because we can't sit alone in silence. Merton's point made decades ago, truer now, that society has mercifully provided distractions so that we can avoid our own company twenty-four hours a day. There are so many forms of morphine that we can't tell if we are high or being euthanized. As Matthew's illness and fear awakened the hidden depths of the psalm, religion should not dull our pain or our awareness of suffering. It should awaken us to joy, to grief, to death, and to life.

What is the pain that makes us yearn to put it out like a fire? What is the paper cut pain of the privileged that makes people react as if they have skin cancer? How can we face our pain, all pain, without benefit of drug or diversion? What is it in our consumer-friendly, constantly self-medicating society that hurts so persistently and so much? True religion, as Buddha said, is to be awake! True religion, as James said, is to act! Heaven ought to sharpen our passion for earth. The awareness of eternity ought to fix and focus our attention on the eternal in each moment.

On the operating table, they opened and closed Matthew's chest in one almost seamless act. The cancer was inoperable. The doctors were helpless. He was dying.

One Sunday afternoon a few months later, after futile phone calls to find me, after he collapsed in the street, Matthew was rushed to the same hospital. They tried to save him. They hadn't cleaned him up. They weren't expecting visitors. I went to see his dead body, to hold his cold hand, to pray, to feel my eyes fill, and to say goodbye.

After his surgery, Matthew had told me he had been disappointed in the morphine. "No mmmmmmMMMMMM."

HOLY TEARS

In a culture that enshrines "the pursuit of happiness" as the goal of government and the way, the truth, and the life for each person, it is hard not to project this secular quest on to the mystic way, the Christian truth, and the activist life. In a culture that turns this pursuit into a sacred mission and happiness into the Holy Grail, any interruption of bliss causes frustration, envy, and rage. In such a culture, it is inevitable that the mystic's yearning and the activist's passion are misconceived and forced to fit into this ideal of happiness, square pegs in a black hole.

Such a culture misdiagnoses mysticism and monasticism as ways to evade the harshness of life in a displaced and mismanaged search for bliss. In reality, monks and mystics experience as much sorrow as joy, tedium as ecstasy, tragedy as comedy. Otto says that experiences of God induce anxiety more than tranquility, a terrifying and yawning abyss as often as ecstasy. There are reasons that Teresa of Ávila often told her sisters to "be strong men."[8] The popular characterization of the harmless sweetness of Franciscan spirituality ignores Francis's exceptional distaste for money and his excessively stringent—but apparently effective—behavioral approach to avert carnal temptations by throwing himself into a ditch full of ice to shoo them away.[9] The common view of Francis forgets that after his vision of Christ crucified, "he could never keep himself from weeping, even bewailing in a loud voice the passion of Christ." For this, he allowed himself no consolation and filled his days with "sighs."[10]

8. Teresa, *Way of Perfection*, 79.
9. Celano, *Saint Francis*, 40.
10. Ibid., 145.

Popular culture also shapes our subconscious predispositions and tempts us to interpret the activist's road as paved with displaced intentions. Those engaged in social change might seek happiness for society instead of themselves, or personal happiness in the very elusiveness of triumph in a particular social cause—the signing of legislation or the surrender of oppressive forces. But "happiness" does not describe the feelings induced by Mrs. Turpin's vision or Rama's experience; the vision violated Mrs. Turpin's hierarchical order; the experience frighteningly fulfilled Rama's revolutionary dream. It takes a rigorous, churning purging to prepare one to celebrate the transfiguring reversal of the realm of God.

Even those profoundly awakened to the need for the revolution of God sometimes find themselves baffled by doubt, confusion, and the apparent meaninglessness of their best efforts to respond to God's grace. As she shared the deprivations and degradations of the homeless, Dorothy Day felt humiliated when she was pushed beyond her limits and driven to tears.[11] Martin Luther King, Jr. is remembered for speeches about mountaintops, yet the majority of his journey—tactical fragmentation, strategic failure, personal doubts and bouts of depression, public attacks on his intelligence and integrity from enemies and allies alike—was spent in an almost endless wilderness. Like Moses, to whom he was so often compared, King found his leadership ability and his political sense of direction constantly doubted. He was subjected to public vitriol, physical assault, and the constant threat of murder.

Desmond Tutu apologizes because he is by nature almost as quick to cry as to laugh. Chairing South Africa's Truth and Reconciliation Commission, its official attempt to address and heal the nation's hideous past, he heard story after story of torture, cruelty, indifference, and loss. Finally, when one witness broke down in tears at his inability to describe the methods by which he had been tortured, Tutu responded in kind: "I was too full from all that I had heard and it was all too much for me too. I could not hold back the tears, I just broke down and sobbed like a child. The floodgates opened. I bent over the table and covered my face with my hands." Afterwards, he "wondered whether I was the right person to lead the commission since I knew I was so weak and vulnerable." He begged God not to let it happen again, and he was relieved he had no further public breakdowns.[12] Tutu, Day, and King did not pursue and certainly did not find happiness.

If anything, to seek first the realm of God or to seek God in and above all things is a very different quest. It is, rather, a pursuit of holiness that may

---

11. Day, *Houses of Hospitality*, 87–88.
12. Tutu, *No Future*, 143–44.

incidentally, accidentally, or fortuitously include happiness, but only as a fleeting puff in a dense cloud of uncertainty. One need only study more rigorously the witness of mystics and activists, and their traditions, to realize that their journeys do not conform to the world's expectations.

It is precisely the painfulness (and holiness) of awakening that is so well chronicled in the parables, anecdotes, short stories, and legends Martin Buber treasured. Better than philosophical discourse that leads to a bottomless quagmire of micromanaged colloquy—an endless end in itself—a myth reveals what a treatise cannot. In a world in which it is almost impossible to untie an endless series of contradictory-but-prized values, one hyperbole, question, or metaphor can cut through truth like a diamond. Like Jesus' pregnant questions, stories sometimes assemble good things in order to discern the better from the best, the holy from the holiest, the one thing necessary for life and love.

Two desert Christian stories illustrate the point. People came to Abba Agathon hoping to tease or torment him, to see if their words could detonate his temper or puncture his sanctity.

> "Aren't you the Agathon who is a fornicator and a proud man?"
> "Very true," he replied.
> "Aren't you the one who always talks nonsense?"
> "I am."
> "Aren't you 'Agathon the heretic'?"
> He said, "I am not a heretic."[13]

Libels and slanders, misperceptions and rumors, insults and lies do not disturb Agathon. He doesn't mind being accused of promiscuity, self-righteousness, or of being a babbling fool. But he cannot abide being called someone who propagates dangerously infectious beliefs. Abba Theodore of Pherme makes the same point: one can befriend a fornicator, but not a heretic.[14] You can reach out your hand to try to rescue from judgment a promiscuous and exploitative person without worrying about the contact infecting you. But if you reach out to a heretic, you may be dragged into a pit. Taken together, the stories tell us that promiscuity, pride, and irrelevance are redeemable, but *heresy* blasphemes the Holy Spirit; to Abba Agathon it is the sin of sins, the crime of crimes.

Among the legends Buber extols, there is a subgenre—stories and sayings, conversations and monologues that, at the time of death, summarize and illuminate the meaning of life. Sometimes these brief narratives are warnings. Often they offer spiritual direction. Always, their intent is clear.

---

13. Ward, *Sayings of the Desert*, 20–21.
14. Ibid., 74.

A person seeking to enter heaven alone is asked, "Where are the others?" Then one suddenly realizes that salvation is not as individualistic as Western Christianity has averred. Perhaps you cannot enter alone; maybe you can enter *only* with others. Or, as in the Hasidic saying where Zusya of Hanipol anticipates the moment of his judgment: "In the coming world, they will not ask me: 'Why were you not Moses?' They will ask me, 'Why were you not Zusya'?"[15] You don't have to aspire to singular prominence or to be remembered as one of the greatest religious figures of history. But why were you not yourself? Why were you not the person God created you to be? How did you miss the personalized purpose of *your* life?

In the same end-of-life genre, John Climacus makes a point that might comfort Tutu: "When we die, we will not be criticized for having failed to work miracles. We will not be accused of having failed to be theologians or contemplatives. But we will certainly have some explanation to offer to God for not having mourned unceasingly."[16] Where would the world be without those who heal its wounds or those who put into words the mystery of faith or those who directly experience God? Ah! But where would the world be without tears? Not to weep is as serious a sin as being a heretic. In the sacred death-judgment setting when one's life is measured against one plumb line or another, Climacus ranks three highly regarded vocations— miracle worker, theologian, and contemplative—lower than the common, uncontrolled, unintentional human act of crying. Contemplation, theology, miracles, grief; these four abide, but the greatest of these is grief.

Thomas à Kempis links grief to spiritual maturity—not personal grief at the death of a loved one, but a lifelong discipline of mourning: "the more spiritual" someone is, he says, "the more painful" it is to live.[17] Any image of holiness as a spiritual state above or beyond suffering is disastrously askew. Spiritual resources may enable us to absorb and cope with grief, but spiritual wisdom breeds and multiplies sensitivity. Rumi's awakened person who hears the far-off cry of a sparrow and the zaddik who feels the pain of a woman in labor reveals a long-distance empathy that makes it impossible not to ache. One need not be a spiritual master to realize that if only we could see, we would weep.

According to traditional spiritual writers tears are a divine imperative. There is no fear of anguish; in fact, we are warned against detours that avoid it. Rumi counsels us not to look sourly on sourness; instead, he says, hold

---

15. Buber, *Tales: Early Masters*, 251.

16. Climacus, *Ladder of Divine Ascent*, 145. An interesting twist on Paul's "pray without ceasing" (1 Thess 5:17).

17. à Kempis, *Imitation of Christ*, 61.

meanness to your chest like a healing root.[18] Climacus says that Christians weep when reborn into the age to come just as newborn babies weep when they enter this world. Adult baptism, he says, cleanses Christians from the ghosts of sins past; tears purify us from the specter of sins future.[19] Mourning is a "golden spur," a proper disposition of the seeker's heart.[20] Grief, and the prism of emotions to which grief gives birth, is the beginning of a new spiritual path. Faith does not goad persons to soothe their own anguish, but to comfort and undo the moaning and mourning of the world.

The desert tradition prepared the way for the insights of Climacus. It commends Abba Arsenius because "he had a hollow in his chest channeled out by the tears which fell from his eyes all his life."[21] Tears respond to a myriad of stimuli. They are shed for one's soul; so Abba Poemen says, "Whoever who does not weep for themselves here below will weep eternally hereafter."[22] Poemen also teaches that tears purify our faults and prepare us to acquire virtues.[23] But tears have a broader function than as a spur to repentance. Weeping is a way of life. Abba John the Dwarf looks into the face of a woman and weeps for *her* sins.[24] Abba Joseph confides that he wishes "I could always weep" like Mary, the mother of God, "as she wept by the cross of the Savior."[25] Theognius, an early bishop, was "drenched in tears" interceding with God on behalf of the world.[26] We weep for ourselves, for others, for the world, for Christ. Some early Sufi women believed that those who submit to God's will cannot help but "live with sighs and burning grief." Anticipating Thomas à Kempis, they say, "The amount a person weeps depends on the amount of fire in the heart."[27] Like Abba Arsenius, one Sufi woman wept her way to blindness and holiness.[28] If one becomes the flame, one may also become a waterfall of tears.

One tradition attributes Francis of Assisi's eye ailments—like those of Abba Arsenius and the Sufi women—to his constant weeping. When told by a doctor to restrain his tears, he said that he preferred blindness, for tears

---

18. Rumi, *Delicious Laughter*, 32.
19. Climacus, *Ladder of Divine Ascent*, 137.
20. Ibid., 136.
21. Ward, *Sayings of the Desert*, 18.
22. Ibid., 18.
23. Ibid., 184.
24. Ibid., 94.
25. Ibid., 187.
26. Vivian, *Journeying into God*, 159.
27. Helminski, *Women of Sufism*, 40–41.
28. Ibid., 36.

"cleansed his interior vision so that he could see God."[29] Francis's tears were signs that he saw and a means by which he was enabled to see. So moaning, mourning, and weeping are not for the spiritual novice, the morally distracted, or the emotionally childish. They are for the Buddha, the zaddik, the mahatma, the saint, the holy ones of the world.

The commendations of holy tears scroll on and on. Symeon the New Theologian gives anguish an honored place in the life of faith. Christians, he says, should never receive communion "without tears." Weeping is a basic spiritual discipline: "Let no one say that it is impossible to weep daily!"[30] George Herbert's poetry exalts our prayerful inarticulate groaning.

> I sent a sigh to seek thee out,
> Deep drawn in pain,
> Wing'd like an arrow: but my scout
> Returns in vain.
> I turn'd another (having store)
> Into a groan;
> Because the search was dumb before:
> But all was one.[31]

Following Paul's depiction of the Spirit as the interpreter of sighs too deep for words, Herbert considers inarticulate moans spiritual pioneers straining toward God. Again, he invokes the power of the heartfelt moan.

> All Solomon's sea of brass and world of stone
> Is not so dear to thee as one good groan
> But groans are quick, and full of wings,
> And all their motions upward be;
> And ever as they mount, like larks they sing;
> The note is sad, yet music for a king.[32]

Jerusalem's temple, all of the world's cathedrals, and all their gold and finery are not as precious to God as "one good groan." The "brass and stone" are rare, but inanimate; the common groan is active, alive, engaging, and vital. The sound may be plaintive, like the cry of slaves in Egypt, but like that desolate lament it is fit "for a king," Israel's divine monarch.

His eye ever keen to uproot all forms of spiritual positivism, John of the Cross treasures tears. In *The Spiritual Canticle* he labels the soul's moans

---

29. Bonaventure, *Soul's Journey*, 224.
30. Symeon, *Discourses*, 70, 83.
31. Herbert, "The Search," in *Country Parson*, 287.
32. Herbert, "Sion," in *Country Parson*, 226–27.

"shepherds" to guide it.[33] John takes his place in the chorus of mystics' voices proclaiming the value of grief. He says that God communicates with us, communes with us, pastors us, and leads us through our emptiness, our failures, and the world's heartrending tragedies, through all that is *not* right with the world. As often as faith may ameliorate grief, just as often it accentuates loss because it gives us an inkling of the infinite image that is always being defaced, degraded, and destroyed. The person fully awake to God and the world will be deeply, perhaps devastatingly, immersed and overcome, yet paradoxically set right, by grief.

When any person of faith surveys the relentless history of evil, and one's place in it, moaning is not the final defeat of God's revolution, but a beginning. Grief fuels moral outrage. It is a primal protest against the status quo. It is the psalmist's "how long," the people's cry in Egypt. Isaac of Nineveh says that it is an "infinite pity which reigns in the hearts of those who are becoming united with God."[34] In words that resonate equally with activist and mystic, Isaac describes a merciful or "charitable heart" as

> a heart which is burning with charity for the whole of creation, for people, for the birds, for the beasts, for the demons—for all creatures. Those who have such a heart cannot see or call to mind a creature without their eyes becoming filled with tears by reason of the immense compassion which seizes their heart; a heart which is softened and can no longer bear to see or learn from others of any suffering, even the smallest pain, being inflicted upon a creature. This is why such a person never ceases to pray also for the animals, for the enemies of Truth, and for those who do them evil, that they may be preserved and purified.[35]

"The fruits" of our inner being "begin only with the shedding of tears." Whoever reaches "the place of tears" has "come out from the prison of this world and has set . . . foot upon the path that leads toward the new age."[36] For Isaac, grief—not fear—is the beginning of wisdom.

There is no path to the realm of God untouched by tears. Isaac's vision of being born again or "from above" is the inverse of exiting Symeon's spiritual prison in order to enter Rumi's magnificent world. If Isaac spoke with Rumi's embryo, he would add that the world of wonder is also a cosmos of sorrow. If only we could see we would hear the cry of the sparrow from a thousand miles a way, and feel the pain of every woman in labor. To enter

---

33. John of the Cross, *Collected Works*, 425.
34. Lossky, *Mystical Theology*, 111.
35. Ibid.
36. Cited in Climacus, *Ladder of Divine Ascent*, 26.

the revolutionary life one must, like a baby at birth, cry. When tears fall you begin to breathe—in this case, inhaling the Spirit. An abundant life includes an abundance of tears.

As Tutu lamented his public display of anguish, Merton sometimes chastised himself for being "too anguished and too excited" to be useful to others. He worried that his writings on racism and war were tainted, distorted, muddled, disjointed, or out of touch because of his emotionalism.[37] Yet his anguish—as much the product of his contemplative practice as his emotional demeanor—may have been his greatest gift. In Walter Brueggemann's interpretation of "the prophetic imagination," he argues that *anguish* engages the world in ways that social analysis cannot.[38] To Brueggemann, anguish would not disqualify Merton from social criticism. It corroborates his acuity.

So when Tutu confessed that he cries when he hears stories of cruelty and terror, he is not acknowledging a weakness, as he thinks, but a spiritual strength. Tutu's tears accompany revelations of extraordinary evil, and of individuals willingly, perhaps gladly, possessed by a demonic system. He weeps for the past. When Day records one night's hardships in a Catholic Worker House of Hospitality and the trials besetting those who slept willy-nilly on the floors, she writes of the daily dislocation in a run-of-the-mill system of oppression in which it is hard to hold anyone accountable. In effect, her anguish is as much the creative source of the Catholic Worker as the result. And when she wrote of being overcome with tears, it was no failure. According to the mystical tradition, it was an enactment of the most profound holiness. King momentarily cowered in the face of racist violence. He was later hospitalized for depression. He felt like a failure when his faith seemed inadequate to overcome the weapons of evil knocking him off balance like the blast of one fire hose after another. But he felt weak because his chest was hollowed out by holy grief.

So grief may not be something to fear or avoid or dread. Rather it may be a sign and source of faith and life.

SPLITTING TEARS

Sometimes falsely stereotyped as an escape from the travails of human affairs into an ethereal self-directed ecstasy, the mystical tradition has also been rebuked for unnecessarily and gratuitously imitating the physical hardships of Christ tortured and crucified. These critics accuse mystics of wallowing

---

37. Merton, *Dancing in the Water*, 216.
38. Brueggemann, *Prophetic Imagination*, 57, 79.

too easily in mires of mud and bogs of blood in a cheerfully cheerless, self-congratulatory, powerless masochism, as mystics falsely absolve themselves from lifting a pinkie to alleviate even one child's misery. But even as the mystical tradition extols tears, it casts an analytical eye on them. While it quite willingly engages pain, it is too spiritually supple to make blanket assumptions about reality. For every truth there is a countertruth, for every experience a counterexperience, for every spiritual thesis a spiritual antithesis. Sometimes this gives birth to a new synthesis. Sometimes it merely reaffirms the resolutely contradictory and paradoxical nature of reality.

Heralding the sanctity of tears can encourage a renewal of some of the distortions of mysticism and activism. The Christian spiritual tradition has at times inadvertently nurtured a masochistic streak that has led countless figures—from Macarius to Benedict to John of the Cross—to urge prudence in the pursuit of holiness. The activist tradition has also fostered self-righteousness among its constituents. As a wag in the Catholic Worker put it, you have to be a saint to put up with the martyrs![39] It is not enough to praise the sanctity of tears. Sorrow can be self-absorbed instead of redemptive. Sacrifices can bless a neurotic self-importance that becomes self-serving and inner-directed, a way to massage personal insecurity instead of loving God.

In modern discussions about redemptive suffering, Audre Lorde draws a distinction between *suffering* and *pain*. To her, suffering is a raw experience untouched by introspection or analysis. Suffering in itself has no innate power to educate, edify, transform, or redeem. It merely hurts, disables, and dehumanizes. Pain, as she defines it, begins with the same experience but through reflection and introspection can become extraordinarily transformative.[40] William Stringfellow draws a different distinction. Writing personally after the death of his partner, Anthony Towne, he contrasts mourning with grief. To him, grief is a personal, solitary experience of shattering brokenness; mourning a public, communal, and liturgical expression that celebrates life. A year after Towne's death, Stringfellow realized that he needed to let go of his grief or it would become terminal.[41]

Like these modern writers, the mystical tradition does not blindly commend tears without delineating the diversity of grief. In many ways, grief parallels guilt. Guilt can be self-reforming and constructive as it leads to metanoia. It can also be self-condemning, merely another subtly self-destructive way to multiply guilt to new heights and depths of grandiosity

---

39. Piehl, *Breaking Bread*, 108.
40. Lorde, *Sister Outsider*, 171–72.
41. Stringfellow, *Simplicity of Faith*, 115.

(for who else in human history has *ever* been so depraved?). As with guilt, the value of grief can be assessed only by its fruits: when you grieve, do you lose yourself in order to find yourself, or merely to feign the loss of self in a perverse narcissism?

Paul constructs a foundational dichotomy when he discerns a distinction between "godly grief" that produces "earnestness" and "eagerness" and leads towards salvation, and a "worldly grief" that "produces death" (2 Cor 7:9–11). Amma Syncletica builds on this distinction: some grief is "useful"; some "destructive." Useful grief weeps over human faults in order to "attach oneself to the perfect good." Destructive grief "comes from the enemy, full of mockery," and leads to accidie, a down-spiraling spiritual weariness in which one's inner strength ebbs away.[42] Similarly, Esther de Waal contrasts the "purifying grief" and "true tears" of sorrow, repentance, and conversion with an "inward-looking" grief whose chief concern is self-centered comfort.[43] One kind of grief—to use Martin Luther's phrase—curves in on itself; the other serves God's transforming grace. One kind of grief surrenders to life as it is, the other seeks life as God crafts it.

Sounding like Audre Lorde, Thomas Kelly addresses Christians too quick to see all thorns in the flesh easily twisted into crowns of thorns. He warns that, while the Christian tradition values redemptive suffering, there is "nothing automatic about suffering, so that suffering infallibly produces great souls." The same misery can just as easily "blast and blight an earnest but unprepared soul, and damn it utterly to despair."[44] Symeon the New Theologian, while commending tears, also says they are sometimes beneficial and sometimes harmful.[45] Like Syncletica, Teresa of Ávila attributes some types of pain to the devil—those that lead away from resolution, reconciliation, tranquility, and joy.[46] Francis de Sales takes the position that more often than not tears have a harmful effect. To him, only two good things can come from tears—"compassion and repentance"—while he counts six "evil effects": "anxiety, sloth, wrath, jealousy, envy, and impatience." He believes that "the evil one" enjoys human melancholy and grief because this is his everlasting condition, and he wants everyone to be like him.[47]

---

42. Ward, *Sayings of the Desert*, 235.
43. de Waal, *Celtic Way*, 123.
44. Kelly, *Eternal Promise*, 54–55.
45. Symeon, *Divine Eros*, 263.
46. Teresa, *Interior Castle*, 137.
47. de Sales, *Introduction*, 253–54.

Taking a positive approach, Meister Eckhart affirms that suffering can give birth to love.[48] Also stressing the positive, John Ruusbroec, anticipating John of the Cross's fuller exploration into the "wounds of love," calls grief a sign of healing and "both the sweetest feeling and the sharpest pain that anyone can experience." Sometimes this wound results from "the struggle of love" between divine and human spirits in which "each spirit is wounded by love."[49] In his thinking, human grief becomes intertwined with God's grief, a union with God that is far from ecstatic but profoundly holy.

A few mystics consider moaning and mourning the inseparable flip sides of joy and love. John of the Cross describes spiritual pain as an ache of unfulfilled anticipation. Ruminating on the story of Moses seeing God's backside from a cleft in the rocks (Exod 33:17–23), he says that many see God through such a fissure, but—to their disappointment—find themselves unable to fully grasp divine goodness.[50] While John describes this as frustrated yearning, others—primarily women—speak of a sorrow that *follows* an ecstatic epiphany. For them, this is a natural letdown after the intensity of divine intimacy. Angela of Foligno describes being "filled with love and an inexpressible contentment" then by a cry because her soul languished after losing that intense closeness.[51] Likewise, Julian of Norwich describes a "supreme spiritual delight in my soul," a condition in which "nothing on earth could have afflicted me," that lasted only "for a time." Afterwards, "there was no ease or comfort for me except hope, faith, and love, and truly I felt very little of this."[52] Others share the same insight: the pain of God's absence is made "more bitter" when one has experienced God's presence.[53] So common is this experience that the alternation of joy and sorrow, "inspiration and deflation,"[54] feeling love/loved and bereft/lonely are a normal facet of the spiritual journey.[55] Hadewijch summarizes this alternation, saying that "satiety and hunger" are inseparable from each other.[56] In light of these mystical witnesses and the peaks and valleys of King's life, it would appear the highs and lows of activism simply mirror the rhythms of the ascetical life.

---

48. Eckhart, *Sermons & Treatises II*, 65.
49. Ruusbroec, *Spiritual Espousals*, 85, 115.
50. John of the Cross, *Collected Works*, 424.
51. Buber, *Ecstatic Utterances*, 99.
52. Julian, *Showings*, 139.
53. Underhill, *Mysticism*, 390.
54. *Christian Faith*, 112.
55. Underhill, *Mysticism*, 178.
56. Hadewijch, *Complete Works*, 222.

In addition to the fluidity of peaks and plateaus, dark nights and transfiguring lights, there is an inevitable contrast that mystical experience sharpens. Underhill describes it as "the discord between Perfect Love and an imperfect world."[57] The more directly you experience God's love, the more deeply disturbed you become with the world's envy, hatred, and violence. The more you are awake to God and the world, the more you are driven to shape the world according to God's loving design. Catherine of Siena contrasts the experience of God's truth and love with humanity's "ingratitude and blindness."[58] Julian says that when we realize that sin and evil make Christ suffer, it amplifies the dissonance of faith.[59] This "discord" can either sap us with despair or inspire us to bear God's love into a destructive world.

The same people who warn about grief dissipating faith paradoxically commend the significance of life's bruises: "Only if we look long and deeply into the abyss of despair do we dare to speak of hope. Only as we know a deeper ground of uncertainty, that can stand every privation and atrocity of which we have read, can stand them as *committed upon ourselves and upon our families*, and can still rise radiant and triumphant, dare we speak of hope."[60] While Kelly *looks into* the abyss, Julian *prays within* it. Revealing her familiarity with the topography of John of the Cross's dark night, she sees that there are times when someone prays "wholeheartedly" while feeling nothing, in "dryness and barrenness, in sickness and in weakness," when words are rendered meaningless and God seems deaf or dead. While this might simply be part of the alternation of *inspiration* and *deflation*, according to Julian an invisible grace is present precisely when God seems absolutely absent. It was "then," God said to her, that "your prayer [is] most pleasing to me, though you think it almost tasteless to you."[61]

Catherine provides elaborate modes of discerning when mourning is a spiritual path to God or a detour into a blind alley. Her multilayered description begins with the lowest spiritual level of grief, "tears of damnation, the tears of this world's evil ones." These entirely selfish and mean-spirited tears mean nothing and lead nowhere. At the second level are "tears of fear" created by anxiety over divine wrath. While including God in their spiritual calculations, these tears are still shed from crude, almost bestial self-interest. In both stages, the same corruption that infects people's actions empties all positive power from their tears. But in the third stage people's

---

57. Underhill, *Mysticism*, 196.
58. Catherine, *Dialogue*, 30.
59. Julian, *Showings*, 280.
60. Kelly, *Eternal Promise*, 52 (italics his).
61. Julian, *Showings*, 249.

tears become signs that they "weep tenderly"; at this point, they begin to serve God. Yet as their love is "imperfect," "so is their weeping." Yet they have risen above fear—they weep from love and hope. At this level, God tells Catherine, people "grieve only for offenses committed against me, for they see how deserving I am of love and service." In the final two stages, people weep with "great tenderness"; these are the tears of those who love God and their neighbors "without any self-interest." People weep with "heartfelt love, grieving only for the offense done to [God] and the harm to [their] neighbors." These tears, like the oil that leaked from the Tomb of the Saints, "are a fragrant ointment that sends forth a most delicate perfume." Beyond even the fifth stage are "tears of fire, shed without physical weeping" and with a "holy longing." The chief characteristic in Catherine's tearful ladder of perfection is the maturity of love. Is it sporadic—human and frail, honest but irregular—or is it constant in its compassion?[62]

Such dichotomies measure the maturity and health of grief, discerning whether it is self-centered or self-transcending, destructive or creative. Yet even healthy grief can be further defined in the contradiction of fulfilled and unfulfilled hopes. The Beatitudes praise the *not yet*: "those who hunger and thirst for righteousness . . . *will* be filled" (Matt 5:6). In the more eschatologically realized Gospel of John—in which present and future mingle wildly—Jesus' sayings bypass the *not yet* for the satisfaction of the *already*: "Those who drink of the water I give them will never be thirsty" (John 4:14); "Whoever comes to me will never be hungry, and whoever believes in me will never be thirsty" (John 6:36); "Whoever eats of this bread will live forever" (John 6:51).

Are the faithful, then, to be hungry or filled? Are we to be thirsty or quenched? Are we to mourn or are we already and always comforted? A simplistic stereotype might consider mystics those already filled and activists always hungry for justice, mystics celebrating God's presence in creation—the *already*—and activists thirsty for the defeat of evil—the *not yet*. But activists have moments when their thirst is at least temporarily quenched, and the mystical tradition is thick with commendations of tears and weeping, moaning and mourning, and yearning and hungering for personal and social metanoia. It is Bernard of Clairvaux, in one of his sermons on the Song of Songs, who sounds like a modern activist: "In tears I ask, 'How long shall we smell and not taste, gazing toward our homeland but not grasping it, hailing it from afar with sighs?'"[63] As Underhill points out, mys-

---

62. Catherine, *Dialogue*, 161–68, 179, 306.

63. Quoted from McGinn, *Growth of Mysticism*, 188; also in Bernard, *Song of Songs III*, 37.

tics experience the disjunction between God's perfect love and the world's angry chaos. Likewise, activists do not live by hunger alone. *Something* tangible sustains them in their endless quest for a less violent world and a more just social order. Merton has something to say to both groups. Mystics who no longer hunger for a new earth will find that their solitude has turned into a terrible solitary confinement: "If you go into the desert merely to get away from people you dislike, you will find neither peace nor solitude; you will only isolate yourself with a tribe of devils."[64] Likewise, he warns activists that without prayerful reflection, their actions will be muddied by "the frenzies and impulsions of human ambition," hurdles and hindrances to the realm.[65] The contradiction of hunger and satiety, as Hadewijch puts it, is "ever well known by those whom Love has touched."[66] Bernard says that whoever drinks of God will "thirst for more."[67] Fulfillment does not quench thirst; it breeds it. Nicholas of Cusa sees this as a constant contradiction: "the blessed are forever drinking and are forever filled, but never have they drunk or been filled."[68] Symeon confirms his intuition: "When I am satiated, I hunger. . . . When I drink, I also thirst."[69] We are always *and* never to hunger and thirst.

Sorting through life-giving and death-dealing suffering, personal grief and public mourning, stages of healthy grief, and the contradiction of blessings present and yet to come do not exhaust the ways in which tears need to be scrutinized. Even within healthy grief, we find another dichotomy in the contrast between two great biblical mourners—Job and Qoheleth. What has been called "wisdom in revolt"[70] might also be called *grieving wisdom*. Job, Ecclesiastes, Lamentations, and many of the psalms are immersed in horror, agony, and sorrow, and could easily be called texts of the terrorized.[71]

In their literary settings, Job and Qoheleth come from the same social location.[72] Job is rich, but he is also—stunningly—truly innocent and resolutely faithful, something so improbable (can the rich squeeze through the eye of a needle?) that one wonders if only the rich can believe such a

64. Merton, *New Seeds*, 52.
65. Merton, *Life and Holiness*, 8.
66. Hadewijch, *Complete Works*, 222.
67. Bernard, *Song of Songs III*, 40.
68. Nicholas, *Selected Spiritual Writings*, 203.
69. Symeon, *Divine Eros*, 175.
70. Scott, *Way of Wisdom*, 136–89.
71. A variation of Trible, *Texts of Terror*.
72. Clines, *Interested Parties*, 125–26 discusses Job.

miracle.[73] Qoheleth is the king of prophets' dreams and psalmists' prayers (Isa 11:1–3, Jer 23:5–6, Ps 72:1), someone whose every day is spoiled by injustice, oppression, and the suffering of the nameless (Eccl 1:13, 3:16, 4:1, 5:8, 6:1–2, 7:7). Qoheleth has been called the Eeyore of the Old Testament,[74] but that is to make of him an effete and ineffectual whiner (like Woody Allen's character who, after witnessing a horrible mine disaster, is unable to complete "a second helping of waffles").[75] While his observations and experiences of life lead Qoheleth to become a rare biblical advocate of existential angst, to him there are no perpetrators, only direct and indirect victims. In contrast to one of the themes in Merton's writings,[76] Qoheleth never worries about being a guilty bystander; complicity never occurs to him. He does not feel implicated by injustice or in collusion as a silent partner in the physical and psychic stripping of the dispossessed. Instead, he is saturated with unfiltered meaninglessness. Qoheleth cannot enjoy life unless the common lot of the common person is no more than futility and a chasing after the wind. *Their* suffering despoils *his* life and pollutes the possibilities of purpose, belonging, meaning, and joy in *any* life.

While the primary intended audience for Job and Qoheleth may be the privileged, it is hard to imagine that the dispossessed could not find common cause with both characters. While the oppressed have not experienced what it is to be rich-and-righteous, they would like to imagine that *someone*—a monarch? A landowner? A lord? A CEO? They if they had the money!—could be both. And having once imagined what it is to *have everything* that Job had—family, prosperity, security, wisdom, compassion, respect, and recognition—it would not be difficult to relate to *having lost everything*. Almost anyone can imagine what it is to bemoan, "how the mighty are fallen" (2 Sam 1:25, 27). The ordinary person, whose *everything* may be far less, can still imagine what it is to lose security, family, health, and dignity. One can lose far less than Job and still lose *all*. Such ruminations just as easily can be the dread dreams of those without social status. Job's tragedy may approach Shakespearean heights, but the despair of Qoheleth may be more poignant. He *has* everything that Job lost, yet he has aborted any and all of his pursuits of faith, hope, and love as chasing after wind.

While the privileged background of the main characters, writers, and intended audience might be the same, Job's first-person familiarity with

---

73. Ibid., 126.

74. Wright, *Resurrection*, 108.

75. Allen, *Side Effects*, 4.

76. Merton, "Letter to Innocent Bystander," in *Raids on the Unspeakable*, 53–64, and *Conjectures*.

agony and Qoheleth's third-person survey of suffering make it is easier for the oppressed—however they are oppressed—to identify with Job. The privileged more easily identify with Qoheleth. His horror is based on observation. Like Thomas Kelly's recommended gaze into the abyss, Qoheleth suffers because he sees. Job's losses implode into the more personal—possessions, loved ones, physical pain. Job *feels*.

Qoheleth *sees*. He even observes himself—his pursuits of pleasure, justice, and faith that never alleviate pain. He parodies the positivist Proverbs that claims that right living leads to blessings, and wrong living to curses.[77] Qoheleth wants only to make peace with senselessness. Job, like Jacob, feels the pain in his flesh and is left limping. Indirect pain is Job's starting point; it is Qoheleth's finish line. The knot in Job's hunger for justice leads him on a long, lonely, frequently stymied verbal pilgrimage toward God where he is ambushed and assaulted along the way by his so-called friends and their so-called orthodoxy. For Qoheleth, as Elsa Tamez says, the horizons have closed.[78] For Job the heavens open; God answers Job.[79] The encounter leaves him even more bewildered than divine silence. Job is blessed because he hungers for righteousness. Qoheleth is blessed because he mourns.

Like anyone who seeks social change, Job demands justice, and not only for himself; like Job, the reformer finds a world of creation/chaos willfully in noncompliance with human hope. The scales of justice are dwarfed by a cosmic whirlwind. As Job's lament transforms from the purely personal to the social, *his* ruined life becomes one with *every* suffering life. Like Lorde's ideal of the one who transforms her suffering into pain, Job finds solidarity through his identification with the suffering of others. He becomes a prophet, an intercessor advocating with God on behalf of the human race. In identifying with others, in sorrow and in protest, he discovers the purpose of his life.[80] He becomes the advocate, a Christlike, Spirit-filled prototype for the crucified messiah suffering with a suffering human race.

"When horizons close,"[81] Qoheleth becomes a minimalist who shrinks hope. Pessimist, realist, or existentialist, he equates hope with spiritual survival. Job is angry; Qoheleth depressed. Job howls. Qoheleth surrenders, convinced that there is no counterfriction to the machine. Job hears God's answer. Darkness is Qoheleth's only companion (Ps 88:18). Hearing and

---

77. Alter, *World of Biblical Literature*, 76.

78. Tamez, *When the Horizons Close*.

79. For the rhetorical connections between Job 3 and 38, see Alter, *Art of Biblical Poetry*, 96–97.

80. Gutierrez, *On Job*, 39, 48.

81. Tamez, *When the Horizons Close*.

seeing nothing from God, Qoheleth creates an answer drawn entirely from nontranscendent human experience in an ordered catalogue of yins and yangs—to *everything* there is a season (Eccl 3:1–8). It is Qoheleth's way of bringing order to God's final answer to Job, in which the poetry of God's answer implies that reality can be brilliantly expressed but never fully encapsulated in neat couplets. Job moans in earsplitting protest, Qoheleth in a whispered surrender. Job wants pain to end. Believing in pain without end, Qoheleth shrugs and says in defeated resignation: Amen. While for the real Christian that spiritual assent can only be temporary, it may sometimes be necessary. When lacerated by horrendous evil, our search for the best tone, tenor, and timbre for grief can be ever elusive.

WRINGING GOOD FROM EVIL

Amma Syncletica says that grief can distort or transform. With Lorde, she says suffering can stagnate or create. The negative effects of suffering are stunningly obvious. It becomes a never-ending, ever-descending helix—an inward and spiritual version of Dom Helder Camara's "spiral of violence,"[82] except that instead of a parallel stepladder of escalation from oppression to counterviolence to repressive violence, the oppression implodes into internalized paralysis until it extinguishes all light and snuffs out the inner spark.[83] The positive impacts of pain and grief are hard to demonstrate and even harder to embrace. Yet faith asserts a potential sacramental quality to suffering that *can* lead to spiritual and social transformation. The idea that grief can be a "golden spur,"[84] like pairing the words *redemptive suffering*, is either a ludicrous oxymoron or a profound insight.

A Sufi tradition, akin to Eckhart, likens weeping to giving birth to Jesus: "The body is like Mary, and each of us has a Jesus within. If the pain appears, our Jesus will be born. But if no pain comes, Jesus will return to his Origin on that same hidden road by which he came."[85] Without labor pain, there can be no birth. Without suffering, the Word has no flesh; the preexistent Christ remains a nonexistent Christ. The Sufis link grief to compassion; with a period of introspective gestation, suffering has the capacity to create a new person, community, or nation. Moaning can give birth to mercy.

---

82. Camara, *Spiral of Violence*.
83. Soelle, *Suffering*, 12, 22, 68.
84. Climacus, *Ladder of Divine Ascent*, 136.
85. Helminski, *Women of Sufism*, 183.

Theognius says simply that tears lead to love;[86] John Climacus that mourning prepares the way for "blessed dispassion,"[87] while selfishness yields to a commitment to the needs of others, Gutierrez's description of Job.[88] Hard hearts are softened; self-reliance, emotional insularity, and spiritual isolationism begin to crumble. William McNamara says prayer is most often jump-started by our experience of "Godlessness or Godforsakenness."[89] Rabbi Shmelke of Nikolsburg draws parallels between Esau's loss of his birthright to two stories of Israel's collective grief—the loss of the ark of the covenant in battle and its abduction at the destruction of the temple. In a twist on modern biblical scholarship on the realm, these, he says, are the tears we shed not so much for what is *already* lost (like Job) as for what is *not yet* lost. The Messiah, he says, "will not come until such tears have ceased to flow, until you weep because the Divine Presence is exiled, and because you yearn for its return."[90] We pray, McNamara says, not so much out of the richness of our personal spiritual depth as at the world's endless dislocation:

> How can we sincerely pray for the coming of the Kingdom, a radical transformation of our lives—not an improvement but a revolution—if we are already fairly satisfied and feel pretty good? . . . Anyone who is at all in touch with reality will be fundamentally dissatisfied with the way things are, with the brokenness of our world and our lives, with the rape of the earth, with the absence of God and the delay of God's Kingdom.[91]

When we no longer sense God's presence and/or blessing, we pray. The impetus to pray can be to something as singularly traumatic as a tsunami or ethnic cleansing. Alternately, as Climacus says, it can be a "melancholy of the soul, a disposition of an anguished heart that passionately seeks what it thirsts for, and when it fails to attain it, pursues it diligently and follows behind it lamenting bitterly."[92] This backbreaking heavyheartedness can ironically prod people to intercession and intervention.

Julian, feeling her own yawning hunger for righteousness, echoes Climacus's idea that moaning incites people to prayer and action: "we can never cease from mourning and weeping, sighing and longing" until we see Christ face to face. "This weeping does not only mean the outpouring of tears from

86. Vivian, *Journeying into God*, 159–60.
87. Climacus, *Ladder of Divine Ascent*, 143.
88. Gutierrez, *On Job*, 39.
89. McNamara, *Earthy Mysticism*, 25–27.
90. Buber, *Tales: Early Masters*, 186.
91. McNamara, *Earthy Mysticism*, 27.
92. Climacus, *Ladder of Divine Ascent*, 136.

our mortal eyes; the natural desire of our soul is so immeasurable that if all the nobility which God ever created in heaven and on earth were given to us for our joy and our comfort, if we did not see God's own fair blessed face, still we should never cease to mourn and to weep in the spirit."[93] We need to be able to differentiate between sorrow for oneself, empathy for others, and compassion for God. Hinting that the suffering of Qoheleth might be holier than the mourning of Job, Catherine hears God say that souls can measure their spiritual maturity when someone "grieves more over the offense given to [God] and the harm done to the other than over her own hurt."[94] Catherine hints that God plants grief in our hearts to sow our prayers; and when we intercede with these prayers, God finds them irresistible. As God said to her, "Dearest daughter, because your tears are joined to my charity and are shed for love of me, your weeping has power over me and the pain in your desire binds me like a chain."[95]

Tears even have the power to break through fossilized dogma and redeem the past. The fourteenth-century poem *St. Erkenwald* may be based on the legend of Pope Gregory the Great, who with his prayers released Emperor Trajan from hell.[96] The poem describes seventh-century London in terms that echo the visions of the Hebrew prophets—people come from the ends of the earth to learn God's word and walk in God's ways (Isa 2:2-4, Mic 4:1-4). So in London, "such a crowd of all kinds came there eagerly,/ Like all the world's dwellers swarming there at once."[97] What is about to take place is a revelation the whole world needs to see.

The city's cathedral is built on the site of an ancient pre-Christian temple (just as the Dome of the Rock is built over the site of the second temple). The cathedral has now been renamed, "cleansed," and the idols of the past "hurled out."[98] As part of an excavation, workers discover a tomb embellished with marble with an inscription written in an indecipherable ancient language. When opening the tomb, they find a "body of blissful appearance," arrayed nobly, with a "mighty mantle," "coruscating crown," and "splendid scepter."[99] Even more striking, the uncorrupted body's garments are unstained. Nothing "moldy or marked or moth-eaten" mar them, as if the burial has been a day and not a thousand

---

93. Julian, *Showings*, 320-21.
94. Catherine, *Dialogue*, 304.
95. Ibid., 50.
96. Stone, comp. and trans., *Owl and the Nightingale*, 28-42.
97. Ibid., 31.
98. Ibid., 28.
99. Ibid., 31.

years before.[100] The flesh on the corpse's face suggests someone in good health who has gently fallen asleep. The workers wonder if this might have been a king. More amazing, the man would better be described not as a corpse, but as undead.

Word leaks to mayor and magistrate. The bishop, Erkenwald, is away, but he too hears the strange news. Upon returning to the city, he spends a night in prayer. He wants earnestly to help the people understand this mystery. In the morning Erkenwald attends matins and mass. When he goes to the tomb, he is told that no chronicle reveals the corpse's identity. The bishop reassures everyone that when human wisdom cannot illuminate the truth, divine grace can. Erkenwald announces, "Jesus has judged that his joy shall be shown today." He asks the dead man what religion he practiced, "whether you are bound for bliss or banished to damnation."[101]

The corpse answers that he had been a master of judges who practiced pagan law and religion. Because he administered justice "as perfectly as a pagan can," in an act of extraordinary recognition he was given the scepter.[102] As they listen to the dead man's tale, the people around Erkenwald became "still as stones," and "many wept."[103] When asked why his body has not decayed, he replies, "The Lord who most loves right has allowed me to last."[104] But when Erkenwald asks him about the state of his soul, the dead man "lying there murmured and moved his head/And gave a great groan" because even God's mercy could not undo his pagan status. His soul remains cut off from the Lord's Supper because, during his lifetime, he never heard the gospel. Because he was not baptized, when Christ harrowed hell, he was left in limbo.

As the judge describes his eternal anguish, "all wept for woe," and the bishop "sobbed without ceasing." But Erkenwald resolves to grace the corpse with holy water so that God will allow his life to return. Then Erkenwald's "tears trickled down and touched the tomb,/One fell on the face, and the body sighed," and in an epiphany the pagan judge realizes that his soul can now be seated at the great supper. Anguish gives way to bliss. The bells in the city "boomed out together," and "mourning and merriment mingled together."[105] The pagan's groan and the bishop's tears meet together

---

100. Ibid., 32.
101. Ibid., 36.
102. Ibid., 38.
103. Ibid., 37.
104. Ibid., 39.
105. Ibid., 40–43.

to redeem the past. Holy justice is overwhelmed by divine mercy. And the earth rejoices.

To believe in redemptive suffering is to embrace the possibility that the future can transform the past. Martin Luther King, Jr., one of the great modern advocates of redemptive suffering—the meeting of groans and love—often ascribed an irreplaceable role to suffering in the cause of social transformation. Like Lorde, he wanted to transform personal suffering into collective redemption. In his "I Have a Dream" speech, he exhorts the "veterans of creative suffering" to "continue with the faith that unearned suffering is redemptive."[106] And in his "Letter from Birmingham Jail," he lauds Birmingham's black protesters for "their willingness to suffer" for the sake of justice.[107] In this, King was in tune with both the African American faith experience and the mystical tradition. Underhill writes that Jesus himself redeems things, "not by shirking any of the dreadful accidents of existence, but by absorbing every bit of it—suffering, treachery, disillusion, death—into the scheme" of life and salvation.[108] This faith in the transformational power of suffering is also characteristic of Gandhi's innovative interpretation of the Hindu tradition. In Hinduism, traditionally and practically, one simply wants to be free of pain, but Gandhi believed that suffering has an intrinsic value and contains a unique power; the "voluntary assumption" of suffering could become a means to convert the hearts of the oppressor. The spiritual power of intentional suffering far exceeds the connivance of reason to achieve historical change. Nations, as he says, can be forged and reformed only "through the agony of the Cross." A satyagrahi does not care for his or her self-purification except as prelude and preparation to cleanse society.[109]

King took Gandhi's insight as an incisive analysis of spiritual and political power and as the gospel for civil rights strategy as he addressed his people's oppressors: "We will match your capacity to inflict suffering with our capacity to endure suffering. We will meet your physical force with soul force. . . . We will soon wear you down by our capacity to suffer. And in winning our freedom we will so appeal to your heart and conscience that we will win you in the process."[110] If Erkenwald's tears could redeem a pagan and the Sufi's labor pains can give birth to Jesus, redemptive suffering could deliver racial equality.

---

106. King, *Testament of Hope*, 219.
107. Ibid., 301.
108. Underhill, *Modern Guide*, 80.
109. Chatterjee, *Gandhi's Religious Thought*, 83.
110. King, *Stride Toward Freedom*, 217, *Strength to Love*, 54.

The intensity of social movements and King's sense of urgency reveal one of the great flaws in Qoheleth's pain: it lacks Job's passion. Because Qoheleth believes the horizons have closed, and because he writes from a position of privilege, he can afford to tinker with reform and leisurely fritter away days, months, and years until a more propitious time arrives as a gift; privilege can always wait. Such patience is the antithesis of perseverance. To King, people couldn't wait because the pain of everyday life was too debilitating; people had suffered too long, and every proposed legislative reform was but a baby step toward true justice. When he was a slave, Frederick Douglass said that he could endure slavery's lash temporarily, but if slavery were permanent, he would despair.[111] King felt the same way about discrimination.

While King believed that suffering contains the power to overcome injustice, he also knew what could happen when injustice soured a community and turned its grief into rage. He sensed the mood in Birmingham's African American community after white terrorists bombed the Sixteenth Street Baptist Church in September 1963, killing Addie Mae Collins, Carole Robertson, Denise McNair, and Cynthia Wesley. In the ensuing days, African Americans in the city started mouthing threats and carrying guns. King sent a telegram to President Kennedy demanding that he send the National Guard to avert "the worst racial holocaust this nation has ever seen."[112] In spite of Kennedy's tepid response, violence was averted—at least in Birmingham. But King's fears were soon realized over the next five years as one American city after another erupted in spontaneous street rebellions, rage that would culminate in a firestorm of grief and fury that followed King's assassination: riots in 168 towns and cities that left forty-three people dead, 3,500 injured, and 20,000 incarcerated. As if engaging in another mid-sixties troop escalation in Vietnam, President Johnson sent an army of 72,000 troops into *American* cities to quash the rebellion.[113] The bombing that murdered the four girls—ages eleven through fourteen—took place only a month after the emotional mountaintop at the March on Washington and came on a day when the theme of the church's Youth Day was "The Love that Forgives."[114] The bombing put King's faith in redemptive suffering to the test.

Racist terrorism was a societal norm. It was, in truth, part and parcel of the law and order King's detractors espoused. Birmingham was the Bible

---

111. Douglass, *Life and Times*, 92.
112. Garrow, *Bearing the Cross*, 292.
113. See Commins, "Is Suffering Redemptive?," 68.
114. Ibid., 62.

Belt's heart of terrorism, earning it the colloquial epithet "Bombingham." Over the previous decade, the city had felt the shock waves of fifty unsolved explosions. Eruptions of violence were no longer random acts of brutality. They had become the expected racist reflex to every inch of progress—intimidating potential voters, beating Freedom Riders, jailing demonstrators, murdering community organizers, and assassinating leaders. Even in that atmosphere, the murders of the four girls ignited a new depth of grief from a movement built on foundations of pain and tears. While the nation's focus fell on the four girls, twenty others were wounded in the bombing. Two other forgotten black youths died in Birmingham the same day: one at the hands of whites returning from a KKK rally, another shot after he threw rocks at police in a Southern-style intifada. The dynamics at the girls' memorial services foreshadowed those at a heartrending series of South African funerals during the apartheid era when most public gatherings were banned. As Stringfellow suggests, grief and mourning are not the same thing. You can minister to persons in their grief. And you can use mourning as a public expression that links grief to faith, hope, and love. Religious leaders in both South Africa and Birmingham used the occasions to link grief with political action and faith with social revolution.

At the funeral for three of the girls, after offering pastoral comfort to their families, King proclaimed that even in the shadow of such a bleak horror, redemption was still possible. That hope rested in the hands of those present at that service, those not yet engaged in the movement, and elected leaders who remained unmoved by cries for justice. All of them could bring meaning—if not solace or comfort—to the deaths of the innocent girls. In a defiant phrase, King insisted that God always has a way of "wringing good from evil. History has proven over and over again that unmerited suffering is redemptive. The innocent blood of these little girls may well serve as the redemptive force that will bring new light to this dark city."[115]

Diane Nash, who had spent her young adult life in the civil rights movement, had not waited for King's words. For her, the murders left her with but two choices. She could become a vigilante and kill the killers, or remain an activist and envision a new political initiative to get African Americans the right to vote and keep black children safe. On the night of the funeral, Nash presented the Southern Christian Leadership Conference (SCLC) leadership with a plan to form the nonviolent army of Gandhi's dreams that civil rights leader Jim Lawson had proposed two years before. Nash proposed an army of 20,000 to 40,000 volunteers who would register people to vote. The electoral power of newly enfranchised voters would

---

115. King, *Testament of Hope*, 221–22.

drive the likes of George Wallace and other demagogues from office. In her plan, the Gandhian army would lie down on railroad tracks, runways, and bus driveways, surround Wallace's office, cut Montgomery's lines of communication, and shut down transportation all across Alabama. Either the emotional weight of the day or the ingrained sexism of the movement kept King from taking her seriously. But Nash persevered. Leaders of the Student Nonviolent Coordinating Committee (SNCC) embraced her plan. In revised form, it came to fruition in the marches from Selma to Montgomery two years later.[116]

The Selma action in 1965 endured another series of terrorist reactions—the nationally televised police riot and beatings on the Pettis Bridge, and the offscreen murders of one northern Anglo and one local African American.[117] Yet in broad outline Nash's strategy succeeded. It achieved precisely what King had preached: it brought justice from the night soil of murder and triumph from mindless tragedy. It redeemed innocent suffering and useless death. It had wrung good from evil. It was in fact a microcosm of the overall purpose of the civil rights movement: to redeem a living legacy of slavery, segregation, exploitation, denigration, and oppression, and save the soul of America. It created a rereading of the past, as Erkenwald's tears brought mercy to the pagan judge. The civil rights movement offered a "love that forgives," transcending the welfare of one moral person (Erkenwald's pagan) for a universal salvation for the enemies of God.

The tactical success of using grief to wring good from tragedy and justice from grief can also be turned into a constant posture. Stringfellow not only endured the death of his "sweet companion" Towne and the emotional evisceration of personal grief.[118] In all his writings, he uses the term *death* to refer to a demonic power—other than God's Word the most potent force in the world. *Death*, for him, is synonymous with cosmic evil. To him, one's physical demise is only a small part of *death's* reality.[119] To him, *death* is the source of a disease that almost took his life *and* the cause of oppression in Harlem, a power that brutalized, dehumanized, and humiliated a whole community.[120] When constantly confronted and frequently defeated by *death*, mourning becomes not a fleeting feeling, but a constant condition.

---

116. Garrow, *Bearing the Cross*, 292–5; Branch, *Parting the Waters*, 893; Lee, *4 Little Girls*.

117. King's sermon for Jimmie Lee Jackson was virtually identical with the one he preached in Birmingham (Branch, *Pillar of Fire*, 600).

118. Stringfellow, *Simplicity of Faith*, 115.

119. Stringfellow, *Instead of Death*, 12, *Simplicity of Faith*, 30, *Conscience and Obedience*, 30, *Ethic for Christians*, 69.

120. Stringfellow, "Harlem," 1346.

Stringfellow says that he read, pondered, and meditated literally a thousand times on a verse in Revelation (13:7) describing "the defeat of the saints."[121] He had meditated on the grotesque power of evil and wondered why God allowed the faithful to be consistently confounded and vanquished. *Death* reigned over inner cities, the margins of society, and the heartland of power. In many ways, grief was Stringfellow's daily bread; sorrow at suffering and powerlessness, heartache at every form of oppression, anguish at the defeat of the saints, misery because *death* dominates the world. His grief fed a cold, clinical rage that crafted his theologically precise prophetic social analysis with a fine-pointed blade. His experience of *death* and mourning gave his writings a "tone of grieving compassion."[122] By birth part Qoheleth (white, educated) and part Job (working class, gay), by vocation he adopted the clinical dispassion of Qoheleth and the passionate rage of Job.

While Stringfellow embraced an apocalyptic world view, he did not believe in a single, final cataclysmic defeat of death nor, to the consternation of his liberal allies, that social evolutions or revolutions could conquer evil. Even during the relative success of the civil rights movement when as a self-described "empirical theologian"[123] he might have been tempted to trust in the potential for social change, he rejected the post-Enlightenment fallacy of progress. Throughout his writings, he insists that people and movements can do nothing to uproot the power of *death* in the world. He drew on his young adult experience meeting members of the resistance under Nazism, who found strength in small group Bible study and prayer.[124] This, he says, is the way—the only way—to conquer death: to deploy the smallest, most ordinary spiritual disciplines. Electoral politics, community organizing, and micromanaged tactics are no match for the elastic, slimy-smooth power of death; but prayer and Bible study enable people in the community of faith to withstand and counter its most obnoxious invasions. As John of the Cross finds intimacy with God at the heart of the dark night, in Stringfellow's paradoxical theology and personal experience, it is in the midst of death that one finds the power of resurrection at work: "Encircled by the manifoldness of death—the death so impatiently at work in my own body; the death so militant in my own country; the death so idolized by my own race; the death which seems to be the moral sovereign in the world; the death incarnate in all existence . . . I felt alive: very much alive: never more alive."[125] So, in a

---

121. Stringfellow, *Conscience and Obedience*, 110.
122. Hutchinson, "Review of *An Ethic*," 396.
123. Stringfellow, *Second Birthday*, 40.
124. Stringfellow, *Ethic for Christians*, 118–20.
125. Stringfellow, *Second Birthday*, 99.

sense it was natural that after he died, an anonymous acquaintance placed a plaque at Eschaton, the home he shared with Towne on Block Island: "Near this cottage, the remains of William Stringfellow and Anthony Towne await the Resurrection. Amen. Alleluia."[126]

Tears are not only a necessity among mystics. They are also handmaids of activism. Moaning and mourning are often the spiritual leaven from which activism arises. While grief can just as easily undermine, erode, dissipate, and defeat social movements, it can also spark them. Grief for a suffering world can keep alive the commitment of the overprivileged to the working out of God's purposes in the harsh realities of unjust structures. When it can be transformed from amorphous, enervating, everlasting, self-defeating suffering to a pain that is understood, analyzed, rejected, and acted upon, it contains the power for world change. When it awakens people to the proliferation and intransigence of evil (Stringfellow), when it reminds people why we can't wait to end injustice (King), when it makes people determined to abort future white terrorism (Nash), when it inspires people to wring good from evil, it has the potential to heal the moaning of the world.

A CHORUS OF GROANS

During the Great Depression, when hopelessness fueled revolutionary fervor for sudden, radical, and violent change, the Catholic Worker built itself as a gradualist movement without watershed moments. Its actions would never register on anyone's Richter scale of social transformation. It was an anarchic community formed to heal both "the long loneliness"[127] of personal life and the longer loneliness of unjust oppression. The Worker's work was incremental, interpersonal, determinedly small-scale, an evolutionary revolution in contradistinction to the secular leftist movements of its era. Its Catholic founders were evangelical in method and tone—one day at a time, one person at a time—but less intrigued by final salvation than daily redemption. The hands-on grind of soup kitchens, houses of hospitality, and farming communes created an environment in which community members sometimes experienced "the Catholic Worker Blues": "The sadness, the weariness, the sense of futility runs very deep at times. The romance of living on the front lines wears thin. If the sadness worms its way into you, it's not romantic or dramatic, it's spiritual catastrophe."[128] Whatever the condi-

---

126. Berrigan, *To Dwell in Peace*, 258.
127. The title of Day's autobiography.
128. Brodhead, "Maryhouse II," 272.

tion of the global economy or the national political topography, Workers faced the wide-swath shadow side of the prosperity of the few. Sometimes historical trauma shatters souls. Sometimes souls splinter slowly.

Those souls do not have to be on "the front lines" of social dislocation. In the humdrum of academic life in the everyday, nontraumatic, nondramatic world, horizons slowly close on hope as we know it. This malaise is expressed, sans label, by Dorothee Soelle, who, when she subtitled *The Silent Cry*, her book on mysticism and politics, christened it *Mysticism and Resistance*. Had it not been the 1990s in the US during the Clinton administration, had it not been in the decade bookended by the fall of the Berlin Wall and the crumbling of the Twin Towers, had it been the 1960s in the US or Europe or Latin America or Africa, had it been earlier, she remembered, or "had it been later," she hoped, she would have called it Mysticism and *Revolution*: "For us who live in the transition to the third millennium of the common era, however, 'resistance' seems to be the formulation that is more accurate and closer to reality."[129] "Revolution" evokes eager hope for shalom incarnate, utopia found, the day dawned, the realm established. "Resistance" evokes endurance—a common theme in an apostolic era faced with seemingly omnipotent principalities. The New Testament preaches a refusal to surrender, accommodate, or compromise, the stubbornness of the powerless as they cling to the grim hope that the world will not slide even further, ever downward into an endless whirlwind of exploitation and defeat. Resistance was Frederick Douglass's posture: he could survive as a slave for *now*; he could not live with *anyone's* slavery forever. Soelle wrote in a decade of receding hope and a quiet suffocating grief when groaning had become part of society's white noise.

"We Shall Overcome" sings of revolution. The music of resistance is the blues, a broad phenomenon of public, sometimes almost liturgical moaning. James Baldwin's Harlem-based "Sonny's Blues,"[130] like the parable of the Prodigal Son, tells the story of two adult brothers. One has found his niche as a teacher. The other—Sonny—has found no niche at all. Sonny's return from a seven-year prison sentence for using and selling heroin is one more broken branch in a knotted family history overwhelmed by death. Their parents have died. An uncle died young in a racial incident. The teacher's daughter died at the age of two. The Harlem the teacher lives in is still the eviscerated and self-destructive community of their childhood: the children he teaches will "have the same things to remember."[131] Sonny comes to live

---

129. Soelle, *Silent Cry*, 4.
130. Baldwin, *Going to Meet*, 86–122.
131. Baldwin, "Sonny's Blues," 96.

with the teacher, his wife Isabel, and their two sons, his musician lifestyle's proximity to drugs disturbing to his stable brother.

As Sonny watches a singing street preacher, he tells his brother, "Her voice reminded me for a minute of what heroin feels like sometimes—when it's in your veins. It makes you feel sort of warm and cool at the same time. And distant. And—and sure." Something in the timbre of her voice speaks of suffering. There is no way to avoid it, Sonny laments, but "that's never stopped anyone from trying . . . has it?" Try to avoid it or give it a reason, "*any* reason," but no reason sticks.[132]

The teacher doesn't know much about music, but when he hears Sonny play at a nearby club, he knows Sonny "is dealing with the roar rising from the void" within, something "of another order, more terrible because it has no words, and triumphant too, for that same reason."[133] When Sonny plays, his music enshrines all of the moaning and mourning, the sadness, the weariness, the sense of futility in the nontraumatic suffering common in life. The wordless music tells the story of Sonny's family, a story of oppression, the human story. When he hears Sonny play, his brother knows he is hearing an epiphany.

> For, while the tale of how we suffer, and how we are delighted, and how we may triumph is never new, it always must be heard. There isn't any other tale to tell, it's the only light we've got in all this darkness.
>
> And this tale, according to that face, that body, those strong hands on those strings, has another aspect in every country, and a new depth in every generation . . . .
>
> I saw my mother's face again, and felt, for the first time, how the stones of the road she had walked on must have bruised her feet. I saw the moonlit road where my father's brother died. And it brought something else back to me, and carried me past it. I saw my little girl again and felt Isabel's tears again, and I felt my own tears begin to rise. And I was yet aware that this was only a moment, that the world waited outside, as hungry as a tiger, and that trouble stretched above us, longer than the sky.[134]

Sonny's blues were cathartic. The Catholic Worker is a cathartic community. In a world in which lives are short, brutal, and—to all appearances—wasted, in which the mighty do not fall and the lowly are not lifted up, in which sacred reversals are rare, in which the first are first and the last last, blues

---

132. Ibid., 113–15.
133. Ibid., 119.
134. Ibid., 121–22.

communities are perhaps the only ones telling the only tale worth telling. There is an incarnational quality to that tale, a tale of God entering a world as ferocious as a tiger and becoming one with the trouble that stretches longer than the sky. The blues are heard in unique forms in every country, culture, and generation. Black Elk speaks of his people's moaning and mourning, Julian of Christ's. Activists hear the world's groans and either try to staunch the flow of tears or dam the tears at their source. The blues belong to the generations of Black Elk and Jeremiah and Qoheleth, a barely audible moan that drowns out all music but its own.

It is as if there are two songs that fill the universe. In Revelation, one of Stringfellow's primary biblical sources, songs of praise ripple and crescendo as first the four living creatures around God's throne sing, then the twenty-four elders, then countless angels, and finally "every creature in heaven and on earth and under the earth and in the sea" (Rev 5:8–14). The song begins closest to the Lamb and spreads like an antiphonal tidal wave of joy to the farthest corner of the cosmos, filling every wrinkle and crevice until all creation is overflowing with the victory of the Lamb. This is the song heard and sung most often by mystics. The groaning of creation has its own arc. With random, unsynchronized starting points, it is disorderly, nonliturgical, and unpredictable. It begins with one voice, any voice, anywhere at any time, lamenting anything. That creates a ripple that turns into a wave until all of creation moans and mourns together for any and every person who suffers. The antithesis of Revelation's irradiating explosion of holy joy, it is a constant dissolution in human tears that is equally infectious and equally divine. Sharing George Herbert's intuition about the power of the groan, the usually ebullient Thomas Traherne says, "one deep and serious groan is more acceptable to God than the creation of the world."[135] All of creation is good; some of it very good, as Traherne unflaggingly attests, but the common groan is better than a planet.

Cries and groans often stimulate sacred stories. At times they are the only psalm worth singing. While biblical writers draw neat distinctions between moaning (seeking God) and murmuring (complaining about God) as acts of faith and faithlessness, both begin with the same pain. The cries of slaves in Egypt are like the prayers God tells Catherine and Julian about, prayers planted in people's hearts so God cannot resist them when they are uttered. Perhaps the Exodus story's blessing on people's cries explains the proliferation of biblical laments; the cry of *the people*, like the prayers of Hannah, Deborah, and Jeremiah, seems often irresistible. Yet sometimes, those tears come from the selfish lower reaches of Catherine's typology of

---

135. Traherne, *Centuries*, 156.

tears. Sometimes, while the agony is real, it masks complicity: "We all growl like bears; like doves we moan mournfully. We wait for justice, but there is none; for salvation, but it is far from us," Isaiah says, mouthing the people's seemingly poignant words except that the same people are the authors of their own foul fate (Isa 59:11). "Writhe and groan, O daughter of Zion, like a woman in labor," Micah says, for all the good it will do a people doomed by their addiction to injustice (Mic 4:10). Yet the same messages of doom announce a possibility of salvation: as they denounce false and shallow piety, they announce the possibility of conversion and sanctification. God, like the zaddik who feels human pain, hears even the cries of *oppressors*. A psalmist even imagines their God as an intercessor among many deities beseeching them to use their powers to create justice, and hoping that these deities can no more resist than Catherine's God (Ps 82).

When the prophets speak, sometimes their words are their own, sometimes their people's, and sometimes their God's. Sometimes the prophet becomes "an enfleshment of the emotion of God. . . . God and prophet speak with one voice,"[136]

> My joy is gone, grief is upon me, my heart is sick
> Hark, the cry of my poor people
> From far and wide in the land:
> "Is the Lord not in Zion?
> Is her King not in her?"
> ("Why have they provoked me to anger with their images, with the foreign idols?")
> "The harvest is past, the summer is ended, and we are not saved."
> For the hurt of my poor people I am hurt, I mourn, and dismay has taken hold of me.
> Is there no balm in Gilead? Is there no physician there?
> Why then has the health of my poor people not been restored?
> O that my head were a spring of water, and my eyes a fountain of tears,
> So that I might weep day and night for the slain of my poor people (Jer 8:18–9:1).

In one breath Jeremiah condemns his people, in the next he weeps for them. In his long and tangled relationship with the divine, when God judges, Jeremiah tries to intercede; when God weeps or waffles, Jeremiah condemns. Jeremiah and God are sickened by the duplicity of the people yet they are heartsick at their people's fate.

---

136. Fretheim, *Suffering of God*, 160–61.

Mystics and activists can share the emotional ambiguity, the blues, of the prophets. Hildegard of Bingen writes that when Abel's blood was shed, "the entire Earth sighed and at that moment was declared a widow," for in that moment "the Earth was robbed of its holy totality by the murder committed by Cain."[137] Even before Israel moans, the earth has sighed, stricken with creation's first innocent blood. Less concerned with the primordial past than his own era, Rauschenbusch notes, "those whose ears are attuned to hear the deepest organ note of the universe, hear a groan of travail from the under deep."[138] The cries ring out in every generation and country. Paul, too, writes of this labor pain, begun by the people of Israel but shared across the cosmos. Paul says that the first generation of Christians did not suffer alone. Rather, like the songs of praise of the four living creatures around God's throne, the cries of Christians have been taken up by the cosmos. Creation itself "waits with eager longing" for the age to come. Subjected to futility, slavery, and endless waiting to be free "from the bondage of decay," creation longs to share what the children of God and before them the people of Israel already had—Freedom: "We know that the whole creation has been groaning in labor pains until now" (Rom 8:19–23). Wherever the groan George Herbert describes begins, the song has been fruitful and the chorus has multiplied.

Black Elk observed his people bereaved because a force of chaotic destruction assaulted their civilization. But human moans are never only human. Julian says that Christ is also and always "moaning and mourning." Love never allows Christ to be without pity. Whenever people sin or fail to practice remembrance (*dhikr*) of God, or fail to stay awake (*buddh*), "then Christ bears all alone the burden of us."[139] And so he remains, moaning and mourning, making his grief one with the people of Black Elk's village. Yet even while their moaning becomes one, there remains a difference. Human suffering is by nature temporary and finite; grief naturally progresses from open wound to jagged scar. God's grief, as Catherine says, is permanent, "for God who is infinite, would have infinite love and infinite sorrow."[140] When one of Muhammad's early companions was groaning loudly, others—like Jesus' disciples keeping an Afrikaner's uitlander (outsider) at arm's distance—rebuked him. But Muhammad intervenes and says, "Let him groan,

---

137. Hildegard, *Book of Divine Works*, 54.
138. Rauschenbusch, *Social Gospel*, 156.
139. Julian, *Showings*, 336.
140. Catherine, *Dialogue*, 28.

for groaning is one of the names of God."[141] People never groan alone, nor does creation. Groaning is intrinsic to the nature of the divine.

Likewise, something sacred takes place when we join our moaning to God's. Rauschenbusch hears a divine cry at the root of the world's suffering so that *we* will respond to *God's* cry. Our grief, Julian and Catherine tell us, is finite like the slavery Douglass said he could not endure; God's is infinite. Perhaps, as Catherine infers, God's moaning inspires our groaning, and our groaning stokes the fires of God's empathic pain. If so, we pray that God will relieve our suffering as we work to end God's.

THE DRILL DRILLS ON

In his memoir of mourning after his wife's premature death, C. S. Lewis confesses that he had lost the certainty, clarity, and solidity of his faith. For this brilliantly effective apologist who once coolly and philosophically—and unsympathetically—dismissed "the problem of pain,"[142] his faith had become "a house of cards."[143] He could grieve with faith. He could grieve without faith. Either way, he was decimated. Lewis compares grief to sitting in the dentist's chair of an earlier, less anesthetized, more primitive, more painful era. One can hold onto the arms of the chair or let go, just as one can grieve with or without faith, but with or without faith, holding on or letting go, the dentist's "drill drills on."[144]

Oppressed, exploited, and decimated peoples through the centuries may resonate with the privileged Lewis's personal grief as they and their loved ones endure an agonizingly normal ache. The Trail of Tears was not limited to the Cherokee, Creek, Chickasaw, Choctaw, and Seminole nations in the 1830s, or to Native Americans in general, or to the leaders of ancient Israel as they were swept into their Babylonian exile. It is a well-worn path. Likewise, the oppressed might hear the words of Black Elk as their own as he endured the sometimes sudden, sometimes languid destruction of his people and the land by the wanton Wasichus (whites), their political and military leaders, and their culture. The Wasichus were nineteenth-century North American barbarians sacking Rome, Saracens assaulting the sacred shrines of Greece, Babylonians looting Jerusalem and desecrating its temple. Of course, as usual, the Wasichus—their self-righteous sense of manifest

---

141. Nicholl, *Holiness*, 131.
142. Lewis, *Problem of Pain*.
143. Lewis, *Grief Observed*, 42.
144. Ibid., 38.

destiny both their vision and their blinders—saw themselves as civilizers. So Nebuchadnezzar saw himself. Black Elk remembers them differently.

Black Elk's words are another culture's confessions of Jeremiah, another book of Lamentations in the multilingual, multigenerational annals of unrelenting grief.[145] He bemoans the deaths of individuals and villages, but even more the dissolution of a way of life and a way of faith. As it was for the Hebrew prophets, Black Elk's visions merge with reality: "It was like rapid gunfire and like whirling smoke, and like women and children wailing and like horses screaming all over the world. I could see my people yonder running about, setting the smoke-flap poles and fastening down their tepees against the wind, for the storm cloud was coming on them very fast and black, and there were frightened swallows without number fleeing before the cloud."[146] Centuries before on another continent, King Zedekiah sent for the oft-imprisoned Jeremiah to beg, "Is there any word from the Lord" (Jer 37:17)? Zedekiah hoped that in spite of the prophet's drumbeat pronouncements of doom, a new word from the divine would reverse the visible and obvious direction of history. There were moments when Jeremiah would have liked nothing better than to alter his manic prophecies to oblige Zedekiah with a managed vision of hope, but no such word came. Among his people, Black Elk yearned for a new vision to offset his historical-spiritual nightmares so that he "could save that country for my people, but I couldn't see anything clear."[147]

Black Elk had the power and gift to heal individuals, "but my nation I could not help." He was living in Sobrino's antimerciful world in which personal healing dangles like a bauble, a false promise of shalom in an era of desecration. In time, Black Elk lost satisfaction in healing men, women, and children because social death so outweighed personal life: "If a man or woman or child dies, it does not matter long, for the nation lives on. It was the nation that was dying."[148]

For Black Elk's people, the hoop was the symbol of created and social order, John of Patmos's vision of the holy city with the tree of life at its center (Rev 22:2), Merton's "hidden wholeness."[149] Black Elk's hopeful vision "was to save the nation's hoop and make the holy tree to bloom in the center of it, [but] I felt like crying, for the sacred hoop was broken and scattered. The life

---

145. See especially Lam 1:3–5, 15–6, 2:10–2, 18–9, 4:6, 17, 5:2–3, 15.
146. Black Elk, *Black Elk Speaks*, 39.
147. Ibid., 82.
148. Ibid., 184.
149. Merton, *Collected Poems*, 363.

of the people was in the hoop,"[150] and no one's laughter or any single blessing could obscure the loss of coherence and meaning. The people were scattered; the nation had unraveled. Black Elk could have been observing one of the destructions of Jerusalem, or Nazi Germany's Anschluss of Austria, or the genocides in Rwanda or Bosnia, or merely sitting beside Conrad's Kurtz (or Qoheleth) as he is absorbed in the horror and the heart of darkness.

Like Black Elk, Jeremiah sees in the historical destruction of his people the ruination of the cosmos and a reversal of the neat liturgical creation story in Genesis.

> I looked on the earth, and lo, it was waste and void
> And to the heavens, and they had no light
> I looked on the mountains, and lo, they were quaking
> And all the hills moved to and fro.
> I looked, and lo, there was no one at all
> And all the birds of the air had fled.
> I looked, and lo, the fruitful land was a desert
> And all its cities were laid in ruins (Jer 4:23-26).

Writing from prison in the twelfth year of a Thousand Year Reich, Dietrich Bonhoeffer saw what he believed was true of all times and places. He asserted that we must grieve with God for the godlessness of the world: "we must live our lives without God. The God who is with us is the God who forsakes us.... Before God and with God we live without God.... God is weak and powerless in the world, and that is precisely the way, the only way, in which God is with us and helps us." Bonhoeffer rejects any answers, comfort, or theodicy to soften God's powerlessness. We do not need reasons or explanations but courage and action. We "must therefore really live in a godless world, without attempting to gloss or explain its ungodliness in some religious way or other. We must live a secular life, and thereby share in God's sufferings." Prefiguring Catholic liberation theologians a generation later, he contends, "It is not the religious act that makes the Christian, but participation in the sufferings of God in secular life." In this very "secular" witness, and *only* in this witness, can Christians articulate their faith: "we must speak of God in such a way that the godlessness of the world is not in some way concealed, but rather revealed, and thus exposed to an unexpected light."[151] In this testament of faith, Bonhoeffer presages Baldwin's narrator: "There isn't any other tale to tell, it's the only light we've got in all this darkness."

---

150. Black Elk, *Black Elk Speaks*, 218.
151. Bonhoeffer, *Letters and Papers*, 360-62.

While it may be an overlooked voice in dominant culture, Black Elk's words represent the prevailing human experience. Unrelenting chaos, the obliteration of a people, and the annihilation of hope may belong primarily to exiles and refugees, the displaced and oppressed peoples of the world, but they are not their private property. For every culture of Job, there is a culture of Qoheleth. When there is disease anywhere, there is unease everywhere. Nowhere in the world's whirlwind is there experienced the shalom that passes all understanding. Writing from a socially coddled experience, T. S. Eliot, a Qoheleth of the lost generation, evokes imagery Black Elk would have recognized.

> There is no end of it, the voiceless wailing,
> No end to the withering of withered flowers,
> To the movement of pain that is painless and motionless
> To the drift of the sea and the drifting wreckage,
> The bone's prayer to Death its God. Only the hardly, barely prayable,
> Prayer of the one Annunciation.[152]

For Black Elk, as for Eliot, there was still an annunciation. For Black Elk, it was not the angel's annunciation to Mary, although a similar rumor enthralled his people in one last gasping grasp at hope. Like an apocalyptic flash, Black Elk's people believed that the Son of the Great Spirit who had come among the Wasichus long before—the one the Wasichus had murdered—was now to come to them. When he did "there would not be any Wasichus in the world that would come like a cloud in a whirlwind and crush out the old earth that was dying."[153] Black Elk's people starved for a redeemer to fulfill visions like Isaiah's and the Songs of Zechariah and Mary, and to halt the relentless assaults of an endlessly devouring civilization, but their dreams remained unfulfilled.

At times dreams are fulfilled, at times delayed, at times crushed and buried. In September 1906, a white race riot scourged Atlanta's African American community, killing dozens, maiming more, and terrorizing an oft-scarred people calloused by fear. Away in Alabama during the riot, W. E. B. DuBois rushed home fretting for the welfare of his wife and child who, unknown to him, were safe. On the train DuBois wrote his searing "Litany at Atlanta." In March 1965, Atlanta-born Martin Luther King, Jr. was in Alabama for the consummation of the seminal Selma march, the fruit of Diane Nash's imagination. On Montgomery's state house steps, in an atmosphere of fulfillment, King delivered one of his most buoyant speeches.

152. Eliot, "Dry Salvages," in *Complete Poems and Plays*, 132.
153. Black Elk, *Black Elk Speaks*, 239.

DuBois's and King's *sitz im leben* could not have been more starkly different: DuBois writing after thousands of whites ran amok in black neighborhoods in yet another mass lynching; King speaking after an integrated group of thousands marched in ordered procession to secure another spoonful of racial justice. For King, there had never been a moment "so honorable"; to DuBois, there had never been a day or night more brutal. For King, it was a moment of divine intoxication; DuBois's times demanded detoxification.

In the public light of Montgomery, King was society's mullah—awakening the nation again to justice and reconciliation. In the privacy of his train ride, DuBois's litany was a priestly intercession on behalf of a muzzled people. The pastor's speech is strikingly secular, the prayer of the future Communist profoundly religious. King commends proactive nonviolence; DuBois prays to resist seductive revenge. DuBois considers his self-characterized near-hysterical litany potentially heretical, but it is a magnificent extension of a lament shared by Job and a string of psalmists. Invoking "The Battle Hymn of the Republic," King's speech is an echo of victory songs that stretch from the Song of Miriam to the cadences of John of Patmos.

King's mid-century elation might be taken as an answer to DuBois's turn-of-the-century despair, but the march of history King trumpeted has not proven as rhythmic or as linear as he envisioned. More recent decades have dulled the bright luster of King's luminous rhetoric—as revolution has drooped into drawn-out resistance—and made more apt DuBois's "hysterics." Neither document, neither sentiment, supersedes the other. They accompany each other, as do triumphant songs (Rev 5:8–14) and creation's groans (Rom 8:19–23).[154]

DuBois and King jointly proclaim a self-evident theological truth that white America fervently, flagrantly, subtly, and systematically denies. Against waves of assaults on human dignity, they announce yet again: African Americans are God's children. Yet they direct their shared message to different audiences. King boosts civil rights marchers, defies racist propagandists, and challenges the complicity of national leaders: *we are God's children; did you not know?* DuBois reprimands an apparently dithering God: *we are your children; have you forgotten?* King speaks in a time when civil rights legislation delivered partial dignity, "dignity without strength,"[155] but legislation had hinted at racial equality. DuBois debunks the whitest of white lies—and with it, Booker T. Washington's accommodationist ideology—that whites would ever allow blacks to earn their dignity: "They told

---

154. See King, *Testament of Hope*, 227–30, and DuBois, *Darkwater*, 14–16 for the full texts.

155. King, *Testament of Hope*, 227.

[the African American]: *Work and Rise!* They worked." But did it get them anywhere? "Nay... this man lieth maimed and murdered, his wife naked to shame, his children to poverty and evil."[156] King sees blacks assert their own dignity. DuBois sees whites dangle pride like a tantalizing gem and then maliciously rip it away.

Cross-examining the divine like Job, DuBois decries the riot's racism as visible proof of systemic evil's steady pulse: "Is this Thy Justice, O Father... ?/Doth not this justice of hell stink in Thy nostrils, O God?"[157] King foresees a "season of suffering"[158] but he also imagines evil is on its last legs, "choking to death in the dusty roads and streets" of Alabama. Segregation lies on its "deathbed": "the brutality of a dying order shrieks across the land."[159] The only shrieks DuBois hears rise from his own people: "Bewildered we are and passion-tossed, mad with the madness of a mobbed and mocked and murdered people." He can pluck not a single bud of hope from an uninterrupted history of cruelty told "by the blood of our stolen fathers, by the tears of our dead mothers, by the very blood of Thy crucified Christ."[160]

Near the end of King's speech, he deploys four of his favorite quotations: "truth pressed to earth will rise again," "no lie can live forever," "you still reap what you sow," "the arc of the moral universe is long but it bends toward justice."[161] *If* he had prayed, eyes closed, with his audience *"thy kingdom come,"* they might have expected to open their eyes to see it. DuBois sees truth crushed, lies reigning, the wicked prospering, and the spine of a moral universe snapped. As he struggles to find meaning in the rubble of a riot, a primal petition becomes the unstated undertone of DuBois's litany and the puny pinnacle of his low-slung hope: at least, at most, if nothing else, *deliver us from evil*.

Together King and DuBois rebuke political leaders who feebly bemoan violence, repression, and exploitation. DuBois anticipates King's accusation of elected leaders after the bombing of Sixteenth Street Baptist Church as DuBois spreads blame beyond the rioters: "Who made these devils? Who nursed them in crime and fed them on injustice?" The white Southern aristocracy might "wag their heads and leer and cry with bloody jaws: *Cease*

---

156. DuBois, *Darkwater*, 15.
157. Ibid., 14–15.
158. King, *Testament of Hope*, 229.
159. Ibid., 228.
160. DuBois, *Darkwater*, 15.
161. King, *Testament of Hope*, 230.

from Crime!"[162] But such words were "mockery, for thus they train a hundred crimes while we do cure one."[163]

In Selma, King's speech came shortly after President Johnson's televised endorsement of the civil rights movement, the strongest support any president has given to racial justice. Johnson lauded demonstrators "for awakening the conscience of the nation" and he embraced the movement's signature language as he promised that with congressional action "we shall overcome."[164] In that afterglow, King thanks white Americans "who cherish their democratic traditions over the ugly customs and privileges" of generations.[165] He graciously promises bigoted opponents: "our aim must never be to defeat or humiliate" you.[166] With so much blood so recently spilled, DuBois makes no room for mercy, forgiveness, reconciliation, or love. He will not dissect his hatreds of sin and sinner nor restrain himself to the lex talionis's eye or tooth. Instead, he exhales the wrath of the psalmist who blesses those who crush the heads of their oppressors' children (Ps 137:9): "When our devils do deviltry, curse Thou the doer and the deed—curse them as we curse them, do to them all and more than ever they have done to innocence and weakness, to womanhood and home."[167]

While DuBois grapples with helpless hopelessness, King revels in fleeting empowerment. Forty years after slavery's end, DuBois sees his people's "shackled hands."[168] Sixty years later King celebrates: "the battle is in our hands."[169] In one refrain, King envisions more challenges, more campaigns, and more victories: "let us march on segregated housing . . . let us march on segregated schools . . . let us march on poverty . . . let us march on ballot boxes." Then King repeats, "We are on the move now":

> We are not about to turn around. We are on the move now. Yes, we are on the move and no wave of racism can stop us. We are on the move now. The burning of our churches will not deter us. We are on the move now. The bombing of our homes will not dissuade us. We are on the move now. The beating and killing of our clergy and young people will not divert us. We are on the

---

162. DuBois, *Darkwater*, 14.
163. Ibid., 15.
164. Garrow, *Bearing the Cross*, 408.
165. King, *Testament of Hope*, 228
166. Ibid., 230.
167. DuBois, *Darkwater*, 14.
168. Ibid., 15.
169. King, *Testament of Hope*, 229.

move now. The arrest and release of known murderers will not discourage us. We are on the move now.[170]

King praises his people's mobilized power. DuBois faces their disjointed weakness with Gethsemane's prayer: "let the cup pass from us, tempt us not beyond our strength."[171] In King's Montgomery, people "transformed dark yesterdays into bright tomorrows,"[172] but DuBois's Atlanta is shrouded in never-ending "midnight." King quotes the spiritual, "We ain't goin' to let nobody turn us around."[173] DuBois's prayer foreshadows King's first foray above the Mason-Dixon Line, "Show us the way and point us to the path! Whither? North is greed and South is blood."[174] Turned around or not, there is nowhere to go.

DuBois asks an age-old question made new by fresh wounds, "How long?" King discerns the same question in his audience and answers with his penultimate rhetorical flourish. "However difficult the moment, however frustrating the hour, it will not be long." And then, attaching his favorite quotations, four times he repeats "How long? Not long."[175] The day, the hour, the realm will not be long because King's God, the God of the exodus, hears and heals people's suffering. Darkness his only companion, DuBois's prayer ends with a decrescendo into oblivion, his grief rasping, his cries exhausted, his tears spent: "Our voices sink in silence and in night. . . . In night, O God of a godless land! . . . In silence, O Silent God."[176]

King's "God is marching on,"[177] but DuBois inhabits Bonhoeffer's "godless land."[178] DuBois splatters anxious images of God like an abstract expressionist throwing paint at a worn canvas: he wonders if God is "deaf to our prayer and dumb to our dumb suffering." Worse, God's silence is "white terror to our hearts." Worse than silent, God has "flown afar." Worse still, God is "dead." But in his spiraling rhetoric he fears something still more terrifying than celestial silence, divine distance, or the deity's death. He wonders if God is "a pale, bloodless, heartless thing!" Worse than Bonhoeffer's godless world, worse than a deaf, dumb, blind, silent, dead, weak, or

---

170. Ibid., 228–29.
171. DuBois, *Darkwater*, 16.
172. King, *Testament of Hope*, 229.
173. Ibid., 227.
174. DuBois, *Darkwater*, 16.
175. King, *Testament of Hope*, 230.
176. DuBois, *Darkwater*, 16.
177. King, *Testament of Hope*, 230.
178. Bonhoeffer, *Letters and Papers*, 361.

indifferent deity, DuBois conjures up the most horrific image he can imagine and asks, could God be "white"?[179]

In Montgomery, King predicted it would not be long before the coming of racial equality. Decades have passed. He envisioned injustice dying before his eyes. Millennia come and go, and we sail toward no beachhead of a promised land; no horizon, mountain, island, desert, or even an oasis is in sight. King assumed what New Testament scholars teach about God's realm. There are signs of the *already,* but God's final triumph on earth has *not yet* come, and Christians wait in restless anticipation for the day of its consummation. King pointed to political stepping-stones leading toward a victory over systemic evil, but the final triumph keeps receding over the horizon.

While DuBois's anguish and King's self-assurance may seem to wedge their messages apart, John of the Cross asserts that "moaning is connected to hope."[180] He may have known this from personal experience. Imprisoned and tortured by members of his own church and his own order, he traversed the dark night of the soul before he described it. To assert, with Thomas Kelly and Thomas Merton, just *how close to hope despair is*, is also to admit how *close to despair hope is*, and how close King in Selma is to DuBois on his way to Atlanta.[181]

Systemic discrimination, sporadic acts of violence, and centuries of chameleonlike oppression have always deepened a hunger for righteousness, escalated eschatological fervor, and stretched slave songs deep into the night. But the experiences of DuBois and Black Elk and countless millions demand harsh questions of dreamers and their dreams: what if those hopes are not holy visions but placebos or pipe dreams? What happens when the chorus of groans envelops the agents of social change, when the moaning starts with one person, one village, or one people and spreads until it encompasses creation? What happens when faith and hope shrivel up and love is left without its comrades in activism?

There are questions one must ask with Bonhoeffer and Black Elk and Job and all the company of earth whose deepest dreams have been perennially deferred or persistently dashed. The questions must be shouted with many persons of many oppressed peoples, with moaning and with mourning. They are the queries to which sighs give voice and grief demands answers: what if the reality of God's realm is not summarized by *already/ not yet*? What if, as empirical evidence all too often attests, the reality of God's realm is *not now/never*? What if the revolution of God is permanent

---

179. DuBois, *Darkwater*, 14–6.
180. John of the Cross, *Collected Works*, 422.
181. Kelly, *Eternal Promise*, 52; Merton, *Hidden Ground*, 145, *Monastic Journey*, 221.

only because it never succeeds? What if Frederick Douglass's worst fears are realized and oppression goes on *forever*? What if we are all—T. S. Eliot and C. S. Lewis and W. E. B. DuBois, John of the Cross and Jeremiah and Dorothee Soelle, privileged and oppressed—spiraling down through chaos into a bottomless abyss? What if violence, injustice, and chaos will *always* reign? What if we *are* so enslaved?

And: if God's realm is never to come, will anyone seek it as if it could?

AFTER THE RIOT

Rodney King. The police. The beating heard 'round the nation. The truth seen 'round the world.

Not guilty. Outrage. Rage. Hatred. Beatings. Burning. Looters. Shootings. Arrests. Terror. The four horsemen set free for a three-day ride through the streets of Los Angeles.

It's the Sunday after, the Second Sunday of Easter, but there is no empty tomb here. Just a gloomy parish hall, always dimly underlit, a muted monument to a collective limited income, more noticeable today with the seasonal low clouds, or simply more noticeable today. It's been three days since empty shoe boxes covered the front lawn of the church, the only physical blemish on our property, nothing compared to the burnt hulks of dozens of buildings or the bloodied clothing of hundreds of people or the bruised hearts of communities.

We come to church to pray together on the Sunday morning after, and after each service we gather in the inadequate light of the parish hall. In our church, unlike so many, black and brown and yellow and white faces are used to seeing each other, greeting each other, befriending each other, used to praying together, laughing together, struggling together. What has been for the city reduced to faces without features, people without names, skin as an end in itself, an insignia and a sign and a uniform showing whose side you are on, is, for us, only the surface. In the city people of different races do not know how to "get along." In our church it is our primary spiritual practice.

It is especially after the first service among our predominantly older, African American parishioners that emotions uncork, a voice quivering and a head shaking, "I never thought this could happen *again*."

"We haven't made any progress."

An elderly Southern-born white woman with racially privileged blinders and personally rose-colored corneas interjects, "I was proud of *our* neighborhood. People took care of each other."

Nodding, someone tries to build us up when so much has torn us to shreds. "Not many people were shot around here. And only a couple of buildings were burned."

On Friday and Saturday night, both priests, Josh and I, telephoned parishioners in "the riot area." Picking up our church directories without coordination, we asked, "Are you all right?"

"There was shooting down the street."

"We spent some time on the floor, but we're OK."

A moment of humor, a flower amidst the rubbish heap, from Ken, an eighty-year-old African American parishioner: "During the riot, Josh wanted to walk me across the street to my car. There were a bunch of young guys in the parking lot. I know he wanted me to be safe, and I know I'm old, but I had to tell him, 'You're white.' I hope I didn't insult him."

"No," I replied, laughing. "I think he knows he's white." In the flurry of chaos there were few dispensations and no eye of the storm. It would not have been a good time to forget.

The hymns have not lifted or lightened our mood. The prayers are quiet, subdued, resigned, but also more specific, more insistent, more heartfelt. The peace has been passed with longer and tighter hugs, reassuring with genuine affection, grasping at hope, grasping at straws.

In the parish hall, someone says insistently, "That isn't what we're about *here*."

"But how do we change what's out *there*?"

The Sunday after. A Sunday without resurrection.

"How long?" How long indeed. How very long. How very, very, very, very long.

4

A Great Light

This word, which is none other than "see," is the generation and birth of . . . the eternal light, in whom all blessedness is seen and known.
—John Ruusbroec[1]

If looking at the sun you be deprived of sight,
Your eyes are then at fault and not the dazzling light.
—Angelus Silesius[2]

The light is the garment of the bare eye.
—Ephrem the Syrian[3]

To praise the sun is to praise our own eyes.
—Rumi[4]

---

1. Ruusbroec, *Spiritual Espousals*, 146.
2. Silesius, *Cherubinic Wanderer*, 46.
3. Ephrem, *Hymns*, 462.
4. Rumi, *Essential Rumi*, 105.

Blessed are the pure in heart, for they will see God.
—Matthew 5:8

You are not the oil, you are not the air—merely the point of combustion, the flash-point where the light is born. You are merely the lens in the beam. You can only receive, give, and possess the light as a lens does.
—Dag Hammarskjöld[5]

God is the Sun of the sun.
—Marsilio Ficino[6]

O Light that never fades, as the light of day now streams through these windows and floods this room, so let me open to You the windows of my heart, that all my life may be filled by the radiance of Your presence.
—John Baillie[7]

The Buddha shines by day and by night—in the brightness of his glory shines the one who is awake.
—The Dhammapada[8]

Your eye is the lamp of your body. If your eye is healthy, your whole body is full of light;
but if it is not healthy, your body is full of darkness.
—Luke 11:34

Let us then lay aside the works of darkness and put on the armor of light.
—Romans 13:12

---

5. Hammarskjöld, *Markings*, 155.
6. McGinn, *Varieties of Mysticism*, 262.
7. Baillie, *Diary of Prayer*, 33 (modernized).
8. *Dhammapada*, 26:387.

A Great Light

> The people who walked in darkness have seen a great light.
> —Isaiah 9:2

MEDITATION: LIGHT AND DARKNESS DOWNTOWN

We're going to a football game. UCLA vs. USC. In our family creed, light vs. darkness. It's a father-son, refreshing evening of mind-freeing recreation. Be immersed in the physicality. Ponder only the strategic battle on the field. Relax. Play. Seize the game. Let the creased canyons in my brow smooth over for a while. Let the tension that gathers in my shoulders dissolve. Blot out all sociological, political, economic, and theological reference points. Let the rest of the world turn on its axis, lick its own wounds, make its own peace. For three plus hours, make this my world.

I've been going to the Coliseum for fifty years—Dodgers games when they first migrated from Brooklyn, UCLA games when I was young. I've been parking in these South LA neighborhoods for five decades. During the 1984 Olympics, we parked in the same front yard every day; by the end of the Olympics—a festival that turned imagined night terrors of gridlock into open highways in the urban wilderness—strangers had become friends. But it has been a long time since I've been here at night in November.

We do the usual reconnaissance through the neighborhood west of the Coliseum. We drive back and forth on a few familiar blocks looking for free parking on the street. When that option fails, as it usually does, we have already scouted out the front and backyard options—the least expensive and the most secure.

Driving through the neighborhood we notice that the blocks immediately adjacent to the Coliseum are brightly lit, spectacularly bright, weirdly bright, an almost otherworldly bright, like a surrealistic scene from *Apocalypse Now*, or as if the streets were prepared for the surreptitious descent of a UFO in *Close Encounters of the Third Kind*. The message of the brightness is clear. The absurdly brilliant lights are crying out to football fans: this place is safe! You can park here without being mugged!

Continuing our search for parking and our short course in urban planning, we turn down an unlit street; not dimly lit, unlit; not streetlights at street corners with nothing in between; nothing. The only lights here peek through curtains, blinds, and uncovered windows. They are murky and yellowish—like eyes certainly jaundiced and possibly bloodshot. On the UFO streets, the streetlights overwhelm these: klieg lights vs. candles. On these streets, even the moonlight seems dimmed. Not a single block marks the transition. There are only two kinds of streets, only well-lit and unlit, only this side and that side of the 38th Parallel, the 17th Parallel, the Great Wall.

The LA City Council has chosen which voters to serve. It has made no effort to blur the obvious. The well-lit streets reassure the suburbanite spectators who anxiously rubberneck and tippy-toe into the neighborhood a few times a year. The unlit streets belong to the residents with limited incomes, the families that can't afford tickets to this game. People residing close enough to the Coliseum live on the UFO streets. From city management they receive an inadvertent, indirect, collateral blessing. But cross the planners' line and it is a twelve-hour uninterrupted midnight. If muggings or drug deals or burglaries or beatings happen here, call 911.

This sharp division, this bifurcated apocalyptic urban landscape, light and darkness, blessing and curse, reminds me of a city council meeting in Long Beach. A group of us were advocating elected leaders enamored of civic salvation by gentrification for mixed-income housing. We spoke of the advantages of shades of gray, but they would have none of it. One council member said that some people "work hard," "make money," and "deserve" to choose their neighbors. We pointed out that the working poor work equally hard for lower wages and fewer rewards, and have little choice where they live or who lives next door. Our argument failed to capture the sociological imagination of the council. Only one council member made this class demarcation so blatant, bold, and insulting, and he would soon abdicate rather than be dethroned, but the council's vote revealed his sentiment's surreptitious reign.

Light and darkness so neatly distributed. Rich and poor so clearly divided. Father and son can't help but register our disgust at the design of city designers. We can't help but allow our anticipated reverie to be invaded by reality. It diverts our conversation and affects our game. It momentarily deepens the creases in my brow. We can't help but keep the sociological light and darkness squarely before our eyes even when we are simply trying to enjoy a football game. And we park in the backyard of one of the homes on a well-lit street.

IN AND OF THE LIGHT

If Abba Joseph counsels Abba Lot to *become the fire* then Seraphim of Sarov shows Nicholas Motovilov he has *become the light*. The content of Motovilov's story would have resonated with the desert Christians, but the digressive, didactic style of the storytelling would have been foreign to their preference for haiku-like gems that encapsulate a universe. In a dialogue with much in common with the stories of the rich young man and Abba Lot, there is one startling difference: Motovilov is not *told* what to do. He does not merely *see*. He *becomes* the answer.

When Motovilov goes to Seraphim in the Russian winter in 1831, he seeks an answer to a question, like the rich young man, the lawyer, and Abba Lot, but Seraphim anticipates the question before Motovilov can blurt it out: what is "the goal of our Christian life?"[9] Growing up, Motovilov learned to expect clichéd, stilted, half-helpful answers: maintain a spiritual practice, love your neighbor, and live in peace with everyone. When he asks his local religious figures, he gets even more institutionally artificial, morally tepid advice: go to church, pray, and obey the commandments. Some of the authority figures he approaches are annoyed at his precocious impertinence. Unlike these institution-bound religious leaders, Seraphim answers that spiritual practices, prayers, alms, fasting, and vigils are means, not the goal; the path, not the prize: *"The true goal of our Christian life consists in the acquisition of the Holy Spirit of God."*[10]

Motovilov interrupts Seraphim's long amplifications: How would Motovilov know if the Holy Spirit is in him? Seraphim points to his own experience—a theologian must be a mystic—and offers a rhetorical question; if the grace of the Holy Spirit did not enlighten him, how "could I receive a spark of light to lighten my way along the road of life?" God reveals how the Spirit works. On Mt. Sinai, Moses shone with an "extraordinary light." On Mt. Tabor, "a great light surrounded [Jesus] and 'his garments became shining, exceedingly white like snow.'" So the Holy Spirit "manifests itself in an ineffable light."[11] Motovilov's curiosity is piqued again. He wants "to understand this completely." How can you know you are "in the Spirit of God?"

Then Seraphim takes him by the shoulders and says, "We are both, you and I, in the Spirit of God at this moment, my son. Why do you not look at me?"

Motovilov says, "I cannot look, Father, because great flashes of lightning are springing from your eyes. Your face shines with more light than the sun, and my eyes ache from the pain."

"Don't be frightened, friend of God," Seraphim replies calmly. "You yourself have now become as bright as I am. You are now yourself in the

---

9. Cavarnos and Zeldin, *St. Seraphim*, 93.
10. Ibid., 94; italics theirs.
11. Ibid., 109–10.

fullness of the Spirit of God: otherwise you would not be able to see me like this."[12] As Motovilov later recalls,

> At these words, I looked at his face and was seized with an even greater sense of trembling awe. Imagine in the center of the sun, in the most dazzling brilliance of its noontime rays, the face of a man talking to you. You see the movements of his lips, the changing expression of his eyes, you hear his voice, you feel that someone is holding his hands on your shoulders. Yet you do not see his hands or his body, but only a blinding light spreading around for several yards, illumining with its brilliant sheen both the bank of snow covering the glade and the snowflakes that fall on me and on the great Starets.[13]

Now Seraphim plies Motovilov with questions: how do you feel? "Extraordinarily well." "An extraordinary sweetness." "An extraordinary joy in all my heart." "An extraordinary warmth," there in the snowy Russian forest, "The kind [of warmth] as there is in a bath-house when they pour water on the stone and the steam rises."[14] The fragrance is superior to any perfume. Seraphim affirms each of Motovilov's rapt answers with another long exegesis. Motovilov frets that he might forget this epiphany, but Seraphim promises that God would forever emblazon it in his mind.

James Baldwin calls human companionship the only light we have in this darkness,[15] but the mystical tradition insists there is more than huddled warmth against the chill and a communal glow against the cosmic night. Like Birgitta and Julian, Motovilov's experience "is not given to you for you alone to understand, but through you for the whole world, so that you may yourself be confirmed in God's work and can be useful to others."[16] Finally, as if the revelation has reached its liturgical denouement, Seraphim blesses and dismisses Motovilov. And Seraphim's face remains illuminated in a vision of "the ineffable brilliance of light."[17]

There is more in the world than the light that keeps us from losing hope in isolating darkness. Symeon the New Theologian reports more than one such epiphany à la Merton, or several reflections on the same epiphany à la Julian. In one of his hymns, he describes a meditation that reflects both the light of Seraphim and the flame of Abba Joseph.

12. Ibid., 112.
13. Ibid., 113–14.
14. Ibid., 114–16.
15. Baldwin, "Sonny's Blues," 121.
16. Cavarnos and Zeldin, *St. Seraphim*, 119.
17. Ibid., 122.

> As I was meditating, Master, on these things
> Suddenly you appeared from above, much greater than the sun
> And you shone brilliantly from the heavens down into my heart
> . . . .
> O what intoxication of light, O what movements of fire.
> O what swirlings of the flame in me, miserable one that I am
> coming from you and your glory. . . .
> . . . while I was there surrounded by darkness
> You appeared as light, illuminating me completely from your total light
> And I became light in the night.[18]

Elsewhere, Symeon renders an epiphany in prose. As he draws near to Christ in a vision,

> in penitence and faith [I] took hold of his feet. At once I perceived a divine warmth. Then a small radiance that shone forth. Then a divine breath from his words. Then a fire kindled in my heart, which caused constant streams of tears to flow. After that a fine beam went through my mind more quickly than lightning. Then there appeared to me as it were a light in the night and a small flaming cloud resting on his head. . . . Afterwards it moved away and shortly after appeared to me as being in heaven.[19]

Like Merton's seeds of contemplation, the light that shines in moments with bewildering generosity is always there. Even when unseen, it is as clearly known by faith.

There is something common and uncommon about this light. In the Orthodox tradition, the transfiguration, not the stigmata, is the ultimate sign of sanctity. Had Francis of Assisi been nurtured in this tradition, his spiritual aspirations would have been bright, not bloody. Yet this tradition is not foreign to the West. If, as John Ruusbroec says, the spiritual journey begins when Christ says "see," it reaches its fruition when we are drawn into the divine light: "All persons who have been raised above their creaturely status into the contemplative life are one with this divine resplendence and are this resplendence itself." Like Motovilov, they see and become the light. Through this divine light, "they see, feel, and find themselves to be the same simple ground from out of which the resplendence shines." The "eternal act of gazing" combined with an "inborn light" makes it possible to "become one with that same light with which they see and which they see."[20]

---

18. Symeon, *Hymns*, 256–58.
19. Symeon, *Discourses*, 363.
20. Ruusbroec, *Spiritual Espousals*, 150.

Not only does the concept of divine light pierce the East-West divide, so does the experience. In a story similar to Merton's Havana awakening, Catherine of Siena hears God remind her of an epiphany during the Eucharist when she gazed at the priest during the words of consecration:

> I revealed myself to you. You saw a ray of light coming from my breast, like the ray that comes forth from the sun's circle yet never leaves it. Within this light came a dove, and dove and light were as one and hovered over the host by the power of the words of consecration the celebrant was saying. Your bodily eyes could not endure the light, and only your spiritual vision remained, but there you saw and tasted the depths of the Trinity, wholly God, wholly human, hidden and veiled under that whiteness.[21]

As this light is not reserved for the Orthodox, so it is not solely for mystics. At age thirteen, as A. J. Muste took a walk on an Easter Sunday afternoon, "the world took on a new brightness."[22] When as a young man he decided to leave behind the conservative Calvinism of his youth, he had a confirming vision of light in New Jersey: "I was walking late one morning down the corridor of [the] hotel. Suddenly came again that experience of a great light flooding in upon the world making things stand forth 'in sunny outline brave and clear' and of God being truly present and all-sufficient."[23]

Muriel Lester describes her conversion to pacifism in mystical terms. She had been what she called "an absurdly militarist young woman,"[24] "but once your eyes get opened to pacifism, you can't shut them again. Once you see it, you can't unsee it. You may bitterly regret the fact that you happen to be one of the tiny minority of the human race who have caught this angle of vision but you can't help it."[25] For Lester it was as unexpected as Motovilov's vision of Seraphim, and she knew that nonviolence was not for her alone.

Some feel compelled to explain the inexplicable, yet, like the midnight voice Gandhi heard, no explanation satisfies the skeptic. But even the person of faith asks, how does this happen? And with Motovilov, how can we understand it? Like Eckhart, Ruusbroec believes we have two eyes. Short-armed reason cannot wrap itself around such an experience:

> This infinite resplendence so blinds the eyes of reason that they have to give way before this incomprehensible light. However,

---

21. Catherine, *Dialogue*, 210.
22. Robinson, *Abraham Went Out*, 8
23. Ibid., 18.
24. Wallis, *Mother of World Peace*, 20.
25. Lester, *Ambassador of Reconciliation*, 9.

that simple eye which dwells above reason in the ground of our understanding is always open, contemplating with unhindered vision and gazing at the light with the light itself—eye to eye, mirror to mirror, image to image."[26]

Ephrem the Syrian amplifies the unknowable nature of unbegotten light: "If the visible light is intangible, how can the hidden Light be comprehended?"[27] Anticipating Ruusbroec, he says God's "Light fills us but is unable to be grasped."[28] This light is not to be examined under an entomologist's pins. It is to be entered, or it is to enter us. As Symeon says:

> Again the light shines for me, again it is seen clearly,
> again it opens the heavens, again it divides the night,
> again it creates all things, again the light alone is seen,
> again it transports me outside all visible things,
> and likewise it separates me from perceptible things—what a surprise!
> Again the light is above all heavenly things
> that no one among human beings has ever seen,
> not opening the heavens, not splitting the night,
> nor dividing the air, nor the roof of the house
> it becomes wholly indivisible with me the wretch
> within my cell, within my mind,
> and the middle of my heart—oh awesome mystery![29]

Teresa of Ávila found herself making a fumbling attempt to match words to a revelation. Her experience not only eluded reason; it was "beyond the scope of any possible imagination."[30] Yet, of course, she tried.

> The whiteness and brilliancy alone are inconceivable. It is not a brightness which dazzles, but a delicate whiteness, an infused brightness, giving excessive delight to the eyes, which are never wearied thereby nor by the visible brightness which enables us to see a beauty so divine. It is a light so different from any light here below, that the very brightness of the sun we see, in comparison with the brightness and light before our eyes, seems to be something so obscure that no one would ever wish to open his eyes again.[31]

26. Ruusbroec, *Spiritual Espousals*, 238.
27. Ephrem, *Hymns*, 464.
28. Ibid., 467.
29. Symeon, *Divine Eros*, 288.
30. Quoted in Underhill, *Mysticism*, 290.
31. Quoted in Underhill, *Mysticism*, 290; see also Teresa, *Life of Teresa*, 260.

Infused contemplation is a gift. Eyes can be open or shut. When God wants us to see—as when God wills a toad to fly—we see.

Just as epiphanies and theological postmortems transcend the Orthodox tradition (Catherine and Teresa) and the company of mystics (Muste), so this light transcends the church. The Zohar text says that God revealed "the light of the eye" to Adam at the beginning of creation, and with this light Adam could see "from one end of the world to the other." But because of the wicked generations of Enoch, Noah, and Babel, God "hid the light away."[32] Theophan the Recluse says that Adam's spirit "saw God and all things divine—as clearly as with normal eyes we today see an object before us." The fall closed our spiritual eyes; we are now like those "whose eyelids have become stuck together. The eye is intact, it thirsts for light, it longs to see the light . . . but the eyelids . . . do not allow the eye to open and to enter into direct contact with the light."[33] But by grace some see. Gregory the Great attributes this spiritual eyesight to Benedict: "The whole world was brought before his eyes, gathered together, as it were, in a single ray of light."[34] While the Zohar myth begins with Adam, Ephrem contrasts the vision of Eve with that of Mary,

> The world, you see, has
> two eyes fixed in it:
> Eve was its left eye,
> blind,
> while the right eye,
> bright, is Mary.
> Through the eye that was darkened
> the whole world has darkened
> and people groped
> and thought that every stone
> they stumbled upon was a god,
> calling falsehood truth.
> But when it was illumined by the other eye,
> and the heavenly Light
> that resided in its midst,
> humanity became reconciled once again,
> realizing that what they had stumbled on
> was destroying their very life.[35]

32. Zohar, *Book of Enlightenment*, 51.
33. Chariton of Valamo, *Art of Prayer*, 179.
34. McGinn, *Growth of Mysticism*, 71.
35. Brock, *Luminous Eye*, 72.

Like Zohar, Ephrem is equally concerned with original *light* and original *sight*.

Later Jewish writers built on Zohar's insight. Uri of Strelisk says that God created a great light so that people "might be able to look from one end of the world to the other."[36] Unlike Zohar's myth of enduring blindness, Uri asserts that sin never completely obscures the light. The founder of Hasidic Judaism, the Baal Shem Tov—like Abba Joseph and Seraphim—appeared as both fire and light. When Rabbi Dov Baer begged heaven to show him a person whose every fiber was holy, heaven showed him the Baal Shem Tov, whose soul "was all of fire. There was no shred of substance in it. It was nothing but flame."[37] When he ascended into heaven, his soul arose as a "blue flame": "The burning light was the Baal Shem himself."[38]

Yet to this sense of fresh wonder the Jewish tradition adds a warning—Buber's ecstasy linked with Otto's dread: uncreated light is wonderful *and* terrible to behold. Like Moses veiling his eyes before entering the tent of meeting (Exod 34:33–35), we are bidden and forbidden to see this light. One of the Hasidim went to see rabbi Jacob Yitzkak of Lublin, the seer. At first, the pilgrim saw only the rabbi seated at a table with an opened book, "but then a vast light began to shine in the narrow room, and when he saw it the Hasid became unconscious." When he regained consciousness, he was alone. As he heard others saying Evening Prayer, he realized that the candles were lit, but he was blind. Frightened, he went to experts in another city who told him, "There is no cure for you. . . . You have seen the original light, the light on the days of creation, which empowered the first people on earth to see from one end of the world to the other, which was hidden after their sinning, and is only revealed to zaddikim [the righteous] in the Torah. Whoever beholds it unlawfully, his eyes will be darkened forever."[39]

The Jewish mystical tradition democratizes original light and original sight with a principle similar to Buddhism's "original mind" and Dorotheos's spark. In an inversion of Rumi's skeptical embryo clinging to ignorance, the Talmud teaches that in the womb children are given a light that reveals all of the world's teachings so they can look "from one end of the world to the other."[40] But the instant they are born an angel strikes them on the mouth, and they forget everything. The entirety of their lives becomes a relearning.[41]

---

36. Buber, *Tales: Later Masters*, 146.
37. Buber, *Tales: Early Masters*, 49.
38. Ibid., 84–85.
39. Ibid., 304.
40. Ibid., 144.
41. Ibid., 96.

This is the original light, sight, spark, and mind that is lost and can be found. In this retelling of creation and fall, original mind and primordial sin are reinterpreted as original seeing and primeval blindness.

Catherine and Teresa see the light. Symeon, Seraphim, Motovilov, and the Baal Shem Tov become the light. Greek philosophy gifted later generations with the proposition that no one can see the divine without becoming divine.[42] Gregory Palamas explains that whoever "participates in the divine energy . . . becomes, in a sense, Light." In this experience, the one "united to the Light and with the Light" sees that which remains hidden to others.[43] William of St. Thierry recapitulates this theme: "To see or know God then is to be like God, and to be like God is to see or know God."[44] Still later, Angelus Silesius distills this claim into a couplet:

> Because in its real nature, the true light I should see,
> Itself I must become, or else this cannot be.[45]

If only we would see the light, we would become the light.

The same words describe the discovery of a different light that gave birth to the Society of Friends. Rather than basing the movement on rare epiphanies, George Fox uncovered light's omnipresent hiddenness in all people, the Seed, the Principle, Christ. In one of Fox's "openings," God "opened to me" that everyone was "enlightened by the divine Light of Christ, and I saw it shine through all." In strikingly Johannine imagery (John 1:11–13), he says that those who believe in the light "became the children of it"; but those who "hated it, and did not believe in it, were condemned by it."[46] As in Jesus' time, you could subscribe to outward forms, rituals, and creeds—yet, like the rich young man, lack the one crucial thing. You could be both zealously religious and spiritually clueless. It is one thing to see the divine light, another to see it in people, and yet another to become the light. If only we could see, Fox says, the light within us would enable us to see the light in all.

As early Christians were taught to clothe themselves in compassion, kindness, humility, patience, forgiveness, and love (Col 3:12–17), God told Catherine of Siena to clothe herself in light.[47] Created and uncreated, resplendent and hidden, the light blurs together as one. The first century

---

42. "People cannot see anything in the real realm unless they become it" (McGinn, *Foundations of Mysticism*, 94).

43. Lossky, *Image and Likeness*, 61.

44. McGinn, *Growth of Mysticism*, 263–64.

45. Silesius, *Cherubinic Wanderer*, 59.

46. Fox, *Journal*, 101.

47. Catherine, *Dialogue*, 363.

Qumran and Johannine communities never try to parse the spiritual from the ethical, being in and of the light. The light is united and whole: spiritual, moral, personal, and social. It is not enough to *see* the light; you must *become* it.

Symeon describes how an ordinary prayer led to a mystical breakthrough. Entering his place of prayer, he was moved to tears and a "loving desire for God" and felt an indescribable delight: "I fell prostrate on the ground, and at once I saw, and behold, a great light was immaterially shining on me and seized hold of my whole mind and soul, so that I was struck with amazement at the unexpected marvel and I was, as it were, in ecstasy." In his elation, he forgets "who I was, and where." He does not know whether he is in or out of the body (2 Cor 12:2-4), but his whole being is transfixed with a light that "invigorated and strengthened my limbs and muscles." Like Motovilov, he is left with sensations of joy and "sweetness."[48] And like Motovilov, he knows that awakenings are not private property. The contemplative, he says, is "wholly united to the light." The contemplative's "mind is itself light and sees all things as light."[49] "The light envelops me and appears to me like a star, and is incomprehensible to all. It is radiant like the sun and I perceive all creation encompassed by it. . . . I am hemmed in by roof and walls, yet it opens the heavens to me." Like Merton's cell, his enclosure had done its work. Fulfilling Maslow's analysis, Symeon sees "all creation encompassed" by light.[50]

If, as Symeon implies, seeing all things bathed in light bids the mystic to embrace the world, then it is Jeremiah's misshapen pot of a world, a prickly pear cactus of a world that the mystic embraces—Stringfellow's world as it is, Bonhoeffer's lightless world, Black Elk's crumbling world, a nonmerciful, antimerciful world, Job's whirlwind of a world. This is the world the desert Christians stepped away from to strip themselves of their housed oppressors and to focus a cocked, suspicious, and redemptive eye back upon it. It is *this* world, made and marred, that the mystics of light embrace.

Those who have never seen or imagined uncreated light might legitimately ask, is it wise to so wholeheartedly and unabashedly embrace a world so chaotic, corrupt, and corrosive? Are these visionaries perhaps blinded or numbed or knocked nonsensical by the *uncreated* light to be so entranced by the *created* world? They do not hoard their experiences; the light is not for them alone. But when they share the light, does that sharing do anything to remold the misshapen world?

48. Symeon, *Discourses*, 200-1.
49. Ibid., 56.
50. Ibid., 202.

STUPID CHILDREN OF LIGHT

Augustine may have come "late" to his wistful love for God, but he never extended the same affection or courtesy toward the human race. He read in Genesis that human beings are "good," but his empirical observations skewered any likelihood that he would draw the same conclusion. In fact, he might have amended the verdict, distinguishing ontological from moral goodness. Like an angel in a playful midrash, he might have questioned God's wisdom in creating the human race.

Augustine never shared his desert contemporaries' enthusiasm for sanctification. He would have lowered the bar, aiming for less than fire or light; he would have been satisfied with a modicum of kindness, a dollop of justice, and a thimbleful of integrity in the personal, political, and ecclesiastical spheres. His assessments were thorough. Even though he delighted in "a certain light,"[51] to him there was no original light or spark or mind, only original conscience-compromising, judgment-bending, soul-snapping sin. Not even babies escaped his austere diagnosis; they evoked affection not through innate innocence but by their physical fragility. He saw the seeds of envy, greed, and violence when a baby, "pale and bitter in the face," spied another infant nursing.[52] Augustine was even less sympathetic with adults: "nobody in this flesh, nobody in this corruptible body, nobody on the face of this earth, in this malevolent existence, in this life full of temptation—nobody can live without sin."[53] He concedes that "there is indeed *some light in people*: but let them walk fast, walk fast, *lest the shadows come*."[54] This was not Seraphim's blazing light; in humankind Augustine saw a bush that would not burn.

Unlike today's dominant American ideology that divorces the doctrine of sin from institutions as if they could miraculously elude its allure, Augustine was cheerlessly consistent. Today's purveyors of capitalism grant nations then and corporations now immunity and impunity from sin. Avarice is not mitigated; it is only and always to be satiated. But for Augustine, there is no special capitalist dispensation to soften the bite of the tenth commandment not to covet. When it comes to the nature of institutions, Augustine asks, "Justice removed, then, what are kingdoms but great bands of robbers? What are bands of robbers themselves, but little kingdoms?"[55] Both bow to

---

51. Augustine, *Confessions* 10.6.
52. Ibid., 1.7.
53. Brown, *Augustine of Hippo*, 363.
54. Ibid., 178 (italics his).
55. Augustine, *City of God*, IV.4.

authority figures. Both add to human suffering in their bald-faced quests for naked power. Both, when dominant, divide spoils at the expense of their victims, a particularly avaricious form of Ellacuría's social necessity. To make his point, Augustine retells a dialogue between a pirate and Alexander the Great. Alexander asks the pirate why he infests the seas with disorder and greed. The pirate replies dryly that he is a "robber" only because he has only one ship; had he a fleet, he would be an "emperor." Augustine discerns no moral difference between them. The attainment of power may fabricate moral legitimacy and the fantasized blessing of Greek gods, but Augustine labels it a transparent sham.

Based on Augustine's keen eye for evil, he would not have qualified as one of William James's *once-born* people. The *once-born*, like many mystics, "see God, not as a strict Judge, not as a Glorious Potentate, but as the animating spirit of a beautiful, harmonious world, Beneficent and Kind, Merciful as well as Pure."[56] While aware of sin, the once-born give greater weight to gradual sanctification, thrilling breakthroughs, and ladders climbing toward perfection. According to James, the once-born live by a "simple algebraic sum of pluses and minuses"; "happiness and religious peace consist in living on the plus side" of life.

Augustine was one of James's *twice-born*. They are often horrified and sometimes paralyzed by their own moral defects, feeling less gradually blessed than dramatically saved. "In the religion of the twice-born . . . the world is a double-storied mystery. Peace cannot be reached by the simple addition of pluses and elimination of minuses from life." The twice-born find something false in the idea of natural goodness—let alone original sight, light, or mind—perhaps even something bogus in natural theology. The once-born life is one of "naturalism," the twice-born life one of "pure Salvationism";[57] the once-born concentrate on the light; the twice-born on darker shades of gray. The once-born consider the twice-born dour and anxious; the twice-born see the once-born as childishly foolish.

Augustine—who has spawned theological offspring as numerous as the stars and the sand—would have been well pleased with Reinhold Niebuhr, a dyed-in-the-wool twice-born disciple. As James would have expected, Niebuhr frowned on mysticism (or his stereotype of it)[58] and scorned the gentle hopefulness of the once-born. The two groups Underhill identified as

---

56. James, *Varieties of Religious*, 80.
57. Ibid., 143–44.
58. Niebuhr, *Moral Man*, 55–56, 60.

pioneers—mystics and pacifists[59]—are the ones Niebuhr portrays tempting people with sand castle hopes and pipe dream promises.

When Muste died in 1967, Niebuhr penned an obituary for his theological and political antagonist. Both had led the Fellowship of Reconciliation in the 1920s. Each in turn abandoned pacifism; Muste's later return in the 1930s flummoxed Niebuhr. In the 1960s, Muste became an early opponent of the Vietnam War, an outward and deadly sign of Niebuhr's Cold War politics. In the last year of his life, Muste was arrested at an antiwar protest in Saigon and went with a small delegation of religious figures to meet with Ho Chi Minh in Hanoi. He died a week before a major antiwar rally he had coordinated in New York City. Niebuhr admired Muste for his audacity, not his sagacity. While lauding Muste's courage, Niebuhr adds that "academic critics" are "obsessed with logical consistency."[60] Muste was brave, but if only he had been astute, he might have had a more profound impact.

Even without knowing of Muste's spiritual experiences, Niebuhr would have classified him as a "child of light." For Niebuhr this was no compliment. He based his interpretation of the children of light on the saying in Luke's Gospel attached to one of Christendom's least favorite parables—the resilient and amoral steward: "the children of this age are more shrewd in dealing with their own generation than are the children of light" (Luke 16:8). Niebuhr much preferred this clear-eyed synoptic sobriety to Johannine loose-lipped effusiveness. With this orphan verse—minisermon, aphorism, proverb, Zen koan—Luke seems to lob a stone at the beautifully crafted glass house of Johannine sectarian idealism: come forth from your ingrown community and engage the real world! In spiritual sensibility, it harmonizes with one of Niebuhr's other favorite Gospel directives: be clever as serpents and innocent as doves (Matt 10:16), a verse that finds an antecedent in Psalm 18:26–27: "With the faithful you show yourself faithful, O God; with the forthright you show yourself forthright. With the pure you show yourself pure; but with the crooked you are wily." If God can be *wily* then to be holy means less to be guileless than sly. What Niebuhr deemed the pacifist's sheer guilelessness renders the works of the children of light an epic tragedy of Shakespearean magnitude.

As Luke 16:8 subverts John's *sectarian* idealism, H. Richard Niebuhr joined his brother in decrying liberal Protestantism's *political* idealism. To them, these theologians were Luke's naïve, ineffectual children of light. They may have fantasized that they saw a light encompassing creation or an inner light in others, but their ideals did not help them more closely follow

---

59. Underhill, *Modern Guide*, 16, 208.
60. Niebuhr, "Christian Revolutionary," 6.

Jesus or better reverence God. Rather, to the Niebuhrs these idealists were not judicious enough to make the *realistic* choices necessary to bring into being practical and positive social change in a world in which babies gurgle in sin, adults dance in it, and systems vary only in the size of their sulfuric footprint. The Niebuhrs prized empiricism and pragmatism—fidelity to world-as-it-is reality—as greater goods than light and love.

In *The Kingdom of God in America*, H. Richard Niebuhr traces the way liberal and conservative Christians mistakenly confuse God's realm with the United States. People conflate faith in the age to come with a bland confidence in Enlightenment "progress." They abandon any notion that the nation would be judged or the church transformed: "Whether conceived in political or ecclesiastical or economic or cultural terms, the coming kingdom is never regarded as involving both death and resurrection, both crisis and promise, but only as the completion of tendencies now established." To these Christians, the realm would not arrive with a big bang, but as the logical outcome of a gentle and genteel evolution. No ax would strike the root of the trees. The trees barely need pruning! To H. Richard Niebuhr this was antithetical to the gospel: this "romantic conception of the kingdom of God involved no discontinuities, no crises, no tragedies, or sacrifices, no loss of all things, no cross and resurrection."[61] Instead of cataclysmic personal and social metanoia, this progressivism prefers the enchanted thinking of inevitable progress. In these patterns of wish fulfillment, the twisted self-interests of individuals and the even more bedeviled self-centeredness of groups and institutions would be reconciled with a magic wand of "benevolent altruistic character." Injustice, exploitation, class division, and international rivalries would suddenly evaporate like a morning fog into sunny good wishes: "Evolution, growth, development, the culture of the religious life, the nurture of the kindly sentiments, the extension of humanitarian ideals and the progress of civilization took the place of the Christian revolution." American idealism made no room for conflict, dialectic, repentance, or self-sacrifice. As Niebuhr famously summarized this fantasy, "A God without wrath brought people without sin into a kingdom without judgment through the ministrations of a Christ without a Cross."[62]

While this chastisement might seem a sufficient intellectual lash, Reinhold Niebuhr more directly chides the once-born children of light. They are

---

61. Niebuhr, *Kingdom of God*, 183.
62. Ibid., 191–93.

naïve. They are romantic.⁶³ They are "foolish."⁶⁴ They are "stupid."⁶⁵ For Reinhold Niebuhr, *the children of light* are dupes in the face of human sin and institutional evil. Liberal Protestants are certainly among the chief culprits, but so are "secularized idealists"⁶⁶ and a bourgeoisie that had mistaken "its own progress for the progress of the world."⁶⁷ Niebuhr branded Hegel and Marxists children of light.⁶⁸ Whatever their ideological trademark, the children of light "underestimate the power of self-interest among the children of darkness. They underestimate this power among themselves."⁶⁹

Between World Wars Reinhold Niebuhr debunked every dream but his own: "In spite of the disillusionment of the World War, the average liberal Protestant is still convinced that the Kingdom of God is gradually approaching, that the League of Nations is its partial fulfillment and the Kellogg Pact its covenant, that the wealthy will be persuaded by the church to dedicate their power and privilege to the common good . . . that the conversion of individuals is the only safe method of solving" social problems.⁷⁰ At the same time, the Marxist "romantic" dream of people living "in perfect accord with the collective will of society" is doomed by its naïve view of humanity "and its mystical glorification" of a communist society.⁷¹

Even Niebuhr's beloved democracies are robber nations. "Complex societies" invariably increase the "centralization of power." Leaders "hide the nakedness of their greed" and obscure "the true character of their collective behavior" with "romantic and moral interpretations" of facts.⁷² Since every society distributes its goods unfairly⁷³ and since the reign of God is a Never Never Land, Niebuhr instructs reformers to pursue tangible progress. His prescription is simple: instead of believing in "the creation of an ideal society in which there will be uncoerced and perfect peace and justice," seek first "a society in which there will be enough justice, and in which coercion will be sufficiently non-violent to prevent" unmanageable mayhem

---

63. Niebuhr, *Moral Man*, 164, 194.
64. Niebuhr, *Children of Light*, 144, 149,
65. Ibid., 38.
66. Ibid., 12.
67. Ibid., 2, 112, 149.
68. Ibid., 32, 38, 112, 149.
69. Ibid., 11.
70. Niebuhr, *Moral Man*, 79.
71. Ibid., 194.
72. Ibid., 8–9.
73. Ibid., 1.

and injustice.[74] Niebuhr disputes the attempt to mitigate racial prejudice by challenging negative stereotypes.[75] Awareness does not transform hearts. Self-interest is too deeply entrenched.

The children of light do not notice that even patriotism, which challenges citizens to rise above petty self-interests, is yet another form of collective "selfishness."[76] Even in a democracy patriotism is but the cumulative effect of the individual's "lust for power and prestige" projected on the nation where people indulge their "anarchic lusts vicariously." The combination of the individual's "unselfishness and vicarious selfishness" gives "tremendous force to national egoism."[77] A psalmist counsels, "Put not your trust in rulers, nor in any child of earth";[78] Niebuhr warns: do not trust institutions.

While intellectually abusing them with one hand, Niebuhr offers the children of light a set of remedies with the other: be "armed with the wisdom of the children of darkness but remain free from their malice"[79]; comprehend the power of self-interest without justifying it; seek divine wiliness in order to "beguile, deflect, harness and restrain self-interest, individual and collective, for the sake of the community";[80] "borrow some of the wisdom of the children of darkness; and yet be careful not to borrow too much."[81]

While a generation earlier Rauschenbusch speaks of the conversion of institutions, and "saved and unsaved organizations,"[82] Niebuhr says, "collective power . . . can never be dislodged unless power is raised against it."[83] He rejects the ideas that improved pedagogy, reformed education, and distilled reason can end exploitation.[84] Sounding like an advocate of apophatic spirituality, Niebuhr says that educators are too enamored of "reason" which has no effect on corporations.[85] Just as *The Cloud of Unknowing* says that reason does not bring people nearer to God, Niebuhr insists that reason alone never budges a nation or institution nearer to God's realm. To him, "the illusions and sentimentalities of the Age of Reason" still dominate American

---

74. Ibid., 22.
75. Niebuhr, *Children of Light*, 114.
76. Niebuhr, *Moral Man*, 48.
77. Ibid., 93–94.
78. Ps 146:2, *Book of Common Prayer*, 803.
79. Niebuhr, *Children of Light*, 40.
80. Ibid., 41.
81. Ibid., 176.
82. Rauschenbusch, *Social Gospel*, 111–12.
83. Niebuhr, *Moral Man*, xii.
84. Ibid., xiii.
85. Ibid., xvi.

culture in spite of ample historical evidence to the contrary.[86] Echoing Augustine's banished optimism and burnished skepticism, Niebuhr says that the moral conversion of corporate leaders is refuted by "the entire history of humankind." To the contrary, collective entities are "incapable of acquiring" detachment or reason. Reformers are blind to "the power of self-interest and collective egoism," and "the brutal character of all human collectives."[87] They have not measured the distance between personal charity and social justice, between moral individuals who can be persuaded and amoral groups that must be coerced. In politics, faith moves no mountains; ethics have no effect; only power, pushing with all its might, can nudge hardhearted leaders and self-interested institutions toward reform.[88]

Voices in greater sympathy with mysticism and idealism still find common ground with Niebuhr's sin-soaked analyses. Peter Maurin agrees about the pedigree of capitalism and communism in spite of their claims to be polar opposites and their pledges of mutual destruction:

> The bourgeois capitalist
> Tries to keep
> What he has,
> And tries to get
> What the other fellow has.
> The Bolshevist Socialist
> Tries to get
> What the bourgeois capitalist has.
> The Bolshevist Socialist
> Is the son
> Of the bourgeois capitalist,
> And the son
> Is too much
> Like his father.
> All the sins of the father
> Are found in the son.[89]

Leech agrees that idealists are unsophisticated about the pain of social transformation, writing of the Magnificat, "People believed that the mighty would be put down from their thrones so gently that they would not feel the bump when they hit the ground."[90] He considers it incredibly naïve to

---

86. Ibid., xxv.
87. Ibid., xix–xx.
88. Ibid., xxii–xxiii.
89. Maurin, *Easy Essays*, 115.
90. Leech, *Eye of the Storm*, 129, paraphrasing Conrad Noel.

believe that simple data collection, facts, and information can initiate social change.[91] More kindly than Niebuhr, he also addresses those who think that consciousness-raising alone can usher in racial equality, and pines, "if only this were true."[92]

A century before Niebuhr's influence peaked, Frederick Douglass anticipated Niebuhr's belief in the use of brute force against entrenched interests. In a speech during the abolitionist struggle, he used what became a famous proverb in the spirit of Niebuhr: "Power concedes nothing without a demand. It never did and it never will."[93] In spite of the best efforts of abolitionists to quicken consciences and introduce legislation, decades of activism had moved the nation no closer to emancipation. Douglass came to believe that slavery's "peaceful annihilation is almost hopeless"; perhaps envisioning a massive slave uprising he said that slaveholders were inadvertently training their own "executioners."[94] While his Niebuhrian quote about power is often cited out of context, in that 1857 speech Douglass grounded it in gory reality as he praised escaped slaves who armed and defended themselves—and killed and died in shootouts against those who would reenslave them; he claimed that Nat Turner's rebellion brought Virginia closer to emancipation than anything the abolitionist movement had done.[95]

Whatever one thinks of Niebuhr's heavy-handed bludgeoning of the children of light, the children of light have been as wrong about the coming of the realm as—for centuries—Adventist Christians have erred in conceiving odd raptures and over-eagerly anticipating the parousia. Early in the twentieth century, Tolstoy wrongly predicted that the coming revolution would be led by "the less civilized Russians, . . . the agricultural workers, who are less intellectually corrupt and still adhere to a vague concept of the idea of a Christian faith." The agricultural workers "will finally understand where the means of salvation lie and be the first to make use of it."[96] In 1908, Tolstoy says he "can boldly write that this awakening is taking place. I, with my eighty years, know that I will not see it, but as surely as I know that spring follows winter and day follows night, I know that the time has come for Christian humanity."[97] In this anarchist utopia,

---

91. Leech, *Doing Theology*, 10.
92. Leech, *Race*, 123.
93. Douglass, *Life and Writings (Vol. II)*, 437.
94. Ibid., 406.
95. Ibid., 437–39.
96. Tolstoy, *Confession*, 182.
97. Ibid., 203.

> There would be no private landownership, no taxes spent on things unnecessary to the nation, no division of nations, no enslavement of some by others, no more wastage of the nation's best resources on war preparation, no more fear on the one hand of the bombs, on the other of the gallows; and there would be none of the senseless luxury of some, and still more senseless poverty of others.[98]

Ellacuría's social necessity would fade away as in a Marxist dream, and Isaiah's new earth would be born. Of course, the revolution that came less than ten years later was not Christian, humanitarian, or utopian, but virulently antireligious Leninism.

Writing from his intentional Christian community in Weimar Germany in 1923—the year of Hitler's aborted Munich Putsch—Eberhard Arnold foresees that "the kingdom of love, which is free of mammon, is drawing near." Like John the Baptist, he urges his readers to "change your thinking radically so that you will be ready for the coming order!"[99] Five years later, he envisions a coming spiritual and social paradise: "All the various movements of the past decades will one day converge in a radical awakening of the masses that leads the way to social justice and to God's unity. . . . Like a volcanic eruption, a spiritual revolution needs to spread through the country, to spur people to crucial decisions. . . . The new awakening must therefore be both religious and social, a Christ-centered communist awakening, an awakening to God's kingdom." Arnold was not so naïve as to believe this could occur without bumps. Capitalism will not euthanize itself. He predicts a painful transition. This Christian revolution "will be paid for with bitterest pain. The suffering of Jesus, which he experienced to the full for the sake of this future joy, will be our suffering. . . . When the movement has reached its peak, it will be so dangerous that capitalism will see itself imperiled by it." He admits that his vision seems farfetched, but "this image of the future appears fantastic only to the unbelieving."[100] Less than five years later, Hitler was Germany's führer.

In Martin Luther King, Jr.'s posthumously published *Playboy* interview, he calls it "the keystone of my faith in the future" that the US would become "a thoroughly integrated society" by the end of the twentieth century.[101] In hindsight, 1968 was not only the year of the assassination; the 1968 election launched a racial counterrevolution that set out to erase the gains of the

---

98. Ibid., 210.
99. Arnold, *Writings*, 121.
100. Ibid., 153.
101. King, *Testament of Hope*, 375.

civil rights movement. Was it naiveté that led Tolstoy, Arnold, and King astray? Are they the once-born children of light Niebuhr derides? Did they fail to understand the depth, intransigence, and ferocity of evil? However someone wants to explain it or explain it away, they were wrong.

Even though Niebuhr, like Muste,[102] dismisses mysticism and monasticism, mystics are not uniformly the one-dimensional once-borns he imagines. Underhill says that awakenings to God do not blind the mystic to the world's complex contradictions; quite the contrary: "New knowledge of beauty must reveal the ugliness" of social and political evil. She suggests a dialectic: every spiritually aware person believes in "the possible perfection of every soul and so of every society" *and* mystics must formulate a "definite attitude" toward war, prisons, capital punishment, capitalism, sex work, international relations, and economics. Because mystics regard "the whole world as a religious fact," they must do "all work in the spiritual light, the judging of all economic problems by its standards, not those of expediency."[103] Underhill maintains that the mystic bears a relevant light on the grimness.

Mystical visions are not always filled with beauty and light; they also see the world's worst corruptions. Birgitta of Sweden had visions of dishonest ecclesiastical leaders, the henchmen of corruption and the handmaids of injustice. In one epiphany, Birgitta hears Christ tell her how he sees bishops and abbots looking "like pigs dress[ed] in pontifical or sacerdotal ornaments." In her parable of the pigs, the pigs' gluttony ironically bars them from the banquet.[104] The Franciscan tradition, likewise, scowls broadly at power, prestige, wealth, and status. Francis calls possessions "sand,"[105] and money "flies."[106] He "cursed money more than all other things" and shunned it "as the devil himself."[107] The man who threw himself into ice at each carnal temptation disciplined his followers with a similar flare. When a potential disciple sold his possessions but gave the profits to his family instead of the poor, Francis dismissed him as "brother fly."[108] When another brother casually touched money, Francis "commanded him to lift the money . . . with his mouth and to place it with his mouth on the asses' dung outside."[109] In

---

102. Robinson, *Abraham Went Out*, 188.
103. Underhill, *Modern Guide*, 84.
104. Birgitta, *Life and Revelations*, 214–15.
105. Celano, *Saint Francis*, 12.
106. Ibid., 202.
107. Ibid., 192.
108. Ibid., 204.
109. Ibid., 193.

an instructive parable, as a wave of covetousness swept over one of Francis's brethren, the brother had a dream in which he saw the wealthy "eating from a very foul and unclean pigs' trough, from which they were eating peas mixed with human dung."[110] He quickly lost his taste for the comforts of the royal court. George Fox had an even more unnerving vision of "all the religions of the world." The clergy were a company of cannibals "eating up the people like bread, and gnawing the flesh from off their bones" (cf. Mic 3:2–3).[111] Less spectacularly but in harmony with Niebuhr and Leech, Merton's "Letters to a White Liberal" say that when liberals balance racial equality against property values, property always wins.[112]

Niebuhr was certainly skeptical of the mystics' uncreated light, but what drove him was the harsh reality of power. Eckhart's inner eye might have an obscure value, but the analytical eye shows people how to live in a twisted and broken world. Niebuhr saw contemplation as an irrelevant distraction from the real business of faith. The powers that be—empires, systems, and nations—are not teetering on the brink of a cliff in terror of being nudged over the edge by a bright light or a good scolding. Mystical vision has a built-in blind spot. It might critique cultures (Merton), but it does not recognize the inherent irrationality of institutions. If mystics want light to touch the world's darkness, they need more conscientization, more analysis, and more realism.

Mystics see evil almost exclusively through the lens of personal sin and repentance. In spite of the massive corruption envisioned by Birgitta and George Fox, they never suggest a collective remedy. At times mystics even come close to the heresy Stringfellow abhors as they ignore the self-exalting self-interested power of ideologies, images, and idols. Underhill says that if we wish to redeem something, we must love it. Niebuhr counters, if we want even to reform something, we must understand it. As Underhill says, mystics see the ugliness and the need to engage it. But Niebuhr says: *they do not know how.*

DUELS WITH DUALISM

Light presumes darkness. Goodness assumes evil. Extraordinary light presupposes an ordinary palette of grays. In their communities of faith, people of light draw lines in sand and Scripture to form identity and define salvation—who are we, who are they, who is in, who is out. Loving *your neighbor*

---

110. Ibid., 237.
111. Fox, *Journal*, 479.
112. Merton, *Seeds of Destruction*, 33.

means identifying who your neighbor is not. Loving *one another* requires the inking of borders around the community of the true believers, the real followers, the faithful, the saved, the beloved. A beloved community separated from, surrounded by, perhaps threatened by, and possibly damning those not among the beloved, loves *only* one another.

At our worst, we people of faith inject ourselves with mirages of sanctification and salvation—innocence by association—by comparing ourselves to others; we are in *because* they are out. Latent even in the most profound texts of mysticism and most committed communities of activism is the potential for corrosive dualism. We can smell the same noxious fumes of smug judgmentalism here as among those who reduce salvation to a formula or who specify the number of the saved. Dualism is the shadow side, an inherent temptation, and a constant bugaboo for those in and of the light. The magnificent wonder of the light and the inherent danger of dualism are as difficult to separate as wheat and weeds. Oversimplifying the world and overidentifying with the light leads to the self-serving, self-soothing, and sanctimonious fundamentalist claim that others are in darkness. In the first-century Palestinian environment, priestly purity codes separated clean from unclean (ritual). Pharisaic teaching separated righteous from sinners (moral). Zealots separated Jews from their Gentile Roman overlords (ethnic, national, ideological). Essenes separated the children of light from the children of darkness (spiritual). Christians would quickly sow the seeds of anti-Semitism by exaggerating their differences with Jews. The light was one. The light was all. There was no parsing of light into categories. People were all in or all out. The light became a rhetorical tool used as often to exclude and vilify as to embrace and welcome.

The apostolic era's seeds of dualism spread like dandelions. This dualism is innate among mystics who declare that God *is* light and love (1 John 1:5, 4:16). Like Lester's nonviolence, once mystics see transcendent light, they can't unsee it, or its consequences. The idea, "if only others could see," begins as an eager invitation, but innate in it is the capacity to turn elitist, pitying, Gnostic, and sour. The faithful are divided into distinct classes—those who see and those who don't—and a spiritual hierarchy is born: mystics, monks, and clergy; and the unenlightened, barely initiated masses. Merton and Underhill initially wrote admiringly of that upper crust of mystics, but later stressed God's egalitarianism and the universal accessibility of spiritual experience. The Merton of *The Seven Story Mountain* not only succumbed to dualism; he splashed delightedly in it, awash in dualistic and hierarchical negativity. The more mature Merton publicly buried the rigid, disdainful young Merton who had confused *his* path with *the* path, *his* way to conversion with *the* way.[113]

Because they are awake to the world, dualism is also innate for activists. Grieving for the world and hopeful for its transformation, their dualism is innate because oppression, war, and poverty have ineradicable moral dimensions. It is innate to activists because of their twin passions for justice and truth. It is innate because there really *are* powers in the world that are antihuman, anticreation, and anti-Christ. Dualism is innate in activism's very rubrics, its preferred texts of Scripture—prophetic denunciations, the karmic Deuteronomic choices of life and death (Deut 30:15–20), and the separation of sheep and goats based on their response to the poor, the sick, the hungry, the naked, and the incarcerated (Matt 25:31–46). Activists rightly demand that people choose moral light, the common good, and human rights; mystics that they choose transcendent light, unconditional love, and eternal life.

The writings of Symeon the New Theologian contain the spiritual DNA of the Johannine and Pauline traditions, John's intuition of the present fruition of God's reign, the *already* dwarfing the *not yet*, and Paul's cheerful obituaries for the still-breathing old order (1 Cor 1:18, 2:6, 15:42, 50, 53, 54, 2 Cor 2:15, 4:3). A great, enchanting, and enlivening light shines. Mrs. Turpin's parade is on earth as it is in heaven. The Mad Farmer's loony beatitudes are fulfilled. El Hadji's beggars have overthrown the *ancien régime*. But in the moment's very ecstasy there is a clinging, cloying dualism. Thus Symeon: "Those who have become the children of light walk at all times in the light." For them, "the day of the Lord will never come, for they are always with God and in God." To those already "enlightened by the divine light," the day the realm is established will be just another day, but "to those who live conformed to this world, attached to the things that are perishing," the day of the Lord "will come suddenly, unexpectedly, and it will be terrible to them, terrible as fire."[114] There are two ages, two kinds of people, two fates.

The whole Johannine tradition assumes dualism. A later Christian legend says that before his death, John repeated over and over to his gathered disciples: "My little children, love one another."[115] The first, last, and paramount thing is love. But the Johannine corpus has bequeathed a more complex and conflicted heritage of light and darkness.[116] Even the command to

---

113. Merton, *Sign of Jonas*, 247; Rice, *Man in the Sycamore*, 100.

114. Lossky, *Mystical Theology* 233.

115. Rensberger, *Johannine Faith*, 124.

116. Brown, *Community of the Beloved*: the Gospel of John is dualistic between insiders and outsiders, the Epistles within the Johannine community.

A Great Light

love one another can be the ingrown love of sectarian believers who love only their own country, their own cronies, or members of *la familia*.

The Synoptics ask: what kind of inferior love is that (Luke 14:12–4)!? Paraphrasing the Sermon on the Mount (Matt 5:46–7), William Law says "a love which is not universal" is neither righteous nor even love. It may have "tenderness and affection," but it is the shriveled and deforming love of "publicans and heathens."[117]

> For if religion requires me to love all persons, as God's creatures, that belong to God, that bear God's image, enjoy God's protection, and make parts of God's family and household; if these are the great and necessary reasons why I should live in love and friendship with any one person in the world; they are the same great and necessary reasons why I should live in love and friendship with every person in the world; and, consequently I offend against all these reasons, and break through all these ties and obligations, whenever I want love towards any one person. The sin, therefore, of hating, or despising any one person, is like the sin of hating all God's creation; and the necessity of loving any one person, is the same necessity of loving every person in the world.[118]

While we may perceive some people as "sinful, odious, or extravagant in their conduct," we still cannot justify "contempt or disregard of them." Rather, that merely arouses "greater compassion" for their "pitiable condition." As Christ is the "compassionate suffering Advocate for all humankind, so no one is of the Spirit of Christ, but those that have the utmost compassion for sinners."[119] There is no greater sign of spiritual maturity than to have compassion towards the morally weak and mightily defective.

Yet the Johannine school struggles to reach such universalism. Beginning in the prologue, the theme of light weaves through John's Gospel in Jesus' ill-fitting dialogue with Nicodemus[120] that leaps into pirouetting, poetic monologue, to announcements and demonstrations of light, to the Last Supper. The great light is also a dividing line: people love darkness or light; they are true believers or tragic refuseniks (John 1:11–3, 3:16, 11:9–10, 12:35–36, 46). The light of the world brings wonder and reveals division. In 1 John, God is "light" and "love," and the beloved community is to "walk in the light" (1 John 1:7). Darkness is passing away, and the true light shines (1

---

117. Law, *Serious Call*, 279.
118. Ibid., 284.
119. Ibid., 285.
120. Countryman, in *Mystical Way*, calls them "obnoxious discourses" (41).

John 2:8). But claiming to be of the light is not enough. The simple litmus test is love. Whoever loves is in and of the light (1 John 2:9–10). Whoever says "I am light" but hates is a "liar" (1 John 4:20).

There is dualism in Paul's dying age, John's emerging one, and Luke's pivotal historical hinge on Jesus. Black Elk calls this world a shadow of the real one: "That is the real world behind this one, and everything we see here is something like a shadow from that world."[121] It is natural when a culture is crumbling to shift the focus of hope elsewhere in time or space to paradise or heaven. But in ordinary times of ordinary horror, to focus on heaven in order to neglect earth, using the transcendent to disregard the material, is a pernicious evasion, the opiate and fantasy Marx and Freud correctly diagnose.

All dualisms assume good guys and bad guys. An unforeseen consequence of John Winthrop's *city on a hill* is Ronald Reagan's *evil empire*. Stalinist paranoia found its mirror image in McCarthyism, the un-Americanism trials settling for prison sentences, public disgrace, and personal ruin only because they lacked the legal infrastructure to build labor camps and order executions. Each fed off the other, deriving presumed light from the other's presumed darkness. During the Cold War, Reinhold Niebuhr fell victim to his own *realistic* projections of the Soviet threat, forgetting his own formulas about the nature of *all* collectives, that as a nation the US is as prone to messianic megalomania as any other.[122] For Niebuhr, the US became the de facto nation of light, the Soviet Union the chief cornerstone of a satanic and monolithic communist threat. The children of realism had in fact become children of dualism, but they were not alone. As with their first-century forebears—Zealots, Pharisees, priests, and purists—activists with their own ideological purity codes projected their own overidentification of evil onto anti-communists, reactionaries, conservatives, militarists, and defenders of the American way, truth, and life.

Because the problem of dualism is intrinsic, spiritual strategies to defeat it proliferate. The spiritual tradition is as full of commendations of humility as Solomon's temple was of God's glory. Esther de Waal points out that the word *humility* is derived from *humus* and invites us to be "profoundly earthed."[123] Humility means being grounded in reality. Sayings honoring humility abound: to live without humility is "to see without eyes, or live without breath";[124] the truly righteous are so humble that they do not

---

121. Black Elk, *Black Elk Speaks*, 85.
122. Niebuhr, *Irony of American History*, 160.
123. de Waal, *Seeking God*, 45.
124. Law, *Serious Call*, 209.

consider humility a virtue;[125] as there are no ships without nails, there is no hope of salvation without humility;[126] prayer and fasting cannot defeat demons, only humility can.[127]

Self-awareness is never isolated from other-awareness. In one desert story, when a man unsuccessfully seeks to woo a married woman, he asks a magician to punish her. The magician weaves a spell around her so that everyone sees her as a mare. Her distraught but loyal husband fasts, tears his clothes, and mourns for her as if she has died. He feeds her hay that, of course, she won't eat. After priests fail to help, he bridles her and leads her through the desert to Macarius. Macarius's brothers try to shoo them away because of their community's ban on females of all species. Like Jesus frustrated with his disciples, when Macarius hears this, he scolds them, "It is you who are horses." Like the husband, they assumed that the magician's spell was on the woman when, in fact, the problem is their spiritual blindness. Macarius prays and makes the sign of the cross over water, blesses it, sprinkles it over *her* head, and *their* eyes are opened. Macarius takes bread, blesses it, and gives it to the famished woman, reviving her with symbols of baptism and Eucharist.[128] Merton ends his poem "Macarius and the Pony":

> Your own eyes
> (Said Macarius)
> Are your enemies.
> Your own crooked thoughts
> (Said the anchorite)
> Change people around you
> Into birds and animals.
> Your own ill-will
> (said the clear-eyed one)
> Peoples the world with specters.[129]

It is less what people *are* than our distorted image of them that causes injustice and war. These distorted views boomerang and distort our self-image. *They* are subhumans in East London, so *we* are civilized; *they* are evil in Germany or Japan or Russia or Vietnam or Iraq or Afghanistan, so *we* are good. Merton complains that the Cold War "puts the root of the evil thousands of miles away, it exonerates our own system from all defect and all guilt, and

---

125. Buber, *Tales: Early Masters*, 180.
126. Dorotheos, *Discourses*, 203.
127. Swan, *Forgotten Desert Mothers*, 67 citing Amma Theodora.
128. Vivian, *Four Desert Fathers*, 106–8.
129. Merton, *Collected Poems*, 318. In Merton's poem, it is a father and daughter.

makes us forget to look for the solution where we have to find it: in our own backyard. In fact, in our own heart."[130]

> We seek the cause of evil and find it here or there in a particular nation, class, race, ideology, system. And we discharge upon this scapegoat all the virulent force of our hatred, compounded with fear and anguish, striving to rid ourselves of our fear by destroying the object we have arbitrarily singled out as the embodiment of all evil.[131]

> The enemy is not just one side or the other. The enemy is not just Russia, or China, or Communism, or Castro, or Khrushchev, or capitalism, or imperialism. The enemy is on both sides. The enemy is in all of us. The enemy is war itself, and the root of war is hatred, fear, selfishness, lust. . . . We have got to arm not against Russia but against war. Not only against war, but against hatred. Against lies. Against injustice. Against greed. Against every manifestation of these things, wherever they may be found.[132]

> The tragic thing about Vietnam is that, after all, the "realism" of our program there is so unrealistic, so rooted in myth, so completely out of touch with the needs of the people whom we know only as statistics and to whom we never manage to listen, except where they fit in with our own psychopathic delusions.[133]

Like a tape on an endless reel, a circular logic justified and blessed the American war in Vietnam; it "fought to vindicate the assumptions upon which it's being fought."[134] In truth, the US was merely replaying its racist assumptions and its childhood games of cowboys and Indians.[135] In truth, the human race had a "fatal addiction to war."[136] It was not rationalism or realism that reigned: "we are completely obsessed with the fury and the fantasies of the cold war,"[137] a war "*equally immoral on both sides, equally*

---

130. Merton, *Faith and Violence*, 168.
131. Merton, *Nonviolent Alternative*, 221–22.
132. Ibid., 220.
133. Merton, *Faith and Violence*, 92.
134. Merton, *Nonviolent Alternative*, 244.
135. Merton, *Seeds of Destruction*, 75, *Nonviolent Alternative*, 253.
136. Merton, *Nonviolent Alternative*, 67.
137. Ibid., 109.

inhuman and incompatible with Christian ethics."[138] The US and USSR were "myths" to each other and therefore to themselves.[139]

Even as he poked holes in the American ideological dualism that ran amok across the face of the earth like thousands of horsemen of the apocalypse, Merton's wisdom shone brightest in his pastoral advice to activists who opposed this insanity, cautioning them against the seductions of dualism in the antiwar movement. He warns them against self-righteousness,[140] and against turning nonviolence into a form of moral aggression.[141] He warns them not to allow their "holy zeal" for an abstract cause to nurture indifference towards those with whom they disagree,[142] never to elevate the holiness of a cause above people,[143] and never to love fabricated ideas more than real people.[144] If activists try to do things for others "without deepening their own self-understanding, freedom, integrity and capacity to love, they will not have anything to give others. They will communicate to them nothing but the contagion of their own obsessions, their aggressiveness, their ego-centered ambitions, their delusions about ends and means, their doctrinaire prejudices and ideas."[145]

Like Merton, Gandhi sought to offset the twin temptations to exalt one's side and to demean enemies. He chose the classic way of self-examination. Rather than magnifying *their* evil, whoever they are, people need to see their "own mistakes with a convex lens."[146] Spiritually aware activists followed suit. Day could be scathing of oppressors and warmongers, bishops and presidents, but she could just as quickly create a list of her own sins: "vanity, pride, cruelty, contempt of others,"[147] hyper-sensitivity, "lack of charity,"[148] criticism of neighbors, friends, and enemies, impatience, "pride and presumption," and willfulness.[149] In his Cold War prayers, Merton turned Gandhi's convex lens on a whole nation:

---

138. Ibid., 221 (italics his).
139. Merton, *Cold War*, 29.
140. Merton, *Nonviolent Alternative*, 213.
141. Ibid., 208.
142. Ibid., 211.
143. Merton, *Disputed Questions*, 115.
144. Merton, *Faith and Violence*, 163.
145. Merton, *Contemplation in World*, 178–79.
146. Gandhi, *Non-violent*, 75.
147. Day, *All is Grace*, 113.
148. Day, *Houses of Hospitality*, 79.
149. Day, *On Pilgrimage*, 174.

> When I pray for peace I pray for God to pacify not only the Russians and the Chinese but above all my own nation and myself. When I pray for peace I pray to be protected not only from the Reds but also from the folly and blindness of my own country. When I pray for peace, I pray not only that the enemies of my country may cease to want war, but above all that my own country will cease to do the things that make war inevitable. In other words, when I pray for peace I am not just praying that the Russians will give up without a struggle and let us have our own way. I am praying that both we and the Russians may somehow be restored to sanity and learn how to work out our problems, as best we can.[150]

Turning the convex lens on the nonviolent community, Muste contrasts love and humility with ideology and truth and asks pacifists to end their self-ingratiating pseudosanctity. When Muste's only son entered the military in 1944, Muste took it as a stinging personal defeat,[151] but his deeper commitment to the virtue of humility and the practice of self-examination led him to combat ideological purity. In the early 1960s, amidst antiwar debates about choosing allies from among the morally pure and the ideologically purest, Muste advocated complete inclusion, welcoming communists into the liberal-pacifist mix when the goose bumps of McCarthyism were still raised and tingling and there were respectable reasons for moral revulsion. To be inclusive Muste had to lick his own past wounds that made him forever wary of the dishonest cynicism and casual, calculating manipulation of the secular Left.

Rufus Jones reverses Gandhi's convex lens to see the other anew. He refuses to wash his hands of the so-called children of darkness. George Fox considers the inner light "a capacity" in everyone to "divine intimations and openings."[152] Each person has "a moral searchlight," everyone can learn "the absolute distinction between right and wrong."[153] No wealthy exploiters of the poor, bigots, or communists, no Nazis, neo-Nazis, or neocons, no terrorists, imperialists, or militarists could ever be completely separated from their inner light.

Day affirms human unity not in shared light, but in common darkness. Following the Memorial Day Massacre in Chicago in 1937 when police shot and killed ten unarmed demonstrators and injured dozens more,

---

150. Merton, *New Seeds*, 121.
151. Robinson, *Abraham Went Out*, 85.
152. Steere, ed., *Quaker Spirituality*, 276.
153. Ibid.

A Great Light

Day put her advocacy for workers' rights and her outspoken opposition to exploitation into theological perspective: the massacre was "One more sin, suffering Christ, worker Yourself, for You to bear." Christ "bore the sins of all the world," including the sinful massacre: "You took them on Yourself, the sins of those police, the sins of the [industrialists]. . . . You took them on Yourself, and You died to save us all." As if to gauge how far Christ could reach—from the powerful to the powerless—and how specific salvation could be, she adds, "Your Precious Blood was shed even for that policeman whose cudgel smashed again and again the skull of that poor striker, whose brains lay splattered on the undertaker's slab."[154] Christ lived and died not only for victims of oppression or advocates of justice, or for progressives or peacemakers or the meek or the merciful or the pure of heart or the children of light. Christ was the light of *the world*.

The perennial language of sin and redemption binds Day and Merton to Symeon. While in 1 John the litmus test for being of the light is love, for Symeon it is repentance. "Penitence," Symeon says, "is the gateway that leads out of darkness into light. Whoever does not enter into the light has not properly gone through the gate of repentance."[155] Cassian's observation that it is easier to exorcise someone else's unclean spirit than to "root out the tinder of luxury from one's flesh"[156] might have awakened Niebuhr and reshaped his Cold War realism. Niebuhr's hermeneutic of suspicion, it turns out, went far and wide without going near and deep. Unconsciously, Niebuhr had made American democracy *the moral society*, undoing his own logic, his own reason, and his own realism.

This Augustinian leveling of sin, repentance, redemption, prayer, and humility also extends to those who might be ironically dehumanized by presumptions of *goodness*. César Chávez, less sanguine about California farmworkers than Tolstoy was of their Russian counterparts, suggests a subtlety of evil more sophisticated than Niebuhr's. Chávez loathed the romanticizing of the poor. In his initiation speech to volunteers, he says: "the farm worker is only a human being. You take the poorest of these guys and give him that ranch over there, he could be just as much of a bastard as that guy sitting there right now." Chávez recognized an inverted, condescending racism. The noble savage—presumed innocence enmeshed with presumed ignorance—now dressed in the ragged clothes of farmworkers. Just as he didn't want to exalt farm workers, he didn't want "pity" for them: "treat them as human beings, because they have just as many faults as you have."

---

154. Day, *By Little*, 246.

155. Symeon, *Discourses*, 298; 1 John 1:8–10 uses penance as a litmus test for love.

156. Cassian, *Conferences*, 180.

At the same time, he refused to dehumanize even the most unscrupulous growers—"if you think that all growers are bastards, you're no good to us either."[157]

Although a cause could separate the just from the unjust, people on both sides were equally human. On the day seminarian and civil rights volunteer Jonathan Daniels was murdered by special deputy Thomas Coleman in Alabama, an anguished Will Campbell telephoned the Department of Justice, the American Civil Liberties Union, and an attorney about "the death of my friend." In those calls, he referred to the murder "as a travesty of justice, as a complete breakdown of law and order, as a violation of Federal and State law." In those calls, he "used words like redneck, backwoods, woolhat, cracker, Kluxer, ignoramus and many others." A journalist-friend with him reminded him of the time he had goaded Campbell into boiling down "the Christian message" to ten words. Campbell did it in eight: "We're all bastards but God loves us anyway." Now the journalist cold-heartedly asked Campbell to apply this message to his murdered friend.

"Was Jonathan a bastard?"

Campbell said Daniels "was one of the sweetest and most gentle guys I had ever known."

The journalist raged, "But was he a bastard? . . . Now that's your word. Not mine. You told me one time that everybody is a bastard. That's a pretty tough word. I know. Cause I *am* a bastard. A born bastard. A real bastard. My Mamma wasn't married to my Daddy. Now, by god, you tell me, right now, yes or no, and not maybe, was Jonathan Daniels a bastard?"

Finally, Campbell said, "Yes."

"Is Thomas Coleman a bastard?"

That, Campbell says, was easier. "Yes."

"Which one of these two bastards do you think God loves the most?"[158]

It was a galling "conversion" for Campbell, who had become "a doctrinaire social activist"[159] with "a ministry of liberal sophistication . . . worshiping at the shrine of enlightenment and academia." With a jolt, he recalled that the Thomas Colemans of the world are loved "and if loved, forgiven. And if forgiven, reconciled."[160] Campbell had stopped being a Christian for whom all bastards need redemption, and "unless that is precisely the case then there is no Gospel, there is no Good News.[161]" In the previous years,

---

157. Dalton, *Moral Vision*, 81–82.
158. Campbell, *Brother to Dragonfly*, 220–22.
159. Ibid., 225.
160. Ibid., 222.
161. Ibid., 224.

Campbell had taken sides in the ferociously racist South. But when we only *take* sides, we become dualists, and sooner or later we want our enemies named, identified, cornered, judged, convicted, or crucified. For years, Campbell had been impatient with so-called white moderates. When we only *transcend* sides, we become mealymouthed quasineutrals. Christians, he realized, have to take *and* transcend sides, and to do that—as did Day and Chávez—is to walk a spiritual tightrope in a political sandstorm.

If only our vision could be healed and we could find human unity more binding than ideology. If only we could find commonality in sin, prayer, humility, redemption, and our capacity for light, we would see through our dehumanizing visions of others and our habitual self-exaltation—as nations, systems, peoples, and movements. Know that you are in and of the light *only* when you love one another, your neighbor, the stranger, *and* your enemy. Take sides. Transcend sides. And dualism will be drained of its sinister power.

That could be said easily and often. As a Buddhist story has it, the demands of the enlightened life are straightforward: shun evil, do good, have a pure mind. These demands are so simple that a five-year-old knows them, but an eighty-year-old finds them hard to practice.[162] The remedies for dualism are easy to name: humility, confession, and charity. But, as individuals, we find them hard to do. They are harder still for communities of faith and advocates of causes. For nations, corporations, and institutions, they are impossible.

READINGS IN REALISM

Niebuhr claimed neither the mystic's enlightenment nor the saint's high moral ground; instead he chose for himself the mantle of realism. He cedes transcendence to mystics and purity to idealists. He seizes the secular world for himself. This concern of the religious for the secular is as ancient as commandments about what to eat, what to wear, and what to do when an ox stumbles into a ditch. As the Epistle of James attests, true religion means caring for the vulnerable, controlling one's tongue, and using one's wealth responsibly (Jas 1:26–27). Stringfellow insists that meaningful theology is "inherently practical";[163] the theologians at Medellín say that faith is enacted

---

162. *Dhammapada*, 22.
163. Stringfellow, *Dissenter*, 126.

primarily in the secular realm;[164] and F. D. Maurice says, "The highest theology is the most closely connected with the commonest practical life."[165]

Realism is a provocative word and a constant quandary. Like normalcy, how does one describe, locate, or return to realism? Realism is entirely subjective and inherently in the eye of the beholder. Realism is an *ism* and, as such, is an ideology and an idol—in Stringfellow's analysis—something that claims absolute devotion. The idea that *realism* exists assumes that someone can manufacture a blue light of truth that reveals things hidden from the naked eye, mystical intuition, or ordinary faith. Realism can be a much-needed awakening for the dreamy, the otherworldly, the narcissistic, or the ineffectually good-willed. But it is also a temptation: ordaining yourself a realist can make you as self-righteous as the most sanctimonious purist. Dostoevsky's Grand Inquisitor claims to be realistic, as opposed to Jesus, whom he has awaiting execution. The Grand Inquisitor's condescension expands geometrically beyond Jesus. *Everyone* is childish, "weak, pathetic," and "stupid."[166] At its worst, ideological realism denies mystery, shrinks possibilities, and narrows horizons. If mysticism can err on the side of over-realized eschatology, realism can err toward its underrealized opposite. As Dostoevsky suggests, at its worst, realism becomes an alternative to and enemy of Jesus.

The narrowing drive of realism can aver the nonexistence of the transcendent. From Bultmann to the Jesus Seminar, biblical scholars have enshrined post-Enlightenment, modernist modes of knowing. In some intellectual circles, snide comments about ignorant savages of other races have been replaced by disdain for the so-called primitive mind-sets of pre-Marxian pre-Freudians. In such circles, offensive racism has been displaced by academically blessed *time-ism*. The illusion of social progress H. Richard Niebuhr decries has been replanted in the delusion of intellectual progress. So, since Thomas Jefferson's edit of the Gospels, Western thinkers have wanted to cut and paste and leech and purify the New Testament by ridding it of signs and wonders as if, by doing so, they would not also lose the wonder and promise of the revolution of God. If you cannot believe in the blind seeing and the lame leaping—what Jesus does, the already—you can hardly pray for what Jesus teaches—the not yet, the realm—and you are left praying for God's will being done on an unchanging earth as it is in a nonexistent heaven. To deny that the blind see and the deaf hear is to imply the next obvious edit: delete the prophets who envision such an age. In this

---

164. Hennelly, *Liberation Theology*, 98.
165. Vidler, *F. D. Maurice*, 14.
166. Dostoevsky, *Brothers Karamazov*, bk. 5 ch. 5.

sense, *realism*—fidelity to what is and only to what is—can balloon the deflated hope and the world-weary word of Qoheleth into the only orthodoxy. Worse still, it can become a concession to a hopelessness that serves the more-realistic-than-thou needs of the ever-realistic, never-ending status quo.

Niebuhr's primary concern is pragmatism, an essential ingredient in making sure one's principles and visions are not to remain aloft in ineffective abstractions. The rabbis could describe the transmission of light from the uncreated to the works of the righteous to the words of teachers,[167] but Niebuhr asks if light always moves in such a clear path. Niebuhr insists that depravity and the demonic regularly defeat the best plans and intentions of the most beatific saints. If light does not enter the world as it is, it is all for show and all for naught. Niebuhr wants to know how the light changes societies. Like Gregory of Nyssa, he embraces Leah's usefulness over Rachel's aesthetic beauty. The light, if it exists, Niebuhr says, is not for you—the mystic, the idealist, the revolutionary—alone.

Who, then, is realistic? In the aftermath of Israel's exile, is it Nehemiah, Ezra, or Second Isaiah? For Nehemiah, it is enough to rebuild the city; for Ezra, enough to rebuild the temple; for both, enough to rebuild a survivors/surviving/survivalist community. Their horizons are narrow; their accomplishments built in stone. Theirs is the realism of Niebuhr; you can only do so much. What then of Second Isaiah, whose extravagant visions yank horizons apart? For him, the return of exiles to Jerusalem—greater than the first exodus—is "too light" a thing to hope for, dream of, or bring to pass (Isa 43:18–9). In his visions, heaven breaks open and pours down blessings like a piñata. The return of exiles is *not* enough; he must be a light to the nations (Isa 49:6). Yet in truth, he too is urging realism: God has again made a way in the wilderness; you can go home again! His awe-awakening visions, themselves turning the mind's desert into a garden, are *needed*—realistically—to move people who had read, marked, learned, inwardly digested, and ultimately enshrined Jeremiah's earlier, temporary memo to settle in and pray for the welfare of Babylon (Jer 29:4–7). Niebuhr, inching forward like Ezra and Nehemiah, urges pragmatic, brick-building reform; Isaiah preaches visionary, eye-opening revolution.

Niebuhr played realism as if it were the joker in a deck of cards. He argued it harshly, the way arguments are made within sectarian communities, and it is hard to argue with Augustine and Niebuhr about sinful humans and idolatrous nations. It takes no great faith to believe in personal sin or collective evil. What requires faith is that people and peoples can change.

---

167. Buber, *Tales: Early Masters*, v.

Yet, in spite of his acidic rhetoric, it was not Niebuhr's purpose to freeze progressive hopes beneath an avalanche of ice, as if they were like Francis's carnal desires writ large. Niebuhr searched for practical ways to achieve social transformation. In a moment of prescience he conjectures that Gandhi's 1930s nonviolent activism might be a successful pattern for African Americans seeking racial justice.[168] Niebuhr even recognizes the realistic need for dreams: "Without the ultrarational hopes and passions of religion no society will ever have the courage to conquer despair and attempt the impossible; for the vision of a just society is an impossible one, which can be approximated only by those who do not regard it as impossible."[169] The realist, it turns out, could dream dreams. But when Niebuhr contrasts liberal *optimism* with sober *realism*, he demands that the harbingers of hope not neglect the depths of institutional intransigence or the human capacity for sin.

Rauschenbusch was to Niebuhr what the Epistle of James was to Martin Luther—straw. Niebuhr may have branded Rauschenbusch the antirealist, but Rauschenbusch's theology is more limber than Niebuhr wants to admit. Rauschenbusch says that both World War I and social oppression were born from "the same lust for easy and unearned gain." Against H. Richard Niebuhr's caricature, he affirms "the sinfulness of the social order" and "the sins of all individuals within it,"[170] and he warns, "the coming of the Kingdom of God will not be by peaceful development only, but by conflict with the Kingdom of Evil." But Rauschenbusch also believes in "the social repentance of nations."[171] He thinks organizations "drift into evil under sinister leadership" but are not innately immune to grace.[172] He believes that when nations practice "real democracy" they can "step out of the Kingdom of Evil into the Kingdom of God."[173]

Having started the realism game, Niebuhr had to let others play their cards as well. Having denounced nonviolence as quaintly illusory, he had to allow the nonviolent to respond. Gandhi, for one, says, "I am not a visionary. I claim to be a practical idealist. The religion of nonviolence is not meant for rishis and saints. It is meant for the common people as well."[174] Like Gandhi, Andre Trocmé was impatient with the critics of nonviolence:

---

168. Niebuhr, *Moral Man*, 252–54.
169. Ibid., 81.
170. Rauschenbusch, *Social Gospel*, 4–5.
171. Ibid., 226.
172. Ibid., 72.
173. Ibid., 117.
174. Gandhi, *Way to God*, 57–58.

people were wrong to accuse "pacifists of wanting to keep their hands clean. Nonviolence engages evil, it does not withdraw from it."[175] During World War I, when idealism was caught on and torn by barbed wired, Lester announces, "we refuse to pronounce a moratorium on the Sermon on the Mount for the duration of war."[176] To surrender principle to war is to negate the realism of Jesus.

While the principle-based Lester and Day would want Niebuhr to amend, broaden, or revolutionize his view of realism, others question Niebuhr's definitions of realism on their own terms. Gandhi gives a nod to Niebuhr in preferring violent resistance to cowardly complicity,[177] yet he insists on the practical superiority of nonviolence. Muste refuses to cede the analysis of evil to Niebuhr or to exclude the *reality* of hope. In contrast to the self-sanctifying isolationist *and* to Niebuhr, Muste describes the true pacifist as the "supreme realist,"[178] and accuses his Niebuhrian antagonists of "secularist and nationalist sentimentalism."[179] Muste agrees with Niebuhr that it is foolhardy to believe that one's enemy is really a "good fellow,"[180] but he thinks it equally half-witted to believe that one can use evil to overcome evil (Mark 3:23–24). An incredulous Muste charged Niebuhr's self-proclaimed Crisis Realists with blind sentimentality when they asserted, *after* Hiroshima and Nagasaki, that the US would never use nuclear weapons![181] In the 1930s, less than two decades after Woodrow Wilson's *war to end all wars* supposedly slew Mars, Moloch, and their minions, Muste offers a scathing attack on Niebuhr's alleged cold, clear logic: "We have to be romanticists, sentimentalists, capable of flying in the face of all the evidence, to believe that another general war, or series of wars" can generate justice.[182] It was as clear to Muste that war did not bring peace as it was to Niebuhr that the League of Nations could not avert war. Bristling with sarcasm, Muste ridicules the "childish assumption that it might be possible in our day and in our world to have a nice, short, snappy war, or maybe a half dozen of them, and thus achieve peace and social justice."[183] In hindsight, Muste has

---

175. Trocmé, *Jesus and the Nonviolent*, 153.

176. Lester, *Ambassador of Reconciliation*, 153; Day, *By Little*, 262, made the same announcement during the next World War.

177. Gandhi, *Non-violent*, 132.

178. Muste, "Where 'Crisis Realism' Fails," 5.

179. Muste, "Love in Action," 7.

180. Muste, "Muste Testifies," 22.

181. Muste, *Not by Might*, 166.

182. Muste, "Fight the Good Fight?" 340.

183. Ibid., 342.

proven the more prophetic—and realistic—of the two: the generations after the World Wars have never been without a "short, snappy war," or a series of proxy wars without inching the world one millimeter closer to a sustainable peace.

The conflict between Niebuhr and Muste played out a century earlier in the abolitionist movement in a confrontation between the erudite Frederick Douglass and the plainspoken Sojourner Truth. In the 1850s, Douglass became accustomed to making fiery addresses that argued for abolition (to retroactively inject Malcolm X's phrase) *by any means necessary*, including violence. Like a story beginning in oral tradition that has two punch lines, after Douglass gave one of these speeches, Truth stood up and said either, "Frederick, is God gone?" or "is God dead?"[184] Muste thought that Niebuhr, like Douglass, had circumscribed the power of God and channeled it into a particular form of realism.

If Muste found Niebuhr's realism farsighted (overlooking the irrationality of war), nearsighted (obscuring hope), and shortsighted (prioritizing short-term goals over the long haul of history), Stringfellow attacks Niebuhr on his self-assessed strength, insinuating that Niebuhr is unrealistically naïve about institutions. When it comes to institutional evil, he considers Niebuhr a theological yokel, as quaint as Billy Graham.[185] Stringfellow expands the height, depth, breadth, and length of Niebuhr's critique of institutions. He takes the Bible's occasional description of nations as "predatory beasts" and turns it into a universal rule.[186] Friend and coconspirator Daniel Berrigan calls the power of death embodied in institutions "all but universal, all but omnipotent, all but omnivorous, carnivorous in its intention and method, claiming all flesh for itself."[187] Rumi invites people to stop devouring; according to Stringfellow, institutions can do nothing else. While Niebuhr maintains that institutions can be reformed by coercion, Stringfellow believes they can *never* reform. Every institution is a principality and principalities have no principles. They do not serve people; people serve them.[188]

In *The Grapes of Wrath*, John Steinbeck weaves such observations into the story of tenant farmers being ruined during the Depression, not by landowners who might be swayed by a hard luck story even during an economic twister, but by inhuman institutions:

184. Douglass, *Life and Times*, 275; Mabee, *Sojourner Truth*, 83; DuBois, *Darkwater*, 102–3.

185. Stringfellow, *Conscience and Obedience*, 64–65.

186. Stringfellow, "Lamentation for Easter," 6.

187. Stringfellow and Towne, *Suspect Tenderness*, 5.

188. He held out an olive branch of hope that the church could be an "exemplary principality" (Stringfellow, *Ethic for Christians*, 57).

> If a bank or a finance company owned the land, the owner said, The Bank—or the Company—needs—wants—insists—must have—as though the Bank or the company were a monster, with thought and feeling.... And the owner explained the workings and the thinkings of the monster that was stronger than they were.... You see, a bank or a company... those creatures don't breathe air, don't eat side-meat. They breathe profits; they eat the interest on money. If they don't get it, they die the way you die without air, without side-meat. It is a sad thing, but it is so.... The bank—the monster has to have profits all the time. It can't wait. It'll die. No, taxes go on. When the monster stops growing, it dies. It can't stay one size.... The bank is something else than people. It happens that everyone in a bank hates what the bank does, and yet the bank does it. The bank is something more than people, I tell you. It's the monster. People made it, but they can't control it.[189]

Steinbeck's monsters want, need, must grow, regardless of their impact on people. It is a *systemic necessity*; institutions are enriched; most people are impoverished. Stringfellow maintains that every principality pledges sole allegiance to the power of death. Political reform is quixotic. The Oval Office possesses whoever sits in the Oval Office; the Kremlin possesses whoever occupies the Kremlin. While he urged Nixon's impeachment *before* Watergate, he later earnestly prayed for Nixon's exorcism from systems beyond his control.[190] In effect, Stringfellow displaces Calvin's view of human depravity onto institutions. Yet, in spite of Stringfellow's dour demeanor and his puzzlement at the defeat of the saints, unlike Niebuhr he believes wholeheartedly in God's eschatological triumph and in proximate daily victories.

While activists challenge Niebuhr's notions of realism, the mystical tradition subverts even his predilection to focus on evil. The *Theologia Germanica* warns the credulous of those "obsessed by the devil."[191] Teresa of Ávila adds, "I am more afraid of people who are themselves terrified of the devil than I am of the devil himself."[192] Niebuhr no doubt deemed himself too sophisticated for devil-talk, but Teresa might have found him transfixed by evil and thus as hazardous to people's spiritual health as the very real dangers he exposes.

---

189. Steinbeck, *Grapes of Wrath*, 31–32; Wink, *Engaging the Powers*, 50, uses this passage.

190. Stringfellow, *Conscience and Obedience*, 98; *Keeper of the Word*, 275–79.

191. *Theologia Germanica*, 86.

192. Teresa, *Life of Teresa*, 243–44.

Whatever the legitimate criticisms of Niebuhr, he thought he was offering corrective lenses to the children of light. If nothing else, he insists that visions of light—mystical and moral—must be grounded in incarnational reality, genocide, starvation, and exploitation. If the post-World War II era has proven anything, it is not only the banality of evil (Arendt) but the *banality of Hitler*, not only in the likes of Milosevic, Idi Amin, Pol Pot, Saddam Hussein, and a host of dictators, not only in places like Rwanda, Sudan, Burma, and a host of nations, but in the totalitarian foreign policies of Niebuhr's most precious democracy acted out in Guatemala, Nicaragua, Vietnam, Chile, Afghanistan, and Iraq. Ethnic cleansing may take its most vicious form against Jews and Armenians, in Bosnia or Rwanda, but as Jesus uncovers seeds of murder in anger (Matt 5:21–2), the seeds of genocide are found in nativism's antagonism against undocumented immigrants in the US. Mystics and moralists need to bring light to *this* world.

William James divides people into once-born and twice-born, and Niebuhr could not resist a derogatory tone toward the once-born, often-fooled, cheerily naïve children of light. In contrast, Eckhart has his own dichotomy, not of people, but of knowledge. Eckhart says that those who know "creatures as they are in themselves" have *twilight knowledge*. Those who know creatures as they are "known in God" have *daybreak knowledge*. In daybreak knowledge, we perceive creatures without distinctions, comparisons, prejudices, or even the taint of ideas; they are known only in their oneness with the One God.[193] Instead of prioritizing one kind of knowledge over the other in another meaningless dualistic competition, we need to value the gift of twilight knowledge to assess systemic evil, and the gift of daybreak knowledge to prevent the world as it is from looking like a one-dimensional tragedy devoid of hope. We need a faith that practices fidelity to the hard realities *of* the world (Niebuhr) without being imprisoned *by* the world (Rumi).

AN OCEAN OF LIGHT

Philip Hallie studied evil for a living, so he was not amused when smart-alecky students annoyed him with gimmicky metaphysical tricks to magically make the philosophical category of evil disappear. In response to their abstract arguments, an incensed Hallie whipped up a quick behavioral experiment. He "would pick them up against the wall and say, 'I'm going to kick ya. Now is that good or bad'?"[194] To him, they were children of light

---

193. Eckhart, *Meister Eckhart: Modern Translation*, 79.
194. Hallie, "Cruelty," 135.

A Great Light

living within a shroud of darkness. Hallie hoped to be forgiven his zealous indiscretion but—after all—he had researched "the cruelty perpetrated in the death camps of Central Europe." And, like living near a toxic dump, the study had taken its toll.

> For years I had been studying cruelty, the slow crushing and grinding of a human being by other human beings. I had studied the tortures whites inflicted upon native Indians and then upon blacks in the Americas, and now I was reading mainly about the torture experiments the Nazis conducted upon the bodies of small children in those death camps.
>
> Across all these repeated studies, the pattern of the strong crushing the weak kept repeating itself and repeating itself, so that when I was not bitterly angry, I was bored at the repetition of the patterns of persecution. When I was not desiring to be cruel with the cruel, I was a monster—like, perhaps, many others around me—who could look upon torture and death without a shudder, and who therefore looked upon life without a belief in its preciousness. My study of evil incarnate had become a prison whose bars were my bitterness toward the violent, and whose walls were my horrified indifference to slow murder. Between the bars and the walls I revolved like a madman. Reading about the damned I was damned myself, as damned as the murderers, and as damned as their victims. Somehow over the years I had dug myself into Hell, and I had forgotten redemption, had forgotten the possibility of escape.

While reading an anthology of documents from the Holocaust, Hallie chanced upon a short article about a small village in southern France: "I was trying to sort out the forms and elements of cruelty and of resistance to it in much the same way a veterinarian might sort out ill from healthy cattle."

> About halfway down the third page of the account of this village, I was annoyed by a strange sensation on my cheeks. The story was so simple and so factual that I had found it easy to concentrate upon *it*, not upon my own feelings. And so, still following the story, and thinking about how neatly some of it fit into the old patterns of persecution, I reached up to my cheek to wipe away a bit of dust, and I felt tears upon my fingertips. Not one or two drops; my whole cheek was wet.

Miffed with his self-diagnosed overreaction, he closed the book and walked home to dinner with his family.

> But that night when I lay on my back in bed with my eyes closed, I saw more clearly than ever the images that had made me weep. . . . I saw the police captain facing the pastor of the village and warning him that if he did not give up the names of the Jews they had been sheltering in the village, he and his fellow pastor, as well as the families who had been caring for the Jews, would be arrested. I saw the pastor refuse to give up these people who had been strangers in his village, even at the risk of his own destruction.

Hallie envisioned other scenes—the pastor's thirteen-year-old son handing a piece of chocolate to a prisoner under the watchful gaze of twenty police, the villagers passing gifts through a prison window as they showered generosity on someone presumably doomed to death.

> Lying there in bed, I began to weep again. I thought, Why run away from what is excellent simply because it goes through you like a spear? Lying there, I knew that always a certain region of my mind contained an awareness of men and women in bloody white coats breaking and rebreaking the bones of six- or seven- or eight-year-old Jewish children in order, the Nazis said, to study the processes of natural healing in young bodies. All of this I knew. But why not know joy? Why not leave root room for comfort? Why add myself to the millions of victims? Why must life be for me that vision of those children lying there with their children's eyes looking up at the adults who were breaking a leg for the second time, a rib cage for the third time? Something had happened, had happened for years in that mountain village. Why should I be afraid of it?
>
> To the dismay of my wife, I left the bed unable to say a word, dressed, crossed the dark campus on a starless night, and read again those few pages on the village of Le Chambon-sur-Lignon. And to my surprise, again the spear, again the tears, again the frantic painful pleasure that spills into the mind when a deep, deep need is being satisfied, or when a deep wound is starting to heal.
>
> That night, I decided to try to understand all this. I decided to understand it so that I could hold it more firmly than one can hold a tear, or an image. Since I was a student and a teacher of ethics, I would use what I had learned about human standards of ethical excellence to help me understand the blessing—at least for me—of Le Chambon. Those involuntary tears had been

an expression of moral praise, praise pressed out of my whole personality like the juice of a grape.[195]

An exercise in historical research—a study of the world at its most godless—had become an epiphany, a light shining in darkness, as profound as a mystical vision. Hallie, who had lost the capacity to shudder (Otto), had been awakened. His endless forced march through mass viciousness led him, like Tutu, to shed sacred tears, not of grief, but of spiritual resurrection. Somehow, in the congregation of André Trocmé, he had seen "goodness." Like Motovilov and Birgitta and Julian, he had *seen*, and he knew that this was not a revelation for him alone. Niebuhr might say that the children of light were naïve, sheltered from a raging storm of cruelty. But historical evidence as clear as Hallie's shows that Niebuhr did not read all of the documentation. His *realism* lacks the methodological rigor he insists is required for intellectual integrity. In his focus on darkness, Niebuhr had missed the light.

Augustine's biographer Peter Brown says that the Bishop of Hippo delivered "a hard message for a hard age."[196] True enough. Some eras are more heartrending and brutal than others. People living in such times might wisely—like a Qoheleth—scale back their hopes and mute their expectations. And yet there is harshness in every age. There is always famine, disaster, and war somewhere. Poverty flourishes almost everywhere—there is always another ghetto, another barrio, another favela, another township, another Appalachia. In the ecology of social systems, injustice and oppression are perennials.

Seventeenth-century England was a hard age, rocky soil for the hopeful message of George Fox. Kings gave way to Cromwell and Cromwell to kings. Intrigue, suspicion, paranoia, and violence multiplied until England was awash in blood. Fox and his companions suffered ferocious persecution as they were chastised, beaten, imprisoned, and executed for their outrageous preaching that was heard either as courageously poised or obnoxiously self-righteous. It was in *that* most unpropitious soil, when evidence of conscience was remarkably slim, that Fox's faith in the inner light spread. In the misery of English gulags the gospel of the Christ within took root. Whatever someone like Niebuhr might think of Quaker theology, facile optimism usually wears thin after a few days of gruel and filth. Somehow, in spite of tangible evidence and personal experience, the cruelty of prisons never kept Friends from remaining fixed on the inner light: "Though it was a cruel, bloody, persecuting time, yet the Lord's power went over all, God's

---

195. Hallie, *Lest Innocent Blood*, 2–4.
196. Brown, *Augustine of Hippo*, 406.

everlasting Seed prevailed; and Friends were made to stand firm and faithful in the Lord's power."[197]

The seventeenth-century Friends movement offered an alternative theology to the bleak Calvinistic assessment of human depravity at a time when depravity was more often the midwife to moaning and mourning than to resistance and revolution, a time when human depravity seemed a simple empirical observation with little need for references, footnotes, or faith. But, as Rufus Jones puts it, the Quaker tradition "met the pessimism of depravity with a rival optimism about human potentiality."[198] Later Quaker writers sheepishly admit that Fox had an underdeveloped sense of sin—his own and others—[199] but the numberless conflicts and beatings the Friends endured belie a Pollyannaish theology of human nature. James Baldwin says that Martin Luther King, Jr.—another religious leader accused of a too-sunny disposition—"had looked on evil a long, hard, lonely time."[200] Like King, Fox was no Qoheleth watching as a spectator; he preached in a time of suffering, and felt suffering's teeth in his own life.

In the face of brutality, the first Friends were determined to flood the darkness with even brighter light: "Now it was a time of great suffering; and many Friends being in prisons, many other Friends were moved to go to the Parliament, to offer themselves up to lie in the same prisons where their friends lay, that those in prison might go forth, and not perish in the stinking jails. This we did in love to God and our brethren that they might not die in prison." Yet one edge was not enough for this sword of love. They also acted "in love to those that cast them in that they might not bring innocent blood upon their own heads, which we knew would cry to the Lord, and bring God's wrath, vengeance, and plagues upon them."[201] Like Trocmé, they were concerned lest innocent blood be shed, and worried not only for innocent victims; they were troubled for the guilty perpetrators who would spill it. The first Friends not only reversed the panicked flight of Jesus' disciples, none of whom rushed to take Jesus' place on the cross. They also cared for their era's Caiaphases, Herods, and Pilates. They refused to celebrate vengefully the religious leaders who took responsibility for Jesus' innocent blood even on their descendants (Matt 27:25).

Even as they sought to overcome darkness with light, they also trusted that, whether or not *their* light prevailed in the short term, God's light would

---

197. Fox, *Journal*, 479.
198. Steere, ed., *Quaker Spirituality*, 277.
199. Introduction to Fox, *Journal*, 15.
200. Baldwin, "Highroad to Destiny," 104.
201. Fox, *Journal*, 322–33.

ultimately triumph. In letters to his fellow Friends, Fox writes, "Do not think that anything will outlast the Truth. For the Truth stands sure, and is over that which is out of the Truth. For the good will overcome the evil; the light, darkness; the life, death; virtue, vice; and righteousness, unrighteousness."[202] Gandhi pulls this futuristic vision of the triumph of goodness back into the present: "For I can see that in the midst of death, life persists; in the midst of untruth, truth persists; in the midst of darkness, light persists."[203] Invoking the spirit of John of Patmos, also writing in hard times, Fox enjoins the endurance of the apostolic age: "Therefore be valiant for God's truth upon the earth, and look above that spirit that makes you suffer, up to Christ, who was before it was, and will be when it is gone."[204] Fox reiterates God's promise to Julian of Norwich: all shall be well. Whatever disturbs people of faith or distresses the human race, it is temporary. Nothing outlasts the light. Even if they could not flood the darkness with light, their light would shine in that darkness.

As Catherine of Siena would say, human suffering is finite, God's love infinite. Fox applies the same logic. In Nottinghamshire, "The Lord showed me that the natures of those things, which were hurtful without, were within, in the hearts and minds of the wicked. The natures of dogs, swine, vipers, of Sodom and Egypt, Pharaoh, Cain, Ishmael, Esau . . . the nature of these I saw within, though people had been looking without." Fox asks God why the world should be so evil, and why he should have to see this panorama of depravity, and God answers that Fox needs to have "a sense of all conditions." He could not be sheltered or suckled in ignorant bliss. Right in the midst of this horror, as Hallie saw something glorious in the midst of the Holocaust, Fox sees "that there was an ocean of darkness and death; but an infinite ocean of light and love, which flowed over the ocean of darkness. In that also I saw the infinite love of God."[205]

Three centuries later, if Niebuhr had read Thich Nhat Hanh's writings, he would undoubtedly have tarred him as a child of light. Nhat Hanh, after all, facing the aggressive intransigence of pro- and anti-communist ideological rigidity and the dehumanization of war claims that even in the midst of such chaos and death, "strategies, tactics, and techniques for a nonviolent struggle arise naturally" from "love and the willingness to act selflessly."[206] While his work for nonviolent social change would be swallowed up amidst

---

202. Ibid., 480 (modernized).
203. Gandhi, *Way to God*, 34.
204. Fox, *Journal*, 565; cf. Rev. 1:8.
205. Fox, *Journal*, 86–87.
206. Nhat Hanh, *Love in Action*, 39.

napalm and body counts, he insists, "the success of a nonviolent struggle" is measured in "love and nonviolence," not "political victory."[207] Even in an ocean of darkness *not* swallowed up in an ocean of light, the Buddhist counterparts to the Friends invoked the language of spiritual and moral light.

Niebuhr would have had the same disdain for the pacifism of Day, his fellow Manhattan resident (although in a harder and more hardened neighborhood). He would have deigned her nonviolence naïve about uprooting collective evil without the sharp scythe of power. Merton once leapt to Day's defense after she had been arrested, stripped, and had to borrow "a light wrap" from sex workers to receive communion in jail. Given the lengths to which her solidarity took her, Merton says, "I lose all inclination to take seriously the self-complacent nonsense of those who consider her kind of pacifism sentimental."[208] Day, of course, needed no defenders since she would have no truck with any form of paternalism.

> Let those who talk of softness, of sentimentality, come to live with us in cold, unheated houses in the slums. Let them come to live with the criminal, the unbalanced, the degraded, the perverted.... Let them live with rats, with vermin, bed bugs, roaches, lice.... Let their flesh be mortified by cold, by dirt, by vermin; let their eyes be mortified by the sight of bodily excretions, diseased limbs, eyes, noses, mouths. Let their noses be mortified by the smells of sewage, decay, and rotten flesh.... Let their ears be mortified by harsh and screaming voices, by the constant coming and going of people living herded together with no privacy. Let their taste be mortified by the constant eating of insufficient food cooked in huge quantities for hundreds of people.... Then when they have lived with these comrades, with these sights and sounds, let our critics talk of sentimentality.[209]

Such a bombardment of the senses left no room in any inn for dreamy ideals.

Many popular ideals crumble in the face of hard truths. While others portrayed the US as a new Zion in a hard-edged age, Stringfellow painted Nixon's America—like all nations—as an apocalyptic, cataclysmic Babylon.[210] Principalities and powers, institutions and ideologies, nations and cultures could not be redeemed, and the power of death held sway over the world. Even so, he always offered hope. No esoteric wisdom, no magical

---

207. Ibid., 47.
208. Merton, *Nonviolent Alternative*, 226.
209. Day, *By Little*, 263–64.
210. Stringfellow, *Ethic for Christians*, 54; Niebuhr hints at the same, *Irony of American History*, 160.

formula, no strategic genius could defeat evil, but Christians like Trocmé reminded Stringfellow that the simplest spiritual practices had the power to resist Nazi hegemony. For Stringfellow, the Word did not triumph over death and its principalities only in some final conflagration; paradoxically, the Word triumphed daily. At the height of the apartheid system in South Africa, when it seemed historically impossible, Tutu prophesied that the racist regime would fall. Trocmé, Stringfellow, and Tutu agree with Fox that light outlasts darkness, with Julian that all will be well, and that governments that defy God will inevitably find themselves in the junkyard of history.

Rauschenbusch may have been at times lost in effusiveness, but his ebullient dreams—like King's two generations later—were not for any lack of thorns in his flesh. On the contrary, his hope was fed by his pastoral work—as hard as Day's—in an impoverished community. It was kindled in physical pain and personal suffering, including hearing loss at an early age.[211] Muste chose hardship after hardship, risk after risk. Enacting Gandhi's idea that "non-violence laughs at the might of the tyrant,"[212] Muste urged smiles to combat machine guns and remained calm when beaten physically or bombarded by ridicule. In spite of Niebuhr's contentions, there are no correlations between a hard life and his kind of hard message.

Yet years later Hallie revised his assessment of Trocmé's village of Le Chambon. If he does not completely unsee it, he at least resees it. On his initial discovery, he thought "that by becoming interested in it—assimilating it, imitating it, mimicking it—I might be saved." It made him "a different person for a while." The villagers' love even for their enemies awed him. But he believed as well that not even a thousand such villages would defeat Nazism. Hallie, with his three Battle Stars for his military service in World War II, says, "It took decent murderers like me to do it. . . . The cruelty that I perpetrated willingly was the only way to stop the cruel march that I and others like me were facing."[213] He admires the excellence of Le Chambon but also the efficiency of the US army. For him, Le Chambon was a light shining in darkness, but also a light that could not undo darkness.

Compared to Day, Rauschenbusch, Stringfellow, and Muste, Niebuhr led most of his professional life in an ivory tower. Given the chance, Niebuhr might have rebutted that academia (like Merton's desert) gave him a perspective others lacked. But for them, as for Tutu, Chávez, Gandhi, and Lester, human depravity and collective power were cruelly and daily obvious. They would have quibbled with Niebuhr and Augustine with their one-note

---

211. Minus, *Walter Rauschenbusch*.
212. Gandhi, *Non-violent*, 57.
213. Hallie, "Cruelty," 127–28.

view of human nature, but ultimately their argument, like Sojourner Truth's, was less about the breadth of human nature than the depth of *God's* nature and the unpredictable power of God's love. Their point, like Hallie's original observation, is that light shines in the darkness, and the darkness does not, cannot, and will not overcome it. And that *alone* is a stirring revelation of a very great light.

Ruusbroec says that what is writ large in the world is found in small print in the soul. The light in the human soul is thoroughly mixed with evil, but "in the abyss of this darkness in which the loving spirit has died to itself, God's revelation and eternal life have their origin, for in this darkness an incomprehensible light is born and shines forth. . . . In the simple bareness which envelops all things," people "feel and find" themselves "to be nothing other than the same light" they see.[214] People see and feel and become the light. Underhill mirrors Ruusbroec: what is true of the soul is true of the world. She asserts, in 1939, "Even this pain and evil and the world's dark future we are to realize as enfolded in a deeper, imperishable life; and it is when we see it thus, from God's side, that we deal with its problems best."[215] Even as history's most destructive war was beginning, she saw the cruel, violent, and hateful world as Julian's hazelnut—created, preserved, and loved.

This is *mystical resistance*, not only to the world, but to the twice-born's one-dimensional worldview. The mystic's love for the world is not an aloof blessing of the world's social structures, still less codependence with or coronations of status quos. But to the mystic the world bathed in light is also the world as it is. Mystics like Seraphim, Symeon, George Fox, and Teresa experience light as *overwhelming*. They insist that light is not overcome by darkness. Catherine praises God because "even in the darkness of hell your mercy shines."[216]

But they leave unanswered the follow-up questions: does light overcome darkness? In a world of pirates and princes, principalities and powers, corporations and nations—bands of robbers, one and all—is the great ocean of uncreated light an *overpowering* light or an *enduring* one?

MEDITATION: KEYNOTES, CONFERENCES, AND WORKSHOPS

The eternal keynote speaker is at it again. The speaker's name changes. The speaker's face changes. The keynote speech remains the same. The speaker

---

214. Ruusbroec, *Spiritual Espousals*, 147.
215. Underhill, *Modern Guide*, 201.
216. Catherine, *Dialogue*, 72.

is going the way of many a keynote speaker—the way of all fleshly hopes—at many a conference on justice, at many a workshop on peace. He is saying, if only we can get others to believe as we believe, peace will be at hand. If only this happens, if only that takes place, if only this person is elected, if only that cause succeeds, *the* breakthrough we have awaited for all of the millennia will be upon us. The nation will realize its deepest vocation. The world will be made new.

I have heard too many keynote addresses to believe in salvation by conference. I have attended conferences and workshops. I have organized them. I have spoken at them. We gather at a spiritual-political revival meeting. We hear good news. We renew our faith. We rededicate ourselves at the altar call and are sent out on a divine mission. I know the practical reasons to be here—to learn, to alleviate isolation, to build community, to repair despair. But I wonder if the distance between information and transformation is not wider than even the greatest skeptic can gauge.

Yet I recall people: a thirty-something Anglo at a racial awareness conference two decades ago. A self-identified conservative who enjoyed the visible contradiction of his appearance—his long, jet-black ponytail intentionally belied his politics. He was there because he had been ruffled by the apparent contradiction of seeing an African American man jogging in his 99.9 percent lily-white neighborhood. What particularly disturbed him was yet another contradiction between his reaction and his prejudice-free self-image. He had silently asked himself, "What's *he* doing here?" So he asked us, where did that thought come from?

I recall a conference in 1984 when Orwell's imagination unnerved me less than Reagan's reality. Two keynote speakers advocated radical social change. One spoke glowingly of a new Spirit about to dramatically sweep the land, the other of the cross and the peacemaker's resilient witness. In the next decade, I never saw the Spirit sweep the land, but I certainly saw many a cross.

Now, decades later, it is hard to get keyed up for a speech, a conference, or a workshop. I'm an old dog; I suppose I can learn new facts. Maybe I don't need the renewal. Maybe I need it more than I know.

But I remember a workshop leader telling a story of being a teenager on a youth retreat. Nothing remotely spiritual happened during the retreat, maybe for others, but not for him. Then—as he addressed us, his voice hushed and his eyes glistened—on the ride home from the retreat, when the bus stopped and the youth disembarked for a snack, he saw each person near him suddenly drenched in divine light—light around them, in them, shining through them.

He told us the story and invited us to share. Others, voices also hushed, shared memories of epiphanies that illumined our lives. Voices equally honest, equally sacred, equally still said they had never had any kind of epiphany—no great light, no profound opening, no sudden awakening. I shared my teenaged experience in our youth group when, as the priest shared his faith simply, directly, and plainly, I felt a warm shower in me, passing through me, staying in me, an extraordinary warmth. It was assurance that I was listening to the truth, direct, plain, and simple. Other experiences followed in other years that have taken my breath away and made me sit bolt upright in the middle of the night—epiphanies, warmth, words. Each of them, even without uncreated light, was undeniably a light given to me, and although I had never told the story before, not given for me alone.

Maybe that is why we need speeches and conferences and workshops. Whether it is the analytical eye or the spiritual eye or the one that sees whether or not it is open, we gather because *no light*, whatever its nature, whatever its source, is given to any of us alone.

5

Footprints on the Water

Fix your gaze on the orb of the sun according to the degree of your visual power, only to enjoy its rays and not to investigate its course, lest you be deprived even of your modest vision.
 —Isaac of Nineveh[1]

It is God alone who has immortality and dwells in unapproachable light, whom no one has ever seen or can see.
 —1 Timothy 6:16

We look not at what can be seen but at what cannot be seen; for what can be seen is temporary, but what cannot be seen is eternal.
 —2 Corinthians 4:18

Go where you cannot go; see where you cannot see;
Hear where there is no sound, you are where God does speak.
 —Angelus Silesius[2]

---

1. Isaac of Nineveh, *On Ascetical Life*, 72.
2. Silesius, *Cherubinic Wanderer*, 47.

We do not have technical solutions or infallible remedies. We wish to feel the problems, perceive the demands, share the agonies, discover the ways, and cooperate in the solutions.
—Medellín Conference[3]

Where there is love, there is seeing.
—Richard of St. Victor[4]

Then I saw all the work of God, that no one can find out what is happening under the sun. However much they may toil in seeking, they will not find out; even though those who are wise claim to know, they cannot find it out.
—Ecclesiastes 8:17

One knows not what God is. Not spirit and not light,
Not one, truth, unity, not what we call divine,
Not reason and not wisdom, not goodness, love, or will,
No thing, no no-thing either, not being or concern.
God is what I or you, or any other creature
Has never come to know before we were created.
—Angelus Silesius[5]

One who knows does not speak,
One who speaks does not know.
—Tao te Ching[6]

One who sees grows silent.
—Rumi[7]

My God,

3. Hennelly, *Liberation Theology*, 92.
4. Richard of St. Victor, *Twelve Patriarchs*, 65.
5. Silesius, *Cherubinic Wanderer*, 88.
6. Tzu, *Tao Te Ching*, 25.
7. Rumi, *Essential Rumi*, 198.

how near You are to me
and how far I am from You!
—Ibn 'Ata' Illah[8]

Cease from measuring heaven with a tiny piece of reed . . .
—D. T. Suzuki[9]

God is a desert to be entered and loved, never an object to be grasped or understood.
—Belden Lane[10]

MEDITATION: DRIVING IN THE FOG

Morning coastal fog is nothing unusual but—wispy, clingy, and gray—today it is unusually thick. There is nothing to grasp, nothing to hold, but something very real obscures my vision. There is a transient, ephemeral quality to fog, but trying to see through it is daunting and worrisome. Driving through it this morning I could easily miss seeing a jogger, a toddler, even a car. When I teach Zac how to drive, I will have to tell him about driving in the fog. Go slow. Prepare to stop.

A few months ago I was taking a few of his fifteen-year-old friends to a movie as one of them fretted about learning to drive. I said: don't worry; it's like *Batman Begins*: be aware of your surroundings. He said, "But on the road there aren't any ninjas jumping out at you with swords." So true! But in fog normal street traffic is more than enough to make you squint and wrinkle your brow.

One Sunday night long, long ago, as I drove seventy miles back to college, I entered fog thicker than any I had ever seen. Growing up near the coast, I had assumed a kind of predictability about fog: mornings, near the coast, burning off before noon. But this inland fog, late at night, was new to me. It invoked anxiety as thick as the fog. I had no idea what to do. My familiar highway had turned into an uncertain path. Once in, it made no sense to turn around; the fog could break in 500 miles or 50 feet. It made no sense to stop; some car might ram into mine. It made no sense to pull over to the side of the road; would I find it and park or steer blindly into a

---

8. Illah, *Book of Wisdom*, 121.
9. Suzuki, *Manual of Zen*, 103.
10. Lane, *Solace of Fierce Landscapes*, 12.

ditch? It also didn't make sense to keep going. I cut my speed from 65 miles an hour to 10 and less, inching forward timidly, worried that even at 3 miles an hour I was courting disaster.

I couldn't see the road, the lanes, or the lines. I couldn't see the end of the hood. Only the fog illumined by my headlights was visible. My windshield wipers wagged back and forth uselessly. I rolled down my window and stuck my head out like a panting dog as if desperation would be its own reward. Finally, after an eternity five minutes long, I spied the small red taillights of another car as I crept up behind it. Once there, I relaxed. That was all I needed: another lemming. In a few minutes, someone else joined our lost caravan and I was no longer the caboose.

A few years later I found myself with two friends in a Wisconsin thunderstorm. We were at a picnic and when the downpour began, we leapt up in a Californian's panic, jumped into the car, and tried to flee. Of course, the locals stayed in place knowing that the storm front would pass in thirty, forty, or sixty minutes. We knew little of the meteorology of the Midwest, and not much more of the meteorology of life. We drove down a two-lane road with open fields below us on both sides. The cosmic percussion of thunder accompanied blinding sheets of lightning. Stripping off our shirts, we wiped the inside of the windshield, fogged up by our sweat and fear.

Of course I survived both times and other times, humbled, chastened, and best of all, alive. When I teach Zac to drive, I must mention fog—the blind explaining blindness to the blind.

In centuries past, explorers without maps crossed continents and oceans not knowing what was beyond the next mountain range or the next swell, not knowing if this particularly trying portion of the journey—the storm, the strait, the forest, the wilderness—would ever end or lead somewhere better or worse, sooner or later. In some sense, each of us has to find our way, but there is something comforting in knowing that we are not the only ones getting lost. Even if we cannot see them, our neighbors are with us. And so, unseeing and unknowing, in fog and downpour, in cloud and night, in uncertainty and anxiety, we make our way, not knowing if we are making our way.

THE UNKNOWABLE GOD

They are like warning signs rising from silence to a scream: Construction Zone, Hard Hat Area, Enter at Your Own Risk, Do Not Enter, Narrow Road, Winding Road, No Trespassing, Danger Ahead, Wrong Way, Yield, Slow,

Stop. Each sign alerts us to the fact that we are trying to map a black hole with a surveyor's antique tools.

There are awakenings, openings, and epiphanies: a voice at midnight, calm in the kitchen, a piercing light, a penetrating darkness, a wrenching from our half-tied vision, and the most ordinary faith that enables us to see as clearly as the most profound mystical enlightenment. These are the steps on the stairways to the summits of the kataphatic tradition. But the apophatic tradition negates all ladders, all spiritual benchmarks, and all measurable progress. It insists that every revelation is both an icon and an idol, and that the sum total of all epiphanies will not tear heaven open a single millimeter or illuminate the earth with multiplying shafts of light connecting all dots in a brilliant tightly knit truth.

Evagrius sums up these warning signs: "Never define the divine."[11] Pseudo-Dionysius, the iconic pioneer of iconoclasm whose own slippery identity is a parable for the elusiveness of God's, says "the more [my argument] climbs, the more language falters, and when it has passed up and beyond the ascent, it will turn silent completely, since it will finally be at one with God who is indescribable."[12] Pseudo-Dionysius says that God's light "drives from souls the ignorance and the error" and prepares us with the spiritual weeding of purgation. This light "clears away the fog of ignorance from the eyes of the mind and it stirs and unwraps those covered over by the burden of darkness." Then, right then, as we feel our "longing for light begin to grow," God gives more—darkness.[13]

Images help us in the early stages of our pilgrimage, but at some point we realize that God is beyond definition, allusion, articulation, or even sighs or cries or moans too momentous for words. As Stringfellow renounces all ideologies as idolatrous, Pseudo-Dionysius insists that all theologies, images, and icons are at best shaky fingers pointing at a sliver of the moon. The great treasure of Jesus' parable (Matt 13:44) is ever out of sight and never within reach of our minds. Even after the most revealing epiphany, God remains inexplicable. As Bernard says, we gaze at God's majesty "in admiration, not in scrutiny."[14] If the mystics' stammering explanations of openings defy clarification, so much more so does their Source. Gregory of Nazianzus, irritated with the arrogance of speculative thinkers, turns angrily against constructive theology itself as he warns that people can be

---

11. McGinn, *Foundations of Mysticism*, 155.
12. Pseudo-Dionysius, *Complete Works*, 139.
13. Ibid., 75.
14. Bernard, *Song of Songs III*, 155.

"stricken with madness for prying into the mystery of God."[15] Ruusbroec coolly counsels that whoever wants to know "what God is . . . would be doing something forbidden and would go mad."[16] The mystical tradition tucks a nascent Icarus story within every holy quest. We know the unknown. We know nothing else. In it we live and move and have our being.

In a clever rhetorical flourish in his Athens sermon (Acts 17:22–31), the Lukan Paul praises its citizens for believing in anything and everything, and he exalts their "unknown God." Then he tries to hook and reel in the unformed faith of his listeners to something innovative, bold, shocking, and new. Having given their unknown gods their rhetorical due, he proclaims that God has appeared in Jesus Christ. But even the known includes dimensions of the unknown, like space between planets. As the historical Paul says: we see God in part, not face to face (1 Cor 13:12). As Gregory and Ruusbroec broadly warn, to do so is dangerous. So God tells Moses to push the people away from Mt. Sinai lest they perish (Exod 19:12). To see, touch, or know too much of the divine can be less a sweet treat or a pleasant after-dinner drink than a shortcut to rigor mortis (Exod 33:20). So in his enthusiastic entrance into Jerusalem David plans to keep the ark of the covenant nearby until Uzzah stumbles against it and drops dead. Sobered on the spot, David starts to explore the whereabouts of a more distant storage facility (2 Sam 6:1–11).

The apophatic tradition does not debate the Lukan Paul, nor diminish the iconic, the incarnational, or the Abrahamic recital of revelations. But it maintains that there is a God beyond all gods, the inaccessible Godhead, the kabbalist's *ein sof* that is eternally beyond human comprehension. Nicholas of Cusa compares human knowledge to a polygon that tries to reshape itself to fit a circular God; no matter how many angles we add to the polygon, it never fits the circle.[17] He says that the most we can hope for is "learned"[18] and "sacred ignorance."[19] Symeon, the recipient of such powerful epiphanies, calls God "invisible, unapproachable, inapprehensible, and intangible,"[20] or on second thought "incomprehensible . . . inexpressible . . . uncontainable . . . unapproachable,"[21] or on still further consideration, "completely unexplainable, invisible, unapproachable, and unknowable, untouchable,

---

15. Lossky, *Mystical Theology*, 55.
16. Ruusbroec, *Spiritual Espousals*, 62.
17. Nicholas of Cusa, *Selected Spiritual Writings*, 91, 180.
18. Ibid., 87, 89, 107, passim.
19. Ibid., 126, 131.
20. Symeon, *Divine Eros*, 84.
21. Ibid., 127–28.

impalpable, wholly inapprehensible."²² In another recital of negatives, John Chrysostom describes our unknowing in untraceable spirals: "We call God the inexpressible, the unthinkable God, the invisible, the inapprehensible; who quells the power of human speech and transcends the grasp of mortal thought; inaccessible to the angels, unbeheld of the Seraphim, unimagined of the Cherubim, invisible to principalities and authorities and powers, and, in a word, to all creation."²³ In staccato couplets, Angelus Silesius summarizes the practical ramifications of Chrysostom's observation:

> God is pure naught, untouched by time and space
> The more you reach for God, the more God will escape.²⁴

> The more you know of God, the more you will confess
> That what God is God's self, you can name less and less.²⁵

Pseudo-Dionysius even conjures up a term for God that sounds like a comic book action hero: "the Superunknowable."²⁶ Intermixed with the Abrahamic sequence of revelations of divine presence are the mysteries of agonizing absence; alongside episodes of divine speech are instances of bewildering silence. We can know something of God's sporadically self-revealing *energies* but nothing of God's unchangeably unknowable *essence*.

It is not only God who is masked in obscurity. Everything around God consumes clarity like a sun's corona erupting with fiery opaqueness. The intimate, inner geography of God, and the way into it, is utterly confounding. This way is not neatly laid out with manicured mazes or straight-arrow signs pointing to holy mountains, or even to ladders leading to other ladders to yet more ladders like an Escher drawing. The way to God is to be rid of all ladders, all images, all knowledge, all ways. As Ephrem writes:

> God has names that are perfect and exact,
> and God has names that are borrowed and transient;
> these latter God quickly puts on and quickly takes off.²⁷

Every step is tentative; every definition erasable; every conclusion inconclusive. The fabric of every epiphany has the potential for fabrication. The same illumination that can lead toward God can also, when decontextualized,

---

22. Ibid., 337.
23. Otto, *Idea of the Holy*, 180.
24. Silesius, *Cherubinic Wanderer*, 40.
25. Ibid., 105.
26. Pseudo-Dionysius, *Complete Works*, 53.
27. Brock, *Luminous Eye*, 63.

misinterpreted, or universalized, lead to circuitous, dangerous, and endless detours.

Gandhi would call this, and all of life, an "experiment with truth." Neither a philosophical hobby nor academic research, it is an exploration poles apart from the pretentious Marxist delusion of scientific social analysis. When it comes to truth, there are no specimens to pin under a microscope. Gandhi's personal-communal-spiritual-political experiment with "Truth" (God) is less like climbing Jacob's ladder than Jacob's wounding wrestling match with an unnamed stranger (Gen 28:10–17, 32:22–31). Borrowing a familiar Pauline phrase, Gandhi describes the adequacy of his inadequate efforts: "We neither know God nor God's law, save through the glass darkly. But the faint glimpse of the law is sufficient to fill me with joy, hope and faith in the future."[28] His peeks do no more to define God than a handheld camera can capture a continental expanse, but they reveal enough: "The fleeting glimpses that I have been able to have of truth can hardly convey an idea of the indescribable luster of truth, a million times more intense than that of the Sun.... In fact, what I have caught is only the faintest glimmer of that mighty effulgence. I feel the warmth and sunshine of Truth's presence."[29]

Gandhi was raised to repeat God's name simply, like the instruction of *The Cloud of Unknowing* to choose a "single syllable" in prayer like *God* or *love*[30] and pray it with the intensity of someone crying *fire* or *help*.[31] So Gandhi learned to pray with the singular focus of a terrified child: "When a child, my nurse taught me to repeat Ramanama [a god] whenever I felt afraid or miserable, and it has been second nature with me, with growing knowledge and advancing years"; the word "is in my heart, if not actually on my lips" twenty-four hours a day—"It has been my savior."[32]

If Augustine experiences this intense love *in* all things, Bernard finds it *above* all things.[33] Bernard says that although God entered his soul many times, he could not say when it happened: "I have felt God present, I remember God has been with me, I have sometimes even had a premonition of God's coming, but never have I felt God's coming or departure."[34] It did not happen by the eyes, he says, because God has no color, nor by

---

28. Gandhi, *Way to God*, 86.
29. Ibid., 93.
30. *Cloud of Unknowing*, 76. One syllable is twice as good as two (147).
31. Ibid., 148.
32. Gandhi, *Way to God*, 84.
33. The Collect for the Sixth Sunday of Easter speaks of "loving you in all things and above all things" (*Book of Common Prayer*, 225).
34. Underhill, *Mystics of the Church*, 86.

the ears, because God's approach is silent. God does not enter by the nostrils or the mouth or by touch. Like a Zen master, Bernard says that God's path is "traceless"; yet he knows when God has entered because God "has quickened my sleeping soul, and aroused, softened, and goaded my heart, which was torpid and hard as a stone."[35] Hugh of St. Victor says that the "Beloved" visits but "in an invisible shape," "incomprehensibly," and "disguised": "God comes to touch you, not to be seen by you; to arouse you, not to be comprehended by you. God comes not to give God's self wholly, but to be tasted by you: not to fulfill your desire, but to lead upwards your affection." God gives "a foretaste" of the delights to come, not the "plenitude of perfect satisfaction"; God allows us to learn "how sweet" God is, but the real treasure is not yet "seen and possessed."[36]

In spite of her humorous images of flying toads and her formidable personal store of soul-rousing epiphanies, Teresa of Ávila stresses the subtlety and mystery of divine awakenings. The experience of God, she says, is as if food enters your stomach even though you have not eaten. It is like an illiterate person suddenly acquiring "all existing knowledge," not knowing how, having never learned the alphabet.[37] It is not as if God waits passively and patiently (or impatiently) for us to seize the initiative in a game of hide-and-seek. The ninth-century Sufi Bayezid Bistami writes, "For thirty years I went in search of God, and when at the end of that time I opened my eyes, I discovered that it was God who had been looking for me."[38] Julian of Norwich bases all her theological insights on a powerful "showing," Christ crucified, the most corporeal and indelible image in the Christian tradition; exploring that revelation was her life's work. Yet, like Teresa, she says we need to be as satisfied with what God conceals as with what God reveals. We "rejoice" in *God*; we don't revel in revelations or lament the unknown.[39]

When Ramon Lull asks where the Beloved has been, the answer is: "In the absence of your memory and in the ignorance of your understanding."[40] Ibn 'Ata' Illah contrasts the contradictions of the knowable and the unknowable.

> How can it be conceived that something veils God,
>   Since God is the One who manifests everything?
> How can it be conceived that something veils God,

---

35. Ibid.; cf. Ezek 11:19.
36. Underhill, *Mysticism*, 245.
37. Teresa, *Life of Teresa*, 251–52.
38. Buber, *Ecstatic Utterances*, 19.
39. Julian, *Showings*, 235.
40. Lull, *Romancing God*, 18.

> Since God is the One who is manifest *through* everything?
> How can it be conceived that something veils God,
> Since God is the One who is manifest *in* everything?
> How can it be conceived that something veils God,
> Since God is the Manifest *to* everything?
> How can it be conceived that something veils God,
> Since God was the Manifest *before* the existence of anything?
> How can it be conceived that something veils God,
> Since God is more manifest than anything?
> How can it be conceived that something veils God,
> Since God is the One alongside of whom there is nothing?
> How can it be conceived that something veils God,
> Since God is nearer to you than anything else?
> How can it be conceived that something veils God,
> Since, were it not for God, the existence of everything would not have been manifest?[41]

Another contradiction brings this point to its paradoxical conclusion:

> Only God's extreme nearness to you
> is what veils God from you.[42]

The Abrahamic faiths share chronicles of revelations yet they find the invisible and incomprehensible equally profound.

No matter how overpowering our experience of God, there is something *beyond* it. Pseudo-Dionysius says there comes a point in the mystical quest when we break free "from what sees and is seen" as we plunge into the "darkness of unknowing." Here we cast off all conceptions and ideas; here we are received into what is impossible to grasp or contemplate. Then we belong completely to God "who is beyond everything."[43] The anonymously written *The Cloud of Unknowing* follows the pseudonymous Dionysius in saying, "we know by unknowing"; we find God in a "cloud of unknowing."[44] If God is to be understood at all, it is never by thought, only by love.[45] Citing Aristotle, John of the Cross notes: "as the sun is total darkness to the eyes of a bat, so the brightest light in God is complete darkness to our intellect."[46]

---

41. Illah, *Book of Wisdom*, 50 (italics his).
42. Ibid., 88.
43. Pseudo-Dionysius, *Complete Works*, 137.
44. *Cloud of Unknowing*, 230.
45. Ibid., 72.
46. John of the Cross, *Collected Works*, 128.

The "divine essence" is "alien to every mortal eye and hidden from every human intellect."[47]

Gregory of Nyssa's model of the spiritual pilgrimage unfolds in image after image of obscurity. We move from a moonlit desert night to a fog-covered mountain into an impenetrably thick cloud.[48] Johannes Tauler offers the paradox that mystical knowledge is "ineffable darkness and yet it is essential light." It is a trackless wasteland. There are no "landmarks." There is "no road." "To come there the soul must be led above itself, beyond itself, beyond all its comprehension and understanding." Here in a blessed wasteland far from T. S. Eliot's, the soul "can drink from the stream at its very sources, from those true and essential waters. Here the water is sweet and fresh and pure, as every stream is sweet at its source, before it has lost its cool freshness and purity."[49]

Building on the contradictions imbedded in these layers of obscurity, Lull says that even as a cloud separates us from God, "Love shone through the cloud that had come between the Lover and the Beloved, and it made the cloud as bright as the moon is at night and as brilliant as the midday sun."[50] *The Cloud* witnesses to the same reality: "No matter what you do, this darkness and this cloud is between you and your God and because of it you can neither see God clearly with your reason in the light of understanding, nor can you feel God with your affection in the sweetness of love."[51] What then are we to do?

> Leave this everywhere and this something alone and choose this nowhere and this nothing. Do not be concerned if your mind cannot reason about this nothing; for certainly I love it much the better. It is so valuable a thing in itself that no one can reason about it. This nothing can be felt more easily than it can be seen, for it brings a blinding darkness to those who look at it for even a little while. Nevertheless, to tell the truth, we are more blinded in our feeling for it when we have great spiritual light than when we are in darkness and lack physical sight.[52]

---

47. Ibid., 417.
48. Lane, *Solace of Fierce Landscapes*, 26.
49. Leech, *Experiencing God*, 177–78.
50. Lull, *Romancing God*, 23. *The Cloud of Unknowing* says sometimes God will "send out a beam of spiritual light piercing the *cloud of unknowing* that is between you and God, and God will show you some of God's secret ways of which we neither can nor may speak" (125, italics mine).
51. *Cloud of Unknowing*, 62.
52. Ibid., 224.

The Cloud questions even its own definitions: "And who is it that calls this nothing? Surely it is our outer self and not our inner self. Our inner self calls it All, for it teaches [us] to know the essence of all things."[53] Reflecting on the *via negativa*, Vladimir Lossky says that divine incomprehensibility is not a matter of "prohibitions" against knowledge; rather, the apophatic tradition seeks to "transcend all concepts, every sphere of philosophical speculation" and reach a point in which "knowledge is transformed into ignorance, the theology of concepts into contemplation, [and] dogmas into experience of ineffable mysteries."[54]

This is Pascal's "fire" that disdains philosophy; this is Rumi seeing flames erupt from philosophy books like Moses's burning bush or Abba Joseph's fingers. This reality is beyond harmful things, beyond holy things, beyond perception, beyond concepts, beyond comprehension, beyond theology, beyond faith, beyond sight, beyond feeling, beyond imagining, beyond horizons. Vision begins when we lose sight. Pseudo-Dionysius says that "above Light" we enter darkness; "beyond all vision and knowledge" we begin to see.[55] We do not seek enlightenment or virtue, still less ecstasy or insight. Shneur Zalman of Ladi interrupted his prayers to tell God, "I do not want your paradise. I do not want your coming world, I want You, and You only."[56]

Struck blind, we begin to see. John of the Cross says we are illumined by darkness more than light.[57] Like the blind, we "lean on dark faith" and "rest on nothing" we test, taste, touch, or understand; perceptions become "a darkness" that leads us astray.[58] The heart of his poem *Dark Night* is filled with images of clandestine secrecy.

> One dark night,
> Fired with love's urgent longings . . . I went out *unseen* . . . .
> In *darkness* . . . .
> By the *secret* ladder, *disguised* . . . .
> In *darkness and concealment* . . . .
> In *secret*, for no one saw me,
> Nor did I look at anything.[59]

---

53. Ibid., 224–25.
54. Lossky, *Mystical Theology*, 238.
55. Pseudo-Dionysius, *Complete Works*, 138.
56. Buber, *Tales: Early Masters*, 267.
57. John of the Cross, *Collected Works*, 111.
58. Ibid., 113.
59. Ibid., 68–69 (italics mine).

Yet even in this uncharted terrain, no one—not John or Dionysius or the author of *The Cloud*—can resist the temptation to scotch-tape images to a greased God. Like Gregory of Nyssa delineating one form of obscurity after another, Ruusbroec, without defining the divine, describes three phases of unknowing. In the first we "*rest*" in God; in the second we are "*falling asleep* in God"; in the third we feel we have "*died* and . . . become one with God."[60] How do we progress? What methods do we use? Rest, sleep, and death.

Pseudo-Dionysius provides the primary image for this hidden way. Like a sculptor, we seek an anti-image as we "carve a statue"—we "remove every obstacle to the pure view of the hidden image, and simply by this act of clearing aside" we find its hidden beauty.[61] John says we can carve an image of God (apophatic) but never paint it (kataphatic).[62] Eckhart adds, "If artists want to make an image from wood or stone, they do not put the image into the wood, but they cut away the chips that had hidden and concealed the image: they *give* nothing to the wood but *take* from it, cutting away the overlay and removing the dross, and that which was hidden under it shines forth."[63] We move forward not by accumulation and addition but by subtraction. Instead of adding image to image, insight to insight, and epiphany to epiphany to create a picture of God from the edges of a billion-piece, city-sized jigsaw puzzle, we remove images, knowledge, and wisdom to enter a beautiful, blind, and blinding intimacy.

Ruusbroec has the chutzpah not only to describe the spiritual black hole where we meet God as "Darkness and Nakedness and Nothingness," he tells us what happens in this climactic meeting. In this Darkness we get lost; in this Nakedness, we lose perception and are "transfigured and penetrated by a simple light"; in this Nothingness, all activity comes to naught, as we are "vanquished by the working of God's [abyss of] love."[64]

The mystics have their own version of the African American song "keep your eyes on the prize": settle for nothing other than God. This is not some esoteric ideal too alien and pure for the harshness of history. In practical terms, in the midst of persecution, George Fox advises Friends not to look at "temptations, confusions, corruptions, but at the Light which discovers them and makes them manifest; and with the same Light you may . . . receive power to stand against them."[65] Were the Light constant and

---

60. Ruusbroec, *Spiritual Espousals*, 183 (italics mine).
61. Pseudo-Dionysius, *Complete Works*, 138.
62. John of the Cross, *Collected Works*, 632.
63. Eckhart, *Sermons & Treatises III*, 109 (italics original).
64. Happold, *Mysticism*, 87.
65. Fox, *Journal*, 320.

overwhelming, this would be easy. But the mystics knew that sometimes we see only darkness and hear only silence. What do we do then? Enter the abyss! Be grounded in the black hole! As *The Cloud* (anticipating Shneur Zalman) says to both the persecuted and the privileged, "if a thought should arise . . . between you and that darkness, and if it should ask you, 'What are you seeking and what do you wish to have?' you are to answer that it is God that you wish to have. 'God I covet, God I seek, and nothing but God.'"[66]

We prefer reassurance, encouragement, landmarks, benchmarks, signs, and maps. But in an image like Tauler's, Ephrem insists that God's bottomlessness is a blessing: "A thirsty person rejoices because he has drunk: he is not grieved because he proved incapable of drinking the fountain dry. Let the fountain vanquish your thirst, your thirst should not vanquish the fountain! If your thirst comes to an end while the fountain has not been diminished, then you can drink again whenever you are thirsty; whereas if the fountain had been drained dry once you had had your fill, your victory over it would have proved to your own harm."[67] The truth that God is wrapped in clouded obscurity is as splendid a mystery as the most piercing and penetrating light. In one of Ephrem's hymns, he offers a surprising refrain: "Glory to Your hiddenness!"[68] The dense cloud, the dark night, and the unknowable God are in no way regrettable. They *magnify* God's glory.

Merton gives modern voice to this ancient tradition in prayer, prose, and poetry. In his "Fire Watch" he confesses that questions become glassy smooth and answers icy slick. In *Thoughts in Solitude*, in one of his most plainspoken prayers, he captures the integrity, the reality, and even the *need* to be lost:

> My Lord God, I have no idea where I am going. I do not see the road ahead of me. I cannot know for certain where it will end. Nor do I really know myself, and the fact that I think I am following your will does not mean that I am actually doing so. But I believe that the desire to please you does in fact please you. And I hope I have that desire in all that I am doing. I hope that I will never do anything apart from that desire. And I know that if I do this you will lead me by the right road, though I may know nothing about it. Therefore I will trust you always though I may seem to be lost and in the shadow of death. I will not fear, for you are ever with me, and you will never leave me to face my perils alone.[69]

66. *Cloud of Unknowing*, 74.
67. Brock, *Luminous Eye*, 51.
68. Ephrem, *Hymns*, 386.
69. Merton, *Thoughts in Solitude*, 103.

More analytically, Merton says that trying to assess one's spiritual progress is like a child riding on a night train through a tunnel: you can't tell whether you are going forward or backward.[70] Yet Merton did not find the unknowable disconcerting. Indeed, it is a dwelling place as holy as a temple:

> Night is our diocese and silence is our ministry
> Poverty our charity and helplessness our tongue-tied sermon.[71]

Merton was immersed in this tradition, yet this tradition turns Merton's epiphanies—and all epiphanies—on their collective ears. Awakenings claim insight into ultimate truth, but the apophatic tradition demands a humbling purging—neither our thirst nor our epiphanies drain a fountain; each is but one sip of a boundless ocean! Lester says that once you see pacifism you cannot unsee it, but the apophatic tradition mutters softly that it is only by *unseeing* that we find anything. Merton says that "if only we could see," the world would be transformed. The apophatic tradition counters: the only way toward God and God's realm is to *unsee*.

THE UNSEEN REALM

When we "seek first" the realm of God we grope toward the unseen. We know what discrimination looks like—but equality? We know what exploitation looks like—but justice? No one has lived in a just society; no eye has seen it; no ear has heard of it. What is freedom? It means different things in different nations and cultures; it means one thing when Moses sets people free and another when Christ does it. We know what war's devastation looks like, but peace? We have seen victims of violence, hollow-eyed whether living or dead, on battlefields and street corners and shelters and in the discomfort of their own homes. Unless we live in incredibly privileged insularity, we see the daily damage of unjust structures; to truly *see* it is as much a spiritual discipline as prayer. Prophetic visions paint images of justice but, in practice, most activism carves away at injustice and only then do we see what lies beneath. We may yearn for a beloved community, but in practice we scoop away one form of injustice at a time. And we think, we hope, that when we are finished, what is left will look like our hopes. We are drawn forward by a hunger and a thirst for a righteousness we have barely touched, tasted, sensed, or seen.

Before the reformist thrust of Lyndon Johnson's administration was consumed by its war in Vietnam, and Johnson became a recalcitrant Jonah

---

70. Merton, *Ascent to Truth*, 228–29.
71. Merton, *Collected Poems*, 201.

refusing even in the belly of the whale to admit he was going the wrong way, visions of a "Great Society" seemed to fulfill decades of liberal yearning.[72] It was a brief attempt to legislate justice that progressives may regard with head-turning and heart-aching nostalgia. Johnson initiated his hopes for social transformation with a slew of programs in a "war on poverty."[73] Well-intentioned and often ill-conceived, the war on poverty was meant to be a new New Deal. It launched initiatives that got stuck in wads of sticky red tape and, in the long run, helped fuel a reactionary counterrevolution that still dominates American politics.

Writing in Harlem at the time, Stringfellow labeled himself a *Dissenter in a Great Society*. In his typically polemical style, Stringfellow lacerated both the intentions and the results—the heart and hands—of Johnson's reforms. But beyond his sociological critiques, his most profound unease with the Great Society was theological. His theological distress was anything but neoconservative or separatist-sectarian; he advocated "the orthodoxy of radical involvement,"[74] an incarnational ministry of the institutional church and individual Christians. His primary problems with the Great Society were its limits.

Writing of the sixties race crises—the civil rights movement, race "riots," and economic inequalities—Stringfellow criticized a popular liberal goal: integration. His was not a white man's amen to black separatism. To him, the proximate goal of *integration* fell well short of the ultimate goal of *reconciliation*. Reconciliation, he argues, is not "some occasional, unilateral, private happening" but a "profoundly political" reality. Sounding like Isaac of Nineveh, he says that reconciliation with God is impossible without reconciliation with oneself, with all people, "and with all things in the whole of creation."[75] There was no, is no, and can be no separate peace with God; there was no, is no, and can be no flight of the alone to the Alone. To Stringfellow, that is heresy, a blasphemy, and an abomination. Ever an ally of the civil rights movement, he maintains that even if other citizens are content with the "genuine integration of American public life," "Christians will not be satisfied"; Christians, he says, want more than a Great Society—they want a "*new* society."[76] Segregation was indeed "one of the works of death," but "integration is not the same thing as freedom from death."[77] As Under-

72. Branch, *Pillar of Fire*, 291.
73. Ibid., 488.
74. Stringfellow, *Dissenter*, 125–64.
75. Ibid., 130–31.
76. Ibid., 135 (italics mine).
77. Ibid., 139.

hill says that real Christians are always revolutionaries, Stringfellow says that even when a just cause prevails, Christians "will not be content but will be the first to complain against the 'new' status quo."[78] This is no accident of a particular moment in history: "The inherent, invariable, unavoidable, intentional, unrelenting posture of the Church in the world is one of radical protest and profound dissent toward the prevailing status quo of secular society, whatever that may be at any give time," even if some label it "a great society."[79] Christians insatiably seek first the realm of God.

Although his intense criticism was spurred by his creed that ideology always turns its adherents into pitiable stooges, Stringfellow's is not a lone voice. It is, in fact, a common Christian cry. Jacques Ellul gave voice to Stringfellow's demand for radical ideological fluidity even against the West's epitome of evil. Christians, Ellul says, must change sides as soon as "the revolutionary party assumes power; for the party will immediately begin to oppress the former oppressors." So when Allied forces and the French Resistance defeated Nazi occupiers and their Vichy confreres, liberation devolved into revenge. At that moment Christians should have moved "to the side of the erstwhile 'enemies'—the capitalists, the bourgeoisie, the collaborators, the Nazis . . .—because they are now the victims, they are now the poor and the humiliated."[80]

Oscar Romero professed a similar skittishness toward ideology. In the 1970s, as El Salvador skidded further into a collective heart of darkness, Romero, like Stringfellow, asserts that Christians cannot settle for anything less than the reign of God. The church, Romero says, ought to support progressive organizations, but the church also says to such movements: "it's not enough," only "redemption" is enough; political and social liberation is incomplete without personal and spiritual liberation.[81] In saying this, he was in synch with the Latin American theology of his time. At Puebla, the bishops assert that while the realm "comes to pass through historical realizations" it is not fully realized nor "exhausted" in them.[82] At Medellín, the bishops affirm the inherently unknowable quality of the realm: "This era requires clarity in order to see, lucidity in order to diagnose, and solidarity in order to act."[83] But as it is for Stringfellow, the revolution is endless: "Conversion ever remains an unfinished process on both the personal and

---

78. Ibid., 162.
79. Ibid., 142–43; see also Dancer, *Alien in Strange Land*, 154.
80. Ellul, *Violence*, 138–39.
81. Romero, *Violence of Love*, 102.
82. Eagleson and Scherper, *Puebla and Beyond*, 193.
83. Hennelly, *Liberation Theology*, 91.

societal levels."[84] No social structure ever fulfills the Christian's yearning for the realm. No policies ever win a Christian's ultimate loyalty. Romero not only sought a good society; like Maurin, he yearned for a society that makes it easier for people to be good.[85] Romero knew that it is not enough to amend political policies or tweak social structures. Because he vociferously opposed specific policies he was assassinated. But, as Stringfellow would dissent in every situation, Romero would be dangerous to *any* status quo. A bishop, he was also an agitator. Tutu—another bishop, another agitator—gives further witness to the Christian as a perpetual dissenter. He opposed apartheid. When apartheid fell, he criticized South Africa's new democratic government. He took part in the Truth and Reconciliation Commission because the death of apartheid and a new multiracial regime was not enough. South Africa needed *restorative* justice, redemption, and reconciliation.

King's political-spiritual growth reflects this common cry for more than historic social change. Even as he pressed for specific reforms—racial integration in the South, economic equality across the nation—as years passed, an antsy King grew increasingly "militant." The civil rights movement of the fifties slowly pried from the cold, white-sepulchered fingers of the status quo an end to the gratuitously abusive "indecency" of segregation, but as the movement advocated "equality,"[86] its popularity waned.

A master of rhetoric, King employs an unusual refrain in a Presidential Address to the Southern Christian Leadership Conference: "Let us be dissatisfied."[87] Compared to his ringing choruses in other speeches, it is a clarion clank. The structure of the phrase is grammatically passive, not active. The tone of the phrase is negative, not positive. But in its insistent resistance to the status quo and its rephrasing of his earlier call to the "creative maladjustment"[88] of "transformed nonconformists"[89] are the roots of perpetual revolution.

Siding with those who believe that the faithful are always hungry (Matt 5:6) against those who claim that believers never thirst (John 4:14, 6:35), King calls for constant dissent. With what are Christians dissatisfied? He identifies a familiar litany: the abyss between rich and poor; a dearth of decent housing and safe neighborhoods; a two-tiered, dysfunctional school

---

84. Eagleson and Scherper, *Puebla and Beyond*, 193.

85. Day, *Long Loneliness*, 170.

86. King, *Where Do We Go*, 4.

87. He repeats the phrase nine times in one paragraph. King, *Testament of Hope*, 251.

88. King, *Strength to Love*, 24.

89. Ibid., 17–25.

system; racial inequality. After addressing these easily observed phenomena, King moves from the real to the surreal. He envisions governors in their statehouses following Micah's dictum to do justice, love kindness, and walk humbly with God, and mayors fulfilling the prophecy of Amos as justice rolls down like waters and righteousness like a mighty stream from city halls (wine from a rock)! Then, citing Isaiah and Micah, King's words become purely visionary—"let us be dissatisfied until that day when the lion and the lamb shall lie down together, and everyone will sit under their own vine and fig tree and none shall be afraid." Let people be dissatisfied until the day when everyone recognizes that "out of one blood God made all people to dwell upon the face of the earth."[90] King was ultimately dissatisfied with reforms and realism. Like the psalmist's wishful prayer that a monarch would administer God's justice (Ps 72:1), King suggests that political officials—the elected aristocracy of their time—could administer justice. Like Stringfellow, Ellul, Romero, and Tutu, King would be satisfied with nothing less than the realm of God.

As in his SCLC address, King's 1967 "Christmas Sermon" evolves from the real to the surreal to the visionary. Contrasting dreams and "nightmares," he recalls that only weeks after the mountaintop moment of the March on Washington, "I saw that dream turn into a nightmare" in the white supremacist terrorist bombing of Birmingham's Sixteenth Street Baptist Church. As he saw African Americans "perishing on a lonely island of poverty in the midst of a vast ocean of material prosperity," inner city despair spur violence, and the war in Vietnam escalate, his dreams metamorphosed into new nightmares. "I am personally the victim," he says, "of deferred dreams, of blasted hopes." Of course, King could no more conclude a sermon with a nightmare than John of Patmos could end his revelation with Babylon ascendant. So King reiterates his dreams of racial justice, economic equality, the abolition of hunger, and the end of that era's guerre du jour.[91] As in his address to the SCLC, he traverses the same continuum from the historical to the indefinably transcendent.

Like the unquenchable thirst for reconciliation, redemption, and justice, the mysterious quality of the realm should be no surprise. As Gregory of Nyssa notes that all things in creation share in the ineffable nature of their Creator,[92] so the realm is as indefinable as its God. The warnings (Yield, Detour, Stop) against neat definitions are not limited to God. The realm, when imagined at all, is seen primarily in the surreal, in fiction, legends, poetry,

---

90. King, *Testament of Hope*, 251.
91. Ibid., 257–58.
92. Otto, *Idea of the Holy*, 194.

and song, in mad beatitudes, in a vision of outcasts processing from earth to heaven, in an uprising of freaks casting down the mighty from their thrones. The realm is envisioned as a land of promise and a life of blessings (Lev 26:3–13, Deut 28:1–14), but always as more than words can convey. The apophatic intuition extends not only to God's creatures and human society; it includes the realm.

The testimonies of Stringfellow, Romero, and King raise a question: is activism inherently apophatic? Apophatic spirituality contends that no collage of images fully portrays God; apophatic activism denies that any constitution, legislation, or amendment fully embodies the realm. Just as our finite nature keeps us from envisioning an infinite God, so we as social beings cannot visualize every contour of the realm. A vision of true justice only begins to form as we expose and carve away what we see—innumerable forms of oppression, a legion of injustices, hydra-headed violence, and a constant combustible splintering of sectarianism, tribalism, and nationalism. True peace can only be found when we shear away every form of political, economic, international, interpersonal, psychological, and spiritual violence. As Merton says that we cannot end war until we uproot the seeds of fear in our hearts, Thurman says: "What I seek to eradicate in society . . . I must first attack in my own heart and life."[93]

Not all activists embrace the apophatic. Just as the mystical tradition has its kataphatic wing, so there are conflicting voices among those seeking God's realm. In the 1970s, when *revolution*—not *resistance*—in Latin America seemed possible, when acute exploitation seemed to be the labor-pain prelude to the birth of movements to overcome omni-oppressive systems, Juan Luis Segundo challenged a group of European theologians and their standoffish, know-nothing apolitical theology. European theology of the time, he said, differentiated Christian eschatology from contemporary ideologies not because "it knows more, but that it knows less about that future . . . and that it persists in its lack of that knowledge."[94] To Segundo, such abstractions become cheap absolution for quietism. How could people be inspired to act against injustice—in the US in the sixties, in Latin America in the seventies, or anytime, anywhere—if what they seek is vague? Mocking the terminology of his European contemporaries, he asks, "Who consecrates their life to an 'analogy'? Who dies for an 'outline'? Who moves a human mass, a whole people, in the name of an 'anticipation'?"[95] The civil

---

93. Thurman, *Deep is the Hunger*, 99.
94. Segundo, "Capitalism-Socialism," 110.
95. Ibid., 112.

rights and anti-apartheid movements had concrete goals: simply, to end racial injustice. Specifics inspire action. Abstractions abort it.

Part of this theological conflict is rooted in the distance between First World/third-person and Third World/first-person experiences of oppression.[96] In the First World, Job's false comforters mask themselves with Qoheleth's cushioned despair while millions of Jobs in the Two-Thirds World suffer. To those European theologians, *revolution* implies totalitarian socialism. In Latin America, revolutionary socialism became a dream of liberation from orgiastic oligarchic exploitation. In Western Europe, privileged theologians could afford to prattle on about patience. In Latin America, every day was a crisis of faith and a matter of life and death; people needed their utopianism to be raw and unedited.

Segundo was right. People do not act or risk or devote their lives to abstractions. They are more typically motivated by immediate possibilities than indistinct ideals. Given the opportunity, Segundo would hug close King's immediate goals and honor his surrealistic visions. As the magnetic pull of King's rhetoric continues to show, we need the real, the surreal, *and* the purely visionary. Segundo and King combat the same hopelessness—passive surrender to oppression *and* reactive, undirected violence that is the complicit love-hate dance partner of every oppressive system. Their problem is posed in Langston Hughes's famous poem to which King so often alluded:

> What happens to a dream deferred?
>
> Does it dry up
> like a raisin in the sun?
> Or fester like a sore—
> And then run?
> Does it stink like rotten meat?
> Or crust and sugar over—
> like a syrupy sweet?
>
> Maybe it just sags
> like a heavy load.
>
> Or does it explode?[97]

African American–mid-sixties dreams exploded and then imploded. Latin American-seventies dreams in the past generation have alternated between frenetic activity and embalmed defeat.

---

96. Ibid., 120–21.
97. Hughes, *Langston Hughes Reader*, 123.

Ironically, Reinhold Niebuhr—the skeptic of light and advocate of realism—promotes the value of the unseen when he affirms the necessity of "ultrarational hopes" to conquer despair; only by attempting "the impossible" do people create a more just society.[98] People, Niebuhr says, do not act against "the inertia of society" unless they believe "that it can be more easily overcome than is actually the case." "No one," he says, "will suffer the perils and pains involved in the process of radical social change" unless they believe "in the possibility of a purer and fairer society than will ever be established."[99] As in the mystic's way of unknowing, reason leads only so far. Then a hunger for justice takes over.

The net result of activist unknowing is something like the dark night of the soul—living without clarity is like walking without gravity. Where we might expect to be blessed, we feel queasy. Where we might hope for fulfillment, we sense a void. The eighteenth-century prison reformer Elizabeth Fry found satisfaction elusive in her work: "at times feeling as if I went [to prisons] more as a machine moved by springs than in the lively state I desire."[100] Likewise, Day often found her work unrewarding and fretted that it was in vain. Substituting "work" for "pray" glosses their experiences with God's words to Julian: "Pray [work] wholeheartedly, though you may feel nothing, though you may see nothing, yes, though you think that you could not, for in dryness and barrenness, in sickness and in weakness, then is your prayer [work] most pleasing to me, though you think it almost tasteless to you."[101]

King shared Fry's ill-at-ease ambivalence. His malleable dream evolved partly because of more sophisticated social analysis, and partly because of a changing focus—from homegrown Southern segregation to the frontiers of national injustice and foreign wars. But his dreams also changed in response to the ghoulish injustices of his time. John of the Cross speaks of a "guiding night";[102] King's ministry was shaped by guiding nightmares. His kitchen epiphany resonates with the unknowing intimacy of John's dark night, but King, who carved dreams from nightmares, spent much of his ministry in a spiritual vertigo. In some ways, his experience was less a dark night than acedia, a spiritual malaise and endless wilderness that is the sickly sister of emotional depression.[103]

98. Niebuhr, *Moral Man*, 81.
99. Ibid., 221.
100. Fry, *Quaker Life*, 182.
101. Julian, *Showings*, 249.
102. John of the Cross, *Collected Works*, 68–69.
103. Lossky, *Mystical Theology*, 225–26; the Orthodox tradition, unlike its Western

Perhaps King's greatest pastoral gift was his uncanny ability to calm *collective* nightmares with surreal dreams. His visions function in the social sphere as Underhill's prescriptions work in the spiritual realm: "In the long run, we shall find that we grow best, not by direct conflict with our difficulties and bad qualities, but by turning to and gazing upon the love and joy and peace of the saints."[104] To move nearer to God, she says, we need "to lift our hearts from . . . the heart-breaking poverty, squalor, pain, and hopelessness of human lives gone wrong . . . to turn from all that to join for a moment the love and adoration of Beauty, Wisdom, and Power."[105] Underhill offers no opiates. She does not suppress holy grief. She commends praise to squeeze the self and self-pity out of us.[106] Adoration of the unseen God, she says, more effectively undoes sinfulness than confession. It is easier to "crowd" out sin with goodness than to "kick" it out with a frontal assault.[107] In the same way, King's visions crowd out and leave no room for injustice.

This tension between *crowding out* and *kicking out* lay at the heart of an early dispute between the founders of the Catholic Worker. Day, her hawk eyes eager to spy every societal and personal sin, embraced *denunciation*; the gentle, visionary Maurin preferred *annunciation*. Like asceticism's purgation without illumination, denunciation without annunciation is labor without productivity or purpose. The Catholic Worker had a view of the seen and unseen common to faith-based movements. King's critics in segregated Birmingham believed that the status quo—the seen—was peaceful; he saw only its chaotic, catastrophic underside. Many American Christians assume that the US is a modern Zion; Stringfellow insists it more closely resembles biblical Babylon.[108] While the Roman Catholic hierarchy cheerily appeased the wealthy, Maurin portrayed the status quo as unrelenting bedlam. And in "an age of chaos," he says, people want "to create order out of chaos."[109] What the status quo calls "law and order," activists see as *oppression and systematized mayhem*. This early scuffle within the Catholic Worker led Maurin to retreat from leadership, but *annunciation* became a key component of the movement's witness.[110] Maurin would have agreed

---

sibling, finds no one and nothing to love in the darkness.

104. Underhill, *Ways of the Spirit*, 75.
105. Ibid., 58.
106. Ibid., 175.
107. Ibid., 56.
108. Stringfellow, *Ethic for Christians*, 14, 33.
109. Maurin, *Easy Essays*, 182–83.
110. Ellis, *Peter Maurin*, 46–47, 137–38.

with Underhill: denunciations cannot exorcise injustice. Injustice is better crowded out by dreams.

The power of dreaming comes alive in Rauschenbusch's vigorous intuitive sense of the impending future. Like King, he vacillated in his grasp of the realm.[111] When Jesus says the realm is near, is it near in the same sense that Ibn 'Ata' Illah speaks of God's extreme proximity veiling God's presence? Is it like a planet whose oblong orbit sometimes brings it close to the sun? Or is it like an unpredictable asteroid passing by? In words that would have gladdened Segundo, Rauschenbusch says that Christians "see the Kingdom of God as always coming, always pressing in on the present, always big with possibility, and always inviting immediate action."[112] Sometimes that vision left Rauschenbusch in a state of holy intoxication as the real, the surreal, and the visionary blurred in his own mind as he started to fantasize that the "great day of the Lord" was about to dawn.[113] Romero was more sober about the distance between ideology and theology, between nightmares and dreams. Only by tying political liberation to Christ's Spirit could El Salvador be saved.[114] In contrast to Rauschenbusch's occasionally overrealized eschatology, the Friends World Conference in 1937—at the doorstep of history's most devastating war and most hideous ethnic cleansing—was plainly and humbly realistic: "We are not going to usher in the millennium."[115] Yet the gospel compels people of faith to work for justice no matter how distant the realm might be.

What motivates people to chisel justice from the marble of the world's injustice? To say that the work is not done in a generation is an understatement. Never one to lose sight of proximate gains in a dehumanized soul, a local cause, or a lone voice, Day believed in the ripple effect of the Catholic Worker.[116] To shave away a tiny, daily slice of injustice was her way of meticulously and tediously bringing the realm nearer.

On this continuum from the grassroots to the grand scheme, and from the real to the surreal, there is something even beyond the visionary. Julian of Norwich leaps past King's purist prophetic visions when she hears Jesus say: "all will be well, and all will be well, and every kind of thing will be well":[117] "I may make all things well, and I can make all things well, and I

---

111. Rauschenbusch, *Social Gospel*, 227.
112. Ibid., 141.
113. Rauschenbusch, *Christianity and the Social*, 422.
114. Romero, *Violence of Love*, 17.
115. *Christian Faith*, 536.
116. Day, *By Little*, 98.
117. Julian, *Showings*, 225.

shall make all things well, and I will make all things well; and you will see yourself that every kind of thing will be well."[118] In Julian's repeated mantra, we hear the alpha and the omega, the most simple and most elegant of eschatologies. There are no parameters and no predictions, merely the unadorned substrata of every prophetic vision—all shall be well with vine and fig tree, for wolf and lamb, in city and wilderness, forever and ever. Eschatology is, by its nature, loosely defined, ill-defined, and undefined. Like heaven, the day to come is imagined, unseen, and, along with God, our deepest yearning. As with Rauschenbusch and Tolstoy, imbibing the belief that all shall be well inebriates discourse and can make expectations for a Christian revolution as absurd as the anticipation of those who sit on a hilltop awaiting a skewed-in-imagining, never-to-come rapture. But Julian makes no Tolstoyan claims. She does not say whether the day to come will arrive through Enlightenment progress or an infinite series of social reforms or on clouds of glory. She simply says: all shall be well.

If Qoheleth muses in response to closing horizons, King and Julian write of heaven bursting open. But even Qoheleth's proposal is only one response to shriveling hopes. The apocalyptic tradition from Daniel to the Ghost Dance movement offers another. Like emergency workers, apocalyptic writers inflate hopes—as if they were lungs—with the promise of God's sudden intervention into earthly affairs with divine finality. For them, when horizons close, the faithful imagination forces them back open with jaws of hope. Like Julian and King, apocalyptic writers address what happens when pure grief meets naked glee. But unlike the apocalyptic tradition, King—like Mrs. Turpin—sees a line from earth to the realm in the interaction of divine and human initiative.

In the world as it is, with its chameleon principalities and inconstant human nature, we are left to ruminate: will the day to come be achieved step by step or in an apocalyptic Great Leap Forward? Will we find that, after centuries of our living in the myth of Sisyphus, God finally gives one magnificent shove, or will every holy thought, word, and deed have been critical to world transformation? Some paint the day with visions; others carve it from a gargantuan block of dense chaos. But until it comes the only way to see the realm is in its glorious hiddenness.

THE UNRESOLVED PARADOX

Some believe that to see is to know and to know is to see, others that to unsee is to enter the mystery of love and to enter the mystery of love is to

---

118. Ibid., 229; see also 152, 236, 305.

unsee. As if to respond to both assertions, Pseudo-Dionysius divides the angels into two groups: seraphs aflame with perfect love and cherubs plump with sublime knowledge.[119] In spite of his ability to honor both love and knowledge, there is an enduring, unfortunate, and unnecessary argument in ascetical theology about which takes priority.[120] Like Rolle's assumption that the contemplative life is superior to the active life (Mary's reign), or the liberation theologian's claim that spirituality without activism is sterile (Martha's revenge), the dispute sometimes acquires the feel of many a theological spat: the tinier the head of the pin, the greater the number of arguments.

Traversing the abyss between the advocates of love and the proponents of knowledge can be akin to mending a cultural gulf. Wole Soyinka, for example, not only ridicules Descartes's overrationalistic breed, he opposes negritude's inverted neoracist dichotomy in which Europeans "think" and Africans "feel." Rather, Soyinka imagines an early meeting of archetypes in which an African punctures the arrogant and empty rationalism of a European explorer-exploiter: "You think, therefore you are a thinker. You are one-who-thinks, white-creature-in-pith-helmet-in-African-jungle-who-thinks and, finally, white-man-who-has-problems-believing-in-his-own-existence."[121] To Soyinka, the Cartesian theory is born of a perpetually unraveling anxiety that fabricates an intellectual albatross to justify its existence and exalt itself.

Reinhold Niebuhr, a proud thinker, probably would not have known how to respond to Soyinka's slap of the mind, but it is unlikely he would have turned the other cheek. Niebuhr's insistence on realism over idealism is an argument for the primacy of knowledge-filled cherubs over love-inflamed seraphs. To him, the children of light see through rose-distorting lenses of love without the correctives of reason and logic. To him, the occasional, decisive use of violence is more rational than a pillow-fight-soft pacifism. For Underhill, you cannot redeem without love; for Niebuhr, you cannot reform without knowledge. Knowledge seeks clarity and truth. Love seeks intimacy. Knowledge is innately kataphatic; love inherently apophatic. In each argument for one or the other we find the penultimate power of a partial truth.

Among proactive apologists for knowledge, Eckhart says, "Knowledge is better than love" because it "includes" and leads love; it "detaches and strips off and runs ahead [of love], touches God naked and grasps God in God's essence."[122] Symeon, another advocate for knowledge, spent an hour

---

119. Pseudo-Dionysius, *Complete Works*, 160–62.
120. Happold, *Mysticism*, 40.
121. Soyinka, *Myth, Literature, and the African*, 38–39.
122. Eckhart, *Sermons & Treatises I*, 258.

with God whose face was "a light like a sun without form." Symeon was "struck with wonder at the greatness of the glory—what it was, or whose it was, I know not." Yet, while "totally awestruck," he did not recall the epiphany because of what he saw.[123] When he remembered it, "I wept and lived in an unutterable joy, because I had known" God. His knowledge gave birth to love: "from then onwards I loved You" because God "truly is love."[124]

Eckhart and Symeon were not apologists for Cartesian logic or Niebuhrian realism, but proponents of experience. Spiritual knowledge gives birth to theologians; academic knowledge trains scholars. So Catherine of Siena praises Aquinas because he knew God through prayer rather than study,[125] a sentiment that would have raised an eyebrow from Niebuhr but no dissent from Eckhart. Symeon shares Evagrius's position: you cannot speak of God without experiencing God. Someone standing on the seashore "sees the limitless ocean." Just as one can see only a tiny part of the ocean, so neither the sharpest intellect nor the most marvelous contemplative gaze can penetrate God's glory. Such an attempt inevitably confuses an eddy or a swell with the infinite whole. Someone not content to *look* at the ocean can *enter* it by participating in God's life. As every theology of baptism insists: seeing water is one thing, immersion another. Those who leap into the reality of God "advance into the knowledge of God." Revealing an affinity with Pseudo-Dionysius, Symeon says that this knowledge of God comes "the more deeply they plunge into unknowing"; some wade in waist deep while others "plunge into the depths and become wholly submerged under the waters."[126] For Symeon, the *thinker* puts a toe in the water. The *contemplative* dives in.

Apologists for love are equally adamant. Ambrose Autpert says to God, "When we seek to investigate you, we do not discover you as you are; you are apprehended when you are loved."[127] The *Theologia Germanica*, like many writings stimulated by First Corinthians 13, concedes that knowledge can help us discover God, but without love, no one can be united to God.[128] The argumentative Rolle makes a stinging distinction when describing his intended audience as those "who are seeking rather to love God than to

123. Symeon, *Discourses*, 373.
124. Ibid., 376.
125. Catherine, *Dialogue*, 339.
126. Leech, *True Prayer*, 16.
127. McGinn, *Growth of Mysticism*, 140.
128. *Theologia Germanica*, 122.

amass knowledge."[129] Citing Paul (1 Cor 8:1), he says that knowledge puffs up but does not edify.[130]

At times love and knowledge become theological apples and oranges. Unlike Eckhart, Rolle compares *academic* knowledge with *experiential* love. The more nuanced Ruusbroec favors love: there comes a point in one's journey when "love goes in while understanding remains outside."[131] Yet even then, "although we are above reason, we are not without reason, and therefore feel that we are both touching and being touched, loving and being loved."[132]

For these mystics, life's goal is love. Traherne says, "By Love alone is God enjoyed, by Love alone delighted in, by Love alone approached or admired."[133] Still mulling over her vision of Christ crucified, Julian was given its meaning fifteen years later: "What, do you wish to know your Lord's meaning in this thing? Know it well, love was God's meaning. Who reveals it to you? Love. What did God reveal to you? Love. Why does God reveal it to you? For love."[134] Hadewijch, who often calls God "Love," says,

> What seems to the loved soul the most beautiful encounter
> Is that it should love the Beloved so fully
> And so gain knowledge of the Beloved with love
> That nothing else be known by it
> Except: "I am love conquered by Love!"[135]

The Cloud of Unknowing insists that God is "incomprehensible" through knowledge:[136] God "may be reached and held close by means of love, but by means of thought never."[137] *The Cloud* speaks repeatedly of *stirrings of love*— a "blind stirring of love,"[138] a "devout stirring of love,"[139] a "meek stirring of love,"[140] and a "blind and devout and desirous stirring of love"[141]—that inflame our desire to seek, find, and enter into God. *The Cloud* finds a hidden

---

129. Rolle, *Fire of Love*, 46.
130. Ibid., 58.
131. Ruusbroec, *Spiritual Espousals*, 114.
132. Ibid., 240; see also 70.
133. Traherne, *Centuries*, 36.
134. Julian, *Showings*, 342.
135. Hadewijch, *Complete Works*, 151.
136. *Cloud of Unknowing*, 64.
137. Ibid., 71–72.
138. Ibid., 91, 158, 179.
139. Ibid., 173.
140. Ibid., 175, 177.
141. Ibid., 174.

unity in "this perfect stirring of love that begins here in this life" and the love "which shall last eternally in the bliss of heaven."[142] Never a lone spirit in flight, this love—like all mystical love—benefits the seeker *only* if it blesses others: "it is of greater value to the health of your soul, more worthy in itself, and more pleasing to God and to all the saints and angels in heaven—yes, and *more helpful to all your friends, physical and spiritual, living and dead.*" Love is greater than any revelation: "It is better for you to have this and to feel it in your spiritual desires than it is for you to have the eyes of your soul opened in contemplation or in the perceiving of all the angels or saints in heaven, or in hearing all the mirth and melody they possess in bliss."[143]

"Love" in our contemporary lingua Americana is confused with lust, conflated with covetousness, and enmeshed with ephemeral whimsies. This is not even a distant cousin of mystical love. Julian, as is her wont, speaks of the incredible tenderness of God's "familiar love." God, she says, "is our clothing": God's "tender" love "wraps and enfolds us, embraces us and guides us, surrounds us."[144] But the effects of love sometimes bloom slowly. Remembering the "day the door of Heaven swung back and God's Face was revealed" to him, Rolle says that "the door remained open for nearly a year longer before I could really feel in my heart the warmth of eternal love."[145] Love develops. It evolves. It expands. Traherne, following the Sermon on the Mount (Matt 5:46–47), says that it is a "poor and miserable" thing to love only a few. As Tutu and Merton point out, when the apparatchiks of apartheid and extermination went home, they loved their families as if they had spent their day working in an orchard, an office, or a retail outlet. Even the godless love a few. To love a few is nothing. To love all is glorious: "To love all persons in all ages, all angels, all worlds, is Divine and Heavenly. To love all cities and all kingdoms, all kings and all peasants, and every person in all worlds with a natural intimate familiar love . . . is Blessed."[146] Ruusbroec draws a distinction between "natural love" that circles itself in self-sainted contentment, and "charity" that "raises us up above ourselves."[147] Like Merton's dichotomy of the *crowd* that lowers our behavior and the *community* that raises it,[148] false love soothes us and leaves us unchanged; true love serves God and transforms us. According to Traherne, if only we could

142. Ibid., 110.
143. Ibid., 83–84 (italics mine).
144. Julian, *Showings*, 130.
145. Rolle, *Fire of Love*, 92.
146. Traherne, *Centuries*, 201.
147. Ruusbroec, *Spiritual Espousals*, 138.
148. Merton, *Silent Life*, 43.

love we would overcome class barriers, ideological boundaries, and national borders. True love is to have Isaac of Nineveh's merciful heart.

It is for this mature love that the mystical tradition strings together a chain of rhapsodies. Thomas à Kempis says that love begins to show itself when we care more about the love of the giver than the gift of the lover.[149] John of the Cross, like Hadewijch, says that sooner or later we will not be satisfied until we love as much as we are loved.[150] In another reverberation from First Corinthians 13 and a foretaste of King's midrash on the same passage, John says that what matters is less the quantity or quality of our good deeds, but "the love of God practiced in them."[151] Similarly, Hadewijch notes, "love is not to be measured by sweetness but by the possession of virtues":[152]

> O Love, were I but love,
> And could I but love you, Love, with love!
> O Love, for love's sake, grant that I,
> Having become love, may know Love wholly as Love![153]

Bernard says that we begin by loving ourselves for our own sake; then we love God for our own sake; then we love God for God's sake; and finally we love ourselves for God's sake.[154] Augustine shortens Bernard's orbit: only those who deeply love God can truly love themselves.[155] But love is never meant to merely boomerang. It is supposed to fan out. As God tells Catherine of Genoa in Traherne-like sentiments, whoever "loves Me, loves all that I love."[156] Mysticism, contrary to its critics, is the *perfect opposite* of self-absorption.

Love is also more than the sum total of divine tenderness. Dostoevsky is not alone in discerning its severity. Like a Hindu god, love purges as it creates. John of the Cross calls the work of the Holy Spirit "the very fire of love" consuming human imperfection. As a fire penetrates a log—wounding it, drying it, and stripping it of impurities—so love hurts as it cleanses us of our personal selfishness, our distorted allegiances, our political corruption, and our share in systemic injustice. With laser-like precision, this "dark"

---

149. à Kempis, *Imitation of Christ*, 112.
150. John of the Cross, *Collected Works*, 553.
151. Ibid., 262.
152. Hadewijch, *Complete Works*, 67.
153. Ibid., 352.
154. Williams, *Wound of Knowledge*, 121.
155. Ibid., 93.
156. Underhill, *Mystics of the Church*, 164–65.

fire of love locates the "miseries and defects" of each person, and when it finds them "it is not gentle, but afflictive," "consuming and contentious," and makes us feel "wretched and distressed."[157] This cauterizing cures us: as "love touches the wound of love, it causes a deeper wound of love." The more it wounds, the more it heals. As a dermatologist freezes precancerous growths with liquid nitrogen—burns bubbling into scabs—love inflicts "wound upon wound" until one's entire soul is "dissolved into a wound of love" and finally "transformed in love."[158]

In its political manifestations, this *inflictive* love resonates with the Hebrew prophets and with modern activists. To parse it more carefully, Julian's *tender* love enfolds the oppressed while *inflictive* love rains down a transfiguring fire on oppressors. The same love tenderly caresses the broken while thoroughly ravaging the systems that break them. This is Day's dreadful love. This is Merton's resetting of broken bones. This is the mother bear love of God (Hos 13:8) that inspires prophets and revolutionaries.

It is a daring exercise in faith to embody this love in the midst of ideological Manicheanism, political conflict, and the shadow of violence. The Commitment Cards signed by Birmingham civil rights protesters in 1963 challenged demonstrators to love in the midst of an economic boycott:

1. Meditate daily on the teachings and life of Jesus.
2. Remember always that the nonviolent movement in Birmingham seeks justice and reconciliation—not victory.
3. Walk and talk in the manner of love, for God is love.
4. Pray daily to be used by God in order that all people might be free.
5. Sacrifice personal wishes in order that all people might be free.
6. Observe with both friend and foe the ordinary rules of courtesy.
7. Seek to perform regular service for others and for the world.
8. Refrain from the violence of fist, tongue, or heart.
9. Strive to be in good spiritual and bodily health.
10. Follow the directions of the movement and of the captain on a demonstration.[159]

Providing spiritual direction (the imitation of Christ, the love of God), the highest moral expectations (love in thought, word, and deed), and obedience (a quasimonastic ceding of autonomy for the greater good), the

---

157. John of the Cross, *Collected Works*, 586.
158. Ibid., 597.
159. King, *Why We Can't Wait*, 63–64.

Birmingham movement's leaders argued not only for love's morality, but its efficacy.

The primacy of love was absurd to Niebuhr, and pragmatic to Gandhian nonviolence, but Merton reveled in life's absurdities. Instead of trying to justify his vocation as functional, practical, productive, or expedient, he liked to subvert people's antagonism by simply admitting that being a monk is "damned stupid."[160] Whether speaking of nature or vocation or culture, the cumulative effect of some of his writings creates an enchanting ode to blessed uselessness. He praises the countercultural uselessness of rain over the productivity of the business world's "rhinoceros."[161] He salutes the "sweet whistling" of quails, the "absolutely useless" quality of the noise, and "the delight I take in it."[162] He celebrates the antimessage of poets that preach no sermon and proffer no prescription.[163] To Merton, "If one does not understand the usefulness of the useless and the uselessness of the useful, one cannot understand art."[164] To him, "the highest form of contemplative life is a life that has absolutely no practical use or purpose whatsoever."[165] He echoes Chuang Tzu's saying: the "useless has its use."[166] Art, poetry, rain, quails, and Merton's monastic life itself are all, for better or worse, useless. Niebuhr, who esteemed his close proximity to power, might argue that in so exalting useless love, Merton and his ilk became irrelevant. But Merton, for one, *chose* to be "deliberately irrelevant."[167] Love can be useful or useless. It can be anarchic like Ammon Hennacy's lone protests or Tolstoy's deeply principled and wildly inaccurate visions of the future. It can be paradoxical like Stringfellow's absolutist commitment to anti-ideological dissent. It can even be unsound, eccentric, or silly like the subversive, contrarian love of the Mad Farmer. Love can assault the abusive and enfold the exploited. Love can do all this and more. Or love can simply be.

In mysticism as in activism, the primacy of love or knowledge is ultimately an unresolved paradox. It is absurd to imagine angels aflame with perfect love and angels filled with holy knowledge anathematizing each other. The cherubs would have more sense, the seraphs more charity. Instead of

---

160. Merton, *Hidden Ground*, 507; a description Niebuhr and the Grand Inquisitor would have embraced.

161. Merton, *Raids on the Unspeakable*, 9–23.

162. Ibid., 23.

163. Ibid., 155–64.

164. Ibid., 21.

165. Merton, *Monastic Journey*, 203.

166. Tzu, *Basic Writings*, 137.

167. Merton, *Asian Journal*, 306.

encouraging nonsensical polemical crusades, Catherine of Siena sees love and knowledge working hand in hand: "The more they know, the more they love; the more they love, the more they know."[168] Gregory the Great redefines them: "love itself is a form of knowledge";[169] and William of St. Thierry weds them: "there are two eyes in this sight, love and reason, always throbbing with a natural intention to see the light that is God. When one makes an effort without the other, it doesn't get very far. When they help each other, they accomplish much."[170] To William, love and reason encourage each other: "While love strengthens reason so that it can be drawn along, reason does the same for love so that it can be embraced. Love is protected by reason, reason illuminated by love."[171] It is foolish to separate them, yet many have and many do. William's synthesis might have saved Frederick Douglass and Sojourner Truth, Niebuhr and Muste, competing voices in reform movements—and conflicting progressive ideological voices in every era—energy for the battle against injustice. We might as well try to parse fire.

There is a yin and yang quality to love and knowledge. While different from each other, they belong together. They need each other. True love loves knowledge and true knowledge knows love. Like the meeting of divine traits—steadfast love and faithfulness, righteousness and peace—in Psalm 85, knowledge and love are not rival forces. They meet, kiss, and complete each other.

THE UNTRACEABLE PATH

Journalist Stanley Karnow's cynicism escalated geometrically in the early years of the US intervention in Vietnam. The South Vietnamese government, marketed as a democracy, was led by a series of venal dictators. The American military presence, advertised as advisory, grew exponentially. As if to encapsulate the habitual half-truths and official lies, in the middle of a conversation with an Army press officer in the *advisory* period of 1961, a stunned Karnow pointed to an aircraft carrier turning a bend in the Saigon River; his companion replied with an ironic double negative: "I don't see nothing."[172] Disgusted by American denials and lies, Karnow might have been swayed by apologists who portrayed Ho Chi Minh and the Viet Cong

---

168. Catherine, *Dialogue*, 157.
169. McGinn, *Growth of Mysticism*, 58.
170. Ibid., 233.
171. Ibid., 236.
172. Karnow, *Vietnam*, 254.

as noble nationalists. But the Communists' consistent savagery toward enemies and innocents alike snapped any such temptation.

Even when Buddhist monks occasionally became alternative voices in the cacophony of mayhem, Karnow remained skeptical. In a variation on a theme of an Anglo stereotype of Asians, Karnow wrote that Tri Quang—a leading monk—"defied easy comprehension." Tri Quang told him that monks wanted a government to end oppression and "satisfy the aspirations of the people." Pressed for specifics, Tri Quang replied, "I am merely a monk. Those are questions for politicians." Karnow concluded that the monk was being either disingenuous or coy.[173]

Merton's critics shared Karnow's cynicism about monks who dared to discuss politics. Here was a monk writing scathing critiques not only of the sin of segregation but the flimsiness of white liberalism. Here was a monk damning the nuclear arms race and comparing America's elected leaders to Nazi mass murderers. Here was a monk skewering American policy in Vietnam as a variation of a racist game of cowboys and Indians. But if someone asked Merton how to reform historically ignorant, morally corrupt, and politically counterproductive policies, he would have intoned Tri Quang's answer. He was a monk, not a politician! Monks cannot even describe themselves! A monk, Merton explains in Zen overtones, is "a bird who flies very fast without knowing where he is going. And always arrives where he went, in peace, without knowing where he came from."[174] If that was as clear as an astute student of monasticism could be about himself, how could he guide nations to finding peace?

Merton's "Message to Poets" could have just as easily applied to contemplatives: "Let us be proud of the words that are given to us for nothing, not to teach anyone, not to confute anyone, not to prove anyone absurd, but to point beyond all objects into the silence where nothing can be said."[175] Merton saw a world caught in prickly branches of innumerable obsessions and delusions; his role was simply to awaken people.[176] To do less would abrogate the contemplative's responsibility to the world. To attempt more would be pure hubris.

Just as no one can diagram a trail to God, no one can chart a path to peace or faith or life. When a member of the Catholic Worker's Chicago House of Hospitality describes how a homeless person's "life came back," the most apt words are "slowly, painfully, almost shyly." People who came to

---

173. Ibid., 448–49.
174. Merton, *Courage for Truth*, 198.
175. Merton, *Raids on the Unspeakable*, 160.
176. Commins, *Spiritual People*, 324–26.

the soup kitchen for months and were seen as "dour, wordless, dull people gradually took on a completely new (new to us, that is) character." Routine helps: food to eat, a place to sleep, work to be done, as does the "casual but very real fellowship of the everchanging household"; gradually guests become "useful to others." Their identity shifts. "It was often as if you could see a change taking place before your eyes, like something visible happening—color returning to a face after a faint." The dispossessed find respect, a purpose, and belonging. Without a visible threshold or turn, the zigzagging miracle occurs. We "can rekindle hope, bring back the zest for living, inspire plans for the future, restore self-respect and pride . . . even mirror dimly the infinite charity of God"; we "can raise other people from the dead."[177] The resuscitation's *how* is as obscure as the dimness of an empty tomb, but the new life is unmistakable.

Just as there are limits to our transient images of God, there are random and erratic fluctuations in every spiritual path. At some point, our practices become rigid, harmful distractions, dead-end ends in themselves. This is an apophatic commonplace. What is not a commonplace is to see the dimensions of unknowing in the hopes of Rauschenbusch and the dreams of King. What is not a commonplace is to see the parallel truths in the *hows* of spiritual practice and political strategy. Just as we do not know what it is to meet God face to face, we cannot describe the realm or how the revolution transports us there. We cannot trace that journey; no one has made it.

This truth is deeply embedded in the gospel. Jesus' parables are fingers pointing to the seen and the unseen, the already and the not yet. The parables balance immanence and transcendence with dramatic discoveries, complex reversals, and subversive proposals. In many parables there is a hint of the unknown—seeds suddenly bear fruit; characters behave unpredictably—but the parable of the Seed Growing Secretly is blatantly apophatic (Mark 4:26–9). Something has happened; we don't know *how*. How did the seed grow? How do we draw nearer to God? How is a person's humanity restored? How could peace come to Vietnam? Not to know is not disingenuous. Sometimes the only wisdom is nonwisdom.

Merton says that making contemplative faces in front of a mirror has no impact on our relationship with God—the "way of contemplation" is not a way.[178] Buddhists speak of being "empty of emptiness,"[179] and Ibn al-'Arabi writes of "the station of no station."[180] While John Climacus and Walter

---

177. Cornell, Ellsberg, and Forest, *Penny a Copy*, 56.
178. Merton, *Inner Experience*, 2, 5.
179. Nhat Hanh, *Diamond that Cuts*, 56.
180. al-'Arabi, *Meccan Revelations*, 223–38.

Hilton describe ladders, others claim that if you climb high enough, you enter an impenetrable cloud. Then, and only then, do you enter the mystery of God. Johannes Tauler describes a desert in which you cannot see "any landmarks"—there may be light ahead, but "no road . . . leads to it."[181]

The mystics generously construct images of the imageless. John of the Cross describes a night of the senses when the plug is pulled on perceptions and a night of the spirit when mystical sensibilities grow numb. There is nothing to cling to or grasp for. Precisely then, when we are lost, we find. John *prescribes* this way of no way and encourages us to *seek* it—release everything that keeps us hugging a teddy-bear image of God. The path to God cannot be painted. It can only be carved from false paths.

> To reach satisfaction in all
>   Desire its possession in nothing
> To come to possess all
>   Desire the possession of nothing.
> To arrive at being all
>   Desire to be nothing.
> *To come to the knowledge of all*
>   *Desire the knowledge of nothing*
> To come to the pleasure you have not
>   You must go by a way in which you enjoy not
> *To come to the knowledge you have not*
>   *You must go by a way in which you know not*
> To come to the possession you have not
>   You must go by a way in which you possess not.
> To come to be what you are not
>   You must go by a way in which you are not.[182]

In John's precision-sliced theological explications, detachment is the beginning. Detach yourself from spiritual poisons and deadly sins; then detach yourself from the good to reach the godly. Never a pure iconoclast, John says that images remind us of God, but when we languish too long on "the means"—images in prayer or "supernatural visions"—they can cause "delusions and dangers" and become "an impediment."[183] What begins as an oasis becomes a swamp. Images and knowledge are "as far from the reality [of God] as is a painting from the living object" it represents.[184] Images can help us "toward union with God," as long as we allow ourselves "to soar" past

---

181. Leech, *Experiencing God*, 177.
182. John of the Cross, *Collected Works*, 103–4 (italics mine).
183. Ibid., 236.
184. Ibid., 577.

them, from "the painted image to the living God."[185] Beginners "desire to feel God . . . as if God were comprehensible and accessible."[186] This is the first blind alley. God "weans"[187] us "from the breasts of these gratifications and delights" as we enter into "pure dryness and interior darkness." This "purgation of the night"[188] is not the exiles' homeward way from Babylon on which valleys are raised, mountains lowered, and rough places smoothed. This is not a desert turning into a paradise. It is a road that seemingly has no end.

John says that in this hard way "spiritual persons suffer considerable affliction," less because of the "aridities" themselves than our "fear of having gone astray."[189] We are all children on a night train passing through a tunnel. Uncertainty becomes our companion; anxiety becomes our guide. The night of the spirit, "narrow, dark, and terrible," evokes greater misery, yet its spiritual "benefits . . . are incomparably greater than those of the night of sense."[190] Like the seed growing secretly, love kindles an inner "fire . . . without knowing how nor where this attraction and love originates."[191] Only when compass is lost and constellations disappear do we draw near "divine union." John's "dark and pure faith"—*The Cloud's* naked intent—prepares the way for "the union of love."[192] Referring again to Aristotle, John maintains that "the more one looks at the brilliant sun, the more the sun darkens the faculty of sight, deprives it and overwhelms it in its weakness."[193] Twisting Hosea's image of the protective mother bear (Hos 13:8), John compares the exhausted, disillusioned, and "wounded soul" to "the lioness or she-bear that goes in search of her cubs when they are taken away and cannot be found"—it is then that "it anxiously and forcibly goes out in search of its God."[194]

Merton applies this indifference about spiritual formulas to political strategy. We do not find a great light; we enter a bewildering darkness. Yet, like Tri Quang, his nonanswers did not keep him from decrying bad answers. Merton finds the true path by eliminating false paths, and the most

185. Ibid., 237.
186. Ibid., 309.
187. Ibid., 353.
188. Ibid., 311.
189. Ibid., 316.
190. Ibid., 320.
191. Ibid., 318.
192. Ibid., 332–33.
193. Ibid., 335.
194. Ibid., 359.

notorious and seductive myths and ideologies commend violence as a way to the realm.

Ever since the story was first told, every malevolent Goliath believes he is an underdog David; every tribe and nation sees itself as God's people defending themselves against an irredeemably vile enemy. For many people grief-stricken at injustice, violence presents itself as a quick and decisive slingshot shot, a shortcut to hope, a be-all and end-all of solutions. In a decade fraught with acting out masked as revolution, Merton criticizes the temptation to violence: people using violence "have changed nothing, they have simply enforced with greater brutality the anti-spiritual and anti-human drives that are destructive of truth and love."[195]

The broad non-dogmatic lineage of nonviolence continually repeats this assertion. James Nayler calls his seventeenth-century uprising the "Lamb's war."[196] Two hours before he died, he catalogued the weapons of that "war":

> There is a spirit which I feel that delights to do no evil, nor to revenge any wrong, but delights to endure all things, in hope to enjoy its own in the end. Its hope is to outlive all wrath and contention, and to weary out all exaltation and cruelty, or whatever is of a nature contrary to itself. It sees to the end of all temptations. As it bears no evil in itself, so it conceives none in thoughts to any other. If it be betrayed, it bears it, for its ground and spring is the mercies and forgiveness of God. Its crown is meekness, its life is everlasting love unfeigned; it takes its kingdom with entreaty and not with contention, and keeps it by lowliness of mind. . . . It is conceived in sorrow, and brought forth without any to pity it, nor does it murmur at grief and oppression. It never rejoices but through sufferings; for with the world's joy it is murdered.[197]

Violence calculates means and ends. It exults. It is quick. It is irreversible. Nonviolence is a seed growing secretly. It grieves. It takes time. It endures.

King took this invisible path in the late 1960s when nonviolence had lost its fleeting cachet. King did not merely take the obvious, if controversial, antiwar stance—he opposed all violence. In the mid-1960s, abetted by the martyred Malcolm X, the Black Power movement, and the Black Panther Party, the ideological debate among African Americans, ever mirroring the dominant culture, tilted toward violence as self-defense or as a means to

---

195. Merton, *School of Charity*, 112.
196. Wellman, *Belief and Bloodshed*, 102.
197. Steere, ed., *Quaker Spirituality*, 96 (modernized).

justice. It was not only a foreign and foolhardy war King objected to. He rejected *that* supposedly revolutionary violence popular in urban and academic settings. To oppose violence in the African American community in the late sixties was tantamount to advocating a nonviolent response to Japan after December 7, or to Al Qaeda after September 11, or to any and every Simon Legree any and every day of any and every year. To oppose violence was to be seen as passé, an Uncle Tom, a Judas. Yet King says:

> The ultimate weakness of violence is that it is a descending spiral begetting the very thing it seeks to destroy. Instead of diminishing evil, it multiplies it. Through violence you may murder the liar, but you cannot murder the lie, nor establish the truth. Through violence you murder the hater, but you do not murder hate. In fact, violence merely increases hate. Returning violence for violence multiplies violence, adding deeper darkness to a night already devoid of stars. Darkness cannot drive out darkness; only light can do that. Hate cannot drive out hate; only love can do that.[198]

Two decades earlier, shortly after World War II, when the triumph over Nazism seemed to place a crowning wreath around the myth of violence, Howard Thurman argues not only that history shows that people never tire of proclaiming the presumed blessings of violence, but also a simple reality: violence never works. Violence, he says, is deceptive because it seems "efficient" and "effective." In reality "it stampedes, overruns, pushes aside and carries the day." It is "the ritual and the etiquette of those who stand in a position of overt control in the world." People "resort to violence" because they are unwilling to be patient or unable to be creative.[199]

This twentieth-century–African American testimony echoes George Fox's message to Cromwell. In hindsight, reassurance about Quaker nonviolence seems redundant, but some contemporary continental Anabaptist sects had embraced the purported purging force of violence, and Cromwell, like all of England, was suspicious of the Friends. So Fox told him, "The Spirit of Christ, by which we are guided, is not changeable, so as once to command us from a thing as evil and again to move toward it; and we do certainly know, and so testify to the world, that the spirit of Christ, which leads us into all Truth, will never move us to fight and war against anyone with outward weapons, neither for the kingdom of Christ, nor for the kingdoms of this world."[200]

198. King, *Where Do We Go,* 72.
199. Thurman, *Deep is the Hunger,* 34–35.
200. Steere, ed., *Quaker Spirituality,* 106 (modernized).

Whenever revolutionaries or warriors or academics or religious leaders propose violence as a solution, they lose sight of the infinite value of each life. Jesus declares that all that is holy rejoices in the salvation of one person (Luke 15:7, 10). The Talmud argues that to kill one person is to destroy a world; to save one person is to save a world.[201] The intrinsic value of each life is the essence of Ivan Karamazov's protest: the suffering of one child blots out the goodness of creation. Every violent death is a sacrifice to Moloch, the triumph of Mars, and a holocaust. Every cruelty is as toxic as Chernobyl, polluting planner, perpetrator, witness, and victim through time and space.

Merton and King reject violence as the quintessential destroyer. Nothing else so irreparably obliterates the innate value of human dignity. No other human activity so desecrates the spirit. Nothing else we do is so primly, proudly, and bloodily Manichean. No other extension of politics by other means (von Clausewitz) is so bloated with a mythology of redemption. Ideologies of violence argue that we can diminish evil by destroying life. The logic of calculating Caiaphas in urging Jesus' execution (John 11:50) is the cornerstone of every war, every witch trial, every act of terrorism, every revolution and counterrevolution. *Every war* is thought to be *the war to end all wars,* yet every act of violence contains within it the seeds of the Final Solution.

Jacques Ellul offers a damning condemnation when he says that every violent revolution is loyal to society's "dominant ideology."[202] Revolutionary violence mirrors and mimics its repression and exploitation. It is the alter ego and accomplice of the status quo. It is not a dangerous orthodoxy; it is a complicit banality. Such revolutionaries are not the enemies of the dominant society—they are its superficially rebellious but deeply devoted offspring.

Whatever our legitimate doubts about the true path, the realm cannot be reached through oppression, domestic abuse, or drones any more than God can be reached through power, technology, or technocracy. There are no shortcuts to the realm built on the skulls of the condemned. God's revolution does not usher in the realm in days or weeks or years. It is the desperate need for a quick fix that gives birth to violence. Nonviolence unshackles itself from short-term success. As Chávez says, nonviolence has a profoundly different sense of time.[203] As Merton notes, "The true revolution must come slowly and painfully,"[204] emerging from a bizarre, loose, and superficially ineffective coalition. Gandhi disdains "the temptation of a desire

---

201. Maimonides, *Commentary on Mishnah,* 4:5.
202. Ellul, *Violence,* 66.
203. Dalton, *Moral Vision,* 142.
204. Merton, *School of Charity,* 112.

for results" in politics.²⁰⁵ Nonviolence, then, is a nonpath, and it is only by a nonpath that one can come near the realm.

Yet there are temptations for the nonviolent, snares Karnow stretched before Tri Quang. Merton identifies the quandary: "if nonviolence is too political" it becomes identified with one side (flesh without Word); "While if it is totally apolitical it runs the risk of being ineffective or at best merely symbolic" (Word without flesh).²⁰⁶ Nonviolence can mask a rigidity that justifies puerile hatred or a purity code that sanctifies withdrawal. So Merton warns, "If we love our own ideology and our own opinion instead of loving our neighbor, we will seek only to glorify our ideas and our institutions."²⁰⁷

If violence is not the path and if nonviolence is a nonpath, how can Christians construct a political stratagem? Theological assumptions underlie every strategy: the capacity of persons to change and institutions to reform, and the fused jumble of good and evil in each culture, each person, and every action, as hard to sort as wheat from chaff. Niebuhr objects to nonviolence as naïve love without a navigating knowledge. The use of coercion or violence, conversely, is self-satisfied, self-sanctifying knowledge without love. Knowledge only takes sides; nonviolence also transcends them. Knowledge seeks only proximate justice; nonviolence also yearns for ultimate reconciliation. The Birmingham protesters' Commitment Cards declared social and spiritual transformation, justice and redemption interlocking goals.

Echoing apophatic warnings, King and Merton demand the opposite of violence. In the trash heap of things the apophatic tradition casts aside, Merton even renounces argument, one of the seeds of violence (Matt 5:21–2 2). After all, not only are visions and revelations transient, *all ideas of God, God's realm, and revolution are merely stations to pass through.* The apophatic tradition commends Underhill's "humble agnosticism"²⁰⁸ about what we can know about God's will *and* realm. Niebuhr rightly brands a certain kind of idealism foolish when it thinks it can chart a "straight path" toward health or happiness.²⁰⁹ King claimed he had seen the promised land, but he never said he knew how to get there.

This agnostic unknowing makes endless debates about transient ideologies, strategies, and tactics as inherently debilitating as disputes about knowledge and love. The heated rivalries within the civil rights movement

---

205. Gandhi, *Non-violent*, 381.
206. Merton, *Faith and Violence*, 21.
207. Ibid., 163.
208. Underhill, *Worship*, 263.
209. Niebuhr, *Irony of American History*, 133.

embody the ideological competition of every generation. Arguments between the NAACP, SCLC, Urban League, SNCC, and CORE about the best or most direct or most propitious path to justice—grassroots organizing *or* national organizations, confrontation *or* negotiation, legal action *or* civil disobedience, economic development *or* legislative reforms *or* electoral politics, the courts *or* the streets *or* the ballot box—exhausted valuable energy, generated unnecessary bile, and turned mutual respect into rancid animosity. Similar arguments about pragmatism and ideological purity turn allies into competitors. Saul Alinsky spurns altruism as unrealistic, embracing a Calvinistic view of self-interested human nature. His is a way of knowledge. Gandhi addresses the best in human nature—ahimsa from his followers, respect for his opponents. His is a way of love.

It ought to be an axiomatic apophatic principle that it is far easier to identify ideologies that do not lead to the realm than to discern which ones do, let alone which ones offer the widest path or the quickest shortcut. Instead of offering clarity about the path toward the realm, faith offers a stunning undefined openness. Rauschenbusch and Muste were both inspired by Hebrews 11:1: "Faith is the assurance of things hoped for, the conviction of things not seen." To Rauschenbusch, this shows "faith launching life toward the unseen future."[210] In Gatsbyesque terms, he describes faith as "a groping quest" toward "the occasional flitting of a distant light."[211] As Maurin contrasts chaos and order and King nightmares and dreams, Muste speaks of the city which is and the city to be.[212] Muste was inspired by his namesake's uncertain migrations: "Abraham . . . set out, not knowing where he was going. . . . For he looked forward to the city that has foundations, whose architect and builder is God" (Heb 11:8–10). There is a *here* and a *there*, but no map, no compass, no sun by day or moon by night that offers a sure way to get from one to the other.

This spiritual-political iconoclasm requires a stripping of ideas and self. Eckhart retells the story of Diogenes's meeting with Alexander the Great. The philosopher stood naked before the world conqueror—as Francis of Assisi later stood before his father—and told Alexander, "I have rejected more things than you have ever possessed. What you think it a great thing to possess is too petty for me to scorn."[213] Merton says it is absolutely necessary to renounce materialism. If you renounce war, you must renounce the

---

210. Rauschenbusch, *Social Gospel*, 101.

211. Ibid., 168.

212. Muste, *Essays*, 375, 415.

213. Eckhart, *Sermons & Treatises III*, 55. In a Sufi story, a sultan bows to a dervish who has renounced more than the sultan possesses (Fadiman and Frager, *Essential Sufism*, 85).

things that lead to war.[214] If you seek justice, you must distance and detach yourself from exploitation.

As Rauschenbusch describes a flitting light and John of the Cross a dark night, Underhill, using a homely metaphor, says it is a pitiful faith that cannot enter darkness until it knows where to find the light switch.[215] Whether praying or doing justice, there is no way to fully assess our direction. Underhill had her own version of keeping our eyes on the prize. When walking "a plank bridge," if we focus on "its narrowness and our own uncertain footsteps" we court disaster—but we cross it "easily" if "we look at the bank on the other side, and let ourselves go towards it."[216] As *The Cloud* recommends paying more attention to "the worthiness of God than to your own sinfulness,"[217] so Underhill urges us to envision the realm, King's surrealistic vision, rather than focusing on injustice. Hope links the unknowable God, the unseen realm, and the untraceable path. Underhill says, "Hope is supremely the virtue of the incomplete; of the creature stretching out in love and prayer to the complete Reality of God, the final object of Hope."[218]

This Magellan-like spirit of ideological fluidity characterized Muste's long career. Like a Sufi moving from one station to the next, Muste found temporary vocational homes in pacifism, labor organizing, labor education, secular leftist politics, and finally in antiracist, antinuclear, and antiwar activism. Muste shared with Gandhi a tireless exploration of nonviolence, constantly searching for alternative coalitions. To counter Cold War dualism, he sought a "third force" among nonaligned nations;[219] to counter the split between pacifism and violent activism, he sought a "third way."[220] Like Tri Quang, Muste admits that he can't outline a clear political path for the US to get out of Vietnam, but he knows that when someone is driving deeper into a swamp, the first step is to back up![221]

Often our commitment to a strategy or to a set of tactics or to charity or development or justice says more about our *vocation* than the path to the realm. If too much ideological clarity is as dangerous as prying into the essence of God, the world as it is needs more than *random acts of kindness* just as it needs more than infrequent, erratic prayer. Day speaks of increasing

---

214. Merton, *Secular Journal*, 110–11.
215. Underhill, *Ways of the Spirit*, 73.
216. Underhill, *Modern Guide*, 101.
217. *Cloud of Unknowing*, 117.
218. Underhill, *House* and *Concerning*, 64.
219. Muste, "Prospect for Peace in 1953," 9.
220. Robinson, *Abraham Went Out*, 51.
221. Muste, "Visit to Saigon," 10.

the sum total of goodness[222] in the world, but the spirits of the Niebuhrs and the practice of Freire cry out for conscientization. Discussions of strategy are never absolute but always necessary. There is a dialectical relationship between strategy and spontaneity. We seek to find *a* way if not *the* way.

Rather than dismissing the need for these debates, apophatic activism demands simply they take place in community—Clarence Jordan's Koinonia Farm, Lester's Brethren of the Common Table, Muste's The Comradeship, Gandhi's ashram, the Catholic Worker's roundtable discussions, Latin America's base communities, or the Fellowship of Reconciliation's chapters. Borrowing from the Wobblies, Maurin writes of creating "a new society within the shell of the old," of workers and scholars—bearing gifts of pragmatism and perspective—"making a path from the things as they are to the things as they should be."[223]

From a more Himalayan perspective, Dag Hammarskjöld expresses the same yearning for a community seeking the realm: "Hunger is my native place . . . hunger for fellowship, hunger for righteousness—for a fellowship founded on righteousness, and a righteousness attained in fellowship."[224] Activism, like mysticism, is never the flight of the alone to the Alone. Community is Baldwin's light in the darkness, Day's antidote to the "long loneliness," and our foretaste of the realm.

In and out of the ashram, Gandhi's pioneering socio-spiritual experiment with truth has that groping, Gatsby-like character of Hebrews 11. In his time, nonviolence was a new field, like psychoanalysis or quantum physics. Gandhi says candidly, "I claim to be making a ceaseless effort to find [Truth]. But I admit that I have not yet found it." He found it refreshing to be "painfully conscious of my imperfections," grounding to know his limitations.[225] The most famous theoretician and practitioner of nonviolence claims he has found the first steps toward truth, but freely confesses that he had "not mastered the whole technique of nonviolence." It is the nature of an experiment to take "one step at a time"; the distant goal remains beyond the horizon.[226]

Gandhi does not stand alone on this pinnacle of unknowing. After all of John of the Cross's flowing poetry, stifling prose, and theological craftsmanship, he assesses his work like a Zen novice who has been measuring heaven with a tiny reed: "the reason I undertook this task was to explain this

---

222. Day, *By Little*, 335.
223. Maurin, *Easy Essays*, 27, 37, 77, 83.
224. Hammarskjöld, *Markings*, 53.
225. Bondurant, *Conquest of Violence*, 17.
226. Gandhi, *Non-violent*, 385.

night.... Now the nature of this night has been explained *to some extent*."[227] His careful depiction of the dark night is an unfinished experiment with truth. After all, "pure contemplation is indescribable" and "secret." This is not a Gnostic secret whispered among a self-congratulatory elite. It is *God's* secret, unspoken because unspeakable. When all is said and done, the way to God is still no way. It cannot be mapped or traced. As John says, the "way and road of God, by which the soul travels toward God" is like the sea; "the way to God is as hidden and secret . . . as are *the footsteps of one walking on water* imperceptible."[228] If the land of the Spirit is a land without ways,[229] the revolution of God is an unseen path.

Merton reassures us that unknowing need not be unnerving: "It should not disconcert anyone who knows, from the Bible and from the mystics, that the silences of God are also messages with a definite import of their own."[230] Thus Silesius says:

> God far exceeds all words that we can here express
> In silence God is heard, in silence worshiped best.[231]

John adds, "The only language God hears is the silent language of love."[232]

There are parallels between the ways of no-violence and no-speech. Both are ways of no way, and in their unknowing they convey what we need to know. So when the archbishop of cosmopolitan Alexandria sought out Abba Pambo in the desert, his fellow monks encouraged him to share his wisdom, but Pambo replied, "If he is not edified by my silence, he will not be edified by my speech."[233]

The Egyptian desert stops there, but not the Russian forest. Seraphim of Sarov, reportedly so loquacious in his meeting with Motovilov, is also known as the "saint of silence."[234] A pilgrim, a student from Kiev troubled by a spiritual conundrum, treks for weeks to see Seraphim. Arriving at the monastery, he is directed to Seraphim's hermitage several miles further into the forest. The student finds the hut, but Seraphim is still nowhere to be seen. Then the student spies the hermit curled up sleeping like a squirrel in the thick grass. As the student gazes at Seraphim for a long time, he begins

---

227. John of the Cross, *Collected Works*, 382 (italics mine).
228. Ibid., 370–71 (italics mine).
229. Lane, *Solace of Fierce Landscapes*, 219.
230. Merton, *Faith and Violence*, 211.
231. Silesius, *Cherubinic Wanderer*, 49.
232. John of the Cross, *Collected Works*, 689.
233. Vivian, *Becoming Fire*, 86.
234. Nicholl, *Holiness*, 68.

to feel a great peace. He does not awaken Seraphim. He does not speak to Seraphim. He does not hear from Seraphim. But the spiritual conflict that burdened him and inspired his pilgrimage to Sarov is resolved, and he immediately begins the four-hundred-mile journey back to Kiev.[235] Like Motovilov, he sought Seraphim with a burning question. But unlike Motovilov, this pilgrim has no life-changing, jaw-dropping epiphany. Yet like a seed growing secretly, this apophatic revelation satisfies his spiritual hunger. He is edified by silence.

Just as God is unknowable and the realm is unseen, so the road to God's realm is like trying to trace the path of an arrow or follow footprints on the water. It is less like walking a path than wading into an ocean. The apophatic testimony is this: there are no footprints. There is no path. There are no ideological answers. What we think is *the* path is really *my* path. What we think is *the strategy* is really *my vocation*. What we think is *the truth* is only *my experiment*.

If only Karnow and all of the French and American and Communist forces of Armageddon arrayed in Vietnam in the mid-twentieth century could have heard that truth in the silent shrug of a monk's nonanswer, two million worlds might not have been destroyed. If only we, who kill even more breezily with drones that obscure the polluting effects of violence, could listen more deeply to such iconoclastic nonanswers, maybe a few million worlds can be saved.

MEDITATION: HOW SHOULD I PRAY?

How should I pray? What should I say? So often it's clear. The situation inscribes the words. The heartfelt, heartsick, heartbreaking needs of the person, the people, the loved ones, the collective need of those gathered; the needs of the parishioner, the patient, the family, the stranger invoke the words in my mind before they move my lips. Sometimes I pray for a clear and dramatic turning point. For the man with cancer—the father of teenagers—at the end of one of our long walks; for the baby in NICU; for the two-year-old in the ER; for my oldest, closest friend recovering from his second surgery: for powerful, out-of-this-world healing in this world this very day.

Sometimes I pray for calm, sometimes for surrender—contentedly when something truly is God's will, begrudgingly when out of horrific, inalterable necessity. For the mother weeping over her twelve-year-old daughter who has a bullet lodged in her brain: wisdom. For the raging, bedridden old bigot living in the psych ward with a five-minute memory: give her this day

235. Nicholl, *Holiness*, 68–69.

her daily blessings. There are times when grief and celebration mingle in a sacred embrace—holding hands around the hospital bed as the elderly man, his life complete, exhales his last breath during our prayer: receive him into the arms of your mercy; comfort his family at their loss. Visiting that same dear old friend in a hospice surrounded by snow, his blue eyes, lightning wit, and still-water faith still vibrant, praying together in thanksgiving for the last time for life and love and what is to come.

But right now I can't even feel or see the steamy breath of the Spirit. There is always the fallback position: your will be done, but half the time—*half* the time?—I admit to myself, who knows what that is? For the couple at the edge of divorce: reconciliation or resurrection? For the man in a coma as ready to die as to live: what words for him whether he hears me or not?

I pray for peace all the time: for people in Sudan or Israel or Palestine or Iraq or Iran or Afghanistan or Pakistan or Sri Lanka or Syria or Egypt or Libya or Ivory Coast or Colombia or Mexico or Mali or American city streets, wherever on any continent the violence is chronic or erupting. But when I pray for peace, what do I seek? Not only an end of violence, but the start of something unseen and unknown—the salaam, the shalom, the new creation, the wolf with the lamb, the child playing with the asp, the vine and fig tree, no one making anyone afraid. What else? When I pray for an end of oppression, what do I have in mind? That every homophobic tongue will cleave to the roof of its venomous mouth? That everyone has a job, a living wage, food, clothing, shelter, access to skilled teachers and competent health care? That any and every exploitative system will be replaced? By what? By something never clearly envisioned, yet always imagined?

I have just seen Irene for the first time in thirty years. When her sixteen-year-old daughter Allison was in that accident, in the days that followed in the hospital when they said her brain was irreparably damaged, in the months that dragged on when she couldn't speak, when she couldn't feed herself, when eye contact meant nothing, how was I to pray? When she died, what was I to say? Irene sent me a note after seeing me again, thanking me for my kindness. She says: "I miss her still."

How should I pray? What should I say?

6

Wounds, Forever Fresh

Fix your eyes on the Crucified, and nothing else will be of much importance to you.
—Teresa of Ávila[1]

Let us look with the hidden eye
and see Christ hanging from the Tree;
Let our eyes behold the Blood
that flowed from Christ's side.
—Ephrem the Syrian[2]

But all his acquaintances, including the women who had followed him from Galilee, stood at a distance, watching these things.
—Luke 23:49

I once was lost, but now am found,
Was blind but now I see.
—"Amazing Grace," John Newton

---

1. Teresa, *Interior Castle*, 229.
2. Brock, *Luminous Eye*, 83.

Wounds, Forever Fresh

Blessed are you when people revile you and persecute you and utter all kinds of evil against you on my account. Rejoice and be glad, for your reward is great in heaven.
  —Matthew 5:11

The Cross says just as much about Zen, or just as little, as the serene face of the Buddha.
  —Thomas Merton[3]

The Cross of Christ is the Jacob's ladder by which we ascend into the highest heavens.
  —Thomas Traherne[4]

There is but one road to the kingdom of God—a cross, voluntary or involuntary.
  —Theophan the Recluse[5]

Is this the Place of Skulls?
How can it happen then
That rose and lily here in fadeless beauty stand?
And there, the Tree of Life, the fount of the four rivers?
Yes, it is Paradise; Whatever be its name
Skull place or Paradise, I value them the same.
  —Angelus Silesius[6]

Do not seek Christ without the cross.
  —John of the Cross[7]

---

3. Merton, *Courage for Truth*, 271.
4. Traherne, *Centuries*, 29.
5. Chariton of Valamo, *Art of Prayer*, 231.
6. Silesius, *Cherubinic Wanderer*, 90.
7. John of the Cross, *Collected Works*, 702.

MEDITATION — OKLAHOMA CITY

Easter Week 1995. The afterglow of the resurrection. Christ is Risen! The Federal Building in Oklahoma City has been bombed. One hundred sixty-eight are dead, nineteen of them children. Nineteen new Holy Innocents on this day in that place. Liturgical life and real life are out of synch. Perhaps we ought to say, "Christ has died. Christ is risen. Christ has died again." Stories of the risen Lord suddenly seem out of context and out of tune. We have been forced to march back to the cross. Racist reactionaries have engaged in what they consider purposeful violence—an oxymoron in every season. We might have thought that the malevolent spirit of the Birmingham bombings had melted into the ether. Why did we think that? Why would we ever think that those bad old days, whatever the "badness," whichever the "days," would ever be behind us?

Events don't often dictate my preaching. I'd be a yo-yo if they did. I plan the basic content of my sermons months in advance. Liturgical life has a rhythm of its own, but it needs to intersect and interact with real life. Sometimes life in the world or in the congregation or in my heart intervenes, and I shift or tilt or reverse the sermon's direction. This week life—rather, death—has erupted to disrupt my neat plans. But before I redirect the sermon, I have to reconsider my thoughts. Once again sickened, I need to look and listen to the readings for the Second Sunday of Easter.

The end of the book of Job is speaking. A floored Job responds to the vertigo of the *mysterium tremendum*: "I had heard of you by the hearing of the ear, but now my eyes see you; therefore I despise myself, and repent in dust and ashes" (42:5–6). Like many others, I find this prose postscript a weak anticlimax and an artistic afterthought to the brilliant poetry that precedes it. Job has copped out. His torch is blown out. He has compromised his nonnegotiable demands. He has abandoned his quest for answers to the top tier of unanswerable questions. He may have known at a given moment that his Redeemer lives (19:25–7), but *we* know that Job has been *our* advocate, like another Holy Spirit interpreting our gurgling groans, like another Christ voicing our anguish and taking our side. This week, though, the book of Job speaks of a God beyond questions. This God transcends creation in which death and life spin together helplessly in a tornado. I could not maintain my faith unless I believed that God transcends all.

The beginning of the book of Revelation is speaking, the introduction to a series of overlapping visions, a book written in response to persecution, or its threat, or its abatement—systemic violence, real or remembered or feared. Revelation was written for those ready to duck beneath the blind, wild swing of suffering's pendulous blade. Its visions convey a future, a completion, an end that, to paraphrase Paul, will be so filled with glory that the entire history of burning human agony will in hindsight look like nothing more than a rash. Its eschatological "it is finished" speaks of a wholly consummated universe. I could not maintain my faith unless I believed that ultimately God overcomes all.

But I could not maintain my faith with the transcendence of Job and the hope of Revelation alone, not with so many innocents killed again for reasons without reason. I cannot believe in a God who *only* transcends misery, who *only* waits for us at the end with comfort and glory. That is not enough to say the Sunday after a bombing has killed people in Oklahoma City. It is not enough for me to believe in.

The story of Jesus in the Upper Room is speaking. Jesus came there twice to meet his doubtful disciples, Thomas being only the most notorious in a lineup of the usual suspects. The content of Jesus' words and the familiar timbre of his voice failed to convince his friends he was raised from the dead. Appearing inside a locked door did not pierce the armor of their bewildered skepticism. No. Each time the risen presence of God was recognized and recognizable *only* because of his wounds. If the risen Christ is not still wounded, always wounded, forever wounded, he would be an ecclesiastical artifact, a museum piece—do not touch!—partitioned off from real life.

I can believe *only* in a God who is wounded, a God who was crucified again in Oklahoma City. It is that crucified God—transcendent and more, glorious and more—that I need to remember this week and speak of this day.

NEW RICHES EVERYWHERE

Teresa of Ávila says, "Fix your eyes on the Crucified."[8] Watch Jesus bleed. Hear him groan. See the cross, the empire's instrument of social control and psychic castration.[9] See the *crucified God* (Moltmann), even more startling than the *risen Lord*. The scandal still grips our imaginations. The stumbling block still catches beneath our feet. Fix your eyes on the ultimate icon to see through it, an opaque window into eternity, a prism of malevolent darkness and holy light.

Architecturally and liturgically, the cross is the Christian faith's centerpiece. Spiritually, it is the one object upon which all *must* meditate. But even as we gaze at the crucified century after century our collective mind

---

8. Teresa, *Interior Castle*, 229.

9. Baldwin said that for African American men the difference between North and South was the way they were castrated (*Conversations*, 45).

has not settled on a single, paramount, or exclusive way to define its meaning. In fact, the longer we gaze at the cross, the more its meanings multiply. No historical event or religious symbol has accumulated so many connotations and implications. Truths cling to the cross like barnacles to a ship. Half-truths fly to the cross like moths to a flame. No single articulation fully distills its essence. The meanings do not merely flower in an ever-expanding garden; they contradict one another in a never-ending, multidirectional duel. Theologies are made incarnate on crosses; words become flesh and flesh becomes Word. Crosses make profoundly different theological statements, from crucifix—the fusion of Christ and cross—to *Christus Rex*—the *mysterium tremendum* made flesh. The meanings of the cross split, jab, leap, and split again like subatomic particles.

In the 1990s, a French monk—Christian Chergé—asked an Algerian Sufi, "When you look at the cross . . . how many crosses do you see?"

Two, the Sufi answered: one in front and one behind; God created the one in front, the oldest, before people constructed the second. On the front cross, a man extends his arms for "embracing, for loving. . . . The other cross is an instrument of hatred for disfiguring love." Chergé saw a third cross in their midst as a Sufi and a monk met together amidst a sandstorm of religious xenophobia, military brutality, and the rancid leftovers of imperialism: "isn't it perhaps he and I and this common effort we are making to loosen ourselves from the cross of evil and sin behind, so we can bind ourselves to the cross of love in front? . . . Isn't that gesture, the struggle of moving from hatred toward love a third cross?"[10]

This unfolding trinity of meanings is but a beginning. History, hymns, symbols, sculptures, paintings, poems, legends, visions, aphorisms, and stories tell us what we need to know about the cross, just as quick ink strokes unveil what we need to know about a person's character, charism, and faith. A hot coal cleanses Isaiah's lips. Ezekiel swallows a scroll. Jeremiah tastes words in his mouth—sweet, then fiery, then ashen. When Ephrem of Syria was a child, he had a dream braiding together the parable of the Mustard Seed and Jesus' saying of vine and branches, a dream that revealed his vocation: "a vine shoot sprang up from his tongue; it grew, and everywhere under the heaven was filled by it. It bore bunches of grapes in proliferation, and all the birds of the sky came and ate of its fruits; the more they ate, the more the bunches multiplied and grew."[11] The prophets have fire, a scroll, and words. The words from Ephrem's mouth feed multitudes. Brother Sylvester had a dream about the saint of Assisi: "he saw in his sleep a golden

---

10. Kiser, *Monks of Tibhirine*, 134–35.
11. Brock, *Luminous Eye*, 174.

cross coming forth from the mouth of Francis; its top touched the heavens and its extended arms encircled both parts of the world in their embrace."[12] When Francis spoke, his friends saw a cross linking horizons and bridging heaven and earth.

To some, the cross defines Francis's character, charisma, and faith.[13] According to legend, Francis prayed to the crucified Christ for two graces: first, to feel body and soul the pain Jesus "sustained in the hour of Your most bitter Passion"; second, to feel "that excessive love with which You, O Son of God, were inflamed in willingly enduring such suffering for us sinners."[14] Francis did *not* seek to *become* flame or light. To him, there could be no light, flame, sanctification, or transfiguration without humiliation. Theophan the Recluse says that the only way to the realm is through the cross, but that it can be involuntary; we can be drafted.[15] For Francis, taking up the cross is an act of free will, eager volunteerism, even excitement.

Francis prayed before the crucified Christ, and as often happens in meditation the content of his vision shifted, leaping erratically like a capricious deer or dancing like one of the newly-healed lame. In a story of his epiphany before the cross, his prayer swiftly hurdles from the immediate to the transcendent as he sees a Seraph "with six resplendent and flaming wings" descend from heaven. As Francis was "filled with joy and grief and amazement," he understood that he would some day be "utterly transformed into the direct likeness of Christ Crucified, not by physical martyrdom, but by enkindling of the mind." Like Isaiah, Francis is branded with his vocation. Like Isaiah, Francis knows the whole earth is full of God's glory, but Francis makes this discovery through the cross. During this "marvelous apparition, all of Mount Alverna seemed to be on fire with very bright flames, which shone in the night and illumined the various surrounding mountains and valleys more clearly than if the sun were shining over the earth."[16] In a legend foreshadowing Merton's epiphany at Polonnaruwa, Francis sees all matter *becoming fire* through his gaze on the cross. Here was an indelible light—night brighter than noonday, as blinding as Seraphim in the forest—and all things transfigured. Francis found in the crucified the doorway to the new creation.

---

12. Celano, *Saint Francis*, 227–28.

13. Leclerc calls "the humiliation and exaltation" of Christ the "central theme" of Francis's life (*Canticle of Creatures*, 34).

14. *Little Flowers*, 190.

15. Chariton of Valamo, *Art of Prayer*, 231.

16. *Little Flowers*, 190–91.

Visions make hearts sing, but the mind prefers the finite and knowable to fire and night. The mind wants to climb a ladder, not hang from a cross. So to coddle the mind's hubris the church slices up immeasurable truths into sushi-sized nibbles as it reduces the cross to the knowable, the explicable, the mundane, and the clichéd. Seeing less than an Algerian Sufi, historicists—hog-tied by rationalism—limit the cross to a single-sided, one-dimensional instrument of torture, shame, and murder. Superstitionists—enticed and ensnared by prerational magical thinking—rip the cross from history and turn it into a talisman or a jagged rabbit's foot. Yet the cross remains forever iconoclastic as it explodes palliative delusions of a gentle Jesus in a congenial world (H. Richard Niebuhr), hamstrung definitions of a naïve prophet slain by the powers that be, or mythic fantasies of an ahistorical, disembodied sacrifice. The iconoclastic-iconic cross slams false doors closed and opens new windows onto truth.

In one tradition, Francis modestly kept his stigmata in the closet as he "made every effort to hide this wound" from his friends.[17] But in a later legend, he showed his stigmata to Brother John and invited John to touch the nail in his hand, as the risen Christ asked his disciples to touch his wounds in the Upper Room. When Brother John touched the nail, "a scent suddenly came forth from it, spiraling up like smoke, as incense does"; when John smelled the smoke, "it filled his soul and body with such sweetness that he was immediately rapt by God in an ecstasy and became unconscious." For eight days, John ate nothing. For eight days, "everything he saw seemed fetid."[18] Like the Tomb of the Saints, the crucified, the cross, and the nails themselves emitted the sweet smell of sanctity. What could be more divinely natural than for God to transform a weapon of death into a tool of life, swords into plowshares, spears into pruning hooks (Isa 2:4, Mic 4:3), a cross into a tree of life? Why wouldn't God transform a tomb's stench into the holy fragrance of grace?

As Merton hints, the cross is like a perfectly opaque concrete poem,[19] a labyrinth more than a maze, an unanswerable riddle, a Zen koan, an insomnia-inducing parable. Jesus' parables are said to be *pregnant* with meaning, to have a *surplus* of meaning. To study a parable is not to seek a needle in a haystack of theories. It is, as Jesus says, to look with fresh eyes and listen with open ears (Matt 13:13–8). Jewish midrash and African American hermeneutics have been playfully creative in freshly reopening and vividly applying Scripture. In contrast, modern and postmodern rationalism

---

17. Celano, *Saint Francis*, 86.
18. *Little Flowers*, 212.
19. Merton, *Collected Poems*, 1017–30.

sometimes becomes a straitjacketed search for a needle-nosed truth. One of Robertson Davies's characters complains that the problem with atheists is that they do not understand metaphor.[20] The same problem persists in the mirroring opposite reductionisms of literalists and historicists who seem intent on finding *less* in Scripture than meets the eye, ear, mind, and heart. Every historicist and literalist tapering of meaning blunts the revolutionary implications of the cross.

Writing centuries before the first quest for the historical Jesus, John of the Cross says that discovering Christ is like entering "an abundant mine with many recesses of treasures": no matter how deep we go, we "never reach the end or the bottom, but rather in every recess find new veins with new riches everywhere."[21] What is true of Jesus is also true of his cross. Just as all created things share a shard of the ineffable mystery of their Creator (Gregory of Nyssa), so the cross shares in the mystery of Jesus' life: when Jesus was nailed to the cross, the meaning of the cross was nailed to Jesus.

The four evangelists demonstrate the difficulty of defining the meaning of Jesus' crucifixion when they undertake the superhuman task of using narrative theology to unite absurdity to truth and agony to love. Mark's Gospel baldly foreshadows the crucifixion (Mark 8:31, 9:31, 10:33–4) and hints at its purpose (Mark 10:45), but his passion narrative weaves a tale of unrelieved meaningless anguish. Of the Seven Last Words, the only one uttered in Mark is the opening trope of Psalm 22, the distant and formal "*eli*" ("my God") supplanting the intimate "*abba*" ("father"), the "why" unanswered, and the "forsaken" sickeningly redundant (Mark 15:34). While providing no other last words, Matthew implants purpose into the chaos—like a stiff spinal cord into an invertebrate—asserting that the crucifixion fulfills God's aims. Like the parable of the Seed Growing Secretly, Matthew does not say *how* this is true, but he sees almost everything in Jesus' life fulfilling God's designs (Matt 1:22, 2:15, 2:17, 2:23, 3:15, 4:14, 8:17, 12:17, 13:14, 13:35, 21:4, 26:54, 26:56, 27:9). Luke portrays Jesus—arrested, tortured, and dying—as a tireless, selfless caregiver. Luke's Jesus has already wept over Jerusalem in anticipation that it will fulfill its long-standing role as the executioner and cemetery of the prophets (Luke 13:33–34). When his hour comes, Jesus heals the slave's ear like Florence Nightingale, redirects the women's grief like Henri Nouwen's Wounded Healer, and comforts the dying like Mother Teresa (Luke 22:51, 23:28–31, 23:43). John goes even further as Jesus approaches death with Buddha-like calm. John's Jesus presciently knows that he will draw all people to himself (John 12:32–33). He

---

20. Davies, *Fifth Business*, 55.
21. John of the Cross, *Collected Works*, 551.

never flirts with ambivalence. He feels no pain. All is contentment and consummation. John completes a movement in the Gospels from unspeakable suffering to translucent grace.

This foundational interpretive diversity is the antithesis of reductionism, literalism, historicism, or final answers to theological questions. In fact, the Gospels embody what Gershom Scholem calls the "endless interpretability" of Scripture.[22] This open-ended and inventive hermeneutic is *almost* true of the cross, with one defining caveat: the cross is both like and unlike a nonrepresentational painting to which *any* meaning can be attached. On the one hand, the cross invites and welcomes new connotations. In a way, the Seven Last Words has always been a misnomer—they are, in fact, the first seven. Not only do the words of the risen Lord corroborate, correct, and add new strokes of the midrashic brush, but the cross itself continues to speak. Jesus' title was posted on the cross in Hebrew, Latin, and Greek, but the cross has Pentecost's gift of speaking in every dialect in which the Christian message is conveyed. On the other hand, this multiplicity does not deny one critical source of uniformity. Every word about the cross must be consistent with the historical experience and canonical witness of Jesus' crucifixion. From the beginning, Christians have linked the worst human agony with the most amazing grace. In holding together pain and purpose the Gospels avoid the later disastrous divorces of Jesus from his humanity and pain from the cross. Because it is grounded in history, we can speak of the cross as *suffering without meaning,* but never as *meaning without suffering.*

Even so, mystics sometimes steer close to separating Jesus from his humanity. In turn, activists sometimes quail at the opportunity to embrace his divinity. Like the theological trajectories Brueggemann discerns in the Old Testament—toward holiness *or* justice—when mystics and activists fix their eyes on the crucified, their visions can lead down different forks in the road. Mystics construct intricate soteriologies; activists deconstruct earthly suffering. Mystics proclaim God's objective grace; activists promote human synergy that joins God's initiative. Mystics underscore God's action; activists advocate human participation. Yet both mystics and activists believe that in gazing at and taking up the cross we discover an infinite transcendence amidst the most nauseating brutality.

If, as John of the Cross implies, we are engaged in an endless mining for christological meaning, the cross is one opening into the mine. In the Johannine glut of symbols, Jesus is both gatekeeper and gate (John 10:1–3). Silesius refers to Christ's wounds as "celestial gates";[23] Ruusbroec calls them

---

22. Alter, *Canon and Creativity*, 77.
23. Silesius, *Cherubinic Wanderer*, 89.

a "door to eternal life and your entranceway into that living paradise."[24] So the cross, like the nails in Francis's hands, wafts a scent of holiness that enfolds godforsaken pain. Through the cross, the crucified transforms our vision of all things.

While there is a kataphatic quality to the cross—a kernel of history and a lucid kerygma—the cross also has an apophatic essence. It cannot be explained by reason; it makes sense only to love. No one fully grasps it; anyone can carry it. So when Francis sees the crucified Seraph he enters a cloud of unknowing: "The sharpness of his suffering filled Francis with fear. And so he arose . . . sorrowful and joyful. . . . And while he was thus unable to come to any understanding of it and the strangeness of the vision perplexed his heart, the marks of the nails began to appear in his hands and feet, just as he had seen them a little before in the crucified man above him."[25] As Teresa says, we fix our eyes on the crucified, and whether or not we understand what we see, we are marked, scarred, and converted by seeing the one we have pierced.

EVERYTHING SEEMS TO BE BLOOD

Silence is not always golden, edifying (Pambo), or the language of God (John of the Cross). Silence *can* be calming and healing. Even an indifferent silence blessedly reminds us that the rest of the human race is oblivious to our embarrassments; that—in truth—others rarely think of us at all.[26] Nor does God have our phone lines tapped, our computers hacked, or the feces of our thoughts minutely scrutinized. We are saved from self-absorption by the things that silently ignore us.

Silence *can* be a source of tranquility. But there is also a divine silence that spurns our needs and salts our wounds. Silence can be a stake to the mind or a spear in the heart. Shusaku Endo's historical novel *Silence* describes the persecution of Christians and the apostasy of a Portuguese missionary in seventeenth-century Japan. In sentiments befitting Lamentations, the missionary wonders about "the silence of God. Already twenty years have passed since the persecution broke out; the black soil of Japan has been filled with the lament of so many Christians; the red blood of priests has flowed profusely; the walls of the churches have fallen down; and in the face of this terrible and merciless sacrifice offered up to God, God has

---

24. Ruusbroec, *Spiritual Espousals*, 188.
25. Celano, *Saint Francis*, 85.
26. Lane, *Solace of Fierce Landscapes*, 57.

remained silent."[27] The unrelieved suffering had given Japanese Christians "the feeling that while people raise their voices in anguish God remains with folded arms, silent."[28] God's silence is a terrifying divine apostasy, an abandonment of God's beloved people when they most need their beloved God.

In *Silence*, the act of apostasy is sacramentalized when a person steps on a *fumie*, a small metal image or wooden board, like an icon, of Jesus' or Mary's face. But unlike using an icon to deepen devotion, the political authorities use the *fumie* to induce Christians to renounce their faith. Whoever steps on the face of Jesus either has never been a Christian or has discovered the astronomical cost of discipleship. As the Portuguese missionary, his foot aching, readies himself to step on the *fumie*, he hears Jesus speak to him from the bronze cross beneath his foot: "Trample! Trample! I more than anyone know of the pain in your foot. Trample! It was to be trampled on by people that I was born into this world. It was to share people's pain that I carried my cross."[29]

Silence asks: can God forgive our frailties, infidelities, and denials? In a later novel, *Scandal*, Endo's question shifts. *Scandal* is a story of self-exploration, much like a certain famous novel in which the first-person narrator is shocked to see a respected physician secretly meeting with an unsavory thug. Describing this shadowy soul, the narrator says, "There is something wrong with his appearance; something displeasing, something downright detestable. I never saw a man I so disliked, and yet I scarce know why. He must be deformed somewhere; he gives a strong feeling of deformity, although I couldn't specify the point."[30] In time the narrator makes an even more startling discovery—these two people, one good and the other evil, are one and the same, Dr. Jekyll and Mr. Hyde. Later, the narrator reads in Jekyll's journal: "I knew myself . . . to be more wicked, tenfold more wicked—sold a slave to my original evil,"[31] more than he thought anyone could be. And he reveled in it!

As a bystander discovers that Jekyll and Hyde are one, in *Scandal* the protagonist—a Japanese writer (like Endo), a Roman Catholic (like Endo), someone who writes philosophical novels (like *Silence*)—discovers this moral bipolarity in himself. This is not a terrified disciple fleeing the scene of Jesus' arrest. This is someone who rejoices in vileness. This is Pilate ordering

27. Endo, *Silence*, 84–85.

28. Ibid., 93.

29. Ibid., 259.

30. Stevenson, *Dr. Jekyll and Mr. Hyde*, 9. A friend agrees that Hyde is touched by "the haunting sense of unexpressed deformity" (33).

31. Ibid., 84–85.

Jesus to be tortured when he believes Jesus to be innocent. These are the soldiers and the police around Jesus gratuitously adding humiliation to humiliation and blow to blow. This is the raw sadistic exercise of power. This is the faith-hope-and-love wrecking-ball subject matter of Philip Hallie.

In *Scandal*, the protagonist-novelist is told: "In reality all you've written about are people who have betrayed Jesus but then weep tears of regret after the cock crows three times. You've always avoided writing about the mob, intoxicated with pleasure as they hurled stones at him."[32] Sin is not the same thing as evil; in sin there is no sadism; in evil there is no inner debate, no spiritual divide, no remorse.[33] *Scandal* presents a less comforting portrayal of human nature. We may more happily be drawn into Endo's earlier query about weakness, but we must also face the remorseless evil of the ordinary sociopath in ourselves. For Endo, the cross makes us face human frailty, human cruelty, and divine indifference. This is not only the Algerian Sufi's second side of the cross: it is our empirical experience.

In medieval mysticism, as in fiction, portrayals of evil can be overwhelming. In a scene worthy of a contemporary slasher movie—someone tortured until no semblance of human form remains (Isa 52:14)—Julian of Norwich "saw" in her vision of Jesus' scourging, "the body bleeding copiously. . . . The fair skin was deeply broken into the tender flesh through the vicious blows delivered all over the lovely body. The hot blood ran out so plentifully that neither skin nor wounds could be seen, but everything seemed to be blood."[34] His body's attractiveness, its humanity, even its wounds disappear in a swirling red sea. Julian's vision of blood gushing from the "fair skin" and "tender flesh" of a "lovely body" sounds like a pornographic snuff film.

Everything seems to be blood. All else is obscured. Anyone with eyes to see sees suffering. Anyone with ears to hear hears an apathetic silence to anguished cries. If only we could see, we would see blood. The icons of systemic pain embedded in every act of exploitation and enacted in the sadistic norms of every economic system—like a series of living, breathing *fumie*—litter the face of the earth. Wherever we look, we see a revolving, unending, nonlinear, circular, and circuitous Stations of the Cross. All that is good in family, clan, tribe, and culture is obscured by pain. Everywhere activists look, they see blood. It grieves them. It enrages them. They yearn to prevent the next drop of blood from spilling out to mar and scar the goodness of creation.

32. Endo, *Scandal*, 228.
33. Ibid., 146.
34. Julian, *Showings*, 199–200.

"Every time I see lettuce," César Chávez says, "that's the first thing I think of, some human being had to thin it. And it's just like being nailed to a cross. You have to walk twisted, as you're stooped over, facing the row, and walking perpendicular to it. You are always trying to find the best position because you can't walk completely sideways, it's too difficult, and if you turn the other way, you can't thin."[35] It wasn't only lettuce that triggered his thoughts of the cross. So did beets. "That was work for an animal, not a person. Stooping and digging all day, and the beets are heavy—oh, that's brutal work. And then to go home to some little place, with all those kids, and hot and dirty—that is how a person is crucified. Cru-ci-fied."[36] The physicality of agricultural labor coils bodies into inhuman knots. The humiliating mistreatment—work for ox and ass, not a child of God—disfigures psyches. People—working so hard for so little, working like beasts of the field—were being crucified.

If Chávez sees this as a fellow laborer, W. E. B. DuBois imagines the perpetrators of violence discovering they are crucifying their Lord. In his poem "The Prayers of God," a repulsive epiphany shocks a white man lynching an African American.

> For this, too, once, and in Thy Name,
> I lynched a N------—
>
> (He raved and writhed,
> I heard him cry,
> I felt the life-light leap and lie,
> I saw him crackle there, on high,
> I watched him wither!)
>
> *Thou?*
> *Thee?*
> *I lynched thee?*
>
> Awake me, God! I sleep!
> What was the awful word Thou saidst?
> That black and riven thing—was it Thee?
> That gasp—was it Thine?
> This pain—is it Thine?
> Are, then, these bullets piercing Thee?
> Have all the wars of all the world,
> Down all dim time drawn blood from Thee?
> Have all the lies and thefts and hates—

---

35. Dalton, *Moral Vision*, 159.
36. Ibid., 64.

> Is this Thy Crucifixion, God ... ?[37]

Glimpsing evil through one horrific awakening, this fictitious white character awakens to a heart of darkness written on every page of his people's history.

As horrible as are the chronic physical aches of contorted bodies and the violence of civilizations, the psychic sting of twisted spirits may be worse. In a legend about al-Hallaj, when the crowd turns against him (like Jesus) and pelts him with stones (like Stephen), he maintains a Zen master's calm. When his tormentors chop off his hands, he never winces. But when a friend—a fellow teacher—strikes him with a flower, he "screamed as if in torture."[38] It is not the physical agony, or the hatred of the ignorant—those who do not know what they are doing—but the insult of a spiritual peer, that is most excruciating. Day says that the greatest evil perpetrated on the destitute is the "contempt"[39] that "stripped [them] ... of their sense of human dignity."[40] Francis of Assisi calls every insult of the poor "an injury to Christ."[41] Whoever disparages the poor tramples on the *fumie*.

To Merton, the crucifixion business was franchised, globalized, profitable, and invisible in its brazen commonness. Crosses are everywhere, yet few have eyes to see, ears to hear, or the will to respond to a suffering Christ. Corresponding with a nun in Haiti about the people with whom she worked, he remarks that "Christ is most visible among them, in them, in their poverty, in their abandonment, their destitution: why does no one look to see the face of Christ and come to Christ with help?"[42] If people could not see Christ where poverty and misery were blatant and bare, they were even more oblivious to the meaning of the 1960s arms race: "This is purely and simply the crucifixion all over again. Those who think there can be a just cause for measures that gravely risk leading to the destruction of the entire human race are in the most dangerous illusion, and if they are Christian they are purely and simply arming themselves with hammer and nails, without realizing it, to crucify and deny Christ."[43] Caesar and Pilate were alive and well in the mid-twentieth century, in every nation, every pulpit, and every pew. Yet Jesus' disciples could not discern the meaning of their political actions and their personal inaction. They assumed they

37. DuBois, *Darkwater*, 147.
38. Shah, *Way of the Sufi*, 190.
39. Day, *All is Grace*, 124.
40. Day, *Long Loneliness*, 215.
41. Celano, *Saint Francis*, 69.
42. Merton, *Cold War*, 60.
43. Ibid., 10.

could believe in Jesus, worship Jesus, sing to Jesus, follow Jesus, and love Jesus while getting ready to kill Jesus at the same time. Leading a retreat for nuns in the 1950s, Merton says, "A nun who has meditated on the Passion of Christ but has not meditated on the extermination camps of Dachau and Auschwitz has not yet fully entered into the experiences of Christianity in our time. For Dachau and Auschwitz are two terrible, indeed apocalyptic, presentations of the reality of the Passion renewed in our time."[44] Every concentration camp is another Golgotha. The arms race prepares the way for a cosmic crucifixion. Preemptive war mocks and scourges Jesus. Poverty crucifies sadistically, systemically, and silently.

Crosses are everywhere. And if the cross is endlessly interpretable, it is also endlessly applicable. It is not only seen as injustice through Mississippi eyes. The cross also corrects Mississippi eyes that see in the cross only pain crying out for relief. Day's potentially polemical reflection on the Memorial Day Massacre is transformed by the "suffering Christ," "Jesus of Gethsemane," who "bore the sins of all the world," and who "died to save us all."[45] Day believed the rich and powerful always trample the working poor, and she stood with the oppressed. But the cross not only demanded her activism, it transfigured her politics. So she prayed for those killed and those blind to their own sin, for Endo's fragile apostates, for Hallie's sadistic mob, and for the bestial systems that revel in brutality.

What Chávez, Day, DuBois, and Merton see in extraordinary events, ordinary sadism, and the norms of public policy and daily business, Jon Sobrino observes in the systemic deprivation of the poor of their daily bread and their God-given dignity. With Day and Chávez, he sees humiliation as an ever-present handmaid of oppression. Following Ignacio Ellacuría, Sobrino calls the populace of Latin America "crucified people."[46] Thus it has been for centuries: "the truth is that the Latin American people's cross has been inflicted on them by the various empires that have taken power over the continent: the Spanish and Portuguese yesterday, the US and its allies today; whether by armies or economic systems, or the imposition of cultures and religious views, in connivance with the local powers."[47] Sobrino cites Bartolomé de las Casas: "I leave Jesus Christ our Lord in the Indies, scourging him and whipping him and striking him and crucifying him not once but thousands of times, such are the Spaniards who trample and destroy

---

44. Merton, *Spiritual Direction*, 88–89.
45. Day, *By Little*, 246.
46. Sobrino, *Principle of Mercy*, 79.
47. Ibid., 50.

those peoples."⁴⁸ Another land, another century: people are trampled like the same *fumie*.

Sobrino meticulously compares the crucified people to God's "suffering servant" (Isa 52:13–53:12). What was written of Isaiah's suffering servant and later superimposed over Christ's passion is a universal norm. The servant is "a person of sorrows acquainted with grief" (Isa 53:3)—"the normal condition of the crucified people: hunger, sickness, slums, frustration through lack of education, health, employment." This is the condition of the Latin American people even in times of (others') prosperity and (official) peace. In times of rumor or revolution, the powers that be suspect the crucified people of sedition, condemn them, and massacre them like Holy Innocents.

Like the suffering servant, the crucified people have "no form or comeliness, no beauty" (53:2), since "to the ugliness of daily poverty is added that of disfiguring bloodshed, the terror of tortures and mutilations." Like the servant, they "arouse revulsion": "many were frightened by him because he was disfigured and did not . . . look like a human being" (52:14). So others "hide their faces from him" (53:3). The privileged avert their eyes, distract their minds, and stop their hearts because they cannot stand the sight of the poor. Like the servant, crucified peoples are "despised and rejected" (53:3). Sobrino says that this "contempt reaches its height when ideology takes on a religious tinge to condemn them in God's name." As Rauschenbusch says, religiosity sharpens the steel edge of intolerance. As Pascal says, "people never do evil so completely and cheerfully as when they do it from religious conviction."⁴⁹

It was said of the servant: "We esteemed him stricken, smitten by God, counted among the sinners" (53:4, 12). The poor, like Jesus on the cross, are deemed damned. To the powers that be, only those who suffer passively, like an antebellum Uncle Tom, are worthy. Like the suffering servant who "was oppressed and afflicted yet opened not his mouth" (53:7), they die quietly, surrendering to oppression as if it were God's will. Anyone opposing the status quo is a subversive. Hated in life, they are despised in death: "They made his grave with the wicked and his tomb with evildoers" (53:9). This, Sobrino says, is "the crucified people's epitaph"; their absolute "impotence" in life finds its consummation in being "taken away defenseless and without judgment" (53:8). Like lambs, they are slaughtered.⁵⁰

---

48. Ibid., 74.
49. Pascal, *Pensees*, 265.
50. Sobrino, *Principle of Mercy*, 51–53.

When everything seems to be blood, the institutional church occasionally awakens from its self-satisfied slumber to share the fate of the crucified. Oscar Romero's controversial preaching scandalized ecclesiastical authorities in Rome as much as it infuriated political leaders in El Salvador. In such a time, Romero says, priests *ought* to be murdered alongside their people. In such a place, "the church must cry out"; as a consequence, "it takes as spittle in its face, as lashes on its back, as the cross in its passion, all that human beings suffer." Only by joining the health, life, and fate of the church with the health, life, and fate of the poor could the church awaken oppressors to the pain they inflict on God: "Whoever tortures a human being, whoever abuses a human being, whoever outrages a human being abuses God's image, and the church takes as its own that cross."[51]

This is Christ crucified generation after generation, politically, economically, and spiritually. So when the mystical and liturgical traditions envision Jesus' suffering with gratuitous gore, they witness not only to the truth of Jesus' anguish, they make sense of a crucified world in which Christ's suffering becomes all-encompassing: "Every member of your holy body endured dishonor for our sakes; your head, the thorns; your face, the spitting; your cheeks, the buffeting; your mouth, the taste of gall mingled with vinegar; your ears, the impious blasphemies; your back, the scourging and your hand, the reed; your whole body, the stretching on the cross; your limbs, the nails; and your side, the spear."[52] In a mystical vision, Jesus says, "Now behold how my life was on earth!" This Jesus has "sunken" eyes, "and his cheeks were pitiful to see from the immense sorrow that he suffered"; he looks like one of Chávez' farm workers: "he was very weary from heavy labor, for his back and all his limbs cracked and he groaned within himself."[53] For Stringfellow, the crucifixion is simply the "summation of Christ's ministry."[54] Teresa says Jesus "is always being wronged and offended."[55] And she asks: what was Jesus' "whole life but a continuous death?"[56]

Liturgy links the crucified to human suffering. In the early twentieth century, as the Anglo-Catholic movement began its long push to reemphasize the sacraments within Anglicanism, Bishop Frank Weston put liturgical reforms in social perspective. Anticipating Merton's message to nuns, he

---

51. Romero, *Violence of Love*, 31.
52. Allchin, *Living Presence*, 120.
53. Buber, *Ecstatic Utterances*, 88.
54. Stringfellow, *Free in Obedience*, 15.
55. Teresa, *Life of Teresa*, 241.
56. Ibid., 274.

asserts that the liturgical and the holy must be wed to the political and the daily.

> If you are prepared to fight for the right of adoring Jesus in his Blessed Sacrament, then you have got to come out from before your Tabernacle and walk, with Christ mystically present in you, out into the streets of this country and find the same Jesus in the people of your cities and villages. You cannot worship Jesus in the Tabernacle if you do not pity Jesus in the slum. . . . And it is folly, it is madness, to suppose that you can worship Jesus in the Sacraments and Jesus on the throne of glory, when you are sweating him in the souls and bodies of his children. . . . Go out and look for Jesus in the ragged, in the naked, and in the oppressed and sweated, in those who have lost hope, in those who are struggling to make good. Look for Jesus. And when you see him, gird yourselves with his towel and try to wash his feet.[57]

Weston's address on the sacraments, Romero's sermons on the church, and Sobrino's analysis of the crucified all demand a response to Christ's suffering. Sobrino joins Ellacuría in saying that "the marrow of liberation theology," the essence of Christian dogma, and the primary demand from the crucified people is to end their exploitation.[58]

Mystics also hear Christ crying out for justice. With an activist's sensibility, Julian says that our sins wound Jesus.[59] Birgitta hears the crucified Christ say, "Those who scorn me and neglect my love: they have done this to me."[60] Sobrino's insight is anticipated by Pascal's mystical-ethical aphorism: "Jesus will be in agony even to the end of the world. We must not sleep during that time."[61] So Sobrino adapts the Ignatian questions Underhill used on retreats—"What have I done for Christ? What am I doing? What ought I to do?"[62]—to the crucified people: "What have I done to crucify them? What am I doing to take them down from their cross? What ought I to do that a crucified people may rise again?"[63] In a world in which Christ is always being crucified, Sobrino and Ellacuría echo Pascal: the single demand is "to take them down from the cross."[64]

57. Leech, *Social God*, 9–10.
58. Sobrino, *Principle of Mercy*, 53, 180.
59. Julian, *Showings*, 280.
60. Birgitta, *Life and Revelations*, 73.
61. Pascal, *Pensees*, 148.
62. Underhill, *Ways of the Spirit*, 103, 123.
63. Sobrino, *Principle of Mercy*, 96.
64. Ibid., vii.

In framing human suffering like this, Sobrino and DuBois reverse our unconscious expectations. Instead of powerless people crying out to an almighty God for divine intervention, we hear a helpless God in a godless universe cry out for human help. This brings a particular meaning to Teresa's guidance to enter prayer "with one sole determination, to help Christ bear his Cross."[65] It is one thing to be Simon of Cyrene (Teresa). It is another to unplug systemic power and ban crucifixions, whether as a means of social control or as a norm of economics. Teresa assumes, like Reinhold Niebuhr, that our power is limited; we can only suffer with Christ. Sobrino and Ellacuría insist we have both the choice and the power to *save* Christ.

Ellacuría remembered Romero's prophecy that when he was murdered, he would rise again in the Salvadoran people. When Ellacuría and his colleagues were murdered, Sobrino claimed that their deaths—crucifixion while seeking social transformation—also had a mystical meaning. But then there is the crucifixion of a whole people. Are martyrs' deaths only for the famous few? Do the deaths of common people lose their redemptive spring? This genealogy of death has its own polyphonic interpretability. Perhaps death redeems only when consciously risked as a way toward the realm. In that light, what of the unnamed and unremembered who bear the cross involuntarily? Who do they die for? As W. H. Auden quipped: if we are here to do good to others, why are the others here? To interpret the murders of the powerless in this way heightens the premythologized role of the cross as an instrument of law and order, cruelty and humiliation without meaning or purpose. Such a linear and exclusive reading of martyrdom is yet another emasculation of the crucified. Worse than Auden's critique, to Freire this is trickle-down redemption. As bad as losing life and limb, we again soul-strip the crucified people when we portray them as passive victims instead of as active agents empowered to transform life and death.

A more circular reading of this communion of martyrs starts with Romero's words to the citizens of Aguilares after they were victimized—murdered and tortured—by rampaging military forces. Visiting the town a month after the incident, Romero identified the village with Christ: "You are the image of the divine one who was pierced." Even as Romero protested the military's actions, he petitioned the villagers, "If your suffering . . . is given a redemptive meaning, then Aguilares is singing the precious stanza of liberation. . . . For God there is only the mystery of pain, which if accepted with a sense of sanctification and redemption, will be like that of Christ our Lord, a redemptive pain."[66] If they could voluntarily fuse their involuntary

---

65. Teresa, *Life of Teresa*, 160.
66. Brockman, *Word Remains*, 53–54.

victimization to the cross, their suffering would transform El Salvador. If they could link their suffering with the anguish of Christ, *they*—ordinary peasants—could liberate their nation. Sobrino says that when Romero died, he mixed his blood with the blood of his people, and joined his sacrifice to *theirs*:[67] "crucified people themselves are bearers of salvation."[68] The martyrdoms of the few are only the most visible signs of salvation arising from the crucified people.

Redemption begins and ends with the crucified people from whom Romero and Ellacuría arise and to whom they belong. Populist synergy precedes the redemption that comes from singular martyrs. Populist synergy is Isaiah's rain of grace that brings life from the earth (Isa 55:10). This egalitarian redemption arises from ordinary people. From this perspective, everywhere you look, you see crosses, but you also see some of the crosses faithfully embraced as the way to the realm.

REDEMPTION EX NIHILO

The irresolvable conundrum of Christian faith became its central symbol. How could a first-century Palestinian Jew explain the judicial execution of a fellow Palestinian by the Roman authorities with the complicity of the Jewish religious establishment? Not: how could it be explained as a historical event? That was simple: for the Roman Empire—like all empires and nations—savagery was a norm of its civilization aimed to quell any and all political opposition, any and all conscientious objection—real or imagined. For Stringfellow, the intrinsically bloodthirsty nature of principalities is as much an article of faith as the infinite grace of God. Even the homicidal behavior of religious leaders—preoccupied with ritual purity while lobbying for human blood—falls within the norms observed by Rauschenbusch and Pascal. So Stringfellow refers to the first-century Sanhedrin as "ecclesiastical authorities"[69] as he prods the bishops of his time so deft at silencing criticism, critics, and Christ.[70]

That side of the cross, the Sufi's second side of unabashed, institutional cruelty and human frailty is empirical. For that, there is no theological

67. Sobrino, *Archbishop Romero*, 196.

68. Sobrino, *Principle of Mercy*, 53.

69. Stringfellow and Towne, *Suspect Tenderness*, 64; Stringfellow, *Count It All Joy*, 86.

70. Stringfellow was harshest with bishops of the Episcopal Church ("State of the Church," 4), but when a Roman Catholic bishop said he "washed his hands" of Daniel Berrigan and his antiwar compatriots, Stringfellow sarcastically said he was glad the bishop knew his Bible, as the bishop quoted Pontius Pilate (*Second Birthday*, 131–32).

problem. But to insert cosmic significance into the defeated silence of Calvary requires a different kind of gall. The New Testament laid the first cornerstone in a theological edifice on which tradition continues to build. Sometimes extravagant mental paraphernalia even obscures the cross just as blood covers Jesus' body in Julian's vision. But with clarity and simplicity, Julian summarizes the questions to be asked of the crucifixion: 1) who suffered, 2) what he suffered, 3) why he suffered, and 4) for whom he suffered.[71] Never even in the first century was there a temptation to attribute martyrdom—the usual spin—to Jesus' death.[72] So when the most routine explanation was casually chucked aside, there was a need for both new wineskins and new wine.

Historically, Jesus' death refutes his life. In the face of his message of truth, love, and forgiveness, he was libeled, despised, and shamed in methods as thorough as Roman and Jewish cultures could devise. In the face of his beatitudes, he was visibly cursed. When Paul calls the cross a "stumbling block" (1 Cor 1:23), he is guilty of an incredible, and incredibly rare, understatement. If ever there has been a theological train wreck, this is it. Yet from the apostolic era, Christians embraced the cross instead of shunning it, running hands, hearts, and minds through its gelatinous theological consistency and its logical inconsistencies. In early centuries, pilgrims to the Holy Land, like modern paparazzi, were so visibly star struck by the cross that when the bishop of Jerusalem exposed pieces of the True Cross for veneration, he held it firmly while his deacons—like secret service agents—surveyed the crowds to make sure that when pilgrims kissed it, they didn't bite off a piece.[73] So Christians still drawn to the cross chew on its ancient slivers.

Sometimes theology pairs the cross and resurrection as a built-in solution to quickly fix and round off the serrated cross into a speed bump in God's divine plan. But more often than not, the cross stands alone. The most debasing and debased of all cruel and usual ancient punishments became, in the eyes of Christians, the paradoxical cure for everything that ails the human race. As Julian hears God say, "I have set right the greatest of harms, then it is my will that you should know through this that I shall set right everything which is less."[74] It is by the peculiar logic of the cross that King could say that God can "wring" good from the deaths of innocent girls. So the cross became a sign of *redemption ex nihilo*; redemption not only from nada, but from chaos, the sadistic, and the satanic.

71. Julian, *Showings*, 213.
72. Williams, *Resurrection*, 74.
73. Wilken, *Land Called Holy*, 116.
74. Julian, *Showings*, 228.

This is not to say that the cost of the cross is lost to tradition. Upon further theological review, the human tragedy is merely the first layer of horror. If, as Christian theology claims, Jesus is one person of the Trinity, it heightens the crucifixion's hideous perversity. If, as the Gospel of John (John 1:1–18), and the Epistles to the Colossians (Col 1:15–20) and the Philippians (Phil 2:5–11) (and Christian theology after them) proclaim, the logos-the-source-of-life is also the logos-killed, then the cost of the cross is exponentially greater than the political murder of a brilliant and charismatic first-century rabbi—it is the calamity of the crucified God. Augmenting the ironic tragedy of the cross, an Orthodox hymn for Good Friday says that the one "who suspended the earth upon the waters is hung on the tree. The King of Angels is crowned with a crown of thorns. The One who adorned the heavens with clouds is arrayed in the purple of mockery. The One who freed Adam in the Jordan, bears to be struck."[75]

A medieval mystery play dramatizes the paradox. It is characteristic of these plays to parody Satan by showing that the best laid plans of devils and demons oft go astray.[76] So in one play, demons initiate the crucifixion, but when the redemptive significance of Christ's death dawns on them, they try and fail like comic silent movie figures to keep Jesus from being crucified.[77] Attributing redemption to the cross takes Audre Lorde's distinction between pain and suffering a great leap forward. Not only could affliction contain the power to heal; the cross—suffering simmered to its essence—could renew the universe. The cross became a symbol of gratuitous cruelty and God's graceful mercy. It was as if God, puzzled and paralyzed like a world-weary Qoheleth, decided like Malcolm X that redemption would be achieved *by any means necessary*.

Mystics have long given voice to this contradiction as human evil and demonic intent (Luke 22:3) ally in sinful synergy only to collide with divine purpose. In that collision, divine intentions overwhelm the evil of the cross like a cleansing wave sweeping through barbed wire. If the *cost of messiahship* is the excommunication, annihilation, and damnation of God, the purpose of the cross makes that price a bargain. Laying out these contradictions, Anselm of Canterbury—seeing both sides of the Sufi's cross—focuses on Julian's question: why. He explains why *they*, the authorities, wanted Jesus dead, and how God—letting Jesus die—is the antithesis of a silent bystander.

> They chose you [Christ]

---

75. Lossky, *Mystical Theology*, 150.
76. Russell, *Lucifer*, 259.
77. Ibid., 266–67.

> That they might carry out their evil deeds;
>> God chose you
> That God might fulfill the work of God's goodness.
> They that by you
>> They might hand over the righteous to death;
>> God that through you God might save sinners from death.
> They that they might kill life;
>> God that God might destroy death.
> They that they might condemn the Savior;
>> God that God might save the condemned.
> They that they might bring death to the living;
>> God to bring life to the dead.
> They acted foolishly and cruelly; God wisely and mercifully.
>> Therefore, O Cross, to be wondered at,
>> We do not value you
>> Because of the intention of their cruel folly,
>> But according to the working of mercy and wisdom.[78]

Struggling to avoid early heresies that nullify Jesus' humanity and insulate God from pain, the mystics speak of Jesus being pulled in two directions. But contrasting the human and the divine within his nature, at times they seem to stray into ante- and anti-Nicene Christology. Founded on the contrasts within the Gospels and their own vision, they describe Jesus' human nature as betrayed and befuddled as his divine nature remains still and serene. In daring theological language, they elucidate the paradox of godforsaken meaninglessness *and* the crowning work of salvation in visualizations of the atonement.

In Johannine fashion, Julian reports Jesus' "patience," his "joy and delight,"[79] and Catherine that he was both "happy and sad" as he went to the cross.[80] Like the grammatically limited but eloquent African American woman during the Montgomery bus strike who said "my feets is tired but my soul is rested,"[81] so, according to Catherine, Jesus' *body* suffered, but "because his divine nature joined with his human nature" his "soul was happy."[82] The *Theologia Germanica* makes a similar distinction, claiming that Jesus' "outer" person suffered while the "inner" one "rested in the same bliss and joy as it did after the Ascension."[83] Ruusbroec, perhaps harmoniz-

---

78. Anselm, *Prayers and Meditations*, 102–3.
79. Julian, *Showings*, 168.
80. Catherine, *Dialogue*, 146.
81. King, *Testament of Hope*, 227.
82. Ibid., 193.
83. *Theologia Germanica*, 67.

ing Gospel accounts, says that Jesus' "tender nature was oppressed by fear of suffering," but in "the higher part of his being Christ was always of one will" with God.[84]

Always focused on the *why* of the cross, Julian says that the degree of Christ's suffering measures the magnitude of his extravagant love. Love, she says, gave Jesus strength "to suffer more than all people could," not only more than someone could endure in a lifetime, but "more pain than would all people together, from the first beginning to the last day."[85] In spite of this torment, the crucified tells her, "If I could suffer more, I would suffer more." If he needed to die once for each person so that all could be saved, "love would never let him rest till he had done it." Christ did not say to her, "If it were necessary to suffer more," but that he would willingly suffer regardless of the necessity. When she tried to imagine how many times Christ would be willing to die, "the number so far exceeded my understanding and intelligence that my reason had not leave or power to comprehend or accept it." Just as his suffering was greater than that of the whole human race through history, so his "love was without beginning, it is and shall be without end."[86]

Human sin, mystics believe, hurt Christ more than the nails of the cross, and Christ would rather die to destroy sin than live and let it reign.[87] No matter how the mystics calculate their theology, the equations always show the divine purpose of the cross far exceeding its cost. Catherine contrasts Jesus' "finite" suffering with his "infinite" longing for the human race.[88] His torture lasted unendurable hours, but his yearning for the human race is eternal. Playing on this contrast, *The Mirror of Simple Souls* says that even the tiniest drop of Jesus' blood could redeem 100,000 worlds.[89] In light of the infinite significance of Christ's blood, Teresa struggles to gauge the significance of *our* actions: "For the sum total of all we can do is worthless by comparison with a single drop of the blood which the Lord shed for us."[90] As a tireless reformer, Teresa is not denigrating human effort—she expended all she had. She is simply measuring human effort against God's.

Eckhart hints at a connection between the crucifixion and *becoming the flame* when he says that Jesus bore his suffering because "on the Cross

---

84. Ruusbroec, *Spiritual Espousals*, 197.

85. Julian, *Showings*, 144.

86. Julian, *Showings*, 217–18; see also Birgitta, *Life and Revelations*, 196, Pseudo-Dionysius, *Complete Works*, 280.

87. *Theologia Germanica*, 109–10.

88. Catherine, *Dialogue*, 138, 139, 278.

89. Porete, *Mirror of Simple Souls*, 141–42.

90. Teresa, *Life of Teresa*, 383.

his heart burnt like a fire and a furnace … so he was inflamed on the Cross by his fire of love for the whole world."[91] Catherine insists that Jesus *chose* to be crucified: he was held on the cross not by physical nails but by "nails of love."[92] She contrasts Jesus' terrible pain and the "fruit" of the cross: "Had it not been infinite the whole of humankind, past, present, and to come, would not have been restored."[93] Salvation is not imparted to "just half of the world but the whole human race, past, present, and future."[94] Universal salvation, hardly in theological vogue in the fourteenth century, is the only logical purpose for Jesus' death, the only purchase—to use one tradition's language—that would make it worth the price. And just as purpose far exceeds price, so, she says, God's mercy is "incomparably greater than all the sins that have ever been committed in the world."[95] Insisting that Jesus' energized soul overcame his exhausted body, Catherine and Julian say that Jesus, knowing what his death would achieve, "ran" to take up his cross.[96]

Activists face the same contradictions and often arrive at the same conclusion. Sobrino acknowledges the "absurdity and meaninglessness of suffering" but also asserts its "salvific possibilities."[97] While Jesus' suffering is never fully grasped intellectually, Christians say "in the Suffering Servant of Yahweh there is light and salvation, and that in the crucified Christ lies the wisdom of God."[98] Echoing mystical tradition, Sobrino claims: "The cross on which God is placed is the most eloquent proclamation that God loves the victimized of this world."[99] Writing more personally of his friends' deaths, he says that in their lives, work, and fate they unite the human and the divine.[100] For Christians, the incarnation and the atonement—two distinct theological strands—both seek the same end: the reunion of the divine and the human. As Christ's death draws all people to him, so "from their crosses, the martyrs unite us as a Salvadoran people and as a Christian people." Like the prophets' visions of the nations on pilgrimage to Jerusalem (Mic 4:1–4, Isa 2:2–4) or the gathering of all creation around God's throne (Rev 7:9–17), he says, "Around their crosses have gathered Salvadorans and

91. Leech, *True Prayer*, 150.
92. Catherine, *Dialogue*, 143.
93. Ibid., 139.
94. Ibid., 247.
95. Ibid., 260.
96. Ibid., 239, 327; Julian, *Showings*, 273.
97. Sobrino, *Principle of Mercy*, 28.
98. Ibid., 78.
99. Ibid., 9.
100. Ibid., 183.

people from many other countries, Christians of different churches, and even nonbelievers."[101] So, for Sobrino, not only does Christ's cross reveal God's love, redeem from violence, restore creation, and unite all people—whenever we join our work, life, and death to the work, life, and death of Jesus, we cocreate salvation from the sadistic and satanic with the nothingness of our own deaths.

BLESSED WOUNDS

Artistic renderings of the cross sometimes glory in prurient spectacle, religious masochism, and insatiable sadism. Each drop of blood from hands, feet, side, brow, and even eyes is portrayed in minute detail. In such depictions, the crucified Jesus becomes another freak, to be observed or perversely enjoyed, but not emulated. The stigmata are reduced to ritual tattoos. Jesus' death is severed from a Christlike life. Feminists and womanists rightly protest that meanings blur destructively as false pastors, like false prophets saying "peace, peace, when there is no peace," tell women that they should endure domestic violence and forgive their abusers as Jesus did. When we get lost in the gore alone *or* the grace alone, we disconnect empathy from the foulest of human experiences. Christ suffers, not with us or for us, but instead of us.

If activists see the cross primarily as a political reality, mystics see it as a merciful sacrifice, a revelation of divine love, and a source of glory. The mystics, as Underhill notes, are not only grounded in biblical tradition, they are rooted in the religious expressions of their culture, embedded in what Merton calls the unique "logos" of time and place.[102] Pentecost was a one-time event in which people heard the good news in the language of their culture and class, but the ongoing interpretive movement of the Spirit makes that singular event a common norm. So the mystics rooted in their age and touched by the Spirit use culture-bound and time-honored norms to express the meanings of the cross.

Julian's vision of the crucified contains enough gruesomeness to satisfy any sadist. At the same time, the *meaning* of the grotesque incarnates a divine ardor to share the most horrid of circumstances—cruelty, abuse, torture, injustice, poverty, disease, and starvation. The point of such visions is not to get *lost* in Christ's wounds but to be *found* in them. Julian sees Jesus' body obscured by a grisly flood, but she draws a distinction between her spiritual vision and our physical reality. The blood dripped down from Jesus'

---

101. Ibid., 184.
102. Merton, *Courage for Truth*, 186.

body, but then "disappeared"; if her vision had been physical, "the bed and everything all around it would have been soaked in blood." No vision of the crucifixion can be bloodless, yet Julian is less concerned with the physical details than the personal and universal significance of Christ's wounds. So when she sees that Christ's blood "descended into hell and broke its bonds, and delivered all who were there and who belong to the court of heaven," she envisions a universal liberation unbound by space. When she sees that his blood "overflows all the earth, and it is ready to wash from their sins all creatures who are, have been and will be of good will,"[103] she envisions redemption unbound by time. What flows from Christ's side is not merely his "dear blood and precious water" but a "flood of mercy" that restores us in God's image and makes us "fair and clean."[104] Her vision literally embodies Isaiah's words: by his wounds we are healed (Isa 53:5).

For Julian, the bond between Christ's pain and ours began when the world was drawn to *his* suffering. As Christ's suffering draws him into all times and places, so all creation is magnetically pulled toward Calvary. In John's language, Jesus draws the world to himself (John 12:32). To this Julian adds: "We are now on his cross with him in our pains, and in our sufferings we are dying, and with his help and his grace we willingly endure on that same cross until the last moment of life."[105] Such is the personal significance of the cross, but as Stringfellow reminds us, the personal is but one component of faith, and Julian's vision is multidimensional: "When he was in pain, we were in pain, and all creatures able to suffer pain suffered with him," even animals, even "the firmament and the earth failed in their natural functions because of sorrow at the time of Christ's death"; when Jesus was dying, "their nature constrained them to fail with him."[106] If Paul contends that creation groans in labor, Julian adds that creation wailed its most deafening groan when Jesus died.

Among medieval mystics as among modern evangelicals, Jesus' wounds and blood take on a life and power of their own as if salvation is achieved almost apart from the teachings, the actions, even the person of Jesus. Julian says, "the blessed wounds of our savior are open and rejoice to heal us."[107] Silesius describes Christ's blood as "precious dew."[108] Bernard

---

103. Julian, *Showings*, 199–200.
104. Ibid., 302.
105. Ibid., 215.
106. Ibid., 210.
107. Ibid., 302.
108. Silesius, *Cherubinic Wanderer*, 73.

knits together a collage of biblical images to describe his experience of the cross. Through Jesus' hands, feet, and side,

> I can suck honey from the rock and oil from the flinty stone—
> I can taste and see that the Lord is good. . . . [T]he nail that pierced him has become for me a key unlocking the sight of the Lord's will. . . . The secret of his heart is laid open through the clefts of his body; that mighty mystery of loving is laid open, laid open too the tender mercies of our God. . . . Surely his heart is laid open through his wounds![109]

For Ruusbroec, the wounds are like the Tomb of the Five Saints healing and intoxicating the human race: "From his wounds balm and wine flow upon us, and their fragrance and taste make the lovers of God drunk."[110] The holy scent emitted from the nails in Francis's hands becomes, in Ruusbroec's reading of the crucifixion, a universal ecstatic experience.

Matthew's attribution of divine purpose to the crucifixion is the fountainhead for these images. To some the cross signifies divine compassion: Francis de Sales says, "it is certain that on the tree of the Cross the Heart of Jesus, our beloved, beheld your heart and loved it."[111] To Ephrem it means the restoration of the human race:

> There came forth from Christ water;
> Adam washed, revived, and returned to Paradise.[112]

Catherine hears God say that Jesus, "by stripping himself of life, clothed you anew in innocence and grace."[113] As God swallows death in the resurrection (1 Cor 15:54), in the crucifixion mercy swallows sin like an annoying insect.

In Traherne's reflections on the "strange paradox" of the crucifixion, human nature stays stubbornly distant from the divine. Usually reveling in the even-keeled goodness of creation, Traherne contrasts the worst in human nature with the inscrutable and incalculable greatness of God's grace: "The worse they are the more they were to be beloved . . . to be pitied, and tendered and desired, because they had more need, and were more miserable." Sin demands divine love. Yet to him, the crucifixion does not restore human goodness. Rather, it magnifies the ever-stretching grandeur of God's mercy. With the crucifixion, and ever after, people "are now worse, yet more

---

109. Bernard, *Song of Songs III*, 143–44.
110. Ruusbroec, *Spiritual Espousals*, 208.
111. de Sales, *Introduction*, 285.
112. Brock, *Luminous Eye*, 83.
113. Catherine, *Dialogue*, 279.

to be beloved. For Jesus Christ has been crucified for them. God loved them more."[114] Thus does Traherne make a lyrical prestatement of Endo's fiction and Will Campbell's "we're all bastards but God loves us anyway." Yet if human nature remains debauched, for Traherne the crucifixion burnishes creation's gleam: "Heaven and Earth are infinitely more valuable than they were before, being all bought with Your precious blood."[115]

Catherine has a personal experience of the cross. In Christ's wounds she finds a place to "hide myself . . . and bathe in his blood" as her sins are "consumed."[116] God invites her to make the wounds "your place of refuge": "Make your home and hiding place in the cavern of his open side." In Christ's "open heart" she finds the source of love that inspires her to love her neighbor.[117] For Catherine the wounds unite as a single nurturing womb; for Thomas à Kempis they are a place of metanoia. If we "entered the bloody wounds of Jesus, and had there tasted a little" of Christ's love, we would "care nothing for the liking or the disliking of the world." Next to Christ's wounds, all that the world offers is infantile, vacuous, tepid, petty, and trite. Entering the wounds of Christ is the first step to spiritual freedom. Dwelling in God's "perfect love," we disarm our selfish self.[118] Where Catherine finds love, and Thomas freedom, Teresa finds divine comfort. In her visions, she usually saw Christ in his "resurrection body"—but occasionally, she says, "to strengthen me when I was in tribulation," Christ revealed his wounds, wore a crown of thorns, carried his cross, or was nailed to the cross.[119] To be awakened to Christ's suffering helps Teresa endure her own anguish.

Ruusbroec finds the doorway to Christ's wounds in the sacraments. When we receive his body and blood we press ourselves "into the wounds and into the open heart of Christ."[120] Rather than being a sanctuary, as the wounds are for Catherine and Julian, for Ruusbroec, as with Thomas, they are the starting line of a Pauline race. And rather than merely being a transforming personal experience, for Julian the wounds are signs of universal salvation perfected in intimate affection: "With a kindly countenance our good Lord looked into his side, and he gazed with joy." He drew her comprehension "into his side by the same wound; and there he revealed a fair and delectable place, large enough for all humankind that will be saved and will

---

114. Traherne, *Centuries*, 180.
115. Ibid., 38.
116. Catherine, *Dialogue*, 125.
117. Ibid., 239.
118. à Kempis, *Imitation of Christ*, 77.
119. Teresa, *Life of Teresa*, 269.
120. Ruusbroec, *Spiritual Espousals*, 109.

rest in peace and in love." Then, with joy, "our good Lord" spoke again, "See how I love you." And he said it "as if he said, my darling." The tender love Julian so often describes becomes even more intimate: "My child, behold and see what delight and bliss I have in your salvation, and for my love rejoice with me."[121]

Remolding and enlivening the tradition they inherited, the mystics turn the wounds of Christ into a "fountain of forgiveness,"[122] a safe haven, a source of healing, a place of awakening, an expression of intimacy, a doorway to eternal life, and a proclamation of universal salvation. For them, the cross becomes what Traherne calls "the throne of delights. That Center of Eternity, that Tree of Life in the midst of the Paradise of God."[123]

This multiplication of meanings does not white out any of the Seven Last Words, staunch the tears of Jesus' loved ones, or mute the heartsick, stricken cry of creation. Each new insight enhances the meaning of the cross as more than a temporal event imprisoned by time and space. Silesius says that the passion "did not end on the Cross; by night and also day" Jesus "suffers still for us."[124] Catherine describes God's "joy" that "Christ's wounds, forever fresh" are "continually crying out for mercy to me."[125] In Hildegard's view, Christ's "wounds will remain unhealed as long as we humans in this world continue to sin"—in fact, Christ's wounds "remain fresh and open, so long as the wounds of the human race's sins are open."[126] Our personal, corporate, and systemic sins continuously bruise Jesus, bind Jesus, tear at Jesus, torture Jesus, and kill Jesus. Following traditional views of the atonement, Hildegard believes that Christ's wounds intercede with a frustrated, conflicted God "disturbed by the evil deeds" of the world. Christ's wounds take the role of Noah's rainbow, so when the divine pain at being bloodied by sin grows too great and God might unleash wrath on humanity for its wanton destructiveness, Christ "shows his wounds" so that God spares us.[127] As Maximus the Confessor concludes, "The death of Christ on the cross is a judgment of judgment,"[128] not a reprieve for the innocent, nor a reversal that condemns those who condemn. It is the undoing of judgment itself. It

---

121. Julian, *Showings*, 220–21.
122. Allchin, *Living Presence*, 121.
123. Traherne, *Centuries*, 27.
124. Silesius, *Cherubinic Wanderer*, 112.
125. Catherine, *Dialogue*, 85.
126. Hildegard, *Book of Divine Works*, 261, 329.
127. Ibid., 261.
128. Lossky, *Mystical Theology*, 152.

is the meaning of Day's Memorial Day prayer for oppressed and oppressors, the murdered and their murderers.

Mystics are not alone in asserting Christ's solidarity with suffering humanity. In a meditation on the Last Judgment (Matt 25:31–46), Rauschenbusch rewrites the words in anticipation of Eugene Debs's identification with the dispossessed: Jesus says, "I am the hungry, the naked, the lonely."[129] But even as we cripple Jesus, God suspends judgment. Only in God's humanly perverse but blessed economy would the violence we inflict on Jesus cry out for God's mercy on the perpetrators. This negation of judgment overrides the verdict that blesses sheep and damns goats. Only a merciful God feeds those who starve the poor, clothes those who strip others naked, welcomes those who ignore strangers, heals those who leave others ill, and frees those who imprison innocent and guilty alike. If Trocmé acted lest innocent blood be shed (Deut 19:10), it not only shielded persecuted Jews—it saved their Vichy and Nazi persecutors.

While Hildegard contends that Jesus' wounds cry out to God for mercy, Pascal and Sobrino argue that they call out to the human race for action. For Pascal as for Hildegard, the blood of Christ has a voice of its own. In DuBois' poem, God cries out from the one being lynched to the ones doing the lynching.

> *Thou* needest me?
> Thou *needest* me?
> Thou needest *me?* . . .
> *Courage, God,*
> *I come!*[130]

If Jesus is forever in agony, as mystics and activists agree, we must hope that God sees his wounds and hears his cries as God hears and sees and knows the suffering of slaves in Egypt (Exod 3:7–8). There is a paradox in God's message to Moses from the burning bush. God says: *I will liberate*. God says: *You will liberate*. Centuries later, God says: *I will be crucified*. God says: *You will be crucified*. In Exodus, grace is both objective and synergistic. So while we pray that God still liberates the oppressed, we must also hear and see and know Christ's suffering if we are to liberate; in fact, if God is to liberate. If only we could see, not only would we see suffering, we would end it.

There is an oral tradition about Clarence Jordan, whose progressive theology and integrationist actions offended his mid-twentieth century Southern white contemporaries. His stress on living his faith befuddled

---

129. Rauschenbusch, *Social Gospel*, 108–9.
130. DuBois, *Darkwater*, 148.

racist and reactionary Christians and ironically made them skeptical about the orthodoxy of his beliefs. So someone asked him: do you believe we are saved by Christ's blood? He answered: I do if it flows in my veins.[131] Centuries earlier, Ephrem anticipated Jordan's answer as he says Christ's "Blood too has been poured out into our veins."[132] For Jordan as for Ephrem there is no salvation without sanctification. Like Underhill, he did not believe that redemption means being magically transported out of the world's tedium into heavenly bliss. We are redeemed when we participate in the world's redemption. As much as any mystic, Jordan believed that Christ's blood contains a power to reconcile sinners and transform the world. But it does not happen as some charming enchantment apart from history, but when kneaded into the realities of everyday life. Jordan did not want Christians to be gawking spectators of the crucifixion: he wanted to make sure that after people fixed their gaze on the cross, they followed the way of the cross.

THE WAY OF LOSING

If Stanley Karnow found the rhetoric of Tri Quang inscrutable, most of the West considered the ritual suicides of Vietnamese monks a form of insanity or blasphemy (as opposed to war, which Buddhists consider insane but most Christians accept as a norm). The willingness of Jesus' early followers to die as a public witness to their faith must have looked equally incomprehensible to the patricians and plebeians of the Roman Empire. Yet North American Christians were puzzled when twentieth-century Buddhists chose to die. Lost in the fire and the ashes were the purpose of these acts. Madame Nhu, Vietnam's Marie Antoinette, dismissively, cynically, and famously described one self-immolation as a "barbecue." While Thich Nhat Hanh disagreed with the method, he knew the acts were not inspired by madness. What others considered an idiotic waste was to these monks a carefully calibrated protest. When Venerable Thich Quang Duc immolated himself, Nhat Hanh said that the senior monk wanted to "awaken the world to the suffering of the war and the persecution of the Buddhists."[133] When Nhat Chi Mai, a student and social worker under Nhat Hanh's tutelage, immolated herself, she said she wanted "to use my body as a torch to dissipate the darkness, to awaken Love among people and to bring peace to Vietnam." In a letter to President Johnson, she presciently warned that his ignorance of Vietnamese

---

131. Jordan, *Writings*, 176.
132. Brock, *Luminous Eye*, 105.
133. Nhat Hanh, *Love in Action*, 43.

history would spell his downfall—the greater the military escalation, the more profound his defeat.[134]

According to Nhat Hanh, Thich Quang Duc's act, "like the crucifixion of Jesus," expressed "the unconditional willingness to suffer for the awakening of others. Accepting the most extreme kind of pain, he lit a fire in the hearts of people around the world."[135] Nhat Hanh stressed Nhat Chi Mai's "willingness to suffer for the sake of enlightenment of the people. In its essence it does not differ from the act of Christ in his death on the Cross."[136] When Nhat Chi Mai called her sacrifice a torch to bring light to darkness she gave new and harsh meaning to *becoming fire*.

The cultural and religious norms of North American Christians blinded them to the meaning of these self-sacrifices. The grotesque manner of death made their antiwar goals elude even American antiwar leaders. When a handful of Americans followed the example of Vietnamese Buddhists, it grieved and confounded the religious antiwar movement. The self-immolation of Roger LaPorte, who had passed through both the Trappists and the Catholic Worker, led the often overreactive Merton to recoil and momentarily recant his involvement in the peace movement. Merton believed that in a Buddhist context, self-immolation might have an internal logic, but outside of that milieu, it was misdirected and "pathological."[137] Day more kindly called LaPorte's suicide "a sad and terrible act." She imagined that LaPorte himself, as he lay dying in a hospital, knew "that he was wrong in taking his own life." But mirroring Nhat Hanh, she respected the intentions of American protesters who willingly chose "to endure the sufferings that we as a nation are inflicting upon a small country and its people, to lay down their lives rather than take the lives of others. It is the teaching of the Church that only in the Cross is there redemption."[138]

Although many martyrs have been burned, the way of self-immolation is foreign to modern Christians. The way of the cross is supposed to be common, but Thomas à Kempis complains that few truly practice it.

> Jesus has many lovers of his kingdom of heaven, but Jesus has few bearers of his Cross. Many desire his consolation, but few desire his tribulation. He finds many comrades in eating and drinking, but he finds few who will be with him in his abstinence and

---

134. Douglass, *Resistance and Contemplation*, 20–21.
135. Nhat Hanh, *Love in Action*, 43.
136. Douglass, *Resistance and Contemplation*, 22.
137. Merton, *Hidden Ground*, 285–87, 422–24, 472.
138. Day, *By Little*, 166–68; The Catholic Worker later named one of its farms in memory of LaPorte (Day, *On Pilgrimage: The Sixties*, 316).

fasting. All people would joy with Christ, but few will suffer anything for Christ. Many follow him to the breaking of his bread, for their bodily refreshment, but few will follow him to drink a draft of the chalice of his Passion. Many honor his miracles, but few will follow the shame of his Cross and his other ignominies. Many love Jesus as long as no adversity befalls them, and can praise and bless him whenever they receive any benefits from him, but if Jesus withdraws a little from them and forsakes them a bit, they soon fall into some great grumbling or excessive dejection or into open despair.[139]

Thomas grumbles about the Christians in his time, a lament applicable to all times, from the "exemplary disbelief" of Jesus' first disciples[140] and the God-nauseating wishy-washy faith in Laodicea (Rev 3:16) to the present. "We want to be crowned with roses," says Charles de Foucauld, when Christ "was crowned with thorns."[141] It has proven to be a problem transcending cultures and generations to encourage, inspire, coax, convince, or cajole Christians to follow Jesus. This is hard enough when *merely* encouraging people to love sister and brother Christians of other denominations and ideologies, let alone a distant or distinctly different neighbor or a sworn enemy. The chosen few become the shrinking fewer when it comes to conscientiously taking up a cross and willingly risking and enduring pain for a higher purpose. Jesus' disciples laid a well-worn path when they boldly proclaimed that nothing could keep them from following Jesus and then slept while he agonized in prayer, sprinted away when he was arrested, and feigned ignorance when people recognized them as his friends. It is one thing to be convinced of the nonrational proposition that Jesus' crucifixion demonstrates God's love. It is harder still—harder than getting a disciple through the eye of a needle—to embrace the idea that our own risks and sacrifices can redeem others, restore peace, and revolutionize society.

It is not only hard to bear the cross: it is even hard to explain it. There are the crosses that line the boulevards, alleys, dirt roads, and ditches of the world with the incidental and accidental suffering of communities, classes, and peoples. Such involuntary suffering is a cross because Christ shares every physical bruise and emotional lash the human race will ever endure. As Julian says, Christ suffers intimately with each person and his cosmic suffering is greater than that of the whole human race through history. But there

---

139. à Kempis, *Imitation of Christ*, 92.
140. Stringfellow, "Exemplary Disbelief," 13–14.
141. Foucauld, *Writings*, 25.

are also the purposeful crosses, those intended to heal nations, resurrect the spiritually dead, and defeat evil by absorbing it.

Only a spiritual logic as counterintuitive as believing that Jesus' crucifixion gives birth to redemption and restoration can motivate us to voluntarily pick up our own cross. Yet it is this very logic that fills the writings of the mystics. Teresa calls love "the measure of our ability to bear crosses."[142] Ruusbroec agrees: only "loving devotion" creates in us the desire "to be nailed with Christ to the cross and to shed [our] heart's blood for the glory of Christ."[143] Julian says her love for Christ had become so great that nothing hurt her more than to see him in pain.[144] Catherine explains that only when people experience greater pain at "the offense done" to God and "the harm done to their neighbors" than in carrying the cross do they lay down their life for their friends.[145] Only when sin is more painful than sacrifice, injustice more painful than prison, and war more painful than fire do the few or the fewer bear the cross. Yet the cross is not taken up stoically as a backbreaking yoke, but as Leonardo Boff says, it is "an essential element to the paschal experience of liberation."[146] Ironically, bearing the cross is a celebration. Traherne calls it "sweeter" to be with Christ in his sufferings "than with princes on their Thrones, and more do I rejoice with You in Your misery, than in all their solemnities."[147]

It is not only in one or two legends that Francis makes the cross his joyful goal. In an expansive jazz riff on First Corinthians 13, the self-effacing leader instructs Brother Leo about "perfect joy."[148] Francis tells Leo that even if they were flawless examples of holiness and integrity they would not know perfect joy. Even if they healed the paralyzed, the blind, and the deaf, or exorcised demons or raised the dead, even if they knew everything there was to know about science or languages, even if they could prophesy the future or unveil the secrets of the conscience, they would not have perfect joy. Even if they could speak with the voice of an angel, if they knew the courses of the stars and the medicinal powers of herbs, if they controlled the treasures of the earth, or if they understood every living being, they would not know perfect joy. Even if—during the Crusades—they converted everyone to Christ, they would not have perfect joy.

142. Teresa, *Way of Perfection*, 213.
143. Ruusbroec, *Spiritual Espousals*, 109.
144. Julian, *Showings*, 209.
145. Catherine, *Dialogue*, 147.
146. Boff, "Salvation in Jesus Christ," 88.
147. Traherne, *Centuries*, 46.
148. *Little Flowers*, 58–60.

But if, suffering from cold, soiled with mud, and famished they went to a church and were angrily rebuffed, they could find perfect joy. If they endured chill and hunger and insults "without being troubled and without complaining" with charity in their hearts for those who turn them away, "perfect joy is there!" If they kept knocking, accepted rejection, and bore insults with love, "that is perfect joy!" And if, being beaten while begging for shelter, they endured the scornful blows with patience, bearing "the sufferings of the Blessed Christ patiently for love of him . . . that is perfect joy!" Perfect joy does not depend on the conversion of the enemy, the healing of the sick, or the awakening of the indifferent. The cross is a *way*, not an end.

As the vision of the cross coming from Francis's mouth brings perspective to his life, so biographer David Garrow puts King's life in the context of the cross. King's views of the cross reflect its *inherent interpretability*. Sometimes he says we bear the cross for our own sanctification (Francis's perfect joy), sometimes for the sake of our allies, sometimes for our enemies, sometimes as an instrument of social change.[149] The cost of discipleship was extraordinarily high for King. As Teresa observes that Jesus' death was visible in his life, so King felt death weighing on him and pursuing him for a dozen years. To say that he gave his life for justice means not only that he died seeking justice, but that he gave each day of his life in that holy cause. We can call his clinical depression and spiritual turmoil a *dark night* or *acedia*,[150] but it was also the way of the cross.

Like King and the Buddhist monks, we are not responsible for how others respond to our crosses. We can only cocreate the possibility of awakenings, openings, and redemption. Meditating on the deaths of his compatriots in Vietnam, Nhat Hanh writes, "When someone stands up to violence in such a courageous way, a force for change is released."[151] Similarly, Gandhi offers a terrifying mystical equation: "the purer the suffering, the greater is the progress."[152] Applying his faith to anti-colonial politics, he says, "I saw that nations like individuals could only be made through the agony of the Cross."[153] This is how people set themselves free. This, he says, was how Jesus sought "to free a sorrowing world."[154]

---

149. King, *Stride Toward Freedom*, 216, *Testament of Hope*, 207, *Strength to Love*, 25, 92, *Where Do We Go*, 54, Garrow, *Bearing the Cross*, 290.

150. Lossky, *Mystical Theology*, 225–26.

151. Nhat Hanh, *Love in Action*, 43.

152. Gandhi, *Non-violent*, 113.

153. Chatterjee, *Gandhi's Religious Thought*, 78.

154. Gandhi, *Non-violent*, 113.

Activists make remarkably bold, utterly unsubstantiated *mystical* claims about the power of redemptive suffering. Nhat Hanh and Gandhi proclaim that suffering sacrifice unleashes an innately transforming power into history. Muste believed in a "law of suffering and crucifixion,"[155] a "law" grounded in the Gospels that seed must fall into the ground so grain can grow.[156] To Muste, this is no historical sideshow. To him, "God's weapon and method is the Cross."[157] To him, "whenever love that will suffer unto death is manifested, whenever a true Crucifixion takes place, unconquerable power is released into the stream of history."[158] "Here is released the power which in the political and social realm is the counterpart of the fission of the atom and the release of atomic energy in its realm."[159] For very different reasons Nietzsche says that whatever does not kill us makes us stronger.[160] Muste says: that which kills us makes us stronger still.

Sobrino saw the way, the work, and the power of the cross in El Salvador's murder-martyrdoms. He believed that the murder of Rutilio Grande converted Romero.[161] Like Romero's assassination, there was nothing surprising about the cold-blooded executions of his University of Central America colleagues. As if the university were somehow linked to the Sixteenth Street Baptist Church, bombs had been planted there fifteen times before.[162] In the week Sobrino's colleagues were murdered, El Salvador endured a thousand other violent deaths.[163] Finding continuity between death and life—as Teresa does of Jesus—Sobrino says, "If so many have died like Jesus, it is because so many have lived like Jesus."[164] "Their deaths, which they met consciously, are what convince the poor, more than any possible words, that they were with them, that in this cruel world there are human beings who have defended them and loved them."[165] Martyrdom, then, not only renews the crucifixion, it re-embodies the incarnation (Phil 2:5-12).

It is eerie to read Ellacuría remembering Romero's murder before his own, recalling that Romero offered "my blood to God for the redemption

---

155. Muste, *Not by Might*, 80.
156. Muste, *Essays*, 293.
157. Muste, "Religious Basis," 6.
158. Muste, *Essays*, 294.
159. Muste, *Not by Might*, 85.
160. Nietzsche, *Twilight*, 6.
161. Sobrino, *Archbishop Romero*, 9.
162. Sobrino et al., *Companions of Jesus*, 14.
163. Ibid., 51–52.
164. Ibid., 45.
165. Sobrino, *Principle of Mercy*, 180.

and resurrection of El Salvador," that he prayed, "May my death, if it is accepted by God, be for the liberation of my people and as a witness of hope in the future."[166] Sobrino asserts with Gandhi, Nhat Hanh, and Muste the mystical-political meaning of sacrifice: "It is a Christian truth that wherever there is death like the death of Jesus on the cross for having defended the victims of this world . . . there is also resurrection, a word continues to resound and the crucified endure through history."[167]

The activists' mystical kerygma of purposeful suffering is mirrored in the action-oriented mysticism of Teresa of Ávila. Negating the stereotype of the mystic as ahistorical, isolated, and self-indulgent and *spirituality* as an escape pod from worldly grittiness, Teresa writes in the spirit of the Epistle of James, Puebla, and Medellín. She hints that *only* those who try to change the world have prayed: "Do you know when people really become spiritual? It is when they become the slaves of God and are branded with God's sign, which is the sign of the Cross." When do people become spiritual? Only when God "can sell them as slaves to the whole world" as Christ himself was sold.[168] *How* we embody Teresa's words may vary from one place, path, and person to the next. That is a matter of social location and personal vocation. But, according to Teresa, there is no way to follow Jesus unless it leads your broken heart to heal a broken world.

It was with a breaking heart that Albert Luthuli faced a personal quandary. Nine years before he won the Nobel Peace Prize in 1961, the South African government stripped him of his status as a chief because he refused to resign from the African National Congress or distance himself from the liberation movement. As he girded himself to face an uncertain future, he gave an address called "The Road to Freedom is Via the Cross." In a message foreshadowing Tutu's, he insists that a government that debases anyone's God-given humanity has to be "relentlessly opposed in the spirit of defiance."[169] Accepting the Peace Prize, Luthuli said that "as a Christian and patriot" he "could not look on while systematic attempts were made, almost in every department of life, to debase the God-factor" in people "or to set a limit beyond which the human being in its black form might not strive to serve their Creator to the best of their ability. To remain neutral when the laws of the land virtually criticized God" for creating black people "was the sort of thing I could not, as a Christian, tolerate."[170] Like Julian's assurance

---

166. Sobrino et al., *Companions of Jesus*, 65.
167. Sobrino, *Principle of Mercy*, 173.
168. Teresa, *Interior Castle*, 229.
169. Luthuli, *Speeches*, 43.
170. Ibid., 111.

that all will be well, and like the phrase King borrowed from abolitionists that *the arc of the moral universe is long but it bends toward justice,*[171] Luthuli believed that the "road to Freedom may be long and thorny," but it would have a "glorious end."[172]

Just as his contemporary, King, was aware that the movement would outlive him,[173] Luthuli knew that the road to equality could be deadly as he reflected on the personal cost of his discipleship.

> What the future has in store for me I do not know. It might be ridicule, imprisonment, concentration camp, flogging, banishment and even death. I only pray to the Almighty to strengthen my resolve so that none of these grim possibilities may deter me from striving for the sake of the good name of our beloved country, the Union of South Africa, to make it a true democracy and a true union in form and spirit of all the communities of the land. My only painful concern at times is that of the welfare of my family but I try even in this regard, in a spirit of trust and surrender to God's will, to say "God will provide."[174]

Acting in a more open, concerted, and aggressive style than the FBI did in tormenting King, the South African government did its damnedest to make Luthuli's life a living hell. After he was banned (with Nelson Mandela and other leaders), later tried for treason, and still later put under house arrest, his health wilted. He died in a suspicious accident six years after receiving the Nobel Prize. He did not avoid prison like fellow Nobel laureate Tutu. He did not experience a resurrection from prison like Mandela. He was, however, a posthumous centerpiece in the polemical 1980s South African play *Woza Albert.*[175] In that play, Christ returns to earth, to South Africa, to raise people from the dead. As Latin American base communities in the same decade invoked the names of the disappeared and then proclaimed, "*presente!*" so Christ says "*woza*" (rise) as he walks through a cemetery and raises South Africa's martyrs from the dead. In spite of *Woza Albert's* poignant wistfulness, Luthuli never saw the fruits of his labors. Like King, he did "not get there with you." Nonracial democracy came into being, but the road to freedom was pockmarked with crosses.

---

171. Branch, *Parting the Waters*, 197.

172. Luthuli, *Speeches*, 76.

173. King said that if someone made a movie about him, it would end with him being killed (Garrow, *Bearing the Cross*, 469).

174. Luthuli, *Speeches*, 43–44.

175. Mtwa, Ngema, and Simon, *Woza Albert!*

Wounds, Forever Fresh

For Luthuli as for Muste, the cross is *the* weapon of social change, yet Luthuli's life reminds us that generations and genealogies of activists and martyrs suffer and die like seeds falling uselessly on stony paths to cultivate an iffy progress. In the 1960s, Merton notes coldly, sadly, that the deaths of the civil rights movements' martyrs did not automatically or magically redeem the Deep South.[176] In South Africa, the day came in Mandela's time, not Luthuli's. In Vietnam, the day for which Thich Quang Duc, Nhat Chi Mai, and Roger LaPorte died never came. If spiritual power was released into history through their deaths, it was the power of unscented, undetected, and soon-forgotten holiness. The day of tranquility, equality, and freedom has never come for Black Elk's crucified people. To take up one's cross is to take a terrible chance. Suffering is certain; spiritual rebirth and social transformation are possible. Whatever the power of the cross, more often than not, as Francis's disciple Brother Giles notes, "The way of salvation is the way of losing."[177]

In early centuries non-Christians fashioned the crucifix with the head of a donkey perched on it to symbolize the absurdity of the cross.[178] To take up one's cross is to tilt laughably at windmills. It is to make an ass of oneself. Paul says as much—it is less holy, holy, holy, than folly, folly, folly (1 Cor 1:18–25)! Even if every cross willingly borne releases spiritual power into history, it is a power that is paradoxically perfected in weakness (2 Cor 12:9). In truth, every cross is the surest sign that power is made perfect in *God's* weakness.

Tangible results, as Gandhi and Merton so often warn, are addictive and illusory. What matters, they say, is our intention. To Anselm, *destructive* human intentions collide with the *creative divine*; to this we can add our *creative* human intent. Through the cross, by risking and losing, we join our lives to the life of Jesus, our work to the work of Jesus, our faith to the faith of Jesus, and our intention to the intention of Jesus. Powers in every age are "crucifying the Seed."[179] If Franciscan legends and King and Luthuli's witness mean anything, then the way of losing is the way to holiness, transcendence, and transfiguration. These are not pious stories about others. All Christians experience the horror and hope of history through the cross. All Christians see the glory of creation through the cross. All Christians have the cross in our mouths.

---

176. Merton, *Dancing in the Water*, 219.
177. *Little Flowers*, 268.
178. Leech, *We Preach Christ*, 8.
179. Fox, *Journal*, 354.

But if Giles is right about "the way of losing," we must reexamine the lineage that begins with Jesus' nonmartyrdom and continues in the risk, vulnerability, and sacrifices of his followers. Nonviolent activists are sadly aware of the desperate need—and vain foolishness—nations have to bequeath sanctity to war dead, as if every combatant killed in war is posthumously anointed a hero. In our dominant mythology, American soldiers killed in World War II died in a holy cause. The same is said of the Civil War (on both sides!). But what of the Korean stalemate or the Afghanistan stalemate or the World War I stalemate that failed to keep the world safe *from* democracies? What of the catastrophic failure in Vietnam, or even the self-defined success of the Gulf War or Grenada? What of the wars of Manifest Destiny and naked aggression against Native American peoples and Mexico? What of the reestablishment of colonialism under new management in Cuba and the Philippines? Finally, what *of* World War II, the blessed war of carefully crafted memory that reinvigorated colonialism in the future killing fields of Southeast Asia, Eastern Europe, Kenya, and Algeria? It would be more apt and accurate to say with Qoheleth that all of these deaths, like all of these wars, are in vain.

For nonviolent activists, such honesty is comparatively easy—if regrettable—when discerning the pure meaninglessness of sacrifices made in war. It is always easier to identify the folly of others. But what happens if we apply the same ruthless honesty to the nonviolent war on war and injustice? We might be moved to find meaning in the trials of Luthuli or the deaths of Jonathan Daniels and the martyrs of Alabama because of the demise of legal apartheid in South Africa and the American South. But if this is so, then success redeems their deaths. Regime change or political progress or landmark legislation retroactively injects meaning into their sacrifice, and subsequent Supreme Court decisions may drain it away. In other words, whether the goal is to exercise raw national power or to seek first the realm of God, the same desperate need—and folly—exists to validate, justify, even exalt in the risk, the courage, and the sacrifice of those engaged in *la causa*, whatever the cause. But what of Romero and Nhat Chi Mai and other martyrs, remembered and forgotten? Those committed to the way of the cross would do well not to rely on subsequent events to validate their sacrifice. Instead, it must be enough to share Christ's sufferings in Christ's cause—the revolution of God and the redemption and restoration of the world.

Only when success is unrecognizably muddled can we truly grasp the cross. Only when the cross is unmistakably bizarre can we fully embrace it. Merton says as much in one of his favorite essays.[180] In "Notes on a Philoso-

---

180. The thin-skinned Merton was also brutally self-critical; see his chart evaluating

phy of Solitude," he writes: "it is only when the apparent absurdity of life is faced in all truth that faith really becomes possible"—unless we face life's depressingly farcical futility, faith shrinks and shrivels into a mere "diversion, a spiritual amusement," a set of "conventional formulas and approved mental patterns" devoid of transformational truth.[181] In other words, where Anselm tidily bifurcates the meaning of the cross into a clash of divine and human intent, Merton would cover those neatly drawn theological lines beneath layers and layers of absurdity.

What is true of the absurdity of life is also true of the absurdity of *death*. A few months before a freak accident ended his life, Merton fumbled to respond to King's assassination. In part, Merton reflected the *logos* of his time as he shared the sentiments of the media—black and white, religious and secular—that scrounged for hope beneath a national tidal wave of violence.[182] Writing personally with comforting words to Coretta Scott King, Merton tells her that her husband "has done the greatest thing anyone can do. In imitation of his master he has laid down his life for his friends and enemies."[183] In his journal, however, Merton shared in the pathos of his age as he chewed and choked on the faith-chilling absurdity of King's death: "Is the human race self-destructive? Is the Christian message of love a pitiful delusion? Or must one just 'love' in an impossible situation?"[184]

To wrestle with King's death, or Romero's, or so many others, is to grapple with the incongruity of the cross and the realization that all deaths of all martyrs can be *both* a pinnacle of self-sacrifice for love and justice *and* a useless and pathetic mirage. In facing the tragedy of King's death, Merton struggled with the apophatic theological nature of every cross: there is absolutely no way to foretell *how* Point A (suffering and death) leads to Point B (redemption and restoration). We always perceive the future through dark glass and impenetrable fog.

By any standard, the Buddhist monks in Vietnam were failures. Their burning bodies had no influence on Lyndon Johnson or Ho Chi Minh; they failed to make Madame Nhu blanch or blush. And the Martyrs of El Salvador? Is it enough to remind the poor that God is with them as they endure a never-ending, soul-scalding, sadistic-systemic ordeal? And King? Are we to ignore the empirical fact that in the decades since his death his goals of

---

his own books in *Introductions*, 126–27. So when Merton praises one of his own essays, it bears notice: *Road to Joy*, 238, 332, *Courage for Truth*, 103.

181. Merton, *Disputed Questions*, 166.
182. See Commins, "Is Suffering Redemptive?"
183. Merton, *Hidden Ground*, 451.
184. Merton, *Other Side*, 78.

racial, economic, and international justice have receded out of sight and mind? Even Jesus' death is sometimes justified by the subsequent spread of Christendom as if the existence of a big institution corroborates the truth of the gospel. To Jesus, that would be a disappointment of cosmic proportions! According to Christian theology, Jesus died for the redemption of the world, the coming of the realm, and/or the birth of a unified body to carry out God's revolution, not in order to establish a set of petty ecclesiastical fiefdoms. If the tangible results of *Jesus' crucifixion* are still unclear, perhaps we can accept that the way of the cross—every risk for the realm, every sacrifice for the gospel—is the way of losing.

So, as follower of Jesus, we are left to live, to die, to love, and to lose, and to rejoice in it.

MEDITATION: INTO A CROSS

"What do you think happens?" Bob asked.

Pillows propped him up so he could sit upright. Always wiry, with the strong hands of his drumming days, he was now concentration-camp thin. All he could coax out of his baritone voice was a heavy whisper. Forty-seven-years old, his pallor was as gray as his hair. But his blue eyes still sparkled—adventurous and bright—and his startling wit still struck with comic force. When his wife Norma momentarily disconnected his oxygen to reattach it to a mobile tank, he hung his head and dangled his arms like a jellyfish, and shook as if he was dying. I laughed, "You can't help yourself, can you?" We always laughed. No one had a more free-flowing sense of humor; it was in his DNA.

We had known each other over thirty years, and now he looked forty years older than me. We shared churchy teenaged things: youth group, acolyting, and retreats. We shared human teenaged things: a drag race, volleyball games, and sweet sarcasm. As our young adult philosophical palettes broadened we pondered shadings in the meanings of life. In seminary we wrote musical comedies, chortles and guffaws bouncing off our apartment walls as we conjured imaginary future redactors arguing over who wrote which line. There was the morning when I crossed the street and looked up to see him at the seminary dorm's second-story window, an apple in his mouth, lifting his nightshirt to expose himself to me. I shook my head and laughed: he can't help himself, I thought. He sang at my wedding; I was his best man. Months later we puzzled over the conundrum of marriage in one car as our wives psychoanalyzed us in another. Months later he told me to stop complaining and get counseling. Years later, he phoned long distance on the Father's Day after his father died, knowing my estrangement from mine, to say "it's weird."

I had gotten a phone call. I apologized to the class. I knew they had traveled hundreds of miles, but Friday's class was canceled—we would adjust. I needed a two-day window to see Bob in the hospice. A blizzard shrouded the east coast, and my red eye left me stuck in Detroit. As I stood in line defeated, ready to return to LA, a woman asked where I was going. I felt tears rise as precursors to his funeral and my voice choked: to see a dying friend. Her voice shrank in response, "I'm so sorry," and I swallowed back more tears. Only after I had given in to failure did I hear that my flight to Boston would depart in ten minutes. In the rental car, I reminded myself how to skid in the January snow. We would still have a morning together.

I had visited Bob before. After his first surgery, I designed a family vacation to see him. Returning to his home in one car after lunch with our families, he and I took a detour to extend our conversation, leaving our loved ones wondering where we were. He confessed something embarrassing. Trumping him, I confessed the stupidest, damnedest, most destructive thing I had ever done, and—like the voice of God—he laughed, and said "I'm sorry," and I felt my shame cascade away like a melting glacier. After his second surgery, I flew east alone for a long weekend. As part of his recuperation, we played tennis. When one of us threw the ball in the air to serve, the other shuffled his feet and made animal noises—snorts, snuffles, silly birdcalls. I whiffed more than once. At one point we lay on opposite sides of the net laughing too hard to breathe.

His cancer was absurd. He was as intentional about his health as he was about being humanly and humorously holy. Now his eyes pierced through the exquisite but antiseptic surroundings, the silent snow outside completing the picture-perfect place to die, waiting for my answer: what do you think happens?

"I don't know," I said. "All I can think of is John of the Cross: all and nothing."

"I don't know either, but I think it's more than that." And his eyes gleamed again, eager for the next adventure after wave upon wave of weakness, grief, and loss.

The last few months I phoned him every Monday. He said I was "kind." I reminded him it was "love." Once I phoned when he was writing his obituary. He didn't want Norma to have to do it. Another time, he said the family dog—Preacher—had cancer and had to be put down. He grieved for his teenaged children: it wasn't enough that their *father* was dying of cancer?

Another time, he was choreographing his funeral. Nobody else should have to do it. More than that, as I would discover, he would make that service a testimony to his faith in Emmanuel, our loving, present God.

When the oncologist told him there was nothing more she could do, no treatment, no hope, he asked her, "How are *you* doing with that?" She excused herself and left the room to regain her professional composure.

Bob didn't "beat" cancer. He glued his faith to it. And no matter how widespread the malignancy grew, it never outgrew his faith.

We will all find out what happens after death. But what *had* happened was a mixture of human and divine grace. As he was dying, Bob took care of everyone around him. He witnessed to his faith. He filled his dying with life. He turned cancer into a cross.

7

Harijans

The eye is the penetrating love that the soul has for God.
—The Book of Spiritual Poverty[1]

Everything drew me to love and thank God; people, trees, plants, animals. I saw them all as my kinsfolk, I found in all of them the magic of the Name of Jesus.
—The Way of a Pilgrim[2]

The best person, the one who sees.
—The Dhammapada[3]

Blessed are the eyes that see what you see!
—Luke 10:23

1. McGinn, *Harvest of Mysticism*, 389.
2. *Way of a Pilgrim*, 106.
3. *Dhammapada*, 20:273.

From one blood God made all nations to inhabit the whole earth.
—Acts 17:26 (RSV)

As for me, I am establishing my covenant with you and your descendants after you, and with every living creature that is with you, the birds, the domestic animals, and every animal of the earth.
—Genesis 9:9–10

Everything we think, feel, and do has an effect on our ancestors and all future generations and reverberates throughout the universe.
—Thich Nhat Hanh[4]

Is not the sky a father and earth a mother, and are not all living things with feet or wings or roots their children?
—Black Elk[5]

Praised be You, my Lord, through Brother Wind . . . Sister Water . . . Brother Fire . . . Sister Mother Earth.
—Francis of Assisi[6]

It is a strange awakening to find the sky inside you and beneath you and above you and all around you so that your spirit is one with the sky, and all is positive night.
—Thomas Merton[7]

MEDITATION: A BUSY DAY IN A LIFE

He looked forty, a tall, slender man with an afro time warped from the past in quest of a retro future. He had a shy, sweet manner and an apologetic smile. A quasi-Quaker quiet enfolded him. He didn't quite look me in the eye. The second time he came to church, he asked to meet with me. Sometimes an agenda accompanies such verbal memos. This time not. We made an appointment. He gave me his address.

4. Nhat Hanh, *Touching Peace*, 45.
5. Black Elk, *Black Elk Speaks*, 3.
6. Francis of Assisi and Clare of Assisi, *Francis and Clare*, 38–39.
7. Merton, *Sign of Jonas*, 329.

The appointed time landed on a busy day in a busy week in a job I made more hectic by compulsively seeking new ways to do *more*. If the coming of the kingdom relied on my workload, it was coming soon and coming *here*! It was not my "cup" that runneth over; it was my "plate." Never one to be tempted by substance abuse, my chronic body aches drove me to two Tylenol every four waking hours, every day of the ever-blessed week.

Driving to see him, I utilized another coping device—music. Except for random visits to NPR, in my car I seek music to match my mood—simple melodies when relaxed, foot-tapping beats when happy, and when stressed, intricate, loud, dissonant rock and roll; the greater the stress, the louder the music. The volume that day was all my speakers could handle. The windows were down; they had to be as I flipped from one rock station to the next in search of something louder and more grating.

But the music didn't drown out my internal chatter: why was I seeing this guy? He had been to church *twice*! I barely had time to visit my usual shut-ins, to write decent sermons, or to attend every sacred meeting and to invent the need for more. And here I was wasting time, pouring my last canteen of water into desert sand.

I pulled up next to the motel—weekly and monthly rates, not daily, thankfully not hourly. I double-checked the address. Turning off the car shut off the music and quieted the earth. The aging motel had two long parallel strips, like dislocated wings, each with six rooms. His was the last one on the left. When he opened the door the gas fumes were overwhelming. I hadn't taken enough Tylenol for this; there wasn't enough in the world. The room was dingy; the window bolted shut. I wasn't sure what distasteful or apocalyptic horrors might unfold if the antediluvian curtains moved.

He laid out his agenda. He wanted to help people. He wanted to be a teacher. He didn't know how to go about it. The longer he spoke, the more I saw the gap widen between fantasy and reality. He hadn't gone to college. There had been mental health issues. He was on disability. He moved around town. Estranged from his family, he could name no friends. He turned to me to be his vocational counselor. What should he do?

What *could* he do? My heart broke. I had no answer to give, no referral to make, no program to offer, just a church to attend, people to meet, people who might—inspired by Jesus or bullied by me—reach out in the ambiguous ineffective kindness of an unfocused family. I could tell he had had this conversation before, a conversation that started and ended in hopelessness without roaming far afield. He wanted to help; I couldn't help him. And he seemed resigned, maybe perversely content, with my helplessness.

Leaving, as I sucked in LA's "fresh" air, I also choked on shame. It was almost overpowering, like the fumes in his room. As pressed for time as I had felt, I sat silently in my parked car. Here was this sweet, good-hearted, lonely, lost man, and, in spirit if not practice, I worked for the one who came to seek and save the lost. In the mayhem of ministry, I had forgotten what I am supposed to be and do. I felt sad and sick and guilty. I blushed with shame.

When I started the car, the radio blasted one word: "forgiveness!" from a song by Don Henley. I knew the rest of the song, and it didn't matter. I heard the word; I'd heard enough. I turned off the engine and sat still, sponging up the message.

I don't like neat stories: problem named, problem solved, sins noted, passport stamped. My spiritual home turf is furnished with paradox, contradictions, and conundrums, not happy-faced coincidental thunderbolts. But that is what I got that day—a message as subtly apocalyptic as lightning. That is what stayed with me after that busy day—the most indelible memory from a busy year.

He came to church twice after that and then disappeared. The only reason I remember him is that not knowing who he was, forgetting who I am, ignoring who we are—God's people, God's family—I dismissed him before I knew him. And I was forgiven.

THE PRIME MINISTER AND THE HYENA

In *The Inheritors*, William Golding tells a story of a small band of Neanderthals. In their rugged and rudimentary existence, they communicate without words. Having no concept of memory, they form pictures in their minds. They live a predefined social existence: they may be a family; they do not seem to be part of a clan. They stay together out of affection, necessity, and habit. Though they are few, they consider themselves *the people.*

But they cross paths with a more intelligent group, the next step up on the evolutionary ladder: homo sapiens, *new people*. In a reversal of our evolved and sophisticated expectations, the *new people* are more aggressive and violent than *the people*. The *new people* anticipate eighteenth- and nineteenth-century Western European attitudes toward Asians, Africans, Native Americans, everybody but themselves—noble savages to a romantic few, but savages first, last, and always in popular opinion and public policy. The *new people* find it natural to dominate, subjugate, quell, and kill with or without reason. At the end of *The Inheritors, the people* have been kidnapped, murdered, or left moaning and mourning at the deaths of their loved ones and the blotting out of their social world. One of the *new people* looks ahead: he "could see the low hills and the green of trees with the darkness under them. The darkness stretched along above the water like a thin line." Then, gazing into the future, he "looked at the line of darkness. It was far away and there was plenty of water in between. He peered forward . . . to see what lay at the other end of the lake, but it was so long . . . that he could not see if the line of darkness had an ending."[8]

Like Golding's *The Lord of the Flies*, *The Inheritors* is a parable of original sin. But *The Lord of the Flies* tells the story of a homogeneous band of civilized English boarding school boys who—given freedom—turn on one another in unfettered savagery. In the end, they are saved and returned to a world consumed in its own unfettered savagery, a world at war.[9] Whoever they are, wherever they live, and however civilized they think they may be, *the people* turn first against other peoples, then, inevitably, against one another. And the line of darkness shows no signs of ending.

Golding's sobering fables complement the biblical witness about human nature. If the goodness of creation is intrinsic *in* the beginning, destructive human compulsions have shadowed creation *from* the beginning. And the line of darkness, the lust for dominion, and the alluring magic of violence that can make people disappear are ever with us. What has been true from the beginning is now, and ever shall be. What has been true, and is now, is that *some* people assume they are *the* people, singularly unrelated to other peoples, essentially different, inherently better. In the modern and postmodern West when some find the concept of original sin unworthy of civilization's evolution,[10] mystics and activists consistently restate this truth: *original sin* is not an obscure superstition or a one-time, precedent-setting, prehistoric event. It is a line of darkness without end.

The Bible's pre-Abrahamic fables echo *The Inheritors* as the misuse of free will twists and deforms relationships—original gullibility (Adam, Eve), original envy (Cain, Abel), original grandiosity (Babel). Even the Exodus, the Bible's story of "ineradicable subversion,"[11] the scriptural foundation of Underhill's permanent revolution, has its shadow side. The spiritual roots of divisiveness turn even this primal tale of liberation into a "text of terror."[12] The shadow side of the Exodus is as long and despicable as its liberating message is enduring and distinguished. As the shadow side of New Testament texts of terror have given warrant to anti-Semitism, pogroms, and the

---

8. Golding, *Inheritors*, 230, 233.
9. Golding, *Lord of the Flies*, 185–87.
10. Menninger, *Whatever Became of Sin?*
11. Walzer, *Exodus and Revolution*, 115.

12. Trible, *Texts of Terror*, singles out gender violence, but Scripture is equally terrifying when it blesses economic exploitation, ethnic cleansing, and military expansionism.

Holocaust, the poisoned roots of the Exodus enmesh liberation with annihilation. No scalpel has yet cut this cancer from its tissue, flesh and bone.

The Exodus story proclaims a God who adopts slaves as *the beloved people*. God hears, sees, and internalizes their suffering like the zaddik who feels the pain of a woman in labor from fifty miles away (Exod 3:7). The moans of slaves inspire the complicit or slumbering or ineffectual God of DuBois's nightmares to act. This newly awakened God promises slaves a dream they can literally taste—milk and honey. More profoundly, God offers a vision of life without inequality or exploitation—an idyllic place, paradise on earth, Shangri-la, Utopia—in which each family lives without fear, contented with its own vine and fig tree, in which *the people* live in peace with all of the families of the earth (Mic 4:4).[13] Like King's dreams that sway fluidly from the pragmatic to the visionary, the Exodus appeals to the common denominators of physical realism—food, shelter, and safety—and to the highest aspirations of human idealism—peace, justice, and equality.

Yet embedded in these liberating texts of God's *new people*, the Exodus story offers a set of sinister promises—tombstones among the lilies of the field—that this land of milk and honey and peace and justice will be seized from *other* peoples—Canaanites, Hittites, Amorites, Perizzites, Hivites, and Jebusites—as if they were not people (Exod 3:17). These peoples are the collateral damage of God's preferential option for slaves. The "ban" is God's warrant to destroy whole peoples—men, women, and children, ox and ass (Deut 2:34-5, 7:1-6, Josh 6:21, 8:24-9, 10:28-40)[14]—like the wholesale demolition of one manger scene after another. This violence against other peoples floods over into internecine violence, dividing groups of God's people against one another. Herod implicitly invokes the ban in a preemptive surgical strike against the male infants of Bethlehem as he tries with smart swords to murder the Christ child (Matt 2:16).[15] Israel has become Golding's *new people* who can, who *should* (Deut 20:17), butcher other peoples without qualm or conscience.

This biblical pattern gives voice to what Walter Brueggemann calls "tribal truth," a "naïve and precritical" theology in which providence shines brightly here, but not there, on us, but not on them, a place in which it does not rain on just and unjust alike.[16] There is a particular intensity to the

---

13. Walzer, *Exodus and Revolution*, 102–3.

14. Niditch, *War*, 28.

15. See ibid., 78–79, regarding the debate in Numbers 31 about killing boys (prospective soldiers), not girls (prospective child bearers).

16. Brueggemann, *David's Truth*, 20.

"partisan narrative" of tribal truth[17]—a depth of wonder and "amazement"[18] that God stoops down to act on the behalf of the marginalized, the uncivilized, the outcasts, the Robin Hoods, the ruffians, the red necks, the banditos. This is not merely some barbaric fantasy: one hears its echoes in the Song of Zechariah and the Magnificat. When accepted as a partial truth, it re-energizes faith; when it becomes the one and only truth, like hoarded manna, it begins to rot.

This typical biblical pattern is also authored by the anxiety of an easily and often dominated Podunk, backwater nation that feels like small stakes in an imperial poker game. Biblical Israel had all the military prowess of modern Luxembourg and all the international stature of modern Albania. Too often overwhelmed by merciless empires—Egyptian, Assyrian, Babylonian, Persian, Greek, and Roman—and its puny neighbors, Israel's dreams seek peace *either* as revealed enlightenment (Isa 2:2–4, Mic 4:1–4) *or* at the end of bloodied swords. Its recurring experience of oppression and humiliation *after* original liberation, like waves of debilitating nausea after a miraculous healing, leads it to negate the humanity of other peoples, a pattern renewed in the small, fragile sect of Jesus' followers who shudder at the thought of persecution and imagine a glorious day—the revenge of the nerds—when they will join Christ as cold, cruel judges of a cold, cruel world. If Jesus' followers failed to judge other peoples, it was not due to a lack of imagination or desire. If the people of Israel failed to dominate other peoples, it was not due to a lack of wish or will or whim, hostility, hubris, or original sin.

Not only were God's new people theologically hell-bent on conjuring up and summoning down divine wrath on other peoples (Isaiah 13–24 is a long but typical series of prophecies against the nations that spills over on Jerusalem and finally encompasses the earth); in time, the circle of exclusion ballooned until it pushed almost everyone away from God's grace. So the taint that was splattered on neighboring nations as if they, like Mr. Hyde, were defined by some inchoate deformity, spilled onto other tribes. So in Judges when liberating battles are not directed at occupying forces, a viral violence ignites intertribal wars between varying sets of Hatfields and McCoys. The rage of the powerless once targeting oppression becomes, like the self-consuming ideological purity of the Jacobins, a guillotine that falls on just and unjust alike. The division of new people from nonpeople that separates Israelites from Amalekites soon stains Ephraimites (Judg 12:1–6). As if there aren't enough *others*, the lust for power becomes the primary plot

---

17. Ibid., 22, 39.
18. Ibid., 39.

line in the Shakespearean conspiracies of the Saul-David-Solomon succession narrative—the Bible's War of the Roses.

The shadow side of the Exodus dismisses other peoples like expendable movie extras in a divine plot. While corrosive when attached to the message of liberation, it becomes even more insidious when merrily embraced in the policies of every *imperium tremendum* that seeks to shock and awe others into submission. It is the Janus-faced ideological façade that has launched 10,000 ships, shibboleths, skirmishes, blitzkriegs, fraudulent preventive wars (Poland, Iraq), and land seizures (the Sudetenland, the West Bank). It is at the heart of every presumed Manifest Destiny, whether the nonpeoples are Hittites, Hivites, Five Nations, First Nation, Zulu, Xhosa, or Palestinian. It is the doctrinal legal fiction of *terra nullius*—a land without inhabitants—that officially blotted out the existence of aboriginal peoples in Australia and appeased the consciences of English imperialists.[19] The legalities of apartheid, imperialism, and free market capitalism forever reinforce it.

This bloated underbelly of the Exodus story inverts the hauntingly beautiful message of Hosea, who addresses Israel with the withering word that they have forfeited the right to receive God's mercy or to be called God's people. They are now Lo-ammi (not my people) and Lo-ruhamah (no mercy) (Hos 1:6–9). But God is foundationally unable to give people what they deserve (Hos 1–3, 11). Instead, no matter how much the people turn to "whoredom" (Hos 1:2, 2:4, 4:11–2, 5:4 6:10), God has Hosea speak "to your brother Ammi (people), and to your sister, Ruhamah" (mercy) (Hos 2:1). But perverting the amazing grace of Hosea, biblical Israel and every *imperium tremendum* since declares that *other* peoples are unworthy of mercy—human or divine, personal or political. As the Old Testament shadow calls others nonpeople who deserve no mercy, the New Testament shadow calls for nonmercy on others, making them not people. The New Testament merely displaces human violence onto God's judgment as Christians, in spite of Jesus' specific instructions (Luke 9:54–5), gleefully call down fire from heaven.

To use the language of modern secular Israel, biblical Israel has a right to exist that it refuses to extend to its Aramean, Edomite, or Palestinian neighbors. This is the universal myth that *they* are not people as *we* are. This is the myth Lester's nurse perpetuates about the poor, a lesson repeated ad nauseam about persons of every race, caste, or country: they are not like us; they do not feel or think as we do; they do not have our capacity for intelligence, refinement, or morality.

---

19. Habel, *Land is Mine*, 7.

While mystics and activists share Golding's vision of the line of darkness, they never succumb to the temptation—a cynical gullibility—that the human race is forever doomed within a web of grim fatalism. In South African history, Afrikaners adopted a deterministic view of their own Manifest Destiny in which they overidentified their history with the Exodus. Theirs was a tribal truth: Afrikaners were God's people; black Africans were nonpeople. Like their North American Jim Crow brothers, apartheid's apologists rationalized their policies as separate-but-equal development; and like its North American counterpart, behind a lingerie-thin veneer, it was a system of bruising and bloodthirsty brutality.

In a poem written after South Africa's 1960 Sharpeville massacre, Dennis Brutus focuses on the police's savage cruelty that killed seventy in an unarmed, panicked, retreating crowd, and the horror that bullets tore through the bodies of a mother and her child. But he contemplates the greater meaning of Sharpeville as if scrawling it on a series of propagandized placards. With its wildly flying bullets, Sharpeville embodied the demonic essence of apartheid's patterns of dominance and oppression. What other governments dared to enact only with practiced subtlety, the apartheid regime disdainfully exposes visibly, nakedly, and bloodily.[20] Brutus knows that when he denounces apartheid, he condemns only one manifestation of original oppression. But as Merton says that God can create "an opening toward peace and love even when the sulphur [sic] and brimstone are at their worst,"[21] Brutus ends his poem with a similar prophetic irony: for all of the terror of Sharpeville, the dead bequeathed to others their unappeasable appetite for freedom.[22]

Sixteen years later, as black South African students protested a fresh insult—the mandatory introduction of Afrikaans, the language of their most noxious oppressor, into school curricula—Desmond Tutu adopted a very different approach. Perfectly capable of Brutus's style of denunciation—his prediction that apartheid would end up in the Gehenna of history[23]—instead of using bullet-in-the-back rhetoric, Tutu sought face-to-face reconciliation. As the Soweto crisis neared its peak, he wrote a letter to John Vorster, South Africa's then-prime minister. With remarkable warmth, Tutu designed this simple epistle to reveal common ground between an elected leader defending multitiered racialism and a bishop advocating racial equality.

20. Brutus, *Stubborn Hope*, 88–89.
21. Merton, *Hidden Ground*, 458.
22. Brutus, *Stubborn Hope*, 89.
23. Tutu, *Hope and Suffering*, 158.

> I am writing to you Sir, because I know you to be a loving and caring father and husband, a doting grandfather who has experienced the joys and anguish of family life, its laughter and gaiety, its sorrows and pangs. I am writing to you Sir as one who is passionately devoted to a happy and stable family life as the indispensable foundation of a sound and healthy society. You have flung out your arms to embrace and hug your children and your grandchildren, to smother them with your kisses, you have loved, you have wept, you have watched by the bed of a sick one whom you loved, you have watched by the deathbed of a beloved relative, you have been a proud father at the wedding of your children, you have shed tears by the graveside of one for whom your heart has been broken. In short, I am writing to you as one human person to another human person, gloriously created in the image of the selfsame God, redeemed by the selfsame Christ who for all our sakes died on the Cross and rose triumphant from the dead and reigns in glory now at the right hand of God; sanctified by the selfsame Holy Spirit who works inwardly in all of us to change our hearts of stone into hearts of flesh. I am, therefore, writing to you, Sir, as one Christian to another, for through our common baptism we have been made members of and are united in the Body of our dear Lord and Savior, Jesus Christ. This Jesus Christ, whatever we may have done, has broken down all that separates us irrelevantly—such as race, sex, culture, status, etc. In this Jesus Christ we are forever bound together as one redeemed humanity, black and white together.[24]

Instead of imbedding a transforming prayer in an article, as Day did after the Memorial Day Massacre, Tutu implants a plea in a letter. And instead of transforming his vision of a political crisis as Day did through the singular act of Jesus of Gethsemane, Tutu appeals to the Christian's everyday faith and to the commonness of family life.

Spiritually, Tutu seeks to massage a stony heart into malleable flesh (Ezek 11:19). Politically, he illegally imports religious language into a dictatorial monologue to reveal blasphemy at the heart of public policy. But he writes not as a prophet condemning the unjust, nor as a preacher censuring the unrepentant, but as one family member to another. It is an astonishing way to address someone so rigidly rooted in a vicious ideology. It would have been easy, even apt, to compare Vorster to Hitler. Yet against a backdrop of barbed wire, bloodshed, insult, and humiliation, Tutu injects a message

---

24. Tutu, *Rainbow People*, 6–7.

of familial wonder to gently awaken Vorster to the reality that the two of them—of different peoples and opposing ideologies—are part of one family.

Yet Tutu's rhetoric is not as surprising as *his* ability to find commonality with Vorster. By appealing to Vorster's humanity, he affirms that the prime minister of a racist government is still brother Ammi receiving sister Ruhamah. As Day creates three-dimensional portraits of the poor to unearth their full dignity for her bourgeois readers, Tutu humanizes a leader who needs no projections for anyone to question his humanity; for that, Vorster could run on his own record. Rather, Tutu's invocation of family is another theme in the language of the realm, an announcement of common humanity that not only subverts every justification for class division or ethnic conflict—it erases every excuse to hate.

As Tutu knew too well, South Africa's "spiral of violence"[25] fueled reverse rage, sometimes aptly subverting apartheid, sometimes flooding uncontrollably against all white persons. The rhetoric of family blunts and channels this escalation as it dulls clear definitions of good vs. evil and light vs. darkness, rehumanizing oppressors that activists are tempted to demonize. Because of its antipharisaical thrust, invocations of family are among the recurring themes of Tutu's multilateral protest. After apartheid's collapse, this font of protest became a source of anguish as he wondered how people could bureaucratically and distractedly humiliate and exploit other people. How could they torture someone and then do as Vorster did: "embrace their wives, and enjoy, say, their child's birthday party?"[26] Merton's observation that at Auschwitz "ordinary respectable people" raised in purportedly Christian households could "put their best energies into making genocide a success"[27] would be no surprise to Tutu.

It is one thing for Tutu to use theological truisms: "all of us, black and white together, belong in the family of God. We are brothers and sisters, we are one. With his Cross God has effected reconciliation among us all."[28] It is one thing to urge an oppressor to see the humanity of the oppressed. It is another to apply familial language to the chief architects of oppression. A few years after his letter to Vorster, with yet another prime minister overseeing apartheid, Tutu asked his black African audience: "Can you imagine what would happen in this land if we accepted that theological fact about ourselves—that whether we like it or not we are members of one family? Whether I like it or not, whether he likes it or not . . . P. W. Botha is my brother

---

25. The title of the book by Dom Helder Camara, *Spiral of Violence*.
26. Tutu, *No Future*, 130.
27. Merton, *Nonviolent Alternative*, 157–58.
28. Tutu, *Rainbow People*, 262.

and I must desire and pray for the best for him."[29] Affection is irrelevant. The gospel demands an icier resolve and a steelier love. Tutu could truthfully have said that he loved his enemies, a resonant enough statement that would implicitly heighten his nobility and question Vorster and Botha's humanity. Instead, Tutu invokes the image of family to place them on the same moral plane and to fine-tune the rhetoric of equality.

When practiced, Tutu's striving for commonality paid political dividends in the most fragile of political transitions. When Nelson Mandela emerged from prison thirty years after Sharpeville and fifteen after Soweto, white South African leaders were caught off guard, and charmed, when they discovered that during his twenty-seven-year imprisonment, Mandela studied Afrikaans and Afrikaner history, the language and lore of his tormentors. This enabled him to sympathize with Afrikaner suffering under British colonialism and draw parallels with the black South African struggle.[30] As Tutu found common ground in stories of family, Mandela unearthed it in the history of peoples.

This liberating theme applied in modern South Africa has, in the Christian tradition, sometimes extended the scope of family even beyond species and genus. When Macarius of Alexandria heals a hyena, it foreshadows Francis of Assisi's sermon to the birds and the story of the Wolf of Gubbio. It also echoes Gospel healing stories, and becomes both a catechesis and a story of repentance. A hyena, like Bartimaeus crying out in need (Mark 10:47), comes to see Macarius in his cell. As Jairus and the Syrophoenician woman came to see if Jesus would heal their daughters (Mark 5:22–23, 7:24–25), the mother hyena, "carrying her cub in her mouth," places her in front of Macarius's door and knocks. Amazed at the sight, Macarius asks, as Jesus asks prospective disciples, "What do you seek" (John 1:38, RSV)? She picks up her cub in her mouth and shows it to the "old man, weeping." Macarius sees that the cub is blind and sighs. Like Jesus with the blind man of Bethsaida (Mark 8:23), he spits, but directly into the cub's face, and makes the sign of the cross on its eyes with his finger: "Immediately the cub could see and left him for its mother and suckled."[31] Together hyena and cub disappear into the marshland.

As most Gospel stories are less about the therapeutic than social implications and religious conflicts—Jesus heals the wrong person on the wrong day or in the wrong place or without proper religious authority—so the healing of the cub is only the beginning. Like the thankful Samaritan among

29. Ibid., 119.
30. Sampson, *Mandela*, 393.
31. Vivian, *Four Desert Fathers*, 140.

the ungrateful lepers (Luke 17:11–9), the hyena returns to "the old man with a sheepskin, very plush and soft, hanging from her mouth as an offering, and knocked with her head on the door." When Macarius sees the mother hyena "holding the skin as an offering," he scolds her as Jesus rebukes his friend who cut off the slave's ear (Luke 22:51): "Where have you come from? Where did you get this unless you ate a sheep? What you have brought has come from violence. I will not accept it from you."

Responding to his censure, "the hyena was hitting her head on the ground and bending her paws, imploring him like a person to take the sheepskin from her." But Macarius is adamant. Not only has she killed; she has stolen from the poor. He refuses to accept the sheepskin "unless you promise me not to hurt the poor by eating their sheep." She moves her head up and down as though making this promise, as the wolf will with Francis. Macarius adds, "Unless you promise me you will not kill any living beast but will eat only carrion from now on, I will not accept the sheepskin." Then, anticipating Francis's prescription for the wolf, he says, "From now on, if you are weary from searching for food and are unable to find anything to eat, come to me here and I will give you bread, and do no violence to anyone from now on." The hyena "prostrated herself to the earth, throwing herself on her knees, bending her paws," and kept moving her head up and down "as though she were giving him her promise"; Macarius realizes that God "gives intelligence even to wild beasts in order to teach us a lesson." He "gave glory to God" that, like the lions in Daniel's den, the hyena understands God's ways. He accepts the sheepskin and the hyena returns to her lair. Every few days thereafter she visits him and if she is hungry, he gives her bread. And "the old man slept on the sheepskin until he went to his rest."[32]

As Macarius affirms his relatedness to the hyena, he also demands that she enter into familial relationship with sheep and the poor. Like the stories of the Syrophoenician woman and Jairus that erase ethnic lines and recycle the scales of power as so much scrap metal, this healing stretches notions of personhood. For Macarius the human family becomes merely a nuclear family in God's larger, more diverse created family and partially fulfills Isaiah's vision of predators and prey living together in peace (Isa 11:6–8). The hyena hears a condensed version of the Sermon on the Mount: she must love more than her cub; she must bless all creatures.

As Macarius instructs the hyena about a binding unity among all creatures, Tutu tries to teach a prime minister a lesson in human family. The Soweto crisis reached its peak after Tutu's letter. In an escalation of Sharpeville, police killed hundreds of protesters and bystanders and the

---

32. Ibid.

government slammed shut the doors to reform. Unlike the hyena, Vorster was not a ready disciple. Perhaps a hyena, more easily than a prime minister, embraces the revolutionary realization that all creatures belong to one family.

Maybe it would have been different had Tutu healed a member of Vorster's family; then again, maybe not.

BEGETTING THE REVOLUTION

Using traditional Father-Son language, Meister Eckhart describes God begetting Christ in the world, "ever anew and fresh"; begetting so delights God that God "does nothing else but this."[33] God's very nature—God's "ground," "essence," and "being"—moves God "to generation."[34] Anyone who sees God "unveiled and bare" inevitably catches God "in the act of begetting."[35] God begets Christ "unceasingly," and God begets in us "the same" Christ.[36] As Augustine maintains that we are restive until we rest in God,[37] Eckhart implies that God is forever fidgety until Christ is born in us.[38] Thus Eckhart complicates the rhetoric of family. Not only are we created in God's image as God's children; God is eternally begetting Christ in us and through us. As Mary bore Christ physically, we bear Christ spiritually. We, both male and female, are eternally pregnant.

With one foot in mysticism and the other in activism, Rufus Jones says that a filial spirit always begets God's revolution. It is this "spirit which has reformed prisons, fought slavery, championed the case of the Indian and freed slave, striven to alleviate suffering everywhere, and quietly wrought in city and country to make peace supplant war, and love hatred."[39] The belief in a *new* people that embraces its relationship to *all* people, Underhill's *new race*,[40] is at the heart of social transformation. When this spirit fills us, we become not only children of God; we become begetters of the revolution.

But, like begetting itself, the rhetoric, poetics, politics, and prayers of God's family is a many-splendored thing. At times, filial rhetoric softens the sharp, clear lines between good and evil, us and them; at times it clarifies

33. Eckhart, *Sermons & Treatises II*, 31–32.
34. Ibid., 100.
35. Ibid., 104.
36. Ibid., 135.
37. Augustine, *Confessions*, 1.1.
38. Eckhart, *Sermons & Treatises II*, 157.
39. Jones, *Essential Writings*, 140–41.
40. Underhill, *Abba*, 34.

and creates new conflicts. Whether Tutu uses the rhetoric to invite Vorster into a multiracial family or reminds Africans that—like it or not—they are related to Afrikaners, familial images help us overcome boundaries of class, caste, religion, ideology, and nationality.

Yet this rhetoric does not emerge spotless, whole, clear, clean, or without blemish at its New Testament sources; they waffle in their characterizations of God's family. At times, faith and ethics determine this relationship: those who believe in the Word have the power to *become* God's children (John 1:12); peacemakers will be *called* God's children (Matt 5:9). In other writings, however, agency rests solely with God, who adopts us as children and makes us heirs of the realm (Gal 4:5–7). In one view, being a child of God is an itching intriguing possibility; in the other it is a bona fide ontological reality. It is, like God's realm, already and not yet.

Jesus' words and deeds functions like Hindu gods, creating and destroying images of family. They expose pharisaical modern North American "family values" that circle wagons to exclude uitlanders [outsiders], excoriate immigrants, and stone gay and lesbian persons. The notion that the nuclear family has a permanent part in the divine order instead of being a sociological by-product of a blink-of-an-eye bourgeois economic circumstance is, of course, mythic fantasy. Nuclear "family values" pervert and reverse gospel values—the gospels expand the idea of family to cross borders, embrace enemies, and encircle all creatures within God's loving arms.

The destroyer-Jesus flails rigid notions of family values as ferociously as he cleanses the temple; the creator-Jesus begets a family with an unflappable sense of universal love. At the beginning of John's Gospel, Jesus rudely distances himself from his mother (John 2:4). Yet from the cross, he forges a new family, as a patriarch might arrange a marriage, between his mother and his beloved disciple (John 19:26–7). In Mark, had it been possible, Jesus' family would have had him institutionalized, or worse (Mark 3:21). As Ephrem of Syria notes, Jesus' kin rush him with "swords," but strangers flock to him with "offerings."[41] When people speak to him of his blood kin, he pointedly describes an embryonic egalitarian counterfamily without patriarch, hierarchy, or lineage, based only on "whoever does the will of God" (Mark 3:35). Throughout the Sermon on the Mount, Jesus lays the foundations for a revolutionary contrast-community whose members are in familial relationships with all. With prophetic insight into South African torturers, Holocaust bureaucrats, and citizens that sip coffee while reading about the drones their government uses to assassinate suspected terrorists,

---

41. Ephrem, *Hymns*, 189.

Jesus teaches that the self-righteous unrighteous care only for their own kin (Matt 5:46–47).

Even so, the boundaries of this contrast-community are often in flux. The Synoptics consistently smuggle love past ethnic, ethical, religious and political borders to include sinner, Samaritan, tax collector, and Roman. In John, Jesus invites the Samaritan woman—a two-strike outcast—into the family of disciples as she simultaneously storms that Bastille. But the greater stress in the Johannine corpus is Ezra-like in drawing thick, dark, clear sectarian lines to separate *us* from *them*, first dividing *us* from a suspect world, and then subdividing *us* from other community members who fail to love the right people or believe the right thing. Members of that community are to love their brothers and sisters *within* the community; they are a quasimonastic or Anabaptist community known for the way *we* love one another. Of all the epistles, 1 John is most filled with the lingo of love and most fraught with nascent hate. So when Underhill says that each Christian "belongs to a new race,"[42] she sides with Synoptic expansiveness. To listen to Jesus, to follow Jesus, to become part of Christ's body, is to have every aspect of our identity deconstructed and reconstructed.

Among activists, the rhetoric of family takes on the characteristics of the Maurin-Day debate that pitted *annunciation* against *denunciation*. Prayers and rhetoric can function as protests against the powers that be or as proclamations of the realm to come. At times, such rhetoric becomes Muste's *third way*, a road barely imagined and rarely taken. Day employs the image of the Holy Family as an annunciation: the Holy Family, like so many families, lives in poverty. Theirs are the struggles of manual laborers and the working poor.[43] When Day uses Paul's image of the mystical body, she inverts her church's frequent abuse of the term that emboldens a self-appointed, self-anointed inner circle to overidentify the contours of the body with the structures of an institution. She bursts this boundary apart until everyone is a "potential" member of the body.[44] So in 1962, the year of the Cuban Missile Crisis, she writes that the body of Christ includes the peoples of Cuba, China, the Soviet Union, and all Marxist-Leninists.[45] After praying at the grave of Karl Marx she notes that the author of *Das Kapital* was known for his compassion; the children of his neighborhood called him "Papa Marx."[46] In an act that would have irritated Communist and Catholic

---

42. Underhill, *Abba*, 34.
43. Day, *On Pilgrimage*, 16.
44. Ibid., 78.
45. Day, *On Pilgrimage: The Sixties*, 94.
46. Day, *On Pilgrimage*, 53.

alike, she prays at Lenin's tomb that in death he find "a place of refreshment, light, and peace."[47]

Gustavo Gutierrez reiterates the truth in 1 John that no one can segregate love of God from love of neighbor, but he uses it to dismantle Johannine walls: Jesus is not only the way to a parental God, "he is also our way to recognition of others as brothers and sisters."[48] Like Lester's spiritual discipline of "remembering the Presence of God" in each person,[49] Gutierrez announces a filial relationship with all people through our child-parent relationship with God. And as Gutierrez announces, Rauschenbusch denounces. For him, when Jesus invokes God's parenthood, it is "only by contrast to the despotic ideas which it opposed and was meant to displace."[50] For him, Jesus exposes and opposes all exploitative systems through the rhetoric of family as he creates a vision of an alternative *order* and a counter*world*.

In Merton's hands, familial language is both iconic and iconoclastic. He tells of an incident in a white Roman Catholic church in New Orleans during the civil rights movement. When the priest preached that the commandment to love one's "brother" applies to integration, a man shouted that he didn't go to church to hear such "junk." Another called it "crap"; a third shouted, "If I miss Mass today *it's your fault*." Merton concludes: you can consider yourself a good Catholic and be, in fact, "an apostate": "To exclude a brother or sister in Christ" is, as Paul says, "to 'eat and drink judgment to oneself'" (1 Cor 11:29).[51] The same lack of filial sensibility reinforced the ways that Cold War superpowers remained "myths" to each other.[52] Both national identities were warped by the kind of crude propaganda that makes the enemy appear bestial, craven, and cruel.[53] Through its cartoonish projections on its enemy, each nation defined itself as the antidote, the anti-antichrist, and therefore a messianic Savior.

Using the image as an icon, Merton links familial language to his Louisville epiphany. In the afterglow of that revelation, he has a goosebump-inducing insight into the power and wonder of the incarnation: "It is a glorious thing to be a member of the human race, though it is a race dedicated to many absurdities and one which makes many terrible mistakes: yet, with all that, God gloried in becoming a member of the human race. A

---

47. Ibid., 54.
48. Gutierrez, *We Drink*, 112.
49. Lester, *Ambassador of Reconciliation*, 125.
50. Rauschenbusch, *Social Gospel*, 175.
51. Merton, *Conjectures*, 109–10.
52. Merton, *Cold War*, 29.
53. Keen, *Faces of the Enemy*.

member of the human race! To think that such a commonplace realization should suddenly seem like news that one holds the winning ticket in a cosmic sweepstake. . . . And if only everybody could realize this! But it cannot be explained."[54] The church teaches it. We hear it. But if only we could see it!

The same spiritual blindness that explains America's apartheid—the Jim Crow status quo, banned ballot boxes, segregated schools, snarling dogs, bruising fire hoses, police beatings, and Sharpeville's bullets in Alabama's byways—also exposes the dominant cowboy-and-Indian ideology in Vietnam[55] that blesses napalm and sanctifies carpet bombings. Announcing an alternative, Merton employs familial language to beget new families. In 1964, early in the antiwar movement, he called then little-known Buddhist activist Thich Nhat Hanh "my brother." In the infancy of interfaith dialogue, when the American media commonly deemed Vietnamese monks inscrutable, Merton declared that he had been adopted into a family with a Vietnamese Buddhist: "He is more my brother than many who are nearer to me by race and nationality, because he and I see things exactly the same way. He and I deplore the war that is ravaging his country. We deplore it for exactly the same reasons: human reasons, reasons of sanity, justice and love. We deplore the needless destruction, the fantastic and callous ravaging of human life, the rape of the culture and spirit of an exhausted people."[56] Nhat Hanh is his brother because they both seek God's will (cf. Mark 3:35).

In Merton's short essay "Taking Sides on Vietnam," written the same year, when Hawks demonized Communists, and Doves projected primordial Leviathan-like evil on the American military, Merton took a *third way*. As someone who sometimes wondered if monks should take sides,[57] Merton was emphatically not neutral, but he chose a particular way to oppose war: "I am on the side of the people who are being burned, cut to pieces, tortured, held as hostages, gassed, ruined, destroyed. They are the victims of both sides. . . . The side I take is then the side of the people who are sick of war."[58]

Merton's siding with "victims" is Stringfellow's consistent ethic: to him, Christians side with "every victim of the rulers of the age," not because the victims are "right" or sympathetic, not because of their economic status, the color of their skin, *or* the content of their character—Christians side with victims simply "because the victim is a victim."[59] These were the people

---

54. Merton, *Conjectures*, 157.
55. Merton, *Nonviolent Alternative*, 253.
56. Merton, *Faith and Violence*, 106.
57. Merton, *Silent Life*, 174.
58. Merton, *Faith and Violence*, 109–10.
59. Stringfellow, *Conscience and Obedience*, 94.

Stringfellow defended as an attorney: "I have been an advocate for the poor, for the urban underclass, for freedom riders and war resisters, for people deprived of elementary rights: children, women, blacks, Hispanics, native [sic] Americans, political prisoners, homosexuals, the elderly, the handicapped, clergy accused of heresy, women aspiring to priesthood."[60]

In sentiments similar to Merton's during the previous episode in the serial American land war in Asia, Day wrote a "Message of Love" at Christmas in 1950. Like Merton, she sided not with North or South Korea or China or the US. She took sides with a previously unacknowledged group as if she could recast the war not as a contest between ideologies or nations but as an example of liberation theology's as-yet-unstated preferential option: "We are on the side of the poor. . . . Who are the poor? They are our soldiers in Korea fighting in zero [degree] weather, thousands of them suffering and tortured and dying. . . . They are the Koreans themselves, north and south, who have been bombed out, burnt out in the rain of fire from heaven." The poor are the "men, women, and children, the old and the sick and the cripples. The innocent, the noncombatant." When napalm killed a thousand Korean soldiers, Day applied the spirit of her Memorial Day Massacre prayer, "God have mercy on them all and those who killed them as well as those who died!"[61]

Lester also uses filial language to subvert the tribal hypernationalism at the root of modern war as she declares every international dispute another family tragedy and every *good war* another shibboleth. Like Day, she found wartime the best time to underline the revolutionary relevance of the Sermon on the Mount. So, as Day says the day after Pearl Harbor "Our manifesto is the Sermon on the Mount,"[62] Lester one World War earlier declares "no moratorium on the Sermon on the Mount."[63] Yet it is not enough to remind people to love their enemies. Lester protests against the very notion that a government can tell its citizens who to hate. During World War I, she protested against the absurd arbitrariness of looking upon "our brother and sister" as "an enemy just because they chance to have been born [on] the other side of a river or a strip of sea."[64] One did not have to be well educated or highly refined to recognize this absurdity. Having a cup of tea with an East London neighbor, the woman, like her Montgomery counterpart

---

60. Stringfellow, *Simplicity of Faith*, 129. His ministry also lumped together Freedom Riders and neo-Nazis simply because they were "outcasts" (*My People*, 40–43).

61. Day, "Message of Love," 1–2.

62. Day, *By Little*, 262.

63. Lester, *Ambassador of Reconciliation*, 39.

64. Lester, *It Occurred to Me*, 61.

whose "feets was tired," spoke the truth without refinement: "When you come to think of it, Miss, those Germans in the zepps, you can't blame 'em. They're only made to do it, same as our men are, pore devils!" Another woman added, "our men are doing the same to them. And every German we kill is only some pore mother's son."[65] Theirs were commentaries on the Golden Rule: do not condemn those who are doing to you what you are doing to them.

After Lester's visit to China during the next *great* war, while Japanese troops raped, pillaged, and murdered Chinese by the hundreds of thousands, she told Christian audiences in Japan that Chinese Christians "refused to consider any one as the enemy because they happened to have been born on a different patch of earth."[66] It might make *some* sense to have personal enemies based on personal experience, but it made no sense to allow others to select your enemies from an international lineup. This abdication of agency fused each citizen of another country into an anonymous mass without name, face, age, character, personality, or moral compass. As the devastating blockade of Germany after World War I caused mass starvation, Lester's East London neighbors "wrote a letter to the Prime Minister saying that 'they knew what it was to be hungry and because of that they and their children didn't want anyone in any part of the world to be hungry.'"[67] Their Prime Minister was as deaf to them as Vorster was to Tutu.

As Lester targets the irrationality of wartime rhetoric, Stringfellow calls John F. Kennedy's famous nationalistic phrase—"ask not what your country can do for you; ask what you can do for your country"—not idealism but idolatry.[68] Idolatry also lay at the root of racism.[69] Run-of-the-mill patriotism, like the most vicious racial pride, is antithetical to a parental God. Both build ziggurats as monuments to themselves and abort our relationship to God's children.

To the ears of a "realist" like Reinhold Niebuhr, Lester's contentions would sound impossibly naïve. But as Day lived on the bleaker streets of Manhattan, Lester lived in bombed-out London and walked among corpses in China; she was hardly a fluffy quixotic idealist. Like Tutu, she wrestled regularly with outrage and grief. Writing of her experience in war-ravaged China, "a wave of bitterness threatened to overwhelm me . . . for I don't

---

65. Ibid., 71.

66. Ibid., 179.

67. Lester, *Ambassador of Reconciliation*, 67.

68. Stringfellow, *Free in Obedience*, 58.

69. Ibid., 63; for a sustained argument of racism as idolatry, see Kelsey, *Racism and Christian Understanding*.

find it easy to be a pacifist. It requires a ceaseless self-discipline, reminding oneself that the enemy isn't any one set of people, Japanese, German or Italian.... The enemy is always the same. Violence, pride, greed, fear, callousness, the things that flourish in our hearts."[70]

To oppose war means transforming one's heart with Christendom's foundational prayer:"To disarm—not only our bodies by refusing to kill, or to make killing instruments in munitions factories—but to disarm our minds of anger, pride, envy, hate and malice. We should stop praying the Lord's Prayer until we can see that 'Our Father' means we are 'tied to the same living tether' not only with fellow citizens but with everybody on this planet."[71] "Unless God meant the human race to be actually one family, we have no right to the phrase 'Our Father.'"[72] So Lester prayed for the day when people would realize that "war was an unscientific way of trying to settle anything; that as cannibalism, chattel slavery, blood-feuds and dueling had one by one been recognized as foolish, old-fashioned, an insult to God and the human race, so war was an outmoded custom and a daily crucifixion of Christ." One can only pray the Lord's Prayer for so long without absorbing the ramifications and, in Lester's case, suffering the consequences. While traveling abroad early in World War II Lester was detained in jail by the British government for two months for threatening the war effort by confessing that England was not without international imperialistic sin and professing that violence is not the way of Jesus.[73] So Jesus' concept of family is not only abhorrent to racists, fascists, and dictators; it is treasonous to "good guys" fighting "good wars."

Merton writes of *victims*, Day of the *poor*, Lester of the *bombed*. In a story mixing elements of foot washing, the Good Samaritan, and Paul's conversion, a Belgian woman shared a memory at a Fellowship of Reconciliation conference in 1923 from the perspective of the *occupied*. Addressing an audience that included German delegates, she confessed that as Belgium suffered cruelly under occupation, she grew to despise Germans, any German, all Germans: "I hated Germans with the bitterest hatred. I wanted the French and the Belgians ... to crush Germany."[74] But one day she and her husband saw a German soldier, faint with hunger, lying in the mud. His bleeding feet peeked through his shoes. He was so dazed that he did not even know which country he was in. They helped him to their home and

---

70. Lester, *Ambassador of Reconciliation*, 162.
71. Ibid., 93.
72. Ibid., 53.
73. Lester, *It Occurred to Me*, 61.
74. Wallis, *Mother of World Peace*, 198.

put him on their bed. While washing his bloodstained feet "something fell down from my eyes, and I saw that he was a brother. A German was my brother. The Germans were our brothers."[75] She was a sister to this soldier and to all Germans. She experienced Lester's annunciation: the nations are not cubbyholes in which people can be pigeonholed as allies or enemies; family transcends all biases and boundaries.

Lester's friend Gandhi—in occupied India—knew well the intricate spiritual complexities of living in peonage under British patronage. He knew Tutu's dilemma as he faced a racist ideology and one intransigent prime minister after another. He knew how difficult it is to convince an *imperium tremendum* to treat nonpeople as God's people, and the mirroring problem of helping Indians see the humanity of the stiff-lipped, stiff-necked, self-righteous British. Gandhi also understood the hydra-headed nature of oppression. True liberation means more than exchanging colonial rulers for an indigenous elite, and more than establishing an independent India with one dominant religion and one submissive caste. Even as he pursued political independence, he worked to correct his culture's blind spots to amplify the deeper meaning of *swaraj* (freedom) as far more than autonomy from the British Raj. Gandhi wanted India to sing a new, noncaste, nonclass, Hindu-Muslim song.

True swaraj demands self-transcendence as much as self-rule. It requires not only the expulsion of an imperialistic power but the resolution of religious rivalries, the dismantling of the caste system, and the end of economic inequality: "Swaraj is impossible if Hindus, Muslims and others do not shed their mutual distrust and do not live as blood brothers and sisters, if Hindus do not purify themselves by removing the curse of untouchability and thus establish intimate contact with those whom they have for ages put beyond the pale of society, if the wealthy men and women of India will not tax themselves" for the sake of the poor, and "if we all will not identify ourselves with the semi-starved millions by giving up" luxurious clothes and "revert to *khadi* ('homespun cloth')."[76] As Christianity's shadow side has enslaved the children of Ham, promotes homophobia, and enshrines the nuclear family, Gandhi saw Hinduism's shadow side blessing the caste system.[77] So as Jesus ate with outcasts and sinners, Gandhi dined with *dalits*.[78] He risked his ashram's unity when he invited a *dalit* family to

---

75. Wink, *Peace is the Way*, 258–59.
76. Gandhi, *Non-violent*, 368.
77. Browne, *Gandhi*, 76, 100.
78. Also known as "untouchables" (Browne, *Gandhi*, 206).

join its fellowship.⁷⁹ And to change people's perceptions of *dalits*, he called them *harijans*, Children of God.⁸⁰ To Gandhi, true freedom is impossible until people of competing faiths recognize each other as part of one family, until caste differences are junked, until the wealthy see their fate tied to the poor. Liberty without reforms against caste distinctions, class structures, and religious intolerance is, like faith without love, a banging gong and a clanging cymbal.

Gandhi's bottom-up view of India's freedom mirrors Abraham Lincoln's top-down view during a Civil War that famously divided families. Lincoln experienced the length of the arc of the moral universe in his internal battle of the principled with the political. Wavering over whether the war was fought for political reasons (restoring the Union) or moral goals (emancipating slaves), by the time of his Second Inaugural Address, his Deuteronomic theology crystallized into a new blend of political expediency, God's judgment, and human freedom. Lincoln considered the Civil War God's judgment on the North for its complicity with slavery.⁸¹ By 1864, he believed that the Union could not be rebuilt on the rotting foundation of injustice. Emancipation was necessary to union, as swaraj could not be built on religious prejudice, social exclusion, or economic exploitation.

If, as Jones says, familial language begets social transformation, it is also the seed of spiritual revolution. Lester says that when a Christian prays the Lord's Prayer—alone in one's room, in monastic solitude, or in solitary confinement—to pray "Our Father" forces us to recognize a kinship with all who use the same prayer. Entering into a relationship with an *abba* or *amma* God transforms all persons into brothers and sisters. Underhill maintains that once we use the phrase "Our Father," we "can never again enter into prayer as a ring-fenced individual, intent on a private relation with God"—Christian prayer "must overflow the boundaries of selfhood to include the life, the needs of the [human] race; accepting as a corollary of its filial relation with God a familial relation with all other souls however diverse, and at every point replacing 'mine' with 'ours.'" Underhill had a deep reverence for the "bracing solitude" that deepens intimacy with God, but solitude finds its true place in the body of the prayerful: "Here my enemies pray by my side, since the world of prayer has no frontiers; and in so doing they cease to be my enemies, because we meet in God."⁸²

---

79. Ibid., 101.
80. Ibid., 268.
81. Morel, *Lincoln's Sacred Effort*, 148, 180, 189.
82. Underhill, *Abba*, 14–15.

The Hasidic tradition also affirms the unifying effect of prayer. Pinhas of Koretz says, "A prayer which is not spoken in the name of all Israel is no prayer at all!"[83] Amplifying on this, Yehiel Mikhal of Zlotchov says that before praying, "I join myself to all of Israel, to those who are more than I, that through them my thought may rise, and to those who are less than I, so that they may rise through my thought."[84] Prayer is not only spoken in the name of all, it has to be of equal value to all. Charles de Foucauld says that when we pray "what we ask for ourselves we ask always for all people without exception."[85] Members of a family cannot pray for one without praying for all. They pray with Isaac of Nineveh's merciful heart.

Just as people allow themselves to be divided by nation and race, religious people destructively and self-destructively build ever higher and steeper border fences between good and evil, saints and sinners. Because the desert tradition was attuned to help people grow in holiness, it often demanded harsh discipline for those who failed miserably, memorably, or visibly. So at one meeting to discuss a "brother" who had sinned, as several *abbas* spoke, Abba Pior, without a word, "got up and went out; he took a sack, filled it with sand and carried it on his shoulder." Then he had a second smaller bag filled with sand. When the other *abbas* asked him what he was doing, he said, "In this sack which contains much sand, are my sins which are many; I have put them behind me so as not to be troubled about them and so as not to weep; and see here are the little sins of my brother which are in front of me and I spend my time judging them. This is not right. I ought rather to carry my sins in front of me and concern myself with them, begging God to forgive me for them." Like Yehiel Mikhal, Abba Pior links himself both to those more and less righteous. And like Tutu, he approaches a sinner on the same moral plane. Responding to Pior, the *abbas*, echoing Jesus at the house of Zacchaeus (Luke 19:9–10), declare, "Truly, this is the way of salvation."[86]

God's people bridge moral and spiritual divides, but how are we reconciled with God? In contrast to the image of a stern patriarch already undercut in Jesus' *abba*, Julian of Norwich sees each person of the Trinity as maternal,[87] nurturing us, and holding us to Jesus' "blessed breast."[88] Macarius the Spiritbearer employs a very different maternal image: "You

---

83. Buber, *Tales: Early Masters*, 126.
84. Ibid., 150.
85. Foucauld, *Writings*, 110.
86. Ward, *Sayings of the Desert*, 199.
87. Julian, *Showings*, 292–305.
88. Ibid., 298.

will see him who is gentle, our Lord Jesus Christ, his face full of joy for you, like a nursing mother whose face is full of joy for her child. When [the baby] raises his hands and his face up to her, even if he is full of all kinds of uncleanness, she does not turn away from that bad smell and excrement but takes pity on him and lifts him up and presses him to her breast, her face full of joy, and everything about him is sweet to her." What Isaiah envisions as a contrast metaphor for God—one who cannot forget Israel even if a nursing mother can (Isa 49:15)—becomes, for Macarius, the very image of the divine. If a nursing mother, "a created person," can show this much love "for her child, how much greater is the love of the creator, our Lord Jesus Christ, for us!"[89] The Mishnah insists that to save a life is to save a world. Traherne says that redeeming one soul is greater than creating a world. For his part, Eckhart marvels that God's mercy changes us "from an enemy into a friend. And that is more than creating a world."[90] To be human is to be part of a body of sinners without borders.

The significance of the one, the last, and the least is at the root of the spiritual direction to the Catholic Worker community: We love God only as much as the person we love least.[91] Without knowing this saying, A. J. Muste put it to the test when, at a Quaker meeting in 1940, as Nazi troops conquered Europe, he stood up in the midst of the gathering and said, "If I can't love Hitler, I can't love at all."[92] Yet this counsel is not only for an alternative community like the Catholic Worker or a moral rigorist like Muste; it is Tutu's message to his whole people.

It is also at the heart of James Baldwin's open letter to his fourteen-year-old nephew. Famous for his blunt and bruising rhetoric,[93] and his precise prophetic dissections of American racism, Baldwin, writing *The Fire Next Time* in the early 1960s, describes a damnable national sin, a "crime of which . . . neither I nor time nor history will ever forgive," for white Americans "have destroyed and are destroying hundreds of thousands of lives and do not know and do not want to know it."[94] Sarcasm bristling, his *j'accuse* says the US is committing this crime against his nephew and every black teen that has ever lived within its borders:

---

89. Vivian, *St. Macarius*, 104.
90. Otto, *Mysticism*, 211.
91. Day, *By Little*, 301.
92. Robinson, *Abraham Went Out*, 75.
93. Preaching at New York's St. John the Divine Cathedral in the early 1970s, he referred to Richard Nixon as a "motherfucker" (Leeming, *James Baldwin*, 332).
94. Baldwin, *Fire Next Time*, 15.

> This innocent country set you down in a ghetto in which, in fact, it intended that you should perish. Let me spell out precisely what I mean by that, for the heart of the matter is here, and the root of my dispute with my country. You were born where you were born and faced the future that you faced because you were black and *for no other reason*. The limits of your ambition were, thus, expected to be set forever. You were born into a society which spelled out with brutal clarity, and in as many ways as possible that you were a worthless human being. You were not expected to aspire to excellence: you were expected to make peace with mediocrity.[95]

The most insidious, self-immolating disaster for his nephew would be to believe what *they* say about *him*. Even as the US had the gall to celebrate the centenary of the Emancipation Proclamation, Baldwin tells his nephew, "You know and I know, that the country is celebrating one hundred of years of freedom one hundred years too soon."[96]

Yet for all that and more, these "lost" white people were his brothers and sisters.[97] His privileged oppressors might think that they had the power to choose if and when they wanted to integrate society, if and when they wanted to be so liberal and noble as to accept his nephew, "but the really terrible thing, old buddy, is that *you* must accept *them*. . . . You must accept them and accept them with love."[98] *They*, in trying to dehumanize him, had dehumanized themselves; *they* were the ones in need. In a variation on Tutu's "like it or not" and on Will Campbell's nutshell of theology, "we're all bastards but God loves us anyway," Baldwin creates a summation of ethics: *they're* all bastards but *you* must love *them* anyway. In spite of everything they do (to you!), they too are harijans. This, of course, is the gospel of the civil rights movement. Even as its political goals evolved, it reiterated: as evil and oblivious as white Americans are, they must be loved. You could not be black, Christian, and seek justice without loving your oppressors into freedom and reconciliation.

Everyone's norms are shaken; everyone's categories shattered. The prayers and politics of the filial replace puny, exclusivist divisions with Jesus' expansive vision. The rhetoric of family is the *grund* of denunciation and protest, the font of annunciation and hope, and the inspiration to take unimagined paths. It denounces the despoilers of earth, prime ministers,

---

95. Ibid., 17–18 (italics his).
96. Ibid., 22.
97. Ibid., 21.
98. Ibid., 19 (italics his).

white America, and anyone who turns a single nation or race into *the people*. It erases boundaries separating castes and classes, and cancels every purity code as God begets and multiplies a newly liberated and liberating family.

REPAIRING THE SACRED HOOP

In 1855, Young Chief, a Cayuse leader, refused to sign the Treaty of Walla Walla, not because of the usual American government cheating, conniving, swindling, and stealing, nor the crumbling clay promises that seemed written in disappearing ink, and not because the *new people* continually and contemptuously sneered at his nonpeople. He refused because one of the key negotiators had been excluded from the diplomatic process. Young Chief asked if "the ground is listening" to the wheeling and dealing, if "the ground" had anything to say, if "the ground would come alive," or if it had become another unnamed, unacknowledged victim of Manifest Destiny's hubris.[99] Young Chief thought he knew what the ground, the grass, and the water—muted or mute—were saying.

> The ground says, It is the Great Spirit that placed me here. The Great Spirit tells me to take care of the Indians, to feed them aright. The Great Spirit appointed the roots to feed the Indians on. The water says the same thing. The Great Spirit directs me, Feed the Indians well. The grass says the same thing, Feed the Indians well. The ground, water and grass say, The Great Spirit has given us our names. We have these names and hold these names. The ground says, The Great Spirit placed me here to produce all that grows on me, trees and fruit. The same way the ground says, It was from me people were made. The Great Spirit, in placing people on earth, desired them to take good care of the ground and to do each other no harm.[100]

Western Christians expect Native Americans to refer to all created things as mother, father, sister, and brother. We expect Black Elk to lament that the Wasichus [white people] "had forgotten that the earth was their mother."[101] Only people who forget their relationship with creation could be so ceaselessly voracious and calculatingly vicious.

In Native American spirituality, the world is held together in circles. As Black Elk says: "That is because the Power of the World always works

---

99. Deloria, *God is Red*, 82.
100. Ibid., 81–82.
101. Black Elk, *Black Elk Speaks*, 221.

in circles, and everything tries to be round. In the old days when we were a strong and happy people, all our power came to us from the sacred hoop of the nation, and so long as the hoop was unbroken, the people flourished. The flowering tree was the living center of the hoop, and the circle of the four quarters nourished it." The sky and the earth are round. "The wind, in its greater power, whirls. Birds make their nests in circles, for theirs is the same religion as ours." The sun and moon rise and set in circles. "Our tepees were round like the nests of birds, and these were always set in a circle, the nation's hoop, a nest of many nests, where the Great Spirit meant for us to hatch our children."[102] Even as he endured the destruction of countless hoops, Black Elk had a vision akin to that of Isaiah (2:2–4) and Micah (4:1–4):

> I was standing on the highest mountain of them all, and round about beneath me was the whole hoop of the world. And while I stood there I saw more than I can tell and I understood more than I saw; for I was seeing in a sacred manner the shapes of all things in the spirit, and the shape of all shapes as they must live together like one being. And I saw that the sacred hoop of my people was one of many hoops that made one circle, wide as daylight and as starlight, and in the center grew one mighty flowering tree to shelter all the children of one another and one father. And I saw that it was holy.[103]

Black Elk's vision could fit neatly into the Apocalypse: everything in creation circles the center (cf Rev 7:9); at the center of creation is a garden; at the heart of the garden is the tree of life (Rev 21:22—22:5).

As Western Christians assume this filial spirituality of Native Americans, we also expect it from Buddhists. Thich Nhat Hanh says bluntly that "whether we can wake up or not depends on whether we can walk mindfully on our Mother Earth."[104] In his book subtitled *Jesus and Buddha as Brothers*, he offers a way to see this: "[I]f you look around, you do not see anyone or anything that is not your father or your mother. A pebble is also your mother, a cloud is also your father. A squirrel is also your father, a deer is also your mother." All living creatures and inanimate creations belong to the family. Amending Eckhart's view of a begetting God, Nhat Hanh says, "there is an umbilical cord linking us with all the other phenomena around us. There is an umbilical cord joining us with the cloud. The cloud is really a mother. If we cut the cord, we have no relationship or connection with the

---

102. Ibid., 198–200.
103. Ibid., 43.
104. Nhat Hanh, *Love in Action*, 131.

cloud, and," because we are made of water, "we will not survive."[105] We are one family, true. But even more, we are part of the same organism, a single life.

Until recently, modern activism has ignored earth, air, fire, and water. Young Chief would protest, but it is an excusable lacuna. It has always required inexhaustible energy and an unyielding commitment to stand up for *human* dignity against crushing economic, political, and psychological exploitation. So even for Romero, Tutu, King, Day, and Muste, Young Chief, Black Elk, and Nhat Hanh are voices for the voiceless. They ask contemporary activists: how can you negotiate for justice when creation is muted or mute? How can you be complicit in ecological segregation, environmental domestic violence, and the war on creation? Lester, in spite of her boundary-erasing awareness that transcends nations, laughingly recognized her anxious shortcomings and spiritual immaturity while visiting an ashram in India.

> A spider of intimidating girth lodged in the crack of the rough-boarded door which separated my bath shed from the rest of the sheds. When a centipede fell out of my wall, I told the superintendent [of the ashram], gently, so as not to appear to grumble. Unmoved, he answered, "Of course, sister, this Ashram is bounded on three sides by the jungle. The creatures naturally come through our place. It is their short cut. But have no fear. They do not hurt us. They know we are non-violent people." I smiled feebly, knowing I was not, and certain that they knew it, too.[106]

Until recent decades, activists have assumed that human unity and equality are the unclimbed summit, the Mount Everest, of activism. Only recently have they readjusted their vision to see that what appeared to be an ethical pinnacle is but the first low hill in an ascending mountain range. It is precisely here that political activism has stopped. And it is here that traditional spirituality, more than modern activism, finds greater kinship with eco-justice.

There have always been traces of the aboriginal people's motherland,[107] the Native American's sacred hoop, and the Buddhist's inter-being in Christian spirituality. Francis of Assisi's "Canticle of Creatures"—part creed, part psalm—joys in the interrelatedness of all created things. While the canticle enjoys an exuberant effervescence, Eloi Leclerc identifies method in the

---

105. Nhat Hanh, *Going Home*, 147.
106. Lester, *Ambassador of Reconciliation*, 149–50.
107. Sugirtharajah, *Asian Faces*, 134.

mystical. The canticle was not composed in one holy outburst of praise. Francis carefully amended its arrangement more than once. The canticle begins with "the lofty, virile, celestial image of the Lord Sun whose dominion and splendor symbolize the Most High, the Father. And the sequence ends with the solid image of the feminine and the maternal, that of the earth, our mother, who supports and feeds every living thing. All the other elements are set between these two great images of fatherhood and motherhood."[108] The canticle's praise passes from creator to sun and moon and then to the four elements in "a descending movement that is reinforced by the addition of the last four stanzas which praise the religious value of negativity, suffering, physical decay, and death." While Francis infuses every line of the canticle with love and delight, he also integrates fragility and mortality into "the mystery of light and being."[109] He composed the final stanzas—a drop downward rather than a leap forward—as he was dying, and their literary style contrasts sharply with all that goes before.[110] Even the theological tone shifts from intoxicated adoration (frankincense) to severe admonitions (myrrh mingled with vinegar). Yet, if Traherne sees people as "glittering jewels," Francis sees everything in creation shining with glory.

> Most High, all-powerful, good Lord
> Yours are the praises, the glory, the honor, and all blessing.
> To You alone, Most High, do they belong,
> And no one is worthy to mention Your name.
> Praised be You, my Lord, with all your creatures,
> Especially Sir Brother Sun,
> Who is the day and through whom You give us light.
> And he is beautiful and radiant with great splendor;
> And bears a likeness of You, Most High One.
> Praised be You, my Lord, through Sister Moon and the stars,
> In heaven You formed them clear and precious and beautiful.
> Praised be You, my Lord, through Brother Wind,
> And through the air, cloudy and serene, and every kind of weather.
> Through which You give sustenance to Your creatures.
> Praised be You, my Lord, through Sister Water,
> Which is very useful and humble and precious and chaste.
> Praised be You, my Lord, through Brother Fire,
> Through whom You light the night
> And he is beautiful and playful and robust and strong.

108. Leclerc, *Canticle of Creatures*, 20.
109. Ibid., 78.
110. Ibid., 22.

> Praised be You, my Lord, through our Sister Mother Earth,
> Who sustains and governs us,
> And who produces varied fruits with colored flowers and herbs.
> Praised be You, my Lord, through those who give pardon for Your love
> And bear infirmity and tribulation.
> Blessed are those who endure in peace
> For by You, Most High, they shall be crowned.
> Praised be You, my Lord, through our Sister Bodily Death,
> From whom no living person can escape.
> Woe to those who die in mortal sin.
> Blessed are those whom death will find in Your most holy will,
> For the second death shall do them no harm.
> Praise and bless my Lord and give God thanks
> And serve God with great humility.[111]

The canticle is not a stand-alone, shelved-away poem or an abstract statement of Francis's faith. Its spirit is interwoven into every aspect of his life. In truth, it does not begin to capture every dimension of his elation in creation. Nowhere does it mention his ministry to or joy in winged, finned, or two- or four-legged creatures. In the sweet story of Francis's evangelical sermon to the birds, he teaches a litany of thanksgiving: "My little bird sisters, you owe much to God your Creator, and you must always and everywhere praise God, because God has given you freedom to fly anywhere." God dresses them in a colorful and beautiful "double and triple covering" of skin and feathers. Even though birds "neither sow nor reap," God teaches them to sing, multiplies them, and gave them safe harbor—salvation—on Noah's ark. God invites them to live in the realm of the air, gives them rivers and springs from which to drink, and mountains, hills, rocks, crags, and trees as places of refuge. "So the Creator loves you very much. . . . Therefore, my little bird sisters, be careful not to be ungrateful, but strive always to praise God."[112] Francis did not stop with birds. "In the same way he exhorted with the sincerest purity cornfields and vineyards, stones and forests and all the beautiful things of the fields, fountains of water and the green things of the gardens, earth and fire, air and wind, to love God and serve God willingly."[113]

When he referred to them as family members, Francis believed he was "expressing the true reality of these creatures."[114] To him, the minimum creatures owe one another is a Hippocratic oath and a Golden Rule. When a

---

111. Francis of Assisi and Clare of Assisi, *Francis and Clare*, 38–39.
112. *Little Flowers*, 76–77.
113. Celano, *Saint Francis*, 73.
114. Leclerc, *Canticle of Creatures*, 11.

doctor treated his failing eyesight, he brought an iron to cauterize Francis's eyes and ordered it put into the fire "until it should be red-hot." Even though they faced no danger, Francis's brothers, as if in Gethsemane, fled. Francis, wrestling with his own fears, made the sign of the cross over the fire and said: "My brother fire that surpasses all other things in beauty, the Most High created you strong, beautiful, and useful. Be kind to me in this hour, be courteous. For I have loved you in the past in the Lord. I beseech the great Lord who made you that he temper your heat now so that I may bear it when you burn me gently." Then "the iron was plunged into the tender flesh with a hiss, and it was gradually drawn from the ear to the eyebrow in its cauterizing." Afterwards Francis told his friends that the fire treated him like a brother: "I did not feel either the heat of the fire or any pain in my flesh."[115] On another occasion, when a nearby flame starts to burn his clothes, Francis tries to return the favor. Although he risked injury, when one of his companions tries to douse the flames, Francis says, "Dearest brother, do not hurt Brother Fire!"[116] Finally, against his wishes, the flames were extinguished, but Francis had tried to practice reciprocity.

To Francis, if only we could see, we would know that we are related to all created things. Yet the *all*—peoples, stones, plants, animals, planets, stars—endlessly exceeds our imagination. On the last leg of Leonardo Boff's pilgrimage to Assisi, Brother Bonaventure, a Franciscan gardener, drove Boff along a rocky road in an old Fiat. Bonaventure stopped the car and got out, not to give thanks for the magnificent panorama before them, but to revel in the sight of white flowers and the taste of mulberries. As they drove slowly towards Assisi—as if caught in an invisible gridlock—Boff asked the gardener why he didn't drive faster. Bonaventure replied, "There is no reason to abuse the good nature of the car. For eighteen years it has carried me to and fro, and it has always been good to me."[117] For Bonaventure the car has become a mule. Even this polluting post-industrial vehicle with its toxic carbon tire print is part of God's family.

We expect this of Franciscans as we do of Native Americans and Buddhists. Yet this deep sense of relatedness is not a single odd, awkward, protruding wing of Christian spirituality. The Celtic tradition is a "creation-filled spirituality."[118] In Russian Orthodoxy's *The Way of a Pilgrim*, the pilgrim observes: "The trees, the grass, the birds, the earth, the air, the light seemed to be telling me that they existed for our sake, that they witnessed

---

115. Celano, *Saint Francis*, 271.
116. Leclerc, *Canticle of Creatures*, 112.
117. Boff, *Saint Francis*, 3–4.
118. de Waal, *Celtic Way*, 141.

to the love of God for us, that everything proved the love of God for us, that all things prayed to God and sang God's praise."[119] The New Testament itself offers a Krishna-like Christology: "in Christ all things in heaven and on earth were created . . . all things have been created through Christ and for Christ . . . and in Christ all things hold together" (Col 1:16–7).

This is less a loose strand in tradition than leaven within all mystical theology. Merton, the rejected Franciscan aspirant who never lost his Franciscan bent,[120] writes in a prose poem:

> There is in all visible things an invisible fecundity, a dimmed light, a meek namelessness, a hidden wholeness. This mysterious Unity and Integrity is Wisdom, the Mother of all, *Natura naturans*. There is in all things an inexhaustible sweetness and purity, a silence that is a fount of action and joy. It rises up in wordless gentleness and flows out to me from the unseen roots of all created being, welcoming me tenderly, saluting me with indescribable humility. This is at once my own being, my own nature, and the Gift of my Creator's Thought and Art within me, speaking as Hagia Sophia, speaking as my sister, Wisdom.[121]

While John of the Cross's name has too often been fused with *The Dark Night of the Soul*, he also wrote *The Spiritual Canticle* and *The Living Flame of Love*. His was never a one-chord, minor-key faith. The pall of anxiety and shadow of death that darken the coda of Francis's canticle are John's overture; Francis's empirical afterthought is John's gateway to God. Yet John elatedly embraces the wonder of creation. As psalmists speak of the hills praising God (Ps 65:12, 98:8, 148:9), John proclaims his relationship to those hills (and more) as he links the language of *the Beloved*—his intimate term for God in the dark night—to God's creation.

> My Beloved is the mountains,
> And lonely wooded valleys,
> Strange islands,
> And resounding rivers,
> The whistling of love-stirring breezes.
>
> The tranquil night
> At the time of the rising dawn,
> Silent music,
> Sounding solitude,

---

119. *Way of a Pilgrim*, 31.
120. Merton, *Sign of Jonas*, 208.
121. Merton, *Collected Poems*, 363.

The supper that refreshes, and deepens love.[122]

If Merton in his Louisville vision and Traherne in his prose poems could claim that all people are "mine,"[123] John says the same of the inanimate. Leaping further in his "Prayer of a Soul Taken with Love," John proclaims, "Mine are the heavens and mine is the earth. Mine are the nations, the just are mine, and mine the sinners. The angels are mine, and the Mother of God, and all things are mine; and God is mine and for me, because Christ is mine and all for me."[124] While Lester and Underhill insist that the Christians' *our* trumps every *mine*, John repeats the first person singular over and over again to the same end—to establish an inalienable, intimate, universal, and all-encircling relationship with all that is.

As Francis uses a maternal image for earth, and as Julian uses it for Christ, Teilhard de Chardin employs the feminine to describe the elements. When we become conscious of the cosmos, he says, we realize that "everything that is active, that moves or breathes, every physical, astral, or animate energy, every fragment of force, every spark of life, is equally sacred." Becoming conscious, our "first impulse" is to "be rocked like a child by the great mother in whose arms we have just woken." For some, he says, this is an "aesthetic" experience, an emotion, for others "a rule of practical life."[125] Merton's epiphany before the Buddhist statues in Sri Lanka begins with an aesthetic experience. Then he is jolted to see "clarity, as if exploding from the rocks themselves." Finally he concludes: "The rock, all matter, all life, is charged with dharmakaya [the Buddha nature]—everything is emptiness and everything is compassion."[126] Colossians could not have stated it more concisely, nor Francis with greater wonder.

Francis's canticle envelops even our mortality. His sense of relatedness touches even the bleakest moments of history. Leclerc ends his study of the canticle with a personal reminiscence of the collapse of Nazi Germany when he was one of thousands imprisoned for three weeks on a freight train.[127] Hundreds died; hundreds more lingered near death; hunger made many delirious. Even as Nazism—like another totalitarian lemming—cascaded toward Tutu's scrap heap of history, its cruelty, the perfect refutation of all Francis preached, remained virile.

---

122. John of the Cross, *Collected Works*, 412.
123. Merton, *Conjectures*, 156; Traherne, *Centuries*, 110.
124. John of the Cross, *Collected Works*, 669.
125. Teilhard de Chardin, *Writings*, 46.
126. Merton, *Other Side*, 323.
127. Leclerc, *Canticle of Creatures*, 227–36.

The train meandered and detoured from one concentration camp to another. Its horrors were endless and, like Otto's sense of the holy, indescribable. When one of his fellow Franciscans lay dying, Leclerc asked, "what rises from our hearts to our lips?" Not the dissonant, distancing shrug of Qoheleth nor the wail of Job, not even an invocation of the dark night, but the canticle of Francis: "It rises spontaneously out of our darkness and nakedness, as though it were the only language fit for such a moment.... In this dark world, the brilliant rays of divine love are still to be seen." Whoever acts as a brother or sister "is always a witness" to an *abba* God.[128] This Franciscan brother's death was the last in their car. Francis amended the canticle as he approached death; Leclerc's comrades bore its light into one of evil's most hideous incarnations.

Reinhold Niebuhr lances mysticism and lampoons the children of light with reminders of humanity's stone-cold, sobering capacity for depravity, proclaiming just how dark it is where we want and need light to shine. In counterpoint, Leclerc and his brothers sing of light in darkness and air on an excrement-filled train. Under the bootheel of blasé mass murder and in the shadow of all-consuming furnaces where fire never burned gently, they assert that all genocide is both fratricide and suicide. As the canticle descends from harmonious heights to atonal dank depths, even in one of Dante's circles of hell, one of Black Elk's anticircles, they praise their beloved Creator in this beautiful creation.

BROTHER BARBARIAN AND SISTER LAMB

As nationalism began its Darwinian journey in the Middle Ages, when one's *people* might be a family or a clan, European villages were often embroiled in small-minded, gang-like warfare with their neighboring villages. At this time some saw the Crusades as a way to export unwanted intravillage aggression (as military recruiters today scour inner cities for prospective soldiers among potential gang members). And at this time, a ferocious wolf—like an embodiment of a Jungian shadow—terrorized the town of Gubbio. In this oft-told story, Francis approaches the wolf as a desert monk might address a fellow sinner, or as Tutu writes to Vorster, as a dissolute and volatile family member: "Brother Wolf," he says, "I want to make peace between you and them, so that they will not be harmed by you any more, and," he promises, "after they have forgiven you all your past crimes," neither they nor their dogs will pursue you. As part of this détente, Francis pledges that the townsfolk will treat the wolf as if Christ had said: when I was a hungry wolf,

---

128. Ibid., 234.

you fed me. Francis knows "that whatever evil you have been doing was done because of the urge of hunger." In return for this nonaggression pact, Francis asks the wolf "to promise me that you will never hurt any animal or person. Will you promise me that?"

The wolf nods and raises its front paw.

Then Francis says, "Brother Wolf, I order you, in the name of the Lord Jesus Christ, to come with me now, without fear, into the town to make this peace pact in the name of the Lord." Then, with the wolf at his side, Francis addresses the townsfolk, "Listen dear people, Brother Wolf, who is standing here before you, has promised me and has given me a pledge that he will make peace with you and will never hurt you if you promise also to feed him every day." And "from that day, the wolf and the people kept the pact." For two years, the wolf went door to door like a child playing trick-or-treat on Halloween and "the people fed it courteously." The wolf "hurt no one and no one hurt it." When the wolf died, "the people were sorry, because whenever it went through the town, its peaceful kindness and patience reminded them of the virtues and holiness of Francis."[129]

Another story of Francis is as obscure—and as important—as this one is famous. In what could be a proof text for vegans, a peasant takes lambs to market to sell and butcher them. When Francis hears the lambs bleating, like the Good Samaritan seeing a pilgrim in a ditch, he is moved by pity: "coming close he touched them and showed his compassion for them like a mother over her weeping child." As he once censured the wolf, now he reprimands the peasant: "Why are you torturing my brother lambs tied up and hanging like this?" The answer? Like the shepherds in the story of Macarius and the hyena, he is poor; he needs money. Like the wolf, *he* needs to eat. Francis weighs two sets of needs—those of the poor and those of their victims—then he rebukes the man as Macarius scolded the hyena: "God forbid," he says, "this must not happen." Then, as with the wolf, he pragmatically cuts a deal to ransom the lambs: "Take the mantle I am wearing as their price and give the lambs to me." Francis commands the peasant as the Samaritan instructed the innkeeper (Luke 10:35): do not harm or sell the lambs; "keep them, feed them, and take care of them conscientiously."[130]

In both stories, Francis respects everyone's needs—the townsfolk's security, the wolf's hunger, the peasant's livelihood, and the lambs' lives. He freely interrupts the natural order of creation and the normal flow of commerce. He arranges the release of the lambs as if they were hostages. He sees them as his children and the wolf as his brother. Both stories are told;

---

129. *Little Flowers*, 89–91.
130. Celano, *Saint Francis*, 71.

one is remembered. Tradition's enshrinement of the Wolf of Gubbio and its parallel amnesia about the ransoming of the lambs, a story buried like a lamp beneath a basket, is a commentary on human nature: even when we want to embrace all creatures as brothers and sisters, we more happily lie down with the tamed wolf than the tasty lamb; we are more anxious to be reconciled with our predators than our prey.

A third story of Francis is as famous as the first. His well-documented fear of lepers was a reflex to the deformed, the unclean, and the unknown, an image of lepers revived in fears of contamination and contagion during the early stages of the modern AIDS epidemic. As the *First Life* of Celano reports, "So greatly loathsome was the sight of lepers" that Francis "would look at their houses only from a distance of two miles and he would hold his nostrils with his hands." While still in his secular life everything changed when "he met a leper one day and, made stronger than himself, he kissed him," thus transforming his relationships with all lepers.[131] The *Second Life* of Celano inks its own midrash: Francis gets off his horse to kiss the leper but when the leper reaches out to beg, he "received money along with a kiss." Mysteriously, after remounting his horse, Francis looks around but sees no one. A few days later he went to the "dwelling places of the lepers, and after he had given each leper some money, he kissed his hand and his mouth."[132]

When it comes to lepers, Francis is only one prominent part of a long tradition deeply melded into Scripture. Elisha heals Naaman (2 Kgs 5:1–19); Jesus heals lepers almost by the bundle. Abba Agathon says, "If I could meet a leper, give him my body and take his, I should be very happy."[133] Centuries later, on Molokai, Father Damien completed the half of this transaction he could control, dying among other lepers. As Francis invites lepers into his heart, Elizabeth of Hungary gave lepers her bed. These saying and stories end with noble goosebumps, but—as Father Damien's death illustrates—loving lepers has its risks. Given the usual harsh turns of her ministry, it is unsurprising that Day had two distasteful encounters with social lepers. One woman's face had been eaten away by cancer, so Day kissed the place where her nose and eye had been; and a toothless sex worker returned Day's kiss in a "loathsome" way.[134] Day's heart was not strangely warmed. Her stomach churned.

The ground of Francis's being is to treat perpetrators and victims, predators and prey as harijans. He provides food for the wolf and money for

---

131. Ibid., 18–19.
132. Ibid., 143–44.
133. Ward, *Sayings of the Desert*, 24.
134. Day, *Loaves and Fishes*, 79–80.

the poor; he secures release for the lambs and gives love (and aid) to lepers. Yet Francis is not the only one to massage conflict and calm storms. The restructuring and restoration of relationships are also at the core of Buddhist lore. As Hasidic rabbis measure righteousness by someone's ability to overcome the fear of disease and suck pus from a child with the plague,[135] so the Buddha sucks pus from a child's finger to heal his infection.[136] He calms a charging elephant known for its erratic and aggressive behavior: at the sound of the Buddha's voice, the elephant comes to an abrupt halt, kneels on all fours and lowers its head to the ground while he strokes its head.[137] In a story similar to the Wolf of Gubbio, the Buddha meets Angulimala, a violent antisocial human predator. Unlike the quick acquiescence of the elephant and the wolf, when Angulimala meets the Buddha on the road, they debate. As the hyena converts more easily than the prime minister, the same duplicity of soul and multiplicity of self-justification impedes Angulimala's reconciliation. His bitter rage is fueled by a boiling cauldron of angry despair at the dark cruelty of human nature. In reply, the Buddha gently witnesses to the oft-hidden human potential for goodness. Personalizing the philosophical dispute, Angulimala argues that it is too late for him to change, but he succumbs to the Buddha's compassion, and the murderer (like the wolf, the hyena, and the elephant) converts.[138]

Whoever or whatever the predator—contagious infection, wayward animal, vicious thief, unctuous prime minister—the awakened person restores harmony. Among the desert's stories of what Merton jokingly calls "tame lions and all that jazz,"[139] Abba Bes orders a hippo and a crocodile to stop ravaging the countryside.[140] It is as if we could say: even winds and seas and wolves and elephants and hippos and crocodiles obey them. Macarius the Spiritbearer meets an antelope with three deformed young. Like the hyena, she weeps before the saint. With Isaac of Nineveh's merciful heart, Macarius prays, "You who care for all of creation, our Lord Jesus Christ, who have numerous treasuries of mercy, take pity on the creature you made."[141] Speaking with tears, he makes the sign of the cross over them and they are healed. Merton had his own unforgettable, inexplicable desert-like interaction. One morning as he was praying "under the pine trees in

---

135. Buber, *Tales: Later Masters*, 87.
136. Nhat Hanh, *Old Path White Clouds*, 525.
137. Ibid., 506.
138. Ibid., 352–55.
139. Merton, *Hidden Ground*, 503.
140. Vivian, *Becoming Fire*, 73–74.
141. Vivian, *St. Macarius*, 14.

front of the hermitage, I saw a wounded deer limping along in the field, one leg incapacitated. I was terribly sad at this and began weeping bitterly. And something quite extraordinary happened. I will never forget standing there weeping and looking at the deer standing still looking at me questioningly for a long time, a minute or so. The deer bounded off without any sign of trouble."[142]

This creaturely harmony is captured in the traditional manger scene that, for Stringfellow, is much more than a quaint and sentimental depiction of the baby Jesus. Rather "the manger scene itself is a political portrait of the whole of creation restored in the dominion of Jesus Christ in which every creature, every tongue and tribe, every ruler and authority, every nation and principality is reconciled in homage to the Word of God incarnate."[143] It is linked as closely to the eschaton as the incarnation; it is as much a multidimensional prophetic vision of the realm as a grainy black-and-white photo of the revolution.

While such visions and stories depict peaceful coexistence, smooth reconciliation, and fully mature, newborn new life, like two of Isaiah's prophecies they also offer distinctly different paths to the peaceable realm. In his famous vision liturgically enshrined in Advent, children play over the holes of asps (Isa 11:8) just as lamb, calf, and cow graze cheerfully beside leopard, lion, and bear. Yet in another vision, people tread on the heads of snakes (Isa 65:25, Ps 91:13; cf. Mark 16:18). One vision is rooted in the reconciliation of equals, the other in domination and subjugation, as if the Isaiah tradition could not decide if Eden is most efficiently re-entered, and the manger scene most handily constructed, with the snake restored as a harijan or subdued as a *dalit*. This same tension exists in the desert. When an asp bites Macarius of Alexandria, he immediately inverts the Golden Rule, returning violence for violence, doing "to you [the snake] according to your own evil nature" as he seizes the "two lips of the asp in his two hands, pulled them apart, and tore it in half down to its tail."[144] In contrast, Macarius the Spiritbearer meets a wounded, more quiescent serpent that "bent its neck and venerated" the saint. Noticing something lodged in the serpent's eye, Macarius "thought about the compassion of my Lord Jesus Christ and the invincible power of the cross." Following Jesus' example of using saliva to heal (John 9:6), Macarius prays, "My Lord Jesus Christ, who opened the eyes of the man born blind, have pity on this beast's infirmity and heal it." The fragment falls from the serpent's eye and it bends its neck three times, kisses the saint's

---

142. Merton, *Dancing in the Water*, 315–16.
143. Stringfellow, *Conscience and Obedience*, 79.
144. Vivian, *Four Desert Fathers*, 143.

feet, and the saint glorifies "our Lord Jesus Christ for his numerous acts of compassion, for he even cares about wild beasts."[145]

This hopscotch pattern—part double-edged sword, part high priest's empathetic intercession (Heb 4:12–16)—is also present in Francis. As gently as he announces filial relationships with wolf, leper, and lamb, he just as indignantly denounces materialism and the systems that enshrine it. Francis abhors money as much as Macarius loathes the biting asp: he calls money and those who love it "flies."[146] As Underhill notes, Francis "hated property" because it seduces its victims with greed; "it split an attention which should be devoted to the one object of worship and love, and turned the relation of brotherhood and sisterhood within which all living things should adore their common Abba into a relation of ownership."[147] To Francis, private property creates public chaos. It puts neighbor second to acquisition and God second to gain. It reverses his achievements with wolf and lamb and leper by prioritizing individual aggrandizement over mutual respect.

This tension is personified in the story of a "simple man" named John. While plowing his family's field, John asks Francis to make him a "brother." With echoes of the story of the rich young man (Mark 10:17–22), a passage that inspired Francis's conversion,[148] the saint happily informs the peasant that he should "give to the poor whatever you may have, and I will receive you after you have given everything away." Calculating his years of labor for his father, John decides it is fair to give away one of the family oxen. But when John's family hears this, "they came running with tears, unhappy, however, about losing the ox rather than about losing" their brother! When Francis tells them they can keep the ox as long as their brother John can join him, they eagerly agree.[149]

In this distorted world, saints sometimes reconcile or subdue wolves, hyenas, snakes, hippos, elephants, and murderers. But what happens when saints fail to persuade prime ministers? What happens when it is not in their control or part of their charism to calm a storm but rather to endure it? Desert *Abbas* sometimes faced a conundrum: how to respond to barbarians deaf to religion and reason. People so illogical and unmerciful must be of a different kind and kin. Whether an old or a new people, they are unlike *our* people. When Daniel of Scetis tries to confess that he murdered a barbarian, one religious figure after another assures him he has not sinned since he

---

145. Vivian, *St. Macarius*, 142–43.
146. Celano, *Saint Francis*, 201, 202, 204.
147. Underhill, *Mystics of the Church*, 92.
148. Celano, *Saint Francis*, 149.
149. Ibid., 289.

has only killed a "wild beast"; they wish he had murdered more![150] Facing barbarians—like Darfur's modern murderous Janjaweed—some monasteries doubled as fortresses that could raise a drawbridge to keep *abbas* safe from marauding bands. Even so, the *abbas* felt a sacred obligation to feed the hungry; each monastery could lower bread from behind the gate to barbarians below—as Gubbio less cautiously fed the wolf.[151]

When no gates barred the barbarians, monks had to decide whether to flee as refugees or die as martyrs. Given the choice, John the Dwarf anticipated Trocmé's concern about innocent blood, but shifted the focus from the victim's safety to the perpetrator's salvation. John flees rather than let them more indelibly stain their already blood-soaked hands. Empirically, the barbarians are worse than beasts because they kill without necessity, but John insists, "This barbarian, even if he is separated from me by faith, nevertheless is an image and creature of God in the same way that I am. If I resist this barbarian he will kill me and will go to punishment because of me."[152]

A similar dilemma faced a group of French Trappists in their Algerian mountain monastery in the 1990s. Living in the broad, murky shadow of imperialism, Christian Chergé and his brothers reversed the theology and practice of their recent forebears who suffered unknowingly from the common-as-a-common-cold conflation of religion and culture. Chergé's nineteenth-century predecessors believed in the messianic colonial assumption that all people secretly want to be French (like British imperialist's theory that, in their heart of hearts, everyone wants to be a merchant), and that all *ought* to want to be Christian. But as Merton rebelled against the suggestion that he should convert D. T. Suzuki as a "terrible infidelity to Truth, to myself and to Christ,"[153] Chergé and his brothers refused to proselytize; rather they sought "the notes that are in harmony" between Christianity and Islam.[154] To find those notes, they entered into a symbiotic relationship with their Muslim neighbors.

Each monk found a different set of notes from which to build relationships. One of the monks, a doctor, had little intellectual interest in Islam.[155] The common transcending notes that preoccupied him were the health needs of villagers. When people came to him with gunshot wounds, he saw neither soldiers of an oppressive regime nor guerrillas of an unstable cause.

---

150. Vivian, *Witness to Holiness*, 45.
151. Vivian, *Words to Live By*, 42.
152. Vivian, *Becoming Fire*, 82–83.
153. Merton, *Search for Solitude*, 273.
154. Kiser, *Monks of Tibhirine*, 40.
155. Ibid., 55.

Like Stringfellow, not even the content of a person's character was important if he or she were a victim. To him, "A sick person is neither a terrorist nor a soldier; he is a sick person."[156] As Lester transcended national boundaries, the monks bridged religious and ideological divisions.

The decade's violence began when Algeria's government negated the results of a democratic election that would have brought an Islamist party to power. Algeria then descended into chaos in a decade fit to share Merton's anguished question after King's assassination: is love in the midst of violence a pitiful delusion? Among dozens of splintered factions, one group of xenophobic, revolutionary reactionaries/zealous patriots announced that foreigners had thirty days to leave Algeria or take responsibility for their own death.[157] Armed guerrillas approached one imam after another as if each were another pope to demand that each issue a fatwa—in effect, a ban—against infidels, Europeans, Christians, monks, nuns, priests, even Muslims of other ideological stripes, to give divine sanction to their murders. One respected Muslim leader, when kidnapped, said, "I will give you all my blood before I will issue a fetwa which will justify the spilling of one drop of innocent Algerian blood." His courage proved prophetic; his body was found two months later with his throat slit.[158] Many Muslim leaders faced the same perilous death-or-death choice.

As danger lurked nearby, the monks—like John the Dwarf—debated whether or not to stay in Algeria. One Christmas Eve a gang of rebels, having recently murdered a group of Croats familiar to the monks, invaded their monastery. While held at gunpoint, Chergé confronted them: "Both your religion and mine forbid weapons in places of worship." If they were going to talk, the invaders had to leave their guns outside or go outside themselves. In the end, Chergé agreed to help the guerrillas, but only on the monks' terms.[159] Soon afterward, when the army killed these guerrillas and dragged their corpses through the streets, Chergé objected that the dead had been treated as "filthy beasts":[160] even murderers are children of God created in God's image.

As with the Jesuits at the University of Central America, the surrounding violence finally engulfed the Trappists: seven of the eight brothers were kidnapped, held hostage, and finally beheaded. Protests in France were not

---

156. Ibid., 164.
157. Ibid., 138.
158. Ibid., 140–42.
159. Ibid., 146–47.
160. Ibid., 155.

surprising, but even so-called "terrorists" denounced the monks' murders.[161] Algeria's Minister of the Interior called them "our brothers too."[162] Chergé, preparing himself for his fate, and concerned that his death might "reinforce people's stereotypes and false images of Islam and Algeria,"[163] wrote a testament in anticipation of their murders. Like Francis, he had a deep sense of interrelationship. Like Baldwin, he knew *you* must love *them*. Going beyond John the Dwarf, he did not even want his innocent blood to besmirch his murderers' reputations.

> If the day comes, and it could be today, that I am a victim of the terrorism that seems to be engulfing all foreigners living in Algeria, I would like my community, my Church, and my family to remember that I have dedicated my life to God and Algeria . . .
>
> My life is not worth more than any other—not less, not more. Nor am I an innocent child. I have lived long enough to know that I, too, am an accomplice of the evil that seems to prevail in the world around, even that which might lash out blindly at me. If the moment comes, I would hope to have the presence of mind, and the time, to ask for God's pardon and for that of my fellowman, and, at the same time, to pardon in all sincerity he who would attack me. . . .
>
> I know the contempt that some people have for Algerians as a whole. I also know that caricatures of Islam that a certain (Islamist) ideology promotes. It is too easy for such people to dismiss, in good conscience, this religion as something hateful by associating it with violent extremists. . . .
>
> Obviously, my death will justify the opinion of all those who dismissed me as naïve or idealistic. . . . But such people should know my death will satisfy my most burning curiosity. At last, I will be able—if God pleases—to see the children of Islam as God sees them, illuminated in the glory of Christ, sharing in the gift of God's Passion and of the Spirit, whose secret joy will always be to bring forth our common humanity amidst our differences.
>
> I give thanks to God for this life, completely mine yet completely theirs, too, to God, who wanted it for joy against, and in spite of, all odds. In this Thank You—which says everything about my life—I include you, my friends past and present, and those friends who will be here at the side of my mother and father, of my sisters and brothers—thank you a thousandfold.

161. Ibid., 237.
162. Ibid., 242.
163. Ibid., 245.

And to you, my friend of the last moment, who will not know what you are doing. Yes, for you, too, I wish this thank-you, this "A-Dieu," whose image is in you also, that we may meet in heaven, like happy thieves, if it pleases God, our common Father. Amen! Insha Allah![164]

Like Merton, Chergé knows he is a "guilty bystander." Like Macarius, he carries his sins like sand before him. As John of the Cross sees the hills, as Merton sees the people of Louisville, Chergé sees Algerians as "mine." Like Stephen and Jesus, he knows that the violent do not know, never know, what they are doing.

The Gospel of John says that there is no greater love than to lay down your life for your friends (John 15:13). Paul disputes this, saying that Jesus died for us while we were "weak," "sinners," even "enemies" (Rom 5:6–11). Chergé redefines his enemy, his murderer, as his "friend of the last moment." His Algerian Muslim tormentors—like Serbian Christians in their mirroring ethnic cleansing in Bosnia and Kosovo in the same decade—could not understand that their relationship with God irrevocably redefines all relationships and transcends all religious divisions.

In a political firestorm in which movements splintered into sharp shrapnel-like fragments, the Trappists took no ideologically identifiable side, and thus became enemies to all sides. They sided with victims (Merton). They sided with the poor (Day). They saw all as harijans (Gandhi). Like Francis, they allied themselves with lepers and lambs, and like Father Damien, they paid the price for exposing themselves to the contagion of violence. If Leclerc could sing Francis's canticle over his dead brother to affirm that darkness never obliterates light, Chergé more insistently asserts that the light shines even in the most murderous heart as he applies to his own murder all three dimensions of the cross: human evil, divine redemption, and a bridge between peoples (enemies, friends) as if they were one family.

If John the Dwarf's conviction that all barbarians are harijans gives context to the deaths of the Trappists, a story of Abba Moses serves as an unscientific postscript. Unlike John, Abba Moses and his comrades choose to risk death. As with Chergé, when the barbarians were at the door, one monk had time to hide. After the early desert monk saw the barbarians murder Abba Moses and his six companions, "he saw seven crowns descending [from heaven] and crowning the others."[165] The surviving Trappist monk of Algeria reports no such vision. So we are left to imagine or wonder or hope

---

164. Ibid., 244–46.
165. Vivian, *Becoming Fire*, 348–49.

that seven crowns of glory adorn their heads, for they risked everything for *the people* (Algerians) so often treated by the *new people* (French) as *nonpeople*, and for barbarians who considered them infidels, all of them sisters and brothers who never know that the people we kill are part of the one and only family of God.

MEDITATION: BEFORE THE BIRTHDAY

I look at Zac. He's going to be three in less than a month. It's been a pleasurable and peaceful evening. We're lying on his bed, heads on pillows at opposite ends, head to toe. He's said his prayers, which he doesn't always do: "thank (you) God" for toys, TV shows, pizza, and loved ones—in that order.

The three words that embedded themselves in my mind the day after his birth—delight, adore, and good—still ring true. It becomes more complex as he gets older, and it will get far more complicated and contradictory in the years to come. But I still delight in him. I adore him.

Through him, I have learned the meaning of "goodness"; I have tasted the reality of the goodness of creation. It isn't that he acquiesces easily or always behaves as I would like—I had that reminder earlier in the evening. But he is "good," existentially, ontologically, in his very being and existence, like all persons, places, and things are good because God created them. I didn't know how good everyone and everything was until Zac was born.

Shortly after his birth, a friend of mine wanted to know if being a father would affect my politics. I think he was implying that I might become more conservative. What I've found is that I hate violence more; I become more upset when I see children suffer, even at a distance; I grieve physically for parents who can do even less than I can to keep their children safe and healthy and warm.

When I look at Zac's blond hair, his blue eyes, his pale skin, I know that his hair, eyes, and skin give him privileges in this society that the babies with whom he was baptized—with their chocolate skin, coal eyes, and black hair—will not share. These are privileges he did not ask for, privileges that I do not want to exist, privileges that no one should have because they always bring a terrible cost to those who do not have them, and even to those who do. It sickens me that he is growing up in such an insidious and vicious world.

When Zac was eight months old, we met my brother Neil for dinner on Third Street in Santa Monica. Afterwards, we meandered and sat down outdoors for dessert, enjoying the balmy evening air. Sitting nearby smoking a cigarette, a homeless man started telling us about his children, and the happiest days of his life now years past. Wells of joy and loss filled his eyes and constricted his throat. Another homeless man, sitting against a wall, a cardboard sign propped on his knees asking for money, told us not to give our money to him, but to keep it for the "worthwhile cause" I was carrying on my shoulders. Other random conversations followed because of the goodness they saw in this baby, and the abyss between rich and poor briefly narrowed in sympathy if not in fact.

For me, Zac is a bridge between others and myself, a window into the feelings of parents around the world, a lesson in how we are all related to one another, and a joy that spreads into a smile on my face—that spreads my delight, my adoration, my awareness of goodness—when I see other children, other people, at church, on the street, anywhere and everywhere.

Thank you, God, for Zac.

8

Holy Communists

We need nothing but open eyes, to be ravished like the Cherubims.
—Thomas Traherne[1]

I've seen the promised land.
—Martin Luther King, Jr.[2]

All knees shall bow to thee; all wits shall rise,
And praise God who did make and mend our eyes.
—George Herbert[3]

What we are is what we see, and what we see is what we are . . .
—John Ruusbroec[4]

---

1. Traherne, *Centuries*, 18.
2. King, *Testament of Hope*, 286.
3. Herbert, "Love II," *Country Parson*, 169.
4. Ruusbroec, *Spiritual Espousals*, 171.

The eye with which I see God is the same eye with which God sees me: my eye and God's eye are one eye, one seeing, and one knowing and one love.
—Meister Eckhart[5]

God then is the Seer and the Seeing and the Seen.
—Thomas Merton[6]

... for you are the seer, the seeable, and the seeing ...
—Nicholas of Cusa[7]

Awake, O north wind, and come, O south wind!
Blow upon my garden that its fragrance may be wafted abroad.
Let my beloved come to his garden, and eat its choicest fruits.
I come to my garden, my sister, my bride;
I gather my myrrh with my spice,
I eat my honeycomb with my honey,
I drink my wine with my milk.
Eat, friends, drink, and be drunk with love.
—Song of Songs 4:16—5:1

Love and loving, Lover and Beloved are so united in the Beloved that they are unity in Essence.
—Ramon Lull[8]

The place to which we are going is one in which the knower, the knowing, and that which is known are all one.
—Thomas Keating[9]

---

5. Eckhart, *Sermons & Treatises II*, 87.
6. Merton, *Monastic Journey*, 221.
7. Nicholas of Cusa, *Selected Spiritual Writings*, 257.
8. Lull, *Romancing God*, 36.
9. Keating, *Open Mind*, 74

MEDITATION: THE COMMON FLASK

I smiled. Chuck was on the phone. When we worked together, he started our church thrift store and then turned it into a food and clothing ministry. With his bald head and gray mustache, his lips pursed around a cigarette, his discreetly leering eye and under-his-breath lurid remarks, and a heart equal parts sly one-liner and joy-in-giving almsgiver, Chuck made a paradoxical Santa Claus. It had been four years.

My smile wilted when he told me that Dan, Chuck's frequent-if-irregular assistant, was dead. Dan's recklessness, his drinking, his motorcycle, and his flirtatious self-destructiveness had been long skid marks toward a drink-and-drive "*que será será,* whoever will die will die" accident. Chuck wasn't asking for a prayer. He wasn't sharing information. This was business. There needed to be a memorial. Would I come?

There would be no vestments, no music, no bread, no wine, no chalice, no church, not even a building—none of the usual niceties. To get to the service I would drive fifty miles to the edge of my normalcy zone. I had no idea what they wanted or needed. I wore my collar. I took my prayer book. I would meet Chuck at 11 o'clock at a parking lot in Ventura and he would drive me to the homeless hamlet where Dan had lived.

Ten of us—Dan's friends, neighbors, and a priest—met in a clearing. They were passive. I was the professional. I was supposed to magically assess the situation—their faith, their grief, their relationships with Dan, with each other, and with God—and improvise. An Episcopal priest's specialty, improvisation! As if each liturgy were a dazzling never-to-be-repeated jazz riff.

We stood in an awkward semicircle like inexperienced summer campers away from home for the first time. I put my prayer book down and said two prayers, then invited those who so wished to share a memory of Dan. Some did. Some didn't. I said a closing prayer that closed nothing. One person from an unclassified liturgical tradition had brought a flask of whiskey. Returning to the idea that we could toast Dan, we passed the flask, each taking a swig after saying something or nothing. Even though I equate whiskey with swill, I did my part. The flask was our chalice, the whiskey our sacrament. In a way more tangible than usual because it was so unusual, it made us one the way the common chalice is supposed to.

Afterwards we walked to their exurban village for a reception—part wake, part coffee hour, part afternoon tea. Most of the half-dozen dwellings were three-quarters-built huts, shacks, with battery power for light, walls of uneven height, doorways without doors, 360-degree sky roofs, and natural air conditioning. We sat in perfectly unmatched chairs, dumpster decor, yesterday's rummage, yesteryear's Ikea. A concerned voice asked if anybody had seen a missing-in-inaction neighbor. No. His shopping cart—like a station wagon in an empty driveway—was gone. He must have gone out.

The reception could have been any reception and every repast I have ever attended. Our hosts fawned over me, thanking me again and again for driving so far, for taking time out of my busy day and my important life to pray for Dan, to break bread, sip punch, and eat finger food. The attention was embarrassing. Why shouldn't I be there? Who was I to think that Dan's death was less important than my life?

Their welcome exceeded the two most extravagant experiences of hospitality I had ever known—a four-day friends-from-out-of-town Jewish wedding in Toronto and a ten-day family-to-family wedding in Damascus. The cuisine in this unmapped, uncounted hamlet didn't compare to Toronto or Damascus. But the heartfelt generosity and humble hospitality were unparalleled.

There was no need for hymns, for ceremony, for formalities, not even for a church. We remembered Dan. We prayed. There was sacred hospitality. There was the common flask, the communal germs, the terrible taste, the usual physical uncleanness of the chalice accentuated by the wrenching destructiveness of the flask in Dan's life, a meaning oddly parallel to the cup in Jesus' life. For us that day there was no Jew or Greek, no male or female, no slave or free, no homeless or housed, just one flask, and one humanity. On that one day, for those select moments, we were one.

HOLY EROTICA

For much of its history, Christianity has been hijacked and held hostage to an asexual, anti-sexual, puritanical, prudish-yet-prurient, repressed, distorted, and demeaning hermeneutic of sexuality. The inquisitors of asexuality, whatever their internal conflicts and ranting demons, are perennially armed and ready to edit or expunge any positive connotations of what God empirically and obviously created us to be and to do. Typical of such repression, Richard Rolle speaks of a divine intervention into his budding sexuality: God "curbed my youthful lust and transformed it into a longing for spiritual embrace."[10] But while anti-sexuality may demand perfect chastity, Rolle, in seeking God, never uses images of a deer panting for flowing streams (Ps 42:1) or a soul fainting for God like a light-headed pilgrim in the desert (Ps 63:1). Rather, in place of human sexual desire, Rolle substitutes an image-metaphor-experience of people panting, aching, yearning, longing, and *lusting* for God.

10. Rolle, *Fire of Love*, 91.

The language of holy lust permeates holistic spirituality. In a common observation about our everyday half-awake experience of the sacraments, Dorothy Day phrases an insight in an uncommon way. Each sacrament, she says, is like a couple's kiss, something done "casually," "absent mindedly," and like any couple's every kiss, it often remains just a kiss, easily enacted and quickly forgotten. Yet, she says, "that kiss on occasion turns to rapture, a burning fire of tenderness and love."[11] Writing of the sacraments like an old movie's fade-out during a kiss, Day doesn't say what passion looks like. Some things we imagine without seeing. Some things we know.

Merton never framed his Havana epiphany with romanticism or eroticism but in that Eucharist he felt a "great joy"[12] as the Christian mystery was made real for him.[13] Yet Day is hardly the first to use such imagery. At age eleven, Thérèse of Lisieux, Day's favorite saint, calls her first communion a "first kiss . . . a lover's kiss." In turn, she tells Christ: "I loved You and was giving myself to You for all eternity."[14] The Eucharist, it turns out, is often a jumping-off point—a lover's leap—into passion. The more mature Hadewijch had a more erotic eucharistic epiphany: "After that [Christ] came himself to me, took me entirely in his arms, and pressed me to him; and all my members felt this in full felicity, in accordance with the desire of my heart and my humanity. So I was outwardly satisfied and fully transported."[15]

The Eucharist is but one starting point for mystical passion. Like the door to heaven,[16] there is no lone gate to ecstasy; the way to union is everywhere. Yet the ease of access belies the constricting limitations of language. Nowhere do the blind lead the deaf more than when describing divine union. Some things cannot be spoken; others cannot be known. Teresa of Ávila says that anyone who truly experiences divine union confesses the fraudulence of crystalline descriptions.[17] Yet, while this apophatic assertion blurs all ink, mystics—like smitten adolescents—invariably pen and pin words to quicksilver. In fact, the very fruitlessness of words breeds descriptions like rabbits. So Symeon the New Theologian speaks of union's incontestable incomprehensibility:

> God was suddenly completely there,
> united with me in an ineffable manner,

---

11. Day, *Long Loneliness*, 199–200.
12. Merton, *Turning Toward the World*, 111.
13. Merton, *Courage for Truth*, 236.
14. Day, *Thérèse*, 84.
15. Hadewijch, *Complete Works*, 281.
16. Merton, *Conjectures*, 158.
17. Teresa, *Life of Teresa*, 174.

joined to me in an unspeakable way
and immersed in me without mixing
as the fire melds one with the iron,
and the light with the crystal.
And God made me as though I were all fire,
and God showed me myself as light
and I became that which before I saw
I had contemplated only from afar.[18]

Symeon uses images of iron and fire, crystal and light, while others speak of being knitted and knotted together,[19] wax candles melting together,[20] God and soul breathing into each other,[21] a drop of water in a vat of wine taking on wine's color and flavor.[22] Inverting a stereotype of hell, Ruusbroec uses the counterintuitive image of an eternally enjoyable fire[23]—and, since one image never says enough, he also speaks in the philosophical language of double entendre: being enveloped "in fathomless love" and flowing "forth into the wild darkness of the Godhead."[24] *The Cloud of Unknowing*, like al-Hallaj, says that in union we are made a God.[25] All of these linguistic experiments with truth are warm-ups, trial runs, and forerunners to the most popular image of union, the one that begins with a kiss.

Bernard of Clairvaux encapsulates our relationship with God with three kisses. We start as a penitent beggar kissing Christ the Master's feet in an axis of evil transformed in sin-confession-forgiveness. Grateful but dissatisfied with mercy alone, we become "restless again," "eager for greater familiarity." "With renewed insistence" we seek "the second grace, the kiss of the hand," the kiss of the servant-disciple wanting to please God. While service is good, the soul, like a breathless bride, "cannot rest" with this chaste, polite, platonic kiss. Even the satisfaction of being recognized as a good and faithful servant (Matt 25:21, 23) stokes urgent hunger more than placid rest. We are not satisfied until we taste "the kiss of [Christ's] mouth." This is not ingratitude. As the soul says, "It is simply that I am in love. The favors I have received are far above what I deserve, but they are less than what I long for." We are driven on by "desire," "not reason" and the soul yields "to

---

18. Symeon, *Hymns*, 168.
19. Julian, *Showings*, 284.
20. Teresa, *Interior Castle*, 214.
21. Ruusbroec, *Spiritual Espousals*, 240; John of the Cross, *Collected Works*, 558.
22. Eckhart, *Sermons & Treatises III*, 42; Leech, *Experiencing God*, 337–38.
23. Ruusbroec, *Spiritual Espousals*, 129.
24. Ibid., 132.
25. *Cloud of Unknowing*, 221.

this impulse of love."²⁶ Mercy and ministry lead us to Christ, but only desire lures us to the fullest expression of love.

But what kind of love? Martin Luther King, Jr.—following his era's biblical scholarship—argues in a didactic sermon that the un-self-conscious, non-self-seeking love of *agape* is superior to familial *philia* or yearning *eros*.²⁷ To King, *eros* merely distracts from the revolution. For him, *philia* is the ethic of social change, and *agape* its soul force. To him, *philia*, *eros*, and *agape* all abide, but the greatest of these is *agape*. Mystics take a dramatically different view. Origen says he could not blame anyone for calling God "Passionate Love" (*eros*) as much as "Charity" (*caritas*).²⁸ In contrast to King, the mystical tradition suggests that to everything there is a season and a *love* for every purpose under heaven—a time for *philia*, a time for *agape*, and a time for *eros*—and if mystics prize one most of all, it is the love for which we ache: God's intense *eros*.

Like a genre of literature that moves gingerly from the discreet to the explicit, the *eros* hinted at in the medieval language of the troubadour and the liturgical lexicon of God's tender love blossoms into the naked vocabulary of sexuality. As early as Origen, the Song of Songs began its formative role in Christian spirituality.²⁹ The spiritualization of the Song of Songs can be interpreted as a forced march detour around the discomforting embarrassment the pious feel at hearing suggestive descriptions of sexuality and their devout need to tidy up morally loose ends. Yet the Song of Songs, like a subtly seductive Holy Wisdom, can call us to revel in spiritual *and* physical *eros*. It may have been a very different need that made that most passionate of biblical books a primary source of metaphors for divine intimacy: the experience of divine *eros* launched a search for apt language. In truth, the projection of the Song of Songs' passion into the divine-human realm does less to sanitize its sexual imagery than it luridly whispers that our relationship with God can be more suggestive, saucy, lewd, racy, randy, raw, even more raunchy than puritanical theology allows. Instead of elevating chastity as the virtue of virtues, mystical erotica ennobles fleshly passion. John Climacus cries out to God: "You have ravished my soul, and I cannot contain your flame."³⁰ Gregory Palamas redefines Paul's mystical experience (2 Cor

---

26. Bernard, *Song of Songs I*, 53–54.
27. King, *Strength to Love*, 50, *Stride Toward Freedom*, 104–6, *Testament of Hope*, 19–20.
28. McGinn, *Foundations of Mysticism*, 119.
29. Ibid., 118.
30. Lossky, *Mystical Theology*, 212.

12:2–4) as being "ravished to the third heaven."[31] John Donne wants, needs, and expects to be "ravished."[32] They cannot fathom a mystical experience *without* passion.

The tradition that uses the Song of Songs to describe the unthinkable but not unknowable conjures up a rich series of homo- and heteroerotic images. There ought to be nothing surprising in this holy eroticism that likens divine union with sexual acts, no "blinking" about it, not to mention blushing. To the puritanical, such descriptions seem blasphemous. But can the intensity of union with God be described *without* referring to the most ecstatic human experience?[33] Even this, however, begs one question and begets others. We can say it is natural to use sexual imagery—like any anthropomorphism—to describe divine intimacy. But is this a culturally acceptable, perhaps even prescribed, *metaphor,* or is this an *experience*? Is it the product of empiricism, autosuggestion, or a culturally induced hallucination? Or is divine *eros* any more or less a metaphor than seeing an obscuring cloud, a dark night, a wound in Christ's side, hearing God speak, or being enveloped in light? Is it, in fact, any more a theological—and mystical—abstraction than solidarity with the poor?

Literarily, these homo- and heteroerotic accounts vary as much as richly nuanced biblical stories that describe the divine as an angel in one verse and God in the next. So for mystics crying out a lover's name in the throes of divine ecstasy, the lover can be an angel, Christ, the Trinity, an earthy, walking, talking anthropomorphic God, or the much more unreachable, untouchable Godhead. Like the oscillation in a prophet's voice in which it becomes impossible to tell who is speaking—the prophet, the people, or God—mystics vacillate between first-, second-, and third-person accounts of their experiences.

Perhaps because such accounts became popular (why wouldn't they?), some writers warn against scandalous fantasies. Just as some caution against the pursuit of visions, others wag a finger at visions that include hugging, kissing, and "being caressed in other less decent ways" by Jesus or, even more shamefully, by his virgin mother![34] Such warnings were as readily ignored as parental admonitions ordering adolescents to abstain from sex.

Erotic mystical accounts shift in tone between gauzy romance and brazen pornography as lovers pass through fantasy, furtiveness, and foreplay to fulfillment. For Bernard, this succession turns hierarchical relationships

31. Palamas, *Triads*, 50.
32. Donne, Holy Sonnet xiv, *Selections*, 10.
33. Leech, *Experiencing God*, 339–40.
34. McGinn, *Flowering of Mysticism*, 115.

of beggar-almsgiver and servant-master into lover-lover. For others, passion begins in a Song of Songs-like flirtatious dialogue with Christ.[35] For still others the kiss begins in adolescent fantasy—Thérèse wanted to be a princess to Christ, her Prince Charming: "I want to be the prey of Your love. I hope that one day You will swoop down on me, carry me off to the furnace of love, and plunge me into its burning depths so that I can be its ecstatic victim for all eternity."[36] For still others, there is a longing as stinging as the psalmist's and as conflicted as Langston Hughes's dream deferred. In a variation on Augustine's "what do I love when I love you," Richard Rolle asks,

> what am I to do? How long have I to wait? To whom shall I flee to enjoy what I am longing for? For I am needy and famished, tortured and afflicted, wounded and wan because my Love is not here; for this immense love torments me, and the hope deferred afflicts my soul. And so the cry of my heart goes up, and in the midst of the heavenly choir there moves my music and my musing, eager to be raised to audience with the Most High.[37]

Some describe this passion as unpredictable, unpremeditated, and spontaneous; others as the steady heartbeat of Augustine's restless heart until it rests in God: "O soul, before the world was I longed for you: and I still long for you, and you for Me. Therefore, when our two desires unite, Love shall be fulfilled."[38] For Gregory of Nyssa yearning begins in voyeurism as we gaze "on the infinite beauty of God." Instead of progressing by kisses, we progress by sight: "As God continues to be revealed, we . . . never exhaust our desire to see more, since what we are waiting for is always more magnificent, more divine, than all we have already seen"; our "yearning for further vision" never ends.[39]

Yearning fantasy becomes furtive desire. Imagined in daydreams, intimacy begins under cover of darkness: "One dark night, Fired with love's urgent longings . . . I went out unseen. . . . In darkness, and secure, By the secret ladder, disguised. . . . In darkness and concealment. . . . On that glad night, In secret, for no one saw me."[40] Like people too embarrassed to say *I did it*, like Paul's account of the third heaven, mystics sometimes talk about a *friend*. When the couple meets, *they* begin *their* foreplay: "The Lover and the Beloved met, and their caresses, kisses, and tears testified to their love for

---

35. Ibid., 165.
36. Thérèse, *Autobiography*, 159.
37. Rolle, *Fire of Love*, 155.
38. Underhill, *Mysticism*, 92 (modernized).
39. Gregory of Nyssa, *From Glory to Glory*, 247.
40. John of the Cross, *Collected Works*, 68–69.

one another."[41] As first- and third-person accounts blur, the Beloved bends down to hold and kiss the lover:[42] "Once I embraced you with both arms and happily breathed in your very pure kiss."[43] Kisses, like a sacrament, begin foreplay: "Upon my flowering breast Which I kept wholly for You alone, There You lay sleeping, and I caressing You. . . . When the breeze blew from the turret Parting Your hair, You wounded my neck With your gentle hand, Suspending all my senses . . . I abandoned and forgot myself, Laying my face on my Beloved."[44]

Passion brews: "I held you, I embraced you, I kissed you for a long time. I felt how deeply you appreciated this sign of love when in the midst of the kiss you opened your mouth so that I could kiss you more deeply";[45] "folding your entire self around me, you tenderly kiss all of me."[46] The once inexperienced lover is inflamed with desire:

> What you gave me once when I neither knew nor understood
> give me again now that I am experienced and am asking for it!
> Fondle me with joyful, heavenly love . . . ![47]

Passion grows. The liturgist's "O God" melts into the lover's "Oh God!" and pillow talk and prayer become one:

> The more your desire grows, the more tightly you hold me. . . .
> The more fervent the embrace, the sweeter the taste of the kisses.
> The more lovingly we gaze at each other, the harder it is for us to
> part. The more you give me, the more I consume, however much
> I have. . . . The hotter I remain, the sooner does my flame die
> down. The more I burn, the more beautifully I shine.[48]

Foreplay leads to fruition, fulfillment, completion, climax, telos, to simultaneous erotic union and agapaic annihilation. None of Otto's dread is here; only Buber's ecstatic cries, now speaking for oneself, now shyly, slyly, as if speaking of another. Like voyeurs or eavesdroppers, these accounts

---

41. Lull, *Romancing God*, 22.
42. Ibid., 18.
43. McGinn, *Growth of Mysticism*, 130.
44. For the sake of the uniformity of voice in this section, I have rendered many of the quotes as direct speech in the first and second person rather than the third person. These are noted as "first person." John of the Cross, *Collected Works*, 69 (first person).
45. McGinn, *Growth of Mysticism*, 332 (first person).
46. Symeon, *Divine Eros*, 92 (first person).
47. Rolle, *Fire of Love*, 191.
48. Buber, *Ecstatic Utterances*, 53 (first person).

embarrass us with a prurient-but-holy curiosity. To hear these accounts is like opening a series of sealed journals or eavesdropping on affairs.

> In the bed that is yours alone, I boil over when driven to it by the fire of [your] love.[49]

> ... when the Beloved is placed between my breasts, I melt completely through desire for you into an expressible infusion of divine sweetness...[50]

> How shall I, the least of souls, take in my arms, eat you and drink you and have my way with you.... No matter how high you dwell above me, your Godhead shall never be so distant that I cannot constantly entwine my limbs with you. And so I shall never cool off.[51]

> ... how we penetrate each other in such a way that neither of us distinguishes ourselves from the other. But we abide in one another in fruition, mouth in mouth, heart in heart, body in body, and soul in soul, while one sweet divine Nature flows through us both...[52]

> For surely nothing can surpass the joy of being within the Beloved when the Beloved is also within us.[53]

> You embrace me wholly, kiss me wholly, and give yourself entirely to me, unworthy as I am; and I take my fill of your love and beauty and am filled with the rapture and sweetness of the Godhead.[54]

> Jesus, when I am in you, and on fire with joy
>   and when the heat of love is surging in,
> I want to embrace you, the most loving, with my whole being.[55]

---

49. McGinn, *Growth of Mysticism*, 302 (first person).
50. Ibid., 410 (first person).
51. McGinn, *Flowering of Mysticism*, 235–36.
52. Hadewijch, *Complete Works*, 66 (first person).
53. Gregory of Nyssa, *From Glory to Glory*, 200 (first person).
54. Buber, *Ecstatic Utterances*, 39 (first person).
55. Rolle, *Fire of Love*, 154.

> In your hands I saw a long golden spear and at the end of the iron tip I seemed to see a point of fire. With this you seemed to pierce my heart several times so that it penetrated to my entrails. When you drew it out, I thought you were drawing them out with it and you left me completely afire with a great love for you. The pain was so sharp that it made me utter several moans; and so excessive was the sweetness caused me by this intense pain that one can never wish to lose it, nor will one's soul be content with anything less...[56]

Images of sexual longing mingle and merge with a thirst for righteousness:

> O Lord, love me mightily and love me often and long; the oftener you love me, the purer I become; the more mightily you love me, the more beautiful I become; the longer you love me, the holier I become here on earth.[57]

> O eternal Trinity! O Godhead!... The more I enter you, the more I discover, and the more I discover, the more I seek you. You are insatiable, you in whose depth the soul is sated yet remains always hungry for you, thirsty for you, eternal Trinity, longing to see you with the light in your light.[58]

> You consume whatever sin and selfishness you find in the soul. Yet your consuming does not distress the soul but fattens her with insatiable love, for though you satisfy her she is never sated but longs for you constantly. The more she possesses you the more she seeks you, and the more she seeks and desires you the more she finds and enjoys you, high eternal fire, abyss of charity![59]

In ascetical theology, purgation and illumination lead to union, but here union rebounds back to purgation and sanctification: "I am totally transformed into you; absorbed into a similar mode of being.... In this third... [bed]... there is no one there but you alone."[60] After fulfillment, mystics thank the skilled divine Lover for ravishing them, and when they part, the lover misses the Beloved.

---

56. Teresa, *Life of Teresa*, 274–75 (first person).
57. Buber, *Ecstatic Utterances*, 53.
58. Catherine, *Dialogue*, 364.
59. Ibid., 273.
60. McGinn, *Growth of Mysticism*, 302.

> At once I rose from my bed, ran to lift the latch, so that my whole house might be open to my lover, and my mind see in all fullness you whom I most longed to see. But you had already gone! You had left the gate. What could I do then, in my misery?[61]
>
> I went about as if in a stupor. I had no wish to see or speak with anyone, but only to hug my pain, which caused me greater bliss than any that can come from the whole of creation. I was like this on several occasions, when the Lord was pleased to send me these raptures, and so deep were they that, even when I was with other people, I could not resist them.[62]

Seeing couples on the street hug and kiss each other "with love and tears" spurs the lover to "recall the Beloved" so "that the Lover almost fainted."[63]

For all of the intensity of these descriptions, fantasy, furtiveness, foreplay, and fulfillment are only part of erotic union. While some see mysticism as a life aimed at union with God,[64] the holy erotic, like sex, aims not only *to* union but *through* it. Like sex, divine *eros* is an ecstatic end in itself, an expression of a more complex love, and an experience that transforms all relationships. In other words, the holiness of holy erotica transcends the erotic. *Eros*, momentarily wrenched away from *philia* and *agape* in divine intimacy, merges with them again, reanimating them in the most intimate of revolutions and the most universal dispersal of love.

King understood *philia* and *agape* better than divine *eros* and the mystic's lust for God, but he continually expressed *eros* for the revolution. Many of his speeches, in fact, bear the fragrance of Buber's ecstatic utterance as they articulate the delight of someone who in intoxicating moments has brushed up against the hem of the realm. Only someone drunk with justice could answer, as he did at the end of the Selma march, his rhetorical "how long" it would take until segregated housing and schools would cease, until all could vote, until poverty would vanish, until the American dream would be fulfilled, with a thunderous "not long."[65] But to a degree this ecstasy spiced his public ministry from start to finish because he had been to the mountaintop and seen the promised land.[66] Every political victory, every

---

61. Ibid., 145.
62. Teresa, *Life of Teresa*, 274–75.
63. Lull, *Romancing God*, 13.
64. Underhill, *Mystics of the Church*, 20.
65. King, *Testament of Hope*, 229–30.
66. King, *Stride Toward Freedom*, 178, *Testament of Hope*, 286; Garrow, *Bearing the Cross*, 89.

oasis of justice in the endless exodus was a moment of ethical voyeurism and mystical union with the realm.

Union with God also leads to the realm but by a different path. John of the Cross and Eckhart insist that erotic ecstasy is a means to a broader, deeper love of all creation. As with all intimacy, the depth of our relationship with God is measured not in ecstatic union but in the convictions and commitments of a God-centered life:[67] "Union with God means every bit of our human nature transfigured in Christ, woven up into God's creative life and activity, absorbed into God's redeeming purpose, heart, soul, mind and strength."[68] That "redeeming purpose" is not only the natural offshoot of erotic union with God; it is its raison d'être as our hunger for God becomes one with our lust for justice. Some seek first the realm of God. Some seek God first. But in finding one, we find both.

THE SUBVERSIVE AFTERGLOW

In dialectical opposition to the tradition of holy tears, Martin Buber says that the purpose of religion is "to beget a life of elation, of fervor which cannot be stifled by any experience."[69] Union begets this life of elation and reintegrates the mystic into the revolution of God. According to Julian of Norwich, the "fruit" of prayer is to be "united and like" Christ *"in all things."*[70] This is Paul's "nothing can separate us from the love of God" (Rom 8:35–9) with an asterisk: nor from one another.[71] Eckhart says that God "intends to lure" us into God's very being to cleanse us, to "love us in God," so God may be "in us."[72] Union changes us. Stunningly, it also changes God. According to John of the Cross, God's postcoital "humility and sweetness" could not be more "solicitous" if God became the soul's slave, and "she God's god."[73] To John, the divine afterglow reverses the direction of Bernard's ascending kisses. After union, it is as if an infatuated, love-struck deity willingly descends from the kissing of the lips, to our hand and to the soul's feet in an enchanting, divine agapaic kenosis.

This divine-human life of unity and elation is the subversive afterglow of erotic union. After union the mystic sees creation through a kaleidoscope

67. McGinn, *Flowering of Mysticism*, 239.
68. Underhill, *Light of Christ*, 23.
69. Buber, *Tales: Early Masters*, 2.
70. Julian, *Showings*, 251 (italics mine).
71. Ibid., 309.
72. Eckhart, *Sermons & Treatises II*, 196.
73. John of the Cross, *Collected Works*, 517.

of beauty no longer narrowed to the Beloved. John of the Cross lauds the night "that has united The Lover with the beloved, Transforming the beloved in her Lover."[74] In stammering prose, he says that the afterglow of *eros* absorbs him "in Your beauty" and enables him to see beauty everywhere:

> ... hence, I shall see You in Your beauty, and You shall see me in Your beauty, and I shall see myself in You in Your beauty, and You will see Yourself in me in Your beauty; that I may resemble You in Your beauty, and You resemble me in Your beauty, and my beauty be Your beauty and Your beauty my beauty; wherefore I shall be You in Your beauty, and You will be me in Your beauty, because Your very beauty will be my beauty; and therefore we shall behold each other in Your beauty.[75]

Underhill's clean bifurcation of mystics as passionate lovers or discerning seers[76] disappears; the two are joined at the hip—or, more precisely, the loins.

Even in his fall-dimmed, sin-drenched *The Seven Storey Mountain* period, Merton reveled in this abiding sense of creation's inherent goodness. If only we could see the world knowing that "everything that is, is good ... we would not be able to look at a flower or a blade of grass or an insect or a drop of water or a grain of sand or a leaf, let alone a whole tree, or a bird, or a living animal, or a human being, without exploding with exultation."[77] In an essay written under the spell of creation and the incarnation (the antidotes to theological obsessions with sin and the fall), Merton writes that in becoming human, Christ wanted to be "anyone and everyone." Those who believe in the incarnation should be "prepared to see, in mystery, the presence of Christ" in anyone, anything, everyone, and everything.[78]

> When we are alone on a starlit night; when by chance we see the migrating birds in autumn descending on a grove of junipers to rest and eat; when we see children in a moment when they are really children; when we know love in our own hearts; or when, like the Japanese poet Basho we hear an old frog land in a quiet pond with a solitary splash—at such times the awakening, the turning inside out of all values, the "newness," the emptiness and the purity of vision that make themselves evident, provide a glimpse of the cosmic dance.

74. Ibid., 68–69.
75. Ibid., 547.
76. Underhill, *Mysticism*, 195.
77. Merton, *Thomas Merton Reader*, 316.
78. Merton, *New Seeds*, 296.

> For the world and time are the dance of the Lord in emptiness. The silence of the spheres is the music of a wedding feast. The more we persist in misunderstanding the phenomena of life, the more we analyze them out into strange finalities and complex purposes of our own, the more we involve ourselves in sadness, absurdity and despair. But it does not matter much, because no despair of ours can alter the reality of things, or stain the joy of the cosmic dance which is always there. Indeed, we are in the midst of it, and it is in the midst of us, for it beats in our very blood, whether we want it to or not.[79]

Merton's eyes dance. John of the Cross sees beauty. Eckhart sees the universal divine: "All things become simply God to you, for in all things you notice only God, just as someone who stares long at the sun sees the sun in whatever they afterwards look at."[80] In his eisegesis of Paul on the road to Damascus, Eckhart inserts this view into his retelling of the story. When Scripture says "Paul rose from the ground and with open eyes saw nothing," it has a "fourfold sense": (1) "when he rose up from the ground with opened eyes he saw Nothing, and the Nothing was God; for when he saw God he calls that Nothing"; (2) "when he got up he saw nothing but God;" (3) "in all things he saw nothing but God"; (4) and "when he saw God, he saw all things as nothing."[81]

The erotic afterglow paints a vision of beauty in some, a vision of divinity in others. It can also create a new sensitivity to the potential unity of all things. Using a common ascetical reference to Hosea (Hos 2:14) in which God considers luring Israel back to the wilderness where, in romanticized memory, the people were newly wedded to God, Eckhart says that there God speaks "to her heart, one with One, one from One, one in One, and in One, one everlastingly."[82] Ruusbroec describes this mystical state as "union with" and "unity in God."[83] Similarly, Silesius says the soul's "tranquility" rests in becoming "a oned one."[84] Isaac of Stella waxes rhapsodic about God in and above all things:

> O One before all things, One above all things, One after all things, One from which all things come, and One for which all things are! It is a strong oneness where two in one flesh are

---

79. Ibid., 296–67.
80. Eckhart, *Sermons & Treatises I*, 45.
81. Ibid., 153.
82. Eckhart, *Essential Sermons*, 247.
83. Ruusbroec, *Spiritual Espousals*, 240.
84. Silesius, *Cherubinic Wanderer*, 123.

> no longer two but one flesh. It is a stronger oneness where two things [body and soul] in one person are no longer two but one person. The greatest oneness is where the spirit that adheres to God is no longer two but one.[85]

If in Eden two become one flesh (Gen 2:24), in union, God and the soul find themselves in inseparable and contagious bliss. Writing during his transforming hajj, Malcolm X sounds Franciscan in his spirituality, or like Merton after his Louisville epiphany, as he speaks of God's family and human unity: "everyone forgets Self and turns to God and out of this submission to the One God comes a [family] in which all are equals." Islam teaches "the Oneness of God, gives the Believer genuine, voluntary obligations toward [others] (all of whom are One Human family, brothers and sisters to each other) . . . the True Believer recognizes the Oneness of all Humanity."[86]

Union, like sexual exhaustion, melts into Sabbath rest. Aelred of Rievaulx says, "let it be one in the One, with the One, through the One, about the One, knowing the One, savoring the One, and because it is always one, always being at rest, and thus enjoying a perpetual Sabbath."[87] This rest, this heavenly peace on earth, becomes a forgotten verse—an arrhythmic addendum—to *Silent Night*:

> In these beds
> Christ sleeps with them:
> Happy the sleep,
> Sweet the rest,
> . . . Of the heavenly Bridegroom,
> With his right arm
> Embracing her as a bride,
> His left arm under her head,
> She falls asleep.
> Wakeful in heart,
> In body she sleeps,
> On the Bridegroom's loving
> Breast she slumbers.[88]

All is calm. All is bright. All is beauty. All is light.

This oneness, now shared with humanity, is innate in divinity. Eckhart says that the first two persons of the Trinity are so inseparable that even the

---

85. McGinn, *Growth of Mysticism*, 295.
86. Marable, *Malcolm X*, 311.
87. McGinn, *Growth of Mysticism*, 322.
88. Ibid., 145.

cherubim and seraphim cannot "find out the difference between them";[89] "God liquefies" and "melts" into Christ and Christ "melts back" into God, just as God and the soul melt into each other.[90] Ruusbroec says that in union "all creatures are in them both."[91] For Eckhart, the soul does not *have* Christ; the soul *is* Christ[92] and in order to know God, one must *become* Christ.[93] Catherine says God and the soul's "loving affection makes them two bodies with one soul, because love transforms one into what one loves."[94] Eckhart, Catherine, and Julian use the same simile: the soul is more united to God than it is to the body.[95]

All is calm. All is bright. All is contentment. All is light. Yet to feel that *all is well with the world* is always a localized, temporary sensation. The subversive afterglow of union leads to Eckhart's trial and al-Hallaj's execution and to one dangerous assertion after another. Eckhart says, God is not there while we are here; "That is not so. God and I are one." Bridging the debate between the comparative value of love and knowledge, Eckhart says, "Through knowledge I take God into myself, through love I enter into God." He is not "similar" to God; he is "one" with God.[96] In Zen-like koans, Eckhart says he has become "free of God, for my essential being is above God;" "I am the cause of God's being God: if I were not, then God would not be God."[97]

Eckhart's claims seem the height of hubris, but Rumi refutes accusations of pride with an even more astonishing claim. Not only did al-Hallaj tell the truth when he said he was one with God,[98] he was in no way "presumptuous"; rather, it would be insolent to say, "I am the slave of God," a perfectly submissive Muslim. To say "I am God" is in fact "an expression of great humility"—if you call yourself a slave of God you not only claim to be fully self-realized in your faith, you assert your existence apart from God; if you say, "I am God" you make yourself "non-existent," you say "I am naught," and "there is no being but God's". This, Rumi says, is an "extreme of

---

89. Eckhart, *Sermons & Treatises III*, 42.
90. Eckhart, *Essential Sermons*, 37–38.
91. Ruusbroec, *Spiritual Espousals*, 148.
92. Otto, *Mysticism*, 215.
93. Eckhart, *Sermons & Treatises I*, 100.
94. Catherine, *Dialogue*, 115–16.
95. Eckhart, *Sermons & Treatises III*, 42; Catherine, *Dialogue*, 295; Buber, *Ecstatic Utterances*, 95.
96. Eckhart, *Sermons & Treatises II*, 136.
97. Ibid., 275.
98. Rumi, *Essential Rumi*, 101.

humility and self-abasement."[99] Rumi's poetic logic takes the Muslim claim of God's oneness to its most radical conclusion. Like Eckhart's insight into Paul's vision on the road to Damascus, there is nothing to see but God because nothing exists except God. Therefore, to declare oneness with God is not only a mystical statement, it is the only theologically credible, spiritually viable, humanly humble statement one can make.

While those who make this claim tread on thin ecclesiastical ice, early Christian theology embraced deification as a natural by-product of the incarnation and the quintessence of orthodoxy. Irenaeus writes that God became human so that humans could become divine,[100] as if incarnation simultaneously sparks union and transformation. Slanting this claim toward a pedagogy of wisdom and word, Clement says the Logos became human so that "you may learn" from a person how a person "may become God."[101] Mystics like Catherine and Ruusbroec echo these assertions.[102] Eckhart says that God became human so "I might be born God," a way of being *born again* that would make the usual purveyors of the cliché wince.[103]

Like Paul's evocation of the kenotic Christ, John of the Cross asserts that an incredibly humble divine self-emptying gives birth to every divine-human interaction. In an image of the incarnation as God's Ash Wednesday, Birgitta of Sweden says that in the incarnation, God wore "the sackcloth of humanity."[104] Eckhart adapts a contemporary story of a lord and a lady to describe God's motivation to become human: a lord and lady live "happily ever *before*" until the lady loses an eye in an accident. Her happiness sinks into grief as she mourns her disfigurement and worries that her husband will love her less. Hearing this, he puts out one of his eyes and says to her, "so you may know I love you I have made myself like you."[105] It is not *eros* that moves this lord, but self-sacrifice, *agape*, maturity heated and leavened in *eros*. Unlike the "beauty" John sees everywhere, for Eckhart the incarnation begins when God gazes at scarred deformity and open-sore anxiety, and becomes one with it in grim-faced, unsentimental love.

The incarnation reminds us that not all is calm, bright, beauty, or light. Not all is well. Not all are one. Not yet. That will be so at the eschaton,

---

99. Rumi, *Poet and Mystic*, 184.
100. Smulders, *Fathers on Christology*, 14–15.
101. McGinn, *Foundations of Mysticism*, 107.
102. Catherine, *Dialogue*, 53, 205; Ruusbroec, *Spiritual Espousals*, 215.
103. Eckhart, *Sermons & Treatises I*, 138.
104. Birgitta, *Life and Revelations*, 121.
105. Eckhart, *Sermons & Treatises II*, 62. In another version of the story, the woman puts out her eye for her husband.

on the day, in the age and realm to come. In the afterglow of union, we see God, beauty, unity. But the afterglow is not as simple as seeing heaven and earth full of God's glory. We also distinguish more sharply between holy and human, gain and loss, treasure and rubbish. Our senses become more sensitive to suffering, injustice, violence, and neglect. We experience a deeper dissonance between beauty and brokenness, elation and injustice, union and indifference. What A. J. Muste calls "the political strategy of the prophets"[106]—profound inner communion with God and a passion for social justice—is also mystical awareness. As with Isaiah and Jeremiah, union enables mystics to smell the dung of the world as if they had just stepped in it. It is precisely when Isaiah sees earth full of God's glory, and when Jeremiah tastes God's word, that God sends them into the world (Isa 6:8–11, Jer 1:10), *not to save the world but to judge it*. Perhaps, oddly, a more acute vision of glory gives birth to *Mississippi eyes*, not as the work of conscientization but of mystical consciousness. Even at the height of mystical ecstasy, bliss is never 100 percent pure, for union makes the soul "gloriously happy and grief-stricken" at the same time.[107]

While maintaining her affinity for the apophatic, Teresa allows that God can grant "an understanding of God's secrets and wonders" that includes "a joy so far above all joys attainable on earth that it fills us with a just contempt for the joys of life, all of which are but dung." This overwhelming delight is, as Teresa says, but "a single drop of the great and abundant river which God has prepared for us."[108] This is the mutual "delight" God and the soul take in one another.[109] This is the joy, tears of joy that overwhelms Pascal, a joy that enthralls Paul—a joy that shrinks and shrivels all of the world's glories to rubbish (Phil 3:8). In ascetical theology, purgation enables union, but here we find that union spurs purgation. Contempt for anything less than elation gives birth to the detachment Eckhart praises in the philosopher Diogenes who "sat naked in his tub" and proclaimed to Alexander the Great that he was "a greater ruler than you, for I have rejected more things than you have ever possessed. What you think it a great thing to possess is too petty for me to scorn."[110]

Assisi eyes never blinded Francis to corruption. After hearing Francis warn them of the corrupting temptations of luxury, one of his brothers has a vision in which he sees his companions at "a very foul and unclean pigs'

---

106. Muste, *Non-violence*, 193.
107. Catherine, *Dialogue*, 57.
108. Teresa, *Life of Teresa*, 254.
109. Teresa, *Way of Perfection*, 119.
110. Eckhart, *Sermons & Treatises III*, 55.

trough, from which they were eating peas mixed with human dung."[111] Birgitta has a prophetic vision in parabolic clothing about the corruption of the ecclesiastical hierarchy:

> ... because they glory and delight in those offices and honors and, for this reason, leave my sheep and their churches, they are, in doing such things, to my eyes like pigs dressed in pontifical or sacerdotal ornaments. This situation might be expressed by means of the following similitude: There was a great lord who had invited his friends to supper. And at the hour of the supper, those pigs—dressed as above—entered into the palace in the sight of that lord and in the sight of the banqueters who sat at the table. The lord, however, wished to give to them some of those precious foods on his table; but then the aforesaid pigs cried out with a loud sound, grunting their opposition with their pig voices and refusing to eat those precious foods, although they were avidly eager to eat, in their usual way, the cheap husks meant for pigs. Then, however when that lord saw and understood this, he loathed their vileness and filth; and at once he said to his servants with great wrath and indignation: "Expel them from my palace and cast them forth to be refreshed and sordidly sated with the pigs' husks of which they are worthy! For they are neither willing nor worthy to eat of my foods, which have been prepared for my friends."[112]

Sounding like a conduit for the prophetic scowling of a chorus of liberation theologians, John Chrysostom scolds and scalds Christians with a more direct prophetic denunciation:

> Your Lord is out there, dying of hunger, and you give yourselves up to gluttony. And the terrible thing is not only this but as you give yourselves up to gluttony you calmly despise him, and it is very little he asks of you: a piece of bread to assuage his hunger. He is out there, dying of cold, and you dress yourself in silk and turn your gaze away from him, showing him no compassion but go on your way without mercy.[113]

For Pascal, Christ is always on the cross. For Chrysostom, Christ is forever on the streets. And Christians, as Chrysostom saw, want nothing more than to ignore Christ's suffering and rest in luxurious, earthly peace.

---

111. Celano, *Saint Francis*, 237.
112. Birgitta, *Life and Revelations*, 214–15.
113. Leech, *Experiencing God*, 414.

So those who find unparalleled fulfillment in mystical union need to be warned: do not seek God unless you are willing to be confounded, bewildered, annihilated, and transformed. Do not pass this way unless you are willing to gain all that you do not yet possess by losing all that seems comfortable and satisfying. When all that is "good" becomes dung, you are left to reassess all of your priorities and rearrange all of your values. Like the Gospel of Mark's messianic secret, like an affair, there is something intrinsically disquieting about intimacy with God.

The experience of union is fleeting. The effects are not. Mystics return to their daily lives, their normal routines, their five senses, their common sense, to the contradictions of the self and the world as-it-is. But having known God in union, mystics know what they did not know before. They see things they did not see before. They love things they did not love before. They rage against machines they had ignored. Yet what they experience is not an occasional, unpredictable, providential intervention in this or that person—lifted away in privatized rapture—into union with God. Ruusbroec reminds us that God's Unity "draws all things to itself." While it may seem wondrously extraordinary to experience union with God, this is merely one instance of God's love that persistently invites us to live in "a state of eternal enjoyment," a life of elation. It is as normal as the Eucharist, as everyday as a kiss. But the experience, while indelible, is not perpetual. In this "we will flow forth and flow out of ourselves into the uncomprehended abundance of God's riches and goodness."[114]

What, then, does it mean to remain one with God in the midst of the run-of-the-mill blandness of the every day world? It means an ongoing sense of union and unity that transforms our way of life. Mechtild von Hackenborn hears God say, "See, I give you my eyes, that you may see all things with them, and my ears, that you may hear all things with them; my mouth I also give you, so that all you have to say, whether in speech, prayer, or song, you may say through it. I give you my heart, that through it you may think everything and may love me and all things for my sake."[115] The only way we can know we love God is by loving our neighbor (Teresa). They are the only ones we can love without being loved (Catherine). The goal of union is never to be taken out of the world any more than the goal of monasticism is to keep a few select souls safe behind secure and cinctured doors. That is not what the Epistle of James calls "true religion" (Jas 1:27). Underhill says that the arc of the spiritual life always returns to the complexities of the world. Those who have known "that interior union with God . . . do not stand aside

---

114. Ruusbroec, *Spiritual Espousals*, 159.
115. Buber, *Ecstatic Utterances*, 63.

wrapped in delightful prayers and feeling pure and agreeable to God. They go right down in the mess; and there, right down in the mess, they are able to radiate God because they possess God."[116]

Union with God provides the most powerful impetus to political engagement. Nowhere else is the mystical vision more demanding of social transformation. Abba Isaac speaks of the transforming effects of union: "This will be the case when every love, every desire, every effort, every undertaking, every thought of ours, everything that we live, that we speak, that we breathe, will be God." The unity of God and Christ is "carried over into our understanding and our mind, so that, just as Christ loves us with a sincere and pure and indissoluble love, we too may be joined to Christ with a perpetual and inseparable love and so united with Christ that whatever we breathe, whatever we understand, whatever we speak, may be God."[117] Union with God is no more an end in itself than the incarnation is a one-way street from the infinite and unsullied into the finite and fallible. Union is like Thurman's description of mundane monastic life—there is always a U-turn that leads us back to re-engage the world in a newly minted way. Union, like the incarnation, leads to deification.

A MORE SACRED UNION

As much as any mystic, Rumi celebrates intoxicating union. But even in his exhilaration, there is a scent, a taste, a creeping shudder, a nod to Otto's awestruck dread. To Rumi, there is no elation without risk, no height without chance of a fall.

> Those of you who are love-drunk on the edge of the roof,
> Sit down, or climb down. Every moment spent in Union
> With the Beloved is a dangerous delight,
> Like standing on a roof-edge.
>   Be afraid up there,
> Of losing that connection, and don't tell anybody
> About it. Keep your secret.[118]

Like "standing on a roof-edge," the "dangerous delight" of union is foolhardy. Subversive ecstasy leads to universal solidarity; intimate revolution ignites prophetic passion.

---

116. Underhill, *House* and *Concerning*, 150–51.
117. Vivian, *Four Desert Fathers*, 44.
118. Rumi, *Delicious Laughter*, 31.

Day experienced God's passion in the sacraments; the oneness of creation begins in the mystical event of baptism, F. D. Maurice's "sacrament of constant union" with God,[119] Stringfellow's "sacrament of extraordinary unity" with all people.[120] The logic of the pneumatology of baptism is that the Holy Spirit is given at baptism to begin the work of deification and solidarity. As Thurman says that mystical and socialist visions are one, Stewart Headlam in late nineteenth century England believed that everything in our faith—Scripture, tradition, reason, the sacraments—leads to utopian socialism: Jesus was "the revolutionary socialist of Galilee"[121] who founded the church as a "Socialist community."[122] When in the Lord's Prayer he taught people to pray for the coming of the realm, that "kingdom" was a "righteous Socialistic order."[123] So all who receive holy communion naturally become "Holy Communists."[124] Everyone dampened by holy water or fed with holy food awakens to solidarity with the human race.

Solidarity, of course, is more than a one-word slogan or an inconsequential commitment. The full extent of solidarity, as Sobrino intones solemnly after the hit-squad murders of Romero and Ellacuría, is to suffer and die at one with the oppressed. Solidarity is a continuing manifestation of incarnation. It traffics in intentional risk, heartrending tragedy, and gasping grief. It is the political equivalent to the Sufi's experience of annihilation at the moment of union.[125] Romero said that in the sociopolitical climate of his El Salvador, the church ought to be scarred and its priests suffer.[126] Yet solidarity is not limited to the theologically trained or ecclesiastically chosen. As she awaited her arrest as part of her generation's Final Solution, Etty Hillesum hinted that suffering is yet another doorway to unity: "I am not alone in my tiredness or sickness or fears, but at one with millions of others from many centuries."[127] Targeted for where we stand or who we are, solidarity is a practice of atonement, a way to be *at one* with suffering humanity.

Solidarity can be a once-in-a-lifetime, eyes-wide-open decision to risk life and limb. More often it is a series of choices to prune away slices of privilege

---

119. Vidler, *F. D. Maurice*, 106.
120. Stringfellow, *Free in Obedience*, 78.
121. Headlam, *Laws of Eternal Life*, 27.
122. Ibid., 5.
123. Ibid., 62.
124. Ibid., 97.
125. al-Kalabadhi, *Doctrine of the Sufis*, 102.
126. Romero, *Violence of Love*, 31.
127. Hillesum, *Interrupted Life*, 165.

or security. César Chávez found it liberating to be paid a pittance.[128] But for most people, solidarity is far more politically complicated and emotionally conflicted. For King, raised during the ascendancy of Jim Crow in an oasis of marginal bourgeois half-privilege, solidarity could mean opportunities to try to shake his status in interactions with the working poor, or bearing a blush of the shame of fame when his family was treated as VIPs at a World's Fair.[129] He practiced solidarity more baldly when he was beaten in Birmingham,[130] stoned in Chicago,[131] did jail time time and again, or weathered bomb threats and bombs, death threats and death.[132] Certainly there were times—unlike the night in his Montgomery kitchen when he heard God's encouraging word—when only the divine silence DuBois decried mimed powerlessly and failed to soothe his terror. In such moments he bore the norm of African Americans in most times and most places in most of America's history of white supremacy. But he was targeted for a lynching in ways few have ever known.

The cost of solidarity may have hit him hardest, though, when he moved his family to the south side of Chicago to share the burden of poverty and urban racism. After just a few days, as their children too quickly assimilated the norms of their peers, he and Coretta reversed direction and moved their children away.[133] Like any parents, they did not want their children twisted by oppression's invisible hand, and what their skin color could not buy, their economic and social privilege could: they chose to cushion their children's lives when others could not. As King discovered, if epiphanies birth Buber's ecstasy and elation, solidarity evokes Otto's anxiety and unease.

When Stringfellow, raised in a working class family and fresh from Harvard Law School, moved to Harlem in 1956 to work in a community-based ecumenical ministry, he went to "honor the Incarnation."[134] The tenement apartment the ministry located for him "was typical of the housing of the neighborhood." He moved in to an incarnational awakening of the senses and the spirit.

> The stairway smelled of piss.
> The smells inside the tenement ... were somewhat more ambiguous. They were a suffocating mixture of rotting food, rancid mattresses, dead rodents, dirt, and the stale odors of human life.

128. Dalton, *Moral Vision*, 101.
129. Garrow, *Bearing the Cross*, 345.
130. Ibid., 221, 232.
131. Ibid., 500.
132. Ibid., 135, 311, 328, 329, 341, 392–5, 619, Oates, *Let Trumpet Sound*, 455.
133. King, *Where Do We Go*, 135–36.
134. Stringfellow, *My People*, 47.

This was to be home. . . .

The place, altogether, was about 25 x 12 feet, with a wall separating the kitchen section from the rest. In the kitchen was a bathtub, a tiny, rusty sink, a refrigerator that didn't work, and an ancient gas range. In one corner was a toilet with a bowl without a seat. Water dripped perpetually from the box above the bowl. The other room was filled with beds: two double-decker military cots, and a big ugly convertible sofa. There wasn't room for anything else. The walls and ceilings were mostly holes and patches and peeling paint, sheltering legions of cockroaches.

This was to be my home.

I wondered, for a moment, why.

Then I remembered that this is the sort of place in which most people live, in most of the world, for most of the time. This or something worse.

Then I was home.[135]

Honoring the incarnation actually took longer than this prosy reflection. On his first day in Harlem, he went to his new apartment. As a precautionary measure, he bought a "DDT bomb." After opening a window with 1950s naïveté, "so as not to DDT myself," he released the poison and sat down. "From everywhere—from every crack and corner, from the ceiling and walls and from underneath the linoleum, from out of the refrigerator and the stove, from in back of the sink and under the bathtub, from every place—came swarms of creeping, crawling vermin." He wondered how an alcoholic could distinguish the sight from delirium tremens, a surreal *delirium tremendum*. Shaken by the skin-crawling seizure of that bizarre vision, he went to a bar, had a drink, and checked into a hotel. He was not yet ready for the incarnation. The next night, encouraged by the knowledge that the high altar of St. John the Divine Cathedral practiced liturgical solidarity—cockroaches lived there as well—he swept up the dead vermin in the apartment and "slept in my new home."[136]

Stringfellow's was no less an awakening than Muriel Lester's childhood train ride through East London. His portraits of poverty have the intensified precision that comes from someone unaccustomed to its sights and smells; in Harlem, he was a de Tocqueville, an immigrant, an extraterrestrial. Poverty, he writes, is a parent whose child dies after being attacked by a rat; poverty is a widow—unlike the parable's (Luke 18:1–5)—who knows her complaints against her landlord will go unheard; poverty is a drug addict who steals from his own family, an adolescent in whom intelligence and

---

135. Ibid., 2.
136. Ibid., 23–24.

illiteracy coexist, a family living in darkness because the electricity is a fire hazard. Poverty is "the enormous burden of waiting" for a doctor, a social worker, at the employment office. Poverty is vulnerability "in its crudest forms."[137] Poverty means adults having no privacy to have sex "out of the sight of their children," whether sex is within marriage or an affair, "and so the children see that too."[138] Poverty is more than an experience of atomized individuals. It is a primordial, chaotic, anarchic, totalitarian, demonic power that seeks to neuter, neutralize, emasculate, and dehumanize. In Harlem's poverty Stringfellow first experienced the principalities and powers in concrete form.[139] Solidarity enlightened Stringfellow to institutional and social norms. He *experienced* Sobrino's words: "From the poor they receive, in a way they hardly expected, new eyes for seeing the ultimate truth of things and new energies for exploring unknown and dangerous paths."[140]

Solidarity means sharing solemn tragedy. It also means participating in divine comedy. Members of the Catholic Worker community, whose voluntary poverty helped them to taste the vulnerability of the oppressed, often found themselves mistaken for the poor. When Peter Maurin would go to deliver an address in a suburb or another city, a message often came to the Worker office that the intellectual was nowhere to be seen—the only person there was a "tramp" or a "bum," who of course, was Maurin.[141] When Day sought clothing for an impoverished woman, she was mistaken for the woman in need. Since the Workers wore donated clothes, this made sense, and Day wore the social slight as a badge of honor.[142] This, after all, was what she called "precarity,"[143] the dicey instability that goes with solidarity, a unity on Rumi's rooftop. But it was not only the Catholic Worker's leaders who practiced precarity. A popular quip said that at the daily soup kitchen the only way you could distinguish volunteers from homeless guests was that the volunteers looked "miserable and worried."[144]

Perhaps bolstering Thurman's mystic-socialist link, Day, as a young adult secular socialist reflects in earth mother, Debs-like solidarity on an early stay in jail: "I was the mother whose child had been raped and slain.

137. Ibid., 6
138. Ibid., 8.
139. Stringfellow, "Living Biblically, 59–60, "Harlem," 1346, 1348; Dancer, *Alien in a Strange Land*, 93.
140. Sobrino, *Principle of Mercy*, 150–51.
141. Day, *By Little*, 127, *On Pilgrimage*, 83–85.
142. It happened more than once: Day, *Houses of Hospitality*, 60, *By Little*, 106, *On Pilgrimage: The Sixties*, 199.
143. Day, *By Little*, 108.
144. Vishnewski, *Wings of the Dawn*, 201.

I was the mother who had borne the monster who had done it. I was even that monster, feeling in my own heart every abomination."[145] In even more dire circumstances, Muriel Lester walked among corpses near Shanghai after the Japanese invasion in 1937. She had visited before when the city was alive; now it was desolate. Packs of dogs meandered about the streets feeding on the dead. Lester wrote, "I roamed about for an hour or two, then I found myself in a part [of the city] to which the dogs had not yet eaten their way. Chinese soldiers lay all over the ground. They lay as they had fallen, as though asleep. Arms flung out, hands relaxed, a peaceful look on their faces. I went from one to another, linking them in thought to their mothers, to their homes, and to God."[146] The pacifist had found solidarity with soldiers; an Englishwoman with Chinese men; the living with the dead.

Even as he wrote of poverty, Stringfellow stood against the ideological cult of *voices for the voiceless*, insisting that the oppressed needed no middle-class white man to speak for them.[147] Against this slanderous fiction, Richard Wright tells a story from his work in a hospital basement where doctors slit the vocal cords of dogs brought from the city pound for experiments—no howls should disturb the patients: "When the dogs came to, they would lift their heads to the ceiling and gape in a soundless wail."[148] Wright found a common bond between the dogs and his fellow African American workers. It was "as though we were close kin to the animals we tended, huddled together down in the underworld corridors of the hospital separated by a vast psychological distance from the significant processes of the rest of the hospital—just as America had kept us locked in the dark underworld of American life for three hundred years."[149] To Wright, the oppressed are not *silent*; they are *silenced*. Romero, King, Day, and Stringfellow may authenticate their voices for the overprivileged that carefully calibrate a deafness that keeps them from hearing the poor. Rather than *voices for the voiceless*, James Baldwin prefers the word "witness" for King and for himself.[150] They see. They speak. They are more easily heard because they are *interpreters* who speak both the lingo of the oppressed and the lingua franca of the dominant class.

While generally deemed the province of activists, solidarity and advocacy are also norms among mystics. Catherine of Siena hears God instruct

---

145. Day, *From Union Square*, 6.
146. Lester, *Ambassador of Reconciliation*, 174.
147. Stringfellow, *My People*, 3; see Romero, *Voice of the Voiceless*.
148. Wright, *American Hunger*, 48.
149. Ibid., 59.
150. Baldwin, *Evidence of Things*, 89.

her to be like the widow with the unjust judge, praying for mercy and demanding justice from God; if Harlem's landlords were deaf, God—at least—would hear. God tells her,

> ... for it is I who gave you the very hunger and voice with which you call to me, and when I see your constancy I fulfill your desires insofar as they are ordered in accord with my will. ...
>
> So I am telling you what I want you to do. Never relax your desire to ask for my help. Never lower your voice in crying out to me to be merciful to the world. Never stop knocking at the door of my Truth. ...
>
> Through this lamentation and crying out it is my will to be merciful to the world. This is what I require of my servants and this will be a sign to me that you love me in truth.[151]

God initiates prayer and then grants the very petitions God has planted.

Union with God leads to human unity, yet union is not only achieved mystically. A second road runs through solidarity and charity. In fact, the straightest path to union with God is through one's neighbor. Gandhi says that if someone is praying and "hears the cry of another who is stung by a scorpion, she is bound to leave the prayer and run to help him"; "[p]rayer," he says, "finds fulfillment in the service of the distressed."[152] Eckhart says that if you are in a state of spiritual ecstasy, and you know a sick person needs a bowl of soup, it is "far better if you were to leave that rapture out of love and help the needy person out of greater love."[153] Bernard of Clairvaux commends the same *contemplatio interruptus*[154] as if in such moments the way to union is best achieved not with *eros* but through *philia*.

A Sufi concurs that saints would rather cast away "both worldly and religious blessings" to give bread or water to someone in need; to do so is more blessed than "one hundred thousand fasts and prayers."[155] In what could be a commentary on Francis's interactions with lepers, another Sufi proposes that when we give alms, before the money touches the poor person's palm it touches the hand of God.[156] Taking the mystical path through union to unity and echoing the pragmatism of the Epistle of James, Teresa tells her spiritual "daughters" that the "aim of prayer" is "good works"—such

---

151. Catherine, *Dialogue*, 201; see Julian's same sentiment in *Showings*, 248.
152. Gandhi, *Prayer*, 78.
153. Eckhart, *Sermons & Treatises III*, 24–25.
154. Underhill, *Mystics of the Church*, 85.
155. Helminski, *Women of Sufism*, 79.
156. Ibid., 294.

actions are the "best proof" that we "have come from God."[157] As God tells Catherine, union "gives birth to charity," the "final stage of perfect union with me. These two stages are linked together, for the one is never found without the other any more than charity for me can exist without charity for one's neighbors.... The one cannot be separated from the other."[158] Ruusbroec, like Thurman, describes an arc to faith: we move "towards God," then dwell "in God," then go "out towards all creatures, in a spirit of love toward all things"—this final stage *is the supreme summit of the inner life.*"[159]

According to this logic, activists reach the summit of the inner life without an interior experience. Vladimir Lossky says we can measure the goodness of an act by how well "it furthers our union with God."[160] John of the Cross adds, "one act done in charity is more precious in God's sight than all the visions ... possible."[161] Like Gregory of Nyssa, they treasure fruitful Leah over beautiful Rachel. Day criticizes "telescopic philanthropy"[162] because hands-on action has intrinsic spiritual power. Yehiel Mikhal of Zlotchov, in fact, argues that it has greater spiritual power than erotic union: as long as the hand of the giver touches the recipient, "Every act of charity can bring about a *sacred union.*"[163] There need be no flight of the soul to God, certainly not of the alone to the Alone. All we need to experience sacred union is one generous act.

In Franciscan lore, Brother Juniper exemplifies the eccentric, comedic, wildly munificent person in constant dervish-like charitable motion, who makes every healthy boundary-seeker grouse. Juniper's runaway compassion and profligate generosity drives him to distribute his own clothes, piece by piece. He gives away ornaments and books from the altar, the cloaks of other friars, even his own habit, "whatever he could lay his hands on." In time his uncontained giving became such a well-known norm that "When people came to beg from Brother Juniper, the other brothers would hide the things they wanted to keep so that Juniper couldn't find them."[164] As annoying as this was to his comrades, the Gita says that when "a person

---

157. Underhill, *Mysticism*, 429.
158. Catherine, *Dialogue*, 137.
159. Underhill, *Mysticism*, 436 (italics hers).
160. Lossky, *Mystical Theology*, 197.
161. John of the Cross, *Collected Works*, 187.
162. Coles, *Dorothy Day*, 145—a term coined by Charles Dickens.
163. Buber, *Tales: Early Masters*, 139 (italics mine).
164. *Little Flowers*, 226–27.

responds to the joys and sorrows of others as if they were their own," this is "the highest state of *spiritual union*."[165]

Charity sparks divine union. Mystical union sparks social action. Yet there are other gateways to communion with God and to become one of Headlam's holy communists. According to Gustavo Gutierrez, solitude sharpens the same hunger and prepares us for communion: "Without the experience of solitude there is no ... union with God or any genuine sharing with others."[166] Evagrius succinctly states this in a dialectical aphorism: "A monk is one who is separated from all and united with all."[167] Monks are "one with all persons" because they see themselves "in every person."[168] So Merton came to understand the place of solitude in reference to political history: "It is clear to me that solitude is my vocation, not as a flight from the world but as my place in the world, because for me to find solitude is only to separate myself from all the forces that destroy me and destroy history, in order to be united with the Life and Peace that build the City of God in history and rescue the children of God from hell."[169]

Underhill says that in solitary prayer we are always in communion.[170] Symeon echoes that anyone

> who has been united to God is not alone even if they are solitary
> even if one is settled in the desert, even if one is in a cave.[171]

James Douglass reflects on the purging and unifying centrality of contemplation for the activist:

> The truth which comes home in solitude is that no movement, no organization, no strategy, no individual, and most certain of all, no power in *me*, is capable of transforming the world. . . . The truth which comes home in solitude is that the struggle for liberation must begin by recognizing the terrifying emptiness and impotence of all that self of mine which is so prepared to pose on the outside as a redeemer of others. The truth which comes home in solitude is that the "I" who resists, who refuses

---

165. *Bhagavad Gita*, 6:32 (italics mine).
166. Gutierrez, *We Drink*, 85–86.
167. McGinn, *Foundations of Mysticism*, 157.
168. Vivian, *Becoming Fire*, 448.
169. Merton, *Sign of Jonas*, 251.
170. Underhill, *Ways of the Spirit*, 182.
171. Symeon, *Divine Eros*, 205.

to live in fear of the state's punishment, is in reality chained to the cell of its own fears and self-fantasies.[172]

As Douglass found, contemplation is a purging desert.

There are not billions of solitudes confined in pods flying into space in billions of directions nor are there a myriad of solitudes crammed inhumanly next to each other like slaves stacked in a ship. For Merton, solitude is not a private possession: "There is One Solitude in which all persons are at once together and alone."[173] In his "Notes on a Philosophy of Solitude," he says the purpose of solitude is not to help us find ways that we are different from or better than other people; rather, perhaps "confusedly," we enter "*a solitude that is really shared by everyone.*"[174] Union with God is a fraudulent fantasy without a binding unity with humanity in which the *shalom* of one depends upon the *salaam* of all. As King wrote from the Birmingham jail in response to accusations that he was an "outside agitator": "Injustice anywhere is a threat to justice everywhere. We are caught in an inescapable network of mutuality tied in a single garment of destiny. Whatever affects one directly, affects all indirectly."[175] Indeed, we are even closer to one another. Julian asks: "what can make me love my fellow Christians more than to see in God that loves all who will be saved, all of them as it were one soul?"[176] Shmelke of Nikolsburg, pondering how to love a pain-in-the-neck neighbor, says, "Love your neighbor like something which you yourself are":

> For all souls are one. Each is a spark from the original soul, and this soul is wholly inherent in all souls, just as your soul is in all the members of your body. It may come to pass that your hand makes a mistake and strikes you. But would you then take a stick and chastise your hand, because it lacked understanding, and so increase your pain? It is the same if your neighbor, who is of one soul with you, wrongs you for lack of understanding. If you punish him, you only hurt yourself.[177]

Seraphim of Sarov, linking Edenic intimacy, universal solidarity, and human physicality, says, "your neighbor is your own flesh."[178]

---

172. Douglass, *Resistance and Contemplation*, 140.
173. Merton, *Love and Living*, 17.
174. Merton, *Disputed Questions*, 174 (italics his).
175. King, *Testament of Hope*, 290.
176. Julian, *Showings*, 241.
177. Buber, *Tales: Early Masters*, 190.
178. Moore, *St. Seraphim*, 123–24.

When he speaks of human unity, Eckhart inverts the meaning of loving others as yourself: until you love others as yourself, you don't yet love yourself.[179] If you favor someone, anyone, even (or especially) yourself, over others, "you have never for a single instant looked into this simple ground" that is God.[180] Contradicting the evangelical claim that our number one awakening is to know Christ as our personal savior, Eckhart says that it is far more wondrous that God is "the common Savior of the entire world"; we are more deeply indebted to God for loving and saving the world than if God "had saved me alone."[181]

Union with God, while unforgettable, is a beginning. What Dag Hammarskjöld calls "God's marriage to the soul" is also "a union with other people."[182] King had his metaphorical dream, Gandhi a literal one. In one of Hammarskjöld's dreams, "I walked with God through the deep places of creation; past walls that receded and gates that opened, through hall after hall of silence, darkness and refreshment—the dwelling place of souls acquainted with light and warmth—until, around me, was an infinity into which we all flowed together and lived anew, like the rings made by raindrops falling upon wide expanses of calm dark waters."[183] The same ebb and flow that moves to God alone and God in-humanity encompasses God-in-creation. The movement Gutierrez describes between solitude and communion applies equally to that which lies beyond activism's humanocentric hermeneutic—communion with creation. Gershom Scholem notes that in Hebrew Scripture and Jewish history *redemption* is a purely political concept. But in Jewish mysticism redemption becomes a cosmic reality.[184]

Just as *eros*, *philia*, and *agape* are interrelated, love of God, neighbor, and creation know no single spark from a big bang. Just as the incarnation hints at deification, creation points toward panentheism. Teilhard de Chardin says that when he first contemplated the proposition that God is still creating the world, "I looked around and I saw, as though in an ecstasy, that through all nature I was immersed in God."[185] As Eckhart says the soul is pregnant with Christ, Teilhard says that "the universe is physically impregnated to the very core of its matter" by Christ's nature.[186] Krishna is in every

---

179. Eckhart, *Sermons & Treatises II*, 84.
180. Eckhart, *Sermons & Treatises I*, 116.
181. Eckhart, *Sermons & Treatises III*, 34.
182. Hammarskjöld, *Markings*, 160.
183. Ibid., 118.
184. Scholem, *Major Trends*, 305.
185. Teilhard, *Writings*, 49.
186. Ibid., 96.

creature;[187] the kabbalist's divine sparks are in all beings. When Traherne writes that God's "Glory," "Goodness," and "Wisdom" shine everywhere,[188] he sees through the eyes of the rabbis and the Gita.

Union with God can create a sense of the universe as "an integrated and unified whole."[189] Our alienated, insular self becomes self-in-relationship.[190] We discover and revel in God as the single center, Underhill's "Magnet of the Universe."[191] In rising prose, the usually plain-spoken scholar says, "Thus does Dante, initiated into Paradise, see the whole Universe laugh with delight as it glorifies God: and the awful countenance of Perfect Love adorned with smiles. Thus the souls of the great theologians dance to music and laughter in the Heaven of the Sun; the loving seraphs in their ecstatic joy, whirl about the Being of God."[192]

Union, though, is always on a roof-edge. It is the *already* that demands the *not yet*, a revelation that demands the revolution. Describing God as the "one who consummates all things," Teilhard says, "the universal convergence of all created spirit is effected in sweat and tears,"[193] the sweat of activists, the tears of those who pray. The union experienced by a few mystics at a few times in human history will, at the omega, be shown to be a foretaste for all creation. It is *then* that all things shall be well. Until *then* moments of ecstatic *eros*, extraordinary mystical leaps, and common every day charity are the doorways to sacred union.

ANOTHER ME

What *eros* enacts in ecstasy, and *philia* and *agape* embody in action, the rhetorical imagination realizes with words. In ethical pronouncements and mystical prayers, the New Testament blurs pronouns to heighten both divine union and human unity. In Jesus' farewell discourse he says that he is in God, "and you in me, and I in you" (John 14:20); in his high priestly prayer, he prays that his followers may be one as he is one with God (John 17:11). In an ecstatic insight, Paul says, "it is no longer I who live, but it is Christ who lives in me" (Gal 2:20). When, in his personal letter seeking manumission for Onesimus, he asks Philemon to "welcome him as you would welcome

---

187. *Bhagavad Gita*, 10:39, 15:12–4.
188. Traherne, *Centuries*, 18.
189. Maslow, *Religions*, 59.
190. Happold, *Mysticism*, 53.
191. Underhill, *Ways of the Spirit*, 57.
192. Underhill, *Mysticism*, 438.
193. Teilhard, *Writings*, 91.

me" (17), Paul is not appealing to lacy etiquette; he seeks Philemon's wholesale conversion—the faith to see a social inferior as a peer or even a spiritual master. In a recitation on "mutual love," the Epistle to the Hebrews offers a sanctifying anamnesis: "remember those who are in prison, as though you were in prison with them; those who are being tortured, as though you yourselves were being tortured" (Heb 13:3). In a passage envisioning Christ perpetually on the streets, Jesus says that nations are judged according to what they do to "me" (Matt 25:31–45). Pronouns blur. Ethical injunctions are mystical utterances.

One of the themes of *The Theologia Germanica* is the transformation of the I-me-mine axis. Adam's primary sin is his assumption of his "'I' and his 'Me' and his 'Mine.'"[194] "The I, self-will, self-serving, egoism, Mine, nature, false light, devil, sin" are all "one and the same thing."[195] The I-me-mine was the first "apostasy" and remains the primary cause of sin. Silesius writes that nothing casts us as deeply "into hell's very jaws/As two detested words, and they are *mine* and *yours*."[196] The I-me-mine is so deviously subtle that it even twists our desire for sanctification. Instead of seeking to become Christ, we want to be an unmoved mover, a disengaged deity, an eternally imperturbable God. Or if we can *only* be Christ, it is the "postressurection Christ," not Christ sent, Christ homeless, or Christ crucified.[197]

The remedy for the I-me-mine axis of sin lies in the same problematic pronouns as Christ leeches them of their poison and leavens them with grace. "If you want to come to me, then renounce yourself and follow after Me"—anyone who fails to renounce all, loses all, and is "not worthy of Me," nor of being "My disciple."[198] In life freed from its palatial prison of first-person pronouns, "all matters of self and the I and the Me have been surrendered and abandoned." No longer do we assert love for "this or that;" we love goodness solely for goodness' sake.[199] Underhill calls this purifying purgation "the giving up of I-hood."[200] In complex masculinist language, Eckhart prescribes a way toward transformation: "You should wholly sink away from your youness and dissolve into God's Hisness, and your 'yours' and God's 'His' should become so completely one 'Mine' that with God you

---

194. *Theologia Germanica*, 62.
195. Ibid., 129–30.
196. Silesius, *Cherubinic Wanderer*, 117 (italics mine).
197. *Theologia Germanica*, 124.
198. Ibid., 83.
199. Ibid., 104.
200. Underhill, *Mysticism*, 317.

understand God's unbecome Isness and God's nameless Nothingness."[201] The deconstruction of first-person pronouns is the beginning of wisdom, sanctification, and salvation.

The Sufi tradition also decries the I-me-mine triad. Rumi says that only God has the right to say "I."[202] Ibn Al 'Arabi lays out four steps to transformation: 1) in Sharia (Islam's law code), there is yours and mine; 2) on the Sufi path, mine is yours and yours is mine; 3) when we reach Truth, there is no mine and no yours; and 4) in true knowledge there is no me and no you.[203] In fact, "through Me God hears, and through Me God sees."[204] Zeynep Hatun, a fifteenth-century Turkish Sufi woman, writes,

> I am a fountain, You are my water
> I flow from You to You
> I am an eye, You are my light
> I look from You to You . . .
> I am a traveler, You are my road
> I go from You to You.[205]

As if in dialogue with her, God speaks in one of Rumi's poems:

> I am dust particles in sunlight.
> I am the round sun. . . .
> I am morning mist,
> And the breathing of evening.
> I am wind in the top of a grove,
> And surf on the cliff.
> Mast, rudder, helmsman, and keel,
> I am also the coral reef they founder on.
> I am a tree with a trained parrot in its branches.
> Silence, thought, and voice
> . . . I am all orders of being,
> The circling galaxy,
> The evolutionary intelligence,
> The life and the falling away . . .
> What is and what isn't. You
> Who know Jelaluddin, You
> The One in all, say who
> I am. Say I am You.[206]

201. Eckhart, *Sermons & Treatises II*, 333.
202. Rumi, *Poet and Mystic*, 145.
203. Fadiman and Frager, *Essential Sufism*, 13.
204. al-Kalabadhi, *Doctrine of the Sufis*, 116.
205. Helminski, *Women of Sufism*, 87.
206. Rumi, *Say I Am You*, 81.

With God, there is no "I" or "You."[207] God tells Catherine of Siena that her soul is "another me,"[208] precisely what Jesus says of the hungry, the sick, the poor, the stranger, and the prisoner. Mechtild of Magdeburg says that the soul tells God, "your blood and mine is one and undivided; your garment and mine is one and immaculate; your mouth and mine is one bliss."[209] Like Ezekiel's promise that God will replace hearts of stone with flesh (Ezek 11:19) Catherine hears God say, "Just as I took your heart from you the other day, so I am now giving you my heart."[210] Thomas Kelly writes that there comes a time in prayer, like the oscillation of voice in prophetic speech, when "it is not easy to say *who* is speaking, we or, an Other through us."[211] The blurring of pronouns is yet another manifestation of our oneness with all things. Al-Hallaj says, "I am the one I love, and the one I love is I; we are two souls fused in one body. When you see me, you see God. When you see God, You see us."[212] For John of the Cross, love discovers unity: "Love produces such likeness in this transformation of lovers that one can say each is the other and both are one."[213]

To reorder pronouns is to re-envision relationships. Traherne says, "Till you see that the world is yours, you cannot weigh the greatness of sin, nor the misery of your fall, nor prize your Redeemer's love."[214] When pronouns blur, we blur Christ with all people in need; all of them are, to use Catherine's phrase, "another me." When Abba Agathon says he will exchange his body for a leper's, it is because the leper is another Agathon, another Christ, another me. This was Merton's spiritual exercise during the Cold War: "When we love the other, the enemy, then we obtain from God the key to an understanding of who they are, and who we are."[215] Moshe Leib of Sasov shifts our perspective on empathy when he says that we can never "share" another's suffering, not because we lack empathy, but because "It is my own sorrow; how can I help but suffer it?"[216]

The *Theologia Germanica* describes what happens when we enact this oneness: "if someone killed a divinized person a hundred times over and

---

207. Fadiman and Frager, *Essential Sufism*, 118; Buber, *Ecstatic Utterances*, 14.
208. Catherine, *Dialogue*, 26, 181.
209. Buber, *Ecstatic Utterances*, 60.
210. Ibid., 107.
211. Kelly, *Eternal Promise*, 33–34 (italics his).
212. Buber, *Ecstatic Utterances*, 21.
213. John of the Cross, *Collected Works*, 455.
214. Traherne, *Centuries*, 58.
215. Merton, *Cold War*, 30.
216. Buber, *Tales: Later Masters*, 86.

the victim should come to life again," they "would still harbor love for [the] killer, and this despite the injustice, evil and wickedness committed"; they "would wish the assailant well," and give the assailant "the very best, as soon as [the] assailant is ready to receive it and accept it." When Christ calls Judas "friend, it is as if he said: 'You hate Me, you are My foe, but I love you, I am your friend and you wish Me, desire for Me, and do to Me the very worst you can. But I will desire and wish for you the very best and I would give it to you and do it to you, if you were prepared to receive and accept it.'"[217] These are the words King puts in the mouths of those with soul force as they speak to the practitioners of raw force:

> Do to us what you will, and we shall continue to love you. . . . Bomb our homes and threaten our children, and, as difficult as it is, we will still love you. Send your hooded perpetrators of violence into our communities at the midnight hour and drag us out on some wayside road and leave us half-dead as you beat us, and we will still love you. . . . But be assured that we'll wear you down by our capacity to suffer, and one day we will win our freedom. We will not only win freedom for ourselves; we will so appeal to your heart and conscience that we will win you in the process, and our victory will be a double victory.[218]

The journey from selfishness and self-exaltation to communion/communism, from *I-me-mine* to *another me* is encapsulated in a mystical experience: "There came upon me a beyond-seeing, a beyond-desire, and a beyond-understanding. I found in myself a forgetfulness of all things and a self-forgetfulness: a knowing of you alone, God. There came upon me a vision of your eternity and a discovery of your blessedness. I found myself fixed on you alone. I came out of myself and found myself in you and you in me. I found myself one being with you."[219] Eckhart says, "you have never truly learnt to love yourself—unless you love all people as yourself, all people in one person, that person being God and human."[220] Discovering that for God our soul is "another Me," and that Jesus sees each person—in prayer, in prison, at war, at church—as "another me," means that when we share that transforming vision and identity we touch the hem of the realm. If only we could see without the I-me-mine axis, we would become another Me.

---

217. *Theologia Germanica*, 104–5.
218. King, *Trumpet of Conscience*, 74–75.
219. McGinn, *Harvest of Mysticism*, 328.
220. Eckhart, *Sermons & Treatises II*, 84.

MENDING

Someone asks Abba Mius a pharisaic question: does God—do we—accept a sinner's repentance? Like a good rabbi, Mius answers with a question: "if your cloak is torn, do you throw it away?" "No," came the reply, "I mend it and use it again." Question answered. But like Jesus dropping verbal bread crumbs so his dull-witted disciples can catch the full gist of a parable, Mius explains his allegory: "If you are careful about your cloak, will not God be equally careful about every creature?"[221]

If erotic union with God is unthinkable yet not unknowable, the mending of creation is impossible but not undoable. As Golding's *The Inheritors* hints, the need to mend relationships began at the dawn of evolution as creatures claw at the fabric of creation and tear each other limb from limb. In the biblical telling of evolution, Adam and Eve sew fig leaves to try to cover their egocentricity (Gen 3:7), counterproductively tipping God off, and God—before driving them out of Eden—sews garments for the earth's first family/first sinners to cover their shame (Gen 3:21).[222] So Day liked to quote Julian of Norwich: the worst has happened and it has been mended.[223] But this mending is not only the work of God. William Penn says that "true godliness" does not distract people from the world; it "excites their endeavors to mend it."[224] The oft-overlooked pattern begun in Eden is not solely a free fall of frenetically caustic free will; it is creation's repair. The oft-overlooked pattern of mystical union is that it leads not only to a posture of solidarity but also to the menial handiwork of mending.

The kabbalistic tradition of *tiqqun* is an extension of God's handiwork at the frontier of Eden. For the kabbalists, however, mending begins in the act of creation—God contracts to make room for creation, containers of divine sparks shatter, and divinity sprays wildly everywhere, implanting itself into everything.[225] This is what Merton discovers at Polonnaruwa—all matter is charged with divinity. This is Isaiah's realization—heaven and earth are full of God's glory (Isa 6:1–8). Yet the kabbalists go further. From the beginning, redeeming the sparks, *tiqqun*, mending, has been the sacred work of all people of faith.

The Gospels, tales of faith, and hagiographies of saints embody the work of *tiqqun*. Just as Jesus mends wherever he goes—forgiving sinners,

---

221. Ward, *Sayings of the Desert*, 150.
222. Brueggemann, *Genesis*, 50.
223. Day, *By Little*, 105.
224. Jones, *Essential Writings*, 22.
225. Buber, *Tales: Early Masters*, 16, 29.

healing the sick, feeding the hungry, finding the lost, rebuking the judgmental, and teaching the ignorant—so the faithful extend this apostolic work. In the legends of Columba of Iona, the saint's actions mimic the signs and wonders of Moses, Elijah, and Jesus. Like Moses, he brings water from a rock.[226] Like Elijah, he ends a drought[227] and raises a boy from the dead.[228] Like Jesus, he facilitates a huge catch of fish,[229] turns water into wine,[230] calms a storm,[231] and in a twist on Jesus' curse of a fig tree, makes a tree's bitter fruit sweet.[232] Like a zaddik, he relieves a woman in labor of her extraordinary pain.[233] Columba's works are sometimes epic, sometimes intimate. To help the hungry feed themselves, he multiplies a cattle herd[234] and makes a crop grow with miraculous speed.[235] As God toys with the primordial Leviathan like a "rubber ducky,"[236] Columba saves a swimmer from a "water beast."[237] Finding a third way beyond Macarius' blessing *or* curse of snakes, Columba blesses the earth to leech the snakes of their poison.[238] He keeps sailors safe by changing the direction of the wind, sometimes in two directions at once.[239] He even intervenes in a marriage so that a wife will once again have sex with her husband![240]

But mending is more than acting with narrow-beamed, laser-like precision to quench a sacred thirst, heal a dread disease, or soothe a violent demon. Zaddikim redeem sparks wherever they go. Zevi Hirsh of Zhydatchov says that "when travelers walk in the ways of God, then whether they know it or not all the holy sparks which cling to the herbs of the field and the trees of the forest rush forth and attach themselves to such people, and this illuminates them with a great light."[241] Mending takes place in ordinary ac-

226. Adomnán, *St. Columba*, 161–62.
227. Ibid., 199–200.
228. Ibid., 179–80.
229. Ibid., 168.
230. Ibid., 154–55.
231. Ibid., 163.
232. Ibid., 155.
233. Ibid., 194.
234. Ibid., 170.
235. Ibid., 155–56.
236. Jon D. Levenson, quoted in Brueggemann, *Theology*, 538.
237. Adomnán, *St. Columba*, 175–76.
238. Ibid., 177.
239. Ibid., 165–66.
240. Ibid., 194–95.
241. Buber, *Tales: Later Masters*, 217.

tions: "You can mend the cosmos by anything you do—even eating. Do not imagine that God wants you to eat for mere pleasure or to fill your belly. No, the purpose is mending." So before eating, pray. "Then by eating, you bring forth sparks that cleave to your soul."[242] Kabbalism calls us to contemplative awareness: "When you desire to eat or drink or to fulfill other worldly desires, and you focus your awareness on the love of God, then you elevate that physical desire to spiritual desire. Thereby you draw out the holy spark that dwells within. You bring forth holy sparks from the material world. There is no path greater than this. For wherever you go and whatever you do—even mundane activities—you serve God."[243] In Buddhist thought, this is what happens when people master their thinking:

> However many species of living beings there are—whether born from eggs, from the womb, from moisture, or spontaneously; whether they have form or do not have form; whether they have perceptions or do not have perceptions; or whether it cannot be said of them that they have perceptions or that they do not have perceptions, we must lead all these beings to the ultimate nirvana so that they can be liberated. And when this innumerable, immeasurable, infinite number of beings has become liberated, we do not, in truth, think that a single being has been liberated.[244]

This is Origen's restoration of creation.[245] This is Isaac of Nineveh's charitable heart. This is how we redeem sparks. Each act of mending has the same potential for sacred union as erotic ecstasy with God. All mystical-ethical questions become one: how do we mend all that is fragmented, frayed, and torn—every system of oppression, every threat of abuse, every whiff of spiritual superiority, and every inward-spiraling, self-centered, implosive movement in a single soul?

Do all agree the world needs mending? Yes! But do any agree how to do it? Conflicting theologies, ideologies, ethical systems, and theories of social change tear at alliances and coalitions for peace and justice. Perhaps especially among those who engage most passionately in social transformation, there are powerful, even violent, arguments. This was the tragedy of the ideological tensions among civil rights groups. As Pauli Murray says of one conflict among reformist-but-divided African Americans, "self-inflicted wounds within a group deeply committed to the same objective

---

242. Matt, *Essential Kabbalah*, 149.
243. Ibid., 151.
244. Nhat Hanh, *Diamond that Cuts*, 4.
245. McGinn, *Foundations of Mysticism*, 115.

are often more painful and difficult to bear than hurts imposed by enemies, because they have the effect of dividing one against oneself in ways seldom achieved by an outsider."[246] Nothing undermines, erodes, and corrodes unity as effectively. Great minds from Augustine to Marx have sketched widely disparate views about how and why the world is broken, and if and how it can be made whole. In the post-Enlightenment unconscious consciousness of Western civilization, progress—while frustratingly uneven—is deigned inevitable. While sometimes in its thrall, King challenged this assumption, and its head-patting, silky-smooth advice to go slow and wait patiently for Godot.[247] So different theologies and ideologies of social change should not become swords and spears or sticks and stones to turn against one another, but plowshares and pruning hooks with which to mend the earth.

During the anti-Vietnam War movement, A. J. Muste's activism modeled *tiqqun* in building coalitions among startlingly disparate groups. He initiated a policy of nonexclusion among lifelong radicals, first-time protesters, Quakers, anarchists, pacifists, communists, labor organizers, and liberals—as long as they shared a common goal and willingly worked together, he welcomed them.[248] Giving greater integrity to nonexclusion was Muste's lifelong aggravation with the all-talk, no-walk ethical pronouncements of the church and his experiences of deceit and backstabbing betrayal with the secular Left.[249] His younger colleagues marveled that although Muste could have played each card, he never claimed to be more-Left-than-thou, or older-and-wiser-than-thou.[250] Accused by Niebuhr of being rigidly and naïvely principled, he became a master of holistic pragmatism. In this regard, he differed from Gandhi. Unlike Muste, who welcomed skilled and unskilled hands to chip away at injustice, Gandhi insisted that all activists practice complete spiritual consistency. For him there can be no satyagraha [truth force] without ahimsa [a nonviolent heart],[251] no social transformation without an inner revolution, no *basileia* without *metanoia*. For Gandhi, the addictive and seductive need for the holy grail of immediate results is a deluding mirage on the road to Swaraj and its multiple mendings of caste, class, and religion.

Although Day worked with Muste and admired Gandhi, the Catholic Worker's quasievangelical one-person-at-a-time personalist philosophy

246. Murray, *Autobiography*, 226.
247. King, *Testament of Hope*, 292–93.
248. Cornell and McReynolds, Untitled, 8.
249. Robinson, *Abraham Went Out*, 49–61.
250. Ibid., 160, 187; Cornell and McReynolds, Untitled, 8.
251. Gandhi, *Non-violent*, 381.

uses small-scale stitchery to repair the torn cosmic cloak. Day's simple ethic to diminish the sum total of evil and increase the sum total of goodness[252] empowers those with the least social capital: anyone can increase goodness by an inch, an ell, or an iota. Yet the Worker was—and is—multidimensional: Houses of Hospitality practice the traditional physical works of mercy (feeding the hungry, clothing the naked, sheltering the homeless, visiting the sick, ransoming the prisoner), a counterfriction to the machine so gentle that the machine pays it no heed. The Catholic Worker newspaper and its proworker, antiwar protests were spiritual works of mercy (admonishing the sinner, instructing the ignorant, counseling the doubtful, comforting the sorrowful).[253] The Workers' roundtable discussions provided a designated verbal boxing ring to wrestle with social analysis, political strategy, and campaign tactics. But, as Maurin insists, mending requires annunciation—valleys lifted up, mountains laid low, the rich cast down, and the lowly raised. Farming communes—forerunners of ethical land use and environmental sustainability—were the foundation of a society in which it would be "easier for people to be good."[254]

Day's ministry, like her experience of the Eucharist, was often more empty ritual than fulfilling kiss. In mystical union, the divine kiss is heavenly bliss. In Day's experience with lepers, the divine is not a very good kisser. Yet according to Eckhart, Bernard, John of the Cross, and the kabbalists, even without a sense of satisfaction, Day actualized sacred union. As Tutu felt ashamed of his tears, Day often felt disappointed in herself. And this was all *after* the deepest division in Day's soul had been mended. During her secular radical days, her single-minded devotion to justice sustained her with a deep purpose: loving her neighbor as herself. Conversion was conceived with her pregnancy. The visceral conviction that she was being punished with infertility for her sins—divorce, abortion, and nonmarital sex—made her pregnancy more-than-usually profound and drove her to take long devotional walks on beaches thanking God.[255] She had another epiphany when she gave birth.

> If I had written the greatest book, composed the greatest symphony, painted the most beautiful painting or carved the most exquisite figure, I could not have felt more the exalted creator than when they placed my child in my arms.[256]

252. Day, *By Little*, 335.
253. Ibid., 98.
254. Day, *Long Loneliness*, 170.
255. Day, *From Union Square*, 123, *Long Loneliness*, 133.
256. Day, *Thérèse*, v.

> Such a great feeling of happiness and joy filled me that I was hungry for Someone to thank, to love, even to worship, for so great a good that had been bestowed upon me.[257]

> The final object of this love and gratitude was God. No human creature could receive or contain so vast a flood of love and joy as I often felt after the birth of my child. With this came the need to worship, to adore.[258]

But this newly discovered joy created conflict with her atheist partner; baptizing their daughter killed their relationship.

This was torment enough, but Day thought she had lost still more—her principles, her passion, and her ministry. Nothing she knew of religious institutions made her think she could smuggle her hunger for justice through church doors. Her two loves—God and neighbor—like the curtain in the temple, were torn in two. Her soul ached when her activist life died. After covering a 1932 hunger march as a journalist, she broke down, wept, and prayed.[259] Shortly thereafter, she met Maurin, who became a Shams to her Rumi. Maurin instructed her in an entirely new catechism that united her loves of justice, solidarity, precarity, anarchy, protest, prayer, and worship. Day had experienced *philia*, *agape*, and *eros* as discombobulating forces. Only when she discovered that the door to heaven and the way to justice are one could she give birth to a movement. Only then did worship and revolution become one kiss.

In contrast to the Catholic Worker's hands-on work, Muste's grand designs, and Gandhi's strict ethical code, Stringfellow offers a perfect paradox. Adamantly rejecting every ideology as an idol,[260] he believed, with Bonhoeffer, that all ethics are contextual—in perpetually unique circumstances people must act according to their conscience.[261] Stringfellow's view of principalities led him to be absolutely pessimistic about institutional change while being radically hopeful about the power of impractical, purely spiritual resistance—as if agreeing with Merton that the useless has its use. This he learned from European resistance movements to Nazism.[262] While Philip Hallie came to believe that Trocmé and Le Chambon were magnificently

---

257. Ibid., vi.
258. Day, *Long Loneliness*, 139.
259. Ibid., 165–66; Coles, *Dorothy Day*, 11.
260. Stringfellow, *Free in Obedience*, 31, 57–58.
261. Stringfellow, *Dissenter*, 160–63, *Conscience and Obedience*, 24–27.
262. Stringfellow, *Ethic for Christians*, 117–19, 125–26.

inspiring but ultimately ineffective—only brute force could defeat brutality—Stringfellow insists that resistance itself is almighty.

Niebuhr believed that liberals conflate the moral malleability of persuadable people with reason-resistant, conscience-proof institutions that could only be changed by naked, steely force. Stringfellow was convinced that institutions, corporations, and nations could not even be coerced. While in the 1960s he shared for a moment the common civil rights era faith in structural change,[263] in the next decade, his attitude hardened as he came to believe that each institution is an amorally impregnable silo.[264] To him, all principalities are a product of the fall.[265] It is the very nature of every institution to serve only itself; to use Paul Tillich's term, the *ultimate concern* (*only* concern) of each ideology, nation, corporation, and institution is its own wealth, status, and power. If asked if institutions could be mended, Stringfellow would have uttered a resounding *no*. In Stringfellow's universe, institutions serve only death.[266]

Stringfellow would have disdained Muste's dream that the US could repent and become a savior nation.[267] To Stringfellow, the US always deludes itself in its *mirror, mirror on the wall* that we are the fairest, the freest, the greatest, and the most ethical nation of them all. The US, as he says, sees itself as "Zion"[268] when, in reality, it will always be oppressive "Babylon."[269] He supported the civil rights movement but believed racism was indestructible. White supremacy, the dominant ethic in American history,[270] would simply change forms. Harlem might gentrify (something Stringfellow never envisioned), but America would become Harlem—oppressed by principalities beyond its people's control.[271] So, while he supported protests, voting rights, and legislative reforms, he did not believe they could change institutions. Legislative niceties could paint a happy face on human oppression, but there would be no deep or lasting social change, no justice rolling down like waters from city halls, state capitols, or even heaven.

---

263. Stringfellow, *Imposters of God*, 65.
264. Stringfellow, *Ethic for Christians*, 81.
265. Ibid., 71, Stringfellow, *Second Birthday*, 61, *Politics of Spirituality*, 20.
266. Stringfellow, *Ethic for Christians*, 67; Stringfellow and Towne, *Suspect Tenderness*, 67–68.
267. Muste, *Not by Might*, 91–92.
268. Stringfellow, *Ethic for Christians*, 14.
269. Ibid., 32.
270. Stringfellow, *Conscience and Obedience*, 96, *Dissenter*, 120.
271. Stringfellow, "Harlem," 1348.

Ironically, while Stringfellow believed that million man marches, grassroots movements, and electoral politics could not defeat the power of death, death is powerless against a simple, primal reliance on the Word of God.[272] Somehow, inexplicably but empirically, faith confounds death and the Word of God triumphs.[273] So Stringfellow supported the Catonsville Nine, whose antiwar protest—pouring pig's blood on draft files, "a liturgical act to exorcise the hosts of death . . . and proclaim the efficacy of the resurrection"—was, like a spiritual work of mercy, symbolic, capable only of giving the Selective Service System a minor case of institutional indigestion.[274]

While Stringfellow refers to his life with Anthony Towne as "monastic,"[275] Merton's monastic ministry was political primarily in the feminist sense that the personal is political. Often struggling with his vocation's disjointed connection to society, he groped and scrambled to engage issues in politically meaningful ways. He complained that it was "not enough" to practice a "spiritual" witness, or the then-conventional pacifism of sectarian withdrawal. But neither did he find it enough "simply to stand up and say that the world is wicked and is traveling toward an apocalyptic doom and that the Christian is an individual witness, or the Church is a witness purely and simply calling people to repentance before it is too late."[276] Yet even as he complained he was a "political prisoner" of his monastery,[277] he reaffirmed his call to monastic life as one of deep solidarity: "I believe my vocation is essentially that of a pilgrim and an exile in life, that I have no proper place in the world, but for that reason I am in some sense to be the friend and brother of people everywhere, especially those who are exiles and pilgrims like myself."[278] This is what John Howard Griffin saw as Merton's capacity for compassion and why Eldridge Cleaver, in his black power manifesto *Soul on Ice,* called Merton his "brother."[279]

According to Merton, contemplatives understand that "God works in history." They see God less as a "static essence, or as an intellectual light, or as a nameless ground of being"—rather, they find themselves "face to face with the Lord of History and with Christ, the King and Savior, the Light of

---

272. Stringfellow, *Private and Public Faith,* 63. His definition of the Word is elusive (*Conscience and Obedience,* 14).

273. Stringfellow, *Simplicity of Faith,* 32.

274. Stringfellow, "Acts of the Apostles," 341–42.

275. Stringfellow, *Simplicity of Faith,* 52.

276. Merton, *Nonviolent Alternative* 90. Yet at times Merton did precisely this. See Commins, *Spiritual People,* 279–92.

277. Merton, *Turning Toward the World,* 34.

278. Merton, *Cold War,* 129.

279. Cleaver, *Soul on Ice,* 32–34.

the world." To Merton, "we must comfort Christ in the awful paradoxes of our day, in which we see that our society is being judged."[280] This is the God that calls Isaiah and Jeremiah to mend the world by judging it.

On a practical level, Merton became a spiritual director to activists.[281] He wrote voluminously on justice and peace, signed political statements, and pinned a peace button to his monk's robe.[282] But his specifically monastic work was in acts of mystical mending in which he addressed the stale animosity between Christians East and West, the cultural divide of Americas North and South, and the Cold War split between communism and capitalism. Far from the corridors of power and the barricades of protest, Merton returns in one of his journals to the idea that the best way a monk can say *we shall overcome* is to defeat divisions internally. Not in an ecclesiastical position to initiate ecumenical dialogue, Merton says, "If I can unite *in myself,* in my own spiritual life, the thought of the East and the West of the Greek and Latin [theologians], I will create in myself a reunion of the divided Church and from that unity in myself can come the exterior and visible unity of the Church." Unity could not be achieved with ecclesiastical imperialism, one side "imposing" its will on the other; rather, "We must contain both in ourselves and transcend both in Christ."[283]

If that was a difficult task in ecumenism's Jurassic period, it was still viable, since all churches claim a common cornerstone. A more difficult challenge was to unite an ignorant, arrogant North America with its exploited and psychologically strip-mined neighbors to the south. Merton had a long-established sympathy for Latin America—corresponding with its poets and translating their poetry as they translated his. He describes his "vocation" as "American—*to see and to understand and to have in my self the life and the roots and the belief and the destiny and the Orientation of the whole hemisphere.*" This posture was "an expansion of something of God, of Christ, that the world has not yet found out—something that is only now, after hundreds of years, coming to maturity!" One had to embrace "all the extremes and have them in oneself without confusion—without eclecticism, without dilettantism, without false mysticism, without being torn apart." No fragment could be mistaken for the whole: "Not Spanish colonial Catholicism, not 19th century republicanism, not agrarian radicalism . . . not the

---

280. Merton, *Cold War,* 51.

281. Merton, *Hidden Ground,* passim; Forest, "Thomas Merton's Struggle," 15–53; Commins, *Spiritual People,* 341–49.

282. Twomey, *Thomas Merton,* 25.

283. Merton, *Search for Solitude,* 87.

Indianism of Mexico—but all of it, everything. To be oneself a whole hemisphere and help the hemisphere to realize its own destiny."[284]

If churches and continents were fractured, at least they were not caught up in a constant involuntary reflux of hostility. For half a century, the US and USSR battled through surrogates and teetered near cataclysm. Détente provided occasional respite, but entente was unimaginable. Merton, saying "I don't want to be part of either 'we,'"[285] found both sides culpable. In an essay on Boris Pasternak, Merton says the West wanted to aim Pasternak's social critique at communism, but his truths—like a two-edged sword—equally condemned capitalism.[286] If Merton was to find unity for I-me-mine superpowers, he had to understand the Soviet Union, and the only way to understand an enemy is to "love," and not with "a prejudiced and jingoistic love" that gently massages malevolence into condescension. Instead, "I must unite in myself all that is good in both Russia and America, see all that is vain and false in both, in myself, purge that out of myself."[287] Until churches, continents, and ideological antagonists could unite in a person, they could not become one body, one hemisphere, or one world.

Merton, Muste, Day, Gandhi, and Stringfellow all saw the world's need to be mended, but they never tried to reach an agreement about how to mend it. Each in their own way took part in what Maurin would call roundtable discussions for the "clarification of thought,"[288] and each went about their own holy business. Arguing about strategy would have been like having a fistfight to decide the best image for divine union. Rather, each of them found their *political vocation* and each mended. Reconciling rifts, healing hemispheres, brainstorming sophisticated strategies, defeating almost almighty powers with a prayer, in macro- and micromending moments of sacred union, they became, like the ideologies from which Muste forged a broad coalition, allies seeking the realm. The work, after all, is endless, and there are sparks everywhere waiting to be redeemed.

MEDITATION: THE AFRICA DAY DANCE

There were inklings that this was not a typical Episcopal church, moments that leapt like fulfillments of visions—wolf and lamb nestled together, peoples from many nations climbing a mountain to learn God's ways, dancers

---

284. Ibid., 168–69 (italics his).
285. Merton, *Turning Toward the World*, 20.
286. Merton, *Literary Essays*, 80.
287. Merton, *Search for Solitude*, 191.
288. Day, *Loaves and Fishes*, 7.

moving joyfully, nimbly, uninhibitedly around God's throne. There was the conversation I observed my first year as I stood with three young adult parishioners—Julio from Guatemala, Roxanne from Trinidad, and Leng from Singapore—and listened in pleased, dumb ignorance as they conversed in Spanish. There was the appearance of a soccer ball—an earthy, unifying icon—at a parish picnic when two Africans, four Latinos, an Englishman, and two American teenagers kicked the ball around linguistic barriers and into a cross-cultural goal. There were the potlucks after bilingual services when tables along parish hall walls were piled with soul food, Salvadoran food, African food, Jamaican food, goat, greens, *pupusas*, plantains, jerk chicken, rice and beans, *more* rice and beans, and an occasional whiter-than-white cupcake. There was the presentation of the offering at Anna's ordination when the usual Igbo-English songs—translated by Nigerian women and Latinas—became trilingual. Singing songs in three languages was a revelation, the varying numbers of syllables per word creating three distinctly different rhythms within the same song—three languages, three rhythms, one faith, one song.

But the most profound epiphany was our first Africa Day—a celebration first envisioned in a meeting with African parishioners when I asked what would make *this* church *their* church. Our rarely used balcony was packed with family members and friends of Nigerian parishioners. While a later norm, the music's African rhythms seemed to shake some of the too-lily-whiteness out of the northern Europeanized figures on the ornate Stations of the Cross and the pale faces on the stunningly beautiful stained glass windows.

At the reception, deafening African music blared off the walls of the too-small parish hall. Realizing that the noon Spanish service had ended, some Nigerian parishioners invited Spanish speakers, mostly Guatemalans, into the reception. In succeeding years, African and Latino parishioners would say how much they enjoyed each other's music, but that was made immediately clear. In a few minutes our typical American parish hall became a crowded, vibrant, gyrating dance floor, people dancing with no one and everyone—moving in a circle, moving in all directions. Nations and peoples had come to this church to learn the ways of God. People from many nations had come to our altar; now, knowing or unknowing, they surrounded God's throne. Soon, the dance floor was a sea of bright clothing, a rainbow of faces from many nations—Nigeria, Sierra Leone, Ghana, Liberia, Guatemala, Nicaragua, Mexico, El Salvador, Grenada, Trinidad, Jamaica, Belize, Great Britain, Canada, and the US—moving to one rhythm in one celebration. It was a glimpse of the future, a taste of the realm, a truth better danced than spoken. We were caught up in the movement of the universe, a moment of ecstasy, a moment of unity. We felt—we *knew*—that we were, and always would be, one.

9

The Unseeable One Glory

Blessed are the eyes which see and to which God reveals the kingdom and the glory . . .
—John Ruusbroec[1]

Awe is the salve that will heal our eyes.
—Rumi[2]

To see the eternal in the midst of time, to feel and to enjoy the infinite here in the finite,
is one of the greatest blessings life has to offer.
—Rufus Jones[3]

For wherever they turn their eyes on earth, there they see only the sun.
—Thomas Kelly[4]

---

1. Ruusbroec, *Spiritual Espousals*, 239.
2. Rumi, *Delicious Laughter*, 75.
3. Jones, *Essential Writings*, 83.
4. Kelly, *Testament of Devotion*, 63.

How is it, then, that as I look around me, still dazzled by what I have seen, I find that I am almost the only person of my kind, the only one to have *seen*?

—Teilhard de Chardin[5]

If we could but see existence as Christ and those who shared his mind have seen it, that is to say, transfigured and made significant by the light of the "Kingdom of God," we should know how to deal with its problems.

—Evelyn Underhill[6]

Wherever God is, there is Heaven.

—Teresa of Ávila[7]

Enough of phrases and conceits and metaphors!
I want burning, burning: become familiar with that burning!

—Rumi[8]

KING DAVID

The doorbell rang. I stepped away from the computer, from working on the church newsletter. I opened the door, unconsciously measuring a social distance between the two of us. Looking through the metal screen that is supposed to keep the church staff safe, I saw his familiar round face. I caught the familiar smells of bad breath and an unwashed body. The screen did not keep me safe from that. Sometimes he asked for money, sometimes for food, sometimes for directions; twice he asked for a car. Sometimes he was "David," sometimes "King David."

His shopping cart, half full, was parked a few feet behind him in the church driveway. He began a familiar, wandering, confused, and

5. Teilhard, *Writings*, 168 (italics his).
6. Underhill, *Modern Guide*, 80.
7. Teresa, *Way of Perfection*, 183.
8. Rumi, *Poet and Mystic*, 171.

semicoherent monologue. After a couple of minutes, we got around to the idea of food. I tossed some of the church's basic food groups into a bag and handed it to him. A familiar transaction.

A new detail. He often has some kind of gadgetry—I remember a Walkman that didn't have a chance of working. Today I noticed his watch. Digital. All the numbers were the same: 0. I wondered about the significance of all those zeros for him—the seconds, the minutes, the hours, the day, the month, and the year.

Was it the end of time? The beginning? Was he out of time? Outside of time?

Society's judgment, a judgment too easily, too habitually arising out of my heartless heart, is: this man's life is over. Nothing can be done with him or for him. Perhaps something could be done *to* him, whatever good that would do.

How easy it is—in the familiar dehumanizing harshness of our city streets and avenues of power, in the daily digital reminders of time forever passing us by—to lose sight of another person's humanity, another person's dignity, even his fancied royalty, what might have been in his life if he could reset his watch, if something done to him could be undone, if some decision made could be unmade. How easy it is to forget that, whatever the distance between us, we are both loved by the same God.

How easy it would have been to take less than a second on a functioning digital watch to listen more deeply to his confusion and, in listening, to stop denying that he, too, is created in the image of God.

How easy it is for all of us. How easy it would have been to have stayed at the computer writing about faith in my familiar, wandering, semiarticulate way, without going to the door, and seeing not David, or even King David, but Christ. Seeing and smelling Christ, feeling the distance between *us*, and the closeness, the divine dignity that binds us all together.

THE POLITICS OF MT. TABOR

In a terrifying time, Oscar Romero scrambled for apt words to still roiling waters. Like a priest finding a moldy scroll rotting lost and forgotten in the basement of a temple (cf. 2 Kgs 22–23), he sought old wisdom to rouse a people's moribund sense of humanity. Addressing a sermon to an oligarchy—landowners, dictators, generals, soldiers, and death squads—as well as workers, peasants, organizers, reformers, guerrillas, anyone and everyone, he says that the season of Advent has and is a message:

> Advent should admonish us to discover in each brother or sister that we greet, in each friend whose hand we shake, in each beggar who asks for bread, in each worker who wants to use the right to join a union, in each peasant who looks for work in the coffee groves, the face of Christ. Then it would not be possible to rob them, to cheat them, to deny them their rights. They are Christ, and whatever is done to them Christ will take as done to him. This is what Advent is: Christ living among us.[9]

Of course, what Romero says of Advent could as easily be attributed to the Feast of the Incarnation, the season of Epiphany, or the Feast of the Transfiguration. It is a rudimentary Christian assertion: each person, no matter how ordinary, extraordinary, powerful, or powerless, is—for us—another Christ, is—for Christ—another me. Echoing Traherne and Merton, Romero sighs: if only we could see *this*. If Merton calls "mercy" the "bass bell and undersong of the whole Bible,"[10] as unheard as white noise, the Christian faith just as constantly advises us, admonishes us, awakens us "to discover . . . the face of Christ" in all people.[11]

Yet it seems that we need to be rudely shaken and regularly reawakened to this basic tenet of faith. In an anonymous mystic's epiphany, an angel leads a pilgrim to heaven. The pilgrim is bewildered. Heaven isn't as expected. He doesn't see "God sitting on God's golden throne." So, like John of Patmos, who often feels lost, he asks for directions: "Where is the Lord God?" The angel replies, "God is in God's children. . . . For God's sons and God's daughters are temples in which God dwells and which are filled with God's glory." Blinking away the magnetic pull of the heavenly throne, the pilgrim sees: "And I looked around for the thousand times a thousand children of God and became aware that they were shining from the inner truth of God like bright clear suns. There I saw living sapphires and rubies. The light of the Lord sparkled in their bodies and drove them so that they could not stand still, for the clarity of the Lord is a living clarity."[12] This is what Merton saw in Louisville. This was his "clarity" at Polonnaruwa.[13] This is the insight Traherne trumpets as he sees young and old, male and female, as glittering, leaping jewels. While breaking free of the process of Isaiah's epiphany (Isa 6:1–3), this vision reaffirms its meaning: the earth is

---

9. Romero, *Violence of Love*, 125.
10. Merton, *Seasons of Celebration*, 175.
11. Romero, *Violence of Love*, 125.
12. Buber, *Ecstatic Utterances*, 127.
13. Commins, "Thomas Merton's Three Epiphanies," 70; Merton, *Other Side*, 323. He uses variations on the word "clear" eight times.

full of God's glory, perhaps nothing more brimming with grandeur than God's children, these living gleaming jewels and breathing precious stones. Instead of seeking a one-way path to God in heaven, in this vision we see that the angels of heaven may be no more bursting with divine radiance than the people of earth.

On the streets of Louisville, Merton saw the dignity of the human race. In people on the streets, Traherne saw the magnificent splendor of created beings. In those intoxicating realizations, they were awakened to what their faith assured them is always true. No one could sense it in darkness, or see it in light, or cradle it in one's heart and remain blasé about injustice, neglectful of exploitation, indifferent to suffering, or defeated by powerlessness. Visionaries and preachers parse such words differently, but they never fail to reframe our vision, reignite our eyes, and remind us of the infinite value of each person.

To signify this ordinary divinity, Teresa of Ávila describes an "interior castle," a "mansion,"[14] "a palace" within us where God dwells: "Now let us imagine that we have within us a palace of priceless worth, built entirely of gold and precious stones—a palace, in short, fit for so great a Lord." This is a God-given gift, a creation in which we have no hand, yet this, Teresa says, "is partly your doing." God built the palace, but its upkeep is ours. Virtues are the workers that maintain the palace's magnificence, "for there is no building so beautiful as a soul that is pure and full of virtues, and the greater these virtues are, the more brilliantly do the stones shine." In this palace lives a monarch defined by dominion, yet who prefers to be a parent molded by love. This parent-monarch God "is seated upon a throne of supreme price—namely, your heart."[15] Julian of Norwich, who sees the truths of creation in a hazelnut, sees another treasure in herself: "Our good Lord opened my spiritual eye, and showed me my soul in the midst of my heart. I saw the soul as wide as if it were an endless citadel, and also as if it were a blessed kingdom."[16] To Teresa and Julian, the kingdom, the palace, and the glory within, though unseen, are as real and potent as a shining sun. Such visual images and spiritual constructs are not built from scratch. Even as celibate Paul censures pornographic sexual misconduct and amoral indifference to immorality, he never denigrates physicality or sexuality; he consecrates the human body as the temple of the Holy Spirit (1 Cor 6:19). So the roots of Teresa, Julian, and Traherne's esteem for human dignity are not extracted only from Jesus' example; they can be absorbed from Paul's words.

---

14. Teresa, *Interior Castle*, which has seven "mansions."
15. Teresa, *Way of Perfection*, 187–88.
16. Julian, *Showings*, 312–13.

The majesty of creation, the cosmic brothers and sisters Francis praises in his canticle, the first things created in the first chapter of Genesis mesmerize the psalmist. But then the star-struck songwriter asks, who are *we* that God should care so much for *us* (Ps 8:3–4)? Teresa and Julian answer: we are the ones who contain kingdoms, palaces, citadels, and mansions. Traherne answers: we are made of gold and gems. Merton answers: we are the ones shining like Francis's brother sun. Our value is infinitely more than anything we can invent or invoke. God's glory is found less on a heavenly throne than in our hearts and on our skin.

Teresa and Julian share Romero's intuition, but what they draw from breathtaking mystical vision, he extracts from the yellowed pages of a centuries-old liturgical calendar. What they use to help people appraise their infinite worth and spur an inner revolution, Romero uses to revolutionize socioeconomic structures and inspire social transformation. How dare you cheat a sacred kingdom? How could you exploit blinding suns? How can you neglect gleaming jewels? What could make you treat a mansion like a hovel? These are the questions Frederick Douglass asked of slavery, Tutu asked of apartheid, and King asked before the Lincoln Memorial. They are the questions that must always be asked of colonialism, imperialism, capitalism, and racism. Such mystical insights do not lead us to build booths for Jesus, Moses, and Elijah. They prepare us to meet human anguish and senseless bedlam (Mark 9:2–29). To embrace such a high view of human nature does not make us bypass politics. It ups the ante; it deepens the tragedy; it heightens the outrage; it raises the stakes; it makes the revolution even more urgent.

In her travels between world wars, Muriel Lester said she had never encountered anything like the subservient, squeamish peonage she saw in India under the bootheel of the English raj—except, of course, in Mississippi in the Jim Crow South. She found "the servility, the cowering obsequious attitude" in India deeply distressing: "Fear was writ large on so many faces, not just physical fear, but a deep-seated worry, apparently caused by never quite understanding what these big Englishmen wanted done next."[17] The paternalistic assumptions of imperialism were a pure, undiluted, unfiltered denial of human dignity. An ever-threatening, peace-shattering psychological storm, they were a daily norm. As the title of Chinua Achebe's second novel on colonial Nigeria infers, the oppressed are *No Longer at Ease*—they are *never* at ease.

While it is a norm of Christian mysticism in general and the Russian Orthodox tradition in particular to attribute divinity to human nature, it

---

17. Lester, *It Occurred to Me*, 130.

can be theologically jarring to find arguments about abolitionism, apartheid, civil rights, and human rights framed as crimes against the divine. Discussing his visit to Garée, an island off the coast of Senegal where slavers loaded Africans onto ships bound for America, James Baldwin describes his visceral reaction as he takes the staircase down to the slave quarters: "It's narrow and low and it's built of stone and it's wet. On either side of you there are the cells. The manacles are still there, rusted with time. For me, the smell is still there.... And you are going where? Chained together, defecating together, sweating together, unable to speak to each other, going where?" This, he says, is "the crime," the unforgivable sin named in the Gospel of Mark—blaspheming the Holy Spirit (Mark 3:28–29). Challenged to clarify or qualify the off-the-cuff judgment others perceive in his remark, a verdict shared by sainted Francis of Assisi and the sedate book of Proverbs,[18] he calls child labor and anti-Semitism other manifestations of the same blasphemy.[19]

It is one thing to assert human dignity, one of humanism's utterly unsubstantiated faith claims. It is another to assert that human nature is divine, angelic, holy, or sacred. This is the repeated message of the Puebla Conference: systems of oppression deny human dignity; they abuse God's image; they exploit God's children.[20] It would be a quick-but-healthy slap of reality to remind American "originalists" that the Constitution compromised the humanity of African Americans precisely this way. In a document that made it equally disenfranchising to be without property or a penis, as a matter of political expediency African Americans counted as three-fifths of a human being. For the sake of crass economics, of course, they were 100 percent chattel, a trend-setting national disposition that, like Lester's nurse, considers some more human than others and esteems maximized profits over minimized people. To assert that slaves are in any way divine put the lie to such intricate, self-serving calculations. That American culture and American law have subsequently applied a similar calculus to women, workers, immigrants, and gay-lesbian-bisexual-transgender persons highlights the truth that once such metrics are lodged in the collective body-memory and blood, they are hard to purge. It will take more than amendments to expunge originalism's sin.

To assert the divinity of slaves throws a brighter, harsher, more piercing light on oppression, injustice, and violence. Never penurious in his use of exclamation points, David Walker, in his *Appeal*, expresses his shrill

18. Celano, *Saint Francis*, 69; Prov 14:31, 17:5.
19. Baldwin and Mead, *Rap on Race*, 174–76.
20. Eagleson and Scherper, *Puebla and Beyond*, 129, 167, 168, 265.

outrage in his punctuation: they "call us, who are free and next to the Angels of God, their property!!!!!!"[21] Henry Highland Garnet expands, "I would as soon attempt to enslave Gabriel or Michael as to enslave someone made in the image of God," someone "for whom Christ died"; no person, no system, nothing, he says, can "unmake" our created image.[22] Human dignity is inseparable from divine majesty. So ideologies of *La Raza*, black pride, gay pride, and race consciousness are more than political slogans; they are theological tools to transfigure the self-image of the oppressed.

Two generations before DuBois agonized over God's existence, power, presence, justice, and skin color, Frederick Douglass, seeing ships on Chesapeake Bay, reflected in Gatsby-like wistfulness over the distance between slavery and freedom.

> These beautiful vessels, robed in purest white, so delightful to the eye ... were to me so many shrouded ghosts, to terrify and torment me with thoughts of my wretched condition. I have often, in the deep stillness of a summer's Sabbath, stood all alone upon the lofty banks of that noble bay, and traced, with saddened heart and tearful eye, the countless number of sails moving off to the mighty ocean. The sight of these always affected me powerfully. My thoughts would compel utterance. And there, with no audience but the Almighty, I would pour out my soul's complaint, in my rude way ... :—You are loosed from your moorings, and are free: I am fast in my chains, and am a slave! You move merrily before the gentle gale, and I sadly before the bloody whip! You are freedom's swift-winged angels that fly round the world; I am confined in bands of iron! O that I were free! O that I were on one of your gallant decks, and under your protecting wing! Alas! Betwixt me and you, the turbid waters roll. Go on, go on. O that I could also go! Could I but swim! If I could fly! O, why was I born a man, of whom to make a brute! The glad ship is gone; she hides in the dim distance. I am left in the hottest hell of unending slavery. O God, save me! God, deliver me! Let me be free! Is there any God? Why am I a slave? I will run away. I will not stand it. Get caught or get clear, I'll try it.[23]

For Douglass, the contrast between ships and slaves, between sailing freedom and shackled slavery leads him to prayer, to anxious wonder, to Job's questions, and finally to steel himself to steal away.

21. Marable and Mullings, *Let Nobody Turn Us*, 3.
22. Mays, *Negro's God*, 47.
23. Douglass, *Narrative of the Life*, 83–84.

While singularly focused on attaining his own freedom, Douglass's eye was refined enough to see slavery twisting the psyches of slaveholders. The psychological damage of oppression is subtler and even more ruinous to the oppressor than to the oppressed. The unuttered insight of Douglass's juxtaposition of slaves to beautiful vessels is that he never compares the slave's fate to the slave owner's liberty, for slavery also defines, objectifies, and dehumanizes them: "The slaveholder, as well as the slave, was the victim of the slave system."[24] They, too, are never free. In slaveholders, Douglass observes morality underdeveloped, reason imprisoned, and inhibitions unrestrained. They are never Dr. Jekyll; they can only be Mr. Hyde. In a variation on Dennis Brutus's observation that the oppressed too easily absorb the brute traits of their oppressors, Douglass says that in the slave system, all hearts are shriveled; all are made cruel; all have become small. In the antebellum South's hierarchy, masters, overseers, poor white trash, house slaves, and field slaves all hunger for favor and thirst for power: "Everybody in the South seemed to want the privilege of whipping somebody else."[25] It was one massive, abusive, trickle-down social system from which not even people at the top could escape. Owners were slaves of their own whims and wishes—transient moodiness and churlish childish tantrums; they looked unhappy, haunted, and worried.[26] While rare rebellions and random acts of violence targeted slaveholders, Freud would have had all he could handle analyzing their exaggerated anxiety and largely unrealized nightmares of slave revenge.

The slave system not only twisted the oppressors' psyches; it also stunted their souls. In a prophetic denunciation of every oppressor's religion, a free Frederick Douglass draws a sharp distinction between the slaveholders' faith and legitimate Christianity:

> the religion of the south is a mere covering for the most horrid crimes,—a justifier of the most appalling barbarity,—a sanctifier of the most hateful frauds—and a dark shelter under which the darkest, foulest, grossest, and most infernal deeds of slaveholders find the strongest protection. Were I to be again reduced to the chains of slavery, next to that enslavement, I should regard being the slave of a religious master the greatest calamity that could befall me. For all slaveholders with whom I have ever met,

---

24. Ibid., 45.
25. Ibid., 43.
26. Ibid., 43–45.

religious slaveholders are the worst. I have ever found them the meanest and basest, the most cruel and cowardly, of all others.[27]

Even when an owner "converted," all it changed was an imagined affiliation with God; not a flesh-and-blood rapport with their slaves.[28] The masters' religion kept them from "breaking the Sabbath, but not from breaking my skin on any other day than Sunday";[29] they tithed mint, dill, and cumin, but neglected the weightier matters of justice, mercy, and faith (Matt 23:23). Comparing the "slaveholding religion of this land" and "Christianity proper," Douglass voices a holy complaint:

> For between Christianity of this land [and] the Christianity of Christ, I recognize the widest possible difference, so wide, that to receive the one as good, pure, and holy, is of necessity to reject the other as bad, corrupt, and wicked. To be the friend of the one is of necessity to be the enemy of the other. I love the pure, peaceable, and impartial Christianity of Christ; I therefore hate the corrupt, slaveholding, women-whipping, cradle-plundering, partial, and hypocritical Christianity of this land. Indeed, I can see no reason, but the most deceitful one, for calling the religion of this land Christianity. I look upon it as the climax of all misnomers, the boldest of all frauds, and the grossest of all libels.[30]

While slaveholders congratulated themselves for supposedly converting their slaves, they merely exposed the duplicity of their schizophrenic creed. Yet slaves did more than see and critique. They created and redeemed. As Howard Thurman says, "By some amazing but vastly creative spiritual insight slaves undertook the redemption of a religion that their masters had profaned in their midst."[31] Long before the Southern Christian Leadership Conference set out to save the soul of America, slave religion undertook the same Sisyphean task.

To Baldwin, slavery is but one particularly horrific example of blasphemous socioeconomic norms. What was true of slavery and apartheid are now true of the prison system, sweat shops, and human trafficking. What Harriet Beecher Stowe says of the antebellum South's genteel and cruel social norms, Alexander Solzhenitsyn says of the inhumanity of Soviet inquisitions, and Sinclair Lewis says of industrial capitalism's manic indifference

---

27. Ibid., 92.
28. Douglass, *Life and Times*, 108.
29. Ibid., 139.
30. Douglass, *Narrative of the Life*, 120.
31. Thurman, *Deep River*, 36.

to human dignity. They all imply the same questions: how do you get the oppressor to see the oppressed as a castle, a palace, a mansion, and a citadel? How do you get the oppressed to exorcise their constrained, confined, secularized, and constricting imagination and see themselves as little lower than the angels? And how do you enable the oppressed to see their oppressors as fallen angels, sepulchered souls, debased by the same humiliating and dehumanizing system?

Carried by the same Spirit as liberation theology's declaration of dignity and the abolitionist proclamation of divinity, and riding on the wings of Albert Luthuli's rhetorical imagination, Tutu judges apartheid's "bankrupt and barren policies" as antithetical to "the dignity of persons"—for him, people are "of infinite value because they were created in the image of the triune God." Their "intrinsic" value never depends on "extraneous biological factors" like skin color; it matters not if people are bourgeois, or "voracious consumers or producers," or if they have staked out a particular place on the food chain of the means of production. Their worth rests "simply and solely on the fact that God had created them," and creation endows them with "inalienable rights."[32]

Tutu returns to this political dimension of dangerous orthodoxy time and time again. The Bible, he says, asserts that "human beings are created in the image and likeness of God." You need not be a bishop, a scholar, or even biblically literate to see this. You do not have to find an obscure aphorism in Proverbs or delve into an opaque verse in the Minor Prophets to know this. You do not even have to read far into the Bible before your unschooled eyes glaze over with confusion. It is in the first chapter of Genesis. It is a first truth. Dangerous orthodoxy begins in the beginning. And according to Tutu, this first fact of orthodoxy "endows each person with a unique and infinite value," while apartheid—like Jim Crow, like capitalist exploitation, like the British Empire—focuses on "a biological quality, which is a total irrelevancy."[33] Apartheid misses the mark. It skirts the truth. Like abolitionists in another time and place, Tutu uses the revolutionary language of exalted humanity and ordinary royalty to help people resee their socioeconomic world:

> I am God's viceroy on earth, you are God's viceroy ... if only we could believe this of ourselves then we would behave so differently to our usual conduct. Those who are victims of injustice and oppression would not have to suffer from a slave mentality by which they despised themselves and went about apologizing

32. Tutu, *Hope and Suffering*, 119.
33. Ibid., 166.

for their existence. They would know that they matter to God, and nothing anybody did to them could change that fundamental fact about themselves.[34]

If only we believed this, we would see.

Serving on the Truth and Reconciliation Commission after the death of apartheid, Tutu reasserts the same message even as murderers, assassins, torturers, and terrorists are brought to truth, if not punishing justice, for the crimes they committed either in the defense of apartheid or in debased response to its dehumanization: "Each person is not just to be respected but to be revered as one created in God's image." Echoing Baldwin's harsh judgment from Garée, Tutu says it is worse than inhuman or unjust to exploit: "it is veritably blasphemous, for it is to spit in the face of God."[35]

On the surface, Tutu can sound like an advocate of human decency, human equality, and humanistic self-respect. But his are the politics of transfiguration: "The principle of transfiguration says nothing, no one and no situation is 'untransfigurable,' that the very creation, nature, waits expectantly when it will be released from its bondage and share in the glorious liberty of the children of God, when it will not be just dry inert matter but will be translucent with a divine glory."[36] While drawn from a distinct theological source, Tutu's politics of transfiguration mirrors the Quaker inner light and Lester's internal spark. He also enfolds into his kerygma the gist of Romero's Advent—to see Christ's face in all people. As Paul says all are raised with Christ, Tutu and Romero claim that in Christ anyone can be transfigured.

As with the revolution and the realm, transfiguration is *already and not yet*. Intrinsically, it is who we are; potentially, it is what we can be. For Traherne and Merton, we already shine like the sun. For Romero, we are yet to see that truth. Tutu stresses that the already (we are viceroys) gives birth to the nascent (the realm). Just as Day speaks of the potential members of Christ's mystical body, the Orthodox tradition describes our intrinsic and latent value: we are created in God's image (already); we can be sanctified into Christ's likeness (not yet). We are (Gal 3:26, 4:5) and can become (John 1:12, Matt 5:9) God's children. Yet even when nascent, the potential for transfiguration bestows an infinite value on each person. Such a faith wrenches both oppressors and oppressed from a descending spiral of internalized degradation. There is nothing within people, no matter how despoiled they have become as tortured or torturers, colonized or colonizers,

---

34. Ibid., 141.
35. Tutu, *No Future*, 197.
36. Tutu, *Rainbow People*, 121–22.

victims or victimizers, that can stamp their transfiguration null and void. In Teresa's symbology, their interior palace still shines.

The politics of Mt. Tabor—transfiguration politics—not only intensifies the tragedy of what is not and not yet, it teases us to imagine what could be. The politics of Mt. Tabor are an antithesis to Augustine, Niebuhr, and Qoheleth; they never lower the bar; they never settle for reform; they never permit premature contentment. While wielding their own two-edged sword of annunciation and denunciation, like King's speeches, they invite us to envision more than we can ever accomplish as they spice our hopes with the scent of the surreal.

In fleeting glances, Tutu and King each see the realm's transfigured face. During the apartheid era, Tutu repeatedly called South Africa a "rainbow country" and racially mixed crowds a "rainbow people."[37] Asserting black pride almost a decade before it metamorphosed into an ideology, King told his all-black audience in his first public address in Montgomery that future historians would say, "There lived a great people—a black people—who injected new meaning and dignity into the veins of civilization."[38] In 1959 in Washington, D. C., King addressed thousands of students gathered to support the five-year-old Supreme Court decision to desegregate schools. He told his audience that in the thousands of black and white faces "intermingled like the waters of a river, I see only one face—the face of the future"[39]—an interracial, transfigured, eschatological face. In an epiphany like Malcolm X's during his hajj, as King was leaving Alabama after the Selma march; "There was a delay at the airport and several thousand demonstrators waited more than five hours, crowding together on the seats, the floors and the stairways of the terminal building. As I stood with them and saw white and black, nuns and priests, ministers and rabbis, labor organizers, lawyers, doctors, housemaids and shopworkers brimming with vitality and enjoying a rare comradeship, I knew I was seeing a microcosm of humankind of the future in this moment."[40] Including and transcending race, people of many classes and faiths are again the "future."

Just as the transfiguration is one day in the Christian year, just as Mt. Tabor is one peak in a range of high-altitude epiphanies, Jesus does not stand by himself before Peter, James, and John. Like a religious skeptic or a doubting Thomas, Richard of St. Victor says he would believe in the transfiguration only if when he saw Christ transfigured he also saw Moses and

37. Ibid., 187–88.
38. King, *Stride Toward Freedom*, 63.
39. King, *Testament of Hope*, 21.
40. King, *Where Do We Go*, 10.

Elijah.[41] For Richard, there is no such thing as transfiguration untouched by covenantal relationship and prophetic truth. Unless the law and the prophets are linked to this prototypical mystical event, the transfiguration is a worthless interlude spiritually ghettoized from humanity, anxiety, and social responsibility. Left by itself, it becomes a flight of the alone to the nonexistent. And just as Jesus is seen with Moses and Elijah, Mt. Tabor is linked to Mt. Sinai and Mt. Carmel. In this small scrum of intuitions, each revelation brings its own unique political insight. It may be only when we see Moses and Elijah with Jesus that we realize that the transfiguration has its own sociocultural implications alongside the politics of exodus, covenant, law, and prophets.

The politics of Mt. Sinai are God's way to create a new society within the shell of the old world. The covenant is biblical Israel's foundational, communal politics of the common good by the people, for the people, and through the people. The theophany of the law uniquely provides a social structure and a moral musculature that stimulates, regulates, and reinvigorates people to act ethically. Yet the politics of Mt. Sinai has its limits. While strangers and stragglers within the homeland—the few, the others—find themselves on the charitable end of proactive legislated compassion and covenantal noblesse oblige, strangers amassed or imagined at the borders find themselves crudely dehumanized and quickly dispatched.

The renewal politics of Mt. Carmel appear in seasons of the limping (1 Kgs 18:21) and the lukewarm (Rev 3:16) dominated by the half-hearted and those wholly hostile to the God of covenant and creation. These are the zealous reformist politics that grind the golden calf to dust and castigate idolaters for violating commandments. The politics of Mt. Carmel merge radical human fidelity with a purifying, purging divinity who rebukes those blind to the contrast between Baal's GNP/fertility worship and Yahweh's collective common good. When historical forces rake aside devotion to covenant or lead the faithful into corrupting syncretism, the politics of Mt. Carmel declare a Barmen Declaration. As Elijah demonstrates in his contest with the prophets of Baal (1 Kgs 18:20–40), the politics of Mt. Carmel are more efficacious when resisting the powers that be than when whipping defeated enemies with the reins of power.

The politics of Mt. Tabor provide a corrective to the shadow sides of the jingoistic tribalism of the Exodus and the cultural revolution of Elijah, with its Maoist purge of Baal's prophets. To the self-righteous bloodletting of both, Mt. Tabor adds a sword-stopping dimension of transcendence: the realization that neighbors and strangers, idolaters and enemies can be

---

41. Richard of St. Victor, *Twelve Patriarchs*, 138–39.

transfigured. The wonder induced on Mt. Tabor births awe more than affiliation, affection, or even love. How can you stand in awe of enemy, stranger, oppressor, or neighbor if you pity them as children, condescend to them as fools, or abhor them as monsters? But if you realize that they contain an unseen inner spark that might shine like the sun, if you can reverence even the most debased victim or perpetrator, then having absorbed the awe politics of Mt. Tabor, your inner revolution can begin to affect transfiguring social change.

One can imagine potential problems in the politics of Mt. Tabor: quiescent nonresistance, dreamy ineffectiveness, paralyzed inaction, or an apolitical overdose of awe, Niebuhr's children of light too kindhearted, codependent, or thunderstruck to act. Niebuhr would have intuited the connection between Tutu's transfigurable people and the Quaker inner light and scoffed at the imagined near-at-hand utopianism of the Social Gospel and liberation theology. Yet he would have had a hard time calling Tutu and Romero naïve.

These political intuitions lead in different directions: Mt. Sinai and Mt. Carmel to the Nuremburg Trials, Mt. Tabor to the Truth and Reconciliation Commission. Mt. Sinai and Mt. Carmel countenance capital punishment; Mt. Tabor questions a life sentence without parole. These intuitions can also complement, balance, and complete each other. Just as Jesus, Moses, and Elijah need each other at the transfiguration, Sinai and Carmel need Tabor to bear light on their shadow sides; and Tabor needs Sinai's covenant and Carmel's single-mindedness to sharpen the soft, rounded edges of its ordinary wonder. Sinai politics are foundational, structural, covenantal, and communal. Carmel politics fuel resistance, renewal, and reform. Tabor animates both with radical awe.

FRUITFUL AND BURNING

In the litany of bizarre tasks *abbas* assigned to desert monks, John the Dwarf's mentor instructs him to take a dry stick, plant it, and water it "until it bears fruit."[42] The command is not precisely Elijah's (raise the dead)—but it is Gabriel's: make the barren give birth.

Apparently this isn't challenging enough. An additional hurdle multiplies the degree of difficulty. There is no well nearby. To get water, John must leave his cell every evening, walk all night, and return the next morning to water this dead dry stick. It is as if he is *ordered* to sow seeds on rocky ground in windy weather and scorching heat. In spite of the obstacles, after

---

42. Ward, *Sayings of the Desert*, 85.

three years of interminable nights "the wood came to life and bore fruit." In a variation on the Words of Institution, John's *abba* invites the assembly to "Take and eat the fruit of obedience."[43] Unfeeling submissiveness, rigid discipline, and odds-on futile drudgery have a powerful synergistic chemistry. Just as fingers catch fire, dead wood yields fruit.

In the Bible, God works with dead and sterile things as if tutored by a desert *abba*. A barren fig tree can be a prime candidate for urban renewal or, given leeway, receive special dispensation for a yearlong probation (Luke 13:6–9). But failing fig trees are but one divine dilemma. Ambitious Abimelech—the bramble bush that would be king (Judg 9:8–15)—is a thorn in Israel's flesh. And unlike the fig tree, God and history quickly slough him aside. On the other hand, Isaiah foresees a barren desert—as lifeless as Chernobyl or Fukushima's toxic exclusion zones—blossom "abundantly"; and he envisions a dead stump producing a singularly significant shoot (Isa 35:1–2, 11:1–5). Ezekiel sees a valley of disembodied bones revived by God's power and revivified by God's breath (Ezek 37:1–14). Dead wood, the desert, and the dead are the stuff from which God brings the fruit of life and hope.

Just as there are numerous images of implausible birth and mystical union, many metaphors seek to capture the blinking firefly elusiveness of transfiguration. Eucharistic bread becomes Christ's body (Eckhart).[44] Water takes on the color and flavor of wine (Eckhart, Bernard).[45] In nonliturgical imagery, fire changes iron and sunbeams shine through crystal (Symeon, Bernard, John of the Cross).[46] Seeking without finding a board certified textbook image, John of the Cross rotates metaphors as if in a revolving door. In *The Ascent to Mt. Carmel*, he likens God to the sun and the soul to a window. A "smudgy window"/conflicted soul impedes the light; but when a window is cleaned, sunlight transforms and illumines it to shine "just as the sun's ray."[47]

Images of bread and body, water and wine, iron and fire, sunbeams and windows infer sanctification, deification, or transfiguration. But, while less likely to startle us than union's public metaphor number one (sex), the mystics' most common symbol for transfiguration is dead wood burning. In effect, Eckhart turns wood into the protagonist in a rewrite of Abba Joseph becoming fire. Showing theological sensitivity, Eckhart nimbly dodges

43. Ibid.

44. Eckhart, *Sermons & Treatises II*, 135.

45. Eckhart, *Sermons & Treatises II*, 21, *Sermons & Treatises III*, 42; Leech, *Experiencing God*, 337–38.

46. John of the Cross, *Collected Works*, 339; Symeon, *Hymns*, 168–70; Leech, *Experiencing God*, 216.

47. John of the Cross, *Collected Works*, 117.

Pelagianism with a nod to grace: just as we do not sanctify ourselves, wood cannot start a fire; fire "ignites" dry wood and "infuses" it with its nature.[48] Then, flinging caution into the air with a theological slingshot, he declares deification: as fire changes wood into itself, so God changes us "into God."[49]

Even for God, such a transformation takes more than a snap of the divine fingers. The process can be as laborious and excruciating as getting a dry stick to bear fruit: when fire first scorches wood, it emits putrid smoke and a loud crackling sound as human and divine natures meet. As the fire heats up, it becomes more still until "all unlikeness [is] cast out."[50] Wood ceases to be wood; it is fire.[51] Drawing an analogy to spiritual openness, Birgitta says that some logs (souls) are "most apt and efficient for combustion"; so it was, she says, with Mary.[52]

John of the Cross divines the same process. In *The Dark Night of the Soul*, he says God purges "imperfection . . . through the dryness and distress of the dark night."[53] Fire dehumidifies and darkens the wood. Dry wood is ugly. It smolders and stinks. Finally, "the fire transforms the wood into itself and makes it as beautiful as it is itself." Wood *becomes* fire: "it is dry and it dries; it is hot and it gives off heat; it is brilliant and it illumines; and it is also light."[54] In *The Living Flame of Love*, he says that after fire transforms wood and unites it to itself, the fire blazes until "the wood becomes much more incandescent and inflamed . . . flaring up and shooting out flames from itself."[55] So when God transforms the soul "in the fire of love," it becomes a leaping flame.[56] Dead wood becomes living fire; we become divine.

Transfiguration, though, is no natural act, magic trick, or Herculean feat. Human effort is futile. Sometimes even dictatorial divine fiat works no wonders. Although no family recipe or mathematical equation can delimit transfiguration, it may require relational synergy. So, in a parallel analogy, when a guest arrives at the feast of the Beloved, "They asked the Lover: 'From where do you come?' . . . 'From love.' 'To whom do you belong?' 'I belong to love.' 'Who gave you birth?' 'Love.' 'Where were you born?' 'In

---

48. Eckhart, *Sermons & Treatises II*, 62–63.
49. Ibid., 137.
50. Ibid., 159.
51. Eckhart, *Sermons & Treatises III*, 78. Theophan and Symeon describe the same process: Chariton of Valamo, *Art of Prayer*, 156; Symeon, *Divine Eros*, 245.
52. Birgitta, *Life and Revelations*, 116–17.
53. John of the Cross, *Collected Works*, 306.
54. Ibid., 350.
55. Ibid., 578.
56. Ibid., 578, 580.

love.' 'Who raised you?' 'Love.' 'How do you live?' 'By love.' 'What is your name?' 'Love.' 'Where do you dwell?' 'In love.'"[57] As wood becomes fire, the Lover, transformed and transfigured, *becomes* the Beloved.[58] The chief end of the spiritual life, then, is not the pursuit of happiness or ecstasy or even union. Richard of Victor says that just as birth results from sex, love follows mystical ecstasy.[59]

John of the Cross seconds Paul's conclusion that knowledge without love goes nowhere fast, if anywhere at all (1 Cor 8:1, 13:8).[60] As *The Cloud of Unknowing* occasionally breaks into lyrical song about the "stirrings" of love, in chapters 11, 12, and 13 of *The Dark Night of the Soul*, John's rhetoric becomes ripe with a harvest of phrases, many repeated, about love: "loving wisdom," "loving knowledge," "passive love," "esteeming love," the "savor of love," "impassioned love," "impassioned and intense love," the "passion of love," the "desire and anxiety of love," the "urgent longing of love," the "union of love," the "strong union of love," "strong divine love," the "strength and vehemence of love," the "enkindling of love," the "warmth of love," the "burning and warmth of love," the "inflaming of love," the "fire of love," the "purgative fire of love," "burning love," the "dark fire of love," the "dark night of loving fire," and a "dark loving spiritual fire."[61] In the dark night when the senses have lost their way, when we grope intellectually, spiritually, and always blindly, in the very hour when dismay arises in waves, love finds the unmapped nonpath to intimacy, and the lover is transformed—like a burning log—becoming the Beloved. For John, then, union is not merely the culmination of holy flirtation (Thérèse), gazing (Ruusbroec), kissing (Bernard), or increasingly intense pleasure. It is the unexpected companion of floundering clarity and vanished security. For John, the dark night's union sparks transfiguration.

Dorothy of Montau experiences this sensually in the replacement of her heart of stone (Ezek 11:19): after her "old heart" is "extracted," "an extremely hot piece of flesh was shoved into her,"[62] and the transplant is complete. Catherine of Genoa senses a transfiguring power in her new burning heart: "Might but one little drop of what I feel fall into Hell, Hell would be transformed into a Paradise."[63] No one, Catherine discovers, is beyond

---

57. Lull, *Romancing God*, 19.
58. John of the Cross, *Collected Works*, 452; Rolle, *Fire of Love*, 144.
59. McGinn, *Growth of Mysticism*, 418.
60. John of the Cross, *Collected Works*, 461.
61. Ibid., 352–61.
62. McGinn, *Harvest of Mysticism*, 357.
63. Otto, *Idea of the Holy*, 38.

redemption. No one, Ezekiel assumes, is beyond resurrection. No one, Tutu insists, is beyond transfiguration. Gregory Palamas, recalling early church teachings, says that our restoration begins in the incarnation: "the transformation of our human nature, its deification and transfiguration—were these not accomplished in Christ from the start, from the moment in which Christ assumed our nature?"[64] The incarnation sparks union *and* transfiguration.

As if her mystical sexual encounter were not enough, Teresa of Ávila, who considered herself dead wood or worse, has another riveting epiphany. During the Eucharist at a monastery on the feast of the Assumption, while ruminating on the ampleness of her sinfulness "there came upon me a rapture so vehement that it nearly drew me forth out of myself altogether." It so discombobulated her senses that "I could neither see the Elevation nor hear Mass." "While in this state, I thought I saw myself being clothed in a garment of great whiteness and brightness," if not astral apparel, then the very garb Jesus wore at his transfiguration. Perceiving herself a prodigal daughter even though her lifestyle ran truer to the dutiful elder sibling, she receives a robe from "Our Lady" and Joseph. And she understands: "I was now cleansed of my sins." But mercy is only an hors d'oeuvres in an expansive feast. Teresa also receives vocational confirmation. "Our Lady" promises Teresa that her ministry—like John the Dwarf's dead stick—will bear fruit. Finally, instead of being dressed, à la Ephesians, with the full armor of God (Eph 6:10–20), Mary adorns her with a lavish complement of divine gifts—a jewel, a gold collar, and a precious cross: "The gold and stones were so different from earthly things of the kind that no comparison between them is possible: their beauty is quite unlike anything that we can imagine and the understanding cannot soar high enough to comprehend the nature of the garment or to imagine the brightness of the vision . . . by comparison with which everything on earth looks, as one might say, like a smudge of soot." This vision gave Teresa her greatest "bliss and happiness." After Joseph and Mary "seemed to" ascend to heaven with a multitude of angels, Teresa found herself "so greatly comforted and exalted and recollected in prayer, and so full of tender devotion, that I stayed for some time where I was, without moving, and unable to speak, quite beside myself. I was left with a vehement impulse to melt away in love for God."[65] Her sins, like haunting ghosts, evaporate. At that moment, confession becomes small stakes, forgiveness pocket change, and redemption chicken feed. Her vision affirms her ministry, her reforms, her activism, and her life. Holy people

---

64. Palamas, *Triads*, 76.
65. Teresa, *Life of Teresa*, 317–19.

clothe her with holy things. It is one thing to be forgiven, another to be blessed, of another order to be transfigured.

Like Teresa's vision, the subplots of Jesus' transfiguration highlight his identity, vocation, and mission. He has told his disciples that his road leads to Jerusalem, crucifixion, and death; now the voice reasserts his intimate relationship with God and says: listen to him. The message in Jesus' transfiguration is directed to his *disciples* at their most deaf, blind, and dull witted. Teresa's vision is meant for *her* when she is most fiercely self-condemning. If she wants to think of herself as dead wood, fine, but she must also know that her ministry bears fruit and that she is dead wood burning.

The relentlessly buoyant Traherne might look askance at Teresa's compulsive self-examination. His is a rare voice in Christian tradition that says: blessed are the sinful, and blessed is sin. Rather than being ransacked by guilt, he marvels at the gift of free will and bathes in the realization that God has "enabled me if I please to offend You infinitely!" God hungers for us to do God's will and seek divine justice, make no mistake—but God delights in giving us freedom: "Of all the exaltations in all worlds this is the greatest. To make a world for me was much, to command Angels and people to love me was much, to prepare eternal joys for me was more. But to give me a power to displease You, or to set a sin before Your face, which You infinitely hate, to profane Eternity, or to defile Your works, is more stupendous than all these."[66] For Traherne, even sin is transfigured. This does not become a quietist excuse for complacent passivity. There can be no revelry without a cause. We find ultimate fulfillment when we seek God's realm and do God's will. And yet, God so loves the world—John's world, Job's world, Jesus' world—that God gives us freedom to "defile" God's work and to defy God's will.

Dead wood can burn anywhere. The doorway to heaven is everywhere. But Teresa's vision takes place on the traditional front step of transformation—worship. For mystics, worship opens heaven and unveils eternity. For activists, worship reignites a passion to transform the world. It *may* trigger mystical vision; it *always* spurs social action. In worship divine fire licks dead wood.

Romero says worship should change *each of us*. When leaving the Eucharist "we ought to go out the way Moses descended Mount Sinai: with his face shining, with his heart brave and strong to face the world's difficulties."[67] As Moses needed courage to lead his people, the Salvadoran people need faith to follow Jesus. Lester describes worship's social impact on *all of us*:

---

66. Traherne, *Centuries*, 185–86.
67. Romero, *Violence of Love*, 169.

> The practical effect of corporate worship is to weld varying individuals into a unity that can stand against the evil, disruptive forces of the world, its quarreling, its envying, and its war.
>
> You cannot concentrate your mind and spirit in the worship of anything, good or bad, without acquiring something of the nature of the things worshipped. To worship truth is to assimilate a part of truth. To worship beauty is to become in some measure beautiful. To worship courage is to begin to be brave.[68]

For Stringfellow, worship gives us new eyes, a new heart, and a divine commission. Worship illumines "every flaw and injustice, every falsity and offense, every vanity and need of the prevailing social order while notoriously, passionately, incessantly calling for the . . . transfiguring of the incumbent order in society."[69] Two of his favorite images symbolize the transfigured order: the biblical manger and his personal icon, the circus. To Stringfellow, the manger embodies Isaiah's vision of creation reordered (Isa 11:6–9),[70] so when living on Block Island, Stringfellow and Anthony Towne called Towne's outbuilding "the manger."[71] Circus iconography filled Stringfellow's homes: a circus tent motif in his Manhattan apartment, a carousel horse, circus posters, and an elaborate scale-model circus in his study on Block Island.[72] To him, the circus mocks evil—on the high-wire, taming lions, being shot out of a cannon: "the circus performer is the image of the eschatological person—emancipated from frailty and inhibition, exhilarant and militant, transcendent over death—neither confined nor conformed by the fear of death any more."[73] Romero and Lester say that worship infuses courage. Stringfellow says it transforms us into death-defying activists.

For Stringfellow, worship also purges our vision and enables us to expose every lie, deceit, and deception in any and every social order. For Thomas Kelly, worship has a contrasting function: it transfigures our vision as we bear a "sanctuary frame of mind" that opens our eyes to "see all humankind tinged with deeper shadows and touched with Galilean glories."[74] Romero and Lester see worship as a time to *be* transfigured individually

---

68. Lester, *Ambassador of Reconciliation*, 103–4.
69. Stringfellow, *Second Birthday*, 101.
70. Stringfellow, *Conscience and Obedience*, 79.
71. Stringfellow, *Simplicity of Faith*, 33–34.
72. Ibid., 86–91, *Second Birthday*, 167–70; Stringfellow and Towne, *Suspect Tenderness*, 19; Berrigan, J. and C., "Eschaton Hospitality," 26; Donnelly, "Mighty Soul," 26.
73. Stringfellow, *Simplicity of Faith*, 90.
74. Kelly, *Testament of Devotion*, 30.

and as a body, Stringfellow as a time to be given Mississippi eyes, Kelly as a time that gifts us with Assisi eyes. Worship purges. Worship illumines. Worship strengthens. Worship unites. Worship transfigures us to transfigure the world.

Worship contains the seeds of transfiguration, but familiarity with the worshiping community's institutional home sabotages the very transformation worship nurtures. Writing of the fourteenth-century church, Vida Scudder calls this disillusioning "spectacle presented by the visible" church "the sharpest trial to Christian faith throughout the ages."[75] In spite of Protestant and Catholic penchants to romanticize different epochs (once upon a time, we must have gotten it right!), the church resolutely underachieves in every era, past, present, and yet to come. All too commonly the church is fire resistant and sterile, dead wood rotting. Activists know it, and they are not too shy to say it.

Drawing on two too-familiar female archetypes, Day calls the church both "mother" and "harlot."[76] Brutally frank about an insufferable organization, Merton says we must "miserably, honestly" concede the church's corruption, confess our cowardly complicity, and yet push through a bog of institutional mediocrity toward truth.[77] Frequently frustrated by its opposition to activism, King found the church "weak and vacillating,"[78] habitually a pawn of the status quo instead of a power for social change:[79] "How we have blemished and scarred that body through social neglect and fear of being nonconformists."[80]

In a failure of nerve, imagination, vision, and faith, the church downsizes the gospel as congregations and denominations fixate on the institutional navel. The church is impervious to the workings of the revolution and irrelevant to the coming of the realm; it is dead weight burying the realm instead of dead wood burning with the Spirit. The realm, as Rauschenbusch says, is never contiguous with or "confined within the limits of the Church and its activities"—rather, the revolution "embraces the whole of human life. It is the Christian transfiguration of the social order."[81] In a 1940 essay, Underhill asks the church to look beyond its organizational minutiae and even the horrors of war "towards a transfigured world, in which the ener-

---

75. Catherine, *Letters*, 337.
76. Day, *On Pilgrimage: The Sixties*, 290.
77. Merton, *Search for Solitude*, 185.
78. King, *Where Do We Go*, 113.
79. King, *Strength to Love*, 19, *Testament of Hope*, 300, 407.
80. King, *Testament of Hope*, 300.
81. Rauschenbusch, *Social Gospel*, 145.

gies now wasted on conflict shall be turned to the purposes of life"—the church, she says, should call "upon every one of her members to work for this transfigured world."[82]

King's surrealistic rhetoric envisions this transfiguration. When in the final chorus of his "I Have a Dream" speech he plays on the patriotic hook "let freedom ring." He first imagines freedom ringing from mountains in New England, New York, Colorado, and California—everywhere but the South. Only then does he mention the untransfigurable: Lookout Mountain, a Civil War battleground, and Stone Mountain, the Mt. Rushmore of the Confederacy and the re-birthplace of the Ku Klux Klan. King's dream purges, redeems, and transfigures these mountains linked to slavery and terrorism. Only then does he mention a state incapable of mountaintop vision and inoculated against political hope as freedom rings "from every hill and molehill of Mississippi."[83] From toxic mountains and tainted molehills, God's message, he says, will ring. King envisions transfiguring grace in history, in the most hateful and hopeless places, in the deadest of dead wood.

Witnesses to the spiritual power of the early civil rights movement beheld visions moving mountains. Like a mystic expressing the unutterable, journalist Pat Watters describes the civil rights movement as (obviously) anti-cultural but also (elusively) "extra-cultural." To Watters, "culture defines how those in it perceive their reality" (what is normal, what is not) and defines people's "response" (what will change, what cannot). The cry for racial equality punctured cultural walls as it "held forth alternatives which the culture was incapable of accepting and which, therefore, it actively resisted. The movement called this extra-cultural quality 'the power of love.'"[84] Describing his fellow journalists as if they had heard a voice from heaven or seen the dead raised, "these tough-minded and competent, objectivity-seeking professionals became uncharacteristically, unprofessionally emotional. More than once, one of them choked up and was unable to speak when he called in."[85] It happened to Watters as well. When he first heard "We Shall Overcome" it heartened him as the story of Le Chambon stirred Philip Hallie: "I listened and heard them saying in the song that the way things used to be was no more, and was forever ended. And knowing all that that meant for them, and for me, I cried. I cried for the first time in many years, cried unabashedly, cried for joy—and hope."[86] This extra-cultural epiphany led

---

82. Underhill, *Modern Guide*, 214.
83. King, *Testament of Hope*, 220.
84. Watters, *Down to Now*, 10.
85. Ibid., 53.
86. Ibid., 54.

Watters into "a process of alienation" from all that felt normal, conventional, routine, stable, and everlasting: "Suddenly in the South I was seeing what I had not needed or not dared to see before." "We Shall Overcome" gave him "a vision of what humankind and society might be beyond anything that our culture would have allowed us to believe in."[87] He imagined segregation ended, society transfigured, and dead wood fruitful and burning.

As Romero knew, transfiguration is not an all-healing balm or an all-purpose armor. For him as for Tutu, the transfiguration is not an ascent out of harm's way, but a renewal *for* ministry in a dangerous world. For them transfiguration is as real as sin, systemic evil, and human suffering. Yet there are subtle variations in the politics of Mt. Tabor. For Romero, transfiguration strengthens activists to become light. For Tutu, the potential for transfiguration in everyone keeps us from vilifying landowners, slave owners, industrialists, dictators, colonizers, or perpetrators. Transfiguration not only makes radical social action more urgent; it moderates social revolution to avoid puritanical purges and ideological cleansings.

The Theologia Germanica daringly suggests that if the devil ever obeyed God, "he would turn into an angel and all his sin and wickedness would be amended and atoned and all at once forgiven."[88] Even evil incarnate can be transformed. So Tutu *had* to write to Vorster because even the Pilates of apartheid can be forgiven, redeemed, and transfigured. To seek less is to assert that free will is forever more powerful than *ennobling* grace. The transfiguration is, as King says, a double victory that frees oppressors and oppressed.[89] It makes even the deadest of dead wood flower and burn.

ALL MATTER

At Polonnaruwa Merton saw all matter pulsing with the presence of divinity in a once-in-his-lifetime epiphany. For Teilhard de Chardin, that singular awakening was a basic creed. In the last days of his life, Merton saw what he already knew: that God is in everything,[90] that everything on earth plants something of heaven in us,[91] and that everything that is is holy.[92] Teilhard's credo formed early in life, and it became his central contribution to

---

87. Ibid., 57.
88. *Theologia Germanica*, 79.
89. King, *Strength to Love*, 55.
90. Merton, *Thomas Merton in Alaska*, 139–40.
91. Merton, *New Seeds*, 25.
92. Ibid., 21–28.

theology—creation itself is alive. In a revelation tinged with biblical symbols of cloud and light, inanimate creation seems remarkably human.

> And now in the heart of the whirling cloud a light was growing, a light in which there was the tenderness and the mobility of a human glance; and from it there spread a warmth which was not now like the harsh heat radiating from a furnace but like the opulent warmth which emanates from a human body. What had been a blind and feral immensity was now becoming expressive and personal; and its hitherto amorphous expanses were being molded into features of an ineffable face.[93]

Teilhard sees creation itself as personal, living, tender, and warm. He admits that his depictions could be misconstrued as "the essential revelation of paganism" with a dollop of panentheism if not a hint of pure pantheism: "Everything that is active, that moves or breathes, every physical, astral, or animate energy, every fragment of force, every spark of life, is equally sacred; for, in the humblest atom and the most brilliant star, in the lowest insect and the finest intelligence, there are the radiant smiles and thrill of the *same Absolute*."[94] But he also insists that in its exaltation of God's creation this intuition has dual religious citizenship—pagan and Christian. Perhaps there is something in this discovery that extends ecclesiastical theology beyond its more timid borders: Merton uses Buddhist language to say: everything is emptiness and everything is compassion.[95] But Underhill calls it the Christian mystic's vocation and prophetic mission to perceive things that to others remain hidden. So they find "in every manifestation of life a sacramental meaning; a loveliness, a wonder, a heightened significance."[96] What could be more Christian than for Teilhard to experience creation as a living sacrament? As a priest he would "make the whole earth my altar and on it will offer you all the labors and sufferings of the world."[97]

Alongside religion's holy times—feasts, fasts, festivals, and Sabbaths—most faiths are topophilic as they nurture an appreciation, affection, and awe for sacred places. On Mt. Sinai, Moses stands on holy ground. In a cave on Mt. Hira, Muhammad hears Gabriel. Under the bodhi tree, the Buddha receives enlightenment. Native Americans in the American northwest call Mt. Rainier "Tahoma," "The Mountain That Was God."[98] Christians sojourn

93. Teilhard, *Writings*, 44.
94. Ibid., 46 (italics his).
95. Merton, *Other Side*, 323.
96. Underhill, *Mysticism*, 36.
97. Teilhard, *Writings*, 80.
98. Lane, *Landscapes of the Sacred*, 6–7.

to the Holy Land. For Muslims, the hajj to Mecca to circumambulate the Kaaba, the sacred mosque, is one of a few primary religious obligations.

Yet, for this thesis there is an antithesis. While glory is revealed locally, splendor can be accessed globally. When a woman preparing for her hajj visits Rumi, they are awakened and go to the rooftop where they see the Kaaba spinning in the sky.[99] The gate of heaven is everywhere; all places are sacred spaces. So Teilhard reports the universality of specific epiphanies: what is occasionally visible is always true.

> Within every being and every event there was a progressive expansion of a mysterious inner clarity which transfigured them. But, what was more, there was a gradual variation of intensity and color that was related to the complex interplay of three universal components: the cosmic, the human, and the Christic. . . .
>
> Crimson gleams of matter, gliding imperceptibly into the gold of spirit, ultimately to become transformed into the incandescence of a universe that is person—and through all this there blows, animating it and spreading over it a fragrant balm, a zephyr of union—and of the feminine.[100]

God's glory is not only in God's daughters and sons; God is in all places and things. For Teilhard, matter contains more than "the cosmic, the human, and the Christic." There is also a balm of healing, a hint of the feminine, and a doorway to union.

The insight, of course, is not unique to Teilhard. Bede Griffiths finds notes in harmony with Hinduism as Chergé sought them with Islam. Like the cosmic Christology of Colossians (1:15–20), Lord Krishna teaches us to see all things in ourselves and ourselves in all things.[101] And while Hinduism sees each person as a drop of water in a great ocean,[102] Rumi tells his readers to let the ocean splash in their chests.[103] To Thomas Traherne, without an awareness of this interrelationship with creation, we lead impoverished lives.

> You never enjoy the world aright, till the Sea itself flows in your veins, till you are clothed with the heavens, and crowned with the stars: and perceive yourself to be the sole heir of the whole world, and more than so, because people are in it who are every

---

99. Rumi, *Say I Am You*, 44.
100. Teilhard, *Writings*, 31–32.
101. Griffiths, *Return to the Center*, 121.
102. Ibid., 144.
103. Rumi, *Delicious Laughter*, 129.

> one sole heirs as well as you. Till you can sing and rejoice and delight in God, as misers do in gold, and Kings in scepters, you never enjoy the world.[104]

In the spirit of Psalm 8, Traherne says: be aware of the sea within you, the heavens draped over you, and the stars adorned about you. His spiritual outlook is almost anti-Copernican: wonder revolves around the human race; it exists for our delight. For Traherne, the world belongs to each person *and* to all people; and all people belong to the world and its creator. The privatization of religious awareness is selfish, cloying, greedy, and latently hostile, yet unless we embrace God's gift personally, we cannot savor life fully. To do so would be tantamount to saying Christ is an impersonal savior of an immaterial world. Without a personal taste of wonder, corporate spiritual ownership diminishes the value of God's gift, like being one of a billion shareholders in a business whose real estate is heaven, whose profits are nirvana, and whose currency is bliss.

Traherne's writings are antithesis, antidote, and immunization against becoming so spellbound by the godlessness of the world (Bonhoeffer) that we miss its saving beauty (Dostoevsky). If others praise the redemptive value of hallowed tears, Traherne inhales the transfiguring incense of blessed joy. His message is a healing glow against evil's gloom. In the early pages of *Centuries*, Traherne's persistent mandate to enjoy life amasses the force of a commandment:

> Till your spirit fills the whole world, and stars are your jewels; till you are as familiar with the ways of God in all Ages as with your walk and table: till you are intimately acquainted with that shady nothing out of which the world was made: till you love people so as to desire their happiness, with a thirst equal to the zeal of your own; till you delight in God for being good to all: you never enjoy the world.[105]

Traherne's transfigured cosmic awareness has a sharp ethical kick. The joy of all creation rouses us to embrace the equitable distribution of God's grace and to seek a stranger's joy "with a thirst equal to the zeal of your own." Traherne says: make the world's history, the earth's topography, the sky's vast glory part of your daily cell. Discover for yourself the nighttime reach of Theophan's monk. Revel in God's universal grace, and seek the welfare of *Babylon* (Jer 29:4–7) with the same passion you have for your own next

---

104. Traherne, *Centuries*, 14.
105. Ibid., 14–15.

breath. See others as they are; pursue *their* happiness with the urgency of someone grasping for the only handful of joy on earth.

Like Merton's spiritual exercise uniting a hemisphere in himself, Traherne says, "Till you more feel it than your private estate, and are more present in the hemisphere, considering the glories and the beauties there, than in your own house,"[106] your joy is a child's bauble. To enjoy the world, delight in God's love; seek its perfection in beauty and harmony. As Underhill says we cannot redeem anything we do not love, Traherne suggests that we cannot love something we do not enjoy.

Teilhard follows Traherne, Franciscans, psalmists, and a host of witnesses as he carouses in creation. He also reopens the core issue of an eighth-century theological skirmish over representational religious art. With Islam's strict ban on iconography banging on the door and Gnosticism's disdainful disgust for all things physical still nascent and hidden in the flesh of the church institutional, some Christians argued rightly that the first two commandments forbade images. Others insisted that the incarnation implies, promotes, and even demands iconography. In the midst of that fierce debate, John of Damascus invoked the Word made flesh to drive a stake through the heart of Gnosticism's ghostly anti-incarnationalism: "I do not worship matter, but I worship the Creator of matter, who for my sake became material. . . . I will not cease from reverencing matter, for it was through matter that my salvation came to pass."[107] Unless God becomes human in Christ, our link with the divine dangles unhinged, and we are left far from a distant, unidentified floating deity. Unless the Word becomes flesh, there is no salvation. But Teilhard's credo leaps past the theology of John of Damascus. For Teilhard, matter is sacred whether or not it is an instrument of salvation; it is a means for our awakening, and an ever-present epiphany from the beginning without end.

As it was with mystics before him, the force of Teilhard's conversion compelled him to evangelize Christians even if the cost of mysticism meant being silenced—an institutionally cooler way of nailing a witch's tongue to the roof of her mouth—as the church perceived him as another Galileo introducing concepts beyond its comfort zone and control. But, like John of Damascus, Teilhard had the incarnation on his side. The incarnation not only means that when God became human the human could become divine (Irenaeus, Athanasius). It means that when the Word became matter, matter became forever infused with the Word.[108]

106. Ibid., 15.
107. Leech, *True Prayer*, 79.
108. Teilhard, *Writings*, 23.

In his *Hymn to Matter*, Teilhard, like Merton, is completely overawed by the spiritual sovereignty of created things. His hymn is less a ballad to spiritual beauty than a paean to material power. It is also a twist on the story of Job. Confronted by the whirlwind, Job falls into sphinx-like silence. From within the same whirlwind, Teilhard gushes praise. When there is so much that could make him cower in Otto's dread-tinged awe, he roars in ecstatic shouts.

> Blessed be you, harsh matter, barren soil, stubborn rock: you who force us to work if we would eat.
> Blessed be you, perilous matter, violent sea, untamable passion: you who unless we fetter you will devour us.
> Blessed be you, mighty matter, irresistible march of evolution, reality ever newborn, you who, by constantly shattering our mental categories, force us to go ever further and further in our pursuit of the truth.
> Blessed be you, universal matter, immeasurable time, boundless ether, triple abyss of stars and atoms and generations: you who by overflowing and dissolving our narrow standards of measurement reveal to us the dimensions of God.
> Blessed be you, impenetrable matter: you who, interposed between our minds and the world of essences, cause us to languish with the desire to pierce through the seamless veil of phenomena.
> Blessed be you, mortal matter: you who one day will undergo the process of dissolution within us and will thereby take us forcibly into the very heart of that which exists....
> I acclaim you as the divine milieu, charged with creative power, as the ocean stirred by the Spirit, as the clay molded and infused with life by the incarnate Word...[109]

Teilhard's *Hymn to Matter* snubs tender warmth in favor of transfiguring beatitude. Inhabiting Job's wild and wildly indifferent universe, Teilhard delights in creation, not as Young Chief who blesses a symbiotic, nurturing mother earth in its endless suckling of the human race, not as Francis's canticle that senses a kinship with all created things, but simply as a revelation of creation and Creator. Francis describes the sun as *beautiful* and *radiant*, the moon and stars as *clear*, *precious*, and *beautiful*, water as *useful*, *humble*, *precious*, and *chaste*, and fire as *beautiful*, *playful*, *robust*, and *strong*. Teilhard uses adjectives from another lexicon: matter is *untamable*, *irresistible*, *stubborn*, *perilous*, *violent*, *barren*, and *harsh*; "mortal matter" is colder than Sister Death. The Sermon on the Mount blesses the poor in

---

109. Ibid., 44–45.

spirit, the pure in heart, peacemakers, mourners, the merciful, the meek, and those who hunger and thirst for righteousness. Teilhard blesses the violent, the devouring, and the impenetrable. Young Chief speaks of fructifying earth instinctively practicing the Golden Rule toward all creatures; John of Damascus blesses matter because God uses it to achieve salvation. For Teilhard, matter's physical functions and spiritual benefits are irrelevant. For Teilhard, matter itself—not its potential, not its beauty—is a revelation. Matter is blessed even as an antagonistic threat, a harsh and dreadful thing, something as dangerous as orthodoxy. Matter needs no divine confirmation that it is "good." Matter is blessed because it *is*. As Traherne lauds the wildness of human nature—that God so loves the world that God allows free beings to be dense, sinful, and destructive—Teilhard praises the untamable nature of creation.

Throwing humanistic hubris into a tizzy, when we see creation through Teilhard's eyes we are forced to assess human nature not apart from creation, not above creation, but as a fragment of creation, intrinsically and intimately related to the nature of matter. People, like matter, can be hard, harsh, threatening, barren, stubborn, untamable, perilous *and* beautiful, useful, precious, playful, radiant, robust, and strong. It might be as hard (or as easy) for God to transfigure matter as it is to transform people, and as hard (or as easy) for the divine to permeate earth and penetrate rock as it is to pierce hearts of stone. The implacable, obstinate rock that Teilhard praises is perhaps no more malleable or less redeemable than the hard hearts and stiff necks of the human race.

Merton found the gate of heaven in a church, on city streets, in matter. Teilhard's single doorway is creation; he would have approved of Traherne's observation that "when you are once acquainted with the world, you will find the goodness and wisdom of God so manifest therein, that it was impossible another, or better should be made."[110] Without any need for a further agenda—without recognizing all created things as sisters and brothers, without praising creation as a nurturing mother, without believing in matter as a conduit for salvation—Teilhard senses the divine in all things. If only we could see this, we would bless matter, and that blessing would bless us.

IN BEAUTY AND IN UGLINESS

As the "war to end all wars," World War I did not exactly pan out. Rather, much like "the end of history," "the war to end all wars" was merely another vapid, fallacious, pandering, if particularly grandiose bit of sloganeering.

---

110. Traherne, *Centuries*, 6.

Rather than ending war, World War I launched a century of innumerable wars—Muste's "short and snappy wars"—and unparalleled devastation. World War I magnified every false note and clanging gong in myths of heroism and war's nobility; it unveiled the pure tawdriness of patriotism; it confirmed the deepest Augustinian cynicism of robber nations; it exploded myths of Enlightenment progress; it rained havoc on optimistic humanism; it spawned *the* Lost Generation of lost generations; it became a long, loud, but too soon forgotten prelude to the chaotic disillusionment of American soldiers in Vietnam, Afghanistan, Iraq, and wars yet to come. Its muddy trenches, its promiscuous carnage, and the progress of its battles measured in meters came to symbolize the futility of life. Its sludge, filth, and blood gave the lie to Western civilization's very claim of civilization. The Enlightenment's faith, hubris, and self-love were as crudely hacksawed as any crusade has aptly subverted confidence in the church.

Had he considered it, Merton might have called Erich Maria Remarque's *All Quiet on the Western Front* a "devout meditation"[111] on that war, any war, or all war. Sunk conscience deep in mud and muck, the narrator and characters alternately observe themselves, their times, and their nation like so many ants under a magnifying mirror. When the war begins, peasants enlist as quizzical but passive participants, Freire's inert objects senseless to their potential as subjects, trained in a Pavlovian class system that has drained them of free will. Likewise, industrialism's poor enlist in the army without any passion for *la causa*. They are, as always, caught up in and ground down by forces beyond their questioning and control. In contrast, the bourgeoisie, those accustomed to a greater measure—or illusion—of power, are "beside themselves with joy." Whatever their questions or convictions about war, the middle class yields to the voices of authority they associate with "insight" and "wisdom," and insight and wisdom tell them to believe and to fight. But enthusiasm and patriotism quickly shatter: "The first bombardment showed us our mistake, and under it the world as they had taught it to us broke into pieces."[112]

Left to the anarchy of his own ideas, each soldier becomes part political theorist, part philosophical pragmatist, part amateur psychologist, and part moral theologian. One soldier conjures up an innovative approach to international conflict: war in an almost-perfect world matches opposing leaders and generals "dressed in bathing-drawers and armed with clubs" who "have it out among themselves. Whoever survives, his country wins."[113]

---

111. Merton, *Raids on the Unspeakable*, 45–49.
112. Remarque, *All Quiet*, 11–12.
113. Ibid., 28.

Others adopt a Calvinistic-Hobbesian bent: "Man is essentially a beast, only he butters it over like a slice of bread with a little decorum."[114] In war, this bestiality is supremely functional: the military needs the dumbly compliant to obey orders. As soldiers wait in long lines at army-administered brothels, they see every aspect of a soldier's life, a civilian's life, a man's life, a woman's life, and a human life systematically degraded.[115] Turning their psychoanalytical gaze inward, they dispassionately diagnose the "annihilation of all human feeling."[116] Their emotions are numbed at the skin or clogged at the heart. Their principles, values, virtues, ethics, morals, and conscience dissolve into a sewer of relativism: Germans protect our fatherland; the French protect their fatherland; who is right?[117] War, once raised as a trophy and proposed as a solution, is merely a contagion, a "fever"; no one seeks war; no one wants war; all succumb to war.[118] Already sensing that their lives are collateral damage, they fret about survival as much as dismemberment or death—will anyone at home welcome the survivors?[119] As if to test this hypothesis, when the protagonist goes home on leave, he realizes he no longer belongs: "it is a foreign world."[120] Live or die, counted or uncounted among the casualties, "the war," they realize, "has ruined us for everything."[121]

Amid all the horrors of interminable infection, illness, amputation, drawn-out suffering, and sudden death; amid cruelty, predictable cowardice, and fruitless courage, what pierces their hearts is not the sound of wounded soldiers crying for help caught between the lines in no-man's-land; no, they break down when they hear the cries of wounded horses: "It's unendurable. It is the moaning of the world, it is the martyred creation, wild with anguish, filled with terror, and groaning."[122] Such a devout meditation re-enters Job's whirlwind, Job's life, Job's loss, Job's skin, and makes that tumbleweed rootlessness its home.

It is one thing to sit in an ivory tower or a monastic cell and wax theologically rhapsodic about transfiguration. It is one thing for Traherne to esteem people as sparkling jewels or for Merton to observe them as shining suns. It is quite another to write of transfiguration when anguished,

---

114. Ibid., 30.
115. Ibid., 93.
116. Ibid., 119.
117. Ibid., 124.
118. Ibid., 126.
119. Ibid., 55.
120. Ibid., 104.
121. Ibid., 56.
122. Ibid., 41.

martyred creation is filled with "terror and groaning." So we might assume that the gift to *see* transfiguration belongs to the spiritually gifted or the materially privileged, those who may know enough to ask for forgiveness, but nothing of anxieties about daily bread or barbarous drones or cruel bureaucracies or being instantly delivered from evil. Some have time, spiritual time or leisure time, to gaze, to look out from the masts of their ship (Merton) or from mountains or hills—but not from trenches, caves, or valleys, and certainly not from the shadow of death. It would seem easier to see glory while perched in privilege. But such is not the always the case.

Jesus was transfigured, but Jesus' life does not glide without turbulence above the fraught frays of life like a hummingbird flitting from one theological peak experience to another: from incarnation to transfiguration to resurrection to ascension. So, on second thought, we might sympathize with Peter's bumbling attempt to memorialize the transfiguration in booths like one of the paparazzi trying to get Moses and Elijah and Jesus to hold a pose for an old, staged black-and-white photo. Peter tries to bring stasis to a singular flash of beatific bliss, but even before the inner three can heed the voice from the cloud, they are swiftly down the mountain facing demons. No. Transfiguration is not as insular as that. As Catherine of Siena says that Jesus ran to the cross eager to complete the work of salvation, Gregory Palamas reminds us that as Stephen faced martyrdom, his face "shone like the face of an angel" (Acts 6:15).[123] Unless it is sullied by suffering or obliterated by death, transfiguration becomes a demonic temptation. Praise does not arise only from periods of centeredness and serenity. Francis did not write his canticle from a position of luxury, ease, or conventional happiness.[124] Traherne and Merton, prophets of the politics of Mt. Tabor, wrote in chaotic times—the English Civil War, or amid the Cold War, civil strife, and the war in Vietnam. Are there any other times in which to write? Perhaps places, but not times.

If *All Quiet on the Western Front* is a devout meditation on World War I, Underhill's introduction to *Practical Mysticism*, written as that war began, was an apologetic for authoring a book on spiritual practice when grace seemed nothing more than an infant's fable—when we became warriors, we put away our childish faith. Under similar circumstances, Merton wondered about the translation of his book *No Man is an Island* into Vietnamese: "The whole thing brings home the futility of so-called spiritual literature in this day and age. Who is going to have time for pious meditations with the whole

---

123. Palamas, *Triads*, 52.
124. Leclerc, *Canticle of Creatures*, 28.

place getting showered with napalm?"[125] Yet, while admitting that "it is not difficult to sit in a quiet monastery and meditate on love, humility, mercy, inner silence, meditation and peace," he hoped his "meditation on love and peace" could "be realistically and intimately related to the fury of war, bloodshed, burning, destruction, killing that takes place on the other side of the earth."[126]

Underhill, perhaps defensively, perhaps courageously, perhaps with breathtaking naïveté, perhaps with Wendell Berry's ornery hope even though "you have considered all the facts,"[127] justifies her book's publication. She acknowledges that some might find her book "wholly out of place" in such a time. She admits she thought about postponing its publication. She knows that "the cauldron of war" makes mysticism's claims iffy, dodgy, and dubious. Yet she reaffirms her mission to proclaim mysticism "practical" not only in times of "fair weather"—a sunny-day mysticism, after all, would be nothing but a "spiritual plaything."[128] Even so, her comments can be read as astonishingly out of tune—and touch—with all that World War I meant: "It is significant that many [mystical] experiences are reported to us from periods of war and distress: that the stronger the forces of destruction appeared, the more intense grew the spiritual vision which opposed them." She reiterates her recurrent claim that spiritual visions and auditions do not insulate mystics from the pain of the world; they do not provide a "soothing draught" as much as "the most powerful of stimulants" to transform it.[129]

As it turns out, the long-shot bet of Underhill's faith was at least true for Teilhard de Chardin. Teilhard had his first inklings of the transfiguration of matter in World War I's trenches when nothing was quiet on the western front.[130] In the middle of one of history's most blatantly useless, hideous, and meaningless catastrophes in which every muddy mile of progress was a delusion, Teilhard discovered a milieu that would seem almost impossible to perceive in wreck, ruin, muck, and gore. Unlike the epiphany-conducive surroundings of Isaiah in the temple or Merton at Polonnaruwa, Teilhard finds the hem of God's robe in Western Europe's killing fields.

For others, transfiguration takes place in the beauty of holiness (Ps 96:9),[131] or in all things bright and beautiful. Rufus Jones praises beauty

125. Merton, *Hidden Ground*, 298.
126. Merton, *Introductions*, 104.
127. Berry, *Collected Poems*, 151.
128. Underhill, *Practical Mysticism*, vii–viii.
129. Ibid., ix.
130. Teilhard, *Writings*, 15.
131. *Book of Common Prayer*, 726.

even as he challenges its particularity: beauty "breaks through not only at a few highly organized points, it breaks through almost everywhere. Even the minutest things reveal it as well as do the sublimest things"; even "a bit of mold . . . is charged with beauty. Everything from a dewdrop to Mount Shasta is the bearer of beauty." Size does not matter! Jones adds his own emendation to Merton's ode to uselessness: beauty "has no function, no utility. Its value is intrinsic, not extrinsic. It is its own excuse for being. It greases no wheels, it bakes no puddings. It is a gift of sheer grace, a gratuitous largesse." The existence of beauty "must imply behind things a Spirit that enjoys beauty for its own sake and that floods the world everywhere with it. Wherever it can break through, it does break through, and our joy in it shows that we are in some sense kindred to the giver and revealer of it."[132] While Jones stresses the beauty of creation, Hildegard's experience of transfiguring splendor begins in the unseen essence of God: "In the pure and holy Godhead all visible and invisible things shine before all eternity without a temporal moment and without the elapse of time, just as trees and other bodily things are reflected in adjacent waters without being within them in a bodily fashion, even though their outlines may appear in this mirror."[133]

Beauty can ease our apprehension of the divine. Merton reveled in beauty—Shaker furniture,[134] Zen drawings, and photography. His photos rarely seek out anything as spectacular as the carved faces of the Buddhas at Polonnaruwa. Most often his black-and-white photos frame the ordinary: blurs of sunlight, leafless trees, dead wood, cut wood, gnarled wood, wooden wheels, tree stumps, rocks, fences, signs, chairs, bricks, buckets, buildings, cups, nails, staples, a bed, a desk, a kitchen, a typewriter, and an altar.[135] Whether it is the plain, straight lines of his hermitage, or the rounded curved lines of the Buddhas, each and every thing becomes another Zen drawing.

Beauty sparks each of Merton's three core epiphanies. In Havana, distracting street noise hushes alongside the children's chiming voices that strike him "like a thunderclap."[136] Beauty overwhelms the grating, the tinny, and the discordant. In Louisville, his epiphany takes place in a city he does

---

132. *Christian Faith*, 136.
133. Hildegard, *Book of Divine Works*, 13.
134. Merton, *Mystics and Zen Masters*, 193–202.
135. Merton, *Hidden Wholeness*.
136. Merton, *Run to the Mountain*, 218.

not like,[137] in its shopping district,[138] a symbol to Merton of commercialism's quicksand banality of banalities. In his first published account influenced by Traherne,[139] he edits out the source of the shining sun that sparked his epiphany: the nonmonastic beauty of women. Even in the privacy of his posthumously published journals, he seems compelled to clarify his attraction to the "secret beauty" of their hearts instead of the visible beauty of their bodies.[140] Yet later in the same journal, he notes that there is something of sexuality in almost every spontaneous human interaction,[141] so it is unlikely that his epiphany was 99.9 percent asexual. Merton's central epiphany into human nature is sparked by his attraction to women.

At Polonnaruwa, the epiphany's calling card is an aesthetic awakening to the artistic "beauty" of the Buddhas: "The great smiles. Huge and yet subtle." Only as the statues grasp his attention—like the children's voices and the women's beauty—does the revelation become an ode to matter as "[t]he rock, all matter, all life, is charged with dharmakaya." Yet as critical for Merton as *what* he sees is *that* he sees: "I have now seen and have pierced through the surface and have got beyond the shadow and the disguise."[142] Merton, like Traherne, finds the gate of transfiguration in all that is good and true and beautiful.

Of course, these were not Merton's only epiphanies. In January 1964 in a visit to New York City, he felt a reverberation of Louisville (1958) and an anticipation of Polonnaruwa (1968) in an urban jumble. Merton had a natural affinity for New York; on the plane he realizes he is still a "New Yorker" and at JFK he observes the

> enormous rumble of trucks and buildings, a vast congeries of airports, and then in the American Airlines Building fantastic beings, lovely humans, assured yet resigned, some extraordinarily beautiful, all mature and sophisticated actual people, with whom I was in a profound rapport of warmth and recognition—these are my people for God's sake! I had forgotten—the tone of voice, the awareness, the weariness, the readiness to keep standing, an amazing existence, the realization of the fallible human condition, and of the fantastic complexity of modern life.[143]

137. Merton, *Road to Joy*, 171, *Search for Solitude*, 316, *Sign of Jonas*, 97–98, 119.
138. Merton, *Conjectures*, 156.
139. Merton, *Search for Solitude*, 384, *Dancing in the Water*, 298.
140. Merton, *Search for Solitude*, 182.
141. Ibid., 323.
142. Merton, *Other Side*, 323.
143. Merton, *Dancing in the Water*, 114.

Beauty, energy, and affinity reawaken Merton again.

Traherne, concerned to maximize our appreciation of the world, says that we cannot fully enjoy the world "till you so love the beauty of enjoying it."[144] Human beauty—men and women, the elderly and children—left him awestruck. Seeing it, "I knew not that they were born or should die. But all things abided eternally as they were in the proper places. Eternity was manifest in the Light of the Day, and something infinite behind everything appeared." But he is also awakened to the fact that Eden and heaven, alpha and omega, are before us all of the time. Like Francis's credo that all things are related, and John of the Cross's avowal that everything is "mine," Traherne sees sun, moon, and stars, temple, streets, and people, their clothes, their eyes, their skin, and their faces as "mine: and I the only spectator and enjoyer of it."[145]

For the most part, Traherne's string of epiphanies is an unalloyed annunciation while Merton uses the same insights to spur proclamation *and* protest. For Traherne, all can begin to sound like unconditional blessing and bliss. For Merton, *if* we can see, we can end every curse. But Traherne's revolutionary revelation is both comforting and jarring; beauty rubs up against ugliness; his revelation itself is *the rub* against every status quo that quantifies or diminishes human value—three-fifths of a man, acceptable casualties, polite homophobia, permanent poverty. Like all annunciations, it births denunciation. Traherne's elegant praise turns to aggravated protest. Even in the great carnival of beauty,

> [you must] so perfectly hate the abominable corruption of people in despising it, that you had rather suffer the flames of Hell than willingly be guilty of their error. There is so much blindness and ingratitude and damned folly in it. The world is a mirror of infinite beauty, yet no one sees it. It is a Temple of Majesty, yet no one regards it. It is a region of Light and Peace, did not people disquiet it. It is the Paradise of God. . . . It is the place of Angels and the Gate of Heaven.[146]

It is, he cries. It *is*!

Like Teilhard, Edwin Muir sees the divine not in beauty but among the muck. Muir's life was hardly one of starry-eyed privilege or personal tranquility. In his youth, he worked in a factory on the bottom side of the social class divide; he witnessed the communist takeover of Prague; he struggled

---

144. Traherne, *Centuries*, 15.

145. Ibid., 110.

146. Ibid., 15.

with his own mental health.[147] Yet Muir writes "The Transfiguration" about things we might consider foul, crass, distasteful, or destructive. Tutu says that no person is untransfigurable. Muir's poem says the same of places and things.

> Was it a vision?
> Or did we see that day the unseeable
> One glory of the everlasting world
> Perpetually at work, though never seen
> Since Eden locked the gate that's everywhere
> And nowhere? . . .
> The shepherds' hovels shone, for underneath
> The soot we saw the stone clean at the heart
> As on the starting day. The refuse heaps
> Were grained with that fine dust that made the world;
> For he had said, "to the pure all things are pure."
> And when we went into the town, he with us
> The lurkers under doorways, murderers,
> With rags tied round their feet for silence, came
> Out of themselves to us and were with us
> And those who hide within the labyrinth
> Of their own loneliness and greatness came,
> And those entangled in their own devices
> The silent and the garrulous liars, all
> Stepped out of their dungeons and were free . . .[148]

Eden, like the Kaaba seen from Rumi's roof, does not lie behind us in prehistoric lore, or ahead at the end of a million-mile march, or even circling above us in the heavens. It is hidden among the company of liars and lurkers and murderers in the midst of trash, fleapits, rags, and soot. Yet even in these places among these people, to the pure all things are pure (Titus 1:15). People who see are like those released from dungeons (Ps 146:7, Isa 61:1, Luke 4:18). Eden's entrance, like the gate to heaven, is everywhere and nowhere. It is not only in beauty that we discover holiness. The morally disfigured—liars, lurkers, and murderers preparing to violate the innocent—are transfigured. The people we consider unsavory or unsafe—gang bangers, drug lords, terrorists, neo-Nazis, elected politicians, corrupt CEOs—are transfigured. Not only can Dr. Jekyll avoid becoming Mr. Hyde; Dr. Jekyll can be transfigured. *Mr. Hyde* can be transfigured.

Jesus' transfiguration on Mt. Tabor is a once-in-a-messiah's-lifetime affair on the home turf of epiphanies. But just as Teilhard sees matter

147. Allchin, *Living Presence*, 131.
148. Muir, *Collected Poems*, 174–75.

translucent in trenches, Muir sees human and material refuse transfigured. Transfiguration is more than a moment in time, and not merely an *already* and a *not yet*. It is the conviction that the divine is present in all creation all of the time. God's redeeming mercy and unconditional love are neither a subjective discovery nor private property; mercy and love are stuffed into each inch and radiant in every atom. God's love is more than the restorative grace that remolds sinners. It is an empowering grace that turns sinners to saints and makes every creature and all matter glow with divinity. We may most effortlessly see the transfiguration in the good, the true, and the beautiful. But Tutu finds the transfigurable in the midst of apartheid, Teilhard in all matter, and Muir in rubbish and refuse.

Biblical passages liturgically linked to Holy Week, where brutality and ugliness kiss, remind us not of the transfigured but the crucified. But whether Isaiah's suffering servant or the figure in Psalm 22, we hear in the week's wailing grief a distant whisper of wonder. The central character in Psalm 22 is "a worm, and not human," scorned, despised, and mocked (Ps 22:6–7). "Poured out like water," his bones "are out of joint," his "heart . . . like wax . . . is melted" (Ps 22:14). The suffering servant is another Elephant Man: "So marred was his appearance beyond human semblance" (Isa 52:14), "he had no form or majesty that we should look at him, nothing in his appearance that we should desire him" (Isa 53:2). Yet these poetic passages coupled by tradition to Christ crucified are fused by that link to Christ already transfigured just as Francis's vision of the crucified reveals Mt. Alverna—another Mt. Tabor—afire with glory. In trash heaps and trenches, among murderers and lurkers, on the cross as on the mountain, no one, no place, no thing—not even the crucified one, the crucified people, or the crucified world—is untouched by transfiguration.

MEDITATION: MAY DAY

May 1, 2006. Proposed anti-immigrant legislation has aroused millions of people across the country from their stupor of passivity and powerlessness. Zac is 12. He, too, is awakened. He wants to do justice. He wants to go. This will be his first demonstration. But Zac and I will be late. I don't want him to miss any school.

We park at a church a mile from where the march has started. We walk a block, and wait. We stand in the middle of Wilshire Boulevard and look down the street to see a river, a tsunami, of white shirts coming toward us in a sea of flags and festivity. In the afternoon sun, they are transformed, transfigured; the shirts are whiter than anyone on earth could bleach them.

Zac, eyes wide, heart pounding, looks and laughs. He says nothing but I see it in his eyes: "Wow!" I pull out my cell phone to talk to a friend we plan to meet somewhere in this river of half a million people.

We move from the middle of the street to the sidewalk to wait for our friends. The white river rushes toward us, past us. It is more exhilarating than body surfing. These are merely the first waves. We watch from the sidewalk, but the marchers don't stay in the street. They can't. There are too many. Almost immediately, they are in front of us and behind us on the sidewalk. We are standing on a rock of salvation as the overflowing waters of Amos's ever-flowing stream of justice pour by. It takes our breath away. It gives us breath.

Helicopters circle above. Someone is always looking down at the kingdoms of this world, figuring out what movements to manipulate, what dreams to deflate, which nations to rule, which peoples to oppress. They wait for the river of righteousness to run dry, for the transfiguring light to dim. They wonder how long it will take this time.

We have seen block after solid block filled with marchers in their gleaming white shirts. We know that people a mile up the street are walking. The river runs from one urban horizon to the other, seemingly from here to the ends of the earth.

Our cell phones work. We find our friends. We jump into the march and move with the rhythm and the river. We walk and talk, we chant, we sing, surrounded by the signs and the sounds and the undiluted and irrefutable power of the movement and the moment. We are part of this movement, a movement as old as the Exodus, a movement made new. A purposeful circus, a powerful tide. Celebration as much as demonstration. Demonstrating joy as much as power. We wave to people as we pass. Block after block of concrete passes beneath our feet.

Even in Amos's ever-flowing river of righteousness, feet get tired even as souls are rested. Other realities, daily drudgeries, rear their normalcy and rouse us from our ecstatic waking dream. There is homework to do. There is dinner to cook. The river will wind its way to its destination without us. And it will keep flowing in us and through us. We have taken part in the day's transfiguration.

As Zac and I take the long walk back to our car, the parent-mentor emerges. I remember so many times I've marched, walked, sat, or stood. I do not have the credentials—the ID, the green card—to be called an activist, but I recall many times I've carried signs, held a candle, handed out flyers—in front of a retail store (no guns), in front of a grocery store (no grapes), in front of the Federal Building (no death squads, no war), in front of a courthouse (no execution). End this war and that one and that one. Stop this injustice and that one and that one. I've sat and stood and walked with thousands, hundreds, fifties, dozens, with a handful, and all alone.

At the end of this day when tens of thousands of white shirts were transfigured, when the ever-flowing stream overflowed, when we stood on the sidewalk of salvation, I had to tell Zac that this was the largest demonstration in which I had ever taken part. He needed to know that this exhilaration is not the norm. It was my parental responsibility to tell him, "They aren't all like this."

But later I wondered—maybe they are.

10

The Peace that is No Peace

Master, now you are dismissing your servant in peace, according to your word; for my eyes have seen your salvation . . .
—LUKE 2:29–30

Guide us waking, O Lord, and guard us sleeping; that awake we may watch with Christ, and asleep we may rest in peace.
—ANTIPHON FOR COMPLINE[1]

They see everything with an equal eye.
—THE BHAGAVAD GITA[2]

O good Jesus, you are the Tree of Life in the paradise of delights.
—NICHOLAS OF CUSA[3]

---

1. *Book of Common Prayer*, 134–35.
2. *Bhagavad Gita* 6:29.
3. Nicholas of Cusa, *Selected Writings*, 277.

Pure and still,
one can put things right everywhere under heaven.
—Lao Tzu[4]

There is no way to peace; peace is the way.
—A. J. Muste[5]

You ask me to pray for peace for you, my dear; the secret of peace is to love, love, love.
—Charles de Foucauld[6]

Blessed are the peacemakers, for they will be called children of God.
—Matthew 5:9

The peace of God, it is no peace, but strife closed in the sod.
Yet let us pray for but one thing—the marvelous peace of God.
—William Alexander Percy[7]

MEDITATION: MT. CALVARY

Standing, facing the altar from the other side—"and also with you." I feel the ache in my heart, the hunger in my spirit. I look at the celebrant here at Mt. Calvary and see behind him through the bay window the green hills, the low, gray clouds that whisper a drizzle, the great ocean stretching from the beach until it merges with the sky. Eucharist and creation together. Christ in bread and wine. Christ in the hills, the clouds, the sea. I want to take it all in, hug it all close.

Christ on the mountaintop being tempted with all the power and glory the world could offer. The voice descending from the clouds like thunder, like a mist, as Jesus is transfigured before the disbelieving eyes of his disciples. Jesus' voice calming the storm, stilling the waters, bringing peace to voyagers far and near, lost or on their way.

4. Tzu, *Tao Te Ching*, 13.
5. Muste, "Peace is the Way."
6. Foucauld, *Writings*, 113.
7. Hymn 661, *The Hymnal 1982*.

The ache in my heart so often lost among all the other aches—the others' aches—that crowd in and make a home there. They are welcome, truly welcome—have a seat, a bite to eat, a sip to quench a desert of thirst. The hunger forgotten in the rush to feed the others, to gather up the crumbs under the table that not one precious Word of God might go unreceived or unconsumed, that no one should miss the hidden taste of mercy in even a stale crumb or a hurried swallow.

I must remember these next three months on this sabbatical, remind myself each morning not to tell before I have heard, not to lose the ache in my desire to learn, not to miss this feast prepared for me. For soon enough I will be back behind the altar, looking out at the faces, hearing the growl of their unmet, undirected spiritual hunger, sensing, feeling the unvoiced cry of the ache in each heart for God's blessings, God's healing, God's mercy, God's love, God.

"The Peace of the Lord be always with you."

"And also with you."

And also *for* you, Gary. Also *for* you.

SATYAGRAHI IN PARADISE

It is one thing to hunger for justice and thirst for righteousness, another to be without food or water. As in all of history, so today hunger afflicts too many children, spits on too many prayers, and skins too many souls. Today threats to potable water grow, influenced more by climate change, population growth, and perpetual greed than humanist myths of progress. The as-yet-unlearned lesson of the globalization of modern terrorism is that injustice anywhere is a *direct* threat to peace everywhere.

So the dream of a time and a place where there is no hunger, no thirst, no insecurity, no illness, no tears, no fear, and no death is as compelling as it was in slavery, in the wilderness, among the prophets, to the evangelists, to the last dream on the last page of Scripture. There is a promised land of milk and honey and justice and equality. There are promised visions of vine and fig tree, plowshares and pruning hooks. There is a promised paradise to Jesus' neighbor on the neighboring cross. At the center of the city to come there is a tree of life. There is the realm for which we pray, the realm we await, the realm we seek. And there are caresses, touches, tastes, foretastes, scents, sights in the mind's eye of the realm, the promised place, the longed for day, paradise in the here and now. There is a dream that by cultivating an inner peace, an inner realm, we can at least have some solace, some grounding, some sense of equilibrium in the midst of the chaos, the whirlwind, the "cosmic storm."[8] Better yet, perhaps that internal peace cannot be only for us alone; like any run-of-the-mill epiphany, it is a gift to the world. Our inner peace need not create a gargantuan space, like Christ's mystical wounds, large enough for the whole world. But perhaps we can offer enough for many, enough for some, enough for a few, enough.

Rumi writes of a Sufi in "a fair orchard, full of trees and fruit and vines and greenery." In the desert, an orchard is sometimes a shimmering mirage, sometimes a surreal symbol, and occasionally a realization of abundant life, a taste of paradise. Yet in this poem in this fair orchard this Sufi's eyes are closed in meditation, walled off from abundance, shut off from beauty, even the astounding fecundity enfolding him. A bystander is puzzled. The stranger asks the Sufi: Why would you close your eyes and not behold "these signs of God the Merciful displayed around you?" The Sufi answers, "I behold within; Without is naught but symbols of the Signs." All the beauty of the world is but an image "reflected in a stream of that eternal Orchard which abides unwithered in the hearts of the perfect."[9] The world dreams of a paradise we can locate, demarcate, map, enjoy, and return to again. The Sufi sees what matters, what does not wither or weather, the true orchard, true abundance within.

In *The Sabbath*, Abraham Heschel tells a similar story. Instead of a Sufi meditating in an orchard, in a dream a rabbi enters heaven. In the dream, he is given permission to approach "the temple in Paradise where the great sages of the Talmud, the Tannaim" spend "their eternal lives." What do the rabbis of rabbis, sages of sages, wisest of the wise, do in heaven? The rabbi expects to be awestruck. In rapt attention he sees: what they do in eternity is exactly what they did on earth. He sees them "just sitting around tables studying the Talmud"; he is understandably "disappointed." He wonders, "'Is this all there is to Paradise?' But suddenly he heard a voice: 'You are mistaken. The Tannaim are not in Paradise. Paradise is in the Tannaim.'"[10] We can enter paradise—or paradise can enter us.

As the abbas say, saints are like trees of paradise laden with the fruits of life.[11] As Evagrius says, if we cultivate a "pure mind in a gentle soul," we can become like palm trees in paradise.[12] Drawing consciously or unconsciously on this tradition, Merton compares monks to trees. They go unnoticed. They are background, part of the landscape, yet "by their vital presence purify the

---

8. Merton, *Nonviolent Alternative*, 270.
9. Rumi, *Poet and Mystic*, 47.
10. Heschel, *Sabbath*, 75.
11. Vivian, *Becoming Fire*, 421.
12. Evagrius Ponticus, *Mind's Long Journey*, 63.

air."[13] Peace is found within. Paradise lies within. Its effect on the world may be invisible and unquantifiable, and crucial.

Peace may sometimes be a gift, but as the Medellín Conference insists, "peace is a permanent task. . . . Peace is not found, it is built."[14] The desert tradition agrees. In the desert, there are as many directions to find peace as street signs at the most congested and chaotic postmodern urban intersection. In the desert as at the most confusing intersection, the proliferation of signs seems to multiply the possibilities of losing your way, and signifies as many ways to find it: Don't let animosity govern your heart; don't even hate those who hate their neighbor; that is peace.[15] Let go of your sense of righteousness; be at peace.[16] Denigrate no one; condemn no one; slander no one, and God will give you peace.[17] Do not judge yourself; be at peace.[18] Remain silent. Don't take yourself too seriously, and you will have peace.[19] Miles and centuries away, Thomas à Kempis says, "all disquiet of heart and restlessness of mind come from inordinate love and groundless fear."[20] Avoid these. Expel these. Ban these. Be at peace.

On one of the rare occasions when Thomas Traherne's spiritual counsel becomes social criticism, he tells a story reminiscent of the ancient dialogue between Diogenes and Alexander.[21] In Traherne's tale, a prince decides to invade Italy and sends for a philosopher, Cineas, for counsel. Using the Socratic method, Cineas asks the prince why he wants to invade Italy. "To conquer it," comes the unself-conscious reply. Cineas asks the next logical question: "And what will you do when you have conquered it?" Conquer France. "And what will you do when you have conquered France?" Conquer Germany. And then? Conquer Spain. Cineas draws a conclusion that leads to yet another question: "I perceive . . . you mean to conquer all the World. What will you do when you have conquered all?" Then, the prince says, we shall "enjoy ourselves at quiet in our own land." Cineas concludes, "so you may now . . . without all this ado."[22] It is a story worth telling in any nation that has been, is, or aspires to be a world power, an international player, or

---

13. Merton, *Monastic Journey*, 61.
14. Hennelly, *Liberation Theology*, 109.
15. Vivian, *Becoming Fire*, 91.
16. Ibid., 92.
17. Ibid., 242.
18. Ibid., 479.
19. Ibid., 464.
20. à Kempis, *Imitation of Christ*, 147.
21. Eckhart, *Sermons & Treatises III*, 55.
22. Traherne, *Centuries*, 11.

an empire. Such "ado" is much ado—much propaganda, much mobilization, and much destruction—about nothing. The story reminds us that the political is always spiritual. What does it mean to conquer the whole world when one gains nothing and may even lose oneself? If such a conversation could begin with a mustard seed of inner peace, or within a sense of communal well-being, there would be no need for Japan's imperialistic vision of a Greater East Asia Co-Prosperity Sphere, a Nazi vision of a Third Reich, or an American vision of Manifest Destiny.

Cineas politely mentions the obvious—the prince could already live in peace at home, but he is filled with the common delusion that power and control over neighbors and enemies is a prerequisite to peace when, in fact, inner peace is always available, always at hand without need of a meaningless conquest, a circuitous forced march, an external detour. The endless need to conquer and rule reveals a chaotic and conflicted inner abyss, a yawning, gaping hunger—not for righteousness, but for a secret salve, to self-medicate one's soul. Instead of taking a few moments for introspection, instead of seeking genuine peace within, we are driven by an internal impetus to conquer all external stimuli, real or imagined. We would rather control others with guns and butter and armies and foreign aid and drones and free trade than to address the more difficult jihad within. It is, as Cassian says, easier to perform an exorcism on someone else than to reform yourself. It is, as Traherne illustrates, easier still to start a war than to pursue inner peace.

Building on the traditions of the desert, those living in other topographies recommend cultivating an "inner desert," not to flee from "outward things," but to "seize" God in them and beyond them.[23] The rabbis say: go nowhere; make no pilgrimage; seek no paradise; take no prize; "seek peace in your own place."[24] This is what Etty Hillesum did as the Holocaust's shadow closed in around her: "I draw prayer round me like a dark protective wall, withdraw inside it as one might into a convent cell and then step outside again, calmer and stronger and more collected again."[25] This is the inner desert, a hidden cove, an invisible fortress. This is a norm of the spiritual life. The Buddhist says, "I take refuge in the Buddha, the one who shows me the way in this life. I take refuge in the Dharma, the way of understanding and love. I take refuge in the Sangha, the community that lives in harmony and awareness."[26] So the Christian takes shelter in the person of Christ, the way

---

23. Eckhart, *Sermons & Treatises III*, 19.
24. Buber, *Tales: Later Masters*, 264.
25. Hillesum, *Interrupted Life*, 139.
26. Nhat Hanh, *Old Path White Clouds*, 160.

of Christ, and the body of Christ. Writing in her era bursting with ecclesiastical corruption and political upheaval, Catherine of Siena writes of a blessed life for those who humble themselves, obey God, and revel in God's presence: "Here there is peace without any war, every good without any evil, security without any fear, wealth without poverty, satiety without boredom, hunger without pain, light without darkness, supreme Good not finite but infinite, shared by all the truly joyful."[27]

Charles de Foucauld argues that when we see everything "in that great light of Faith," we create a "habit of seeing" that "lifts us above the mists and the mire of the world. It takes us into another atmosphere, into full sunshine, into a calm serenity, into a luminous peace above the cloud and the wind and the storms, a region without twilight or darkness."[28] Yet these visions of concord are not locked away in a castle behind a moat separated from the aches and pains and trials and tribulations of the world. Such visions are one station among many. They are a refuge to which we need to return and a sanctuary from which we must emerge. This "habit of seeing" nurtures a place to sow the seed, Christ, within us. As Thomas Kelly says, "small though this seed be in you, sow your life into the furrows of the world's suffering, and you will return in joy, and the world will arise in hope."[29] Like the visions of Birgitta and Julian, like the revelation to Motovilov, this peace, this vision, is never for anyone alone.

Merton brazenly, even mercilessly warns activists that if they have no inner peace, no spiritual center, no grounding, they have nothing to offer the antiwar movement, the civil rights movement, and the rare-as-rarified air hopes of their age but the contagion of their own anxieties. Lacking spiritual health, "alienated by the violence of their own enthusiasm," all they bring to politics is "a kind of blind and immature zeal,"[30] and a "hidden drive to self-assertion."[31] Framing it more as an annunciation of what some Quakers have called "applied mysticism,"[32] Underhill writes about people "irradiated with love and joy and peace":[33] "the full, mature, spiritual personality radiates love, joy, and peace, and transfers God's redeeming power because it is utterly merged in God's light and love."[34] It isn't difficult to

27. Catherine, *Dialogue*, 333.
28. Foucauld, *Writings*, 100.
29. Kelly, *Eternal Promise*, 56.
30. Merton, *Seasons of Celebration*, 18.
31. Merton, *Nonviolent Alternative*, 214.
32. *Christian Faith*, 661.
33. Underhill, *Ways of the Spirit*, 86.
34. Ibid., 119.

diagnose who has and who lacks this inner health. As Buber commends the anecdotal story as a vessel of infinite truth, so Climacus writes, "a single cup is sufficient to reveal the flavor of a wine, and a single word . . . can reveal" someone's "whole inner condition and activity."[35] One word, one deed is enough to taste a person's inner core.

This spiritual formation is impossible without one of Eckhart's favorite themes: detachment.[36] This, too, is the reason for solitude or an "inward desert,"[37] not "world-flight, running away from things . . . going apart from the world,"[38] but disengaging in order to reengage. Ruusbroec shares Eckhart's perspective: to "enjoy God," we need "true peace, interior silence, and loving adherence"; such "true peace" means that for God's love and glory we "renounce everything . . . that [we] possesses or could possess."[39]

Inner revolution, not social transformation, creates detachment. This is why Gandhi insists that satyagraha (truth force) must be cultivated in ahimsa (no harm/no violence). A detached heart cultivates nonviolent action. Like Chávez, Gandhi knew that nonviolence works only if its practitioners have a different sense of time, a divine and patient persistence, and an alternative interpretation of history. The need for tangible success and political victories always militates for quick-fix violence that is rarely quick and never fixes anything. No political cause or campaign, no success or failure, is more or less than another experiment with truth. Gandhi says that if satyagrahi had or hid guns, they would lose all "inner strength" and, ironically, "cease to feel invulnerable."[40] Even "incivility" could spoil "satyagraha like a drop of arsenic in milk."[41] The rule of life encapsulated in the Birmingham march's Ten Commandments tried to cultivate ahimsa in apprentice satyagrahi and foster attitudes that nurture nonviolent action.

Detachment often begins with material things. Following the Epistle of James's linkage of inner chaos, greed, and conflict (Jas 4:1), John Woolman connects possessions with violence: "May we look upon our treasures, the furniture of our houses, and our garments, and try whether the seeds of war have nourishment" there.[42] At the beginning of his career in the labor movement, Chávez "resigned my job and set out to found a union. At first

35. Climacus, *Ladder of Divine Ascent*, 273.
36. Eckhart, *Sermons & Treatises III*, 117–29.
37. Ibid., 19.
38. Eckhart, *Meister Eckhart: Modern*, 9.
39. Ruusbroec, *Spiritual Espousals*, 182.
40. Gandhi, *Non-violent*, 293.
41. Ibid., 207.
42. Woolman, *Journal*, 241.

I was frightened, very frightened. But by the time I had missed the fourth paycheck and found things were still going, that the moon was still there and the sky and the flowers, I began to laugh. I really began to feel free. It was one of my biggest triumphs."[43] Day, lover of fine art and fine food, did not find it easy to be parted from beauty, yet she practiced voluntary poverty. King gave away the money from his Nobel Peace Prize and his speaking engagements when it might have been prudent to save it for his children's college education.[44] Muste was known for putting wadded-up newspapers in the soles of his shoes to maximize their longevity.[45] Those who do justice practice material detachment.

Detachment may begin with the material, but it must ultimately address materialism. The spiritual revolution is intricately detailed, turning corner after corner, peeling layer after layer, cutting knot after Gordian knot. Dorotheos of Gaza says, "If an eagle gets out of a snare except for one claw which remains caught in the net, it has lost all its power to escape."[46] John of the Cross observes that it does not matter whether a bird is held down by a "cord" or a "thin thread," either way it cannot fly.[47] One claw. One thread. One drop of arsenic. It does not take much to enslave or pollute a soul. It does not take much to keep the spirit from ascending or the satyagrahi from forming. It does not take much to stymie social transformation before it can take flight.

Like Ruusbroec's image comparing mystical experience to a bee seeking honey for itself *and* wax for the common good, Teresa of Ávila says that we should not pray "for our enjoyment, but for the sake of acquiring this strength which fits us for service."[48] "True perfection," she writes, "consists in the love for God and of our neighbor, and the more perfect is our observance of these two commandments, the nearer to perfection we shall be." The entire rule of her order was "nothing but means which enable us to do this the more perfectly."[49] One purpose of the Torah is to spell out love of God and neighbor 613 ways in 613 circumstances. The heart of mysticism is nothing more than a way to fulfill the twin commandment, to seek a way

---

43. Dalton, *Moral Vision*, 101.

44. Garrow, *Bearing the Cross* 357; for King's lack of interest in money, see ibid., 114, 198.

45. Mayer, "The Christer," 2.

46. Dorotheos, *Discourses*, 181.

47. John of the Cross, *Collected Works*, 97.

48. Teresa, *Interior Castle*, 231.

49. Ibid., 42.

of life that makes no distinction between the well being of self, neighbor, citizen, stranger, and enemy. Inner peace exists for the sake of social justice.

But inner peace is not a commodity attained by a book of quotable quotes. It is not a map, sometimes not even a word; sometimes it is merely Pambo's edifying silence.[50] This was tested when the student from Kiev walked hundreds of miles seeking wisdom from Seraphim of Sarov and had his burning question answered by the radiating presence of the sleeping saint. What is true of Seraphim is what was said of Abba Nisterus: he had become like Moses's brass serpent that cured the people in the wilderness: "without speaking, he healed everyone."[51]

The Hasidic tradition underlines the same truth: a pilgrim travels a long distance to the village of Ladi to study under Rabbi Shneur Zalman, admired for his mystical wisdom and his ability to memorize and argue the Talmud. In their parochial pride, the villagers of Ladi ask the visitor which of the great rabbi's greatest gifts he wants to witness: hear the rabbi read Talmud or hear him pray. But all the visitor wants to do is see the great rabbi cut bread or tie his shoes. He then watches the rabbi sitting absently in thought in the light of the afternoon sun. And when he finishes watching the rabbi do nothing, he goes away edified.[52] All it takes to taste what is in a person's heart is one word, one deed, or even a long silence.

As we become detached, as the inner revolution progresses, as we experiment with truth, we cultivate greater stores of compassion and truth. The Dalai Lama tells the story of a Buddhist monk who spent eighteen years in a Chinese prison after the Communist occupation of Tibet. Years after his release, casually chatting with the Dalai Lama, the monk confessed that on two or three occasions he had felt he was in danger. The Dalai Lama's first thought was that even for the spiritually mature, fear of pain and death is an unavoidable reflex. But that was not the problem. There had been rare instances when the monk feared he would lose compassion for his Chinese captors. When the Dalai Lama heard this, he bowed to the monk.[53] This is detachment nurtured in the bosom of compassion. But detachment may also drink from taciturn truth. Frederick Douglass, asked how he endured incidents late in life "when you are hooted and jeered on the street on account of your color," replied, "I feel as if an ass has kicked, but had hit

---

50. Ward, *Sayings of the Desert*, 81.
51. Ibid., 155.
52. Lane, *Landscapes of the Sacred*, 68.
53. The Dalai Lama, *Toward a True Kinship*, 120.

nobody."⁵⁴ Detachment can be rooted in warm compassion *or* dispassionate truth.

Finding, nurturing, and radiating peace is a spiritual exercise not only for Sufis, rabbis, and monks. Detachment is not the work of a chosen few ascending the highest points of a spiritual peak. Ahimsa is not an extra credit course for the satyagrahi. As Merton repeats, it is the work of activists. Gandhi, comparing the relative value of the violent to the nonviolent in the truth's revolution, says that one nonviolent person is worth more than a million violent ones.⁵⁵ So when he advocates for ahimsa, he is not nurturing spiritual purity, a Pharisee's righteousness, or a priestly code's ritual cleanness. It is a matter of pure pragmatic political power.

Such power erupts in the midst of naked vulnerability. When Bayard Rustin was arrested in 1947 during the Journey of Reconciliation, the forerunner of the later, more famous Freedom Rides, perhaps ironically, perhaps not, those on this quest for human dignity met with inhumane treatment, conditions in an American prison that would have tested a Tibetan monk.

> We had chains on us when we left the prison and went out to work on the roads. We were chained to one another while we used picks and shovels. It was a very harrowing and ugly experience. People were hanged on the bars [of jail cells] by their wrists, their feet dangling above the ground. This was a terrible thing, because it could cause your testicles to swell. People were put into a hole—just a hole in the ground—for two or three days if they misbehaved. No toilet, nothing. Every morning they gave you a pail of water, so that you had enough to drink. But no water for washing. On one occasion when the guards insisted that I entertain them by dancing, I refused. They took out pistols and shot at the ground around my feet, trying to make me dance. Of course, I wouldn't do it.⁵⁶

One imagines Gandhi saying: give me a million like this!

When Rustin's mentor, A. J. Muste, died, Day wrote of Muste: "There was no malice in him, and so he found no malice in others."⁵⁷ His conversion at St. Sulpice Church in 1936 that gave him a sense of "deep . . . singing peace"⁵⁸ was a centerpiece in his life, transforming him from the postpastor

---

54. Douglass, *Life and Times*, 463.
55. Gandhi, *Non-violent*, 288.
56. Anderson, *Bayard Rustin*, 135.
57. Day, "A. J.," 14.
58. Robinson, *Abraham Went Out*, 63.

Marxist-Leninist he had become into the kind of activist Gandhi and Merton might bow to. His reconversion, Muste writes,

> came without warning and transplanted me in an instant from one spiritual world . . . into another. . . . [I]n coming back to faith in the way of non-violence and love I had returned to the true center of my own being, to God. Thus there was again peace within whatever might happen outside. In a sense, what I might be able to do no longer mattered very much. I no longer needed to be anxious and preoccupied with the results of this campaign or that, since I was sure of the ultimate nature of the universe. . . . Paradoxically, however, I was able to go to work again with new enthusiasm and assurance, knowing that if there were a way to prevent war it was in total pacifism, the actual practice of Jesus' way of life . . .[59]

This sense of inner peace stayed with him the rest of his life. Barbara Deming tells the story of Muste at age 81 at a small antiwar demonstration after an abortive attempt to protest at the American Embassy in Saigon in 1966. At a press conference, hecklers hurled insults, eggs, and tomatoes at the protesters, then the police dragged them away. At his age, Muste's hands had a tremor and shook almost constantly. It was a miserably hot, humid day, and the protesters were jammed into a paddy wagon and then stuck in a stuffy detention room as they awaited deportation from Vietnam. Concerned about the elderly Muste, Deming "looked across the room at A. J. to see how he was doing. . . . He looked back with a sparkling smile and, with that sudden lighting up of his eyes which so many of his friends will remember, he said, 'It's a good life.'"[60]

It would be seamless to credit Muste's reconversion with his commitment to nonviolence, but he had lost nonviolence before finding it again. As an organizer during post-World War I labor strikes that sparked violence across the US, Muste led a nonviolent protest in Lawrence, Massachusetts. During a demonstration, police knocked one of his comrades unconscious, but perhaps because Muste was a minister, they were careful to systematically beat him only on his legs and body before arresting him. Upon his release, when management had provocatively installed automatic weapons and aimed them at the shanty houses where workers' families lived, Muste encouraged workers, as they passed by, to turn and smile at the machine guns.[61] Gandhi's hope to create a nonviolent army was not intended to

---

59. Muste, "Steamer Letter," 109.
60. Deming, "It's a Good Life," 60.
61. Muste, *Essays*, 63, 70.

create an idealistic, moral-but-meek alternative to violence, but a viable political force.

At the end of a book that would have struck a chord with Stringfellow for thoroughly dispelling every illusion about *good government* and morally neutral organizations, Tolstoy says that people are hypnotized and disempowered by every educational, cultural, and religious institution.[62] One might expect this of godless nations, but to Tolstoy's dismay a godless church chose the Nicene Creed (conformist belief) over the Sermon on the Mount (radical ethics),[63] turning the church against its founder and raison d'être.[64] Following Augustine in his analysis of robber nations, Tolstoy parts ways with the fourth-century theologian when it comes to seeing wider and brighter horizons in human nature. In such a hypocritical and barbaric world in which every institution betrays God's will, Tolstoy reminds his readers, "the kingdom of God is within you."[65] If we find it in no government, ecclesiastical institution, charitable foundation, or nonprofit organization, at least we can feel its beat in the human heart.

Etty Hillesum makes a similar claim in greater detail: "we carry *everything* within us, God and Heaven and Hell and Earth and Life and Death and all of history. The externals are simply so many props, everything we need is within us."[66] Tolstoy's "kingdom" within is the unfinished revolution, not the radiant realm, but it is from that inner revolution that we find the gifts and tools we can offer the world. Underhill speaks of radiating peace and joy, but if the realm is within us we will also exude awe, anguish, learned ignorance, and human solidarity.

To Gandhi, satyagrahi in the world are orchards, oases, and trees. Like the Tannaim, they are not in paradise—paradise is in them. Gandhi would ask: How can anyone hope to engineer any part of God's revolution if we have not already experienced an inner revolution? Gandhi says that in the world as it is, Tolstoy's hypnotizing world, Stringfellow's death-dealing world, Sobrino's antimerciful world, people who nurture paradise within are the hope of the realm.

---

62. Tolstoy, *Kingdom of God*, 200–201, 333, 336.
63. Ibid., 87.
64. Ibid., 71.
65. Ibid., 380. Luke 17:21 in traditional translations.
66. Hillesum, *Interrupted Life*, 162 (italics mine).

EQUAL EYES

Gandhi's beloved Gita says that some people have "conquered themselves" through meditation and attained an "equal eye."[67] Similarly, the Sufi is one "in whose eyes gold and mud are equal."[68] Jesus' words give his disciples equal eyes. The endpoint of the Sermon on the Mount is to see with the same disposition friend, foe, and stranger; to see fellow citizen and undocumented worker, to see the person living on the next street and the one born across a body of water, and to regard them all the same; to see family member, church member, club member, clan member, and Klan member as all deserving the same love. That is the meaning of love, not "private affection"[69] shared among friends, families, and familiars, for those nearest and dearest, but to share it, spread it, cast it like a line out of the other side of the boat, the other side of one's favor, the other side of one's consciousness, even into the depths of the shadow side, as far and farther than one can imagine sharing it.

If only we could see with equal eyes. This is how the Buddha sees, how the Sufi sees, how Christ sees. This is how someone sees who has practiced meditation, who has had a single, life-altering revelation, or who simply has faith. These people have found equilibrium among all people, under every circumstance, in all times and all places. According to the Gita, such people "live in peace, alike in cold and heat, pleasure and pain, praise and blame. . . . To such people a clod of dirt, a stone, and gold are the same. They are equally disposed to family, enemies, and friends, to those who support them and those who are hostile, to the good and the evil alike."[70] They are "not buoyed up by praise nor cast down by blame . . . the same in honor and dishonor, quiet, ever full, in harmony everywhere, firm in faith."[71] They truly see "the Lord the same in every creature," and "seeing the same Lord everywhere," they harm no one; thus they reach "the supreme goal."[72]

Such Hindu ideals are not foreign to Christians. Julian of Norwich describes a lifelong alternation of pain and delight: "In the time of joy I could have said with Paul: Nothing shall separate me from the love of Christ; and in the pain, I could have said with Peter: Lord, save me, I am perishing."[73]

---

67. *Bhagavad Gita*, 6:29.
68. al-Kalabadhi, *Doctrine of the Sufis*, 10.
69. Catherine, *Letters*, 249.
70. *Bhagavad Gita*, 6:9.
71. Ibid., 12:18.
72. Ibid., 13:28.
73. Julian, *Showings*, 140.

Francis de Sales says, "We must be ready, as ready on Mt. Calvary as on Mt. Tabor, to say 'Lord, it is good for me to be with you, whether you are on the Cross or in your glory.'"[74] In a turbulent world, Eckhart praises equilibrium. Those matured by their inner revolution, those who could "give up the whole world as easily as an egg," voice their commitment in marriage-like vows: they "love God in all things equally: . . . as much in poverty as in riches," "as much in sickness as in health," "as much in temptation as without temptation," "as much in suffering as without suffering."[75] Eckhart calls a peaceful life good, a life of patience in pain better, and "peace in a life of pain" best of all.[76]

Hadewijch believes that equal eyes in an uneven world—a world in which valleys are not raised, mountains not brought low, in which the poor sink and the rich are ever ascending—provide steadiness against the drastic swings of life's mad pendulum.

> If [Love] lifts them up, if she knocks them down,
> May it all be equally sweet to them . . .[77]

> But the perfect person . . .
> Should with a humble heart
> Judge sweetness and pain the same,
> And receive [them] as meriting equal glory . . .[78]

> In taking or in giving, in storm or in peace,
> Were it in loving, or were it in hating:
> In which all events would be rated just alike;
> If God willed to come, or if God willed to go,
> We should understand it all in love,
> And see that [God] is Love.[79]

Some view such an immovable posture as the final fruits of spiritual maturity, sanctification, even deification, at least if God is perceived primarily as an unmoved mover. But equilibrium is not the final rung on a spiritual ladder, nor the omega point in a twelve-step program, nor the pinnacle of Mount Olympus—it is the way we want to live here and now. If we have equal eyes, we see the same beauty and the same horrors. We perceive the

---

74. de Sales, *Introduction*, 261.
75. Eckhart, *Sermons & Treatises I*, 151.
76. Eckhart, *Sermons & Treatises II*, 167.
77. Hadewijch, *Complete Works*, 226.
78. Ibid., 346.
79. Ibid., 323.

same transfiguring presence in the desert, the wilderness, in trenches, and under doorways. Prayer gives us new eyes even in the harshest, deadliest landscape:

> I had the feeling that I was resting against the naked breast of life, and could feel her gentle and warm heartbeat. I felt safe and protected. And I thought: how strange. It is wartime. There are concentration camps. I can say of so many of the houses I pass: here the son has been thrown into prison, there the father has been taken hostage, and an 18-year-old boy in that house over there has been sentenced to death. And these streets and houses are all so close to my own. I know how very nervous people are, I know about the mounting human suffering. I know the persecution and oppression and despotism and the impotent fury and the terrible sadism. I know it all.
>
> And yet—at unguarded moments, when left to myself, I suddenly lie against the naked breast of life and her arms round me are so gentle and so protective and my own heartbeat is difficult to describe: so slow and so regular and so soft, almost muffled, but so constant, as if it would never stop.
>
> That is also my attitude to life and I believe that neither war nor any other senseless human atrocity will ever be able to change it.[80]

Etty Hillesum, a young Jewish woman and future Holocaust victim, did not steel herself against "persecution and oppression." She found calm in "*unguarded* moments" in the midst of the most hideous genocide. Paul writes that nothing can separate us from the love of God (Rom 8:35–9). Hillesum senses it in her bones. This is her sanctuary, her equal eye, her mystical resistance to Nazism and the power of death. Neither ambition, nor privilege, nor power grants such inner peace to Traherne's ambitious prince.

Such inner peace can be freely given or rigorously cultivated. The desert's harsh spiritual practices nurtured an equilibrium that would not be swayed by time or place or circumstance, an equal disposition toward good and evil, even to martyrs and murderers, an equanimity that absorbs chaos and stills storms. Like Freire's pedagogy or Evagrius' *praktikos*, these practices are the way to the truth and the life. Abba Anoub teaches monks to live in peace by becoming like a statue "which is not moved whether one beats it or whether one flatters it."[81] Abba Pambo says: to live in harmony people "ought to be like a stone pillar; hurt them, and they do not get an-

---

80. Hillesum, *Interrupted Life*, 141–42.
81. Ward, *Sayings of the Desert*, 33.

gry, praise them, and they are not puffed up."[82] To be at peace, become like an inanimate object. When, like a lawyer or a rich young man, a seeker asks Macarius the Spiritbearer, "How can I be saved?" Macarius responds with a two-day crash course in spiritual formation: "Go to the tombs. Curse the dead. Throw rocks at them." When the aspirant returns, Macarius asks, "They didn't say anything to you, did they?" No. End of lesson one. Then Macarius tells him to go back the next day and "glorify them, saying 'You are apostles, you are saints and righteous.'" Again when the aspirant returns, Macarius asks, "They didn't say anything to you, did they?" No. End of lesson two. Finally, in case anyone needs subtitles beneath the enacted parable, Macarius summarizes his experiment with truth: "You have seen how you cursed them and they did not say anything to you, and how you glorified them and they did not respond at all. It should be the same with you, too: if you wish to be saved, be dead, having no regard for people's contempt nor their honors, and like the dead, you can be saved."[83] How do we inherit eternal life? Develop something thicker than a thick skin. Use plaster. Use marble. Develop rigor mortis. Be a statue. Be a pillar. Die.

John the Dwarf was not given such a crash course. Instead he trains for three years—the period tradition attributes to Jesus' public ministry—to bear insults and to give his possessions to the very people who verbally abuse him. Thus trained, his mentor tells John to leave the desert and go to Athens, the big city, the cosmopolitan heart of sophistication, where an old man at the philosopher's gate has the sacred calling to insult everyone who enters. When the old man insults John, John laughs. Perplexed and annoyed, the old man demands, "Why are you laughing, when I have insulted you?" John replies: Why wouldn't I laugh? "For three years I have paid to be insulted and now I am insulted free of charge."[84]

Eckhart echoes this rigorous tradition in his own teaching on detachment as the primary spiritual route to divine union and new life. As activists seek social change through economic divestment in corporations profiting from injustice, as they boycott buses in Montgomery, businesses in Birmingham, and grapes in California, as they promote sanctions against apartheid and corporations doing business in the West Bank, so people of faith seek spiritual conversion by becoming detached from harmful things. For Eckhart, anyone unaffected by sorrow or slander or honor or vice has become "as a mountain of lead . . . unmoved by a breath of wind." Through detachment, we receive God's simplicity. It is not a self-serving piety or an

---

82. Ibid., 194.
83. Vivian, *St. Macarius*, 61.
84. Ward, *Sayings of the Desert*, 95.

inward-turning purity intended to bless us alone, but a source of power to benefit others. Like God, we move forward from "purity into simplicity and from simplicity into immutability."[85] Those who practice detachment undergo a transformation so elemental that they "cannot pray, for whoever prays wants God to grant them something, or else wants God to take something from them"—but "a detached heart desires nothing at all"; it is "free of all prayers, or its prayer consists of nothing but being uniform with God."[86]

Not everyone, of course, has a three-year spiritual discipline or a two-day short course in detachment; few have a spiritual coach. But life itself can be a harsh teacher. Among the voluminous letters Merton received from strangers, he responded to a few hundred here, a few thousand there. Trying always to be a wise spiritual director, he did not always show equal pastoral sensitivity. In spite of John Howard Griffin's admiration for Merton's empathy, in his letters he could be brusque, blunt, and curt. When a Cuban émigré wrote Merton seeking sympathy and intercessory prayers after her husband was captured in the calamitous Bay of Pigs invasion, he warns her against melodramatic self-pity: "You must not complain if God also asks you to suffer with the rest of the world."[87] Terse and unsympathetic, Merton's message may have been colored by his warm memories of Havana, his distaste for both sides in the Cold War, or his disdain for the Bay of Pigs fiasco, no more because of its dismal failure than its zany anti-Communism. It is hard to imagine Merton using the same callous tone with the wife of an American MIA in Vietnam, let alone a Vietnamese woman with a family member imprisoned by either side. Yet Merton's underlying point might be the same: do you think you can escape the suffering of the world? In a sense, he commends the faith of Hillesum. Even in untenable situations, seek equilibrium.

Teresa of Ávila who had, alongside her moments of peace and mystical ecstasy, a first-hand experience with the hard-heartedness of life, delivers a similar message: "those who attain perfection do not ask the Lord to deliver them from trials, temptations, persecutions and conflicts."[88] In fact, she believed that those who genuinely experience God do not pray for salvation from trouble; akin to Eckhart's view that they would not pray at all. Julian, in words she could have addressed directly to Hillesum or to the Cuban émigré, says that God did not tell her "you will not be troubled, you will not be belabored, you will not be disquieted; but God said, You will not be

---

85. Eckhart, *Sermons & Treatises III*, 121.
86. Ibid., 126.
87. Merton, *Cold War*, 191.
88. Teresa, *Way of Perfection*, 249.

overcome."[89] Merton, perhaps awkwardly, perhaps coldly, sends the same message.

The inner equilibrium so often prescribed, so often sought, may not always result in calm thoughts, soothing words, and temperate deeds. Equability and affability, like Muste's lack of malice, may express someone's personal spirituality. Others may respond to all things with equal rigor, equal vitality, and equal vivacity. During Stringfellow's life-threatening illness in his thirties, two of his prayers embody his lifelong intensity. In this illness, Stringfellow, like Job, felt the world's pain in his own body.[90] Presumably without having read the book, he intuitively adapted the counsel of *The Cloud of Unknowing* to pray in short, forceful words (Help! Fire!). In words the author of *The Cloud* probably did not foresee when giving that holy guidance, Stringfellow reports candidly that when in pain he cried out "Jesus"—"that name was my prayer"; and when he yelled "Fuck! . . . it was a most earnest prayerful utterance."[91] In contrast to stoicism's stiff upper lip, or even a cultivated tranquility, he found an odd equilibrium, his own equilibrium, in the eye of the storm, at the midpoint between blessing and curse.

Equal eyes not only see heat and cold, profit and loss, martyr and murderer in the same light. They are also unscathed by spiritual fear and unmoved by selfish hope. As Merton dissociates himself from both sides in the Cold War, in a famous prayer, Rabia resists all forms of spiritual selfishness: "O my Lord, if I worship You from fear of Hell, burn me in Hell; and if I worship You from hope of Paradise, exclude me from Paradise. But if I worship You for Your own sake, do not withhold from me Your Eternal Beauty."[92] If spiritual anxiety is the lowest common denominator of faith, lust for reward is but a half step up (Matt 6:1–6, 16–18). Climacus compares fear of hell to "burning incense, which begins with fragrance and ends in smoke."[93] Gregory of Nyssa and Dorotheos call those who act from fear mere slaves. Only slightly less offensive are the "hirelings"[94] and their lustful craving for blessings. Gregory considers them mercenaries, self-aggrandizing entrepreneurs, spiritual capitalists who act "as if cashing in on the virtuous life by some business-like and contractual arrangement."[95] Climacus calls this kind

---

89. Julian, *Showings*, 315.

90. He identified the death he experienced in Harlem as the same power he felt in his body (Stringfellow, *Politics of Spirituality*, 87, "Harlem," 1346).

91. Stringfellow, *Second Birthday*, 109.

92. Fadiman and Frager, *Essential Sufism*, 86.

93. Climacus, *Ladder of Divine Ascent*, 76.

94. Dorotheos, *Discourses*, 209.

95. Gregory of Nyssa, *Life of Moses*, 137.

of self-centered quest "a millstone that always turns around on the same axis,"[96] like a myth of Sisyphus circumscribed and traveling hundreds of miles in tight concentric circles. The life of faith breaks through fear and self-centeredness—material and spiritual—to seek and serve God only for God's sake. For Cassian, people who seek God no longer act from fear or greed, but from "delight" in all goodness.[97] Unlike the fire that turns to choking smoke, this fire "creates a conflagration."[98] Dorotheos calls those freed from fear and greed children of God,[99] Gregory, God's friends[100]; Hadewijch says they serve God "only to love with love in Love."[101]

In a Sufi story, Isa (Jesus) passes by three groups on the side of the road. The people in the first group are made miserable by their fear of hell, the second disconsolate by their unsuccessful pursuit of paradise; but the faces of those in the third group shine with joy even though they have endured tribulation: they "have seen Reality, and this has made us oblivious to lesser goals."[102] So to destroy fear and greed Rabia declares it her mission to "light a fire in Paradise and pour water on Hell, so that both veils [hindrances to faith] completely disappear."[103]

At times, inner peace comes through discipline that, like love, can be harsh and dreadful, like the resetting of broken bones. Peace, as the Puebla Conference says, is the work of spiritual and social revolutions. Yet sometimes, when we least expect it, when it is most stunning, peace can be given, heaven-sent, stumbled upon like a treasure in a field, delivered to the door of our hearts by grace. With so much evil around her, such moments embarrassed Hillesum as out of synch with her times, like Underhill's book one World War before. There were moments, Julian says, when "God gave me again comfort and rest for my soul, delight and security so blessedly and so powerfully that there was no fear, no sorrow, no pain, physical or spiritual, that one could suffer which might have disturbed me."[104] Teresa reports "calmness and inner peace."[105] Francis de Sales speaks of an equal heart: "I hold that devotion does not consist in the sweetness, delight, con-

---

96. Climacus, *Ladder of Divine Ascent*, 76.
97. Cassian, *Conferences*, 146.
98. Climacus, *Ladder of Divine Ascent*, 76.
99. Dorotheos, *Discourses*, 110, 209.
100. Gregory of Nyssa, *Life of Moses*, 137.
101. Hadewijch, *Complete Works*, 335.
102. Shah, *Way of the Sufis*, 58–59.
103. Fadiman and Frager, *Essential Sufism*, 86.
104. Julian, *Showings*, 205.
105. Buber, *Ecstatic Utterances*, 112.

solation, and sensible tenderness of heart that move us to tears and sighs and brings us a certain pleasant, relishful satisfaction when we perform various spiritual exercises. No . . . devotion is not identical with such things. Many souls experience these tender, consoling feelings but still remain very vicious. Consequently, they do not have true love of God, much less true devotion."[106] Upsetting our expectations, the blessed are not necessarily good, pure, meek, or merciful. So, according to de Sales, we need more than blessings.

> We must try to keep our heart steadily, unshakably equable during such great inequality of events. Even though everything turns and changes around us, we must always remain unchanging and ever looking, striving, and aspiring toward God. No matter what course the ship may take, no matter whether it sails to the east, west, north, or south, no matter what wind drives it on, the mariner's needle never points in any directions except toward the fair polar star. Everything may be in confusion not only around us, I say, but within us as well. Our soul may be overwhelmed with sorrow or joy, with sweetness or bitterness, with peace or trouble, with light or darkness, with temptation or repose, with pleasure or disgust, with aridity or tenderness, it may be scorched by the sun or refreshed by the dew—for all that, ever and always our hearts point, our spirit, our higher will, which is our compass, must unceasingly look and tend toward the love of God, its Creator, its Savior, its sole and sovereign good.[107]

Even when all things around us and within us are chaos, we can find the peace Julian and Teresa praise. Hillesum had the equal eyes of the Gita and the equal heart of de Sales as she—and her people—were herded toward their deaths.

Equal eyes act as a third set of eyes, or a third eye, along with Mississippi and Assisi eyes. Those two sets of eyes focus separately on sickness or health, inequality or justice, the grotesque or the beautiful. Equal eyes see blessing and curse with an equanimity that stills but does not eliminate our aching, agonized compassion. Equal eyes maintain stability between beauty and horror. This steadiness keeps us from chucking the need for justice when we are drunk with love, and keeps us from losing hope beneath the crushing weight of oppression.

---

106. de Sales, *Introduction*, 257.
107. Ibid., 256–57.

WHEN THERE IS NO PEACE

When peace is too accessible, too simple, or too easy, it is a cheap substitute, a counterfeit, and a fake. False peace has many dimensions and even more devotees. It manufactures deceptions and delusions to distract us from the constant crying need for social transformation. The first dimension of false peace is the one famously decried by Jeremiah (Jer 6:14, 8:11), a declaration of peace when inequality reigns and violence is marching just beyond the horizon. It is the denial of denials. It is a nonpeace that with velvet voice or iron fist forcefully blesses the status quo as God's will. This is the peace that perceives activists as nihilists and social change as antisocial behavior. Activists will inevitably and blessedly disturb this false peace and defy its unjust laws.

After King was arrested and imprisoned during the 1963 Birmingham boycott, local Protestant, Catholic, and Jewish leaders upbraided him for upsetting the peace. Their inquisitorial condemnation spurred King to write his "Letter from Birmingham Jail." His open letter responds to their accusation that the Birmingham boycott was unnecessarily confrontational, and to their empty assurance that the march of time incrementally but inevitably hops and skips toward progress. Not only did King build into the rhetorical architecture of his letter Protestant, Catholic, and Jewish theological rejoinders to their nasty divorce of orthodoxy from danger,[108] he wove into it what he later called the "central quality" of the African American experience: "pain."[109]

While King's kerygma often ascends into the surreal and the visionary, *pain* is another primary theme in his speeches and writings. His career often linked political reform with his personal anguish. He was one African American child among millions stung by one of segregation's cruel rites of passage when at age five he was barred from playing with white children.[110] So when his "I Have a Dream" speech foresees a time when children of different races play together,[111] he envisions a public future to heal his personal past. He was a high school student fuming with a teenager's impotent fury when, with a teacher, he was ordered off of a segregated bus.[112] So when the Montgomery campaign targeted segregated public transportation, it also mended a memory. He was the psychologically emasculated parent he

---

108. King, *Testament of Hope*, 293–94.
109. King, *Where Do We Go*, 122.
110. Garrow, *Bearing the Cross*, 33.
111. King, *Testament of Hope*, 219.
112. Ibid., 342–43.

describes in his "Letter from Birmingham Jail" who has no logical answer to his young daughter's bewilderment that she can never go to the local amusement park, that she is banned not only from "Funtown" but from fun.[113] He must tell her: she is excluded because of her skin. In his "Letter," King uses theologians to parry his opponents' juvenile and unwieldy ideological thrust. But he uses irrefutable empirical evidence, his own experience, to reveal that the "peace" the civil rights movement disturbed was no divine blueprint for societal order or social justice—it was Jeremiah's false peace, a smirking façade. While with tin ears and stained-glass voices his detractors chanted the familiar moderate call to "Wait!"[114] the cumulative effect of his experience, the pain of his race, and the theology religious leaders should have known inspired the title of the book in which the letter was published: *Why We Can't Wait*. King did not need sophisticated social analysis to detect false notes in calls to maintain peace. This false peace was as clear to him as when he was punched in the face in Birmingham and hit in the head by a brick in Chicago.[115] Like Job, King knew this nonpeace in his own flesh.

As King strips away the false peace inherent in the slow makeover of American racism, Merton denounces the bogus hypothesis of the US as a peace-loving nation. In an era more kindly disposed to government-sponsored religious sentimentality, postage stamps could blithely, blandly, and apparently benignly say, "Pray for peace." Noting the cynical sham extolled in those three words, Merton simply points out indisputable line-item evidence in the federal budget: each year the US spent billions of dollars on conventional and nuclear weapons. Given the gap between the Hallmark-sweet soppiness of the stamp and massive military spending on instruments of megamurder, Merton says that it makes as much sense to pray for peace and prepare for war as it does to pray for health and drink poison.[116] The Epistle of James had long before connected the dots of blood between spirituality and violence (Jas 4:1). It does not matter if it is a thief, a pirate, an empire, or a self-proclaimed peace-loving nation that somehow happens to find itself in one war after another: the problem and process are the same. And how does the US find itself in so many wars? Like Aaron's lame explanation about the Golden Calf (". . .and out came this calf!" Exod 32:24), most Americans aver that wars appear out of nowhere without complicity or culpability.

---

113. Ibid., 292–93, 342.
114. Ibid., 292.
115. Garrow, *Bearing the Cross*, 221, 499–500.
116. Merton, *New Seeds*, 119–20.

The Peace that is No Peace 437

Consciously and unconsciously, Merton links the "eggs" hatching from our violent imaginations with the "eggs" (bombs) that fall from bombers built in a false-peace-loving nation.[117] In what could be a theological gloss on Jesus' teaching "ask and you shall receive; seek and you shall find; knock and door will be opened" (Luke 11:9), Merton strips bare the astonishing mindlessness with which people pray.

> If people really wanted peace they would sincerely ask God for it and God would give it to them. But why should God give the world a peace which it does not really desire? The peace the world pretends to desire is really no peace at all.
>
> To some people peace merely means the liberty to exploit other people without fear of retaliation or interference. To others peace means the freedom to rob others without interruption. To still others it means the leisure to devour the goods of the earth without being compelled to interrupt their pleasures to feed those whom their greed is starving. And to practically everybody peace simply means the absence of any physical violence that might cast a shadow over lives devoted to the satisfaction of their animal appetites for comfort and pleasure.
>
> Many people like these have asked God for what they thought was "peace" and wondered why their prayer was not answered. They could not understand that it actually *was* answered. God left them with what they desired, for their idea of peace was only another form of war. The "cold war" is simply the normal consequence of our corrupt idea of a peace based on a policy of "every man for himself" in ethics, economics and political life. It is absurd to hope for a solid peace based on fictions and illusions!
>
> So instead of loving what you think is peace, love other people and love God above all. And instead of hating the people you think are warmakers, hate the appetites and the disorder in your own soul, which are the causes of war. If you love peace, then hate injustice, hate tyranny, hate greed—but hate these things *in yourself*, not in another.[118]

Like a prophet, Merton condemns the usual suspects and the real culprits—consumerism, capitalism, classism, militarism, imperialism, and rugged and bourgeois individualism—but instead of externalizing the problem and excoriating others as scapegoats so that we (the Left, the righteous) can condemn them as Alabama's religious leaders rebuked King, Merton

---

117. Merton, *Hidden Ground*, 283, *Thomas Merton: Spiritual Master*, 215.
118. Merton, *New Seeds*, 121–22 (italics his).

directs peacemakers to hate not warmakers, not *them*, not even people, but the injustice, violence, and greed sprouting out of our *own* hearts. Even in his most political writings, Merton finds the roots of social transformation in spiritual revolution. Reinhold Niebuhr might believe it easier to reform a heart than to coerce an institution (and he might be right), but Merton knew precisely how intricate and infinite that inner detoxification could be.

False peace, as Merton notes, is not only a handy rhetorical henchman of violence—it is woven into every culture's fables and fantasies. In American culture, it resides in "fatness," "the radiance of satisfied bodies,"[119] and the gleam of "success," a word Merton regarded as coldly as Abba Agathon viewed "heretic."[120] Invited to write an article on success, Merton "replied indignantly that I was not able to consider myself a success in any terms that had a meaning to me. I swore I had spent my life strenuously avoiding success"; any resemblance his life bore to it was "due to inattention and naïveté." So Merton rants: "Be anything you like, be madmen, drunks, and bastards of every shape and form, but at all costs avoid one thing: success."[121] Success may not be as blatantly vile as segregation or as shamelessly destructive as nuclear weapons, but to accept society's blessings on their own terms is to roll out the red carpet to an invasion of the housed oppressor.

The devotees of false peace confuse the status quo with divine providence, conflate it with society's tangible rewards, and equate it with the freedom to rob, exploit, and devour. Surrounded and choked off by so many falsehoods, true peace is not automatically found in a monastic cell, much less a big house. The idea that the mystic, the monk, or the prayerful has a perpetual sense of serenity is sheer nonsense. That is a false *inner* peace. Underhill underlines Teresa's observation: if people claim that union with God keeps them "always in peaceful beatitude," don't believe them![122] King's tragically abbreviated life was anything but a perpetual peak experience soothed by a continuously streaming vision of the promised land. Day paid a terrible cost—and made those around her pay—for practicing voluntary poverty. The lives of mystics include trials (Eckhart), intimidation (Teresa of Ávila), political intrigue (Catherine of Siena), torture (John of the Cross), and threats of damnation (Francis of Assisi). Once safely dead, of course, these disturbers of the peace are restored, honored, and even canonized, but if their sanctity were weighed by perpetual inner harmony, they would be counted among the least holy of all. If injustice anywhere is a threat to justice

---

119. Merton, *Hidden Ground*, 138.
120. Ward, *Sayings of the Desert*, 20–21.
121. Merton, *Love and Living*, 11.
122. Underhill, *Ways of the Spirit*, 143.

The Peace that is No Peace

everywhere, it is also a threat to any sense of internal calm. Few commend inner peace more than Thich Nhat Hanh, but he warns: if "some members of the human family are suffering and starving, for us to enjoy false security and wealth is a sign of insanity."[123] An inner *que será será* in the face of pain is equally crazy.

Accepting the label of a whining Jeremiah, Merton points out that Jeremiah was ultimately right about God's judgment, God's mercy, and the course of history.[124] But Jeremiah's acuity never brought him inner peace—and inner peace never sharpened his insight. When Merton's order and his church silenced him with chiding reminders that monks write about prayer, silence, and meditation, not war, racism, and exploitation, he subverted their escapism just as King scolded Birmingham's religious leaders. Not that Merton denied his own need for a permanent inner revolution. He would have agreed with Brother Giles: you could do nothing else for a thousand years, and still never finish work on your own "heart!"[125] Merton was quick to tell those who wanted him to leave the monastery for an activist life that he had a lifetime's worth of material to work on within himself.[126] But the spiritual life, as Merton defines it, is all Evagrius: separate from all to unite with all. So Merton questioned his ecclesiastical superiors: "I sometimes wonder why we think it is noble to concentrate on producing an inner feeling of peace in ourselves, while allowing the wicked world to blow itself to hell."[127] Gutierrez echoes the Puebla Conference document's warning against a "spirituality of evasion"[128] and Merton saw such "evasions" everywhere.[129] Gutierrez never condemns mysticism. Rather, he censures a bourgeois piety that uses inner peace as both cosmetic and narcotic in an atomized, consumerist, "dangerous privatization of spirituality."[130]

In the 1960s, the 1990s, or the early twenty-first century—in any decade because in every decade, parts of the world are going to hell—does anyone have a right to seek inner peace? Is such a quest really so noble? Is its false contentment worth having? Isn't such a peace merely Marx's morphine? Isn't its spiritual elitism parallel to the racial privilege King condemns from Birmingham's jail? The peace people often seek within isn't true

---

123. Nhat Hanh, *Love in Action*, 120.
124. Merton, *Hidden Ground*, 318.
125. *Little Flowers*, 283.
126. Merton, *Hidden Ground*, 502.
127. Merton, *School of Charity*, 192.
128. Gutierrez, *We Drink*, 15.
129. Merton, *Life and Holiness*, 19, 103.
130. Gutierrez, *We Drink*, 15.

peace anyway. Inner peace is not found in a "happiness pill"[131] or "spiritual tranquilizers."[132] Much to his early dismay and later delight, Merton found a strange consistency throughout his monastic life, a brew of "heavenliness" mixed with "anguish,"[133] "anguish and certitude,"[134] "lostness and wonder,"[135] Climacus's "ecstasy without end" and grief "for life."[136]

How can we be content in a violence-stricken, antimerciful world? A. J. Muste, in his elder years a model of inner calm, said the Vietnam War tore at his "guts."[137] Three decades later, in the 1990s, Soëlle's decade of "resistance," Tutu knew well why people lost faith; in fact, he wondered how God contained divine wrath.

> In a bold anthropomorphic vein I can picture God surveying the awful wrecks that litter human history—how the earth is soaked with the blood of so many innocent who have died brutally. God has seen two World Wars in this century alone plus the Holocaust, the genocide in Cambodia and Rwanda, the awfulnesses in the Sudan, Sierra Leone, the two Congos, Northern Ireland, and the Middle East, and the excesses that have characterized Latin America. It is a baneful catalog that records our capacity to wreak considerable harm on one another and our gross inhumanity to our fellow humans. I imagine God surveying it all, seeing how God's children treat their sisters and brothers. God would weep as Jesus wept over hard-hearted and unresponsive Jerusalem, where he had come to his own people and they would not receive him. If God ever wanted to consider the folly of having created us, we have provided God with ample cause to do so.[138]

Unlike Jewish mysticism's primordial Adam who sees light from horizon to horizon, Tutu, like so many activists, sees bloodshed, cruelty, and crosses. How can you nurture inner peace in this world? Shouldn't pervasive horror evoke perpetual *discontent*?

As Day joined Tutu in tears, so she anticipated him in righteous indignation and prophetic fury. During the Depression, after giving a talk

---

131. Merton, *Seeds of Destruction*, 244.
132. Merton, *Nonviolent Alternative*, 112.
133. Merton, *Dancing in the Water*, 99; he puts "heavenliness" in quotation marks.
134. Ibid., 160.
135. Ibid., 172.
136. Climacus, *Ladder of Divine Ascent*, 209.
137. Robinson, *Abraham Went Out*, 193.
138. Tutu, *No Future*, 124.

to a group of wealthy potential donors, Day's audience offered her condescending and discomforting words. While they said they would "give our very souls to help the poor," they claimed that surely Day had to know that unions hurt the working poor; surely she had to know that the best hope for the poor was "sterilization."[139] Day, trying to contain her volcanic ire, reflected on her daily realities:

> We are told always to keep a just attitude toward the rich, and we try. But as I thought of our breakfast line, our crowded house with people sleeping on the floor, when I thought of cold tenement apartments around us, and the lean gaunt faces of the men who come to us for help, desperation in their eyes, it was impossible not to hate, with a hearty hatred and with a strong anger, the injustices of this world.[140]

Tutu, eyeing horrors from which we naturally shield our eyes, wonders how God can rein in the four horsemen. Day, tapering her wrath to shine a laser light on the relentless invisible class warfare that descends like an odorless leak of carbon monoxide, smells things we might otherwise miss.

For Tutu, the broad strokes of history challenge our faith. For Day, any casual incident or hidden attitude can puncture inner peace. James Baldwin considered King's assassination a seminal moment in his personal life and a turning point in American history. For Baldwin, King's death told a tale of two sixties. When King was alive, people "hoped to bring about some kind of revolution in the American conscience." After his murder, "that's gone now. It's gone because the Republic never had the courage or the ability or whatever it was that was needed to apprehend the nature of Martin's dream."[141] Baldwin remembered hope, but could no longer resurrect it: "There was a time in my life not so very long ago that I believed, hoped . . . that this country could become what it has always presented as what it wanted to become. But I am sorry, no matter how this may sound: when Martin was murdered for me that hope ended."[142]

Baldwin's change of heart not only revised his reading of history; it soured his estimation of human nature. Since King's death, he said, "something has altered in me, something has gone away. Perhaps even more than the death itself, the manner of his death has forced me into a judgment of human life and human beings which I have always been reluctant to make." "Every human being," he says, "is an unprecedented miracle. One tries to

---

139. Day, *Houses of Hospitality*, 203.
140. Ibid.
141. Baldwin and Mead, *Rap on Race*, 10.
142. Ibid., 244.

treat them as the miracles they are while trying to protect oneself against the disasters they've become." This, he says, was the practice of the civil rights movement. But now, he says, "the failure and the betrayal are in the record book forever, and sum up, and condemn, forever, those descendants of a barbarous Europe who arbitrarily and arrogantly reserve the right to call themselves Americans."

Baldwin's change of heart embodied itself in less philosophical ways. Shortly before King's assassination, Baldwin bought a new suit to wear for an appearance with King at Carnegie Hall. He wore the same suit to King's funeral and swore he would never wear it again.[143] For him, the suit had been stained; it had become unclean. For him, "that suit was drenched in the blood of all the crimes of my country. . . . I simply could not put it on, or look at it, without thinking of Martin, and Martin's end, of what he had meant to me, and to so many." A childhood friend who lacked Baldwin's financial resources heard about his unused suit, and asked if he could have it. As Baldwin put it: he could not afford my "elegant despair."[144] Nothing would soften the sharpness of his meticulous judgment, so be it; but he could not hide in the oddly comforting arms of hopelessness.

In Qoheleth's way of collating a whirlwind into a tidy list of yins and yangs (Eccl 3:1–8), in his gift for finding the futility in every endeavor—success, wealth, power, and privilege, certainly, but also wisdom, mercy, holiness, and compassion—perhaps he was, as Elsa Tamez says, practicing "historical realism in the context of chronological time,"[145] whittling a sense of inner peace out of a mahogany-hard gloom. Perhaps by giving everything in life its "season," Qoheleth was training himself in his own form of equal eyes, seeing not only gold and mud as equal, but love and hate, and war and peace. But is this equilibrium? Is this inner peace or bitter fatalism? Is this a deeper calm or a false peace that hums a merry tune as the wicked world goes to hell? Is this the pinnacle of his quest or a premature surrender to elegant despair? Is it Qoheleth's spiritual evasion: chic, empirical, existential, sophisticated political and spiritual cynicism? And given his presumed social location and easy access to the opiates of the privileged, could he afford this emotional distance and these healthy boundaries if he were in Birmingham's jail, Cambodia's killing fields, or on any impoverished farm anywhere on the planet? We need to question Qoheleth to sift nonanxious equilibrium from elective paralysis. We need not condemn him and his spiritual kin, but recall that the world is saved through Christ, not Qoheleth.

143. Baldwin, *No Name in the Street*, 9–11.
144. Ibid., 14.
145. Tamez, *When the Horizons Close*, 23.

If false peace permeates society and threatens every spiritual quest with a sequence of mirages, perhaps we could find true peace in the pursuit of holiness. We could draw that lesson from the Tibetan monk who sustains his compassion for his Communist captors. But holiness does not necessarily nurture peace. As Gandhi's personal secretary, Mahadev Desai, wrote,

> To live with the saints in heaven
> Is a bliss and a glory,
> But to live with a saint on earth
> Is a different story.[146]

Gandhi eagerly extended his niggling, nagging self-criticism to his nearest *and* dearest. Are we really comfortable with the boundless demands of holiness, or are we as uncomfortable as at the goodness before us as Ransom in *Perelandra*? Are we paralyzed betwixt and between inner and outer revolutions, as Rama in *Xala*, neither here nor there, not defending the status quo or truly seeking the realm?

This problem of defining, let alone finding, inner peace is hardly the unique conundrum of a particular time, class, or culture. Concerns about the spirituality of evasion go back centuries. Abba John the Dwarf "had prayed God to take his passions away from him so that he might become free from care." In the desert, the consistent message to every abba-in-training is to practice detachment, to get rid of their "passions," the attitudes that tie us by cords or a thin thread to the worst of the world instead of to the heart of God. Like the lawyer and the rich young man, John has good reason to be pleased with himself. He tells an old man, "I find myself in peace, without an enemy." Apparently it is true; the old man does not dispute his claim. But instead of commending him, "The old man said to him, 'Go, beseech God to stir up [spiritual] warfare so that you may regain the affliction and humility that you used to have, for it is by warfare that the soul makes progress.'" John has followed holy orders; he has rid himself of his passions. But when he does, he hears a new commandment: get them back! "So [John] besought God and when warfare came, he no longer prayed that it might be taken away, but said, 'Lord, give me strength for the fight.'"[147] It is not enough to practice detachment; eventually, we must detach from it.

Not only do the travails of the world render peace false; they cleverly craft the illusion that we can find peace, gain peace, inhale peace, possess peace, and live in peace. They tempt us with assurance that we can pass the ultimate test, receive the sweetest blessing, stand on the highest mountain,

---

146. Browne, *Gandhi*, 286.
147. Ward, *Sayings of the Desert*, 87–88.

and arrive at the last Station. True peace, John learns, is found only in struggle. In agitation, heartache, heartbreak, and outrage, in a thirst that is always and never quenched; that is our peace.

The search for inner peace, then, is apophatic to its core. If we ever find inner peace—if it is here or there or somewhere to be found—we will know it first by what it is not: we can nurture no inner cool while the earth is in flames, no calm collectedness when children are crying, no compromise with robber nations, no comfort in holiness, no cynicism so elegant that we can rest in its silky smooth but tissue-thin embrace. There is no rest for the holy, no great and lasting respite for those who do justice, love kindness, and walk humbly with God.

In the Johannine tradition, Jesus promises a peace that the world cannot give (John 14:27). The peace of Christ, then, is not found in spiritual hedonism or rationalized individualism; not in a gated community, a bribe, a high, or a pleasure cruise. Because we are so used to counterfeit forms of peace—distractions, diversions, placebos, and narcotics—when we experience the peace of Christ, it may not feel like what we imagined peace to be. But when we experience a peace that is no peace? *That* might be the real thing.

THE PEACE THAT SURPASSES ALL PARADOX

Just as there is the way of no way and the station of no station, there is also the peace that is no peace. This is true peace, Christ's peace, a peace that surpasses all paradox. Wherever we are in the world's magnificence and mayhem, we can find a sense of equilibrium; an orchard, but also a desert; paradise, but also the world as it is; the work of the realm, done and undone.

Christ's peace—the peace the world does not give—is simultaneously *congruent* with the suffering of the world, *and* with the realm to come, *and* with the revolution as it plays out in the crises and social change of the day. This peace comprehends human sin, institutional depravity, and the twisting, pothole-ridden, hard-to-find, and heavily defended road to progress. It knows that the toll for walking that road is paid in spiritual wounds and physical death. But this peace is also congruent with the realm—with King's surreal visions bundled as one with Julian's most extravagant promise: all shall be well. Finally, it is congruent with the revolution—with the light within that sparks redemption, restoration, and transfiguration. Paul endorses pastoral congruence with his advice: rejoice with those who rejoice, and weep with those who weep (Rom 12:15). Be congruent with human need.

Christ's peace has equal eyes for the sins of the world and the beauty of the earth. It cuts no deals with the domination system. It is not immune from the blues, but the music of its soul also sings arias of intoxicated love and alleluias of awed praise. In truth, Christ's peace is never entirely still, never completely calm, because no one can say of our inner revolution "it is finished," fulfilled, or consummated.

This is the peace of the Catholic Worker movement, where charity is fused with chaos. It is Trocmé's tranquility as he faces down Vichy France, Gandhi's serenity in prison, and Hillesum's contentedness while being squeezed between the tightening vise of evil incarnate. Like Cassian's ecstasy and grief and Stringfellow's blessing and curse, it is not the imperturbability of an unmoved mover, but an inner disposition equally influenced by the jaggedness of the world, the incompleteness of the realm, and the gestation of the revolution. This peace is congruent with faith-breaking realism and with hopes that have been seared and scarred and obliterated and resurrected millions of times for thousands of years.

True inner peace is not only *congruent* with the godlessness of the world and the coming of the realm; it offers *complementarity* to the world's pain. The prayer attributed to the spirit, if not the pen, of Francis of Assisi commends this complementarity: "where there is hatred, let us sow love; where there is injury, pardon; where there is discord, union; where there is doubt, faith; where there is despair, hope; where there is darkness, light; where there is sadness, joy."[148] This complementarity fills every void, the world's pockets of nothingness. As John of the Cross says: where there is no love, put love, and there you will find love; so where there is no justice, no compassion, no reconciliation, no redemption, put justice, compassion, reconciliation, and redemption.

Embodying congruence and complementarity is always a daunting task. Early in World War II, the Yearly Meeting of the Friends in London declared congruence and complementarity in a season of mass murder, a time apparently inoculated against peacemakers' gentle blessings. At a time when it was equally likely that England would lose as win that war, at a time when almost no one in Europe cared a whit about pacifism, the Yearly Meeting struggled to articulate a meaningful word in a time devoid of meaning: "A word of peace and healing can only be spoken by those who have entered deeply into a sense of sin as well as the suffering of the world and have themselves been brought to the place of penitence. . . . Each one who has entered into such a renewed spiritual experience will be enabled to minister

---

148. *Book of Common Prayer*, 833.

to the world's need."[149] The statement commends honesty, introspection, detachment, congruence, and complementarity. Historically, it was an unfelt breeze in the wilderness, useless, but perhaps a uselessness that has its use, or that might have an impact in another place (Le Chambon) or at another time (the civil rights movement).

Recognizable by its congruence and complementarity, inner peace forever rests in restlessness. It never bequeaths freedom from a gnawing, aching hunger for justice. Restlessness, in fact, is a sign of Christ's peace. If the inner revolution is ongoing, we will never be content with proximate justice or approximations of goodwill, with anything less than the realm. The more evolved our inner revolution, the greater our discomfort with the world as it is, and the more we will love everything in it.

Christ's peace is a peace that is no peace, but in moments our consciousness can rise, ought to rise, above the pollution of the world's misery to see it clearly and to decipher ways to repair its wounds. Gregory of Nazianzus says that a true theologian "ought to . . . have a calm from within from the wheel of outward things, so as not like madmen to lose our breath."[150] Ruusbroec describes a "divine freedom" in which

> a person's spirit is raised up in love above its own nature, that is, above suffering, labor, and reluctance, above anxiety and care, above fear of death, hell, and purgatory, and above all the oppressive burdens which can overcome body and soul in time and in eternity, for consolation and desolation, giving and taking, death and life, and everything that can occur for weal or woe all remain beneath that loving freedom in which a person's spirit is united with God's spirit.[151]

Inner peace is a divine gift that cannot be erased by the travails of the world, not even by personal skin-burning pain. And in spite of countless contradictions there are moments like Hillesum's when we are lifted above the world's suffering so as not to be suffocated by it. In these grace-filled flashes we realize again that we do not dwell in a one-dimensional, antimerciful world, that the domination system and Stringfellow's dominion of death can never be more than the world's penultimate power.

There are seasons when, as for a well-trained swimmer, these moments are like breathing in rhythm as we press purposefully ahead. But there are also seasons when the sight and sound of the sorrows of the world, or the feel of them in our flesh, overwhelm us, and we flail, afraid of drowning, and

---

149. *Christian Faith*, 607.
150. Leech, *Spirituality and Pastoral Care*, 19.
151. Ruusbroec, *Spiritual Espousals*, 199.

take panicked gulps of air—deeper, needier, more frantic, less fruitful—as we struggle even to tread water. As if it needed one, this was the function of the early civil rights movement's mystical mass meetings: to schedule times, breathing room, to reconnect with the body and inhale the Spirit in the midst of an almost unendurable struggle. The mass meetings were scheduled breathers when, as Catherine of Siena says, the church became a hostel,[152] a place of refreshment where the inner desert becomes an inner orchard, when we remember that we are never in paradise, but paradise, the realm, and the revolution are always in us.

Thomas à Kempis echoes Augustine's view of restlessness without God: wherever you come from, wherever you are, "you are but a stranger and a pilgrim, and never will find perfect rest until you are fully joined to God."[153] Eckhart considers being "at peace" synonymous with being "in God."[154] His goal is to have our spirit "ever at rest, united in joyous eternity."[155] This, of course, is eternal life, to know God and to love Christ (John 17:3). Yet for Eckhart, being "in peace" is as complex, contradictory, ineffable, indefinable, paradoxical, and unpredictable as being "in God." Eckhart's God is ever active, forever doing, always begetting, an easily moved (Exod 3:7) and always moving God. To be in God is to share God's work of redemption (Underhill), the revolution, to build and scrape and sculpt the realm. To be in God is to share in divine, resolute restlessness. Our goal is not peace, per se; it is God. Whatever happens *in God*, that is our peace.

As Julian reports, God does not promise us we will not be "troubled," "belabored," "disquieted," dismayed, bedeviled, terrified, or terrorized; God says: "You will not be overcome."[156] True inner peace comes when we look into the mirror image of "We Shall Overcome" optimism. With this inner peace we witness the ongoing defeat of the saints (Rev 13:7) with a crucial disclaimer. We may lose. It is our way. We may lose almost all the time. Those are the odds. But God shall not be overcome. In *that* conviction, in *God*, is the beginning of peace. There is something within us, a core, a spark, an abyss, a citadel, a palace, a revolution, a realm, something of God that cannot be overcome even by the greatest malice or the worst chaos.

Howard Thurman says that the African American tradition took Jeremiah's question, "is there no balm in Gilead" (Jer 8:22) and hammered the question mark into an exclamation point to proclaim: there *is* a balm

---

152. Catherine, *Dialogue*, 123.
153. à Kempis, *Imitation of Christ*, 76.
154. Eckhart, *Sermons & Treatises II*, 333–34.
155. Eckhart, *Sermons & Treatises I*, 84–85.
156. Julian, *Showings*, 315.

in Gilead!¹⁵⁷ The same tradition might forge Sojourner Truth's question to Frederick Douglass—"is God dead?"/"is God gone?"—into a proclamation not only to abolitionists and activists, but to slaveholders, bystanders, and every system of oppression: although the world may often be utterly godless, God is not dead! This Christlike inner peace is what we discover with the women at the empty tomb as they wonder where Jesus' body is laid (John 20:2, 13). They think he is *dead* and that his body is *gone*. Then comes the answer to an unuttered question: Christ is not gone. Christ is not dead. Christ is risen!

Such a peace, Christ's peace, is an astonishingly alien thing. Like a beatitude, sometimes it is logical, but just as often it reverses expectations, and as often as both it resurrects impossibilities: blessed are those who die, for they shall be raised. It is King's peace: "I" may not get there with you, but "we" will get to the promise land.¹⁵⁸ We never know in any moment, in any circumstance, which we will get—blessed logic or outright amazement. All that we can count on is divine incongruity and holy unpredictability. In many ways, Christ's peace is a fragile, whispering, power-in-weakness peace, the peace of a few Friends swamped by world war. Yet it is also oddly durable, not easily scuffed, warped, or shattered. It rarely wins, at least in the ways we usually keep score. But it cannot be defeated. It is a peace that does not fear a force that can kill the body unless that power can also slay the soul (Matt 10:28, Luke 12:4).

Neither mystics nor activists are speculative people. They pray. They act. Mystics seek God—not union, not happiness, not even blessings, but God. They are tenaciously, vocationally engaged in permanent inner revolution. Peace may be an occasional by-product of that search, but they will spend more time in the wilderness and in purgation than on mountaintops and in union. Activists seek the realm—not reform, not victories, not acclaim, but the realm. They are doggedly, vocationally engaged in social transfiguration. There may be inches and indicators of progress and rare giddy triumphs, but most activism takes place in hard-time solidarity in the world's daily purgation. Both pursuits are relentless. Either quest may occasionally be buoyed by epiphanies and victories, but what both pursuits need most is steadfastness in the face of stark dark nights, bitter compromises, and demoralizing defeats. In order to be vibrant, we must be as pillars; in order to be dynamic, we must be as statues; in order to have abundant life, we must be as if dead.

---

157. Thurman, *Deep River*, 56.
158. King, *Testament*, 286.

Tolstoy and Underhill say that we have the capacity to radiate the revolution; it is already at work within us. And we see signs of this invisible transformation. Baldwin abandons his articulate despair. Rustin resists intimidation. Hillesum finds serenity in the midst of genocide. Muste's allies smile at machine guns. Stringfellow asserts that the powers of hell will never prevail against Bible study and prayer. King repeats his Christlike mantra even from the grave: you may kill us, but we will still love you. None of this is a day at the park, a walk on the beach, or an oasis. Just as certainly, none of it is a mirage. While sustained by confidence in the coming age when all shall be well, our hope is remarkably earthy, commonplace, familiar, and routine. Introducing his collection of Gandhi's sayings, Merton says: "love triumphs, at least in this life, not by eliminating evil once and for all but by resisting and overcoming it anew every day."[159] That is our spiritual battle. That is our peace.

True inner peace is comfortable with restlessness: in anguish and conflict we grow in faith and love. True peace combats every power that resists, ignores, disdains, and seeks first to destroy the realm. We find our peace in this daily struggle. We nurture our peace in the ultimately unshakable conviction that, in a world that seems ever determined to squelch compassion, justice, and truth, no matter what becomes of us, God is neither dead nor gone.

A CONCLUDING PRAYER

In his commitment to the practice of faith, Jean-Pierre de Caussade notes testily, "we are like absent-minded people who know all about geography but lose their way when going home."[160] This brings a particular slant to Paul's perspective: the eye is not more important than the hand or the foot (1 Cor 12:21). It is not enough to survey the way. It is not enough to map it. We must walk it. Mysticism and activism form and inform each other in countless ways that can inspire us with the wisdom of experienced and enacted orthodoxy so that we can engage and embody its insurrectionary dissidence. Knowing the geography of orthodoxy is a start, but the way is less to be studied than taken. So activists demand that theologians do justice and mystics assert that theologians pray.

Typically, when medieval mystics preached, they directed their congregations toward embodied action: now you know; go and do. It is the same message Jesus conveys to the lawyer after the lawyer has heard of

---

159. Merton, *Gandhi*, 13.
160. de Caussade, *Abandonment*, 49.

a Samaritan who "sees" and has mercy: now you know; go and do (Luke 10:33, 37). In their sermons, medieval mystics present a theological truth, and they conclude with a thematically related blessing.[161] Johannes Tauler developed this it into a mini art form. Writing of Christ's birth, he concludes, "May God help us to prepare a dwelling place for this noble birth, so that we may all attain spiritual motherhood."[162] Preaching on the crucifixion, he says, "May we take up the Cross in such a way that we enter the true ground where Christ has gone before us."[163] In a sermon on the Trinity, he concludes, "May God the blessed Trinity grant us to arrive at this inmost ground where its true image dwells."[164] Preaching on the gifts of the Spirit, he asks, "May God help us to perform the work to which God's Spirit has called us, each according to the revelation we have received."[165] Almost generically, he prays, "May our loving God help us to attain this,"[166] or "share in this,"[167] or "achieve it,"[168] or "experience this."[169]

Having sat at the feet of mystics and activists, now we know. May we wake up. May we mourn. May we see the great light. May we take the way of no way. May we bear and bury ourselves in Christ's wounds. May we love all harijans. May we seek union with God and solidarity with all people. May we see all things transfigured. And may that peace beyond paradox radiate from us. Now may we go and do.

And we will, if only we can see.

---

161. Eckhart, *Essential Sermons*.
162. Tauler, *Sermons*, 40.
163. Ibid., 168.
164. Ibid., 108.
165. Ibid., 157.
166. Ibid., 54.
167. Ibid., 61.
168. Ibid., 144.
169. Ibid., 152.

Glossary of Names

Abbas Agathon, Antony, Arsenius, Bes, Daniel of Scetis, John the Dwarf, Joseph, Longinus, Lot, Mius, Moses, Pior, Poemen, Theodore and Amma Syncletica: among the desert fathers and mothers of the fourth through sixth centuries who left the city and civilization to live in the deserts of Egypt and Syria.

Aelred of Rievaulx (1110–67): English abbot best known for his writings on spiritual friendship.

Al-Hallaj, Mansur (858–922): controversial Persian Sufi mystic arrested and martyred for his spiritual writings.

Al-'Arabi, Ibn (1165–1240): very influential Spanish-born Sufi mystic and theologian known for his subtle and opaque writings.

Alinsky, Saul (1909–72): founder of modern community organizing and author of *Rules for Radicals*.

Angela of Foligno (1248–1309): mystic, spiritual writer, and founder of a Franciscan order for women.

Anselm (1033–1109): spiritual writer, theologian, monk, abbot, and Archbishop of Canterbury.

Arendt, Hannah (1906–75): influential German-American philosopher and political theorist.

Arnold, Eberhard (1883–1935): German theologian and founder of the Bruderhof community rooted in the nonviolent Anabaptist tradition.

Glossary of Names

Auden, W. H. (1907–73): prominent twentieth-century Anglo-American poet.

Augustine (354–430): Bishop of Hippo, prolific writer and preacher, and a foundational thinker in Christian theology.

Autpert, Ambrose (730–84): abbot and spiritual writer.

Baal Shem Tov (1698–1760): rabbi and founder of Eastern Europe's Hasidic spiritual renewal movement.

Bailie, John (1886–1960): Scottish theologian and ecumenist.

Baldwin, James (1924–87): child preacher, playwright, poet, novelist, essayist, and outspoken social critic on issues of race, class, and sexuality.

Basho, Matsuo (1644–94): Japanese poet generally considered a great master of the haiku.

Benedict of Nursia (480–543): author of *The Rule of Benedict*, considered the founder of Christian monasticism.

Bernard of Clairvaux (1090–1153): prominent spiritual writer, builder of the Cistercian order, and advocate for the Crusades.

Berrigan, Daniel (b. 1921): Catholic priest, prolific writer, and well-known activist.

Berry, Wendell (b. 1934): prolific novelist, poet, cultural critic, essayist, and a major advocate of eco-justice.

Birgitta of Sweden (1303–73): founder of a monastic order, mystic, saint, and prophet.

Bistami, Bayezid (804–74): Persian Sufi mystic.

Black Elk (1863–1950): Oglala Lakota (Sioux) visionary and healer.

Boff, Leonardo (b. 1938): controversial former Catholic priest and prolific writer of liberation theology.

Bonhoeffer, Dietrich (1906–45): influential German Lutheran pastor, theologian, and ethicist, founding member of the anti-Nazi Confessing Church, executed in a concentration camp.

Glossary of Names

Brothers Giles, John, Juniper, and Sylvester: among the first generation of "brothers" and disciples of Francis of Assisi.

Brueggemann, Walter (b. 1933): a dominant contemporary biblical scholar and theologian.

Brutus, Dennis (1924–2009): South African poet, educator, journalist, and anti-apartheid activist.

Buber, Martin (1878–1965): scholar, writer, dominant figure in twentieth-century Judaism best known for his philosophy expressed in his book *I and Thou*.

Bultmann, Rudolph (1884–1976): a German Lutheran pastor and a prominent New Testament scholar.

Bunyan, John (1628–88): English writer and preacher best known for his book *The Pilgrim's Progress*.

Camara, Dom Helder (1909–99): Brazilian Catholic Archbishop best known for his active opposition to repression during a military dictatorship.

Campbell, Will (1924–2013): white Baptist minister, author, and civil rights activist.

Cardenal, Ernesto (b. 1925): Catholic priest, poet, liberation theologian, Nicaragua's Minister of Culture for eight years who for a while lived under Merton's tutelage.

Casas, Bartolomé de las (1484–1566): Spanish Dominican friar and writer who protested against the decimation of indigenous peoples by their colonizers.

Cassian, John (360–435): monk, mystic, and theologian whose writings extended the influence of desert monasticism to Western Europe.

Catherine of Genoa (1147–1510): Italian mystic, spiritual writer, and saint remembered for her ministry with the poor and dying.

Catherine of Siena (1347–80): one of history's foremost mystics and theologians who denounced ecclesiastical corruption and engaged in the politics of her era.

de Caussade, Jean-Pierre (1675–1751): French Jesuit priest and spiritual writer.

Chávez, César (1927–93): farm worker, activist, labor organizer, and civil rights leader.

Chergé, Christian (1937–96): prior of a Trappist monastery in Algeria who built bridges with his Islamic neighbors and was martyred during a decade of violence.

Chrysostom, John (347–407): Archbishop of Constantinople and important theologian who advocated for the poor and denounced the abuse of power.

Clausewitz, Carl von (1780–1831): German-Prussian military theorist who pondered the politics of power in his classic *On War*.

Cleaver, Eldridge (1935–98): an early leader of the Black Panther Party in the 1960s.

Climacus, John (c. 579–649): abbot and spiritual writer whose works have had an enduring influence on the Orthodox tradition.

Coleman, Thomas (1911–97): Alabama deputy who murdered seminarian Jonathan Daniels and was acquitted by an all-white jury.

Collins, Addie Mae (1949–63): one of the four girls who died in the bombing of the Sixteenth Street Baptist Church in Birmingham.

Columba of Iona (521–97): abbot and missionary who founded the Iona community and helped spread Christianity to Scotland.

Damien, Father (1840–89): Belgian Catholic priest who died of leprosy after a sixteen-year ministry on the leper colony of Moloka'i.

Daniels, Jonathan (1939–65): Episcopal seminarian and civil rights worker murdered in Alabama trying to protect other unarmed people.

Dante, Alighieri (c. 1265–1321): medieval poet whose *The Divine Comedy* is a classic in Italian and world literature.

Davies, Robertson (1913–95): Canadian novelist, playwright, academic, and journalist.

Day, Dorothy (1897–1980): journalist, political activist, co-founder of the Catholic Worker movement, and a central figure in modern Catholic activism.

Glossary of Names

Debs, Eugene V. (1855–1926): union leader, founding member of the Industrial Workers of the World (IWW), and Socialist Party candidate for president.

Deming, Barbara (1917–84): American feminist, lesbian activist, and advocate of nonviolent social change.

Desai, Mahadev (1892–1942): activist, writer, and Mohandas Gandhi's personal secretary.

Dorotheos of Gaza (c. 506-c. 560): founder of a monastery, hermit, and spiritual writer.

Dorothy of Montau (1347–94): hermit and visionary.

Douglass, Frederick (1818–95): escaped slave, writer, orator, abolitionist, public official, diplomat, and advocate for human equality.

Dov Baer of Mezritch (d. 1772): Hasidic rabbi and disciple of the Baal Shem Tov.

DuBois, W. E. B. (1868–1963): sociologist, historian, polemicist, Pan-Africanist, civil rights advocate, co-founder of the NAACP, joined the Communist Party at age 93.

Eckhart, Meister (c. 1260–1327): influential and controversial German theologian, philosopher, and mystic tried for heresy.

Eichenberg, Fritz (1901–90): German American illustrator whose wood engravings expressed his passions for faith, social justice, and nonviolence.

Elizabeth of Hungary (1207–31): honored for her service to the sick and the poor.

Ellacuría, Ignacio (1930–89): priest, philosopher, and liberation theologian murdered with his colleagues in El Salvador.

Ellul, Jacques (1912–94): prolific French law professor, lay theologian, sociologist, philosopher, and Christian anarchist.

Endo, Shusaku (1923–96): modern Japanese Catholic novelist.

Ephrem the Syrian (c. 306–73): theologian, preacher, and prolific writer of Syriac hymns.

Evagrius Ponticus (345–99): monk, writer, and teacher known for his practical spiritual guidance.

de Foucauld, Charles (1858–1915): French military officer in North Africa who converted and lived among the Tuareg in Algeria until his murder.

Fox, George (1624–91): founder of the Religious Society of Friends (Quakers) during a time of social upheaval and religious persecution.

Francis of Assisi (c. 1182–1226): preacher, reformer, mystic, and founder of the Franciscan movement who had a singular commitment to voluntary poverty and a sense of relatedness to all created things.

Freire, Paulo (1921–97): Brazilian philosopher and educator best known for his *Pedagogy of the Oppressed*.

Fry, Elizabeth (1780–1845): Quaker woman, prison and social reformer.

Galilea, Segundo (1928–2010): Chilean priest and liberation theologian.

Gandhi, Mohandas ("Mahatma") (1869–1948): a towering figure honored for his role in India's independence movement, his commitment to justice and nonviolence, and his spirit of respect for all religions and peoples.

Garnett, Henry Highland (1815–82): former slave, African American educator, minister, orator, and abolitionist.

Garrow, David (b. 1953): historian, author, and biographer of Martin Luther King, Jr.

Golding, William (1911–93): English novelist and Nobel laureate in Literature.

Grande, Rutilio (1928–77): activist priest in El Salvador whose murder influenced Oscar Romero to challenge government oppression.

Gregory of Nazianzus (325–389): Archbishop of Constantinople, orator, theologian, and one of the Cappadocian Fathers.

Gregory of Nyssa (ca. 335-ca. 384): bishop, theologian, and spiritual writer, and another of the Cappadocian Fathers.

Gregory the Great (ca. 540–604): significant pope, theologian, and patron of education and the arts.

Griffin, John Howard (1920–80): white journalist and author who after darkening his skin wrote of living as an African American in *Black Like Me*.

Griffiths, Bede (1906–93): British monk who lived in ashrams in South India and became a leader in Hindu-Christian dialogue.

Gutierrez, Gustavo (b. 1928): Peruvian priest, prolific author, and founder of liberation theology who has lived and worked among the poor.

Hadewijch: influential but obscure thirteenth-century Dutch woman who was a poet, visionary, and mystic.

Hallie, Philip (1922–94): author, philosopher, professor, and ethicist.

Hammarskjöld, Dag (1905–61): Swedish diplomat, economist, author, and Secretary-General of the United Nations who died trying to mediate Congo's first civil war.

Hatun, Zeynep: fifteenth-century Turkish woman, Sufi, and poet.

Headlam, Stewart (1847–1924): Anglican priest and Christian socialist.

Hennacy, Ammon (1893–1970): American anarchist, pacifist, and member of the Catholic Worker movement.

Herbert, George (1593–1633): Anglican priest, orator, and metaphysical poet.

Hildegard of Bingen (1098–1179): abbess, visionary, composer, scientist, and mystic.

Hillesum, Etty (1914–43): Jewish woman, spiritual writer, and Holocaust victim.

Hilton, Walter (d. 1396): English Augustinian monk and spiritual writer.

Hughes, Langston (1902–67): poet, playwright, novelist, social critic, and leading figure in the Harlem Renaissance.

Illah, Ibn 'Ata' (1250–1309): Egyptian Sufi, mystic, and spiritual writer.

Isaac of Nineveh (d. 700): bishop, theologian, and spiritual writer.

Isaac of Stella (c. 1100—c. 1170): monk, philosopher, theologian, and spiritual writer.

Ishiguro, Kazuo (b. 1954): Japanese-born modern English novelist.

Jacob Yitzkak of Lublin (c. 1745–1815): a rabbi and leading figure in the Hasidic movement known as "the Seer."

James, William (1842–1910): educator, psychologist, physician, and one of America's foremost nineteenth-century philosophers.

John of the Cross (1542–91): priest, friar, reformer, mystic, poet, and a central voice in ascetical theology.

Jones, Rufus (1863–1948): philosopher, professor, prolific writer, activist, and influential modern Quaker.

Jordan, Clarence (1912–69): farmer, New Testament scholar, popular writer, founder of the Koinonia Community, and helped to found Habitat for Humanity.

Julian of Norwich (c. 1342–c. 1416): English anchoress and a central mystic in Christian history.

Karnow, Stanley (1925–2013): American journalist and historian known for his writings on the Vietnam War.

Keating, Thomas (b. 1923): Trappist monk and a primary voice in the modern Centering Prayer movement.

Kelly, Thomas (1893–1941): Quaker educator, pacifist, and writer on Christian mysticism.

à Kempis, Thomas (ca. 1380–1471): monk, devotional writer, and author of *The Imitation of Christ*.

King, Coretta Scott (1927–2006): human rights advocate.

King, Martin Luther, Jr. (1929–68): Baptist pastor and preacher, orator, civil rights and anti-war leader, and advocate of nonviolence and civil disobedience assassinated for his activism.

Lane, Belden (b. 1943): professor, theologian, and writer on Christian spirituality.

LaPorte, Roger (1943–65): American anti-war protester who immolated himself in imitation of Vietnamese Buddhist monks.

Law, William (1686–1761): Anglican priest, theologian, mystic, and spiritual writer.

Lawson, James (b. 1928): civil rights leader, activist, and theoretician of nonviolence.

Leclerc, Eloi (b. 1921): French philosopher, Franciscan, and scholar.

Leclerq, Jean (1911–93): monk and scholar of Western monasticism.

Leech, Kenneth (b. 1939): Anglican priest, Christian socialist, contextual theologian, and prolific writer on politics and spirituality.

Lester, Muriel (1885–1968): pacifist, social reformer, founder of Kingsley Hall, friend of Gandhi, and Traveling Secretary of the International Fellowship of Reconciliation.

Lewis, C. S. (1898–1963): medievalist, essayist, literary critic, novelist, Christian apologist, and lay theologian.

Lewis, Sinclair (1885–1951): novelist, playwright, critic of capitalism and materialism, and winner of the Nobel Prize for Literature.

Lorde, Audre (1934–92): Caribbean American poet, essayist, feminist, and activist.

Lossky, Vladimir (1903–58): scholar and Russian Orthodox theologian.

Lull, Ramon (c. 1232–c. 1315): scholar, philosopher, Franciscan tertiary, and spiritual writer.

Luthuli, Albert (c. 1898–1967): nonviolent anti-apartheid activist, President of the African National Congress, and winner of the Nobel Peace Prize.

Macarius of Alexandria (d. 395): monk and desert Christian.

Macarius of Egypt (the Spiritbearer) (d. 390): monk and desert Christian.

Malcolm X (1925–65): African American activist, advocate of black self-defense and self-determination, and minister in the Nation of Islam assassinated after his conversion to Islam.

Maslow, Abraham (1908–70): American psychologist best known for his view of his theory of the "hierarchy of needs."

Massignon, Louis (1883–1962): Roman Catholic, scholar of Islam, and an advocate of Gandhian social action.

Maud, Sir John (1906–82): British diplomat who served in South Africa.

Maurice, F. D. (1805–72): priest, Christian socialist, and central nineteenth-century Anglican theologian.

Maurin, Peter (1877–1949): French peasant and social activist who co-founded the Catholic Worker movement.

Maximus the Confessor (c. 580–662): monk, theologian, and scholar.

McNamara, William: modern monk, mystic, recluse, and spiritual writer.

McNair, Denise (1951–63): one of the four girls murdered in the bombing of the Sixteenth Street Baptist Church in Birmingham.

Mechtild of Hackenborn (1241–98): Benedictine nun and mystic.

Mechtild of Magdeburg (c. 1210–c. 1285): mystic and spiritual writer.

Merton, Thomas (1915–68): Trappist monk, prolific spiritual writer, anti-war and civil rights writer, advocate of nonviolence, and pioneer in inter-religious dialogue.

Mordecai of Neskhizh: a Hasidic rabbi.

Moshe Leib of Sasov (1745–1807): prominent Hasidic rabbi in Ukraine.

Motovilov, Nicholas (1809–79): Russian landowner, businessman, and first biographer of Seraphim of Sarov.

Murray, Pauli (1910–85): lawyer, Episcopal priest, feminist, civil and women's rights activist.

Muste, A. J. (1885–1967): Presbyterian minister, Quaker, labor organizer and educator, pacifist, secular leftist, anti-war leader, and Executive Director of the Fellowship of Reconciliation.

Nash, Diane (b. 1938): civil rights leader involved in Freedom Rides, SNCC, and the SCLC who planned the Selma Voting Rights campaign.

Nayler, James (1616–60): early Quaker leader and social reformer.

Nhat Chi Mai (1934-67): Buddhist anti-war protester who immolated herself in Saigon to protest the war in Vietnam.

Nhat Hanh, Thich (b. 1926): Vietnamese Zen Buddhist monk, leader in Engaged Buddhism, prolific writer, teacher, poet, and advocate of nonviolent action.

Niebuhr, H. Richard (1894-1962): scholar, author, and an influential thinker in modern American theology and ethics.

Niebuhr, Reinhold (1892-1971): professor, theologian, ethicist, and central figure in mid-twentieth-century public affairs

Nouwen, Henri (1932-96): Catholic priest, psychologist, and popular spiritual writer.

O'Connor, Flannery (1925-64): essayist, Catholic layperson, and a major figure in modern American literature.

Oetinger, Friedrich Cristoph (1702-82): Lutheran pastor and Pietist theologian.

Origen (c. 185-253/4): prolific, influential, and controversial theologian, philosopher, biblical exegete, and spiritual writer.

Otto, Rudolf (1869-1937): prominent theologian and scholar of comparative religion best known for his classic *The Idea of the Holy*.

Palamas, Gregory (1296-1359): monk of Mt. Athos, Archbishop of Thessaloniki, and influential theologian.

Pascal, Blaise (1623-62): French mathematician, physicist, inventor, philosopher, and mystic.

Pasternak, Boris (1890-1960): novelist, poet, literary translator, and winner of the Nobel Prize for Literature.

Péguy, Charles (1873-1914): French poet, essayist, socialist, nationalist, and convert to Catholicism.

Pinhas of Koretz (1728-90): Russian rabbi and pillar of the Hasidic movement.

Plotinus (c. 204-270): Greek philosopher whose metaphysical writings have influenced Christian, Jewish, and Islamic mysticism.

Pseudo Dionysius: an anonymous fifth- or sixth-century theologian, philosopher, mystical writer, and pioneer of the *via negativa*.

Rabia (c. 717–801): prominent female Sufi mystic and Muslim saint.

Rauschenbusch, Walter (1861–1918): Baptist pastor, theologian, social reformer, and the central figure in the Social Gospel movement.

Richard of St. Victor (d. 1173): Augustinian prior, mystic, and influential theologian.

Robertson, Carole (1949–63): one of the four girls killed in the bombing of the Sixteenth Street Baptist Church in Birmingham.

Rolle, Richard (d. 1349): English hermit and well-known religious writer and thinker.

Romero, Oscar (1917–80): influential Archbishop of El Salvador, pastoral leader, and advocate for justice assassinated for his public pronouncements.

Rumi, Jelaluddin (1207–73): Persian theologian, mystic, Sufi, and prolific poet whose influence has crossed religious boundaries.

Rupert of Deutz (d. 1129): Benedictine theologian and spiritual writer.

Ruusbroec, John (1294–1381): the most influential Flemish mystic, known for his theologically nuanced approach to mysticism.

Scholem, Gershom (1897–1982): prominent intellectual, historian, theologian, and modern founder of the academic study of Kabbalah and Jewish mysticism.

Scudder, Vida (1861–1954): professor, editor, writer, feminist, lesbian social activist.

Segundo, Juan Luis (1925–96): prominent Latin American liberation theologian.

Sembene, Ousmane (1923–2007): Senegalese author known as a founder of African filmmaking.

Seraphim of Sarov (1759–1833): foremost nineteenth-century Russian Orthodox spiritual guide who wrote on monasticism and contemplation.

Shams Tabrizi (1185–1248): Persian Muslim credited with being Rumi's spiritual mentor.

Shmelke of Nikolsburg (1726–78): early Hasidic rabbi.

Shneur Zalman of Ladi (1745–1812): early Hasidic rabbi.

Silesius, Angelus (1624–77): Catholic priest whose religious poetry popularized mystical ideas.

Sobrino, Jon (b. 1938): priest, theologian, and a central and controversial liberation theologian based in El Salvador.

Soelle, Dorothee (1929–2003): German liberation theologian, professor, and popular writer.

Solzhenitsyn, Alexander (1918–2008): famous Russian novelist and historian, critic of Soviet Communism, and winner of the Nobel Prize for Literature.

Soyinka, Wole (b. 1934): playwright, novelist, essayist, poet, foundational figure in African literature, and winner of the Nobel Prize for Literature.

Steinbeck, John (1902–68): American novelist and winner of the Nobel Prize for Literature.

Stowe, Harriet Beecher (1811–96): abolitionist, social critic, and author of twenty books including *Uncle Tom's Cabin*.

Stringfellow, William (1928–85): attorney, social critic, activist, author, and lay theologian.

Suzuki, D. T. (1894–1966): professor and translator who popularized Zen and Buddhism in the West, and an early participant in interreligious dialogue.

Symeon the New Theologian (949–1022): mystic, poet, and one of three figures in the Orthodox tradition given the title "theologian."

Tamez, Elsa (b. 1950): biblical scholar, writer, and liberation theologian.

Tauler, Johannes (1300–61): Dominican preacher, mystic, disciple of Meister Eckhart, and a leading figure in Rhineland mysticism.

Teilhard de Chardin, Pierre (1881–1955): geologist, paleontologist, philosopher, and Jesuit priest silenced by the Vatican for his controversial writings.

Teresa of Ávila (1515–82): church reformer, spiritual writer, and one of history's most important mystics.

Thérèse of Lisieux (1873–97): popular nineteenth-century spiritual writer known for the simplicity of her piety.

Theognius (425–522): monk, anchorite, and bishop.

Theophan the Recluse (1815–94): priest, monk, translator, and one of the Orthodox tradition's significant spiritual writers.

Thich Quang Duc (1897–1963): prominent monk who immolated himself to protest the South Vietnamese government's persecution of Buddhists.

Thoreau, Henry David (1817–62): poet, essayist, naturalist, abolitionist, tax resister, transcendentalist, and an early advocate of simple living and civil disobedience.

Thurman, Howard (1899–1981): prolific author, influential pastor, preacher, philosopher, theologian, civil rights leader, and advocate for nonviolence.

Tillich, Paul (1886–1965): existentialist thinker and one of the most prominent theologians of the mid-twentieth century.

Tolstoy, Leo (1828–1910): one of history's most acclaimed novelists who, after his conversion, became a social critic, moralist, anarchist, and advocate of nonviolence.

Towne, Anthony (1928–80): poet, activist, and William Stringfellow's partner.

Traherne, Thomas (1637–74): Anglican priest, poet, theologian, and mystical writer.

Tri Quang (b. 1923): Vietnamese monk who stood up for the religious rights of Buddhists in the 1960s.

Trocmé, Andre (1901–71): French Protestant pacifist and pastor who worked with his congregation to save Jews during the Holocaust

Truth, Sojourner (c. 1797–1883): escaped slave, abolitionist, and advocate for women's equality.

Turner, Nat (1800–31): executed leading the most famous slave revolt in the antebellum South.

Tutu, Desmond (b. 1931): Anglican Archbishop of South Africa, anti-apartheid advocate, theologian, social critic, author, and winner of the Nobel Peace Prize.

Tzu, Chuang: Taoist philosopher of the third century BCE.

Tzu, Lao: Chinese philosopher of the sixth century BCE, considered the founder of Taoism.

Underhill, Evelyn (1875–1941): English pacifist, writer, and spiritual director known primarily for her writings on worship, spirituality, and mysticism.

Uri of Strelisk (1757–1826): well-known Hasidic rabbi.

de Waal, Esther: prolific modern spiritual writer primarily focused on the Benedictine and Celtic traditions.

Walker, David (1796–1830): abolitionist influential in nineteenth-century African American thinking.

Watters, Pat (1927–99): white journalist covering the civil rights movement who later taught journalism.

Wesley, Cynthia (1949–63): one of the four girls killed in the bombing of the Sixteenth Street Baptist Church in Birmingham.

Weston, Frank (1871–1924): Anglican Bishop of Zanzibar.

William of St. Thierry (d. 1148): abbot, theologian, and mystic.

Wink, Walter (1935–2012): biblical scholar, theologian, social activist, and advocate of nonviolence.

Winthrop, John (1588–1649): leading figure in the founding of the Massachusetts Bay Colony, popularly known for calling the Puritan colony a "city on a hill."

Woolman, John (1720–72): merchant, tailor, journalist, Quaker preacher, early abolitionist, and a pacifist who urged tax resistance.

Wright, Richard (1908–60): essayist and novelist who wrote extensively on racial inequality.

Yehiel Mikhal of Zlotchov: Hasidic rabbi.

Young Chief (d. 1859): one of several Cayuse leaders to bear this name.

Zevi Hirsh of Zhydatchov (d. 1831): Hasidic rabbi.

Zohar: the name attributed to the disputed author of thirteenth-century books that became the foundation of Jewish Kabbalism.

Zusya of Hanipol (1718–1800): early Hasidic rabbi.

Bibliography

Achebe, Chinua. *No Longer at Ease.* Greenwich, CT: Fawcett, 1960.
Adomnán of Iona. *Life of St. Columba.* Translated by Richard Sharpe. London: Penguin, 1995.
al-'Arabi, Ibn. *The Meccan Revelations, Volume 2.* Edited by Michael Chodkiewicz. Translated by R. W. J. Austin. New York: Pir, 2004.
Alighieri, Dante. *The Divine Comedy.* Translated by H. R. Huse. San Francisco: Rinehart, 1954.
al-Kalabadhi, Abu Bakr. *The Doctrine of the Sufis.* Translated by A. J. Arberry. Cambridge: Cambridge University Press, 1977.
Allchin, A. M. *The Living Presence of the Past: The Dynamic of Christian Tradition.* New York: Seabury, 1981.
Allen, Woody. *Side Effects.* New York: Random House, 1975.
Alter, Robert. *The Art of Biblical Poetry.* New York: Basic, 1985.
———. *Canon and Creativity: Modern Writing and the Authority of Scripture.* New Haven, CT: Yale University Press, 2000.
———. *The World of Biblical Literature.* New York: Basic, 1992.
Anderson, Jervis. *Bayard Rustin: Troubles I've Seen.* Berkeley, CA: University of California Press, 1998.
Anselm of Canterbury. *The Prayers and Meditations of Saint Anselm.* Translated by Benedicta Ward. New York: Penguin, 1973.
Antony of Choziba. *The Life of Saint George of Choziba and the Miracles of the Most Holy Mother of God at Choziba.* Translated by Tim Vivian and Apostolos N. Athanassakis. San Francisco: International Scholars, 1994.
Arendt, Hannah. *Eichmann in Jerusalem: A Report on the Banality of Evil.* New York: Viking, 1965.
Arnold, Eberhard. *Writings.* Edited by Johann Christoph Arnold. Maryknoll, NY: Orbis, 2000.
Auden, W. H. *The Complete Works of W. H. Auden: Prose, Volume II, 1939–1948.* Edited by Edward Mendelson. Princeton, NJ: Princeton University Press, 2002.
Augustine of Hippo. *City of God.* Edited and translated by David Knowles. Middlesex: Penguin, 1972.
———. *The Confessions of St. Augustine.* Translated by John K. Ryan. New York: Image, 1960.
Baillie, John. *A Diary of Private Prayer.* New York: Charles Scribner's Sons, 1949.

Baldwin, James. *Conversations with James Baldwin*. Edited by Fred L. Standley and Louis H. Pratt. Jackson, MS: University Press of Mississippi, 1989.

———. *The Evidence of Things Not Seen*. New York: Henry Holt and Co., 1985.

———. *The Fire Next Time*. New York: Dell, 1962.

———. "The Highroad to Destiny." In *Martin Luther King, Jr.: A Profile*. Edited by C. Eric Lincoln. New York: Hill and Wang, 1970.

———. *No Name in the Street*. New York: Dell, 1972.

———. "Sonny's Blues." In *Going to Meet the Man*, 86–122. New York: Dell, 1948.

Baldwin, James, and Margaret Mead. *A Rap on Race*. Philadelphia: J. B. Lippincott, 1971.

Bernard of Clairvaux. *On the Song of Songs I*. Translated by Kilian Walsh OCSO and Irene Edmonds. Cistercian Fathers Series 4. Kalamazoo, MI: Cistercian, 1981.

———. *On the Song of Songs III*. Translated by Kilian Walsh OCSO and Irene Edmonds. Cistercian Fathers Series 31. Kalamazoo, MI: Cistercian, 1979.

Berrigan, Daniel. *To Dwell in Peace: An Autobiography*. San Francisco: Harper & Row, 1987.

Berrigan, Jerome, and Carol Berrigan. "Eschaton Hospitality." *Sojourners* 14:11 (1985) 26.

Berry, Wendell. *Collected Poems, 1957–1982*. San Francisco: North Point, 1985.

The Bhagavad Gita. Translated by Eknath Easwaran. Tomales, CA: Nilgiri, 1998.

Birgitta of Sweden. *Life and Selected Revelations*. Translated by Albert Ryle Kezel. Mahwah, NJ: Paulist, 1990.

Black Elk. *Black Elk Speaks: Being the Life Story of a Holy Man of the Oglala Sioux*. As told through John G. Neihardt. Lincoln, NE: University of Nebraska Press, 1961.

Bloom, Anthony. *Beginning to Pray*. New York: Paulist, 1970.

Boff, Leonardo. *Saint Francis: A Model for Human Liberation*. Translated by John W. Diercksmeier. New York: Crossroad, 1988.

———. "Salvation in Jesus Christ and the Process of Liberation." In *The Mystical and Political Dimension of the Christian Faith*, edited by Claude Geffré and Gustavo Gutierrez, 78–91. New York: Herder & Herder, 1974.

Bonaventure. *The Soul's Journey into God, The Tree of Life, The Life of St. Francis*. Translated by Ewert Cousins. New York: Paulist, 1978.

Bondurant, Joan. *Conquest of Violence: The Gandhian Philosophy of Conflict*. Berkeley, CA: University of California Press, 1965.

Bonhoeffer, Dietrich. *Letters and Papers from Prison*. Edited by Eberhard Bethge. Translated by Christian Kaiser Verlag, Reginald H. Fuller, Frank Clark, and John Bowden. New York: Touchstone, 1977.

The Book of Common Prayer. New York: The Church Hymnal Corporation, 1979.

Branch, Taylor. *Parting the Waters: America in the King Years, 1954–63*. New York: Simon and Schuster, 1988.

———. *Pillar of Fire: America in the King Years, 1963–65*. New York: Simon and Schuster, 1998.

Brock, Sebastian. *The Luminous Eye: The Spiritual World Vision of Saint Ephrem the Syrian*. Kalamazoo, MI: Cistercian, 1985.

Brockman, James R. *The Word Remains: A Life of Oscar Romero*. Maryknoll, NY: Orbis, 1982.

Brodhead, Meg. "Maryhouse II." In *A Penny a Copy: Readings from The Catholic Worker*, edited by Thomas Cornell, Robert Ellsberg, and Jim Forest, 270–73. Maryknoll, NY: Orbis, 1995.

Brown, Peter. *Augustine of Hippo*. New York: Dorset, 1986.

Brown, Raymond E. *The Community of the Beloved Disciple*. New York: Paulist, 1979.

Browne, Judith M. *Gandhi: Prisoner of Hope*. New Haven, CT: Yale University Press, 1989.

Brueggemann, Walter. *David's Truth in Israel's Imagination and Memory*. Philadelphia: Fortress, 1985.

———. *Genesis*. Atlanta: John Knox, 1982.

———. *Theology of the Old Testament: Testimony, Dispute, Advocacy*. Minneapolis: Fortress, 1997.

———. *The Prophetic Imagination*. Philadelphia: Fortress, 1978.

Brutus, Dennis. *A Simple Lust*. African Writers Series 115. London: Heinemann, 1973.

———. *Stubborn Hope*. Washington, DC: Three Continents, 1983.

Buber, Martin. *Ecstatic Utterances: The Heart of Mysticism*. Edited by Paul Mendes-Flohr. Translated by Esther Cameron. Syracuse, NY: Syracuse University Press, 1996.

———. *Tales of the Hasidim: Early Masters*. Translated by Olga Marx. New York: Schocken, 1947.

———. *Tales of the Hasidim: Later Masters*. Translated by Olga Marx. New York: Schocken, 1948.

Bunyan, John. *The Pilgrim's Progress*. New York: Books, Inc., 1945.

Camara, Dom Helder. *Spiral of Violence*. Translated by Della Couling. Denville, NJ: Dimension, 1971.

Campbell, Will D. *Brother to a Dragonfly*. New York: Seabury, 1979.

Cassian, John. *Conferences*. Translated by Colm Luibheid. New York: Paulist, 1985.

Catherine of Siena. *The Dialogue*. Translated by Suzanne Noffke. New York: Paulist, 1980.

———. *Saint Catherine of Siena As Seen in Her Letters*. Edited and translated by Vida D. Scudder. New York: E. P. Dutton, 1927.

de Caussade, Jean-Pierre. *Abandonment to Divine Providence*. Translated by John Beevers. New York: Image, 1975.

Cavarnos, Constantine, and Mary-Barbara Zeldin. *St. Seraphim of Sarov*. Modern Orthodox Saints 5. Belmont, MA: Institute for Byzantine and Modern Greek Studies, 1980.

Celano, Thomas of. *Saint Francis of Assisi*. Translated by Placid Hermann. Chicago: Franciscan Herald, 1988.

Chariton of Valamo, comp. *The Art of Prayer: An Orthodox Anthology*. Edited by Timothy Ware. Translated by E. Kadloubovsky and E. M. Palmer. London: Faber, 1997.

Chatterjee, Margaret. *Gandhi's Religious Thought*. Notre Dame, IN: University of Notre Dame Press, 1983.

Christian Faith and Practice in the Experience of the Society of Friends. London: London Yearly Meeting, 1960.

Cleary, Thomas. *The Wisdom of the Prophet: Sayings of Muhammad; Selections from the Hadith*. Boston: Shambhala Classics, 2001.

Cleaver, Eldridge. *Soul on Ice*. New York: Delta, 1968.

Climacus, John. *The Ladder of Divine Ascent*. Translated by Colm Luibheid and Norman Russell. New York: Paulist, 1982.

Clines, David J. A. *Interested Parties: The Ideology of Writers and Readers of the Hebrew Bible*. Sheffield: Sheffield Academic Press, 1995.

The Cloud of Unknowing. Translated by Ira Progoff. New York: Delta, 1957.

Coles, Robert. *Dorothy Day: A Radical Devotion*. Reading, MA: Addison-Wesley, 1987.

Commins, Gary. "Is Suffering Redemptive? Historical and Theological Reflections on Martin Luther King, Jr." *Sewanee Theological Review* 51:1 (2007) 61–80.

———. "Thomas Merton's Three Epiphanies." *Theology Today* 56:1 (1999) 59–72.

———. *Spiritual People/Radical Lives*. San Francisco: International Scholars, 1996.

Cornell, Thomas, Robert Ellsberg, and Jim Forest. *A Penny a Copy: Readings from The Catholic Worker*. Maryknoll, NY: Orbis, 1995.

Cornell, Tom, and David McReynolds. Untitled. In *WIN* 3:4 (1967) 8–9.

Countryman, William. *The Mystical Way in the Fourth Gospel: Crossing Over into God*. Philadelphia: Fortress, 1987.

Coy, Patrick G. *A Revolution of the Heart: Essays on the Catholic Worker*. Philadelphia: Temple University Press, 1988.

Cuneen, Sally. "Dorothy Day: The Storyteller as Human Model." *Crosscurrents* 34:3 (1984) 283–93.

The Dalai Lama. *Toward a True Kinship of Faiths: How the World's Religions Can Come Together*. New York: Doubleday Religion, 2010.

Dalton, Frederick John. *The Moral Vision of César Chávez*. Maryknoll, NY: Orbis, 2003.

Dancer, Anthony. *An Alien in a Strange Land: Theology in the Life of William Stringfellow*. Eugene, OR: Cascade, 2011.

Davies, Robertson. *Fifth Business*. Middlesex: Penguin, 1977.

Day, Dorothy. "A. J." *Commonweal* 86:1 (1967) 14–16.

———. *All is Grace: The Spirituality of Dorothy Day*. Edited by William D. Miller. Garden City, NY: Doubleday, 1987.

———. *By Little and By Little: The Selected Writings of Dorothy Day*. Edited by Robert Ellsberg. New York: Alfred A. Knopf, 1983.

———. *From Union Square to Rome*. Silver Spring, MD: The Preservation of the Faith, 1938.

———. *Houses of Hospitality*. New York: Sheed and Ward, 1939.

———. *Loaves and Fishes*. San Francisco: Harper & Row, 1963.

———. *The Long Loneliness: An Autobiography*. San Francisco: Harper & Row, 1952.

———. "Message of Love." *The Catholic Worker* 17:6 (1950) 1–2.

———. *On Pilgrimage*. New York: Catholic Worker, 1948.

———. *On Pilgrimage: The Sixties*. New York: Curtis, 1972.

———. *Thérèse*. Springfield, IL: Templegate, 1960.

Deloria, Vine, Jr. *God is Red: A Native View of Religion*. Golden, CO: Fulcrum, 1994.

Deming, Barbara. "It's a Good Life." *Liberation* 12:6–7 (1967) 60.

———. Untitled. In *WIN* 3:4 (1967) 16.

The Dhammapada. Translated by Juan Mascaró. Middlesex: Penguin, 1973.

Donne, John. *Selections from Divine Poems, Sermons, Devotions, and Prayers*. Edited by John Booty. New York: Paulist, 1990.

Donnelly, Mary. "A Mighty Soul." *Sojourners* 14:11 (1985) 25–26.

Dorotheos of Gaza. *Discourses and Sayings*. Translated by Eric P. Wheeler. Kalamazoo, MI: Cistercian, 1977.

Bibliography

Dostoevsky, Fyodor. *The Brothers Karamazov*. Translated by Andrew R. MacAndrew. New York: Bantam, 1981.

Douglass, Frederick. *Life and Times of Frederick Douglass*. New York: Collier, 1971.

———. *The Life and Writings of Frederick Douglass (Volume II): Pre-Civil War Decade 1850-1860*. Edited by Philip S. Foner. New York: International, 1950.

———. *Narrative of the Life of Frederick Douglass: An American Slave*. Boston: Bedford, St. Martin's, 2003.

Douglass, James W. *Resistance and Contemplation: The Way of Liberation*. Eugene, OR: Wipf & Stock, 2006.

DuBois, W. E. B. *Darkwater: Voices from Within the Veil*. Mineola, NY: Dover, 1999.

Dyson, Michael Eric. *Making Malcolm: The Myth and Meaning of Malcolm X*. New York: Oxford University Press, 1995.

Eagleson, John, and Philip Scherper. *Puebla and Beyond: Documentation and Commentary*. Translated by John Drury. Maryknoll, NY: Orbis, 1979.

Eckhart, Meister. *Meister Eckhart: A Modern Translation*. Translated by Raymond Bernard Blakney. New York: Harper & Row, 1941.

———. *The Essential Sermons, Commentaries, Treatises, and Defense*. Translated by Edmund Colledge and Bernard McGinn. New York: Paulist, 1981.

———. *Meister Eckhart: Sermons & Treatises, Volume I*. Edited and translated by M. O'C. Walshe. Longmead, Shaftesbury, Dorset: Element, 1979.

———. *Meister Eckhart: Sermons & Treatises, Volume II*. Edited and translated by M. O'C Walshe. Longmead, Shaftesbury, Dorset: Element, 1981.

———. *Meister Eckhart: Sermons & Treatises, Volume III*. Edited and translated by M. O'C. Walshe. Longmead, Shaftesbury, Dorset: Element, 1987.

Eliot, T. S. *The Complete Poems and Plays*. New York: Harcourt, Brace & World, 1971.

Ellacuría, Ignacio. "The Crucified People." In *Systematic Theology: Perspectives from Liberation Theology (readings from Mysterium Liberationis)*, edited by Jon Sobrino and Ignacio Ellacuría, 257–78. Maryknoll, NY: Orbis, 1993.

Ellis, Marc H. "Peter Maurin: To Bring the Social Order to Christ." In *A Revolution of the Heart: Essays on the Catholic Worker*, edited by Patrick G. Coy, 15–46. Philadelphia: Temple University Press, 1988.

———. *Peter Maurin: Prophet in the Twentieth Century*. New York: Paulist, 1981.

Ellul, Jacques. *Violence*. Translated by Cecelia Gaul Kings. New York: Seabury, 1969.

Endo, Shusaku. *Scandal*. Translated by Van C. Gessel. Toronto: Lester & Orpen Dennys, 1988.

———. *Silence*. Translated by William Johnston. New York: Taplinger, 1980.

Ephrem the Syrian. *Hymns*. Translated by Kathleen E. McVey. New York: Paulist, 1989.

Erb, Peter C., ed. *Pietists: Selected Writings*. Mahwah, NJ: Paulist, 1983.

Evagrius Ponticus. *The Mind's Long Journey to the Holy Trinity*. Translated by Jeremy Driscoll. Collegeville, MN: Liturgical, 1993.

Fadiman, James, and Robert Frager. *Essential Sufism*. Edison, NY: Castle, 1998.

Ferriss, Susan, and Ricardo Sandoval. *The Fight in the Fields; César Chávez and the Farmworkers Movement*. San Diego: Harvest, 1998.

Forest, James H. "Thomas Merton's Struggle with Peacemaking." In *Thomas Merton: Prophet in the Belly of a Paradox*, edited by Gerald Twomey, 15–54. New York: Paulist, 1978.

de Foucauld, Charles. *Writings*. Edited by Robert Ellsberg. Maryknoll, NY: Orbis, 2003.

Fox, George. *The Journal of George Fox.* Edited by Rufus M. Jones. Richmond, IN: Friends United, 1976.

Francis of Assisi and Clare of Assisi. *Francis and Clare: The Complete Works.* Translated by Regis J. Armstrong and Ignatius C. Brady. New York: Paulist, 1982.

Freire, Paulo. *Pedagogy of the Oppressed.* Translated by Myra Bergman Ramos. New York: Herder & Herder, 1972.

Fretheim, Terence E. *The Suffering of God: An Old Testament Perspective.* Philadelphia: Fortress, 1984.

Fry, Elizabeth. *A Quaker Life: Selected Letters and Writings.* Edited by Gil Skidmore. New York: Altamira, 2005.

Galilea, Segundo. "Liberation as an Encounter with Politics and Contemplation." In *The Mystical and Political Dimension of the Christian Faith*, edited by Claude Geffré and Gustavo Gutierrez, 19–33. New York: Herder & Herder, 1974.

Gandhi, Mohandas K. *An Autobiography: The Story of My Experiments with Truth.* Boston: Beacon, 1957.

———. *Non-violent Resistance.* New York: Schocken, 1951.

———. *Prayer.* Edited by John Strohmeier. Berkeley, CA: Berkeley Hills, 2000.

———. *The Way to God.* Edited by M. S. Desphande. Berkeley, CA: Berkeley Hills, 1999.

Garrow, David J. *Bearing the Cross: Martin Luther King, Jr., and the Southern Christian Leadership Conference.* New York: William Morrow and Company, 1986.

Geffré, Claude, and Gustavo Gutierrez, eds. *The Mystical and Political Dimension of the Christian Faith.* New York: Herder & Herder, 1974.

Golding, William. *The Inheritors.* San Diego: Harcourt Brace & Company, 1955.

———. *Lord of the Flies.* New York: Capricorn, 1959.

Gregory of Nyssa. *From Glory to Glory: Texts from Gregory of Nyssa's Mystical Writings.* Translated by Herbert Murusillo. Crestwood, NY: St. Vladimir's Seminary Press, 1979.

———. *The Life of Moses.* Translated by Abraham Malherbe and Everett Ferguson. New York: Paulist, 1978.

Griffin, John Howard. "The Controversial Merton." In *Thomas Merton: Prophet in the Belly of a Paradox*, edited by Gerald Twomey, 80–91. New York: Paulist, 1978.

Griffiths, Bede. *Return to the Center.* Springfield, IL: Templegate, 1976.

Gutierrez, Gustavo. *On Job: God-talk and the Suffering of the Innocent.* Translated by Matthew J. O'Connell. Maryknoll, NY: Orbis, 1989.

———. *A Theology of Liberation: History, Politics, and Salvation.* Translated by Caridad Inda and John Eagleson. Maryknoll, NY: Orbis, 1973.

———. *We Drink from our Own Wells: The Spiritual Journey of a People.* Translated by Matthew J. O'Connell. Maryknoll, NY: Orbis/Dove, 1984.

Habel, Norman C. *The Land is Mine: Six Biblical Land Ideologies.* Minneapolis: Fortress, 1995.

Hadewijch. *The Complete Works.* Translated by Columba Hart. Mahwah, NJ: Paulist, 1980.

Hallie, Philip. "Cruelty: The Empirical Evil." In *Facing Evil: Light at the Core of Darkness*, edited by Paul Woodruff and Harry A. Wilmer, 119–30. LaSalle, IL: Open Court, 1988.

———. *Lest Innocent Blood Be Shed.* New York: Harper & Row, 1979.

Hammarskjöld, Dag. *Markings*. Translated by Leif Sjöberg and W. H. Auden. New York: Alfred A. Knopf, 1968.
Happold, F. C. *Mysticism: A Study and an Anthology*. Middlesex: Penguin, 1963.
Harvey, Andrew. *The Way of Passion: A Celebration of Rumi*. Berkeley, CA: Frog, 1994.
Headlam, Stewart D. *The Laws of Eternal Life: Being Studies in the Church Catechism*. Whitefish, MT: Kessinger Legacy Reprints, 2010.
Helminski, Camille Adams. *Women of Sufism: A Hidden Treasure; Writings and Stories of Mystic Poets, Scholars and Saints*. Boston: Shambhala, 2003.
Hennacy, Ammon. *The Book of Ammon*. Salt Lake City: N.p., 1965.
Hennelly, Alfred T. *Liberation Theology: A Documentary History*. Maryknoll, NY: Orbis, 1990.
Herbert, George. *The Country Parson, The Temple*. Edited by John Wall. New York: Paulist, 1981.
Heschel, Abraham Joshua. *The Sabbath: Its Meaning for Modern Man*. New York: Noonday, 1979.
Hildegard of Bingen. *Book of Divine Works with Letters and Songs*. Edited by Matthew Fox. Santa Fe, NM: Bear & Company, 1987.
Hillesum, Etty. *An Interrupted Life: The Diaries of Etty Hillesum 1941–43*. Translated by Jonathan Cape. New York: Washington Square, 1985.
Hutchinson, Russell. "Review of *An Ethic for Christians and Other Aliens in a Strange Land* by William Stringfellow." *Religious Education* 69:3 (1974) 396.
Hughes, Langston. *The Langston Hughes Reader*. New York: George Braziller, 1958.
The Hymnal 1982. New York: The Church Hymnal Corporation, 1985.
Illah, Ibn 'Ata,' and Kwaja Abdullah Ansari. *The Book of Wisdom* and *Intimate Conversations*. Translated by Victor Danner and Wheeler M. Thackston. New York: Paulist, 1978.
Isaac of Nineveh. *On Ascetical Life*. Translated by Mary Hansbury. Crestwood, NY: St. Vladimir's Seminary Press, 1989.
Ishiguro, Kazuo. *The Remains of the Day*. New York: Vintage International, 1989.
James, William. *The Varieties of Religious Experience*. New York: Collier, 1961.
John of the Cross. *The Collected Works of St. John of the Cross*. Translated by Kieran Kavanaugh and Otilio Rodriguez. Washington, DC: ICS, 1979.
Jones, Rufus. *Essential Writings*. Edited by Kerry Walters. Maryknoll, NY: Orbis, 2001.
Jordan, Clarence. *Essential Writings*. Edited by Joyce Hollyday. Maryknoll, NY: Orbis, 2003.
Julian of Norwich. *Showings*. Translated by Edmund Colledge and James Walsh. New York: Paulist, 1978.
Karnow, Stanley. *Vietnam: A History*. Middlesex: Penguin, 1984.
Keating, Thomas. *Open Mind, Open Heart: The Contemplative Dimension of the Gospel*. New York: Continuum, 1996.
Keen, Sam. *Faces of the Enemy: Reflections of the Hostile Imagination*. San Francisco: Harper & Row, 1986.
Kelly, Thomas. *The Eternal Promise*. Richmond, IN: Friends United, 1977.
———. *A Testament of Devotion*. New York: Harper & Row, 1941.
Kelsey, George D. *Racism and the Christian Understanding of Man*. New York: Charles Scribner's Sons, 1965.
à Kempis, Thomas. *The Imitation of Christ*. Edited by Harold Gardiner. Garden City, NY: Image, 1955.

King, Martin Luther, Jr. *Strength to Love*. Philadelphia: Fortress, 1981.
———. *Stride Toward Freedom*. San Francisco: Harper & Row, 1958.
———. *A Testament of Hope: The Essential Writings of Martin Luther King, Jr.* Edited by James Melvin Washington. San Francisco: Harper & Row, 1986.
———. *The Trumpet of Conscience*. San Francisco: HarperSanFrancisco, 1967.
———. *Where Do We Go From Here: Chaos or Community?* New York: Bantam, 1968.
———. *Why We Can't Wait*. New York: Signet, 1964.
Kirk, Kenneth E. *The Vision of God: The Christian Doctrine of the Summum Bonum—The Bampton Lectures for 1928*. London: Longmans, Green and Co., 1931.
Kiser, John W. *The Monks of Tibhirine: Faith, Love, and Terror in Algeria*. New York: St. Martin's, 2002.
Lane, Belden C. *Landscapes of the Sacred: Geography and Narrative in American Spirituality*. Baltimore: The Johns Hopkins University Press, 2001.
———. *The Solace of Fierce Landscapes: Exploring Desert and Mountain Spirituality*. New York: Oxford University Press, 1998.
Law, William. *A Serious Call to a Devout and Holy Life*. Philadelphia: Westminster, 1958.
Leclerc, Eloi. *The Canticle of Creatures: Symbols of Union*. Translated by Matthew J. O'Connell. Chicago: Franciscan Herald, 1977.
Leclerq, Jean. "Merton and History." In *Thomas Merton: Prophet in the Belly of a Paradox*, edited by Gerald Twomey, 213–31. New York: Paulist, 1978.
Lee, Spike, dir. *4 Little Girls*. Produced by Spike Lee and Samuel D. Pollard. 40 Acres & A Mule Filmworks and Home Box Office, 1997.
Leech, Kenneth. *Doing Theology in Altab Ali Park*. London: Darton, Longman, and Todd, 2006.
———. *Experiencing God: Theology as Spirituality*. San Francisco: Harper & Row, 1985.
———. *The Eye of the Storm: Living Spiritually in the Real World*. San Francisco: Harper San Francisco, 1992.
———. *Race*. New York: Church, 2005.
———. *The Social God*. London: Sheldon, 1981.
———. *Spirituality and Pastoral Care*. Cambridge, MA: Cowley, 1989.
———. *Subversive Orthodoxy: Traditional Faith and Radical Commitment*. Toronto: Anglican Book Centre, 1992.
———. *True Prayer: An Invitation to Christian Spirituality*. Harrisburg, PA: Morehouse, 1980.
———. *We Preach Christ Crucified: The Proclamation of the Cross in a Dark Age*. Cambridge, MA: Cowley, 1994.
Leeming, David. *James Baldwin: A Biography*. London: Penguin, 1995.
Lester, Muriel. *Ambassador of Reconciliation: A Muriel Lester Reader*. Edited by Richard Deats. Philadelphia: New Society, 1991.
———. *It Occurred to Me*. New York: Harper & Brothers, 1937.
Lewis, C. S. *A Grief Observed*. New York: Bantam, 1976.
———. *Perelandra*. New York: Macmillan, Inc., 1973.
———. *The Problem of Pain*. New York: Macmillan, Inc., 1976.
———. *Surprised by Joy: The Shape of My Early Life*. London: Harcourt Brace, 1955.
The Little Flowers of St. Francis. Translated by Raphael Brown. New York: Image, 1958.
Lorde, Audre. *Sister Outsider: Essays and Speeches*. Trumansburg, NY: Crossing, 1984.

Lossky, Vladimir. *In the Image and Likeness of God*. Edited and translated by John H. Erickson and Thomas E. Bird. Crestwood, NY: St. Vladimir's Seminary Press, 1985.

———. *The Mystical Theology of the Eastern Church*. Translated by the Fellowship of St. Alban and St. Sergius. Crestwood, NY: St. Vladimir's Seminary Press, 1976.

———. *The Vision of God*. Translated by Asheleigh Moorhouse. Crestwood, NY: St. Vladimir's Seminary Press, 1983.

Lull, Ramon. *Romancing God: Contemplating the Beloved*. Edited by Henry L. Carrigan, Jr. Brewster, MA: Paraclete, 1999.

Luthuli, Albert. *Luthuli: Speeches of Chief Albert Luthuli*. Edited by E. S. Reddy. Durban, South Africa: Madiba, 1991.

Mabee, Carleton. *Sojourner Truth: Slave, Prophet, Legend*. New York: NYU Press, 1993.

Maimonides, Moses. *Commentary on the Mishnah, tractate Sanhedrin*. Translated by Fred Rosner. New York: Sepher-Hermon, 1981.

Marable, Manning. *Malcolm X: A Life of Reinvention*. New York: Penguin, 2011.

Marable, Manning, and Leiths Mullings. *Let Nobody Turn Us Around: Voices of Resistance, Reform, and Renewal*. Lanham, MD: Rowman and Littlefield, 2000.

Maslow, Abraham H. *Religions, Values, and Peak-Experiences*. New York: Viking, 1970.

Massignon, Louis. *The Passion of Al-Hallaj, Mystic and Martyr of Islam*. Vol. 1. Translated by Herbert Mason. Princeton, NJ: Princeton University Press, 1982.

Matt, Daniel C. *The Essential Kabbalah: The Heart of Jewish Mysticism*. San Francisco: HarperSanFrancisco, 1995.

Maurin, Peter. *Easy Essays*. Chicago: Franciscan Herald, 1977.

May, Gerald G. *Pilgrimage Home: The Conduct of Contemplative Practice in Groups*. New York: Paulist, 1979.

Mayer, Milton. "The Christer." *Fellowship* 18:1 (1952) 1–10.

Mays, Benjamin. *The Negro's God: As Reflected in His Literature*. New York: Atheneum, 1968.

McGinn, Bernard. *The Flowering of Mysticism: Men and Women in the New Mysticism (1200–1350)*. New York: Crossroad Herder, 1998.

———. *The Foundations of Mysticism: Origins to the Fifth Century*. New York: Crossroad, 1991.

———. *The Growth of Mysticism: Gregory the Great through the 12th Century*. New York: Crossroad Herder, 1994.

———. *The Harvest of Mysticism in Medieval Germany*. New York: Herder & Herder, 2005.

———. *The Varieties of Vernacular Mysticism (1350–1550)*. New York: Herder & Herder, 2012.

McNamara, William. *Earthy Mysticism: Contemplation and the Life of Passionate Presence*. New York: Crossroad, 1983.

Menninger, Karl. *Whatever Became of Sin?* New York: Bantam, 1978.

Merton, Thomas. *The Ascent to Truth*. San Diego: Harcourt Brace Jovanovich, 1979.

———. *The Asian Journal of Thomas Merton*. New York: New Directions, 1973.

———. *The Cold War Letters*. Edited by Christine M. Bochen and William H. Shannon. Maryknoll, NY: Orbis, 2006.

———. *The Collected Poems of Thomas Merton*. New York: New Directions, 1977.

———. *Conjectures of a Guilty Bystander*. New York: Image, 1965.

———. *Contemplation in a World of Action*. Garden City, NY: Image, 1973.

———. *Contemplative Prayer*. New York: Image, 1996.

———. *The Courage for Truth: The Letters of Thomas Merton to Writers*. Edited by Christine M. Bochen. San Diego: Farrar, Straus and Giroux, 1993.

———. *Dancing in the Water of Life: Seeking Peace in the Hermitage*. Edited by Robert E. Daggy. The Journals of Thomas Merton, Volume 5. New York: HarperOne, 1997.

———. "Day of a Stranger." In *Thomas Merton: Spiritual Master; The Essential Writings*, edited by Lawrence Cunningham, 214–22. New York: Paulist, 1992.

———. *Disputed Questions*. New York: Farrar, Straus and Giroux, 1976.

———. *Faith and Violence: Christian Teaching and Christian Practice*. Notre Dame, IN: University of Notre Dame Press, 1968.

———. *Gandhi on Non-Violence*. New York: New Directions, 1964.

———. *The Hidden Ground of Love: The Letters of Thomas Merton on Religious Experience and Social Concerns*. Edited by William H. Shannon. New York: Farrar, Straus and Giroux, 1985.

———. *A Hidden Wholeness: The Visual World of Thomas Merton*. Text by John Howard Griffin. Boston: Houghton Mifflin, 1970.

———. *The Inner Experience: Notes on Contemplation*. Edited by William H. Shannon. San Francisco: HarperSanFrancisco, 2003.

———. *Introductions East and West: The Foreign Prefaces of Thomas Merton*. Edited by Robert E. Daggy. Greensboro, NC: Unicorn, 1981.

———. *Life and Holiness*. New York: Image, 1964.

———. *The Literary Essays of Thomas Merton*. Edited by Patrick Hart. New York: New Directions, 1981.

———. *Love and Living*. Edited by Naomi Burton Stone and Patrick Hart. San Diego: Harcourt Brace Jovanovich, 1979.

———. *The Monastic Journey*. Edited by Patrick Hart. Garden City, NY: Image, 1978.

———. *Mystics and Zen Masters*. New York: Delta, 1961.

———. *New Seeds of Contemplation*. New York: New Directions, 1961.

———. *The Nonviolent Alternative*. Edited by Gordon C. Zahn. New York: Farrar, Straus and Giroux, 1980.

———. *The Other Side of the Mountain: The End of the Journey*. Edited by Patrick Hart. The Journals of Thomas Merton, Volume 7. San Francisco: HarperSanFrancisco, 1998.

———. *Raids on the Unspeakable*. New York: New Directions, 1964.

———. *The Road to Joy: The Letters of Thomas Merton to New and Old Friends*. Edited by Robert E. Daggy. New York: Farrar, Straus and Giroux, 1989.

———. *Run to the Mountain: The Story of a Vocation*. Edited by Patrick Hart. The Journals of Thomas Merton, Volume 1. San Francisco: HarperSanFrancisco, 1995.

———. *The School of Charity: The Letters of Thomas Merton on Religious Renewal and Spiritual Direction*. Edited by Patrick Hart. New York: Farrar, Straus and Giroux, 1990.

———. *A Search for Solitude: Pursuing the Monk's Life*. Edited by Lawrence Cunningham. The Journals of Thomas Merton, Volume 3. San Francisco: HarperSanFrancisco, 1996.

———. *Seasons of Celebration*. New York: Farrar, Straus and Giroux, 1965.

———. *The Secular Journal*. New York: Farrar, Straus and Giroux, 1959.

———. *Seeds of Destruction*. New York: Farrar, Straus and Giroux, 1964.

———. *The Seven Storey Mountain*. San Diego: Harcourt Brace Jovanovich, 1976.
———. *The Sign of Jonas*. Garden City, NY: Image, 1956.
———. *The Silent Life*. New York: Farrar, Straus and Giroux, 1957.
———. *Spiritual Direction and Meditation*. Collegeville, MN: Liturgical, 1960.
———. *Thomas Merton in Alaska: The Alaskan Conferences, Journals, and Letters*. New York: New Directions, 1988.
———. *A Thomas Merton Reader*. Edited by Thomas P. McDonnell. Garden City, NY: Image, 1974.
———. *Thomas Merton: Spiritual Master; The Essential Writings*. Edited by Lawrence Cunningham. New York: Paulist, 1992.
———. *Thoughts in Solitude*. New York: Dell, 1961.
———. *Turning Toward the World: The Pivotal Years*. Edited by Victor A. Kramer. The Journals of Thomas Merton, Volume 4. San Francisco: HarperSanFrancisco, 1996.
———. *The Way of Chuang Tzu*. New York: New Directions, 1965.
———. *The Wisdom of the Desert*. New York: New Directions, 1960.
———. *Witness to Freedom: The Letters of Thomas Merton in Times of Crisis*. Edited by William H. Shannon. San Diego: Harcourt Brace & Company, 1994.
Minus, Paul M. *Walter Rauschenbusch: American Reformer*. New York: Macmillan, 1988.
A Mirror for Simple Souls. Edited and translated by Charles Crawford. New York: Crossroad, 1981.
Moltmann, Jurgen. *The Crucified God: The Cross of Christ as the Foundation and Criticism of Christian Theology*. Translated by R. A. Wilson and John Bowden. New York: Harper & Row, 1974.
Moore, Archimandrite Lazarus. *St. Seraphim of Sarov: A Spiritual Biography*. Blanco, TX: New Sarov, 1994.
Morel, Lucas E. *Lincoln's Sacred Effort: Defining Religion's Role in American Self-Government*. Lanham, MD: Lexington, 2000.
Mott, Michael. *The Seven Mountains of Thomas Merton*. Boston: Houghton Mifflin, 1984.
Mtwa, Percy, Mbongeni Ngema, and Barney Simon. *Woza Albert!* In *Woza Afrika! An Anthology of South African Plays*, edited by Duma Ndlovu, 3–53. New York: George Braziller, 1986.
Muir, Edwin. *Collected Poems of Edwin Muir*. New York: Grove, 1957.
Murray, Pauli. *The Autobiography of a Black Activist, Feminist, Lawyer, Priest and Poet*. Knoxville, TN: University of Tennessee Press, 1989.
Muste, A. J. "The C.P.L.A. States Its Case." *The World Tomorrow* 16 (1933) 569–70.
———. *The Essays of A. J. Muste*. Edited by Nat Hentoff. New York: Clarion, 1967.
———. "Fight the Good Fight?" *The American Scholar* 6:3 (1937) 334–44.
———. "A Look Around." *Fellowship* 14:5 (1948) 3–5.
———. "Love in Action." *Fellowship* 16:6 (1950) 7–13.
———. "Muste Testifies Against Rearmament." *Fellowship* 18:8 (1952) 22.
———. *Non-violence in an Aggressive World*. New York: Harper & Brothers, 1940.
———. *Not by Might: Christianity, The Way to Human Decency*. New York: Harper & Brothers, 1947.
———. "The Pacifist Way of Life." *Fellowship* 7:12 (1941) 198–200.
———. "'Peace is the Way.'" *Liberation* 10:3 (1965) 3–5.
———. "Prospect for Peace in 1953." *Fellowship* 19:1 (1953) 6–9.

———. "The Religious Basis of Pacifism." *Fellowship* 5:9 (1939) 5–6.
———. "Steamer Letter." *Fellowship* 13:7 (1947) 109–10.
———. "Tract for the Times." *Liberation* 1:1 (1956) 4–6.
———. "The True International." *The Christian Century* 56:21 (1939) 667–69.
———. "A Visit to Saigon." *Liberation* 11:3 (1966) 10.
———. "Where Are We Now?" *Fellowship* 22:1 (1956) 12–20.
———. "Where 'Crisis Realism' Fails." *Fellowship* 5:4 (1939) 4–5.
Myers, Ched. *Who Will Roll Away the Stone? Discipleship Queries for First World Christians*. Maryknoll, NY: Orbis, 1994.
Nhat Hanh, Thich. *The Diamond That Cuts through Illusion: Commentaries on the Prajñaparamita Diamond Sutra*. Berkeley, CA: Parallax, 1992.
———. *Going Home: Jesus and Buddha as Brothers*. New York: Riverhead, 1999.
———. *Love in Action: Writings on Nonviolent Social Change*. Berkeley, CA: Parallax, 1993.
———. *Old Path White Clouds: Walking in the Footsteps of Buddha*. Translated by Mobi Ho. Berkeley, CA: Parallax, 1991.
———. *Touching Peace: Practicing the Art of Mindful Living*. Berkeley: Parallax, 1992.
Nicholl, Donald. *Holiness*. New York: Paulist, 1981.
Nicholas of Cusa. *Selected Spiritual Writings*. Translated by Lawrence H. Bond. Mahwah, NJ: Paulist, 1997.
Niditch, Susan. *War in the Hebrew Bible: A Study in the Ethics of Violence*. New York: Oxford University Press, 1993.
Niebuhr, H. Richard. *Christ and Culture*. New York: Harper & Row, 1951.
———. *The Kingdom of God in America*. Chicago: Willett, Clark and Company, 1937.
Niebuhr, Reinhold. *The Children of Light and the Children of Darkness*. New York: Charles Scribner's Sons, 1960.
———. "Christian Revolutionary." *New York Times Book Review* 72:6 (1967) 6.
———. *The Irony of American History*. New York: Charles Scribner's Sons, 1962.
———. *Moral Man and Immoral Society*. New York: Charles Scribner's Sons, 1960.
Nietzsche, Friedrich. *Twilight of the Idols*. Translated by Richard Polt. Indianapolis: Hackett, 1997.
Noel, Conrad. *Jesus the Heretic*. London: Temple Press, Letchworth, 1939.
Nouwen, Henri J. M. *The Wounded Healer: Ministry in Contemporary Society*. Garden City, NY: Doubleday, 1972.
Oates, Stephen B. *Let the Trumpet Sound: The Life of Martin Luther King, Jr*. New York: Plume, 1982.
O'Connor, Flannery. "Revelation." In *Everything That Rises Must Converge*, 191–218. New York: Farrar, Straus and Giroux, 1956.
Otto, Rudolf. *The Idea of the Holy*. Translated by John W. Harvey. London: Oxford University Press, 1958.
———. *Mysticism East and West*. Translated by Bertha L. Bracey and Richenda C. Payne. New York: The Macmillan Company, 1960.
Ousmane, Sembene. *Xala*. Translated by Clive Wake. London: Heinemann, 1976.
Palamas, Gregory. *The Triads*. Edited by John Meyendorff. Translated by Nicholas Gendle. New York: Paulist, 1983.
Pascal, Blaise. *Pensees*. Translated by W. F. Trotter. New York: E. P. Dutton & Co., Inc., 1958.

Péguy, Charles. "Politics and Mysticism." In *Basic Verities: Prose and Poetry*, translated by Ann Green and Julian Green. New York: Pantheon, 1943.
Piehl, Mel. *Breaking Bread: The Catholic Worker and the Origin of Catholic Radicalism in America*. Philadelphia: Temple University Press, 1982.
Porete, Maguerite. *The Mirror of Simple Souls*. New York: Crossroad, 1981.
Pseudo-Dionysius. *The Complete Works*. New York: Paulist, 1987.
Raines, Howell. *My Soul is Rested: The Story of the Civil Rights Movement in the Deep South*. Middlesex: Penguin, 1977.
Rauschenbusch, Walter. *Christianity and the Social Crisis*. New York: Macmillan, 1907.
———. *A Theology for the Social Gospel*. Nashville: Abingdon, 1945.
Remarque, Erich Maria. *All Quiet on the Western Front*. Greenwich, CT: Crest, 1962.
Rensberger, David. *Johannine Faith and Liberating Community*. Philadelphia: Westminster, 1988.
Rice, Edward. *The Man in the Sycamore Tree: The Good Times and Hard Life of Thomas Merton*. Garden City, NY: Image, 1972.
Richard of St. Victor. *The Twelve Patriarchs, The Mystical Ark, Book Three of the Trinity*. Edited and translated by Grover A. Zinn. New York: Paulist, 1979.
Robinson, Jo Ann Ooiman. *Abraham Went Out: A Biography of A. J. Muste*. Philadelphia: Temple University Press, 1981.
Rolle, Richard. *The Fire of Love*. Middlesex: Penguin, 1972.
Romero, Oscar. *The Violence of Love: The Pastoral Wisdom of Archbishop Oscar Romero*. Translated by James R. Brockman. San Francisco: Harper & Row, 1988.
———. *Voice of the Voiceless: The Four Pastoral Letters and Other Statements*. Translated by Michael J. Walsh. Maryknoll, NY: Orbis, 1985.
Ruffing, Janet K. *Mysticism and Social Transformation*. Syracuse, NY: Syracuse University Press, 2001.
Rumi, Jelaluddin. *Delicious Laughter*. Edited by Coleman Barks. Athens, GA: Maypop, 1990.
———. *The Essential Rumi*. Edited by Coleman Barks. Translated by Coleman Barks, with John Moyne, A. J. Arberry, and Reynolds Nicholson. Edison, NJ: Castle, 1995.
———. *Poet and Mystic*. Translated by R. A. Nicholson. London: Mandala, 1978.
———. *Say I Am You*. Translated by John Moyne and Coleman Barks. Athens, GA: Maypop, 1994.
Russell, Jeffrey Burton. *Lucifer: The Devil in the Middle Ages*. Ithaca, NY: Cornell University Press, 1984.
Ruusbroec, John. *The Spiritual Espousals and Other Works*. Introduction by Richard Woods. Translated by James A. Wiseman. Mahwah, NJ: Paulist, 1985.
de Sales, Francis. *Introduction to the Devout Life*. Translated by John K. Ryan. New York: Image, 1989.
Sampson, Anthony. *Mandela: The Authorized Biography*. New York: Alfred A. Knopf, 1999.
Scholem, Gershom G. *Major Trends in Jewish Mysticism*. New York: Schocken, 1965.
Scott, R. B. Y. *The Way of Wisdom in the Old Testament*. New York: Macmillan, 1971.
Segundo, Juan Luis. "Capitalism-Socialism: A Theological Crux." In *The Mystical and Political Dimension of the Christian Faith*, edited by Claude Geffré and Gustavo Gutierrez, 105–23. New York: Herder & Herder, 1974.
———. *The Liberation of Theology*. Translated by John Drury. Maryknoll, NY: Orbis, 1985.

Shah, Idries. *The Way of the Sufi*. London: Arkana, 1990.
Silesius, Angelus. *The Cherubinic Wanderer*. Translated by Maria Shrady. New York: Paulist, 1986.
Smulders, Pieter Frans. *The Fathers on Christology: The Development of Christological Dogma from the Bible to the Great Councils*. De Pere, WI: St. Norbert Abbey, 1968.
Sobrino, Jon. *Archbishop Romero: Memories and Reflections*. Translated by Robert R. Barr. Maryknoll, NY: Orbis, 1990.
———. *The Principle of Mercy: Taking the Crucified People from the Cross*. Maryknoll, NY: Orbis, 1994.
Sobrino, Jon, Ignacio Ellacuría, et al. *Companions of Jesus: The Jesuit Martyrs of El Salvador*. Maryknoll, NY: Orbis, 1990.
Soelle, Dorothee. *The Silent Cry: Mysticism and Resistance*. Translated by Barbara Rumscheidt and Martin Rumscheidt. Minneapolis: Fortress, 2001.
———. *Suffering*. Philadelphia: Fortress, 1975.
Soyinka, Wole. *Myth, Literature, and the African World*. Cambridge: Cambridge University Press, 1976.
Steere, Douglas V., ed. *Quaker Spirituality: Selected Writings*. New York: Paulist, 1984.
Steinbeck, John. *The Grapes of Wrath*. New York: Penguin, 2002.
Stevenson, Robert Louis. *Dr. Jekyll and Mr. Hyde*. New York: Scholastic, 1963.
Stone, Brian, comp. and trans. *The Owl and the Nightingale, Cleanness, St. Erkenwald*. New York: Penguin, 1971.
Stringfellow, William. "The Acts of the Apostles (Continued)." *The Christian Century* 98:11 (1981) 341–42.
———. *Conscience and Obedience: The Politics of Romans 13 and Revelation 13 in Light of the Second Coming*. Waco, TX: Word, 1978.
———. *Count It All Joy: Reflections on Faith, Doubt, and Temptation Seen through the Letter of James*. Grand Rapids, MI: William B. Eerdmans, 1967.
———. *Dissenter in a Great Society: A Christian View of America in Crisis*. New York: Holt, Rinehart, and Winston, 1966.
———. *An Ethic for Christians and Other Aliens in a Strange Land*. Waco, TX: Word, 1973.
———. "Exemplary Disbelief: A Meditation on Holy Week." *Sojourners* 9:3 (1980) 13–14.
———. *Free in Obedience*. New York: Seabury, 1964.
———. "Harlem, Rebellion, and Resurrection." *The Christian Century* 87:45 (1970) 1345–48.
———. *Imposters of God: Inquiries into Favorite Idols*. Eugene, OR: Wipf & Stock, 2006.
———. *Instead of Death*. New York: Seabury, 1963.
———. *A Keeper of the Word: Selected Writings of William Stringfellow*. Edited by Bill Wylie Kellermann. Grand Rapids, MI: Wm. B. Eerdmans, 1994.
———. "A Lamentation for Easter." *The Witness* 64:4 (1981) 4–6.
———. "Living Biblically." *Journal of Religious Thought* 37:2 (1980–81) 59–61.
———. *My People is the Enemy: An Autobiographical Polemic*. Garden City, NY: Anchor, 1964.
———. *The Politics of Spirituality*. Philadelphia: Westminster, 1984.
———. *A Private and Public Faith*. Grand Rapids, MI: Eerdmans, 1962.
———. *A Second Birthday*. Garden City, NY: Doubleday & Company, 1970.
———. *A Simplicity of Faith: My Experience in Mourning*. Nashville: Abingdon, 1982.

———. "The State of the Church." *The Witness* 62:5 (1979) 4.
Stringfellow, William, and Anthony Towne. *Suspect Tenderness: The Ethics of the Berrigan Witness*. New York: Holt, Rinehart, and Winston, 1971.
Sugirtharajah, R. S. *Asian Faces of Jesus*. Maryknoll, NY: Orbis, 1993.
Suzuki, D. T. *Manual of Zen Buddhism*. New York: Grove, 1960.
Swan, Laura. *The Forgotten Desert Mothers: Sayings, Lives, and Stories of Early Christian Women*. New York: Paulist, 2001.
Symeon the New Theologian. *The Discourses*. Translated by C. J. de Catanzaro. New York: Paulist, 1980.
———. *Divine Eros: Hymns of Saint Symeon the New Theologian*. Edited by Daniel K. Griggs. Crestwood, NY: St. Vladimir's Seminary Press, 2010.
———. *Hymns of Divine Love by St. Symeon the New Theologian*. Translated by George A. Maloney. Denville, NJ: Dimension, 1976.
Takaki, Ronald. *Strangers from a Different Shore: A History of Asian Americans*. New York: Penguin, 1989.
Tamez, Elsa. *When the Horizons Close: Rereading Ecclesiastes*. Maryknoll, NY: Orbis, 2000.
Tauler, Johannes. *Sermons*. Edited and translated by Maria Shrady. Mahwah, NJ: Paulist, 1985.
Teilhard de Chardin, Pierre. *Writings Selected*. Edited by Ursula King. Maryknoll, NY: Orbis, 1999.
Teresa of Ávila. *Interior Castle*. Translated by E. Allison Peers. Garden City, NY: Image, 1961.
———. *The Life of Teresa of Jesus*. Translated by E. Allison Peers. Garden City, NY: Image, 1960.
———. *The Way of Perfection*. Translated by E. Allison Peers. Garden City, NY: Image, 1964.
The Theologia Germanica. Translated by Bengt Hoffman. New York: Paulist, 1980.
Theophan the Recluse. *Tales of a Magic Monastery*. New York: Crossroad, 1988.
Thérèse of Lisieux. *The Autobiography of Thérèse of Lisieux: The Story of a Soul*. Translated by John Beevers. Garden City, NY: Image, 1957.
Thurman, Howard. *Deep is the Hunger*. Richmond, IN: Friends United, 1990.
———. *Deep River and The Negro Spiritual Speaks of Life and Death*. Richmond, IN: Friends United, 1990.
———. "Mysticism and Social Change." *Eden Theological Seminary Bulletin* 4:4 (1939) 3–34.
Tolstoy, Leo. *A Confession and Other Religious Writings*. Translated by Jane Kentish. London: Penguin, 1987.
———. *The Kingdom of God is Within You*. Translated by Leo Wiener. New York: Farrar, Straus and Giroux, 1970.
Traherne, Thomas. *Centuries*. New York: Harper & Brothers, 1960.
Trible, Phyllis. *Texts of Terror: Literary-Feminist Readings of Biblical Narratives*. Philadelphia: Fortress, 1984.
Trocmé, Andre. *Jesus and the Nonviolent Revolution*. Translated by Michael Hishank and Marlin E. Miller. Maryknoll, NY: Orbis, 2003.
Troupe, Quincy. *James Baldwin: The Legacy*. New York: Simon and Schuster, 1989.
Tutu, Desmond. *Hope and Suffering*. Grand Rapids: Eerdmans, 1985.
———. *No Future without Forgiveness*. New York: Image, 1999.

———. *The Rainbow People of God: The Making of a Peaceful Revolution*. New York: Doubleday, 1994.

Twomey, Gerald. *Thomas Merton: Prophet in the Belly of a Paradox*. New York: Paulist, 1978.

Tzu, Chuang. *Basic Writings*. Translated by Burton Watson. New York: Columbia University Press, 1964.

Tzu, Lao. *Tao Te Ching*. Translated by Victor H. Mair. New York: Quality Paperback Book Club, 1990.

Underhill, Evelyn. *Abba: Meditations Based on the Lord's Prayer*. London: Longmans, Green, and Co., 1940.

———. *The House of the Soul* and *Concerning the Inner Life*. Minneapolis, MN: Seabury, 1947.

———. *The Light of Christ*. Wilton, CT: Morehouse-Barlow, 1981.

———. *Modern Guide to the Ancient Quest for the Holy*. Edited by Dana Greene. Albany, NY: State University of New York Press, 1988.

———. *Mysticism*. New York: E. P. Dutton, 1961.

———. *The Mystics of the Church*. New York: Schocken, 1964.

———. *Practical Mysticism*. New York: E. P. Dutton, 1943.

———. *The Ways of the Spirit*. Edited by Grace Adolphsen Brame. New York: Crossroad, 1994.

———. *Worship*. New York: Harper and Row, 1936.

Vidler, Alex. *The Theology of F. D. Maurice*. London: SCM, 1948.

Vishnewski, Stanley. *Wings of the Dawn*. New York: Catholic Worker, 1980.

Vivian, Tim. *Becoming Fire: Through the Year with the Desert Fathers and Mothers*. Collegeville, MN: Liturgical, 2008.

———. *Four Desert Fathers: Pambo, Evagrius, Macarius of Egypt, and Macarius of Alexandria*. Crestwood, NY: St. Vladimir's Seminary Press, 2004.

———. *Journeying into God: Seven Early Monastic Lives*. Minneapolis: Fortress, 1996.

———. *St. Macarius the Spiritbearer: Coptic Texts Relating to Saint Macarius the Great*. Crestwood, NY: St. Vladimir's Seminary Press, 2004.

———. *Witness to Holiness: Abba Daniel of Scetis*. Kalamazoo, MI: Cistercian, 2008.

———. *Words to Live By: Journeys in Ancient and Modern Egyptian Monasticism*. Kalamazoo, MI: Cistercian, 2005.

de Waal, Esther. *The Celtic Way of Prayer: The Recovery of the Religious Imagination*. New York: Image, 1997.

———. *Seeking God: The Way of St. Benedict*. Collegeville, MN: Liturgical, 1984.

Waddell, Helen. *The Desert Fathers*. Ann Arbor, MI: University of Michigan Press, 1957.

Wallis, Jill. *Mother of World Peace: The Life of Muriel Lester*. Middlesex: Hisarlik, 1993.

Walzer, Michael. *Exodus and Revolution*. New York: Basic, 1985.

Ward, Benedicta. *The Sayings of the Desert Fathers*. Kalamazoo, MI: Cistercian, 1984.

Watters, Pat. *Down to Now: Reflections on the Southern Civil Rights Movement*. New York: Pantheon, 1971.

The Way of a Pilgrim and *The Pilgrim Continues His Way*. Translated by R. M. French. New York: Seabury, 1965.

Wellman, James K., Jr. *Belief and Bloodshed: Religion and Violence across Time and Tradition*. Lanham, MD: Rowman and Littlefield, 2007.

Wilken, Robert L. *The Land Called Holy: Palestine in Christian History and Thought*. New Haven: Yale University Press, 1992.

Williams, Rowan. *Resurrection: Interpreting the Easter Gospel.* Cleveland: Pilgrim, 2002.
———. *The Wound of Knowledge: Christian Spirituality from the New Testament to Saint John of the Cross.* Cambridge, MA: Cowley, 1990.
Wink, Walter. *Engaging the Powers: Discernment and Resistance in a World of Domination.* Minneapolis: Fortress, 1992.
———. *Peace is the Way: Writings on Nonviolence from the Fellowship of Reconciliation.* Maryknoll, NY: Orbis, 2004.
Woods, Richard O. P. *Eckhart's Way.* Wilmington, DE: Michael Glazier, 1986.
Woolman, John. *The Journal of John Woolman and a Plea for the Poor.* Seacaucus, NJ: Citadel, 1975.
Wright, N. T. *The Resurrection of the Son of God.* Minneapolis: Fortress, 2003.
Wright, Richard. *American Hunger.* New York: Harper & Row, 1977.
Zohar. *The Book of Enlightenment.* Edited and translated by Daniel Chanan Matt. New York: Paulist, 1983.

Names Index

Achebe, Chinua, 378
Aelred of Rievaulx, 339
Agathon (Abba), 93, 313, 359, 438
Alexander the Great, 147, 226, 342, 418
Al-Hallaj, Mansur, 7, 9–11, 21, 78, 245, 328, 340, 359
Alinsky, Saul, 226
Allen, Woody xii, 105
Amin, Idi, 174
Angela of Foligno, 101
Angulimala, 314
Anoub (Abba), 429
Anselm of Canterbury, 253, 271
Anthony (Abba), 24, 79, 81–82
Aquinas, Thomas, 2, 9, 55, 211
Arabi, Ibn al-, 219, 358
Arendt, Hannah, 79
Aristotle, 25, 194, 221
Arnold, Eberhard, 45, 65, 154–55
Arsenius (Abba), 95
Athanasius, 400
Auden, W. H., 250
Augustine, 46, 55, 59, 71–72, 77, 146–47, 152, 165, 169, 177, 181, 192, 214, 290, 331, 364, 385, 403, 426, 447
Autpert, Ambrose, 211

Baal Shem Tov, 143–44
Bailie, John, 134
Baldwin, James, 50, 117, 124, 138, 178, 228, 301–2, 319, 350, 379, 382, 384, 441–42, 449

Basho, 337
Benedict, 99
Bernard of Clairvaux, 89, 103–4, 189, 192–93, 214, 258, 328, 330, 336, 351, 365, 388, 390
Berrigan, Daniel, 172
Berry, Wendell, 81, 406
Bes (Abba), 314
Bessarion (Abba), 1
Birgitta of Sweden, 9, 27, 40, 59, 138, 155–56, 177, 249, 341, 343, 389, 420
Bistami, Bayezid, 193
Black Elk, 89, 119, 121–25, 130, 145, 160, 271, 278, 303–5, 311
Blake, William, 70
Boff, Leonardo, 266, 308
Bonaventure (Brother), 308
Bonhoeffer, Dietrich, 124, 130, 145, 399
Botha, P. W., 287–88
Bouwsma, William J. xii
Brown, Peter, 177
Brueggemann, Walter, 25, 98, 240, 282
Brutus, Dennis, 68, 285, 381
Buber, Martin, 32, 48, 93, 143, 332, 335–36, 347, 421
Bultmann, Rudolph, 168
Bunyan, John, 83

Calvin, John xii
Camara, Dom Helder, 107
Campbell, Will, 166–67, 260, 302
Casas, Bartolomé de las, 246

Cassian, John, 23, 70-72, 76, 78, 165, 419, 433, 445
Castro, Fidel, 162
Catherine of Genoa, 214, 390
Catherine of Siena, 10, 25, 42, 61-62, 89, 102-3, 109, 119-20, 122, 140, 142, 144, 179, 182, 211, 217, 254-56, 259-61, 266, 340-41, 344, 350-52, 359, 405, 420, 438, 447
Caussade, Jean-Pierre de, 36, 40, 449
Celano, Thomas, 313
Chávez, César, 22, 165-67, 181, 224, 244, 246, 248, 347, 421-22
Chergé, Christian, 236, 317-20, 398
Chrysostom, John, 191, 343
Chuang Tzu, 216
Cineas, 418-19
Clausewitz, Carl von, 224
Cleaver, Eldridge, 368
Clement of Alexandria, 2, 341
Climacus, John, 94-95, 108, 219, 329, 421, 432, 440
Coleman, Thomas, 166
Collins, Addie Mae, 112
Columba of Iona, 362
Conrad, Joseph, 124
Cromwell, Oliver, 177, 223

The Dalai Lama, 423
Damien, Father, 313, 320
Daniel (Abba), 24
Daniel of Scetis, 316-17
Daniels, Jonathan, 166, 272
Dante Alighieri, 29, 311, 356
Davies, Robertson, 239
Day, Dorothy, 10, 17, 28, 39, 50-52, 59, 61-62, 67-68, 70, 77-79, 92, 98, 163-65, 167, 171, 180-81, 206-8, 215, 227-28, 245-46, 262, 264, 286-87, 295, 297, 305, 313, 327, 346, 349-50, 352, 361, 364-66, 370, 384, 394, 422, 424, 438, 440-41
Debs, Eugene V., 35, 262
Deming, Barbara, 425
Desai, Mahadev, 443
Descartes, René, 210
Diogenes, 226, 342, 418

Donne, John, 330
Dorotheos of Gaza, 30, 35, 37, 74, 143, 422, 432-33
Dorothy of Montau, 390
Dostoevsky, Fyodor, 13, 168, 214, 399
Douglass, James, 353-54
Douglass, Frederick, 112, 117, 122, 131, 153, 172, 217, 378, 380-82, 423, 448
Dov Baer, 143
DuBois, W. E. B., 125-30, 244, 246, 250, 262, 282, 347, 380

Eckhart, Meister, 7, 9, 11, 15, 19, 21, 28-29, 41, 47, 60, 73, 101, 107, 140, 156, 174, 197, 210-12, 226, 255, 290, 301, 304, 324, 336, 338-42, 351, 355, 357, 360, 365, 388, 421, 428, 430-31, 438, 447
Eichenberg, Fritz, 69
Eichmann, Adolf, 57, 82
Eliot, T. S., 125, 131, 195
Elizabeth of Hungary, 313
Ellacuría, Ignacio, 49, 62, 79, 147, 154, 246, 249-51, 268, 346
Ellul, Jacques, 201, 203, 224
Endo, Shusaku, 241-43, 246, 260
Ephrem the Syrian, 42, 47, 63, 133, 141-43, 191, 198, 232, 236, 259, 263, 291
Erkenwald, 110-11, 114
Escher, M. C., 191
Eulogius the Stonecutter, 24
Evagrius Ponticus, 18, 27, 189, 211, 353, 417, 429, 439

Ficino, Marsilio, 134
Foucauld, Charles de, 26, 58-59, 265, 300, 415, 420
Fox, George, 144, 156, 164, 177-79, 181-82, 197, 223
Francis of Assisi, 54, 56, 63, 91, 95-96, 139, 155-56, 170, 226, 236-38, 241, 245, 259, 266-67, 271, 278, 288-89, 305-14, 316, 319-20, 342, 351, 379, 401, 405, 409, 411, 438, 445

Names Index 487

Freire, Paulo, 66–69, 228, 250, 403, 429
Freud, Sigmund, 55, 160, 381
Fry, Elizabeth, 206

Galilea, Segundo, 18
Galileo Galilei, 400
Gandhi, Mohandas, 10–11, 21, 35, 49–51, 53, 58, 62–63, 111, 113, 140, 163–64, 170–71, 179, 181, 192, 216, 224, 226–28, 267–69, 271, 298–99, 320, 351, 355, 364, 366, 370, 421, 424–25, 427, 443, 445, 449
Garnett, Henry Highland, 380
Garrow, David, 267
(Brother) Giles, 271–72, 439
Golding, William, 280–81, 285, 361
Graham, Billy, 172
Grande, Rutilio, 268
Gregory of Nazianzus, 189–90, 446
Gregory of Nyssa, 26, 30, 55, 169, 195, 197, 203, 239, 331, 352, 432–33
Gregory the Great, 109, 142, 217
Griffin, John Howard, 35, 368, 431
Griffiths, Bede, 398
Gutierrez, Gustavo xii, 26, 108, 293, 353, 355, 439

Hadewijch, 101, 104, 212, 214, 327, 428, 433
Hallie, Philip, 174–77, 181–82, 243, 246, 366, 395
Hammarskjöld, Dag, 134, 228, 355
Hatun, Zeynep, 358
Headlam, Stewart, 346, 353
Hegel, Georg Wilhelm Friedrich, 150
Henley, Don, 280
Hennacy, Ammon, 34, 216
Herbert, George, 96, 119, 121, 323
Heschel, Abraham, 417
Hildegard of Bingen, 121, 261–62, 407
Hillesum, Etty, 346, 419, 426, 429, 431, 434, 445–46, 449
Hilton, Walter, 220
Hitler, Adolf, 57, 79, 154, 174, 286, 301
Ho Chi Minh, 148, 217, 273
Hugh of St. Victor, 193

Hughes, Langston, 205, 331
Hussein, Saddam, 174

Illah, Ibn 'Ata', 187, 193, 208
Irenaeus, 400
Isaac (Abba), 345
Isaac of Nineveh, 97, 185, 200, 214, 300, 314, 363
Isaac of Stella, 338
Ishiguro, Kazuo, 49

Jacob Yitzkak of Lublin, 143
James, William, 8, 11, 21, 33, 147, 174
Jefferson, Thomas, 168
John (Brother), 238
John of the Cross, 15, 17, 21, 31, 75, 96, 99, 101–2, 115, 130–31, 194, 196–97, 206, 214–15, 220–21, 227–29, 233, 239–41, 275, 309–10, 320, 336–38, 341, 352, 359, 365, 388–90, 409, 422, 438, 445
John of Damascus, 400, 402
John the Dwarf (Abba), 95, 317–19, 387–88, 391, 430, 443–44
Johnson, Lyndon, 112, 128, 199–200, 263, 273
Jones, Rufus, 33, 164, 178, 290, 299, 373, 406–7
Jordan, Clarence, 228, 262–63
Joseph (Abba), 39–40, 136, 138, 143, 196, 388
Julian of Norwich, 9, 27–28, 40, 61–62, 89, 101–2, 108, 119, 121–22, 138, 177, 179, 181–82, 193, 206, 208–9, 212–13, 215, 243, 249, 252–58, 260–61, 265, 269, 300, 310, 336, 340, 361, 377–78, 420, 427, 431, 433–34, 444, 447
Jung, Carl, 55
Juniper (Brother), 352

Karnow, Stanley, 217–18, 225, 230, 263
Keating, Thomas, 324
Kelly, Thomas, 23, 100, 102, 106, 130, 359, 373, 393, 420
Kennedy, John F., 112, 296
Khrushchev, Nikita, 162
King, Coretta Scott, 273, 347

King, Martin Luther Jr., 10, 14, 23, 25, 27, 30, 35, 38, 46, 62, 69, 72–73, 78–82, 92, 98, 101, 111–14, 116, 125–30, 154–55, 178, 181, 202–9, 214, 219, 222–27, 252, 267, 270–71, 273, 282, 305, 318, 323, 329, 335, 347, 350, 354–55, 360, 364, 378, 385, 394–95, 422, 435–39, 441–42, 444, 448–49
King, Rodney, 131

Lane, Belden, 187
Lao Tzu, 415
LaPorte, Roger, 264, 271
Law, William, 88, 159
Lawson, Jim, 113
Leclerc, Eloi, 305, 310–11, 320
Leclerq, Jean, 12, 15
Leech, Kenneth, 11–12, 19, 58, 86, 152–53, 156
Lenin, V. I., 45, 293
Leo (Brother), 266
Lester, Muriel, 10, 29, 49–50, 53, 63, 68–70, 80, 140, 157, 171, 181, 228, 284, 293, 295–99, 305, 310, 318, 348, 350, 378–79, 384, 392–93
Lewis, C. S., 71–72, 122, 131
Lewis, Sinclair, 382
Lincoln, Abraham, 299
Longinus (Abba), 19
Lorde, Audre, 99–100, 106–7, 111, 253
Lossky, Vladimir, 16–18, 196, 352
Lot (Abba), 39–40, 136–37
Lull, Ramon, 193, 195, 324
Luther, Martin, 55, 100, 170
Luthuli, Albert, 269–72, 383

Macarius of Alexandria, 99, 161, 288–89, 315–16, 362
Macarius the Spiritbearer, 300–301, 312, 314–15, 362, 430
Malcolm X, 42, 172, 222, 253, 339, 385
Mandela, Nelson, 270–71, 288
Mao Zedong, 14, 386
Marx, Karl, 8, 55, 160, 292, 364, 439
Massignon, Louis, 10
Maslow, Abraham, 54, 145

Maud, Sir John, 14
Maurice, F. D., 168, 346
Maurin, Peter, 46, 69, 152, 202, 207, 226, 228, 292, 349, 365–66
Maximus the Confessor, 261
McCarthy, Joseph, 14
McGinn, Bernard, 88
McNamara, William, 58, 62, 108
McNair, Denise, 112
Mechtild von Hackenborg, 344
Mechtild of Magdeburg, 359
Merton, Thomas, 5–6, 9, 11–13, 23–26, 29, 34–35, 43, 48, 51–55, 57–58, 60–61, 63–66, 70, 74–79, 81–82, 90, 98, 104–5, 123, 130, 138–40, 156–58, 161–65, 180–81, 198–99, 204, 213, 215–16, 218–19, 221–22, 224–26, 229, 233, 237–38, 245–46, 248, 257, 264, 271–73, 278, 285, 293–95, 309–10, 314–15, 317–18, 320, 324, 327, 337–39, 353–54, 359, 361, 368–70, 376–78, 384, 394, 396–97, 400–409, 417, 420, 424–25, 431–32, 436–40, 449
Milosevic, Slobodan, 174
Mius (Abba), 361
Moltmann, Jürgen, 235
Monet, Claude, 33
Mordecai of Neskhizh, 52
Moses (Abba), 63, 320
Moshe Leib of Sasov, 359
Mother Teresa, 239
Motovilov, Nicholas, 136–40, 144–45, 177, 229–30, 420
Muir, Edwin, 409–11
Murray, Pauli, 363
Muste, A. J., 10–11, 23, 60, 62, 77–79, 140, 142, 148, 155, 164, 171–72, 181, 217, 226–28, 268–69, 271, 292, 301, 342, 364, 366–67, 370, 403, 415, 422, 425, 432, 440, 449

Nash, Diane, 113–14, 116, 125
Nayler, James, 222
Newton, John, 232
Nhat Chi Mai, 263–64, 271–72

Names Index

Nhat Hanh, Thich, 42, 73, 179, 263–64, 267–69, 278, 294, 304–5, 439
Nhu (Madame), 263, 273
Nicholas of Cusa, 32, 104, 190, 324, 414
Niebuhr, H. Richard, 58, 148–49, 168, 170, 228, 237
Niebuhr, Reinhold, 8, 11, 21, 33, 55, 61, 147–53, 155–56, 160, 165, 167, 169–74, 177, 179–81, 206, 210–11, 216–17, 225, 228, 250, 296, 311, 364, 367, 385, 387, 438
Nietzsche, Friedrich, 268
Nightingale, Florence, 239
Nisterus (Abba), 423
Nixon, Richard, 173, 180
Noel, Conrad, 152
Nouwen, Henri, 239

O'Connor, Flannery, 80, 84
Oetinger, Friedrich Cristoph, 30
Origen, 329, 363
Orwell, George, 183
Otto, Rudolph, 15, 48, 56, 72, 85, 91, 143, 177, 311, 332, 345, 347, 401
Ousmane, Sembene, 84

Palamas, Gregory, 74, 144, 329, 391, 405
Pambo (Abba), 229, 241, 423, 429
Pascal, Blaise, 32, 90, 196, 247, 249, 251, 262, 343
Pasternak, Boris, 370
Péguy, Charles, 11
Penn, William, 361
Percy, William Alexander, 415
Pinhas of Koretz, 300
Pior (Abba), 300
Plotinus, 8
Poemen (Abba), 15, 95
Pol Pot, 14, 174
Proust, Marcel, 1
Pseudo-Dionysius, 189, 191, 194, 196–97, 210–11

Rabia, 432–33
Rauschenbusch, Walter, 8, 11, 14, 19, 21, 26, 33, 51, 77, 80, 121–22, 151, 170, 181, 208–9, 219, 226–27, 247, 251, 262, 394
Reagan, Ronald, 160, 183
Remarque, Erich Maria, 403
Richard of St. Victor, 186, 385–86, 390
Robertson, Carole, 112
Rolle, Richard, 24, 210–13, 326, 331
Romero, Oscar, 10–11, 19, 51, 80, 201–4, 208, 248–51, 268, 272–73, 305, 346, 350, 375–76, 378, 384, 387, 392–93, 396
Rumi, Jelaluddin, 1, 32, 53, 62, 79–80, 94, 97, 133, 143, 172, 174, 186, 196, 340–41, 345, 349, 358, 366, 373–74, 398, 410, 417
Rustin, Bayard, 424, 449
Ruusbroec, John, 23, 27, 29, 62, 74, 101, 133, 139–41, 182, 190, 197, 212–13, 240, 254, 259–60, 266, 323, 328, 338, 340–41, 344, 352, 373, 390, 421–22, 446

Sales, Francis de, 100, 259, 428, 433–34
Scholem, Gershom, 240, 355
Scudder, Vida, 394
Segundo, Juan Luis, 204–5, 208
Seraphim of Sarov, 136–38, 140, 143–44, 146, 182, 229–30, 237, 354, 423
Shmelke of Nikolsburg, 108, 354
Shneur Zalman of Ladi, 196, 198, 423
Silesius, Angelus, 42, 133, 144, 185–86, 191, 229, 233, 240, 258, 261, 338, 357
Sobrino, Jon, 123, 246–47, 249–51, 256–57, 262, 268–69, 346, 349, 426
Soelle, Dorothee, 117, 131, 440
Solzhenitsyn, Alexander, 382
Soyinka, Wole, 210
Stalin, Joseph, 14
Steinbeck, John, 172–73
Stowe, Harriet Beecher, 382
Stringfellow, William, 13, 37, 53, 99, 113–16, 119, 145, 156, 167–68, 172–73, 180–81, 189, 200–204, 207, 216, 248, 251, 258, 294–96,

315, 318, 346–50, 366–68, 370, 393–94, 426, 432, 445–46, 449
Suzuki, D. T., 187, 317
Sylvester, (Brother) 236
Symeon the New Theologian, 17, 27, 53, 78, 89, 96–97, 100, 104, 138–39, 141, 144–45, 158, 165, 182, 190, 210–11, 327–28, 353, 388
Syncletica (Amma), 100, 107

Tamez, Elsa, 106, 442
Tauler, Johannes, 198, 220, 450
Teilhard de Chardin, Pierre, 29, 310, 355–56, 374, 396–98, 400–402, 406, 409–11
Teresa of Ávila, 17–18, 38, 73, 91, 100, 141–42, 144, 173, 182, 193, 232, 235, 241, 248, 250, 255, 260, 266–69, 327, 342, 344, 351, 374, 377–78, 385, 391–92, 422, 431, 438
Theodore of Pherme, 93
Theognius, 95, 108
Theophan the Recluse, 34–35, 73, 142, 233, 237, 399
Thérèse of Lisieux, 327, 331, 390
Thich Quang Duc, 263–64, 271
Thomas à Kempis, 94–95, 214, 260, 264–65, 418, 447
Thoreau, Henry David, 6
Thurman, Howard xii, 2, 28–30, 33–35, 38, 75–76, 78, 204, 223, 345–46, 349, 352, 382, 447
Tillich, Paul, 367
Tocqueville, Alexis de, 348
Tolstoy, Leo, 153, 155, 165, 209, 216, 426, 449
Torquemada, Tomás de, 14
Towne, Anthony, 99, 114, 116, 368, 393
Traherne, Thomas, 3–9, 41, 60–61, 77, 84, 119, 212–14, 233, 259–61, 266, 301, 306, 310, 323, 356, 359, 376–77, 384, 392, 398–400, 402, 404–5, 408–9, 418–19

Trajan, 109
Tri Quang, 218, 220, 225, 227, 263
Trocmé, Andre, 45, 170, 177–78, 181, 262, 317, 366, 445
Trotsky, Leon, 45
Truth, Sojourner, 172, 182, 217, 448
Turner, Nat, 153
Tutu, Desmond, 10–11, 28, 35, 56, 81, 92, 94, 98, 181, 202–3, 213, 269–70, 285–91, 296, 298, 300, 302, 305, 310, 365, 378, 383–85, 387, 391, 396, 410–11, 440–41

Underhill, Evelyn, 10, 16, 19–21, 23, 33, 45–47, 62, 102–3, 111, 147, 155–57, 182, 200–201, 207–8, 210, 225, 227, 249, 257, 263, 281, 290, 292, 299, 310, 316, 337, 344, 353, 356–57, 374, 394, 397, 400, 405–6, 420, 426, 433, 438, 447, 449
Uri of Strelisk, 143

Vorster, John, 285–88, 290–91, 296, 396

Waal, Esther de, 100, 160
Walker, David, 379
Wallace, George, 114
Washington, Booker T., 126
Watters, Pat, 14, 69, 395–96
Wesley, Cynthia, 112
Weston, Frank, 248–49
William of St. Thierry, 144, 217
Wilson, Woodrow, 171
Winthrop, John, 160
Woolman, John, 421
Wright, Richard, 350

Yehiel Mikhal of Zlotchov, 300, 352
Young Chief, 303, 305, 401–2

Zevi Hirsh of Zhydatchov, 362
Zohar, 2, 142–43
Zusya of Hanipol, 94

Subject Index

"A Devout Meditation on Adolf Eichmann," 57
African National Congress (ANC), 269
Aguilares, 250
ahimsa, 421, 424
Al Qaeda, 223
All Quiet on the Western Front, 403–5
"Amazing Grace," 232
American Civil Liberties Union (ACLU), 166
American Revolution, 45
Anabaptists, 58, 223, 292
anamnesis, 63
Anschluss, 124
antimerciful world, 55, 123, 145, 426
antiwar movement (Vietnam), 24, 69
apartheid, 14, 56, 68, 181, 202, 205, 285, 287, 383, 385, 396
Apocalypse Now, 135
The Ascent to Mt. Carmel, 388
Atlanta, 125, 129–30
Auschwitz, 35, 246, 287

Bastille, 292
Batman Begins, 187
"Battle Hymn of the Republic," 126
Bay of Pigs, 431
Beatitudes, 82, 103
Berlin Wall, 117
Bhagavad Gita, 414, 427, 434
Birmingham, 111–13, 207, 216, 224, 234, 347, 430, 435–36, 439, 442

Birmingham Commitment Cards, 215, 224, 421
Birmingham Jail, 14, 354
Black Panther Party, 222
Black Power, 222
Bodhisattva, 63
The Book of Spiritual Poverty, 277
Brethren of the Common Table, 228
British Empire, 58, 383
The Brothers Karamazov, 61

Canticle of Creation/Creatures, 54, 56, 305–7, 311
Carnegie Hall, 442
Catholic Worker, 18, 58, 68–69, 98–99, 116, 118, 207–8, 218, 228, 264, 301, 349, 364–66, 445
Catonsville Nine, 368
Cayuse, 303
Centuries, 399
Le Chambon sur Lignon, 176, 181, 366, 395, 446
Chernobyl, 224, 388
Cherokee, 122
Chickasaw, 122
Choctaw, 122
Christ and Culture, 57
"Christmas Sermon," 203
civil rights movement, 14, 24, 65, 69, 113–14, 155, 200, 202, 204–5, 215, 224, 271, 302, 436, 442, 446
Civil War (American), 272, 299
Civil War (English), 405
Clinton Administration, 117

Close Encounters of the Third Kind, 135
The Cloud of Unknowing, 15, 151, 192, 194–98, 212–13, 221, 227, 328, 390, 432
Cold War, 57, 65, 148, 160–61, 163, 165, 227, 293, 359, 369, 405, 431–32
communism, 14, 80, 162, 179, 218, 230, 292, 294, 346, 409, 423, 431, 442
Communist Manifesto, 45
The Comradeship, 228
Congress of Racial Equality (CORE), 226
Contemplative Prayer, 70
Creek, 122
Crusades, 311
Cuban Missile Crisis, 65, 292

Dachau, 246
dalits, 298–99, 315
The Dark Night of the Soul, 196, 309, 389–90
Das Kapital, 292
David Walker's *Appeal*, 379
"Desert Protest," 82
The Dhammapada, 134, 277
dharmakaya, 76
dhikr, 63, 121
Dissenter in a Great Society, 200
domination system, 55

El Salvador, 49, 201, 208, 248, 251, 256, 268–69, 273, 346, 392
Emancipation Proclamation, 302
Engaged Buddhism, 33, 58
Essenes, 22, 157
"Everything That Is Is Holy," 76

Fellowship of Reconciliation (FOR), 10, 148, 228, 297
The Fire Next Time, 301
"Fire Watch," 52, 72, 198
Freaks, 84
Freedom Rides, 113, 424
Friends World Conference, 208
French resistance, 201
French Revolution, 45

Friends of Gandhi, 10
Fukushima, 388
fumie, 242, 247
Funtown, 436

Garée, 379, 384
Gethsemani, 75
Ghost Dance Movement, 209
Gnosticism, 25, 30, 157, 229, 400
Going Home: Jesus and Buddha as Brothers, 304
Golden Rule, 296, 306, 315, 402
Grand Inquisitor, 13, 14, 16, 168
The Grapes of Wrath, 172
Great Society, 200
Greater East Asia Co-Prosperity Sphere, 419
Grenada invasion, 272
Gulf War, 4, 6, 9, 272

Hanoi, 148
harijans, 299, 302, 313, 320
Harlem, 114, 117, 200, 347–48, 351, 367
Hasidism, 26, 32, 83, 143, 300, 314, 423
Havana, 74, 76, 78, 327, 407, 431
Hiroshima, 35, 171
Holocaust, 79, 175, 179, 282, 291, 346, 419, 429, 440
Hymn to Matter, 401

"I Have a Dream," 111, 395, 435
The Inheritors, 280, 361
International Fellowship of Reconciliation, 49
International Workers of the World (IWW, Wobblies), 228

Jesus Seminar, 31, 168
Jim Crow, 285, 294, 347, 378, 383
John F. Kennedy Airport, 408
Journey of Reconciliation, 424

kaaba, 398, 410
Kabbalism, 361, 363, 365
Kellogg Pact, 150
The Kingdom of God in America, 149

Subject Index

Kingsley Hall, 49
Koinonia Community, 58, 228
Korean War, 272, 295
Ku Klux Klan, 113, 166, 395, 427

Lawrence strike, 425
League of Nations, 150, 171
lectio divina, 63
Leninism, 153–54, 292, 425
"Letter from Birmingham Jail," 46, 111, 435–36
"Letters to a White Liberal," 156
Lincoln Memorial, 378
Lincoln's Second Inaugural Address, 299
"Litany at Atlanta," 125–29
The Living Flame of Love, 309, 389
locus imperii, 55–56, 58, 65
London, 49, 68, 109, 161, 295–96, 348, 445
Lookout Mountain, 395
Lord of the Flies, 281
Lost Generation, 403
Louisville, 5, 26, 29, 35, 75–76, 78, 81, 293, 310, 320, 339, 376–77, 407–8
"The Love that Forgives," 112

"Macarius and the Pony," 161
"Mad Farmer" poems, 81–83
"Mad Farmer Liberation Front," 82
"Mad Farmer Manifesto," 82
Magnificat, 84, 283
Manifest Destiny, 272, 284–85, 303, 419
Manichaeism, 215, 224
March on Washington, 112, 203
Marxism, 77, 150, 153–54, 168, 192, 292, 425
McCarthyism, 160, 164
Medellín, 41, 167, 186, 201, 269, 418
Memorial Day Massacre, 164, 246, 262, 286, 295
"Message of Love," 295
"Message to Poets," 218
A Mirror for Simple Souls, 255
Mishnah, 301
Molokai, 313

Montgomery, 114, 125–26, 129–30, 295, 347, 385, 430, 435
Montgomery bus strike, 72, 254
Mt. Alverna, 237, 411
Mt. Hira, 397
Mt. Rainier (Tahoma), 397
Mt. Shasta, 407
Munich Putsch, 153–54
mysterium tremendum, 56, 72, 234, 236
"Mysticism and Social Change," 28

Nagasaki, 171
Nat Turner's Rebellion, 153
National Association for the Advancement of Colored People (NAACP), 226
National Urban League, 226
Nazism, 23, 65, 79, 115, 124, 153–54, 164, 175, 181, 201, 219, 223, 262, 301, 310, 366, 410, 419, 429
The New Deal, 200
No Longer at Ease, 378
No Man is an Island, 405
Nobel Peace Prize, 422
"Notes on a Philosophy of Solitude," 272–73, 354
Nottinghamshire, 179
Nuremburg Trials, 6, 387

Oklahoma City Federal Building, 234–35

Parable of the Pharisee and the Tax Collector, 22–23
Parable of the Prodigal Son, 117
Parable of the Seed Growing Secretly, 219, 239
pax americana, 13
pax romana, 13
Pearl Harbor, 295
Pelagianism, 22, 24, 73, 389
Perelandra, 443
(Edmund) Pettus Bridge, 114
Pietists, 30
Polonnaruwa, 76, 78, 237, 361, 376, 396, 406–8
Practical Mysticism, 405

"Prayer of a Soul Taken with Love," 310
"The Prayers of God," 244
Puebla, 201, 269, 379, 433, 439

Qumran, 145

The Remains of the Day, 49
"Revelation," 80–81
"The Road to Freedom is Via the Cross," 269
Russian Revolution, 45

The Sabbath, 417
Saigon, 148, 217, 425
Sanhedrin, 13, 14, 251
satyagraha, 421, 424, 426
Scandal, 242–43
Selma, 114, 128, 130, 335, 385
Seminole, 122
Sermon on the Mount, 45, 82, 159, 171, 213, 289, 291, 295, 401, 426–27
Seven Last Words, 239–40, 261
The Seven Story Mountain, 157, 337
Shaker furniture, 407
Sharpeville massacre, 285, 288–89, 294
shema, 63
Silence, 241–42
The Silent Cry, 117
Sixteenth Street Baptist Church, 112, 127, 213, 268
Society of Friends (Quakers), 144, 177–79, 197, 223, 301, 384, 387, 420, 445, 448
"Sonny's Blues," 117–18
Soul on Ice, 368
South Africa, 14, 113, 202, 270–72, 285, 287, 291
South African Council of Churches, 56
Southern Christian Leadership Conference (SCLC), 113, 202–3, 226, 382
Soweto, 285, 288–89
The Spiritual Canticle, 96, 309
St. Erkenwald, 109–11

St. Sulpice Church, 78, 424
Stalinism, 160
Stone Mountain, 395
Strange Case of Doctor Jekyll and Mr. Hyde, 242
Student Nonviolent Coordinating Committee (SNCC), 114, 226
swaraj, 58, 298, 364

"Taking Sides on Vietnam," 294
Talmud, 20, 143, 224, 417, 423
Tannaim, 417, 426
Tao te Ching, 186
The Theologia Germanica, 173, 211, 254, 357, 359–60, 396
terra nullius, 284
Thoughts in Solitude, 198
Thousand Year/Third Reich, 65, 79, 124, 419
Tomb of the Five Saints, 37–39, 103, 238, 259
Trail of Tears, 122
"The Transfiguration," 410
Treaty of Walla Walla, 303
Truth and Reconciliation Commission, 92, 202, 384, 387
Twin Towers (World Trade Center), 117

University of Central America, 268, 318

Vichy France, 201, 262, 445
Viet Cong, 217
Vietnam (War), 33, 35, 65, 112, 148, 162, 199, 203, 217–19, 227, 230, 263–64, 267, 271–73, 294, 405, 425, 431, 440

War on Poverty, 200
Wasichus, 122, 125, 303
Watts Riot, 35
The Way of a Pilgrim, 277, 308
"We Shall Overcome," 117, 395–96, 447
Weimar Germany, 153–54
Why We Can't Wait, 436
Wolf of Gubbio, 288, 311–14, 317

World War I, 170–71, 272, 295–96, 402–3, 406, 425
World War II, 10, 174, 181, 223, 272, 297, 301, 445
Woza Albert, 270

Xala, 84–85, 443

Zealots, 22, 157, 160

Scripture Index

Genesis
2:24	339
3:7	361
3:21	361
9:9–10	278
28:10–7	192
32:22–31	192

Exodus
3:7	282, 447
3:7–8	262
3:17	282
19:12	190
32:24	436
33:17–23	101
33:20	190
34:33–5	143

Leviticus
19:18	18
26:1–13	204

Deuteronomy
2:34–5	282
6:5	18
7:1–6	282
19:10	262
20:17	282
28:1–14	204
30:11–14	63, 73
30:14	63
30:15–20	158

Joshua
6:21	282
8:24–9	282
10:28–40	282

Judges
9:8–15	388
12:1–6	283

2 Samuel
1:25	105
1:27	105
6:1–11	190

1 Kings
18:20–40	386
18:21	386
21:1–16	85

2 Kings
5:1–19	313
22–23	375

Job
19:25–7	254
42:5	88
42:5–6	254

Psalms
8	399
8:3–4	378
18:26–7	148

Psalms (continued)

22	239, 411
22:6–7	411
22:14	411
42:1	326
63:1	326
65:12	309
72:1	105, 203
82	120
85	217
85:10	60
88:18	106
91:13	315
96:9	406
98:8	309
137:9	128
146:2	151
146:7	410
148:9	309

Ecclesiastes

1:13	105
3:1–8	107, 442
3:16	105
4:1	105
5:8	105
6:1–2	105
7:7	105
8:17	186

Song of Songs

4:16–5:1	324
5:1	25

Isaiah

2:2–4	109, 256, 283, 304
2:4	238
2:12–16	47
6:1–3	376
6:1–8	361
6:8–11	342
9:2	135
11:1–3	105
11:1–5	388
11:6–8	289
11:6–9	393
11:8	315
13–24	283
35:1–2	388
43:18–9	169
45:7	72
49:6	169
49:15	301
52:13–53:12	247
52:14	243, 247, 411
53:2	247, 411
53:3	247
53:4	247
53:5	258
53:7	247
53:8	247
53:9	247
53:12	247
55:10	251
55:10–11	66
59:11	120
61:1	410
65:17–25	22, 80
65:25	315

Jeremiah

1:10	16, 342
4:23–6	124
6:4	435
8:11	435
8:18–9:1	120
8:22	447
23:5–6	105
29:4–7	169, 399
37:17	123

Lamentations

1:3–5	123
1:15–6	123
2:10–2	123
2:18–9	123
4:6	123
4:17	123
5:2–3	123
5:15	123

Ezekiel

11:19	286, 359, 390
37:1–14	388

Hosea

1–3	284
1:2	284
1:6–9	284
2:1	284
2:4	284
2:14	338
4:11–2	284
5:4	284
6:10	284
11	284
13:8	215, 221

Micah

3:2–3	156
4:1–4	109, 256, 283, 304
4:3	238
4:4	48, 282
4:10	120
6:8	18

Zechariah

4:1	42

Matthew

1:22	239
2:15	239
2:16	282
2:17	239
2:23	239
3:15	239
4:14	239
5:4	89
5:6	103, 202
5:8	134
5:9	291, 384, 415
5:11	8, 233
5:21–2	174, 225
5:46–7	159, 213, 292
6:1–6	432
6:16–8	432
8:17	239
10:16	148
10:28	448
12:17	239
13:13–8	238
13:14	239
13:35	239
13:44	189
21:4	239
22:37	18
23:23	382
24:24	28
25:21	328
25:23	328
25:31–45	357
25:31–46	158, 262
26:54	239
26:56	239
27:9	239
27:25	178

Mark

3:21	291
3:23–4	171
3:28–9	379
3:35	291, 294
4:3–8, 14–20	27
4:26–9	219
5:22–3	288
7:24–5	288
8:23	288
8:31	239
8:36	69
9:2–29	378
9:31	239
10:17–21	39–40
10:17–22	316
10:33–4	239
10:45	239
10:47	288
13:37	43
15:34	239
16:18	315

Luke

2:29–30	414
4:18	410
9:54–5	284
10:23	277
10:25–37	39–40
10:33	41, 450
10:35	312
10:37	450
11:9	437
11:34	134

Luke (continued)

12:4	448
13:6–9	388
13:33–4	239
14:12–4	159
15:7	224
15:10	224
16:8	148
17:11–9	289
18:1–5	348
19:9–10	300
22:3	253
22:51	239, 289
23:28–31	239
23:43	239
23:49	232

John

1:1–18	253
1:11–3	144, 159
1:12	55, 291, 384
1:14	28
1:38	288
2:4	291
3:1–21	53
3:3	1
3:16	55, 159
3:17	55
4:14	103, 202
5:2–9	39
6:35	202
6:36	103
6:51	103
9:6	315
10:1–3	240
11:9–10	159
11:50	224
12:32	258
12:32–3	239
12:35–6	159
12:46	159
14:20	356
14:27	444
15:13	320
17:3	447
17:11	356
19:26–7	291
20:2	448
20:13	448
20:29	31

Acts

2:13	25, 79
6:15	405
17:22–31	190
17:26	278

Romans

5:6–11	320
8:19–23	121, 126
8:35–9	71, 336, 429
12:2	34, 60
12:15	444
13:11	42
13:12	134

1 Corinthians

1:18	158
1:18–25	271
1:23	252
2:6	158
6:19	377
7:31	46
8:1	212, 390
11:29	293
12:21	449
13	23, 211, 214, 266
13:8	389
13:11	50
13:12	190
15:42	158
15:50	158
15:53	158
15:54	158, 259

2 Corinthians

2:15	158
4:3	158
4:18	185
7:9–11	100
12:2–4	9, 145, 329–30
12:9	271

Galatians

2:20	356
3:26	384

4:5	384	11	228
4:5–7	291	11:1	226
		11:18–20	226
Ephesians		13:3	357
6:10–20	391		
		James	
Philippians		1:26–7	167
2:5–11	253	1:27	344
2:5–12	268	2:17	36
3:8	342	4:1	421, 436
Colossians		**1 John**	
1:15–20	253, 398	1:5	157
1:16–7	309	1:7	159
3:12–7	144	2:8	160
		2:9–10	160
1 Thessalonians		2:17	46
5:17	48	4:16	157
		4:20	18, 160
1 Timothy			
6:16	185	**Revelation**	
		3:16	265, 386
Titus		5:8–14	119, 126
1:15	410	7:9	304
		7:9–17	256
Philemon		13:7	115, 447
17	356–7	21:4	46
		21:22–22:5	304
Hebrews		22:2	123
4:12–6	316		

www.ingramcontent.com/pod-product-compliance
Lightning Source LLC
Chambersburg PA
CBHW021230300426
44111CB00007B/489